Life Studies

A THEMATIC READER

Life Studies

A Thematic Reader

SECOND EDITION

EDITED BY

David Cavitch
Tufts University

A Bedford Book

ST. MARTIN'S PRESS · NEW YORK

Library of Congress Catalog Card Number: 85-61294
Copyright © 1986 by St. Martin's Press, Inc.
All rights reserved.
Manufactured in the United States of America
9 8 7 6 5
f   e   d   c   b   a
For information, write St. Martin's Press, Inc.,
175 Fifth Avenue, New York, N.Y. 10010
Editorial Offices: Bedford Books of St. Martin's Press,
29 Commonwealth Avenue, Boston, MA 02116

ISBN: 0-312-48487-9

Typography and cover design: Anna Post
Cover photograph: Tom Norton

Part Opening Photographs

Self-Images (page 2): Frank Siteman
Family Ties (page 76): Annie Leibovitz
Love and Longings (page 152): Gilles Peress/Magnum
Group Pictures (page 222): Thomas Höpker/Woodfin Camp
Possessions (page 312): Robert Frank/Pace/MacGill Gallery
Ambitions (page 374): Richard Howard
Convictions (page 452): Jim Richardson
Dilemmas (page 530): Michael Hayman/Stock, Boston

Acknowledgments

Francesco Alberoni, "Two Kinds of Sexuality." Title by the editor. From *Falling in Love,* by Francesco Alberoni, translated by Lawrence Venuti. Translation Copyright © 1983 by Lawrence Venuti. Reprinted by permission of Random House, Inc.
Sherwood Anderson, "The Egg." Reprinted by permission of Harold Ober Associates

(*Continued on page 613*)

TO INSTRUCTORS

◊

This new edition of *Life Studies* reconfirms the premise that students learn to write well when they try to understand things that truly matter to them. Writers learn about themselves and their world by writing attentively, just as artists learn about their subjects by sketching them from different perspectives and in different settings. Hence the title *Life Studies*, for the works included here offer students varied perspectives on topics they care about, encouraging them to read carefully, to respond in class discussions, and to express their feelings and ideas clearly in writing.

The organization of the book into eight thematic sections suggests the growth of human dimensions, treating a progression of experience from personal to general awareness and from concrete to abstract considerations. The topics focus on our self-images, our family relationships, our love for other people outside the family, our behavior in groups, our connection to valued possessions, our aspirations and ambitions, our scientific and religious theories about life, and our moral dilemmas. Each section contains the widest possible variety in views of the topic and in types of writing. The selections are all well written and provocative, and many of them (even those by well-known writers) appear for the first time here in a composition reader along with several classic essays. Each section opens with a number of "Insights" — succinct, often controversial statements by well-known writers whose colloquy of opinions offers a lively approach to the theme. The longer works that follow include contemporary essays, memoirs, social criticism, and journalism; these selections represent such diverse fields of knowledge as law, art, philosophy, computers, sports, and the social, behavioral, and animal sciences. In addition to essays, each section also contains one short story and one poem that develop the theme imaginatively.

To help students appreciate what they read, and especially to generate good writing, *Life Studies* contains detailed and extensive editorial apparatus. Preceding each selection is a biographical and introductory headnote. Following each selection are pointed questions and feasible writing topics. These lead students to reexamine the selection's concepts and rhetorical methods, and they prompt substantive, intelligent responses in class discussions, in short written exercises, and in longer, more carefully planned essays. Additional writing topics at the end of each thematic section encourage analysis of the "Insights" and further written consideration of the theme. This second edition also includes an appendix on reading and writing. The student is offered guidelines for reading with better comprehension, illustrated with specific observations about an annotated sample essay, E. B. White's "Once More to the Lake." A helpful clarification of the themes follows the sample essay, and useful procedures for writing about their own responses encourage students to become intelligently involved in their work. A rhetorical index to the essays appears in the back of the book, and an instructor's manual offers both suggestions for dealing with each piece and more writing assignments.

Many instructors helped improve this book by responding to a questionnaire about the first edition. I am grateful for the careful consideration given by Lewis M. Baldwin, Onondaga Community College; Robert D. Beckett, Southwest Missouri State University; Carl W. C. Beckman, Tufts University; Nancy Bent, Ithaca College; Anne Bower, West Virginia University; Peter Bricklebank, City College, City University of New York; Jane L. Brown, Georgia Southern College; Joan C. Burton, State University of New York, Stony Brook; Mary Cross, Baruch College, City University of New York; Kathryn Earle, West Virginia University; Marilyn Francis, Washington State University; Della Grayson, San Diego State University; Robert A. Hagstrom, Jamestown Community College; Rosemary Henze, Stanford University; Donna Hollenberg, Simmons College; Karen E. Holleran, West Virginia University; Robert O. Johnson, Washington State University; Clyde Jones, Virginia Western Community College; Gloria O. Jones, Youngstown State University; Dorothea Kehler, San Diego State University; Harold Kugelmass, Onondaga Community College; Andrew Lakritz, University of California, Irvine; Charles Lee, Southwest Missouri State University; Lynn Lee, University of Wisconsin, Platteville; Mitzi Lewellen, West Virginia University;

Tamara Lucas, Stanford University; Jaquelyn Lyman, West Virginia University; Pete M. Mann, Wilkes Community College; Marilyn Monaghan, Gwynedd-Mercy College; Jackson Morton, West Virginia University; Terri L. Nelson, West Virginia University; Susan Monroe Nugent, Keene State College; Tamara Jo Prendergast, West Virginia University; Richard Prince, Lewis University; Wayne Scheer, Atlanta Junior College; Deborah Shaller, Towson State University; Nancy S. Sheley, West Virginia University; George Stavros, California Polytechnic University; Isabel F. Steilberg, Virginia Commonwealth University; David Taylor, Moravian College; Douglas M. Tedards, University of the Pacific; Mary L. Tobin, Rice University; Susan Allen Toth, Macalester College; and Marilyn Wanier, University of Connecticut.

Good suggestions for new material to include came from Lin Haire-Sargeant, Donna Hollenberg, Edward Paolella, and the people at Bedford Books. I am particularly indebted to Nancy Lyman, Karen Henry, editor of this edition, and to the publisher, Charles Christensen. Christine Rutigliano obtained permissions to publish the selections, and Elizabeth Schaaf, managing editor, skillfully piloted the endeavor through production.

CONTENTS

◇

1. SELF-IMAGES   3

INSIGHTS: *Susan Sontag, Rom Harre, Helen Keller, Emily Dickinson, Germaine Greer, Rollo May, E. E. Cummings*   4

Nora Ephron SHAPING UP ABSURD   7

A journalist's witty account of feeling tragically misfitted for life by the curse of flat-chestedness.

Garrison Keillor AFTER A FALL   17

A down-to-earth humorist observes that the taller men are, the harder they fall, every time.

Mary McCarthy NAMES   26

A leading novelist and critic tells how in a girls' boarding school, names and nicknames acquire magical powers over the students' personalities.

Susan Brownmiller THE CONTRIVED POSTURES
OF FEMININITY   35

A feminist objects that the body language women are expected to learn signifies shame and weakness.

ix

Louie Crew THRIVING AS AN OUTSIDER,
EVEN AS AN OUTCAST,
IN SMALLTOWN AMERICA   41

A biracial homosexual couple in a small Southern town break all
the social taboos at once — and learn to thrive as valued citizens.

Joan Didion IN BED   51

The chronic suffering brought on by migraine headaches gave
this essayist a deluded view of herself until she separated fact
from fantasy.

James Thurber THE SECRET LIFE OF
WALTER MITTY (*story*)   56

Irrepressible dreams of glory guide American literature's most famous nonentity through the dreariness of his day.

Theodore Roethke OPEN HOUSE (*poem*)   62

A popular American poet says that in order to write he can't
keep any secrets about himself.

John Berger THE CHANGING VIEW OF MAN
IN THE PORTRAIT   64

According to this contemporary art critic, the industrial revolution, the development of photography, and wide acceptance of
the idea of equality all changed how portraitists painted and how
we see ourselves.

Luis Buñuel MEMORY   71

A famous film director begins to lose his memory, and possibly
his sense of self, along with the images of his past.

Additional Writing Topics   74

2. FAMILY TIES   77

INSIGHTS: *Robert Nisbet, Ferdinand Mount, Leo Tolstoy, C. S. Lewis, Francis Bacon, Robert Weiss, Philip Slater*   78

Margaret Mead FAMILY CODES   81

A famous anthropologist explains that American families vary greatly in codes of behavior and ways of communicating them.

Marie Winn THE *MAD* VIEW OF PARENTS   86

Mad magazine turned the generation gap into a wide gulf, according to this authority on childhood.

Nancy Friday COMPETITION   92

The love between a mother and her two daughters is tempered by the fierce competition in beauty, intelligence, and accomplishment among all the three women, says the author of *My Mother/My Self.*

Raymond Carver MY FATHER'S LIFE   99

A successful writer who feels close to working people tries to understand the misfortunes of his ne'er-do-well father.

Adrienne Rich THE ANGER OF A CHILD   109

A poet looks back at the angry, demanding father and the timid mother who dominated her youth.

Jamaica Kincaid A WALK TO THE JETTY   114

In this autobiographical story a Caribbean girl can hardly wait to leave her family and island home, but the day of departure changes her attitude.

Gordon Lish FEAR: FOUR EXAMPLES   127

His daughter's independence leaves this father in the dark with his own fears.

Calvin Trillin IT'S JUST TOO LATE   130

A teenager's wild behavior leads to her death in an accident for which many people are responsible. But who is to blame?

Robert Hayden THOSE WINTER SUNDAYS
        (*poem*)   142

A poet remembers the weekly ritual that perfectly symbolized his father's lonely devotion to his family.

John Updike STILL OF SOME USE (*story*)   144

A man helps his ex-wife and his sons clean out their house on moving day. The artifacts of his former life — toys, games, a kerosene lamp — remind him of all that is over.

Additional Writing Topics   150

3. LOVE AND LONGINGS   153

INSIGHTS: *La Rochefoucauld, St. John, Walker Percy, Anonymous, Selma Fraiberg, Francesco Alberoni, Erich Fromm, D. T. Suzuki*   154

Susan Allen Toth THE BOYFRIEND   158

Having a boyfriend was a requirement in high school — but this one was special. An Iowa woman remembers her adolescence in the 1950s.

Marcelle Clements TERMINAL COOL   166

In the 1960s the style of romance was so understated that love lacked essential elements, says this former flower child.

Robert Solomon "I-LOVE-YOU" 175

What claims and what challenges do we make when we utter those three daring words? A philosopher considers words as actions.

Francesco Alberoni TWO KINDS OF SEXUALITY 180

An Italian sociologist tries to explain the origin and meaning of "ecstasy" and "misery" in sex.

Raymond Carver WHAT WE TALK ABOUT WHEN WE TALK ABOUT LOVE (*story*) 185

When the drinks begin to flow, two couples get more and more upset as they try to discuss what real love means.

D. H. Lawrence COUNTERFEIT LOVE 198

A novelist laments the death of real emotion and its inevitable, terrible consequences.

Margaret Atwood SIREN SONG (*poem*) 202

A leading Canadian writer presents a sardonic view of love on the rocks.

Ernest van den Haag THE INVENTION THAT ISN'T WORKING 204

A psychoanalyst argues that we've got the idea of marriage all wrong, and our lives show it.

Jill Tweedie THE FUTURE OF LOVE 215

A feminist tells us some of the things we mistake for love and imagines what we will need to learn in order to experience *real* love.

Additional Writing Topics 221

4. GROUP PICTURES   223

INSIGHTS: *John Donne, Jean-Paul Sartre, Ralph Waldo Emerson, Theodore Reik, W. E. B. DuBois, Oscar Wilde, Judith Martin, Sigmund Freud*   224

Edward C. Martin BEING JUNIOR HIGH   228

A teacher examines the anxious desire to belong and the beginnings of confusion about authority that characterize his twelve- to fourteen-year-old students.

Maya Angelou GRADUATION   234

A commencement speaker's prejudice threatens but cannot destroy the pride of a black community.

John Cheever EXPELLED (*story*)   247

A student examines the unthinking conformity and unquestioned beliefs that governed the students *and* faculty at a prep school from which he has just been expelled.

John Edgar Wideman BLACK AND BLUES   258

A black student at a prep school has to defend his assumption that black music is his heritage.

Maxine Hong Kingston THE MISERY OF SILENCE   264

The language barrier is the greater wall of China for this immigrant child raised in a small California city.

Paul Fussell "SPEAK, THAT I MAY SEE THEE"   270

The language we use puts us in our place, says this observer of social class in America.

Gloria Steinem THE TIME FACTOR   279

> A leading feminist argues that women are in a class struggle to gain the power to plan their own time.

Marc Feigen Fasteau FRIENDSHIPS
                                     AMONG MEN   283

> Men form friendships with other men through group activities. This writer asks why men avoid more personal companionship.

Desmond Morris TERRITORIAL BEHAVIOR   295

> A zoologist maintains that groups exist in order to protect their own turf and that people realize who they are by noticing where they are.

Linda Pastan MARKET DAY (*poem*)   305

> Instead of appreciating the sights on her holiday in France, this poet keeps thinking of the customs of folks at home.

Alexis de Tocqueville ARISTOCRACY AND
                                       DEMOCRACY   307

> Few observers had a better grasp of what it means to be an American than this nineteenth-century Frenchman. Here he looks at some of the social changes that take place in a society without an aristocracy.

Additional Writing Topics   310

5. POSSESSIONS   313

INSIGHTS: *Matthew, Henry David Thoreau, Henry James, Paul Wachtel, Caskie Stinnett, Thorstein Veblen, John Kenneth Galbraith, Andrew Carnegie, Anonymous*   314

Toni Cade Bambara THE LESSON (*story*)   **318**

> A tough-talking kid from the ghetto begins to understand that in
> this society money talks even tougher.

Harry Crews THE CAR   **327**

> A Southern writer recalls the period when he seemed to live en-
> tirely through his cars: they organized his activities and defined
> his personality.

E. M. Forster MY WOOD   **332**

> An English novelist finds that owning a stretch of forest changes
> his view of it: being a landowner brings out unwelcome attitudes.

William Ryan MINE, ALL MINE   **336**

> A social psychologist finds the whole idea of *ownership* a little
> incredible.

Matthew THE LILIES OF THE FIELD (*poem*)   **343**

> In the Sermon on the Mount, Jesus warns his listeners not to be
> overly concerned about property and gain, lest they lose sight of
> more important things.

John Brooks TELEPHONE GAMESMANSHIP   **345**

> An ordinary phone call involves both people in jockeying for sta-
> tus, says this observer of the American business scene.

Susan C. Carlisle FRENCH HOMES
                   AND FRENCH CHARACTER   **355**

> An observant American traveler notes that French homes tell
> you what not to expect from French people.

Lewis Hyde GIFTS IN MOTION   **366**

> The rituals of giving away possessions can hold a society to-
> gether, according to this critic of our commercial culture.

Additional Writing Topics   **372**

6. AMBITIONS   375

INSIGHTS: *Robert Browning, Sydney J. Harris, The Peter Principle, Vincent van Gogh, Ecclesiastes*   376

Joseph Epstein THE VIRTUES OF AMBITION   380

> The editor of *The American Scholar* makes a large claim for the importance of ambition as the center of individual character and social order.

Russell Baker MY LACK OF GUMPTION   386

> A prize-winning columnist recalls how he got his start in a job he could do sitting down.

Richard Rodriguez READING FOR SUCCESS   395

> The author, raised in a home where English was not the first language, considers his drive to get an education — and the sacrifices he and his family had to make — in order to be a success in America.

Seymour Wishman A LAWYER'S GUILTY SECRETS   401

> What it takes to be a good lawyer isn't always the same as what it takes to be a good person. A successful criminal lawyer reflects on the competition, the conflicts, and the compromises of his profession.

Pete Hamill WINNING ISN'T EVERYTHING   405

> An avid sports fan says that anyone can take victory in stride, but only a true competitor knows the difficult art of losing.

Michael Novak THE METAPHYSICS OF SPORTS   411

> This devout fan argues that winning *is* everything, if you understand the spiritual significance of competitive sports.

Virginia Woolf PROFESSIONS FOR WOMEN   421

> To learn to write truthfully, this novelist had to face inner obstacles, which she explains to other women entering any profession.

Sherwood Anderson THE EGG (*story*)   428

> A boy observes what happens to his father when "the American passion for getting up in the world" takes hold of the family.

Henry David Thoreau WHERE I LIVED,
AND WHAT I LIVED FOR   439

> America's most famous free spirit wants us to recognize that what we *do* in life becomes our life.

William Butler Yeats THE LAKE ISLE
OF INNISFREE (*poem*)   443

> The poet imagines how he might lead a simpler life.

Christopher Lasch SURVIVAL MENTALITY   445

> When people don't expect much of life, they don't expect much of themselves either, says this critic of contemporary American society.

Additional Writing Topics   451

7. CONVICTIONS   453

INSIGHTS: *Emilie Griffin, William James, Napoleon, Robert Frost, Judge Learned Hand, Bertrand Russell, John Newton, Sigmund Freud*   454

Richard Morris HOW REAL IS REAL?   458

> A science writer points out that science is an imaginative map of reality, similar to art and literature.

Stephen Jay Gould NONMORAL NATURE   **463**

A noted paleontologist argues that evolution teaches us nothing about how we should live. The problem of ethics is up to people, not nature.

Robert Nisbet CREATIONISM   **474**

The big bang theory or the Book of Genesis? A leading sociologist finds possible truths in religion's account of the creation of the universe.

Robert Finch VERY LIKE A WHALE   **482**

A beached whale draws hundreds of onlookers, and this nature writer wonders what he and other people came to witness in the mysterious death.

Carl Jung SECRET THOUGHT   **489**

A renowned psychoanalyst recalls how his childhood torment over a forbidden thought led him to adult understanding of human nature from both scientific and religious perspectives.

Barbara Grizzuti Harrison GROWING UP
                                  APOCALYPTIC   **496**

Severe religious dogmas made her early life miserable, says this feminist writer who broke away from one religion to return to another.

Bernard Malamud ANGEL LEVINE (*story*)   **508**

In this story by an acclaimed novelist, a desperate man can scarcely believe his eyes when God finally sends help to him. Why should a person have to believe what is implausible?

James Wright A BLESSING (*poem*)   **520**

A special glimpse of nature has supernatural effects on this poet.

Alan W. Watts SPIRITUAL LIVING   522

> It's not what you do but the way that you do it, according to this popularizer of Zen Buddhist thought.

Additional Writing Topics   529

8. DILEMMAS   531

INSIGHTS: *Konrad Lorenz, Anonymous, Sissela Bok, E. M. For-ster, Woody Allen, Russell Scott, Anna Freud, Fyo-dor Dostoyevski,* The New Yorker   532

Robert Frost THE ROAD NOT TAKEN (*poem*)   536

> The poet looks back on a moment of decision.

Neil Chayet LAW AND MORALITY   538

> A lawyer recounts a case in which what's right and what's legal are not the same.

Leo Rosten HOME IS WHERE TO LEARN
HOW TO HATE   540

> We've got to learn somewhere that anger contributes to our sense of right and wrong, says a leading essayist.

Forum IMAGES OF FEAR   547

> In a panel discussion, widely disagreeing experts examine how to deal with an epidemic of crime in American society.

George Orwell SHOOTING AN ELEPHANT   560

> An incident that might at first seem amusing teaches a young Englishman a lesson about the mutual fear, hatred, and suspicion that a colonial power and a native people feel toward each other.

Tillie Olsen I STAND HERE IRONING (*story*)   568

A working mother who fought off poverty for her family ponders how she might have been a better mother to her troubled daughter.

Jonathan Schell THE CHOICE   577

The nuclear arms race creates a horrifying situation that people do not want to face, but there is no way to avoid the problem.

Robert Jastrow AN END AND A BEGINNING   586

Computers are growing more intelligent than people. It is just a matter of time before they redefine life as we know it.

Additional Writing Topics   592

Appendix: Reading and Writing About Essays, with Reflections on a Sample Essay, E. B. White's "Once More to the Lake"   595

Rhetorical Index   618

Index of Authors and Titles   622

TO STUDENTS

◇

The title of this book, *Life Studies*, alludes to the series of sketches an artist makes of the human figure. Each selection in this book presents a different perspective on the individual in solitude and in society. Taken together, the selections reveal the complexity of the individual in varied and deep connections with other people and also with objects, ideas, and nonhuman things in the natural world. Like the artist's studies, the essays can open up new ideas about your own and other people's experiences. By writing about the topics you can gain a clearer understanding of what you know and who you are, as the artist gains a clearer understanding of his or her subject by sketching it. Grasping what is important about a subject is a creative activity whether you are gazing or reading, for in both kinds of attentiveness you usually discover what you truly see only by trying to express it on paper — by sketching or by writing.

The selections in *Life Studies* examine matters that are probably important to you. They are organized into eight sections, covering our images of ourselves, our family relationships, our love for other people, our behavior in groups, our connection to valued possessions, our aspirations and ambitions, our philosophical theories about life, and our moral dilemmas. Besides offering diverse and fresh perspectives on significant subjects, the readings also present written language of remarkably high quality. Written language is different from spoken language, so it is acquired mainly through extensive reading. The written language is not the spoken "mother tongue" in which we express ourselves easily and directly to others. It is less tied to momentary situations, it is more compact and formal, and it offers a vastly increased vocabulary. In writing we use sentences that are more complex and diversified; even our thinking changes when we take time to develop precisely what we mean. Learning to write originally and effectively requires practice in reading as well as writing. This book guides you in both activities by providing well-written, interesting selections that suggest writing assignments on stimulating topics.

Whether humorous or solemn about their subject, the authors of the selections considered it important to formulate their viewpoint into words. They tried to be precise in their observations, and they seem to find pleasure — sometimes even great delight — in clarifying and sharing their ideas and feelings about the subject. They discover something through writing about it. By drawing on their experience as well as your own, you too can learn to write well.

Life Studies

A THEMATIC READER

PART 1

SELF-IMAGES

Nora Ephron, *Shaping Up Absurd*

Garrison Keillor, *After a Fall*

Mary McCarthy, *Names*

Susan Brownmiller, *The Contrived Postures of Femininity*

Louie Crew, *Thriving as an Outsider*

Joan Didion, *In Bed*

James Thurber, *The Secret Life of Walter Mitty*

Theodore Roethke, *Open House*

John Berger, *The Changing View of Man in the Portrait*

Luis Buñuel, *Memory*

Additional Writing Topics

INSIGHTS

Photographs actively promote nostalgia. Photography is an elegiac art, a twilight art. Most subjects photographed are, just by virtue of being photographed, touched with pathos. An ugly or grotesque subject may be moving because it has been dignified by the attention of the photographer. A beautiful subject can be the object of rueful feelings, because it has aged or decayed or no longer exists. All photographs are *memento mori*. To take a photograph is to participate in another person's (or thing's) mortality, vulnerability, mutability. Precisely by slicing out this moment and freezing it, all photographs testify to time's relentless melt.

— SUSAN SONTAG

◊

The nicknames children bestow on one another can confer power. Like ancient Rome, the playground republic marks off the inner core of citizens from barbarians. Those who have no nicknames have no social existence; they are the nonpeople. . . . To be nicknamed is to be seen as having an attribute that entitles one to social attention, even if that attention is unpleasant. Thus, it may be better to be called "Sewage" than merely John.

— ROM HARRE

◊

I do not know what it is to see into the heart of a friend through that "window of the soul," the eye. I can only "see" through my finger tips the outline of a face. I can detect laughter, sorrow, and many other obvious emotions. I know my friends from the feel of their faces. But I cannot really picture their personalities by touch. I know their personalities, of course, through other means, through the thoughts they express to me, through whatever of their actions are revealed to me. But I am denied that deeper understanding of them which I am sure would come through sight of them, through watching their reactions to various expressed thoughts and circumstances, through noting the immediate and fleeting reactions of their eyes and countenance.

– HELEN KELLER

◊

I'm Nobody! Who are you?
Are you – Nobody – Too?
Then there's a pair of us!
Don't tell! they'd advertise – you know!

How dreary – to be – Somebody!
How public – like a Frog –
To tell one's name – the livelong June –
To an admiring Bog!

– EMILY DICKINSON

◊

Every survey ever held has shown that the image of an attractive woman is the most effective advertising gimmick. She may sit astride the mudguard of a new car, or step into it ablaze with jewels; she may lie at a man's feet stroking his new socks; she may hold the petrol pump in a challenging pose, or dance through woodland glades in slow motion in all the glory of a new shampoo; whatever she does her image sells. The gynolatry of our civilization is written large upon its face, upon hoardings [billboards], cinema screens, television, newspapers, magazines, tins, packets, cartons, bottles, all consecrated to the reigning deity, the female fetish. Her dominion must not be thought to entail the rule of women, for she is not a woman. Her glossy lips and mat complexion, her unfocused eyes and flawless fingers, her extraordinary hair all floating and shining, curling and gleaming, reveal the inhuman triumph of cosmetics, lighting, focusing and printing, cropping and composition. She sleeps unruffled, her lips red and juicy and closed, her eyes as crisp and black as if new painted, and her false lashes immaculately curled. Even when she washes her face with a new and creamier toilet soap her expression is as tranquil and vacant and her paint as flawless as ever. If ever she should appear tousled and troubled, her features are miraculously smoothed to their proper veneer by a new washing powder or a bouillon cube. For she is a doll: weeping, pouting or smiling, running or reclining, she is a doll. She is an idol, formed of the concatenation of lines and masses, signifying the lineaments of satisfied impotence.

Her essential quality is castratedness.

— GERMAINE GREER

◊

This consciousness of self, this capacity to see one's self as though from the outside, is the distinctive characteristic of man. A friend of mine has a dog who waits at his studio door all morning and, when anybody comes to the door, he jumps up and barks, wanting to play. My friend holds that the dog is saying in his barking: "Here is a dog who has been waiting all morning for someone to come to play with him. Are you the one?" This is a nice sentiment, and all of us who like dogs enjoy projecting such cozy thoughts into their heads. But actually this is exactly what the dog cannot say. He can show that he wants to play and entice you into throwing his ball for him, but he cannot stand outside himself and see himself as a dog doing these things. He is not blessed with the consciousness of self.

— ROLLO MAY

◊

To be nobody-but-myself — in a world which is doing its best, night and day, to make you everybody else — means to fight the hardest battle which any human being can fight, and never stop fighting.

— E. E. CUMMINGS

Nora Ephron

SHAPING UP ABSURD*

◊

NORA EPHRON (b. 1941) grew up in Hollywood amid an adult world of screenwriters, entertainers, and celebrities. This background may have had more to do with shaping her self-image than the physical trait of flat-chestedness that she writes about in this essay. She wanted to be a writer, and she began her career as a journalist in New York by writing for *Newsweek* and contributing articles to entertainment magazines. Her essays have been collected in *Wallflower at the Orgy* (1970) and *Crazy Salad* (1975). In this essay Ephron deals frankly with intimate personal experience that is not usually discussed openly. Her candor gives us a view of preadolescent girlhood that is full of humor and sympathy for the young. Furthermore, her observations about her adult experience suggest that people hold very peculiar attitudes, which accounts for some of her personal distress.

I have to begin with a few words about androgyny. In grammar 1 school, in the fifth and sixth grades, we were all tyrannized by a rigid set of rules that supposedly determined whether we were boys or girls. The episode in *Huckleberry Finn* where Huck is disguised as a girl and gives himself away by the way he threads a needle and catches a ball — that kind of thing. We learned that the way you sat, crossed your legs, held a cigarette and looked at your nails, your wristwatch, the way you did these things instinctively was absolute proof of your sex. Now obviously most children did not take this literally, but I did. I thought that just one slip, just one incorrect cross of my legs or flick of an imaginary cigarette ash would turn me from whatever I was into the other thing; that would be all it took, really. Even though I was outwardly a girl and had many of the trappings generally associated

* Editor's title.

7

with the field of girldom — a girl's name, for example, and dresses, my own telephone, an autograph book — I spent the early years of my adolescence absolutely certain that I might at any point gum it up. I did not feel at all like a girl. I was boyish. I was athletic, ambitious, outspoken, competitive, noisy, rambunctious. I had scabs on my knees and my socks slid into my loafers and I could throw a football. I wanted desperately not to be that way, not to be a mixture of both things but instead just one, a girl, a definite indisputable girl. As soft and as pink as a nursery. And nothing would do that for me, I felt, but breasts.

I was about six months younger than everyone in my class, and so 2 for about six months after it began, for six months after my friends had begun to develop — that was the word we used, develop — I was not particularly worried. I would sit in the bathtub and look down at my breasts and know that any day now, any second now, they would start growing like everyone else's. They didn't. "I want to buy a bra," I said to my mother one night. "What for?" she said. My mother was really hateful about bras, and by the time my third sister had gotten to that point where she was ready to want one, my mother had worked the whole business into a comedy routine, "Why not use a Band-Aid instead?" she would say. It was a source of great pride to my mother that she had never even had to wear a brassiere until she had her fourth child, and then only because her gynecologist made her. It was incomprehensible to me that anyone would ever be proud of something like that. It was the 1950's, for God's sake. Jane Russell. Cashmere sweaters. Couldn't my mother see that? "*I am too old to wear an undershirt.*" Screaming. Weeping. Shouting. "Then don't wear an undershirt," said my mother. "But I want to buy a bra." "What for?"

I suppose that for most girls, breasts, brassieres, that entire thing, 3 has more trauma, more to do with the coming of adolescence, of becoming a woman, than anything else. Certainly more than getting your period, although that too was traumatic, symbolic. But you could *see* breasts; they were there; they were visible. Whereas a girl could claim to have her period for months before she actually got it and nobody would ever know the difference. Which is exactly what I did. All you had to do was make a great fuss over having enough nickels for the Kotex machine and walk around clutching your stomach and moaning for three to five days a month about The Curse and you could convince anybody. There is a school of thought somewhere in the women's lib/women's mag/gynecology establishment that claims that menstrual cramps are purely psychological, and I lean toward it. Not that I didn't have them finally. Agonizing cramps, heating-pad cramps, go-down-to-the-school-nurse-and-lie-on-the-cot cramps. But unlike any pain I had ever suffered, I adored the pain of cramps, welcomed it, wallowed in it, bragged about it. "I can't go. I have cramps." "I can't do that. I have cramps." And most of all, gigglingly, blushingly: "I can't swim. I have cramps." Nobody ever used the hard-core word. Menstruation. God, what an awful word. Never that. "I have cramps."

The morning I first got my period, I went into my mother's bed- 4
room to tell her. And my mother, my utterly-hateful-about-bras mother, burst into tears. It was really a lovely moment, and I remember it so clearly not just because it was one of the two times I ever saw my mother cry on my account (the other was when I was caught being a six-year-old kleptomaniac), but also because the incident did not mean to me what it meant to her. Her little girl, her firstborn, had finally become a woman. That was what she was crying about. My reaction to the event, however, was that I might well be a woman in some scientific, textbook sense (and could at least stop faking every month and stop wasting all those nickels). But in another sense — in a visible sense — I was as androgynous and as liable to tip over into boyhood as ever.

I started with a 28AA bra. I don't think they made them any 5
smaller in those days, although I gather that now you can buy bras for five year olds that don't have any cups whatsoever in them; trainer bras they are called. My first brassiere came from Robinson's Department Store in Beverly Hills. I went there alone, shaking, positive they would look me over and smile and tell me to come back next year. An actual fitter took me into the dressing room and stood over me while I took off my blouse and tried the first one on. The little puffs stood out on my chest. "Lean over," said the fitter (to this day I am not sure what fitters in bra departments do except to tell you to lean over). I leaned over, with the fleeting hope that my breasts would miraculously fall out of my body and into the puffs. Nothing.

"Don't worry about it," said my friend Libby some months later, 6
when things had not improved. "You'll get them after you're married."

"What are you talking about?" I said.   7

"When you get married," Libby explained, "your husband will 8
touch your breasts and rub them and kiss them and they'll grow."

That was the killer. Necking I could deal with. Intercourse I could 9
deal with. But it had never crossed my mind that a man was going to
touch my breasts, that breasts had something to do with all that, petting, my God they never mentioned petting in my little sex manual
about the fertilization of the ovum. I became dizzy. For I knew instantly — as naïve as I had been only a moment before — that only
part of what she was saying was true: the touching, rubbing, kissing
part, not the growing part. And I knew that no one would ever want to
marry me. I had no breasts. I would never have breasts.

My best friend in school was Diana Raskob. She lived a block from 10
me in a house full of wonders. English muffins, for instance. The Ras-
kobs were the first people in Beverly Hills to have English muffins for
breakfast. They also had an apricot tree in the back, and a badminton
court, and a subscription to *Seventeen* magazine, and hundreds of
games like Sorry and Parcheesi and Treasure Hunt and Anagrams.
Diana and I spent three or four afternoons a week in their den reading
and playing and eating. Diana's mother's kitchen was full of the most
colossal assortment of junk food I have ever been exposed to. My
house was full of apples and peaches and milk and homemade choco-
late-chip cookies — which were nice, and good for you, but-not-right-
before-dinner-or-you'll-spoil-your-appetite. Diana's house had nothing
in it that was good for you, and what's more, you could stuff it in right
up until dinner and nobody cared. Bar-B-Q potato chips (they were
the first in them, too), giant bottles of ginger ale, fresh popcorn with
melted butter, hot fudge sauce on Baskin-Robbins jamoca ice cream,
powdered-sugar doughnuts from Van de Kamps. Diana and I had
been best friends since we were seven; we were about equally popular
in school (which is to say, not particularly), we had about the same
success with boys (extremely intermittent), and we looked much the
same. Dark. Tall. Gangly.

It is September, just before school begins. I am eleven years old, 11
about to enter the seventh grade, and Diana and I have not seen each
other all summer. I have been to camp and she has been somewhere
like Banff with her parents. We are meeting, as we often do, on the
street midway between our two houses and we will walk back to

Diana's and eat junk and talk about what has happened to each of us that summer. I am walking down Walden Drive in my jeans and my father's shirt hanging out and my old red loafers with the socks falling into them and coming toward me is . . . I take a deep breath . . . a young woman. Diana. Her hair is curled and she has a waist and hips and a bust and she is wearing a straight skirt, an article of clothing I have been repeatedly told I will be unable to wear until I have the hips to hold it up. My jaw drops, and suddenly I am crying, crying hysterically, can't catch my breath sobbing. My best friend has betrayed me. She has gone ahead without me and done it. She has shaped up.

Here are some things I did to help: 12

Bought a Mark Eden Bust Developer. 13

Slept on my back for four years. 14

Splashed cold water on them every night because some French actress said in *Life* magazine that that was what *she* did for her perfect bustline. 15

Ultimately, I resigned myself to a bad toss and began to wear padded bras. I think about them now, think about all those years in high school I went around in them, my three padded bras, every single one of them with different sized breasts. Each time I changed bras I changed sizes: one week nice perky but not too obtrusive breasts, the next medium-sized slightly pointed ones, the next week knockers, true knockers; all the time, whatever size I was, carrying around this rubberized appendage on my chest that occasionally crashed into a wall and was poked inward and had to be poked outward — I think about all that and wonder how anyone kept a straight face through it. My parents, who normally had no restraints about needling me — why did they say nothing as they watched my chest go up and down? My friends, who would periodically inspect my breasts for signs of growth and reassure me — why didn't they at least counsel consistency? 16

And the bathing suits. I die when I think about the bathing suits. That was the era when you could lay an uninhabited bathing suit on the beach and someone would make a pass at it. I would put one on, an absurd swimsuit with its enormous bust built into it, the bones from the suit stabbing me in the rib cage and leaving little red welts on my body, and there I would be, my chest plunging straight downward absolutely vertically from my collarbone to the top of my suit 17 and then suddenly, wham, out came all that padding and material and wiring absolutely horizontally.

Buster Klepper was the first boy who ever touched them. He was 18 my boyfriend my senior year of high school. There is a picture of him in my high-school yearbook that makes him look quite attractive in a Jewish, horn-rimmed glasses sort of way, but the picture does not show the pimples, which were air-brushed out, or the dumbness. Well, that isn't really fair. He wasn't dumb. He just wasn't terribly bright. His mother refused to accept it, refused to accept the relentlessly average report cards, refused to deal with her son's inevitable destiny in some junior college or other. "He was tested," she would say to me, apropos of nothing, "and it came out 145. That's near-genius." Had the word underachiever been coined, she probably would have lobbed that one at me, too. Anyway, Buster was really very sweet — which is, I know, damning with faint praise, but there it is. I was the editor of the front page of the high-school newspaper and he was editor of the back page; we had to work together, side by side, in the print shop, and that was how it started. On our first date, we went to see *April Love* starring Pat Boone. Then we started going together. Buster had a green coupe, a 1950 Ford with an engine he had handchromed until it shone, dazzled, reflected the image of anyone who looked into it, anyone usually being Buster polishing it or the gas-station attendants he constantly asked to check the oil in order for them to be overwhelmed by the sparkle on the valves. The car also had a boot stretched over the back seat for reasons I never understood; hanging from the rearview mirror, as was the custom, was a pair of angora dice. A previous girl friend named Solange who was famous throughout Beverly Hills High School for having no pigment in her right eyebrow had knitted them for him. Buster and I would ride around town, the two of us seated to the left of the steering wheel. I would shift gears. It was nice.

There was necking. Terrific necking. First in the car, overlooking 19 Los Angeles from what is now the Trousdale Estates. Then on the bed of his parents' cabana at Ocean House. Incredibly wonderful, frustrating necking, I loved it, really, but no further than necking, please don't, please, because there I was absolutely terrified of the general implications of going-a-step-further with a near-dummy and also terrified of his finding out there was next to nothing there (which he knew, of course; he wasn't that dumb).

I broke up with him at one point. I think we were apart for about 20 two weeks. At the end of that time I drove down to see a friend at a boarding school in Palos Verdes Estates and a disc jockey played *April Love* on the radio four times during the trip. I took it as a sign. I drove straight back to Griffith Park to a golf tournament Buster was playing in (he was the sixth-seeded teen-age golf player in Southern California) and presented myself back to him on the green of the 18th hole. It was all very dramatic. That night we went to a drive-in and I let him get his hand under my protuberances and onto my breasts. He really didn't seem to mind at all.

"Do you want to marry my son?" the woman asked me.   21
"Yes," I said.   22
I was nineteen years old, a virgin, going with this woman's son, this 23 *big strange woman who was married to a Lutheran minister in New Hampshire and pretended she was Gentile and had this son, by her first husband, this total fool of a son who ran the hero-sandwich concession at Harvard Business School and whom for one moment one December in New Hampshire I said — as much out of politeness as anything else — that I wanted to marry.*
"Fine," she said. "Now, here's what you do. Always make sure 24 *you're on top of him so you won't seem so small. My bust is very large, you see, so I always lie on my back to make it look smaller, but you'll have to be on top most of the time."*
I nodded. "Thank you," I said.   25
"I have a book for you to read," she went on. "Take it with you 26 *when you leave. Keep it." She went to the bookshelf, found it, and gave it to me. It was a book on frigidity.*
"Thank you," I said.   27

That is a true story. Everything in this article is a true story, but I 28 feel I have to point out that that story in particular is true. It happened on December 30, 1960. I think about it often. When it first happened, I naturally assumed that the woman's son, my boyfriend, was responsible. I invented a scenario where he had had a little heart-to-heart with his mother and confessed that his only objection to me was that my breasts were small; his mother then took it upon herself to help out. Now I think I was wrong about the incident. The mother was acting on her own, I think: that was her way of being cruel and competitive under the guise of being helpful and maternal. You have small breasts, she was saying; therefore you will never make him as happy as I have. Or you have small breasts; therefore you will doubt-less have sexual problems. Or you have small breasts; therefore you are less woman than I am. She was, as it happens, only the first of what seems to me to be a never-ending string of women who have made competitive remarks to me about breast size. "I would love to wear a dress like that," my friend Emily says to me, "but my bust is too big." Like that. Why do women say these things to me? Do I attract these remarks the way other women attract married men or alcoholics or ho-mosexuals? This summer, for example. I am at a party in East Hamp-ton and I am introduced to a woman from Washington. She is a minor celebrity, very pretty and Southern and blonde and outspoken and I am flattered because she has read something I have written. We are talking animatedly, we have been talking no more than five min-utes, when a man comes up to join us. "Look at the two of us," the woman says to the man, indicating me and her. "The two of us to-gether couldn't fill an A cup." Why does she say that? It isn't even true, dammit, so why? Is she even more addled than I am on this sub-ject? Does she honestly believe there is something wrong with her size breasts, which, it seems to me, now that I look hard at them, are just right? Do I unconsciously bring out competitiveness in women? In that form? What did I do to deserve it?

As for men.   29

There were men who minded and let me know they minded. There   30 were men who did not mind. In any case, I always minded.

And even now, now that I have been countlessly reassured that my   31 figure is a good one, now that I am grown up enough to understand that most of my feelings have very little to do with the reality of my shape, I am nonetheless obsessed by breasts. I cannot help it. I grew up in the terrible Fifties — with rigid stereotypical sex roles, the insis-tence that men be men and dress like men and women be women and dress like women, the intolerance of androgyny — and I cannot shake it, cannot shake my feelings of inadequacy. Well, that time is gone, right? All those exaggerated examples of breast worship are gone, right? Those women were freaks, right? I know all that. And yet, here I am, stuck with the psychological remains of it all, stuck with my own peculiar version of breast worship. You probably think I am crazy to go on like this: here I have set out to write a confession that is meant to hit you with the shock of recognition and instead you are sitting there thinking I am thoroughly warped. Well, what can I tell you? If I had had them, I would have been a completely different person. I honestly believe that.

After I went into therapy, a process that made it possible for me to   32 tell total strangers at cocktail parties that breasts were the hang-up of my life, I was often told that I was insane to have been bothered by my condition. I was also frequently told, by close friends, that I was extremely boring on the subject. And my girl friends, the ones with nice big breasts, would go on endlessly about how their lives had been far more miserable than mine. Their bra straps were snapped in class. They couldn't sleep on their stomachs. They were stared at whenever the word "mountain" cropped up in geography. And *Evangeline,* good God what they went through every time someone had to stand up and recite the Prologue to Longfellow's *Evangeline: ". . . stand like druids of eld . . . / With beards that rest on their bosoms."* It was much worse for them, they tell me. They had a terrible time of it, they assure me. I don't know how lucky I was, they say.

I have thought about their remarks, tried to put myself in their   33 place, considered their point of view. I think they are full of shit.

CONSIDERATIONS

1. Ephron establishes a very informal, colloquial tone right from the first paragraph. Underline the key words and phrases in the opening paragraph that help set this tone. What is the correlation between this tone of voice and the subject of her essay?
2. As a child Ephron felt sure that her every distress would lead to a large, fateful disaster. In addition to her flat-chestedness, what else does she worry over? How does she express these worries?
3. What is the point of the section about her friend Diana? Does her name fit the effect that she has on Ephron? Similarly, what is the point of the section about Buster Klepper? And what are the connotations of his name? Did they fit his effect on her?
4. Both Nora Ephron and Mary McCarthy (see the third essay in this chapter, p. 26) suffered mortifications in their girlhood that they say affected their adult character. Compare the kinds of humiliation they endured. What were the aspirations that made each girl feel dissatisfied with herself?

5. WRITING TOPIC. Near the end of the essay, Ephron says, "If I had had them, I would have been a completely different person. I honestly believe that." Being unusually tall or short, thin or fat, red-haired, freckled, pretty, or thoroughly average, can seem to be the most important fact in your existence. Write a 500-word essay on how one trait came to have exaggerated importance for some period in your life.

Garrison Keillor

AFTER A FALL

◊

GARRISON KEILLOR (b. 1942) has worked in radio broadcasting in Minnesota since his first job as an announcer for the college radio station at the University of Minnesota. Now broadcasting from St. Paul, Keillor is best known as the host of "A Prairie Home Companion," the Peabody Award-winning radio show that he originated in 1974 for Minnesota Public Radio and continued from 1980 on National Public Radio. Keillor's program of bluegrass and folk music, country anecdotes and down-home whimsy, features a weekly segment on the happenings in the imaginary town of Lake Wobegon, Minnesota. A collection of these tales, *Lake Wobegon Days*, was published in 1985. While not all Keillor's stories and sketches are set in the Midwest, they generally deal with people who have direct and simple good natures, but whose lives nevertheless become humorously complicated. His fiction and other comic pieces were published in *Happy To Be Here* (1982). Most of those works appeared first in *The New Yorker*, where the following sketch also first appeared. In this piece he considers the ups and downs of a comic's oldest, most basic ploy to win a laugh: the pratfall. Taking a fall becomes an image of much of what we experience in life.

When you happen to step off an edge you didn't see and lurch 1 forward into space waving your arms, it's the end of the world for a second or two, and after you do land, even if you know you're O.K. and no bones are broken it may take a few seconds to decide whether this is funny or not. Your body is still worked up about the fall — especially the nervous system and the adrenaline-producing areas. In fact, I am *still* a little shaky from a spill that occurred two hours ago, when I put on a jacket, walked out the front door of this house here in St. Paul, Minnesota, and for no reason whatever took a plunge down five steps and landed on the sidewalk flat on my back with my legs in the air. I am thirty-nine years old and in fairly good shape, not prone to blackouts or sudden dizziness, and so a sudden inexplicable fall comes as a big surprise to me.

A woman who was jogging down the street — a short, muscular 2 young woman in a gray sweatshirt and sweatpants — stopped and asked if I was O.K. "Yeah! Fine!" I said and got right up. "I just fell, I guess," I said. "Thanks," I said. She smiled and trotted away.

Her smile has followed me into the house, and I see it now as a 3 smirk, which is what it was. She was too polite to bend over and hoot and shriek and guffaw and cackle and cough and whoop and wheeze and slap her thighs and stomp on the ground, but it was all there in the smile: a young woman who through rigorous physical training and feminist thinking has gradually been taking charge of her own life and ridding her attic of self-hatred and doubt and fear and mindless competitiveness and other artifacts of male-dominated culture is rewarded with the sight of a middle-aged man in a brown suit with a striped tie falling down some steps as if someone had kicked him in the pants.

I'm sorry if I don't consider this humorous. I would like to. I wish 4 she had come over and helped me up and then perhaps sat on the steps with me while I calmed down. We might have got to talking about the fall and how each of us viewed it from a different perspective; that she perceived it as symbolic political theater, whereas I saw it as something that was actually happening to me at the time. She might have admitted that when she saw me emerge from the house she immediately thought, He earns sixty thousand a year, his secretary earns twelve thousand, and once a year he takes her out to lunch and tells her how much he sympathizes with the women's movement and what a liberating influence it has had on him personally. I might have understood that the sight of a tall man in a suit folding up and waving his arms and falling helplessly and landing flat on his back was the punch line of a joke she had been carrying around with her for a long time.

I might have seen it her way, but she ran down the street, and now 5 I can only see my side of the fall. I feel old and achy and ridiculous and cheapened by the whole experience. I understand now why my son was so angry with me a few months ago when he tripped on a shoelace and fell in the neighbor's yard — a yard where the neighbor's sheepdog had lived for years — and I cackled at him.

"It's not funny!" he yelled.   6

"Oh, don't be so sensitive," I said.   7

Don't be so sensitive! What a dumb thing to say! Who has the 8 right to tell someone else how to feel? It is the right of the person who falls on the dog droppings to decide for himself or herself how he or she will feel. It's not up to a jury. The fallen person determines whether it's funny or not.

My son and I are both tall fellows, and I suppose tall people are the 9 funniest to see fall, because we try so hard not to. We work hard for our dignity, trying to keep that beanpole straight, keep those daddy longlegs coordinated, keep those big boats from tangling with each other. From a chair through a crowded room to the buffet dinner and back to the chair with a loaded plate is a long route for a tall fellow — a route we have to study for tricky corners and edges, low doorways, light fixtures, rug wrinkles, and other low-lying obstacles that we, being tall, don't see at a glance. A tall fellow has got his hands full on a maneuver like that. He is pulling strings attached to all his joints, knowing that if he lets himself go or makes a mistake, it's a long way down.

Short, compact persons can trip and recover their balance quickly, 10 maybe even turn that stumble into a casual Twyla Tharp-type dance move or a Buster Keaton fall, but when tall fellows stumble they go down like cut timber. We're not like Walter Payton, of the Chicago Bears, who bounces right up from the turf when he's tackled. We're more like the tall trees in the National Basketball Association. When they fall, usually there's ligament damage or torn cartilage; the stretcher crew runs onto the floor, and the crowd applauds sympathetically as the debris is stacked and carried away. "The knee feels good," the tree says six months later. "I am lifting weights with it, and I am now almost able to bend over," but he knows that his pro tree career is done gone, that he has begun a new career as a guy who hurts a lot.

All that can happen in one quick fall, and so a tall fellow is cautious 11 when he threads his way through the party to reload his plate with spareribs. One misstep and down he goes, to the vast amusement of all present, who don't realize that he has wrenched something in his back and will be in a body cast for months and not be so good a friend again. Only a tall fellow knows how major his fall might be.

Five years ago, I got on a bus with five musicians and rode around 12 for two weeks doing shows every night. They played music; I told jokes and sang a song. One night, in the cafeteria of a junior college in southern Minnesota, we happened to draw a big crowd, and the stage — four big plywood sheets on three-foot steel legs — was moved back twenty feet to make room for more chairs. The show was late starting, the room was stuffy, the crowd was impatient, and when finally the lights dimmed and the spotlight shone on the plywood, I broke from the back door and made a run for the stage, thinking to make a dramatic entrance and give these fine people the show they were waiting for.

What I could not see in the dark was the ceiling and a low con- 13 crete overhang that the stage had been moved partly under, and then the spotlight caught me straight in the eyes and I couldn't see anything. I leaped up onto the stage, and in mid-leap my head hit concrete and my right leg caught the plywood at mid-shin. I toppled forward, stuck out my hands, and landed on my hands and knees. The crowd drew a long breath. I got right up — I had been doing shows long enough to know not to lie onstage and cry in front of a paying audience — and, seeing the microphone about ten feet ahead, strode up to it and held out my arms and said, "Hello, everybody! I'm happy to be here!"

Then they laughed — a big thunderstorm of a laugh and a big 14 round of applause for what they now saw had been a wonderful trick. But it wasn't funny! My neck hurt! I hurt all over! On the other hand, to see a tall man in a white suit jump directly into a ceiling and then fall down — how often does a person get to see that? Men dive off high towers through fiery hoops into tiny tanks, men rev up motorcycles and leap long rows of trucks and buses, but I am the only man in show business who takes a good run and jumps Straight Up Into Solid Concrete Using Only His Bare Head. Amazing!

Let's see that once more in slow motion: 15

Me in the hallway saying, "Now?" Stage manager saying, "Not 16 yet, not yet," then, "O.K., *now*." He opens door, I take two steps, see bright circle of light on stage, take five long running strides. In mid-run, the circle moves, man is blinded by the light, looks for edge of stage, then leaps — pushing off with left foot, right leg extended. Head hits concrete, stopping upward motion. Forward momentum carries body onto stage but right leg fails to clear plywood. Body falls, lands on hands and knees, stands up — like a dropped puppet picked up by puppeteer — walks forward, speaks. *Laughter & applause.*

Looking at this footage one more time, you can see how hard this poor guy hit. The head jerks, the eyes squeeze shut, the hands fly up like birds, the body shudders.

Look now as the tall fellow who has had a load of bricks dropped 17 on his head starts singing. It's a song he has sung for years and knows by heart, so it doesn't matter that he is senseless; these lyrics are stored not in his head but at the lower end of the spinal cord. "Hello, hello, it's time for the show! We're all dressed up and rarin' to go!" But his eyes are glazed, and it's clear that something is terribly wrong. Stop the show! This man is hurt! Is there a doctor in the house? This fellow may have broken his neck! Friends, this entertainer who always gave you everything he had has now given you too much. His life is now shattered, owing to one last effort to jump head first into a ceiling for your pleasure and amazement.

> — You've now seen in slow motion the play that led to the injury that so tragically ended your career. Tell us in your own words, if you can, what goes through your mind as you see yourself jump into the ceiling.
> — Howard, I've tried to put all that behind me. I have no hard feelings toward the guy who moved the stage or the audience that laughed — they were only doing their job. Right now my job is to regain my sense of humor and go back to work. I feel like I'm making real good progress. Howard, I consider myself to be one lucky guy.

Oh, it is a sad story, except for the fact that it isn't. My ceiling 18 jump got the show off to a great start. The band played three fast tunes, and I jumped carefully back onstage and did a monologue that the audience, which now *knew* I was funny, laughed at a lot. Even I, who had a headache, thought it was funny. I really did feel lucky.

So do I still — a tall man who fell now sitting down to write his 19 memoirs. The body is so delicate, the skeleton so skinny; we are stick men pencilled in lightly, with a wooden stick cage to protect the heart and lungs and a cap of bone over the brain. I wonder that I have survived so many plunges, so many quick drops down the short arc that leads to the ground.

The Haymow Header of 1949: Was playing in Uncle Jim's hay- 20 mow and fell through a hole, landing in the bull's feed trough, barely missing the stanchion, and was carried into the house, where Grandma put brown paper on my head. *The Milk Jar Mishap of 1951:* Tripped on the cellar steps while carrying two gallon glass jars full of milk from the grocery, dropped the jars (which broke), and then landed on them but didn't cut myself. Went to my room and cried. My dad said, "That's all right, it doesn't matter." But it did matter. I had ruined us — my poor family! A week's worth of milk gone bust, and it was my fault. *Miscellaneous Bike Bowls, 1954 —* : Biking no-handed. Going over the bike jump. Going down a steep hill and hitting loose gravel. Practicing bike skids. Swerving to avoid a dog. *The Freshman Composition Class Collapse of 1960:* After staying up all night to write an essay on a personal experience, rose in Mr. Cody's class to read it, blacked out, and fell on top of people sitting in front of me. Got up and went home. *Miscellaneous Sports Spills:* Basketball collision that dislocated left elbow in 1961. Skating, skiing, tobogganing. Two memorable outfield collisions, after one of which a spectator said she could hear our heads hit two hundred and fifty feet away.

Falls of Fatherhood: Walking across the room, thinking long-range 21 thoughts. Suddenly there's an infant at my feet, whom I am just about to step on! And instantly I lift the foot and dive forward, sometimes catching myself short of a fall and sometimes doing a half gainer into the furniture. (I also fall for cats.) *The Great Ladder Leap of 1971:* Climbing up to install a second-story storm window, felt the extension ladder slip to one side, dropped the window and jumped, landing in a flower bed, barely missing my two-year-old boy standing nearby. *Dreams of Falls:* Too numerous, too common, to mention. Always drawn toward the edge by some powerful force, tumble through space, then wake up and go get a glass of water.

The first time I ever went naked in mixed company was at the 22 house of a girl whose father had a bad back and had built himself a sauna in the corner of the basement. Donna and I were friends in college. Both of us had grown up in fundamentalist Christian homes, and we liked to compare notes on that. We both felt constricted by our upbringings and were intent on liberating ourselves and becoming more free and open and natural. So it seemed natural, and inevitable one night to wind up at her house with some of her friends there and her parents gone and to take off our clothes and have a sauna.

We were nineteen years old and were very cool ("Take off my 23 clothes? Well, sure. Heck, I've taken them off *dozens* of times") and were careful to keep cool and be nonchalant and not look at anybody below the neck. We got into the sauna as if getting on the bus. *People do this*, I thought to myself. *There is nothing unusual about it! Nothing! We all have bodies! There is no reason to get excited! This is a normal part of life!*

We filed into the little wooden room, all six of us, avoiding unnec- 24 essary body contact, and Donna poured a bucket of water on the hot rocks to make steam. It was very quiet. "There's a shower there on the wall if you want to take a shower," she said in a strange, nervous voice.

"Hey! How about a shower!" a guy said in a cool-guy voice, and he 25 turned on the water full blast. The shower head leaped from the wall. It was a hand-held type — a nozzle at the end of a hose — and it jumped out at us like a snake and thrashed around exploding ice-cold water. He fell back, someone screamed, I slipped and fell, Donna fell on top of me, we leaped apart, and meanwhile the nozzle danced and flew from the force of the blast of water. Donna ran out of the sauna and slipped and fell on the laundry-room floor, and another girl yelled, "God damn you, Tom!" Donna scrambled to her feet. "God! Oh, God!" she cried. Tom yelled, "I'm sorry!" Another guy laughed a loud, wicked laugh, and I tiptoed out as fast as I could move, grabbed my clothes, and got dressed. Donna grabbed her clothes. "Are you all right?" I said, not looking at her or anything. "No!" she said. Somebody laughed a warm, appreciative laugh from inside the sauna. "Don't laugh!" she yelled. "It isn't funny! It isn't the least bit funny!"

"I'm *not* laughing," I said, though it wasn't me she was angry at. I 26 *still* am not laughing. I think it's a very serious matter, twenty years later. Your first venture as a naked person, you want it to go right and be a good experience, and then some joker has to go pull a fast one.

All I can say is, it's over now, Donna. Don't let it warp your life. 27 We were young. We meant well. We wanted to be natural and free. It didn't mean we were awful. God didn't turn on the cold water to punish us for taking off our clothes — Tom did, and he didn't mean it, either. It was twenty years ago. Let's try to forget it. Write me a letter and let me know how you're doing. I would like to hear that you're doing well, as I am, and that our night of carnal surprise did you no lasting harm. Life is so wonderful, Donna. I remember once, after I lost track of you, I ran on the dock of a summer camp where I worked as a counsellor — ran and slipped on the wet boards and did a backward half somersault in the air and instead of hitting the dock and suffering permanent injury I landed clean in the water head first and got water up my nose and came up sneezing and choking, but *I was all right,* and is that so surprising? It was luck, I suppose, but then two-thirds of the earth's surface is water, so our chances are not so bad, and when you add in the amount of soft ground, bushes, and cushions in the world and the amazingly quick reactions of the body to protect itself, I think the odds of comedy are better than ever. God writes a lot of comedy, Donna; the trouble is, He's stuck with so many bad actors who don't know how to play funny. When I dropped the window off that falling ladder back in 1971, I didn't know that my son had come around the corner of the house and was standing at the foot of the ladder watching me. The window hit the ground and burst, the ladder hit the ground and bounced, and his father landed face first in the chrysanthemums; all three missed him by a few feet. Quite a spectacle for a little boy to see up close, and he laughed out loud and clapped his hands. I moved my arms to make sure they weren't broken into little pieces, and I clapped, too. Hurray for God! So many fiction writers nowadays would have sent the window down on that boy's head as if it were on a pulley and the rope were around his neck, but God let three heavy objects fall at his feet and not so much as scratch him. He laughed to see me and I laughed to see him. He was all right and I wasn't so bad myself.

I haven't seen you since that night, Donna. I've told the sauna 28 story to dozens of people over the years, and they all thought it was funny, but I still don't know what you think. Are you all right?

CONSIDERATIONS

1. In the first few paragraphs, how does Keillor's tone of voice affect our impression of his size? What sort of person does he appear to be? Find phrases and passages that suggest this impression.
2. What is the author's point in the many contrasts between short and tall people? What usual notions about their strengths and weaknesses does he reverse?
3. How many times does he recount his accident during the college show? How do his reactions differ in each "take" of the experience?
4. During the confusion in the sauna, "somebody laughed a warm, appreciative laugh from inside the sauna." How does that response differ from the reactions of the others? How does it differ from young Keillor's at that time?

5. Sum up the author's attitude about maintaining a sense of humor in life. Avoid clichés and commonplaces by trying to state why the author values humor.

6. WRITING TOPIC. In 700 words, describe and explain someone's humorous response to an event or situation that you did not find humorous at the time, clearly differentiating your response from the reaction of the other person. Was the humor appropriate or inappropriate to the situation? What signs of fear, sympathy, embarrassment, or hostility were evident in specific details of the different responses? If your present attitude toward the event has changed, be sure you fully explain the reasons for both your earlier and your later views.

Mary McCarthy

NAMES

◊

MARY MCCARTHY (b. 1912) writes sophisticated, satirical fiction
about college life and young womanhood, such as *The Company She
Keeps* (1942), *The Groves of Academe* (1952), and *The Group* (1963).
She has also written penetrating social criticism and political reportage
in books about the Vietnam war and the Watergate coverup. Educated
at Vassar, she undertook a career in journalism in New York before
turning to fiction writing and to mixing memories and fiction together
in her memoirs. In this chapter from her *Memories of a Catholic Girlhood* (1957), she recalls the importance she attached to names, especially after she moved back from Minneapolis to Seattle, where as an
orphan she was raised by her grandparents. She implies that the early
difficulties of dealing with her names influenced her adult character.

Anna Lyons, Mary Louise Lyons, Mary von Phul, Emilie von Phul, 1
Eugenia McLellan, Marjorie McPhail, Marie-Louise L'Abbé, Mary
Danz, Julia Dodge, Mary Fordyce Blake, Janet Preston — these were
the names (I can still tell them over like a rosary) of some of the older
girls in the convent: the Virtues and Graces. The virtuous ones wore
wide blue or green moire good-conduct ribbons, bandoleer-style,
across their blue serge uniforms; the beautiful ones wore rouge and
powder or at least were reputed to do so. Our class, the eighth grade,
wore pink ribbons (I never got one myself) and had names like Patri-
cia ("Pat") Sullivan, Eileen Donohoe, and Joan Kane. We were inele-
gant even in this respect; the best name we could show, among us,
was Phyllis ("Phil") Chatham, who boasted that her father's name,
Ralph, was pronounced "Rafe" as in England.

Names had a great importance for us in the convent, and foreign 2
names, French, German, or plain English (which, to us, were foreign,
because of their Protestant sound), bloomed like prize roses among a

26

collection of spuds. Irish names were too common in the school to have any prestige either as surnames (Gallagher, Sheehan, Finn, Sullivan, McCarthy) or as Christian names (Kathleen, Eileen). Anything exotic had value: an "olive"complexion, for example. The pet girl of the convent was a fragile Jewish girl named Susie Lowenstein, who had pale red-gold hair and an exquisite retroussé nose, which, if we had had it, might have been called "pug." We liked her name too and the name of a child in the primary grades: Abbie Stuart Baillargeon. My favorite name, on the whole, though, was Emilie von Phul (pronounced "Pool"); her oldest sister, recently graduated, was called Celeste. Another name that appealed to me was Genevieve Albers, Saint Genevieve being the patron saint of Paris who turned back Attila from the gates of the city.

All these names reflected the still-pioneer character of the Pacific ₃ Northwest. I had never heard their like in the parochial school in Minneapolis, where "foreign" extraction, in any case, was something to be ashamed of, the whole drive being toward Americanization of first name and surname alike. The exceptions to this were the Irish, who could vaunt such names as Catherine O'Dea and the name of my second cousin, Mary Catherine Anne Rose Violet McCarthy, while an unfortunate German boy named Manfred was made to suffer for his. But that was Minneapolis. In Seattle, and especially in the convent of the Ladies of the Sacred Heart, foreign names suggested not immigration but emigration — distinguished exile. Minneapolis was a granary; Seattle was a port, which had attracted a veritable Foreign Legion of adventurers — soldiers of fortune, younger sons, gamblers, traders, drawn by the fortunes to be made in virgin timber and shipping and by the Alaska Gold Rush. Wars and revolutions had sent the defeated out to Puget Sound, to start a new life; the latest had been the Russian Revolution, which had shipped us, via Harbin, a Russian colony, complete with restaurant, on Queen Anne Hill. The English names in the convent, when they did not testify to direct English origin, as in the case of "Rafe" Chatham, had come to us from the South and represented a kind of internal exile; such girls as Mary Fordyce Blake and Mary McQueen Street (a class ahead of me; her sister was named Francesca) bore their double-barreled first names like titles of aristocracy from the ante-bellum South. Not all our girls, by any means, were Catholic; some of the very prettiest ones — Julia Dodge and Janet Preston, if I remember rightly — were Protestants. The nuns had taught us to behave with special courtesy to these strangers in our midst, and the whole effect was of some superior hostel for refugees of all the lost causes of the past hundred years. Money could not count for much in such an atmosphere; the fathers and grandfathers of many of our "best" girls were ruined men.

Names, often, were freakish in the Pacific Northwest, particularly 4 girls' names. In the Episcopal boarding school I went to later, in Tacoma, there was a girl called De Vere Utter, and there was a girl called Rocena and another called Hermonie. Was Rocena a mistake for Rowena and Hermonie for Hermione? And was Vere, as we called her, Lady Clara Vere de Vere? Probably. You do not hear names like those often, in any case, east of the Cascade Mountains; they belong to the frontier, where books and libraries were few and memory seems to have been oral, as in the time of Homer.

Names have more significance for Catholics than they do for other 5 people; Christian names are chosen for the spiritual qualities of the saints they are taken from; Protestants used to name their children out of the Old Testament and now they name them out of novels and plays, whose heroes and heroines are perhaps the new patron saints of a secular age. But with Catholics it is different. The saint a child is named for is supposed to serve, literally, as a model or pattern to imitate; your name is your fortune and it tells you what you are or must be. Catholic children ponder their names for a mystic meaning, like birthstones; my own, I learned, besides belonging to the Virgin and Saint Mary of Egypt, originally meant "bitter" or "star of the sea." My second name, Thérèse, could dedicate me either to Saint Theresa or to the saint called the Little Flower, Soeur Thérèse of Lisieux, on whom God was supposed to have descended in the form of a shower of roses. At Confirmation, I had added a third name (for Catholics then rename themselves, as most nuns do, yet another time, when they take orders); on the advice of a nun, I had taken "Clementina," after Saint Clement, an early pope — a step I soon regretted on account of "My Darling Clementine" and her number nine shoes. By the time I was in the convent, I would no longer tell anyone what my Confirmation name was. The name I had nearly picked was "Agnes," after a little Roman virgin martyr, always shown with a lamb, because of her purity. But Agnes would have been just as bad, I recognized in Forest Ridge Convent — not only because of the possibility of

"Aggie," but because it was subtly, indefinably *wrong* in itself. Agnes would have made me look like an ass.

The fear of appearing ridiculous first entered my life, as a governing 6 motive, during my second year in the convent. Up to then, a desire for prominence had decided many of my actions and, in fact, still persisted. But in the eighth grade, I became aware of mockery and perceived that I could not seek prominence without attracting laughter. Other people could, but I couldn't. This laughter was proceeding, not from my classmates, but from the girls of the class just above me, in particular from two boon companions. Elinor Heffernan and Mary Harty, a clownish pair — oddly assorted in size and shape, as teams of clowns generally are, one short, plump, and baby-faced, the other tall, lean, and owlish — who entertained the high-school department by calling attention to the oddities of the younger girls. Nearly every school has such a pair of satirists, whose marks are generally low and who are tolerated just because of their laziness and non-conformity; one of them (in this case, Mary Harty, the plump one) usually appears to be half asleep. Because of their low standing, their indifference to appearances, the sad state of their uniforms, their clowning is taken to be harmless, which, on the whole, it is, their object being not to wound but to divert; such girls are bored in school. We in the eighth grade sat directly in front of the two wits in study hall, so that they had us under close observation; yet at first I was not afraid of them, wanting, if anything, to identify myself with their laughter, to be initiated into the joke. One of their specialties was giving people nicknames, and it was considered an honor to be the first in the eighth grade to be let in by Elinor and Mary on their latest invention. This often happened to me; they would tell me, on the playground, and I would tell the others. As their intermediary, I felt myself almost their friend and it did not occur to me that I might be next on their list.

I had achieved prominence not long before by publicly losing my 7 faith and regaining it at the end of a retreat. I believe Elinor and Mary questioned me about this on the playground, during recess, and listened with serious, respectful faces while I told them about my conversations with the Jesuits. Those serious faces ought to have been an omen, but if the two girls used what I had revealed to make fun of me, it must have been behind my back. I never heard any more of it, and yet just at this time I began to feel something, like a cold breath on

the nape of my neck, that made me wonder whether the new position
I had won for myself in the convent was as secure as I imagined. I
would turn around in study hall and find the two girls looking at me
with speculation in their eyes.

It was just at this time, too, that I found myself in a perfectly ab- 8
surd situation, a very private one, which made me live, from month to
month, in horror of discovery. I had waked up one morning, in my
convent room, to find a few small spots of blood on my sheet; I had
somehow scratched a trifling cut on one of my legs and opened it during the night. I wondered what to do about this, for the nuns were
fussy about bedmaking, as they were about our white collars and cuffs,
and if we had an inspection those spots might count against me. It
was best, I decided, to ask the nun on dormitory duty, tall, stout
Mother Slattery, for a clean bottom sheet, even though she might
scold me for having scratched my leg in my sleep and order me to cut
my toenails. You never know what you might be blamed for. But
Mother Slattery, when she bustled in to look at the sheet, did not
scold me at all; indeed, she hardly seemed to be listening as I explained to her about the cut. She told me to sit down: she would be
back in a minute. "You can be excused from athletics today," she
added, closing the door. As I waited, I considered this remark, which
seemed to me strangely munificent, in view of the unimportance of
the cut. In a moment, she returned, but without the sheet. Instead,
she produced out of her big pocket a sort of cloth girdle and a peculiar
flannel object which I first took to be a bandage, and I began to protest that I did not need or want a bandage; all I needed was a bottom
sheet. "The sheet can wait," said Mother Slattery, succinctly, handing me two large safety pins. It was the pins that abruptly enlightened
me; I saw Mother Slattery's mistake, even as she was instructing me as
to how this flannel article, which I now understood to be a sanitary
napkin, was to be put on.

"Oh, no, Mother," I said, feeling somewhat embarrassed. "You 9
don't understand. It's just a little cut, on my leg." But Mother, again,
was not listening; she appeared to have grown deaf, as the nuns had a
habit of doing when what you were saying did not fit in with their
ideas. And now that I knew what was in her mind, I was conscious of
a funny constraint; I did not feel it proper to name a natural process,
in so many words, to a nun. It was like trying not to think of their
going to the bathroom or trying not to see the straggling iron-gray hair

coming out of their coifs (the common notion that they shaved their heads was false). On the whole, it seemed better just to show her my cut. But when I offered to do so and unfastened my black stocking, she only glanced at my leg, cursorily. "That's only a scratch, dear," she said. "Now hurry up and put this on or you'll be late for chapel. Have you any pain?" "No, no, Mother!" I cried. "You don't understand!" "Yes, yes, I understand," she replied soothingly, "and you will too, a little later. Mother Superior will tell you about it some time during the morning. There's nothing to be afraid of. You have become a woman."

"I know all about that," I persisted. "Mother, please listen. I just 10 cut my leg. On the athletic field. Yesterday afternoon." But the more excited I grew, the more soothing, and yet firm, Mother Slattery became. There seemed to be nothing for it but to give up and do as I was bid. I was in the grip of a higher authority, which almost had the power to persuade me that it was right and I was wrong. But of course I was not wrong; that would have been too good to be true. While Mother Slattery waited, just outside my door, I miserably donned the equipment she had given me, for there was no place to hide it, on account of drawer inspection. She led me down the hall to where there was a chute and explained how I was to dispose of the flannel thing, by dropping it down the chute into the laundry. (The convent arrangements were very old-fashioned, dating back, no doubt, to the days of Louis Philippe.)

The Mother Superior, Madame MacIllvra, was a sensible woman, 11 and all through my early morning classes, I was on pins and needles, chafing for the promised interview with her which I trusted would clear things up. "*Ma Mère*," I would begin, "Mother Slattery thinks. . . ." Then I would tell her about the cut and the athletic field. But precisely the same impasse confronted me when I was summoned to her office at recess-time. *I* talked about my cut, and *she* talked about becoming a woman. It was rather like a round, in which she was singing "Scotland's burning, Scotland's burning," and I was singing "Pour on water, pour on water." Neither of us could hear the other, or, rather, I could hear her, but she could not hear me. Owing to our different positions in the convent she was free to interrupt me, whereas I was expected to remain silent until she had finished speaking. When I kept breaking in, she hushed me, gently, and took me on her lap. Exactly like Mother Slattery, she attributed all my references to the cut to a blind fear of this new, unexpected reality that had supposedly entered my life. Many young girls, she reassured me, were frightened if they had not been prepared. "And you, Mary, have lost your dear mother, who could have made this easier for you." Rocked on Madame MacIllvra's lap, I felt paralysis overtake me and I lay, mutely listening, against her bosom, my face being tickled by her white, starched, fluted wimple, while she explained to me how babies were born, all of which I had heard before.

There was no use fighting the convent. I had to pretend to have 12 become a woman, just as, not long before, I had had to pretend to get my faith back — for the sake of peace. This pretense was decidedly awkward. For fear of being found out by the lay sisters downstairs in the laundry (no doubt an imaginary contingency, but the convent was so very thorough), I reopened the cut on my leg, so as to draw a little blood to stain the napkins, which were issued me regularly, not only on this occasion, but every twenty-eight days thereafter. Eventually, I abandoned this bloodletting, for fear of lockjaw, and trusted to fate. Yet I was in awful dread of detection; my only hope, as I saw it, was either to be released from the convent or to become a woman in reality, which might take a year at least, since I was only twelve. Getting out of athletics once a month was not sufficient compensation for the farce I was going through. It was not my fault; they had forced me into it; nevertheless, it was I who would look silly — worse than silly; half mad — if the truth ever came to light.

I was burdened with this guilt and shame when the nickname fi- 13 nally found me out. "Found me out," in a general sense, for no one ever did learn the particular secret I bore about with me, pinned to the linen band. "We've got a name for you," Elinor and Mary called out to me, one day on the playground. "What is it?" I asked half hoping, half fearing, since not all their sobriquets were unfavorable. "Cye," they answered, looking at each other and laughing. "Si?" I repeated, supposing that it was based on Simple Simon. Did they regard me as a hick? "C.Y.E.," they elucidated, spelling it out in chorus. "The letters stand for something. Can you guess?" I could not and I cannot now. The closest I could come to it in the convent was "Clean Your Ears." Perhaps that was it, though in later life I have wondered whether it did not stand, simply, for "Clever Young Egg" or "Champion Young Eccentric." But in the convent I was certain that it stood for something horrible, something even worse than dirty ears (as far as

I knew, my ears were clean), something I could never guess because it represented some aspect of myself that the world could see and I couldn't, like a sign pinned on my back. Everyone in the convent must have known what the letters stood for, but no one would tell me. Elinor and Mary had made them promise. It was like halitosis; not even my best friend, my deskmate, Louise, would tell me, no matter how much I pleaded. Yet everyone assured me that it was "very good," that is, very apt. And it made everyone laugh.

This name reduced all my pretensions and solidified my sense of 14 *wrongness*. Just as I felt I was beginning to belong to the convent, it turned me into an outsider, since I was the only pupil who was not in the know. I liked the convent, but it did not like me, as people say of certain foods that disagree with them. By this, I do not mean that I was actively unpopular, either with the pupils or with the nuns. The Mother Superior cried when I left and predicted that I would be a novelist, which surprised me. And I had finally made friends; even Emilie von Phul smiled upon me softly out of her bright blue eyes from the far end of the study hall. It was just that I did not fit into the convent pattern; the simplest thing I did, like asking for a clean sheet, entrapped me in consequences that I never could have predicted. I was not bad; I did not consciously break the rules; and yet I could never, not even for a week, get a pink ribbon, and this was something I could not understand, because I was trying as hard as I could. It was the same case as with the hated name; the nuns, evidently, saw something about me that was invisible to me.

The oddest part was all that pretending. There I was, a walking 15 mass of lies, pretending to be a Catholic and going to confession while really I had lost my faith, and pretending to have monthly periods by cutting myself with nail scissors; yet all this had come about without my volition and even contrary to it. But the basest pretense I was driven to was the acceptance of the nickname. Yet what else could I do? In the convent, I could not live it down. To all those girls, I had become "Cye McCarthy." That was who I was. That was how I had to identify myself when telephoning my friends during vacations to ask them to the movies: "Hello, this is Cye." I loathed myself when I said it, and yet I succumbed to the name totally, making myself over into a sort of hearty to go with it — the kind of girl I hated. "Cye" was my new patron saint. This false personality stuck to me, like the name, when I entered public high school, the next fall, as a freshman, having finally persuaded my grandparents to take me out of the convent, although they could never get to the bottom of my reasons, since, as I admitted, the nuns were kind, and I had made many nice new friends. What I wanted was a fresh start, a chance to begin life over again, but the first thing I heard in the corridors of the public high school was that name called out to me, like the warmest of welcomes: "Hi, there, Si!" That was the way they thought it was spelled. But this time I was resolute. After the first weeks, I dropped the hearties who called me "Si"and I never heard it again. I got my own name back and sloughed off Clementina and even Therese — the names that did not seem to me any more to be mine but to have been imposed on me by others. And I preferred to think that Mary meant "bitter" rather than "star of the sea."

CONSIDERATIONS

1. The first paragraph develops two pairs of contrasts: one between two sets of names and another between two sets of girls. What is the correlation between this structure and the main point of the paragraph?
2. How are the mistakes about the author's supposed first menstruation connected to the principal subject of names in this essay?
3. According to McCarthy, names exercise special powers over people's lives in the adult world of religion and society. She further demonstrates that names and nicknames also wield special powers in the children's world of school. To what different purposes do adults and children use the powers of names?
4. What influences did McCarthy's own various names have over her? How well did she accept or reject their powers?
5. WRITING TOPIC. What sort of a child is McCarthy in this essay? Think of three adjectives that describe her personality and then write a 400-word character sketch that presents your view of her as a child.
6. WRITING TOPIC. As a child did you ever create an imaginary name for yourself? If so, write a 700-word essay explaining its attractions and its advantages over your given name. How did you secretly, or openly, make use of your self-chosen name?

Susan Brownmiller

THE CONTRIVED POSTURES OF FEMININITY

◊

SUSAN BROWNMILLER (b. 1935) attended Cornell University before
returning to New York City, her birthplace, and worked as an actress, a
newswriter, and a news editor for *Newsweek, The Village Voice,* and
ABC-TV. In the 1960s she became active in feminism, helping to
found organizations such as the New York Radical Feminists and
Women Against Pornography. She gained national attention with her
book, *Against Our Will: Men, Women, and Rape* (1975), which is a
history of rape. Brownmiller argues convincingly that rape is not a sexual act but an act of sheer power assertion, an intimidation of women
in the only way that men are safe from retaliation. Brownmiller continues to express her controversial views and to organize public opposition against all demeaning attitudes taken toward women. In this piece
she argues that "feminine" postures are meant to suggest women's
shame and dependency.

I was taught to sit with my knees close together, but I don't re- 1
member if I was given a reason. Somewhere along the way I heard
that boys like to look up girls' skirts and that it was our job to keep
them from seeing our panties, but I didn't put much stock in this vicious slur. "Put your knees together" seemed to be a rule of good posture like "Sit up straight," and nothing more. As with other things
that became entrenched in my mind as unquestionably right and feminine, when I thought about it later on I could see an aesthetic reason.
The line of a skirt did seem more graceful when the knees weren't
poking out in different directions. Slanting them together was the way
to avoid looking slovenly in a chair. (Sitting with legs crossed became
an acceptably feminine posture only after skirts were shortened in the
1920s.)

Bending over to pick up a piece of paper was fraught with the dan- 2 ger of indecent exposure during the sixties miniskirt era, and like other women who believed minis looked terrifically dashing when we stepped along the street, I had to think twice, compose myself, and slither down with closed knees if I dropped something. A breed of voyeurs known as staircase watchers made their appearance during this interesting time. Slowly it dawned on me that much of feminine movement, the inhibited gestures, the locked knees, the nervous adjustments of the skirt, was a defensive maneuver against an immodest, vulgar display that feminine clothing flirted with in deliberate provocation. My feminine responsibility was to keep both aspects, the provocative and the chaste, in careful balance, even if it meant avoiding the beautifully designed open stairway in a certain Fifth Avenue bookshop.

But why did I think of vulgarity when the focal point at issue — I 3 could no longer deny the obvious — was my very own crotch? And why did I believe that if I switched to trousers, the problem would be magically solved?

Spreading the legs is a biologically crucial, characteristically female 4 act. Not only does the female have the anatomical capacity to stretch her legs further apart than the average male because of the shape of her pelvis, but a generous amount of leg spread is necessary to the act of sexual intercourse, to the assertive demand for pleasure, and to the act of giving birth. There may have been a time in history when this female posture was celebrated with pride and joy — I am thinking of the Minoan frescoes on Crete where young women are shown leaping with ease over the horns of a charging bull (the sexual symbolism of the woman and the bull has been remarked upon by others) — but in civilization as we know it, female leg spread is identified with loose, wanton behavior, pornographic imagery, promiscuity, moral laxity, immodest demeanor, and a lack of refinement. In other words, with qualities that the feminine woman must try to avoid, even as she must try to hint that somewhere within her repertoire such possibilities exist.

There is nothing hidden about the male sexual organ. It is a mani- 5 fest presence; the legs need not spread to reveal it, nor are they usually positioned as wide apart as the female's to accomplish the sexual act. But while copulation and other genital activity require a generous spread of the thighs in order for a woman to achieve her pleasure, in the feminine code of behavior she is not supposed to take the initiative out of her own desire.

The ideology of feminine sexual passivity relies upon a pair of 6 closed thighs more intently than it does upon speculative theories of the effects of testosterone on the libido, aggression, and the human brain. Open thighs acknowledge female sexuality as a positive, assertive force — a force that is capable of making demands to achieve satisfaction.

Students of Japanese history know that Samurai warriors trained 7 their daughters in the use of weapons to give them the requisite skill to commit hara-kiri when faced with disgrace. As part of the training, girls were taught how to tie their lower limbs securely so they would not embarrass themselves and their families by inadvertently assuming an immodest position in the agony of death. Traditional Japanese etiquette pays close attention to the rules of modest posture for women. In the classic squat position for eating, men are permitted to open their knees a few inches for comfort but women are not. Men may also sit cross-legged on the floor, but women must kneel with their legs together.

Studies by the psychologist Albert Mehrabian show that, despite 8 evidence of superior anatomical flexibility and grace, women are generally less relaxed than men. Mehrabian proposes that attitudes of submissiveness are conveyed through postures of tension. In his analysis of body language among high and low status males, high-ranking men are more relaxed in their gestures in the presence of subordinates. Not surprisingly, men of all ranks generally assume more relaxed postures and gestures when communicating with women.

Today's customary restraints on women's bodily comportment are 9 broadly defined by fingertips and heels, a pocketbook on the shoulder, and a schooled inhibition against spreading the knees. In addition, as the French feminist Colette Guillaumin has noted, women are physically burdened by what she calls "diverse loads," the habitual signs of chief responsibility for the domestic role — children on the arm, their food and toys in hand, and a bag of groceries or shirts from the dry cleaner's hugged to the chest. Rarely does a woman experience the liberty of taking a walk with empty hands and arms swinging free at her sides. So rare is this, in fact, that many women find it physically un-

nerving when they do. Unaccustomed to the freedom, they are beset
by worries that some needed belonging, some familiar presence (a
purse, a shopping bag?) has been forgotten.

Small, fluttery gestures that betray nervousness or a practiced   10
overanimation are considered girlishly feminine and cute. Toying with
a strand of hair, bobbing the head, giggling when introduced, pulling
the elbows in close to the body, and crossing the legs in a knee and
ankle double twist are mannerisms that men studiously avoid.

Jewelry plays a subtle role in delineating masculine and feminine   11
gestures. To drum one's fingers on the table is an aggressive expression
of annoyance and is conspicuously unfeminine, but to fidget with a
necklace or twist a ring is a nonthreatening way of dissipating agita-
tion. Clutching protectively at the throat is not restricted to females,
but corresponding masculine gestures are to loosen the collar and adjust the necktie, actions which indicate some modicum of control.

Quaint postures that throw the body off balance, such as standing   12
on one leg as if poised for flight, or leading from the hips in a debu-
tante slouch, or that suggest a child's behavior (the stereotypic sexy
secretary taking dictation while perched on the boss's knee), fall
within the repertoire of feminity that is alien, awkward, and generally
unthinkable as a mode of behavior for men. Reclining odalisque-style,
such a shocker thirty years ago when Truman Capote posed in this
manner for a book jacket, is a classic feminine tableau of eroticized
passivity with an established tradition in art.

Of course, feminine movement was never intended for solo per-   13
formance. Vine-clinging, lapdog-cuddling, and birdlike perching require a strong external support. It is in order to appeal to men that the
yielded autonomy and contrived manifestations of helplessness become second nature as expressions of good manners and sexual goodwill. For smooth interaction between the sexes, the prevailing code of
masculine action demands a yielding partner to gracefully complete
the dance.

Nancy Henley, psychologist and author of *Body Politics* (Prentice-
Hall), has written, "In a way so accepted and so subtle as to be unnoticed even by its practitioners and recipients, males in couples will
often literally push a woman everywhere she is to go — the arm from
behind, steering around corners . . . crossing the street."

In this familiar *pas de deux*, a woman must either consent to be led   14
with a gracious display of good manners or else she must buck and

bristle at the touch of the reins. Femininity encourages the romance of compliance, a willing exchange of motor autonomy and physical balance for the protocols of masculine protection. Steering and leading are prerogatives of those in command. Observational studies of who touches whom in a given situation show that superiors feel free to lay an intimate, guiding hand on those with inferior status, but not the reverse. "The politics of touch," a concept of Henley's, operates instructively in masculine-feminine relations.

Henley was the first psychologist to connect the masculine custom 15 of shepherding an able-bodied woman through situations that do not require physical guidance with other forms of manhandling along a continuum from petty humiliation (the sly pinch, the playful slap on the fanny) to the assaultive abuses of wife-beating and rape. This is not to say that the husband who steers his wife to a restaurant table with a paternal shove is no different from the rapist, but rather to suggest that women who customarily expect to have their physical movements directed by others are poorly prepared by their feminine training to resist unwanted interference or violent assault. Fear of being judged impolite has more immediate reality for many women than the terror of physical violation.

To be helped with one's coat, to let the man do the driving, to sit 16 mute and unmoving while the man does the ordering and picks up the check — such trained behavioral inactivity may be ladylike, gracious, romantic and flirty, and soothing to easily ruffled masculine feathers, but it is ultimately destructive to the sense of the functioning, productive self. The charge that feminists have no manners is true, for the history of manners, unfortunately for those who wish to change the world, is an index of courtly graces addressed toward those of the middle classes who aspire to the refinements of their betters, embodied in the static version of the cared-for, catered-to lady of privilege who existed on a rarefied plane above the mundane reality of strenuous labor. When a feminist insists on opening a door for herself, a simple act of physical autonomy that was never an issue for servants, field and factory workers, and women not under the protection of men, her gesture rudely collides with chivalrous expectations, for manly action requires manifest evidence of a helpless lady in order to demonstrate courtly respect.

The psychology of feminine movement, as we know and practice 17 its provocative airs and graces, is based on the premise that direct acts of initiative and self-assertion are a violation of the governance of male-female relations, if not of nature itself. In place of forthright action we are offered a vision so exquisitely romantic and sexually beguiling that few care to question its curious imagery of limitations: a Venus de Milo without arms, a mermaid without legs, a Sleeping Beauty in a state of suspended animation with her face upturned, awaiting a kiss.

CONSIDERATIONS

1. In paragraph 2 Brownmiller says: "Slowly it dawned on me. . . ." What attitudes toward herself and others are suggested by that phrase? How are these attitudes also implied in the preceding, first paragraph? Why does she present her views in this indirect way? Is it more feminine?
2. In paragraph 6 Brownmiller calls certain customary attitudes an "ideology." What are the specific ideas, and what is implied by using that term?
3. Do you agree with her point about the psychological meaning of relaxed and tense postures? Think of other examples from daily life that either confirm or refute her generalization. Are such postures likely to have the same meaning in all countries?
4. Paragraph 17 includes a thesis statement that summarizes the entire essay. Using her statement as a guide, what part of her thesis has been most solidly established? Is any part of the argument less than fully convincing?
5. The three feminine images cited in the final paragraph have a powerful, positive appeal to women as well as to men, and to children are well as to adults. Does their universality suggest that they have more significance than Brownmiller says, or does their universal appeal confirm her point?
6. WRITING TOPIC. Write 500 words on the postures of masculinity as you closely observe them in daily life. Are manly stances, gestures, habits, and mannerisms also contrived? Do not fall into the trap of calling anyone's postures simply *natural*. Be less vague and more observant in your descriptions. What attitudes and possibilities do masculine postures express?

Louie Crew

THRIVING AS AN OUTSIDER, EVEN AS AN OUTCAST, IN SMALLTOWN AMERICA

◊

Louie Crew (b. 1936) is a gay activist and religious reformer who is also a college professor. He grew up in Alabama and after his graduation from Baylor University in Texas, he returned to Alabama to earn advanced degrees from Auburn University and the University of Alabama (Ph.D). He has taught in various parts of the United States and is currently teaching English composition in a college in China. He is the founder of Integrity, a national organization for gay Episcopalians, and as a speaker, essayist, and poet, he has worked steadily to win wider social acceptance for gays. The following essay emerged from his contribution to a Wisconsin conference on social problems in small towns. Crew discusses what he had recently learned from being an outsider in a small town in Georgia where he and his spouse were breaking all the social taboos at once.

From 1973 to 1979, my spouse and I lived in Fort Valley, a town 1 of 12,000 people, the seat of Peach County, sixty miles northeast of Plains, right in the geographic center of Georgia. I taught English at a local black college and my spouse was variously a nurse, hairdresser, choreographer for the college majorettes, caterer, and fashion designer.

The two of us have often been asked how we survived as a gay, ra- 2 cially integrated couple living openly in that small town. We are still perhaps too close to the Georgia experience and very much caught up in our similar struggles in central Wisconsin to offer a definite explanation, but our tentative conjectures should interest anyone who values the role of the dissident in our democracy.

41

Survive we did. We even throve before our departure. Profession- 3
ally, my colleagues and the Regents of the University System of Georgia awarded me tenure, and the Chamber of Commerce awarded my
spouse a career medal in cosmetology. Socially, we had friends from
the full range of the economic classes in the community. We had attended six farewell parties in our honor before we called a halt to further fetes, especially several planned at too great a sacrifice by some of
the poorest folks in the town. Furthermore, I had been away only four
months when the college brought me back to address an assembly of
Georgia judges, mayors, police chiefs, and wardens. We are still called
two to three times a week by scores of people seeking my spouse's advice on fashion, cooking, or the like.

It was not always so. In 1974 my spouse and I were denied housing 4
which we had "secured" earlier before the realtor saw my spouse's
color. HUD documented that the realtor thought that "the black man
looked like a criminal." Once the town was up in arms when a bishop
accused the two of us of causing a tornado which had hit the town
early in 1975, an accusation which appeared on the front page of the
newspaper. "This is the voice of God. The town of Fort Valley is harboring Sodomists. Would one expect God to keep silent when homosexuals are tolerated? We remember what He did to Sodom and Go-
morrah" (*The Macon Herald,* March 20, 1975: 1). A year later my
Episcopal vestry asked me to leave the parish, and my own bishop
summoned me for discipline for releasing to the national press correspondence related to the vestry's back-room maneuvers. Prompted in
part by such officials, the local citizens for years routinely heckled us
in public, sometimes threw rocks at our apartment, trained their children to spit on us from their bicycles if we dared to jog, and badgered
us with hate calls on an average of six to eight times a week.

One such episode offers a partial clue to the cause of our survival. It 5
was late summer, 1975 or 1976. I was on my motorcycle to post mail
at the street-side box just before the one daily pickup at 6:00 P.M.
About fifty yards away, fully audible to about seventy pedestrians mill-
ing about the court house and other public buildings, a group of police officers, all men, began shouting at me from the steps of their
headquarters: "Louise! Faggot! Queer!"

Anyone who has ever tried to ease a motorcycle from a still position 6
without revving the engine knows that the feat is impossible: try as I
did to avoid the suggestion, I sounded as if I were riding off in a huff.

About half-way up the street, I thought to myself, "I'd rather rot in jail than feel the way I do now." I turned around, drove back — the policemen still shouting and laughing — and parked in the lot of the station. When I walked to the steps, only the lone black policeman remained.

"Did you speak to me?" I asked him.   7

"No, sir," he replied emphatically.   8

Inside I badgered the desk sergeant to tell her chief to call me as 9 soon as she could locate him, and I indicated that I would press charges if necessary to prevent a recurrence. I explained that the police misconduct was an open invitation to more violent hoodlums to act out the officers' fantasies with impunity in the dark. Later, I persuaded a black city commissioner and a white one, the latter our grocer and the former our mortician, to threaten the culprits with suspension if ever such misconduct occurred again.

Over a year later, late one Friday after his payday, a black friend of 10 my spouse knocked at our door to offer a share of his Scotch to celebrate his raise — or so he said. Thus primed, he asked me, "You don't recognize me, do you?"

"No," I admitted.   11

"I'm the lone black policeman that day you were heckled. I came 12 by really because I thought you two might want to know what happened inside when Louie stormed up to the sergeant."

"Yes," we said.   13

"Well, all the guys were crouching behind the partition to keep 14 you from seeing that they were listening. Their eyes bulged when you threatened to bring in the F.B.I. and such. Then when you left, one spoke for all when he said, 'But sissies aren't supposed to do things like that!' "

Ironically, I believe that a major reason for our thriving on our own 15 terms of candor about our relationship has been our commitment to resist the intimidation heaped upon us. For too long lesbians and gay males have unwillingly encouraged abuses against ourselves by serving advance notice to any bullies, be they the barnyard-playground variety, or the Bible-wielding pulpiteers, that we would whimper or run into hiding when confronted with even the threat of exposure. It is easy to confuse sensible nonviolence with cowardly nonresistance.

In my view, violent resistance would be counter-productive, espe- 16 cially for lesbians and gays who are outnumbered 10 to 1 by heterosexuals, according to Kinsey's statistics. Yet our personal experience suggests that special kinds of creative nonviolent resistance are a major source of hope if lesbians and gay males are going to reverse the physical and mental intimidation which is our daily portion in this culture.

Resistance to oppression can be random and spontaneous, as in 17 part was my decision to return to confront the police hecklers, or organized and sustained, as more typically has been the resistance by which my spouse and I have survived. I believe that only organized and sustained resistance offers much hope for long-range change in any community. The random act is too soon forgotten or too easily romanticized.

Once we had committed ourselves to one another, my spouse and I 18 never gave much thought for ourselves to the traditional device most gays have used for survival, the notorious "closet" in which one hides one's identity from all but a select group of friends. In the first place, a black man and a white man integrating a Georgia small town simply cannot be inconspicuous. More importantly, the joint checking account and other equitable economies fundamental to the quality of our marriage are public, not private acts. Our denial of the obvious would have secured closet space only for our suffocation; we would have lied, "We are ashamed and live in secret."

All of our resistance stems from our sense of our own worth, our 19 conviction that we and our kind do not deserve the suffering which heterosexuals continue to encourage or condone for sexual outcasts. Dr. Martin Luther King used to say, "Those who go to the back of the bus, deserve the back of the bus."

Our survival on our own terms has depended very much on our 20 knowing and respecting many of the rules of the system which we resist. We are not simply dissenters, but conscientious ones.

For example, we are both very hard workers. As a controversial per- 21 son, I know that my professionalism comes under far more scrutiny than that of others. I learned early in my career that I could secure space for my differences by handling routine matters carefully. If one stays on good terms with secretaries, meets all deadlines, and willingly does one's fair share of the busy work of institutions, one is usually already well on the way towards earning collegial space, if not collegial support. In Georgia, I routinely volunteered to be secretary for most committees on which I served, thereby having enormous influence in the final form of the groups' deliberations without monopolizing the forum as most other molders of policy do. My spouse's many talents and sensibilities made him an invaluable advisor and confidante to scores of people in the community. Of course, living as we did in a hairdresser's salon, we knew a great deal more about the rest of the public than that public knew about us.

My spouse and I are fortunate in the fact that we like the enormous amount of work which we do. We are not mere opportunists working hard only as a gimmick to exploit the public for lesbian and gay issues. Both of us worked intensely at our professional assignments long before we were acknowledged dissidents with new excessive pressures to excel. We feel that now we must, however unfairly, be twice as effective as our competitors just to remain employed at all.

Our survival has also depended very much on our thorough knowledge of the system, often knowledge more thorough than that of those who would use the system against us. For example, when my bishop summoned me for discipline, I was able to show him that his own canons give him no authority to discipline a lay person except by excommunication. In fact, so hierarchical have the canons of his diocese become, that the only laity who exist worthy of their mention are the few lay persons on vestries.

Especially helpful has been our knowledge of communication procedures. For example, when an area minister attacked lesbians and gays on a TV talk show, I requested equal time; so well received was my response that for two more years I was a regular panelist on the talk show, thereby reaching most residents of the entire middle Georgia area as a known gay person, yet one speaking not just to sexual issues, but to a full range of religious and social topics.

When I was occasionally denied access to media, as in the parish or diocese or as on campus when gossip flared, I knew the value of candid explanations thoughtfully prepared, xeroxed, and circulated to enough folks to assure that the gossips would have access to the truthful version. For example, the vestry, which acted in secret, was caught by surprise when I sent copies of their hateful letter to most other parishioners, together with a copy of a psalm which I wrote protesting their turning the House of Prayer into a Court House. I also was able to explain that I continued to attend, not in defiance of their withdrawn invitation, but in obedience to the much higher invitation issued to us all by the real head of the Church. In January, 1979, in the first open meeting of the parish since the vestry's letter of unwelcome three years earlier, the entire parish voted to censure the vestry for that action and to extend to me the full welcome which the vestry had tried to deny. Only three voted against censure, all three of them a minority of the vestry being censured.

My spouse and I have been very conscious of the risks of our convictions. We have viewed our credentials — my doctorate and his professional licenses — not as badges of comfortable respectability, but as assets to be invested in social change. Dr. King did not sit crying in the Albany jail, "Why don't these folks respect me? How did this happen? What am I doing here?" When my spouse and I have been denied jobs for which we were the most qualified applicants, we have not naively asked how such things could be, nor have we dwelt overly long on self-pity, for we have known in advance the prices we might have to pay, even if to lose our lives. Our realism about danger and risk has helped us to preserve our sanity when everyone about us has seemed insane. I remember the joy which my spouse shared with me over the fact that he had just been fired for his efforts to organize other black nurses to protest their being treated as orderlies by the white managers of a local hospital. 26

Never, however, have we affirmed the injustices. Finally, we simply cannot be surprised by any evil and are thus less likely to be intimidated by it. Hence, we find ourselves heirs to a special hybrid of courage, a form of courage too often ignored by the heterosexual majority, but widely manifest among sexual outcasts, not the courage of bravado on battlegrounds or sportsfields, but the delicate courage of the lone person who patiently waits out the stupidity of the herd, the cagey courage that has operated many an underground railway station. 27

Our survival in smalltown America has been helped least, I suspect, by our annoying insistence that potential friends receive us not only in our own right, but also as members of the larger lesbian/gay and black communities of which we are a part. Too many whites and heterosexuals are prepared to single us out as "good queers" or "good niggers," offering us thereby the "rewards" of their friendship only at too great a cost to our integrity. My priest did not whip up the vestry against me the first year we lived openly together. He was perfectly happy to have one of his "clever queers" to dress his wife's hair and the other to help him write his annual report. We became scandalous only when the two of us began to organize the national group of lesbian and 28 gay-male Episcopalians, known as INTEGRITY; then we were no longer just quaint. We threatened his image of himself as the arbiter of community morality, especially as he faced scores of queries from brother priests elsewhere.

Many lesbians and gay males are tamed by dependencies upon 29 carefully selected heterosexual friends with whom they have shared their secret, often never realizing that in themselves alone, they could provide far more affirmation and discover far more strength than is being cultivated by the terms of these "friendships." Lesbians and gay males have always been taught to survive on the heterosexuals' terms, rarely on one's own terms, and almost never on the terms of a community shared with other lesbians and gay males.

Heterosexuals are often thus the losers. The heterosexual acquain- 30 tances close to us early on when we were less visible who dropped us later as our notoriety spread were in most cases folks of demonstrably much less character strength than those heterosexuals who remained our friends even as we asserted our difference with thoughtful independence.

My spouse and I have never been exclusive nor aspired to move to 31 any ghetto. In December, 1978, on the night the Macon rabbi and I had successfully organized the area's Jews and gays to protest a concert by Anita Bryant, I returned home to watch the videotape of the march on the late news in the company of eight house guests invited by my spouse for a surprise party, not one of them gay (for some strange reason nine out of ten folks are not), not one of them obligated to be at the earlier march, and not one of them uneasy, as most of our acquaintances would have been a few years earlier before we had undertaken this reeducation together.

Folks who work for social change need to be very careful to allow 32 room for it to happen, not to allow realistic appraisals of risks to prevent their cultivation of the very change which they germinate.

Our survival has been helped in no small way by our candor and 33 clarity in response to rumor and gossip, which are among our biggest enemies. On my campus in Georgia, I voluntarily spoke about sexual issues to an average of 50 classes per year outside my discipline. Initially, those encounters sharpened my wits for tougher national forums, but long after I no longer needed these occasions personally for rehearsal, I continued to accept the invitations, thereby reaching a vast majority of the citizens of the small town where we continued to live. I used to enjoy the humor of sharing with such groups facts which would make my day-to-day life more pleasant. For example, I routinely noted that when a male student is shocked at my simple public, "Hello," he would look both ways to see who might have seen him being friendly with the gay professor. By doing this he is telling me and all other knowledgeable folks far more new information about his own body chemistry than he is finding out about mine. More informed male students would reply, "Hello" when greeted. With this method I disarmed the hatefulness of one of their more debilitating weapons of ostracism.

All personal references in public discussions inevitably invade one's privacy, but I have usually found the invasion a small price to pay for the opportunity to educate the public to the fact that the issues which most concern sexual outcasts are not genital, as the casters-out have so lewdly imagined, but issues of justice and simple fairness.   34

Resistance is ultimately an art which no one masters to perfection.   35
Early in my struggles, I said to a gay colleague living openly in rural Nebraska, "We must stamp on every snake." Wisely he counseled, "Only if you want to get foot poisoning." I often wish I had more of the wisdom mentioned in *Ecclesiastes*, the ability to judge accurately, "The time to speak and the time to refrain from speaking." Much of the time I think it wise to pass public hecklers without acknowledging their taunts, especially when they are cowardly hiding in a crowd. When I have faced bullies head-on, I have tried to do so patiently, disarming them by my own control of the situation. Of course, I am not guaranteed that their violence can thus be aborted every time.

Two major sources of our survival are essentially very private —   36
one, the intense care and love my spouse and I share, and the other, our strong faith in God as Unbounding Love. To these we prefer to make our secular witness, more by what we do than by what we say.

In conclusion, I am not masochist enough to choose the hard lot of   37
sexual outcast in smalltown America. Had I the choice to change myself but not the world, I would choose the easiest roles and return as a white male heterosexual city-slicker millionaire, not because whites, males, heterosexuals, city-slickers, and millionaires are better, but because they have fewer difficulties. Yet, given only the choice of changing the world more easily than changing my color, my biological plumbing, my locale, or my inherited bank account, I am grateful for

the opportunity to be a dissident in a country which preserves at least the ideal of freedom even if it denies freedom in scores of specific instances. I was not told in my eighth-grade civics class in Alabama what a high price one would have to pay for exercising freedom of speech, as when what one speaks is radically confronting the docile and ignorant majority, but I am grateful that I had a good eighth-grade civics class, learning thoroughly the mechanisms one must use to change this government.

Sometimes I think a society's critics must appreciate the society far 38 more than others, for the critics typically take very seriously the society's idle promises and forgotten dreams. When I occasionally see them, I certainly don't find many of my heterosexual eighth-grade classmates probing much farther than the issues of our common Form 1040 headaches and the issues as delivered by the evening news. Their lives seem often far duller than ours and the main adventures in pioneering they experience come vicariously, through television, the movies, and for a few, through books. In defining me as a criminal, my society may well have hidden a major blessing in its curse by forcing me out of lethargy into an on-going, rigorous questioning of the entire process. Not only do I teach *The Adventures of Huckleberry Finn*, my spouse and I have in an important sense had the chance to be Huck and Jim fleeing a different form of slavery and injustice in a very real present.

CONSIDERATIONS

1. In the the first four paragraphs, Crew emphasizes the social significance of his experience. What are the words and phrases that define the key public issues as Crew perceives them?
2. When he thought to himself, "I'd rather rot in jail than feel the way I do now," what were his probable feelings? What was the immediate result of his returning to the police station? What were the long-range results? Which does he emphasize?
3. What specific advice does he offer to help outsiders to thrive in society? Do you think his advice is cautious? restrained? assertive? bold?
4. Which examples does the author use for the kind of courage he values most?
5. The final paragraph includes a somewhat different attitude toward the author's ordeals. What new considerations are introduced, and how do they

affect the tone of the final paragraph? In what way does this change of
tone weaken or strengthen the essay's effect on you?

6. WRITING TOPIC. Suppose that a high government official strongly objects
to the use of some of your students' fees or other forms of taxation to support the activities of lesbian and gay student groups on campus. Does it
really matter to you whether or not these groups can function at your college? How does the issue affect your sense of yourself as a student and a
citizen? In a 500-word letter to the official, develop a reasonable position
for or against the use of public funds for this purpose.

Joan Didion

IN BED

◊

JOAN DIDION (b. 1934) was raised in California and graduated from the University of California at Berkeley in 1956. Her career in journalism has included work as an editor and columnist for such magazines as *Vogue* and *Saturday Evening Post*, and her essays have appeared in such national periodicals as *The American Scholar* and the *National Review*. She has written three novels, including *Play It As It Lays* (1971) and *A Book of Common Prayer* (1977). Her essays are collected in *Slouching Toward Bethlehem* (1969) and *The White Album* (1979). In this essay from the latter volume Didion gives a complex, double view of her suffering from migraine headaches.

Three, four, sometimes five times a month, I spend the day in bed 1
with a migraine headache, insensible to the world around me. Almost
every day of every month, between these attacks, I feel the sudden irrational irritation and flush of blood into the cerebral arteries which
tell me that migraine is on its way, and I take certain drugs to avert its
arrival. If I did not take the drugs, I would be able to function perhaps
one day in four. The physiological error called migraine is, in brief,
central to the given of my life. When I was fifteen, sixteen, even
twenty-five, I used to think that I could rid myself of this error by simply denying it, character over chemistry. "Do you have headaches
sometimes? frequently? never?" the application forms would demand.
"Check one." Wary of the trap, wanting whatever it was that the successful circumnavigation of that particular form could bring (a job, a
scholarship, the respect of mankind and the grace of God), I would
check one. "*Sometimes,*" I would lie. That in fact I spent one or two
days a week almost unconscious with pain seemed a shameful secret,
evidence not merely of some chemical inferiority but of all my bad attitudes, unpleasant tempers, wrongthink.

For I had no brain tumor, no eyestrain, no high blood pressure, 2
nothing wrong with me at all: I simply had migraine headaches, and
migraine headaches were, as everyone who did not have them knew,
imaginary. I fought migraine then, ignored the warnings it sent, went
to school and later to work in spite of it, sat through lectures in
Middle English and presentations to advertisers with involuntary
tears running down the right side of my face, threw up in wash-
rooms, stumbled home by instinct, emptied ice trays onto my bed and
tried to freeze the pain in my right temple, wished only for a neuro-
surgeon who would do a lobotomy on house call, and cursed my imagination.

It was a long time before I began thinking mechanistically enough 3
to accept migraine for what it was: something with which I would be
living, the way some people live with diabetes. Migraine is something
more than the fancy of a neurotic imagination. It is an essentially hereditary complex of symptoms, the most frequently noted but by no
means the most unpleasant of which is a vascular headache of blinding severity, suffered by a surprising number of women, a fair number
of men (Thomas Jefferson had migraine, and so did Ulysses S. Grant,
the day he accepted Lee's surrender), and by some unfortunate children as young as two years old. (I had my first when I was eight. It
came on during a fire drill at the Columbia School in Colorado
Springs, Colorado. I was taken first home and then to the infirmary at
Peterson Field, where my father was stationed. The Air Corps doctor
prescribed an enema.) Almost anything can trigger a specific attack of
migraine: stress, allergy, fatigue, an abrupt change in barometric
pressure, a contretemps over a parking ticket. A flashing light. A fire
drill. One inherits, of course, only the predisposition. In other words I
spent yesterday in bed with a headache not merely because of my bad
attitudes, unpleasant tempers, and wrongthink, but because both my
grandmothers had migraine, my father has migraine, and my mother
has migraine.

No one knows precisely what it is that is inherited. The chemistry 4
of migraine, however, seems to have some connection with the nerve
hormone named serotonin, which is naturally present in the brain.
The amount of serotonin in the blood falls sharply at the onset of migraine, and one migraine drug, methysergide, or Sansert, seems to
have some effect on serotonin. Methysergide is a derivative of lysergic

acid (in fact Sandoz Pharmaceuticals first synthesized LSD-25 while looking for a migraine cure), and its use is hemmed about with so many contraindications and side effects that most doctors prescribe it only in the most incapacitating cases. Methysergide, when it is prescribed, is taken daily, as a preventive; another preventive which works for some people is old-fashioned ergotamine tartrate, which helps to constrict the swelling blood vessels during the "aura," the period which in most cases precedes the actual headache.

Once an attack is under way, however, no drug touches it. Migraine gives some people mild hallucinations, temporarily blinds others, shows up not only as a headache but as a gastrointestinal disturbance, a painful sensitivity to all sensory stimuli, an abrupt overpowering fatigue, a strokelike aphasia, and a crippling inability to make even the most routine connections. When I am in a migraine aura (for some people the aura lasts fifteen minutes, for others several hours), I will drive through red lights, lose the house keys, spill whatever I am holding, lose the ability to focus my eyes or frame coherent sentences, and generally give the appearance of being on drugs, or drunk. The actual headache, when it comes, brings with it chills, sweating, nausea, a debility that seems to stretch the very limits of endurance. That no one dies of migraine seems, to someone deep into an attack, an ambiguous blessing.

My husband also has migraine, which is unfortunate for him but fortunate for me: perhaps nothing so tends to prolong an attack as the accusing eye of someone who has never had a headache. "Why not take a couple of aspirin," the unafflicted will say from the doorway, or "I'd have a headache, too, spending a beautiful day like this inside with all the shades drawn." All of us who have migraine suffer not only from the attacks themselves but from this common conviction that we are perversely refusing to cure ourselves by taking a couple of aspirin, that we are making ourselves sick, that we "bring it on ourselves." And in the most immediate sense, the sense of why we have a headache this Tuesday and not last Thursday, of course we often do. There certainly is what doctors call a "migraine personality," and that personality tends to be ambitious, inward, intolerant of error, rather rigidly organized, perfectionist. "You don't look like a migraine personality," a doctor once said to me. "Your hair's messy. But I suppose you're a compulsive housekeeper." Actually my house is kept even more negligently than my hair, but the doctor was right nonetheless: perfectionism can also take the form of spending most of a week writing and rewriting and not writing a single paragraph.

But not all perfectionists have migraine, and not all migrainous 7
people have migraine personalities. We do not escape heredity. I have tried in most of the available ways to escape my own migrainous heredity (at one point I learned to give myself two daily injections of histamine with a hypodermic needle, even though the needle so frightened me that I had to close my eyes when I did it), but I still have migraine. And I have learned now to live with it, learned when to expect it, how to outwit it, even how to regard it, when it does come, as more friend than lodger. We have reached a certain understanding, my migraine and I. It never comes when I am in real trouble. Tell me that my house is burned down, my husband has left me, that there is gunfighting in the streets and panic in the banks, and I will not respond by getting a headache. It comes instead when I am fighting not an open but a guerrilla war with my own life, during weeks of small household confusions, lost laundry, unhappy help, canceled appointments, on days when the telephone rings too much and I get no work done and the wind is coming up. On days like that my friend comes uninvited.

And once it comes, now that I am wise in its ways, I no longer fight 8
it. I lie down and let it happen. At first every small apprehension is magnified, every anxiety a pounding terror. Then the pain comes, and I concentrate only on that. Right there is the usefulness of migraine, there in that imposed yoga, the concentration on the pain. For when the pain recedes, ten or twelve hours later, everything goes with it, all the hidden resentments, all the vain anxieties. The migraine has acted as a circuit breaker, and the fuses have emerged intact. There is a pleasant convalescent euphoria. I open the windows and feel the air, eat gratefully, sleep well. I notice the particular nature of a flower in a glass on the stair landing. I count my blessings.

CONSIDERATIONS

1. Why did Didion for many years try to ignore her migraines and to deny having them? What realizations finally changed her mind?
2. In paragraphs 4 and 5, Didion gives an objective account of migraines,

and at the same time she also suggests her subjective responses as a migraine sufferer. What words and phrases give us her personal response, despite the air of objective detachment?

3. What is a "migraine personality"? Does Didion believe that she has one?

4. In the final two paragraphs Didion personifies her migraines as she learns to live with her affliction. How does the personification help make her problem more tolerable?

5. WRITING TOPIC. Children generally assume that any emotional or physical pain that they suffer is caused by some fault in themselves. In a 500-word essay, recall a period of illness or affliction in which you felt guilty, or to blame, for being distressed. How did other people reinforce or dispel your feelings?

James Thurber

THE SECRET LIFE OF
WALTER MITTY

◊

JAMES THURBER (1894–1961) was one of a number of urbane, witty writers about metropolitan life — others included Robert Benchley, Dorothy Parker, S. J. Perelman, E. B. White, Alexander Woollcott — whose essays and fiction appeared mainly in *The New Yorker* during the 1930s and 1940s. Thurber also drew cartoons for that magazine, which were memorable for their enormous dogs and for the fiercely battling little men and large-sized women. His essays, stories, and drawings are collected in such books as *The Owl in the Attic and Other Perplexities* (1931), *My Life and Hard Times* (1933), and *Men, Women, and Dogs* (1943). He also wrote a memoir of his career on *The New Yorker* staff, *My Years with Ross* (1959). The story of Walter Mitty, which was first published in 1939, created the character that popularly symbolizes the henpecked husband whose mind drifts away into daydreams of glory. Even his name, like other notorious fictional names — Uncle Tom, George Babbitt — has come to be a commonplace word for his specific type of personality.

"We're going through!" The Commander's voice was like thin ice 1
breaking. He wore his full-dress uniform, with the heavily braided
white cap pulled down rakishly over one cold gray eye. "We can't
make it, sir. It's spoiling for a hurricane, if you ask me." "I'm not asking you, Lieutenant Berg," said the Commander. "Throw on the
power lights! Rev her up to 8,500! We're going through!" The
pounding of the cylinders increased; ta-pocketa-pocketa-pocketa-*pock-
eta-pocketa*. The Commander stared at the ice forming on the pilot
window. He walked over and twisted a row of complicated dials.
"Switch on No. 8 auxiliary!" he shouted. "Switch on No. 8 auxiliary!"
repeated Lieutenant Berg. "Full strength in No. 3 turret!" shouted

the Commander. "Full strength in No. 3 turret!" The crew, bending to their various tasks in the huge, hurtling eight-engined Navy hydroplane, looked at each other and grinned. "The Old Man'll get us through," they said to one another. "The Old Man ain't afraid of Hell!" . . .

"Not so fast! You're driving too fast!" said Mrs. Mitty. "What are 2 you driving so fast for?"

"Hmm?" said Walter Mitty. He looked at his wife, in the seat be- 3 side him, with shocked astonishment. She seemed grossly unfamiliar, like a strange woman who had yelled at him in a crowd. "You were up to fifty-five," she said. "You know I don't like to go more than forty. You were up to fifty-five." Walter Mitty drove on toward Waterbury in silence, the roaring of the SN202 through the worst storm in twenty years of Navy flying fading in the remote, intimate airways of his mind. "You're tensed up again," said Mrs. Mitty. "It's one of your days. I wish you'd let Dr. Renshaw look you over."

Walter Mitty stopped the car in front of the building where his 4 wife went to have her hair done. "Remember to get those overshoes while I'm having my hair done," she said. "I don't need overshoes," said Mitty. She put her mirror back into her bag. "We've been all through that," she said, getting out of the car. "You're not a young man any longer." He raced the engine a little. "Why don't you wear your gloves? Have you lost your gloves?" Walter Mitty reached in a pocket and brought out the gloves. He put them on, but after she had turned and gone into the building and he had driven on to a red light, he took them off again. "Pick it up, brother," snapped a cop as the light changed, and Mitty hastily pulled on his gloves and lurched ahead. He drove around the streets aimlessly for a time, and then he drove past the hospital on his way to the parking lot.

. . . "It's the millionaire banker, Wellington McMillan," said the 5 pretty nurse. "Yes?" said Walter Mitty, removing his gloves slowly. "Who has the case?" "Dr. Renshaw and Dr. Benbow, but there are two specialists here, Dr. Remington from New York and Dr. Pritchard-Mitford from London. He flew over." A door opened down a long, cool corridor and Dr. Renshaw came out. He looked distraught and haggard. "Hello, Mitty," he said. "We're having the devil's own time with McMillan, the millionaire banker and close personal friend of Roosevelt. Obstreosis of the ductal tract. Tertiary. Wish you'd take a look at him." "Glad to," said Mitty.

In the operating room there were whispered introductions: "Dr. 6
Remington, Dr. Mitty. Dr. Pritchard-Mitford, Dr. Mitty." "I've read
your book on streptothricosis," said Pritchard-Mitford, shaking hands.
"A brilliant performance, sir." "Thank you," said Walter Mitty.
"Didn't know you were in the States, Mitty," grumbled Remington.
"Coals to Newcastle, bringing Mitford and me up here for a tertiary."
"You are very kind," said Mitty. A huge, complicated machine, connected to the operating table, with many tubes and wires, began at
this moment to go pocketa-pocketa-pocketa. "The new anaesthetizer
is giving away!" shouted an interne. "There is no one in the East who
knows how to fix it!" "Quiet, man!" said Mitty, in a low, cool voice.
He sprang to the machine, which was now going pocketa-pocketa-
queep-pocketa-queep. He began fingering delicately a row of glistening dials. "Give me a fountain pen!" he snapped. Someone handed
him a fountain pen. He pulled a faulty piston out of the machine and
inserted the pen in its place. "That will hold for ten minutes," he said.
"Get on with the operation." A nurse hurried over and whispered to
Renshaw, and Mitty saw the man turn pale. "Coreopsis has set in,"
said Renshaw nervously. "If you would take over, Mitty?" Mitty
looked at him and at the craven figure of Benbow, who drank, and at
the grave, uncertain faces of the two great specialists. "If you wish,"
he said. They slipped a white gown on him; he adjusted a mask and
drew on thin gloves; nurses handed him shining . . .

"Back it up, Mac! Look out for that Buick!" Walter Mitty jammed 7
on the brakes. "Wrong lane, Mac," said the parking-lot attendant,
looking at Mitty closely. "Gee. Yeh," muttered Mitty. He began cautiously to back out of the lane marked "Exit Only." "Leave her sit
there," said the attendant. "I'll put her away." Mitty got out of the
car. "Hey, better leave the key." "Oh," said Mitty, handing the man
the ignition key. The attendant vaulted into the car, backed it up with
insolent skill, and put it where it belonged.

They're so damn cocky, thought Walter Mitty, walking along 8
Main Street; they think they know everything. Once he had tried to
take his chains off, outside New Milford, and he had got them wound
around the axles. A man had had to come out in a wrecking car and
unwind them, a young, grinning garage man. Since then Mrs. Mitty
always made him drive to a garage to have the chains taken off. The
next time, he thought, I'll wear my right arm in a sling; they won't
grin at me then. I'll have my right arm in a sling and they'll see I

couldn't possibly take the chains off myself. He kicked at the slush on the sidewalk. "Overshoes," he said to himself, and he began looking for a shoe store.

When he came out into the street again, with the overshoes in a box under his arm, Walter Mitty began to wonder what the other thing was his wife had told him to get. She had told him, twice before they set out from their house for Waterbury. In a way he hated these weekly trips to town — he was always getting something wrong. Kleenex, he thought, Squibb's, razor blades? No. Toothpaste, toothbrush, bicarbonate, carborundum, initiative, and referendum? He gave it up. But she would remember it. "Where's the what's-its-name?" she would ask. "Don't tell me you forgot the what's-its-name." A newsboy went by shouting something about the Waterbury trial.

. . . "Perhaps this will refresh your memory." The District Attorney suddenly thrust a heavy automatic at the quiet figure on the witness stand. "Have you ever seen this before?" Walter Mitty took the gun and examined it expertly. "This is my Webley-Vickers 50-80," he said calmly. An excited buzz ran around the courtroom. The judge rapped for order. "You are a crack shot with any sort of firearms, I believe?" said the District Attorney, insinuatingly. "Objection!" shouted Mitty's attorney. "We have shown that the defendant could not have fired the shot. We have shown that he wore his right arm in a sling on the night of the fourteenth of July." Walter Mitty raised his hand briefly and the bickering attorneys were stilled. "With any known make of gun," he said evenly, "I could have killed Gregory Fitzhurst at three hundred feet *with my left hand*." Pandemonium broke loose in the courtroom. A woman's scream rose above the bedlam and suddenly a lovely, dark-haired girl was in Walter Mitty's arms. The District Attorney struck at her savagely. Without rising from his chair, Mitty let the man have it on the point of the chin. "You miserable cur!"

"Puppy biscuit," said Walter Mitty. He stopped walking and the buildings of Waterbury rose up out of the misty courtroom and surrounded him again. A woman who was passing laughed. "He said 'Puppy biscuit,' " she said to her companion. "That man said 'Puppy biscuit' to himself." Walter Mitty hurried on. He went into an A. & P., not the first one he came to but a smaller one farther up the street. "I want some biscuit for small, young dogs," he said to the clerk. "Any special brand, sir?" The greatest pistol shot in the world thought a moment. "It says 'Puppies Bark for It' on the box," said Walter Mitty.

   His wife would be through at the hairdresser's in fifteen minutes, 12 Mitty saw in looking at his watch, unless they had trouble drying it; sometimes they had trouble drying it. She didn't like to get to the hotel first; she would want him to be there waiting for her as usual. He found a big leather chair in the lobby, facing a window, and he put the overshoes and the puppy biscuit on the floor beside it. He picked up an old copy of *Liberty* and sank down into the chair. "Can Germany Conquer the World through the Air?" Walter Mitty looked at the pictures of bombing planes and of ruined streets.
   . . . "The cannonading has got the wind up in young Raleigh, sir," 13 said the sergeant. Captain Mitty looked up at him through tousled hair. "Get him to bed," he said wearily, "with the others. I'll fly alone." "But you can't, sir," said the sergeant anxiously. "It takes two men to handle that bomber and the Archies are pounding hell out of the air. Von Richtman's circus is between here and Saulier." "Somebody's got to get that ammunition dump," said Mitty. "I'm going over. Spot of brandy?" He poured a drink for the sergeant and one for himself. War thundered and whined around the dugout and battered at the door. There was a rending of wood and splinters flew through the room. "A bit of a near thing," said Captain Mitty carelessly. "The box barrage is closing in," said the sergeant. "We only live once, sergeant," said Mitty, with his faint, fleeting smile. "Or do we?" He poured another brandy and tossed it off. "I never see a man could hold his brandy like you, sir," said the sergeant. "Begging your pardon, sir." Captain Mitty stood up and strapped on his huge Webley-Vickers automatic. "It's forty kilometers through hell, sir," said the sergeant. Mitty finished one last brandy. "After all," he said softly, "what isn't?" The pounding of the cannon increased; there was the rat-tat-tatting of machine guns, and from somewhere came the menacing pocketa-pocketa-pocketa of the new flame-throwers. Walter Mitty walked to the door of the dugout humming "Après de Ma Blonde." He turned and waved to the sergeant. "Cheerio!" he said. . . .
   Something struck his shoulder. "I've been looking all over this 14 hotel for you," said Mrs. Mitty. "Why do you have to hide in this old

chair? How did you expect me to find you?" "Things close in," said
Walter Mitty vaguely. "What?" Mrs. Mitty said. "Did you get the
what's-its-name? The puppy biscuit? What's in that box?" "Overshoes," said Mitty. "Couldn't you have put them on in the store?" "I
was thinking," said Walter Mitty. "Does it ever occur to you that I
am sometimes thinking?" She looked at him. "I'm going to take your
temperature when I get you home," she said.

They went out through the revolving doors that made a faintly 15
derisive whistling sound when you pushed them. It was two blocks to
the parking lot. At the drugstore on the corner she said, "Wait here
for me. I forgot something. I won't be a minute." She was more than a
minute. Walter Mitty lighted a cigarette. It began to rain, rain with
sleet in it. He stood up against the wall of the drugstore, smoking. . . .
He put his shoulders back and his heels together. "To hell with the
handkerchief," said Walter Mitty scornfully. He took one last drag on
his cigarette and snapped it away. Then, with that faint, fleeting smile
playing about his lips, he faced the firing squad; erect and motionless,
proud and disdainful, Walter Mitty the Undefeated, inscrutable to
the last.

CONSIDERATIONS

1. Explain the statement "The Commander's voice was like thin ice breaking." Does it quite perfectly fit the impression that Mitty would like to
give?
2. What is a *tertiary*? What is a *coreopsis*? Why does Thurber use these
terms in Mitty's fantasy of being a surgeon?
3. Explain a few implications of Mrs. Mitty's statement, in the next-to-last
paragraph, "I'm going to take your temperature when I get you home."
4. What personal qualities do Walter Mitty's fantasies of himself have in
common? In addition to his wife, what other things in his actual life contradict his daydreams?
5. WRITING TOPIC. Write a 500-word essay on the daydreams or fantasy
ambitions that preoccupied you when you were ten to twelve years old. To
what extent did your daydreams incorporate current events and celebrities, and to what extent did they incorporate legendary or literary material?

Theodore Roethke

OPEN HOUSE

◊

THEODORE ROETHKE (1908–1963) was a poet and an esteemed teacher of young poets (James Wright, whose poem is printed on p. 520, was one of his students at the University of Washington). Roethke was born in Saginaw, Michigan, and he graduated from the University of Michigan. His books include *The Waking* (1953), *Words for the Wind* (1958), and the posthumous volume *The Far Field* (1964), all of which won notable literary prizes. Many of his poems reflect his childhood awe and naiveté in response to nature. While Roethke's adult life was turbulent, he wrote about himself freely: "Myself is what I wear," he said in "Open House," one of his earliest poems.

My secrets cry aloud.
I have no need for tongue.
My heart keeps open house,
My doors are widely swung.
An epic of the eyes
My love, with no disguise.   5

My truths are all foreknown,
This anguish self-revealed.
I'm naked to the bone,
With nakedness my shield.
Myself is what I wear: 10
I keep the spirit spare.

The anger will endure,
The deed will speak the truth
In language strict and pure.
I stop the lying mouth: 15
Rage warps my clearest cry
To witness agony.

CONSIDERATIONS

1. Is the poet's openness deliberate or does he reveal his thoughts and feelings unwillingly? Or is it unwittingly? Do you think he would prefer to be
   a less open person? What details in the poem suggest his pride or discomfort over his open personality?
2. What appears to cause his "anger" and "rage"?
3. WRITING TOPIC. Do you generally take experience in or do you project
   experience out? If you had to live the rest of your life as either a camera or
   a phonograph, which object would you choose? What kind of pictures or
   sounds would you produce or like to produce? In 300 words, describe
   yourself and give an overview of your future life as one of these objects.

John Berger

THE CHANGING VIEW
OF MAN
IN THE PORTRAIT

◊

JOHN BERGER (b. 1926) was born in London and educated in art schools for his first career as a painter and teacher of drawing. He is also a prominent art critic, novelist, and screenwriter, who brings to his work a Marxist interpretation of the way individuals are affected by the basic structures of their society. His fiction includes *A Painter of Our Time* (1958) and the prize-winning *G* (1972); his books on the visual arts include *The Success and Failure of Picasso* (1965), *The Moment of Cubism* (1969), and *The Look of Things* (1974), from which this essay is taken. In comparing painted portraits and photographs, he maintains that photographs reflect a more modern view of human nature.

It seems to me unlikely that any important portraits will ever be 1
painted again. Portraits, that is to say, in the sense of portraiture as we
now understand it. I can imagine multi-medium memento-sets devoted to the character of particular individuals. But these will have
nothing to do with the works now in the National Portrait Gallery.

I see no reason to lament the passing of the portrait — the talent 2
once involved in portrait painting can be used in some other way to
serve a more urgent, modern function. It is, however, worthwhile inquiring why the painted portrait has become outdated; it may help us
to understand more clearly our historical situation.

The beginning of the decline of the painted portrait coincided 3
roughly speaking with the rise of photography, and so the earliest answer to our question — which was already being asked towards the

end of the nineteenth century — was that the photographer had taken the place of the portrait painter. Photography was more accurate, quicker, and far cheaper; it offered the opportunity of portraiture to the whole of society: previously such an opportunity had been the privilege of a very small elite.

To counter the clear logic of this argument, painters and their patrons invented a number of mysterious, metaphysical qualities with which to prove that what the painted portrait offered was incomparable. Only a man, not a machine (the camera), could interpret the soul of a sitter. An artist dealt with the sitter's destiny: the camera with mere light and shade. An artist judged: a photographer recorded. Etcetera, etcetera.

All this was doubly untrue. First, it denies the interpretative role of the photographer, which is considerable. Secondly, it claims for painted portraits a psychological insight which ninety-nine per cent of them totally lack. If one is considering portraiture as a genre, it is no good thinking of a few extraordinary pictures but rather of the endless portraits of the local nobility and dignitaries in countless provincial museums and town halls. Even the average Renaissance portrait — although suggesting considerable presence — has very little psychological content. We are surprised by ancient Roman or Egyptian portraits, not because of their *insight*, but because they show us very vividly how little the human face has changed. It is a myth that the portrait painter was a revealer of souls. Is there a qualitative difference between the way Velázquez painted a face and the way he painted a bottom? The comparatively few portraits that reveal true psychological insight (certain Raphaels, Rembrandts, Davids, Goyas) suggest personal, obsessional interests on the part of the artist which simply cannot be accommodated within the *professional* role of the portrait painter. Such pictures have the same kind of intensity as self-portraits. They are in fact works of self-discovery.

Ask yourself the following hypothetical question. Suppose that there is somebody in the second half of the nineteenth century in whom you are interested but of whose face you have never seen a picture. Would you rather find a painting or a photograph of this person? And the question itself posed like that is already highly favourable to painting, since the logical question should be: would you rather find a painting or a whole album of photographs?

Until the invention of photography, the painted (or sculptural) 7 portrait was the only means of recording and presenting the likeness of a person. Photography took over this role from painting and at the same time raised our standards for judging how much an informative likeness should include.

This is not to say that photographs are *in all ways* superior to 8 painted portraits. They are more informative, more psychologically revealing, and in general more accurate. But they are less tensely unified. Unity in a work of art is achieved as a result of the limitations of the medium. Every element has to be transformed in order to have its proper place within these limitations. In photography the transformation is to a considerable extent mechanical. In a painting each transformation is largely the result of a conscious decision by the artist. Thus the unity of a painting is permeated by a far higher degree of intention. The total effect of a painting (as distinct from its truthfulness) is less arbitrary than that of a photograph; its construction is more intensely socialized because it is dependent on a greater number of human decisions. A photographic portrait may be more revealing and more accurate about the likeness and character of the sitter; but it is likely to be less persuasive, less (in the very strict sense of the word) conclusive. For example, if the portraitist's intention is to flatter or idealize, he will be able to do so far more convincingly with a painting than with a photograph.

From this fact we gain an insight into the actual function of por- 9 trait painting in its heyday: a function we tend to ignore if we concentrate on the small number of exceptional "unprofessional" portraits by Raphael, Rembrandt, David, Goya, etc. The function of portrait painting was to underwrite and idealize a chosen social role of the sitter. It was not to present him as "an individual" but, rather, as an individual monarch, bishop, landowner, merchant, and so on. Each role had its accepted qualities and its acceptable limit of discrepancy. (A monarch or a pope could be far more idiosyncratic than a mere gentleman or courtier.) The role was emphasized by pose, gesture, clothes, and background. The fact that neither the sitter nor the successful professional painter was much involved with the painting of these parts is not to be entirely explained as a matter of saving time: they were thought of and were meant to be read as the accepted attributes of a given social stereotype.

The hack painters never went much beyond the stereotype; the 10
good professionals (Memlinck, Cranach, Titian, Rubens, Van Dyck,
Velázquez, Hals, Philippe de Champaigne) painted individual men,
but they were nevertheless men whose character and facial expressions
were seen and judged in the exclusive light of an ordained social role.
The portrait must fit like a hand-made pair of shoes, but the type of
shoe was never in question.

The satisfaction of having one's portrait painted was the satisfac- 11
tion of being personally recognized and *confirmed in one's position:* it
had nothing to do with the modern lonely desire to be recognized "for
what one really is."

If one were going to mark the moment when the decline of portrai- 12
ture became inevitable by citing the work of a particular artist, I
would choose the two or three extraordinary portraits of lunatics by
Géricault, painted in the first period of romantic disillusion and defiance which followed the defeat of Napoleon and the shoddy triumph
of the French bourgeoisie. The paintings were neither morally anec-
dotal nor symbolic: they were straight portraits, traditionally painted.
Yet their sitters had no social role and were presumed to be incapable
of fulfilling any. In other pictures Géricault painted severed human
heads and limbs as found in the dissecting theatre. His outlook was
bitterly critical: to choose to paint dispossessed lunatics was a comment on men of property and power; but it was also an assertion that
the essential spirit of man was independent of the role into which society forced him. Géricault found society so negative that, although
sane himself, he found the isolation of the mad more meaningful than
the social honour accorded to the successful. He was the first and, in a
sense, the last profoundly anti-social portraitist. The term contains an
impossible contradiction.

After Géricault, professional portraiture degenerated into servile 13
and crass personal flattery, cynically undertaken. It was no longer possible to believe in the value of the social roles chosen or allotted. Sincere artists painted a number of "intimate" portraits of their friends or
models (Corot, Courbet, Degas, Cézanne, Van Gogh), but in these
the social role of the sitter is reduced to *that of being painted.* The
implied social value is either that of personal friendship (proximity) or
that of being seen in such a way (being "treated") by an original artist.
In either case the sitter, somewhat like an arranged still life, becomes

subservient to the painter. Finally it is not his personality or his role which impress us but the artist's vision.

Toulouse-Lautrec was the one important latter-day exception to 14 this general tendency. He painted a number of portraits of tarts and cabaret personalities. As we survey them, they survey us. A social reciprocity is established through the painter's mediation. We are presented neither with a disguise — as with official portraiture — nor with mere creatures of the artist's vision. His portraits are the only late nineteenth-century ones which are persuasive and conclusive in the sense that we have defined. They are the only painted portraits in whose social evidence we can believe. They suggest not the artist's studio, but "the world of Toulouse-Lautrec": that is to say a specific and complex social milieu. Why was Lautrec such an exception? Because in his own eccentric manner he believed in the social roles of his sitters. He painted the cabaret performers because he admired their performances: he painted the tarts because he recognized the usefulness of their trade.

Increasingly for over a century fewer and fewer people in capitalist 15 society have been able to believe in the social value of the social roles offered. This is the second answer to our original question about the decline of the painted portrait.

The second answer suggests, however, that given a more confident 16 and coherent society, portrait painting might revive. And this seems unlikely. To understand why, we must consider the third answer.

The measures, the scale-change of modern life, have changed the 17 nature of individual identity. Confronted with another person today, we are aware, through this person, of forces operating in directions which were unimaginable before the turn of the century, and which have only become clear relatively recently. It is hard to define this change briefly. An analogy may help.

We hear a lot about the crisis of the modern novel. What this in- 18 volves, fundamentally, is a change in the mode of narration. It is scarcely any longer possible to tell a straight story sequentially unfolding in time. And this is because we are too aware of what is continually traversing the story-line laterally. That is to say, instead of being aware of a point as an infinitely small part of a straight line, we are aware of it as an infinitely small part of an infinite number of lines, as the centre of a star of lines. Such awareness is the result of our constantly having to take into account the simultaneity and extension of events and possibilities.

Something similar but less direct applies to the painted portrait. 19 We can no longer accept that the identity of a man can be adequately established by preserving and fixing what he looks like from a single viewpoint in one place. (One might argue that the same limitation applies to the still photograph, but as we have seen, we are not led to expect a photograph to be as conclusive as a painting.) Our terms of recognition have changed since the heyday of portrait painting. We may still rely on "likeness" to identify a person, but no longer to explain or place him. To concentrate upon "likeness" is to isolate falsely. It is to assume that the outermost surface *contains* the man or object: whereas we are highly conscious of the fact that nothing can contain itself.

It seems that the demands of a modern vision are incompatible 20 with the singularity of viewpoint which is the prerequisite for a static painted "likeness." The incompatibility is connected with a more general crisis concerning the meaning of individuality. Individuality can no longer be contained within the terms of manifest personality traits. In a world of transition and revolution individuality has become a problem of historical and social relations, such as cannot be revealed by the mere characterizations of an already established social stereotype. Every mode of individuality now relates to the whole world.

CONSIDERATIONS

1. Berger rejects the opinion that painted portraits are superior to photographs. What are the arguments that favor portraits, and how does Berger refute them?
2. According to Berger, in what specific ways are photographs superior to portraits? Does he have a general preference for one over the other?
3. In the essay, Berger develops three reasons for the decline of portrait painting. Write a one-paragraph synopsis of his argument.
4. Berger maintains that the truly great portraits express the painter more fully than they represent the sitter: "They are in fact works of self-discovery." Does Berger mean that you can deduce the personality of the artist by examining his works? What is your own view of that inference?

5. WRITING TOPIC. In a 700-word essay, describe a painted portrait, or a self-portrait, such as you might find in a book of art prints or at a museum. Try to explain which details in the painting indicate the sitter's social role and which details seem mainly individualizing. Consider whether, in Berger's sense, the painting has "unity," that is, whether every element of the portrait has been fitted into a general effect.

Luis Buñuel

MEMORY

◊

LUIS BUÑUEL (1900–1983), a Spanish film director, screenwriter, and producer, worked in France, Mexico, and Hollywood. His famous first film, "Un chien andalou," opens with the shocking, surrealistic image of a woman's eyeball being sliced by a razor. Buñuel went on to make many films that continued to shock his audiences, usually by mocking the hyprocrisy of middle-class, Christian life. He was most successful with his later films, among them "Viridiana" (1961), "The Diary of a Chambermaid" (1964), and the film that has acquired a cult of admirers among college audiences, "That Obscure Object of Desire" ("Le charme discrèt de la bourgeoisie," 1972). In speaking about his objectives, Buñuel said that the point of all his works is "to repeat, over and over again, in case anyone forgets it or believes the contrary, that we do not live in the best of all possible worlds." This allusion to *Candide*, the satire by Voltaire, suggests the sharply satirical bite in Buñuel's attacks upon conventional and complacent attitudes. But in the following reminiscence, which appeared first in an American literary magazine just before Buñuel died, he takes a gentler tone toward one of the misfortunes of life.

During the last ten years of her life, my mother gradually lost her 1 memory. When I went to see her in Zaragoza, where she lived with my brothers, I watched the way she read magazines, turning the pages carefully, one by one, from the first to the last. When she finished, I'd take the magazine from her, then give it back, only to see her leaf through it again, slowly, page by page.

She was in perfect physical health and remarkably agile for her age, 2 but in the end she no longer recognized her children. She didn't know who we were, or who she was. I'd walk into her room, kiss her, sit with her awhile. Sometimes I'd leave, then turn around and walk back in again. She greeted me with the same smile and invited me to sit

71

down — as if she were seeing me for the first time. She didn't remember my name.

When I was a schoolboy in Zaragoza, I knew the names of all the 3 Visigoth kings of Spain by heart, as well as the areas and populations of each country in Europe. In fact, I was a gold mine of useless facts. These mechanical pyrotechnics were the object of countless jokes: students who were particularly good at it were called *memoriones*. Virtuoso *memorión* that I was, I too had nothing but contempt for such pedestrian exercises.

Now, of course, I'm not so scornful. As time goes by, we don't give 4 a second thought to all the memories we so unconsciously accumulate, until suddenly, one day, we can't think of the name of a good friend or a relative. It's simply gone; we've forgotten it. In vain, we struggle furiously to think of a commonplace word. It's on the tip of our tongues but refuses to go any farther.

Once this happens, there are other lapses, and only then do we un- 5 derstand, and acknowledge, the importance of memory. This sort of amnesia came upon me first as I neared seventy. It started with proper names, and with the immediate past. Where did I put my lighter? (I had it in my hand just five minutes ago!) What did I want to say when I started this sentence? All too soon, the amnesia spreads, covering events that happened a few months or years ago — the name of that hotel I stayed at in Madrid in May 1980, the title of a book I was so excited about six months ago. I search and search, but it's always futile, and I can only wait for the final amnesia, the one that can erase an entire life, as it did my mother's.

So far, I've managed to keep this final darkness at bay. From my 6 distant past, I can still conjure up countless names and faces; and when I forget one, I remain calm. You have to begin to lose your memory, if only in bits and pieces, to realize that memory is what makes our lives. Life without memory is no life at all, just as an intelligence without the possibility of expression is not really an intelligence. Our memory is our coherence, our reason, our feeling, even our action. Without it, we are nothing.

Imagine (as I often have) a scene in a film where a man tries to tell 7 a friend a story but forgets one word out of four, a simple word like "car" or "street" or "policeman." He stammers, hesitates, waves his hands in the air, gropes for synonyms. Finally, his friend gets so annoyed that he slaps him and walks away. Sometimes, too, resorting to humor to ward off panic, I tell the story about the man who goes to see a psychiatrist, complaining of lapses in memory. The psychiatrist asks him a couple of routine questions, and then says:

"So? These lapses?"   8

"What lapses?" the man replies.   9

CONSIDERATIONS

1. In the first two paragraphs, Buñuel's sadness over his mother is mixed with what other responses? What details suggest these elements of his sadness?
2. How does Buñuel discipline himself to face his progressive loss of memory?
3. WRITING TOPIC. In 300 words, describe closely the body movements, the way of speaking, and other observable behavior of someone who has lost the power of sight or hearing, who is partly paralyzed, very feeble, or severely retarded, or who displays in any way the loss of a capacity that other people normally possess. Include details that establish the concrete situation in which you observed your subject. If you find this assignment becoming ghoulish or embarrassing, don't give up but include your feelings as part of the situation.

ADDITIONAL
WRITING TOPICS

◊

SELF-IMAGES

1. Write a 500-word essay on the way people are portrayed in the drawings and paintings that young children do when they are about six to eight years old. (Perhaps you can remember some of your own at that time.) What features are especially prominent? Is there a sense of movement and purpose in the figures? How do you know who they are?

2. In the past, slaves, serfs, peasants, and subjugated minorities often did not have family names, or even first names with legal standing, because such classes did not have full legal rights as national citizens or subjects. At present, everyone residing in the United States, as in most other literate societies, is required by government regulations to have a name. Does such a requirement increase or reduce personal freedom? Write a 500-word essay explaining how your sense of identity is affected — perhaps both positively and negatively — by the legal status of your name.

3. Write an account in 700 words of how your overall view of someone was changed by your recognition of particular new qualities about the person. The person may have been a stranger who gave you an impression that was modified upon further observation; or the person may be someone long familiar to you in a different way. Was the person aware of your earlier view and your later view? Was the person's reaction part of the process or circumstance of the change? Strive to be precise about your former view and your revised view, and be sure to include enough details to show how this change came about.

4. Write a 700-word essay about looking at old photographs. Perhaps you used to look through an album including pictures of yourself among many photographs of other people. What feelings about yourself were stimulated by this assortment of pictures? Since seeing other people in photographs may evoke reactions different from your responses to them as actual people, try to explain the effect of seeing them and yourself as photographic images.

5. What is *self-respect*? Write a 500-word essay that defines this quality of personal experience. Try to write concretely about this abstraction. You

may find it useful to include explanations of how self-respect is lost (did you ever feel ashamed of something that you really are?), and you might consider what role other people have in diminishing or restoring one's self-respect.

6. If you were going to write an autobiography, where would you start? In a 700-word essay, explain your reasons for deciding on a particular beginning for your life story. In other words, do not write the beginning of your autobiography — write an essay explaining why you would begin one at that particular point.

7. In what way have you been stereotyped? Perhaps as "a brain" or "a jock"; or as a black, a Jew, an Italian; or as someone who is always "good-natured," or always "responsible." In a 700-word essay, examine the stereotype that falsifies and denigrates what is true in your nature.

8. Comparisons between people are often called "invidious" or "odious," because they are almost always displeasing in some way — even when they are meant to be favorable, and even when they have a mainly beneficial effect. When younger, were you often compared with other members of your family? Or were you compared with someone at summer camp? Or with other students in high school? What were such comparisons meant to show? Can you recall your response to them? Write a 700-word essay on the comparison to another person that you were fitted into, for better or worse, for an extended time.

9. In about 300 words, describe in clear detail a nonhuman thing that suggests an image of your essential self. When relevant to your purpose, include description of the movements and surroundings of your subject.

PART 2

FAMILY TIES

Margaret Mead, *Family Codes*
Marie Winn, *The Mad View of Parents*
Nancy Friday, *Competition*
Raymond Carver, *My Father's Life*
Adrienne Rich, *The Anger of a Child*
Jamaica Kincaid, *A Walk to the Jetty*
Gordon Lish, *Fear: Four Examples*
Calvin Trillin, *It's Just Too Late*
Robert Hayden, *Those Winter Sundays*
John Updike, *Still of Some Use*

Additional Writing Topics

INSIGHTS

The family, not the individual, is the real molecule of society, the key link in the social chain of being.

— ROBERT NISBET

◊

The family is a subversive organization. In fact, it is the ultimate and only consistently subversive organization. Only the family has continued throughout history and still continues to undermine the State. The family is the enduring permanent enemy of all hierarchies, churches, and ideologies. Not only dictators, bishops, and commissars, but also humble parish priests and café intellectuals find themselves repeatedly coming up against the stony hostility of the family and its determination to resist interference to the last.

— FERDINAND MOUNT

◊

All happy families are alike; but an unhappy family is unhappy in its own way.

— LEO TOLSTOY

◊

We hear a great deal about the rudeness of the rising generation. I am an oldster myself and might be expected to take the oldster's side, but in fact I have been far more impressed by the bad manners of parents to children than by those of children to parents. Who has not been the embarrassed guest at family meals where the father or

mother treated their grown-up offspring with an incivility which, offered to any other young people, would simply have terminated the
acquaintance? Dogmatic assertions on matters which the children understand and their elders don't, ruthless interruptions, flat contradictions, ridicule of things the young take seriously — sometimes of their
religion — insulting references to their friends, all provide an easy answer to the question "Why are they always out? Why do they like
every house better than their home?" Who does not prefer civility to
barbarism?

— C. S. LEWIS

◇

He that hath wife and children hath given hostages to fortune; for
they are impediments to great enterprises, either of virtue or mischief.
Certainly the best works, and of greatest merit for the public, have
proceeded from the unmarried or childless men, which both in affection and means have married and endowed the public.

— FRANCIS BACON

◇

Children become attached to parents whatever the parents' characteristics, so long as the parents are adequately accessible and attentive.
It does not matter to the intensity of the children's attachment,
though it may matter greatly in the development of their personalities, whether their parents are reliable, consistently loving, or consid-
erate of the children's health and welfare. Nor does it matter whether
the children admire their parents or even whether they feel friendly
toward them. Children who are battered and bruised by parents will
continue to feel attached to them. Attachment, like walking or talking, is an intrinsic capacity that is developed under appropriate circumstances; it is not willed into being after a calculation of its advantages.

— ROBERT WEISS

◇

The nuclear family is a social system with two castes — male and
female — and two classes — adult and child. In the class system there

is an avenue of social mobility, which is called growing up. In American families, the lower-class term for the higher class is, in fact, "grown-up" although the higher class itself uses the label "adult."

The adult class has certain privileges and powers. As in all class systems — since the family is the model for all class systems — the basic contract is one involving responsibility and the obligation to protect, in return for power, narcissistic rewards, and a disproportionate share of scarce resources. But . . . all such contracts are in part a protection racket: "If you do as I say I will protect you against my own wrath." It always seems like a terrible bargain, and yet is often accepted with pleasure by the oppressed, so repugnant is the burden of responsibility. If it were not for the extreme intensity of human dependency needs, political oppression would be a rare event.

— PHILIP SLATER

Margaret Mead

FAMILY CODES

◊

MARGARET MEAD (1901–1978) grew up in Philadelphia and went to Barnard College, where she discovered the subject of anthropology. By her mid-twenties she was doing field work studying adolescent girls in Samoa, a research project that led to her first book, *Coming of Age in Samoa* (1928), and to her Ph.D. from Columbia University. She continued writing about adolescence in primitive societies in *Growing Up in New Guinea* (1930), and the topics of sexual development and family life occupy much of her voluminous writing throughout her distinguished career as a professor, field worker, and highly popular author and lecturer. In *Male and Female* (1949) she examines contemporary society with the trained eye of an anthropologist looking at her own culture. In this excerpt from that book she points out that modern Americans face a particularly difficult problem in learning how to live together in families.

In the United States the striking characteristic is that each set of parents is different from each other set, that no two have exactly the same memories, that no two families could be placed side by side and it could be said: "Yes, these four parents ate the same food, played the same games, heard the same lullabies, were scared by the same bogeys, taught that the same words were taboo, given the same picture of what they would be as men and women, made ready to hand on unimpaired the tradition they received, whole, unravelled, unfaded, from their parents."

Every home is different from every other home, every marriage, even within the same class, in the same clique, contains contrasts between the partners as superficially striking as the difference between one New Guinea tribe and another. "In our family we never locked the bathroom door." "In our family you never entered another per-

81

son's room without knocking." "Mother always asked to see our letters, even after we were grown." "The smallest scrap of paper on which one had written something was returned unread." "We were never allowed to mention our legs." "Father said that 'sweat' was a good deal honester word than 'perspiration,' but to be careful not to say it when we went to Aunt Alice's." "Mother said my hands would get rough if I climbed trees." "Mother said girls ought to stretch their legs and get some exercise while they were young." Side by side, next-door neighbors, children of first cousins, sometimes children of sisters or brothers, the ways of each household diverge, one family bringing up the children to prudery, privacy, and strongly marked sex roles, another to an open give-and-take that makes the girls seem tomboys. Then again comes marriage between the children with the different upbringings, and again the clash, the lack of timing, the lack of movement in step, of the new set of parents. Every home is different from every other home; no two parents, even though they were fed their cereal from silver porringers of the same design, were fed it in quite the same way. The gestures of the feeding hands, whether of mother, grandmother, Irish cook, English nurse, Negro mammy, country-bred hired girl, are no longer the assured, the highly patterned gestures of the member of a homogeneous society. The recently come foreigner's hand is unsure as it handles unfamiliar things and tries to thrust a spoon into the mouth of a child who acts and speaks strangely; the old American's hand bears marks of such uncertainties in former generations, and may tremble or clench anew over some recent contact with some newly arrived and little-understood stranger.

But just because every home is different from every other home, because no husband and wife can move effortlessly in step to the same remembered cradle-songs, so also is every home alike. The anthropologist who has studied a New Guinea tribe can often predict down to the smallest detail what will go on in each family if there is a quarrel, what will be said when there is a reconciliation, who will make it, with what words and what gestures. No anthropologist can ever hope to do the same thing for the United States. What the quarrel will be, who will make up and how, will differ in every home; what the highest moment between parents and child will be will differ. But the form, the kind of quarrel, the kind of reconciliation, the kind of love, the kind of misunderstandings, will be alike in their very difference. In

one home the husband will indicate his importunate desire by bringing flowers, in another by kicking the cat playfully as he enters, in a
third by making a fuss over the baby, in a fourth by getting very busy
over the radio, while the wife may indicate her acceptance or rejection
of his erotic expectation by putting on more lipstick or by rubbing off
the lipstick she has on, by getting very busy tidying up the room, or by
sinking in a soft dream into the other overstuffed chair, playing idly
with her baby's curly hair. There is no pattern, no simple word or gesture that has been repeated by all husbands in the presence of all the
small children who are to be future husbands, and all the small girls
who are to be wives, so that when they grow up they will be letter-
perfect in a ballet of approach or retreat.

In America the language of each home is different, there is a code 4
in each family that no one else knows. And that is the essential likeness, the essential regularity, among all these apparent differences.
For in each American marriage there is a special code, developed from
the individual pasts of the two partners, put together out of the accidents of honeymoon and parents-in-law, finally beaten into a language
that each understands imperfectly. For here is another regularity.
When a code, a language, is shared by every one in the village, spoken
by the gracious and the grim, by the flexible-tongued and the stub-
born, by the musical voice and the halting and stammering voice, the
language becomes beautifully precise, each sound sharply and perfectly differentiated from each other sound. The new-born baby, first
babbling happily through his whole possible range of lovely and unlovely noise, listens, and narrows his range. Where he once babbled a
hundred nuances of sound, he limits himself to a bare half-dozen, and
practices against the perfection, the sureness, of his elders. Later, he
too, however stumbling his tongue or poor his ear, will speak the language of his people so that all can understand him. The perfected
model made by the lips and tongues of many different sorts of people
speaking the same words holds the speech of each new-comer clear
and sharp enough for communication. And as with speech, so with
gesture, so with the timing of initiative, of response, of command and
obedience. The toddler falls in step with the multitude around him
and cannot fail to learn his part.

But in a culture like modern America, the child does not see any 5
such harmonious, repetitive behavior. All men do not cross their legs
with the same assured masculinity, or squat on wooden stools to pro-

tect themselves from a rear-guard attack. All women do not walk with little mincing steps, or sit and lie with thighs drawn close together, even in sleep. The behavior of each American is itself a composite, an imperfectly realized version, of the behavior of others who in turn had, not a single model — expressed in many voices and many ways, but still a single model — but a hundred models, each different, each an individually developed style, lacking the authenticity, the precision, of a group style. The hand held out in greeting, to still a tear, or to help up a strange child that has stumbled, is not sure that it will be taken, or if taken, taken in the sense in which it is offered. Where patterns of courtship are clear, a girl knows the outcome if she smiles, or laughs, casts down her eyes, or merely walks softly by a group of harvesting youths cradling a red ear of corn in her arms. But in America, the same smile may evoke a casual answering grin, embarrassed averted eyes, an unwelcome advance, or may even mean being followed home along a deserted street, not because each boy who answers feels differently about the girl, but because each understands differently the cue that she gives.

CONSIDERATIONS

1. Mead maintains that in modern America "Every home is different from every other home." Consider the illustrations she gives in the second paragraph to demonstrate differences among families. Are they superficial or significant details? Can you add others that illustrate her point? Throughout this essay, when Mead generalizes, how does she support her points?
2. Why is it necessary to devise codes and models of expression? From a social scientist's viewpoint, why isn't it sufficient just to say what we mean and do what we intend?
3. If it is true that American families must develop a code of communication that a primitive society provides ready-made for all its families, how are we more "advanced" than New Guinea tribesmen? Are we occupied in reinventing the wheel, so to speak? Are there personal and social advantages in our situation over theirs?
4. WRITING TOPIC. At home, how long can you talk on the telephone without raising objections from your family? Where is your stereo set, and

what is the acceptable volume level around the house? How are you praised for your academic achievements? And for what things can you give praise to your parents? How do you know when you can feel assured of privacy in your home? With the eyes of an anthropologist observing a primal (if not primitive) society, write a 500-word essay that deciphers the code only your family members would fully comprehend regarding one significant issue of family life.

Marie Winn

THE *MAD* VIEW OF PARENTS*

◊

Marie Winn (b. 1936) was born in Prague, Czechoslovakia, and was brought to the United States in 1939, where she attended public schools in New York City. Perhaps this change of cultures in her early life contributed to her special awareness of children's responses to changes in society, which is the topic of most of her work as a writer. She attended Radcliffe College and Columbia University, and she now lives in New York City and is a regular contributor to the *New York Times Magazine.* Her book, *The Plug-In Drug: Television, Children, and the Family* (1977), helped to rekindle national concern over the negative effects of television on childhood development. Her most recent book, *Children Without Childhood* (1983), draws attention to the early end of carefree attitudes in children who are no longer kept in a long period of protected innocence about adult life. Her book is based on many interviews and on her analysis of popular culture, such as the following section that discusses *Mad* magazine.

There was once a time when children believed that adults were in- 1
evitably good, that all presidents were as honest as Abe Lincoln, that their parents' world was wiser and better than their own child world, a time when children were expected to give up their seats to adults in public conveyances, to reserve strong language for the company of their peers, and in every way to treat adults with "respect." Then along came *Mad* magazine. If there is a single cultural force in the last twenty-five years epitomizing the change that has overtaken child-hood, it is that singular publication.

When *Mad* first appeared in the early fifties it was an offshoot of 2
the principal medium of popular child culture of the day — comics. It had a comic-book format, with stories told by cartoon figures speaking

* Editor's title.

via word-filled balloons above their heads. But while comic books of
earlier years ran the gamut from "cute" Walt Disney types to the
gruesome "Tale of the Crypt" variety of horror comics, nevertheless
they all belonged to the category of fantasy, long an accepted adjunct
of childhood. Then *Mad* introduced a new element: satire. Before
Mad, satire traditionally entered young people's lives in late adolescence, often via college humor magazines. *Mad* was the first satirical
magazine for children, a sort of Swift for Kids, dealing with children's
own reality — their parents, school, and culture — in an irreverent
and mocking way. Its readership has grown ever younger, from high-
school-age kids in the sixties to nine- and ten-year-olds today.

In the first years, *Mad's* sharp satirical lance was aimed at the cul- 3
tural media children were exposed to — old classics, comics, radio,
movies, and, with increasing frequency, television. Action comic strips
of the *Superman* variety were ridiculed in a feature called "Super-
duper Man." "Prince Violent" mocked the pseudo-historical genre of
comic strip. "Dragged Net" laughed at the "real-life" police dramas
that were popular on the radio in the fifties. As television began to
take up more of children's free time, a procession of parodies of TV
programs and especially commercials began to appear. "From the
gaudy grille of Ca-dil-lac to the fins of Che-vro-let. We will push
GM's new mo-dels and make obso-les-cence pay!" ran a parody in the
late fifties. By 1960 television's pre-eminent position in children's lives
was noted by *Mad:* in "A Checklist for Baby-Sitters," the most important consideration for whether to take the job was the condition of
the television set. Food, baby-sitting rates, and record player follow
shortly. In the past position, as number 10, was the type and number
of children to be cared for.

While writers for *Mad* in its first decade chose mainly cultural ma- 4
terial to satirize, from the mid-sixties on the focus turned more and
more to the child's social environment: parents and the family as an
institution. Parents were appalled at the mocking, disrespectful attitude the magazine seemed to encourage towards adults; children
adored it, soaked it up like sponges. A feature entitled "If Babies
Could Take Parent Pictures," for instance, captions one of its illustrations: "Here's my idiot father trying to drive and take pictures at the
same time. I was lucky to get home alive." The phrase "My idiot father" hardly has a jarring sound in the 1980s when much of what kids
say to adults is unprintable, but in 1960 the words were shocking. At

some point during those two decades a long-established convention came to an end, one that had compelled children to repress their anger and impatience, forcing them to mutter under their breath, perhaps, but rarely allowing them to be openly abusive towards adults. *Mad* magazine may have been more influential in the move towards free expression among children than has heretofore been acknowledged.

As Al Feldstein, editor-in-chief of *Mad* for the past twenty-five 5 years (sometimes known as Chief Madman), describes the change:

"What we did was to take the absurdities of the adult world and 6 show kids that adults are not omnipotent. That their parents were being two-faced in their standards — telling kids to be honest, not to lie, and yet themselves cheating on their income tax. We showed kids that the world out there is unfair, that a lot of people out there are lying to them, cheating them. We told them there's a lot of garbage out in the world and you've got to be aware of it. Everything you read in the papers is not necessarily true. What you see on television is mostly lies. You're going to have to learn to think for yourself.

A relentless parade of features exposing parental hypocrisies caused 7 shock-waves of admiration to reverberate among *Mad*'s young readers (who were not unaware of their older siblings' embattled protests against the more profound hypocrisies of the Great Society as it engaged in the Vietnam "conflict"). For example, a regular feature of the mid-sixties entitled "What They Say and What It Really Means" portrays a mother and father addressing their teenage daughter and her seedy-looking boyfriend: "We have nothing against the boy, darling," is What They Say. "It's just that you're both so terribly young." Then the writer spells out What It Really Means: "Wait until you find a boy of your own religion who's got money" — parental bigotry and venality and hypocrisy knocked down in one fell swoop.

As the sixties wore on towards the seventies and adult culture grew 8 increasingly sophisticated and sexually open, *Mad*'s parodies grew ever more adult themselves, dealing more and more often with adult sexuality, women's liberation, the drug and alcohol scene, and other unchildlike subjects. Movie satires abandoned Walt Disney and appeared with titles such as "Boob and Carnal and Alas and Alfred." A take-off on the song "Matchmaker" from the musical *Fiddler on the Roof* was called "Headshrinker" and included such lines as "I'm Sheila, a free-sex fanatic, I'm Nancy, a speed freak just now, I'm Joy, who makes bombs in the attic, and answers the phone with quotations from Mao," and ended prophetically, "Headshrinker, headshrinker, this is our fate, kids we can't stand, parents we hate."

Child readers of the mid-1970s were now swept along in adult so-   9 ciety's increasing preoccupation with sex. "Mom and I are proud of you," says a parent to a teenage daughter in a feature of the 1970s. "We heard that you and Steve were the only students in the history of your college who didn't go to bed together on your first date." The daughter answers via a balloon above her head: "That's true, Dad. But we did make out on a couch, on the floor, etc."

As divorce began to reach epidemic proportions in the second half   10 of the 1970s, *Mad* did not fail to comment on it. A 1975 parody called "Broken Homes and Gardens" had a mother and father who declared that they *weren't* going to get a divorce. "Because of the kids," they explained. "Neither of us wants them." In 1976 appeared "Unweddings of the Future," in which invitations were sent out by the parents of the soon-to-be-ex-bride.

Comparing an issue of *Mad* of the 1980s with one from the 1950s   11 provides an almost shocking view of the change that childhood had undergone in those years. The magazine of December 1980, for example, features a parody of the movie *Little Darlings*, a film about two thirteen-year-old girls at summer camp who have a race to see which of them can lose her virginity first. The *Mad* version includes an outdoor salesman hawking a new kind of children's wares: "Get your training diaphragms here!" he cries. "She's starting foreplay now," a little girl observes as she spies on a pair of prospective mini-lovers. When one of the pubescent heroines gets cold feet during her final seduction scene, her gangly swain protests, "I'm getting frustrated! Y'know, there are NAMES for girls like you!" His partner asks, "Is Crazy Teenager one of them?" He replies, "No . . . but you got the INITIALS right!!!" Will *Mad*'s child readership "get" the allusion? An informal survey of several average seventh-graders suggests that the CT epithet is well known to that age group today.

An ironic footnote: *Little Darlings* received an R rating, officially   12 barring admission to unaccompanied children under seventeen — that is, to almost all *Mad*'s readership. Nevertheless great numbers of pre-teenagers gained access to *Little Darlings*, as they do to many other R movies.

It is almost impossible to imagine children of 1955 openly reading   13 about diaphragms and foreplay. But that was still the Golden Age of Innocence. . . .

. . . Children today, even very young ones, are let in on the secrets 14 of their parents' deficiencies, vulnerabilities, failings, weaknesses, long before these might become naturally apparent in the environment of an unbroken family. Early disabused of their normal illusions of parental omnipotence and omniscience, children of divorce are made to understand in specific detail that their parents are often as helpless and confused as they themselves are. In the past, this was a discovery that children made slowly and painfully during the course of their adolescence; when they finally came to grips with the realization that their parents were just normal, fallible human beings, they were often ready to take the last step towards separating emotionally from their parents and starting an independent life. They were on the verge of adulthood.

But for children who have their parents' fallibility thrust upon 15 them, as it were, long before they reach the developmental point of separation and independence, the question that becomes a deep part of the child's life, whether consciously articulated or not, is: Who will take care of me if my parents can't even take care of themselves? In this way the relaxed insouciance of childhood, during which the child can throw all its energies into work or play, is transformed into a more cautious, survival-oriented frame of mind, one, indeed, that is not unlike that which adults must always maintain — except, of course, for those rare times of relaxation, times when they can let go, times when they like to think they "feel like children again."

CONSIDERATIONS

1. This selection begins with broad statements that probably oversimplify the truth. How does the first paragraph lead us to accept its oversimplifications?
2. Describe the kind of subject material comic books presented before *Mad*.
3. What changes in subject material did *Mad* undergo from its inception to the present time?
4. What changes in other entertainment media, such as books, television, and films, would help account for the alleged loss of innocence among today's children?

5. The editor of *Mad*, whom the author quotes in paragraph 6, takes a very positive view of the magazine's effect on children. How does his view differ from the author's assessment of its effects? With whom do you agree more closely? Why?

6. WRITING TOPIC. In 700 words, compare and contrast the presentation of family life in one weekly segment of two television situation comedies or two soap operas. You may want to analyze such matters as the realism of the social settings, the level of personal interactions through dialogues and behavior, the treatment of personal conflicts, and the expression of moral values. Which program develops a more interesting focus on family life?

Nancy Friday

COMPETITION

◊

NANCY FRIDAY (b. 1937) worked as a journalist after attending
Wellesley College. As a feminist writer, she has helped reexamine
woman's identity by writing about the way sexual roles are enforced
and expressed in everyday life. Her first book, *My Secret Garden*
(1973), considered the prominence of fantasies in the sexual development of young people. This excerpt from her autobiography, *My
Mother/My Self* (1977), recounts the way that as an early adolescent
she reacted to the presence of older, more sexually defined and attractive women in her family.

Although I didn't realize it at the time, my mother was getting 1
prettier. My sister was a beauty. My adolescence was the time of our
greatest estrangement.

I have a photo of the three of us when I was twelve: my mother, my 2
sister Susie, and I, on a big chintz sofa, each on a separate cushion,
leaning away from one another with big spaces in between. I grew up
fired with a sense of family spirit, which I loved and needed, with
aunts and uncles and cousins under the omnipotent umbrella of my
grandfather. "All for one and one for all," he would say at summer re-
unions, and no one took it more seriously than I. I would have gone
to war for any one of them, and believed they would do the same for
me. But within our own little nucleus, the three of us didn't touch
much.

Now, when I ask her why, my mother sighs and says she supposes it 3
was because that was how she was raised. I remember shrinking from
her Elizabeth Arden night-cream kiss, mumbling from under the
blanket that yes, I had brushed my teeth. I had not. I had wet the
toothbrush in case she felt it, feeling that would get even with her. For
what? The further we all get from childhood, the more physically af-

fectionate we try to be with one another. But we are still shy after all
these years.

I was a late bloomer, like my mother. But my mother bloomed so 4
late, or had such a penetrating early frost, that she believed it even less
than I would in my turn. When she was a freckled sixteen and sitting
shyly on her unfortunate hands, her younger sister was already a famous beauty. That is still the relationship between them. Grandmothers both, in their eyes my aunt is still the sleek-haired belle of the
ball, immaculately handsome on a horse. My mother's successes do
not count. They will argue at 2:00 A.M. over whether one of my aunt's
many beaux ever asked my mother out. My mother could never make
up a flattering story about herself. I doubt that she so much as heard
the nice things men told her once she had grown into the fine-looking
woman who smiles at me in family photos. But she always gives in to
my aunt, much I'm sure as she gave in to the old self-image after my
father died. He — that one splendidly handsome man — may have
picked her out from all the rest, but his death just a few years later
must have felt like some punishment for having dared to believe for a
moment that her father was wrong: who could possibly want her? She
still blushes at a compliment.

I think she was at her prettiest in her early thirties. I was twelve and 5
at my nadir. Her hair had gone a delicate auburn red and she wore it
brushed back from her face in soft curls. Seated beside her and Susie,
who inherited a raven version of her beautiful hair, I look like an
adopted person. But I had already defended myself against my looks.
They were unimportant. There was a distance between me and the
mirror commensurate with the growing distance between me and my
mother and sister. My success with my made-up persona was proof: I
didn't need them. My titles at school, my awards and achievements,
so bolstered my image of myself that until writing this book I genuinely believed that I grew up feeling sorry for my sister. What chance
had she alongside The Great Achiever and Most Popular Girl in the
World? I even worked up some guilt about outshining her. Pure survival instinct? My dazzling smile would divert the most critical observer from comparing me to the cute, petite girls with whom I grew
up. I switched the contest: don't look at my lank hair, my 5' 10",
don't notice that my right eye wanders bizarrely (though the eye doctor said it was useless to keep me in glasses); watch me tap dance,
watch me win the game, let me make you happy! When I describe

myself in those days my mother laughs. "Oh, Nancy, you were such a darling little girl." But I wasn't little any more.

I think my sister, Susie, was born beautiful, a fact that affected my mother and me deeply, though in different ways. I don't think it mattered so much until Susie's adolescence. She turned so lush one ached to look at her. Pictures of Susie then remind me of the young Elizabeth Taylor in *A Place in the Sun.* One has to almost look away from so much beauty. It scared my mother to death. Whatever had gone on between them before came to a head and has never stopped. Their constant friction determined me to get away from this house of women, to be free of women's petty competitions, to live on a bigger scale. I left home eventually but I've never gotten away from feeling how wonderful to be so beautiful your mother can't take her eyes off you, even if only to nag. 6

I remember an amazing lack of any feeling about my only sibling, with whom I shared a room for years, whose clothes were identical to mine until I was ten. Except for feelings of irritation when she tried to cuddle me when I was four, bursts of anger that erupted into fist fights which I started and won at ten, and after that, indifference, a calculated unawareness that has resulted in a terrible and sad absence of my sister in my life. 7

My husband says his sister was the only child his father ever paid any attention to: "You have done to Susie what I did to my sister," he says. "You made her invisible." Me, jealous of Susie, who never won a single trophy or had as many friends as I? I must have been insanely jealous. 8

I only allowed myself to face it twice. Both times happened in that twelfth year, when my usual defenses couldn't take the emotional cross currents of adolescence. When I did slash out it wasn't very glorious, no well-chosen words or contest on the tennis courts. I did it like a thief in the night. Nobody ever guessed it was I who poured the red nail polish down the front of Susie's new white eyelet evening dress the day of her first yacht club dance. When I stole her summer savings and threw her wallet down the sewer, mother blamed Susie for being so careless. I watched my sister accept the criticism with her mother's own resignation, and I felt some relief from the angry emotions that had hold of me. 9

When Susie went away to boarding school, I made jokes about how 10 glad I was to be rid of her. It was our first separation. Conflicting urges, angers, and envies were coming at me from every direction; I had nothing left over to handle my terrible feelings of loss at her going. It was the summer I was plagued by what I called "my thoughts."

I read every book in the house as a talisman against thinking. I was 11 afraid that if my brain were left idle for even one minute, these "thoughts" would take over. Perhaps I feared they already had. Was my sister's going away the fulfillment of my own murderous wishes against her? I wrote in my first and only diary: "Susie, come home, please come home!!!!!!! I'm sorry, I'm sorry!!!!!!!"

When I outgrew the Nancy Drew books for perfect attendance at 12 Sunday school, and the Girl Scout badges for such merits as selling the most rat poison door to door, I graduated to prizes at the community theater. I won a plastic wake-up radio for the I Speak for Democracy contest. I was captain of the athletic association, president of the student government, and had the lead in the class play, all in the same year. In fact, I wrote the class play. It might have been embarrassing, but no one else wanted these prizes. Scoring home runs and getting straight A's weren't high on the list of priorities among my friends. (The South takes all prizes for raising noncompetitive women.) In the few cases where anyone did give me a run for the money, I had an unbeatable incentive: my grandfather's applause. It was he for whom I ran.

I can't remember ever hearing my grandfather say to my mother, 13 "Well done, Jane." I can't remember my mother ever saying to my sister, "Well done, Susie." And I never gave my mother the chance to say it to me. She was the last to hear of my achievements, and when she did, it was not from me but from her friends. Did she really notice so little that I was leaving her out? Was she so hurt that she pretended not to care? My classmates who won second prize or even no prize at all asked their families to attend the award ceremonies. I, who won first prize, always, did so to the applause of no kin at all. Was I spiting her? I know I was spiting myself. Nothing would have made me happier than to have her there; nothing would induce me to invite her. It is a game I later played with men: "Leave!" I would cry, and when they did, "How could you hurt me so?" I'd implore.

If I deprived her of the chance to praise me, she never criticized 14 me. Criticism was the vehicle by which she could articulate her relationship to my sister. No matter what it was, Susie could never get it right — in my mother's eyes. It continues that way to this day. Difficult as it is to think of my mother as competitive with anyone, how else could she have felt about her beautiful, ripe fourteen-year-old daughter? My mother was coming into her own mature, full bloom but perhaps that only made her more sensitive to the fact that Susie was simultaneously experiencing the same sexual flush. A year later, my mother remarried. Today, only the geography has changed: the argument begins as soon as they enter the same room. But they are often in the same room. They have never been closer.

How often the dinner table becomes the family battleground. 15 When I met Bill he had no table you could sit around in his vast bachelor apartment. The dinner table was where his father waged war; it was the one time the family was together. In Charleston, dinner was served at 2:00. I have this picture of our midday meals: Susie on my right, mother on my left, and me feeling that our cook, Ruth, had set this beautiful table for me alone.

No one else seemed to care about the golden squash, the crisp 16 chicken, the big silver pitcher of iced tea. While I proceeded to eat my way from one end of the table to the other, Susie and mother would begin: "Susie, that lipstick is too dark. . . . Must you pluck your eyebrows? . . . Why did you buy high-heeled, open-toe shoes when I told you to get loafers? . . . Those pointy bras make you look a, like a — " But my mother couldn't say the word. At this point one of them would leave the table in tears, while the other shuddered in despair at the sound of the slammed bedroom door. Meanwhile, I pondered my problem of whose house to play at that afternoon. I would finish both their desserts and be gone before Ruth had cleared the table. Am I exaggerating? Did it only happen once a week? Does it matter?

I was lucky to have escaped those devastating battles. "I never had 17 to worry about Nancy," my mother has always said. "She could always take care of herself." It became true. Only my husband has been allowed to see the extent of my needs. But the competitive drive that made me so self-sufficient was fired by more than jealousy of my sister. If my mother wasn't going to acknowledge me, her father would. If she couldn't succeed in his eyes, I would. It's my best explanation for all those years of trophies and presidencies, for my ability to "reach" my grandfather as my mother never could. I not only won what she had wanted all her life — his praise — I learned with the canniness of the young that this great towering man loved to be loved, to be touched. He couldn't allow himself to reach out first to those he loved most, but he couldn't resist an overture of affection.

I greeted his visits with embraces, took the kisses I had won and sat 18
at his feet like one of his Dalmatians, while my sister stood shyly in the background and my mother waited for his criticism. But I was no more aware of competing with my mother than of being jealous of my sister. Two generations of women in my family have struggled for my grandfather's praise. Perhaps I became his favorite because he sensed I needed it most. The price I paid was that I had to beat my mother and my sister. I am still guilty for that.

In the stereotyping of the sexes, men are granted all the competi- 19
tive drives, women none. The idea of competitive women evokes disturbing images — the darker, dykey side of femininity, or cartoons of "ladies" in high heels, flailing at each other ineffectively with their handbags. An important step has been left out of our socialization: mother raises us to win people's love. She gives us no training in the emotions of rivalry that would lose it for us. With no practical experience in the rules that make competition safe, we fear its ferocity. Never having been taught to win, we do not know how to lose. Women are not raised to compete like gentlemen.

CONSIDERATIONS

1. What sort of person was the author as a twelve-year-old? Describe her appearance and personality. How was she different at that age from Nora Ephron (see "Shaping Up Absurd," p. 7) or from Mary McCarthy (see "Names," p. 26)?
2. Identify some specific signs of a "family code" (see p. 81) that functions for all three generations. To what extent did Friday practice the code, and to what extent, if at all, did she alter it?
3. What does Friday's mother fear? Identify several things in her life that contribute to those fears. Do Friday's insights to her mother's character seem fair?

4. What do you think the author's guiding purpose is in this selection? Does Friday want to influence her reader's attitudes about competitiveness? Or is she mainly interested in understanding her own past? Or is there another purpose that guides the tone and direction of her writing?
5. WRITING TOPIC. Write a 500-word essay that explains the difference between "hating to lose" and "loving to win."

Raymond Carver

MY FATHER'S LIFE

◇

RAYMOND CARVER (b. 1939) graduated from California State University at Humboldt and spent a year at the Writers' Workshop at the University of Iowa. He writes poetry and short stories that have appeared widely in such magazines as *Esquire, Harper's* and *The New Yorker.* His fiction has been collected in *What We Talk About When We Talk About Love* (1981) — see the story on page 185 of this reader — and *Cathedral* (1984). Carver has taught writing at the University of California at Santa Cruz and at Syracuse University. In this memoir of his father, which first appeared in *Esquire* in 1984, Carver emphasizes the hardships that his father faced as a laborer during the Great Depression of the 1930s and later during the years of his psychological depression.

My dad's name was Clevie Raymond Carver. His family called him 1 Raymond and friends called him C. R. I was named Raymond Clevie Carver Jr. I hated the "Junior" part. When I was little my dad called me Frog, which was okay. But later, like everybody else in the family, he began calling me Junior. He went on calling me this until I was thirteen or fourteen and announced that I wouldn't answer to that name any longer. So he began calling me Doc. From then until his death, on June 17, 1967, he called me Doc, or else Son.

When he died, my mother telephoned my wife with the news. I 2 was away from my family at the time, between lives, trying to enroll in the School of Library Science at the University of Iowa. When my wife answered the phone, my mother blurted out, "Raymond's dead!" For a moment, my wife thought my mother was telling her that I was dead. Then my mother made it clear *which* Raymond she was talking about and my wife said, "Thank God. I thought you meant *my* Raymond."

My dad walked, hitched rides, and rode in empty boxcars when he ₃ went from Arkansas to Washington State in 1934, looking for work. I don't know whether he was pursuing a dream when he went out to Washington. I doubt it. I don't think he dreamed much. I believe he was simply looking for steady work at decent pay. Steady work was meaningful work. He picked apples for a time and then landed a construction laborer's job on the Grand Coulee Dam. After he'd put aside a little money, he bought a car and drove back to Arkansas to help his folks, my grandparents, pack up for the move west. He said later that they were about to starve down there, and this wasn't meant as a figure of speech. It was during that short while in Arkansas, in a town called Leola, that my mother met my dad on the sidewalk as he came out of a tavern.

"He was drunk," she said. "I don't know why I let him talk to me. ₄ His eyes were glittery. I wish I'd had a crystal ball." They'd met once, a year or so before, at a dance. He'd had girlfriends before her, my mother told me. "Your dad always had a girlfriend, even after we married. He was my first and last. I never had another man. But I didn't miss anything."

They were married by a justice of the peace on the day they left for ₅ Washington, this big, tall country girl and a farmhand-turned-construction worker. My mother spent her wedding night with my dad and his folks, all of them camped beside the road in Arkansas.

In Omak, Washington, my dad and mother lived in a little place ₆ not much bigger than a cabin. My grandparents lived next door. My dad was still working on the dam, and later, with the huge turbines producing electricity and the water backed up for a hundred miles into Canada, he stood in the crowd and heard Franklin D. Roosevelt when he spoke at the construction site. "He never mentioned those guys who died building that dam," my dad said. Some of his friends had died there, men from Arkansas, Oklahoma, and Missouri.

He then took a job in a sawmill in Clatskanie, Oregon, a little town ₇ alongside the Columbia River. I was born there, and my mother has a picture of my dad standing in front of the gate to the mill, proudly holding me up to face the camera. My bonnet is on crooked and about to come untied. His hat is pushed back on his forehead, and he's wearing a big grin. Was he going in to work or just finishing his shift? It doesn't matter. In either case, he had a job and a family. These were his salad days.

In 1941 we moved to Yakima, Washington, where my dad went to 8
work as a saw filer, a skilled trade he'd learned in Clatskanie. When
war broke out, he was given a deferment because his work was considered necessary to the war effort. Finished lumber was in demand by
the armed services, and he kept his saws so sharp they could shave the
hair off your arm.

After my dad had moved us to Yakima, he moved his folks into the 9
same neighborhood. By the mid-1940s the rest of my dad's family —
his brother, his sister, and her husband, as well as uncles, cousins,
nephews, and most of their extended family and friends — had
come out from Arkansas. All because my dad came out first. The
men went to work at Boise Cascade, where my dad worked, and
the women packed apples in the canneries. And in just a little while,
it seemed — according to my mother — everybody was better
off than my dad. "Your dad couldn't keep money," my mother
said. "Money burned a hole in his pocket. He was always doing for
others."

The first house I clearly remember living in, at 1515 South Fif- 10
teenth Street, in Yakima, had an outdoor toilet. On Halloween night,
or just any night, for the hell of it, neighbor kids, kids in their early
teens, would carry our toilet away and leave it next to the road. My
dad would have to get somebody to help him bring it home. Or these
kids would take the toilet and stand it in somebody else's backyard.
Once they actually set it on fire. But ours wasn't the only house that
had an outdoor toilet. When I was old enough to know what I was
doing, I threw rocks at the other toilets when I'd see someone go inside. This was called bombing the toilets. After a while, though, everyone went to indoor plumbing until, suddenly, our toilet was the last
outdoor one in the neighborhood. I remember the shame I felt when
my third-grade teacher, Mr. Wise, drove me home from school one
day. I asked him to stop at the house just before ours, claiming I lived
there.

I can recall what happened one night when my dad came home 11
late to find that my mother had locked all the doors on him from the
inside. He was drunk, and we could feel the house shudder as he rattled the door. When he'd managed to force open a window, she hit
him between the eyes with a colander and knocked him out. We
could see him down there on the grass. For years afterward, I used to
pick up this colander — it was as heavy as a rolling pin — and imag-

ine what it would feel like to be hit in the head with something like
that.

It was during this period that I remember my dad taking me into 12
the bedroom, sitting me down on the bed, and telling me that I might
have to go live with my Aunt LaVon for a while. I couldn't understand what I'd done that meant I'd have to go away from home to
live. But this, too — whatever prompted it — must have blown over,
more or less, anyway, because we stayed together, and I didn't have to
go live with her or anyone else.

I remember my mother pouring his whiskey down the sink. Some- 13
times she'd pour it all out and sometimes, if she was afraid of getting
caught, she'd only pour half of it out and then add water to the rest. I
tasted some of his whiskey once myself. It was terrible stuff, and I
don't see how anybody could drink it.

After a long time without one, we finally got a car, in 1949 or 1950, 14
a 1938 Ford. But it threw a rod the first week we had it, and my dad
had to have the motor rebuilt.

"We drove the oldest car in town," my mother said. "We could 15
have had a Cadillac for all he spent on car repairs." One time she
found someone else's tube of lipstick on the floorboard, along with a
lacy handkerchief. "See this?" she said to me. "Some floozy left this
in the car."

Once I saw her take a pan of warm water into the bedroom where 16
my dad was sleeping. She took his hand from under the covers and
held it in the water. I stood in the doorway and watched. I wanted to
know what was going on. This would make him talk in his sleep, she
told me. There were things she needed to know, things she was sure
he was keeping from her.

Every year or so, when I was little, we would take the North Coast 17
Limited across the Cascade Range from Yakima to Seattle and stay in
the Vance Hotel and eat, I remember, at a place called the Dinner
Bell Cafe. Once we went to Ivar's Acres of Clams and drank glasses of
warm clam broth.

In 1956, the year I was to graduate from high school, my dad quit 18
his job at the mill in Yakima and took a job in Chester, a little sawmill
town in northern California. The reasons given at the time for his
taking the job had to do with a higher hourly wage and the vague
promise that he might, in a few years' time, succeed to the job of head
filer in this new mill. But I think, in the main, that my dad had grown

restless and simply wanted to try his luck elsewhere. Things had gotten a little too predictable for him in Yakima. Also, the year before, there had been the deaths, within six months of each other, of both his parents.

But just a few days after graduation, when my mother and I were 19 packed to move to Chester, my dad penciled a letter to say he'd been sick for a while. He didn't want us to worry, he said, but he'd cut himself on a saw. Maybe he'd got a tiny sliver of steel in his blood. Anyway, something had happened and he'd had to miss work, he said. In the same mail was an unsigned postcard from somebody down there telling my mother that my dad was about to die and that he was drinking "raw whiskey."

When we arrived in Chester, my dad was living in a trailer that be- 20 longed to the company. I didn't recognize him immediately. I guess for a moment I didn't want to recognize him. He was skinny and pale and looked bewildered. His pants wouldn't stay up. He didn't look like my dad. My mother began to cry. My dad put his arm around her and patted her shoulder vaguely, like he didn't know what this was all about, either. The three of us took up life together in the trailer, and we looked after him as best we could. But my dad was sick, and he couldn't get any better. I worked with him in the mill that summer and part of the fall. We'd get up in the mornings and eat eggs and toast while we listened to the radio, and then go out the door with our lunch pails. We'd pass through the gate together at eight in the morning, and I wouldn't see him again until quitting time. In November I went back to Yakima to be closer to my girlfriend, the girl I'd made up my mind I was going to marry.

He worked at the mill in Chester until the following February, 21 when he collapsed on the job and was taken to the hospital. My mother asked if I would come down there and help. I caught a bus from Yakima to Chester, intending to drive them back to Yakima. But now, in addition to being physically sick, my dad was in the midst of a nervous breakdown, though none of us knew to call it that at the time. During the entire trip back to Yakima, he didn't speak, not even when asked a direct question. ("How do you feel, Raymond?" "You okay, Dad?") He'd communicate if he communicated at all, by moving his head or by turning his palms up as if to say he didn't know or care. The only time he said anything on the trip, and for nearly a month afterward, was when I was speeding down a gravel road in Oregon and the car muffler came loose. "You were going too fast," he said.

Back in Yakima a doctor saw to it that my dad went to a psychia- 22 trist. My mother and dad had to go on relief, as it was called, and the county paid for the psychiatrist. The psychiatrist asked my dad, "Who is the President?" He'd had a question put to him that he could answer. "Ike," my dad said. Nevertheless, they put him on the fifth floor of Valley Memorial Hospital and began giving him electroshock treatments. I was married by then and about to start my own family. My dad was still locked up when my wife went into this same hospital, just one floor down, to have our first baby. After she had delivered, I went upstairs to give my dad the news. They let me in through a steel door and showed me where I could find him. He was sitting on a couch with a blanket over his lap. *Hey,* I thought. *What in hell is happening to my dad?* I sat down next to him and told him he was a grandfather. He waited a minute and then he said, "I feel like a grandfather." That's all he said. He didn't smile or move. He was in a big room with a lot of other people. Then I hugged him, and he began to cry.

Somehow he got out of there. But now came the years when he 23 couldn't work and just sat around the house trying to figure what next and what he'd done wrong in his life that he'd wound up like this. My mother went from job to crummy job. Much later she referred to that time he was in the hospital, and those years just afterward, as "when Raymond was sick." The word *sick* was never the same for me again.

In 1964, through the help of a friend, he was lucky enough to be 24 hired on at a mill in Klamath, California. He moved down there by himself to see if he could hack it. He lived not far from the mill, in a one-room cabin not much different from the place he and my mother had started out living in when they went west. He scrawled letters to my mother, and if I called she'd read them aloud to me over the phone. In the letters, he said it was touch and go. Every day that he went to work, he felt like it was the most important day of his life. But every day, he told her, made the next day that much easier. He said for her to tell me he said hello. If he couldn't sleep at night, he said, he thought about me and the good times we used to have. Finally, after a couple of months, he regained some of his confidence. He could do the work and didn't think he had to worry that he'd let anybody down ever again. When he was sure, he sent for my mother.

He'd been off from work for six years and had lost everything in 25
that time — home, car, furniture, and appliances, including the big
freezer that had been my mother's pride and joy. He'd lost his good
name too — Raymond Carver was someone who couldn't pay his
bills — and his self-respect was gone. He'd even lost his virility. My
mother told my wife, "All during that time Raymond was sick we
slept together in the same bed, but we didn't have relations. He
wanted to a few times, but nothing happened. I didn't miss it, but I
think he wanted to, you know."

During those years I was trying to raise my own family and earn a 26
living. But, one thing and another, we found ourselves having to move
a lot. I couldn't keep track of what was going down in my dad's life.
But I did have a chance one Christmas to tell him I wanted to be a
writer. I might as well have told him I wanted to become a plastic
surgeon. "What are you going to write about?" he wanted to know.
Then, as if to help me out, he said, "Write about stuff you know
about. Write about some of those fishing trips we took." I said I
would, but I knew I wouldn't. "Send me what you write," he said. I
said I'd do that, but then I didn't. I wasn't writing anything about
fishing, and I didn't think he'd particularly care about, or even necessarily understand, what I was writing in those days. Besides, he wasn't
a reader. Not the sort, anyway, I imagined I was writing for.

Then he died. I was a long way off, in Iowa City, with things still to 27
say to him. I didn't have the chance to tell him goodbye, or that I
thought he was doing great at his new job. That I was proud of him
for making a comeback.

My mother said he came in from work that night and ate a big 28
supper. Then he sat at the table by himself and finished what was left
of a bottle of whiskey, a bottle she found hidden in the bottom of the
garbage under some coffee grounds a day or so later. Then he got up
and went to bed, where my mother joined him a little later. But in the
night she had to get up and make a bed for herself on the couch. "He
was snoring so loud I couldn't sleep," she said. The next morning
when she looked in on him, he was on his back with his mouth open,
his cheeks caved in. *Graylooking*, she said. She knew he was dead —
she didn't need a doctor to tell her that. But she called one anyway,
and then she called my wife.

Among the pictures my mother kept of my dad and herself during 29
those early days in Washington was a photograph of him standing in

front of a car, holding a beer and a stringer of fish. In the photograph
he is wearing his hat back on his forehead and has this awkward grin
on his face. I asked her for it and she gave it to me, along with some
others. I put it up on my wall, and each time we moved, I took the
picture along and put it up on another wall. I looked at it carefully
from time to time, trying to figure out some things about my dad, and
maybe myself in the process. But I couldn't. My dad just kept moving
further and further away from me and back into time. Finally, in the
course of another move, I lost the photograph. It was then that I tried
to recall it, and at the same time make an attempt to say something
about my dad, and how I thought that in some important ways we
might be alike. I wrote the poem when I was living in an apartment
house in an urban area south of San Francisco, at a time when I found
myself, like my dad, having trouble with alcohol. The poem was a way
of trying to connect up with him.

Photograph of My Father in His Twenty-Second Year

October. Here in this dank, unfamiliar kitchen
I study my father's embarrassed young man's face.
Sheepish grin, he holds in one hand a string
of spiny yellow perch, in the other
a bottle of Carlsberg beer.

In jeans and flannel shirt, he leans
against the front fender of a 1934 Ford.
He would like to pose brave and hearty for his posterity,
wear his old hat cocked over his ear.
All his life my father wanted to be bold.

But the eyes give him away, and the hands
that limply offer the string of dead perch
and the bottle of beer. Father, I love you,
yet how can I say thank you, I who can't hold my liquor either
and don't even know the places to fish.

The poem is true in its particulars, except that my dad died in June 30
and not October, as the first word of the poem says. I wanted a word
with more than one syllable to it to make it linger a little. But more
than that, I wanted a month appropriate to what I felt at the time I
wrote the poem — a month of short days and failing light, smoke in
the air, things perishing. June was summer nights and days, gradua-

tions, my wedding anniversary, the birthday of one of my children. June wasn't a month your father died in.

After the service at the funeral home, after we had moved outside, 31 a woman I didn't know came over to me and said, "He's happier where he is now." I stared at this woman until she moved away. I still remember the little knob of a hat she was wearing. Then one of my dad's cousins — I didn't know the man's name — reached out and took my hand, "We all miss him," he said, and I knew he wasn't saying it just to be polite.

I began to weep for the first time since receiving the news. I hadn't 32 been able to before. I hadn't had the time, for one thing. Now, suddenly, I couldn't stop. I held my wife and wept while she said and did what she could do to comfort me there in the middle of that summer afternoon.

I listened to people say consoling things to my mother, and I was 33 glad that my dad's family had turned up, had come to where he was. I thought I'd remember everything that was said and done that day and maybe find a way to tell it sometime. But I didn't. I forgot it all, or nearly. What I do remember is that I heard our name used a lot that afternoon, my dad's name and mine. But I knew they were talking about my dad. *Raymond*, these people kept saying in their beautiful voices out of my childhood. *Raymond.*

CONSIDERATIONS

1. In paragraphs 1 and 2 the author implicitly suggests some of the effects of having a name similar to his father's. What were these effects? Define his reaction explicitly.
2. In paragraphs 3 through 6, how does Carver's attitude about both his parents differ from his mother's attitude about her husband and herself? In your opinion who seems to have a better understanding of the past, the mother or the son?
3. What episodes and details in Carver's early life indicate that he and his father felt closely connected?
4. In Carver's poem about his father he writes, "All his life my father wanted to be bold." Do you think that line sums up the father fairly accurately? Does the essay indicate other things that the father also wanted to be? Was he more successful in those other aspirations? or less successful?
5. In the final paragraph Carver again notes the similarity of their names.

How has his final attitude toward this similarity changed from his attitude at the beginning of the essay?

6. WRITING TOPIC. In 700 words, describe the person in your family whom you most closely resemble in physical appearance. Be precise and detailed about his or her features and other concrete personal traits that are like your own. If it is useful, include such matters as the person's tone of voice, way of walking, usual gestures and mannerisms, or other helpful observations. Perhaps you will also want to differentiate yourself at various points in your essay.

Adrienne Rich

THE ANGER OF
A CHILD

◊

ADRIENNE RICH (b. 1929) published her first book of poems before she
was graduated from Radcliffe. Her early volumes, such as *A Change of
World* (1951), *Snapshots of a Daughter-in-Law* (1963), and *The Will
to Change* (1971), reflect her youth and marriage, her growing consciousness of womanhood, and the coming of middle age. In the 1970s
Rich became an activist in the women's movement, and in addition to
poetry she wrote literary criticism and essays on patriarchy in our culture. In this excerpt from her book about motherhood, *Of Woman
Born* (1976), she gives a thumbnail sketch of her parents and her upbringing that left some deep resentments smoldering even in the adult
woman.

It is hard to write about my mother. Whatever I do write, it is my 1
story I am telling, my version of the past. If she were to tell her own
story other landscapes would be revealed. But in my landscape or hers,
there would be old, smoldering patches of deep-burning anger. Before
her marriage, she had trained seriously for years both as a concert pianist and a composer. Born in a southern town, mothered by a strong,
frustrated woman, she had won a scholarship to study with the director at the Peabody Conservatory in Baltimore, and by teaching at
girls' schools had earned her way to further study in New York, Paris,
and Vienna. From the age of sixteen, she had been a young belle, who
could have married at any time, but she also possessed unusual talent,
determination, and independence for her time and place. She read —
and reads — widely and wrote — as her journals from my childhood
and her letters of today reveal — with grace and pungency.

    She married my father after a ten years' engagement during which 2
he finished his medical training and began to establish himself in aca-

demic medicine. Once married, she gave up the possibility of a concert career, though for some years she went on composing, and she is
still a skilled and dedicated pianist. My father, brilliant, ambitious,
possessed by his own drive, assumed that she would give her life over
to the enhancement of his. She would manage his household with the
formality and grace becoming to a medical professor's wife, though on
a limited budget; she would "keep up" her music, though there was
no question of letting her composing and practice conflict with her
duties as a wife and mother. She was supposed to bear him two children, a boy and a girl. She had to keep her household books to the last
penny — I still can see the big blue gray ledgers, inscribed in her
clear, strong hand; she marketed by streetcar, and later, when they
could afford a car, she drove my father to and from his laboratory or
lectures, often awaiting him for hours. She raised two children, and
taught us all our lessons, including music. (Neither of us was sent to
school until the fourth grade.) I am sure that she was made to feel responsible for all our imperfections.

My father, like the transcendentalist Bronson Alcott, believed that   3
he (or rather, his wife) could raise children according to his unique
moral and intellectual plan, thus proving to the world the values of
enlightened, unorthodox child-rearing. I believe that my mother, like
Abigail Alcott, at first genuinely and enthusiastically embraced the
experiment, and only later found that in carrying out my father's intense, perfectionist program, she was in conflict with her deep instincts as a mother. Like Abigail Alcott, too, she must have found that
while ideas might be unfolded by her husband, their daily, hourly
practice was going to be up to her. (" 'Mr. A. aids me in general principles, but nobody can aid me in the detail,' she mourned. . . . Moreover her husband's views kept her constantly wondering if she were
doing a good job. 'Am I doing what is right? Am I doing enough?
Am I doing too much?' " The appearance of "temper" and "will"
in Louisa, the second Alcott daughter, was blamed by her father on
her inheritance from her mother.) Under the institution of motherhood, the mother is the first to blame if theory proves unworkable in
practice, or if anything whatsoever goes wrong. But even earlier, my
mother had failed at one part of the plan: she had not produced a son.

For years, I felt my mother had chosen my father over me, had sac-   4
rificed me to his needs and theories. When my first child was born, I
was barely in communication with my parents. I had been fighting my

father for my right to an emotional life and a selfhood beyond his needs and theories. We were all at a draw. Emerging from the fear, exhaustion, and alienation of my first childbirth, I could not admit even to myself that I wanted my mother, let alone tell her how much I wanted her. When she visited me in the hospital neither of us could uncoil the obscure lashings of feeling that darkened the room, the tangled thread running backward to where she had labored for three days to give birth to me, and I was not a son. Now, twenty-six years later, I lay in a contagious hospital with my allergy, my skin covered with a mysterious rash, my lips and eyelids swollen, my body bruised and sutured, and, in a cot beside my bed, slept the perfect, golden, male child I had brought forth. How could I have interpreted her feelings when I could not begin to decipher my own? My body had spoken all too eloquently, but it was, medically, just my body. I wanted her to mother me again, to hold my baby in her arms as she had once held me; but that baby was also a gauntlet flung down: *my son.* Part of me longed to offer him for her blessing; part of me wanted to hold him up as a badge of victory in our tragic, unnecessary rivalry as women.

But I was only at the beginning. I know now as I could not possibly 5 know then, that among the tangle of feelings between us, in that crucial yet unreal meeting, was her guilt. Soon I would begin to understand the full weight and burden of maternal guilt, that daily, nightly, hourly, *Am I doing what is right? Am I doing enough? Am I doing too much?* The institution of motherhood finds all mothers more or less guilty of having failed their children; and my mother, in particular, had been expected to help create, according to my father's plan, a perfect daughter. This "perfect" daughter, though gratifyingly precocious, had early been given to tics and tantrums, had become permanently lame from arthritis at twenty-two; she had finally resisted her father's Victorian paternalism, his seductive charm and controlling cruelty, had married a divorced graduate student, had begun to write "modern," "obscure," "pessimistic" poetry, lacking the fluent sweetness of Tennyson, had had the final temerity to get pregnant and bring a living baby into the world. She had ceased to be the demure and precocious child or the poetic, seducible adolescent. Something, in my father's view, had gone terribly wrong. I can imagine that whatever else my mother felt (and I know that part of her *was* mutely on my side) she also was made to feel blame. Beneath the "numbness" that she has since told me she experienced at that time, I can imagine the guilt of Everymother, because I have known it myself.

But I did not know it yet. And it is difficult for me to write of my 6 mother now, because I have known it too well. I struggle to describe what it felt like to be her daughter, but I find myself divided, slipping under her skin; a part of me identifies too much with her. I know deep reservoirs of anger toward her still exist: the anger of a four-year-old locked in the closet (my father's orders, but my mother carried them out) for childish misbehavior; the anger of a six-year-old kept too long at piano practice (again, at his insistence, but it was she who gave the lessons) till I developed a series of facial tics. (As a mother I know what a child's facial tic is — a lancet of guilt and pain running through one's own body.) And I still feel the anger of a daughter, pregnant, wanting my mother desperately and feeling she had gone over to the enemy.

And I know there must be deep reservoirs of anger in her; every 7 mother has known overwhelming, unacceptable anger at her children. When I think of the conditions under which my mother became a mother, the impossible expectations, my father's distaste for pregnant women, his hatred of all that he could not control, my anger at her dissolves into grief and anger *for* her, and then dissolves back again into anger at her: the ancient, unpurged anger of the child.

My mother lives today as an independent woman, which she was 8 always meant to be. She is a much-loved, much-admired grandmother, an explorer in new realms; she lives in the present and future, not the past. I no longer have fantasies — they are the unhealed child's fantasies, I think — of some infinitely healing conversation with her, in which we could show all our wounds, transcend the pain we have shared as mother and daughter, say everything at last. But in writing these pages, I am admitting, at least, how important her existence is and has been for me.

CONSIDERATIONS

1. According to the author, why didn't her mother continue to develop her extraordinary talents and potentials for a creative, artistic life? What became of her mother's abilities?

2. Given what Rich mentions, what concrete details would you like to see filled into this portrait of Rich's mother? How might such details affect our view of the mother? Or of the author?

3. What is the author's view of her father? Was he important in her early life?

4. Describe the kind of mothering that the daughter received. Explain why the author still feels "the ancient, unpurged anger of the child." What is she angry about?

5. WRITING TOPIC. In 500 words, compare Rich's sketch of her parents with Nancy Friday's sketch (p. 92) of her mother and grandfather. In which family does life seem more bearable to the child?

Jamaica Kincaid

A WALK TO THE JETTY

◊

JAMAICA KINCAID (b. 1949) was born in Antigua in the West Indies. As a child she felt that her Caribbean surroundings were "almost overwhelming," and much of her fiction reflects her early life on the island. She came to the United States at seventeen. Her stories have appeared in the *Paris Review, Rolling Stone,* and *The New Yorker.* They were collected in *At the Bottom of the River* (1984). Her interrelated stories about Annie John, a fictional character much like herself, have been collected in *Annie John* (1985). The following selection is about the day of Annie's departure from Antigua.

"My name is Annie John." These were the first words that came 1 into my mind as I woke up on the morning of the last day I spent in Antigua, and they stayed there, lined up one behind the other, marching up and down, for I don't know how long. At noon on that day, a ship on which I was to be a passenger would sail to Barbados, and there I would board another ship, which would sail to England, where I would study to become a nurse. My name was the last thing I saw the night before, just as I was falling asleep; it was written in big, black letters all over my trunk, sometimes followed by my address in Antigua, sometimes followed by my address as it would be in England. I did not want to go to England, I did not want to be a nurse, but I would have chosen going off to live in a cavern and keeping house for seven unruly men rather than go on with my life as it stood. I never wanted to lie in this bed again, my legs hanging out way past the foot of it, tossing and turning on my mattress, with its cotton stuffing all lumped just where it wasn't a good place to be lumped. I never wanted to lie in my bed again and hear Mr. Ephraim driving his sheep to pasture — a signal to my mother that she should get up to prepare my father's and my bath and breakfast. I never wanted to lie in my bed and hear her get dressed, washing her face, brushing her teeth, and gargling. I especially never wanted to lie in my bed and hear my mother gargling again.

Lying there in the half-dark of my room, I could see my shelf, 2 with my books — some of them prizes I had won in school, some of them gifts from my mother — and with photographs of people I was supposed to love forever no matter what, and with my old thermos, which was given to me for my eighth birthday, and some shells I had gathered at different times I spent at the sea. In one corner stood my washstand and its beautiful basin of white enamel with blooming red hibiscus painted at the bottom and an urn that matched. In another corner were my old school shoes and my Sunday shoes. In still another corner, a bureau held my old clothes. I knew everything in this room, inside out and outside in. I had lived in this room for thirteen of my seventeen years. I could see in my mind's eye even the day my father was adding it onto the rest of the house. Everywhere I looked stood something that had meant a lot to me, that had given me pleasure at some point, or could remind me of a time that was a happy time. But as I was lying there my heart could have burst open with joy at the thought of never having to see any of it again.

If someone had asked me for a little summing up of my life at that 3 moment as I lay in bed, I would have said, "My name is Annie John. I was born on the fifteenth of September, seventeen years ago, at Holberton Hospital, at five o'clock in the morning. At the time I was born, the moon was going down at one end of the sky and the sun was coming up at the other. My mother's name is Annie also; I am named after her, and that is why my parents call me Little Miss. My father's name is Alexander, and he is thirty-five years older than my mother. Two of his children are four and six years older than she is. Looking at how sickly he has become and looking at the way my mother now has to run up and down for him, gathering the herbs and barks that he boils in water, which he drinks instead of the medicine the doctor has ordered for him, I plan not only never to marry an old man but certainly never to marry at all. The house we live in my father built with his own hands. The bed I am lying in my father built with his own hands. If I get up and sit on a chair, it is a chair my father built with his own hands. When my mother uses a large wooden spoon to stir the porridge we sometimes eat as part of our breakfast, it will be a spoon that my father has carved with his own hands. The sheets on my bed my mother made with her own hands. The curtains hanging at my window my mother made with her own hands. The nightie I am wearing, with scalloped neck and hem and sleeves, my mother made with her own hands. When I look at things in a certain way, I suppose I should say that the two of them made me with their own hands. For most of my life, when the three of us went anywhere together I stood between the two of them. But then I got too big, and there I was, shoulder to shoulder with them more or less, and it became not very comfortable to walk down the street together. And so now there they are together and here I am apart. I don't see them now the way I used to, and I don't love them now the way I used to. The bitter thing about it is that they are just the same and it is I who have changed, so all the things I used to be and all the things I used to feel are as false as the teeth in my father's head. Why, I wonder, didn't I see the hypocrite in my mother when, over the years, she said that she loved me and could hardly live without me, while at the same time proposing and arranging separation after separation, including this one, which, unbeknownst to her, *I* have arranged to be permanent? So now I, too, have hypocrisy, and breasts (small ones), and hair growing in the appropriate places, and sharp eyes, and I have made a vow never to be fooled again."

Lying in my bed for the last time, I thought, This is what I add up to. At that, I felt as if someone had placed me in a hole and was forcing me first down and then up against the pressure of gravity. I shook myself and prepared to get up. I said to myself, "I am getting up out of this bed for the last time." Everything I would do that morning until I got on the ship that would take me to England I would be doing for the last time, for I had made up my mind that, come what might, the road for me now went only in one direction: away from my home, away from my mother, away from my father, away from the everlasting blue sky, away from the everlasting hot sun, away from people who said to me, "This happened during the time your mother was carrying you." If I had been asked to put into words why I felt this way, if I had been given years to reflect and come up with the words of why I felt this way, I would not have been able to come up with so much as the letter "A." I only knew that I felt the way I did, and that this feeling was the strongest thing in my life.

The Anglican church bell struck seven. My father had already bathed and dressed and was in his workshop puttering around. As if the day of my leaving were something to celebrate, they were treating it as a holiday, and as if nothing usual would take place. My father would not go to work at all. When I got up, my mother greeted me with a big, bright "Good morning" — so big and bright that I shrank before it. I bathed quickly in some warm bark water that my mother had prepared for me. I put on my underclothes — all of them white and all of them smelling funny. Along with my earrings, my neck chain, and my bracelets, all made of gold from British Guiana, my underclothes had been sent to my mother's obeah woman, and whatever she had done to my jewelry and underclothes would help protect me from evil spirits and every kind of misfortune. The things I never wanted to see or hear or do again now made up at least three weeks' worth of grocery lists. I placed a mark against obeah women, jewelry, and white underclothes. Over my underclothes, I put on an around-the-yard dress of my mother's. The clothes I would wear for my voyage were a dark-blue pleated skirt and a blue-and-white checked blouse (the blue in the blouse matched exactly the blue of my skirt) with a large sailor collar and with a tie made from the same material as the skirt — a blouse that came down a long way past my waist, over my skirt. They were lying on a chair, freshly ironed by my mother. Putting on my clothes was the last thing I would do just before leaving the house. Miss Cornelia came and pressed my hair and then shaped it into what felt like a hundred corkscrews, all lying flat against my head so that my hat would fit properly.

At breakfast, I was seated in my usual spot, with my mother at one end of the table, my father at the other, and me in the middle, so that as they talked to me or to each other I would shift my head to the left or to the right and get a good look at them. We were having a Sunday breakfast, a breakfast as if we had just come back from Sunday-morning services: salt fish and antroba and souse and hard-boiled eggs, and even special Sunday bread from Mr. Daniel, our baker. On Sundays, we ate this breakfast at eleven o'clock, and then we didn't eat again until four o'clock, when we had our big Sunday dinner. It was the best breakfast we ate, and the only breakfast better than that was the one we ate on Christmas morning. My parents were in a festive mood, saying what a wonderful time I would have in my new life, what a wonderful opportunity this was for me, and what a lucky person I was. They were eating away as they talked, my father's false teeth making a *clop-clop* sound like a horse on a walk as he talked, my mother's mouth going up and down like a horse eating hay as she chewed each mouthful thirty-two times. (I had long ago counted, because it was something she made me do also, and I was trying to see if this was just one of her rules that applied only to me.) I was looking at them with a smile on my face but disgust in my heart when my mother said, "Of course, you are a young lady now, and we won't be surprised if in due time you write to say that one day soon you are to be married."

Without thinking, I said, with bad feeling that I didn't hide very 7 well, "How absurd!"

My parents immediately stopped eating and looked at me as if they 8 had not seen me before. My father was the first to go back to his food. My mother continued to look. I don't know what went through her mind, but I could see her using her tongue to dislodge food stuck in the far corners of her mouth.

Many of my mother's friends now came by to say goodbye to me, 9 and to wish me God's blessings. I thanked them and showed the proper amount of joy at the glorious things they pointed out to me that my future held and showed the proper amount of sorrow at how much my parents and everyone else who loved me would miss me. My body ached a little at all this false going back and forth, at all this taking in of people gazing at me with heads tilted, love and pity on their smiling faces. I could have left without saying any goodbyes to them and I wouldn't have missed it. There was only one person I felt I should say goodbye to, and that was my former friend Gwen. We had long ago drifted apart, and when I saw her now my heart nearly split in two with embarrassment at the feelings I used to have for her and things I had shared with her. She had now degenerated into complete silliness, hardly able to complete a sentence without putting in a few giggles. Along with the giggles, she had developed some other schoolgirl traits that she did not have when she was actually a schoolgirl, so beneath her were such things then. When we were saying our goodbyes, it was all I could do not to say cruelly, "Why are you behaving like such a monkey?" Instead, I put everything into a friendly, plain wishing her well and the best in the future. It was then that she told me that she was more or less engaged to a boy she had known while growing up early on in Nevis, and that soon, in a year or so, they would be married. My reply to her was "Good luck," and she thought I meant her well, so she grabbed me and said, "Thank you. I knew you would be happy about it." But to me it was as if she had shown me a high point from which she was going to jump and hoped to land in one piece on her feet. We parted, and when I turned away I didn't look back.

My mother had arranged with a stevedore to take my trunk to the 10 jetty ahead of me. At ten o'clock on the dot, I was dressed, and we set off for the jetty. An hour after that, I would board a launch that would take me out to sea, where I then would board the ship. Starting out, as if for old time's sake and without giving it a thought, we lined up in the old way: I walking between my mother and my father. I loomed way above my father and could see the top of his head. I wasn't so much taller than my mother that it could bring me any satisfaction. We must have made a strange sight: a grown girl all dressed up in the middle of a morning, in the middle of the week, walking in step in the middle between her two parents, for people we didn't know stared at us. It was all of half an hour's walk from our house to the jetty, but I was passing through most of the years of my life. We passed by the house where Miss Lois, the seamstress that I had been apprenticed to for a few years, lived, and just as I was passing by a wave of bad feeling for her came over me, because I suddenly remembered that the first year I spent with her all she had me do was sweep the floor, which was always full of threads and pins and needles, and I never seemed to sweep it clean enough to please her. Then she would send me to the store to buy buttons or thread, though I was only allowed to do this if I was given a sample of the button or thread, and then she would find fault even though they were an exact match of the samples she had given me. And all the while she said to me, "You'll never sew, you know." At the time, I don't suppose I minded it, because it was customary to treat the first-year apprentice with such scorn, but now I placed on the dustheap of my life Miss Lois and everything that I had had to do with her.

We were soon on the road that I had taken to school, to church, to 11 Sunday school, to choir practice, to Brownie meetings, to Girl Guide meetings, to meet a friend. I was five years old when I first walked on this road unaccompanied by someone to hold my hand. My mother had placed three pennies in my little basket, which was a duplicate of her bigger basket, and sent me to the chemist's shop to buy a pennyworth of senna, a pennyworth of eucalyptus leaves, and a pennyworth of camphor. She then instructed me on what side of the road to walk, where to make a turn, where to cross, and to look carefully before I crossed, and if I met anyone that I knew to politely pass greetings and keep on my way. I was wearing a freshly ironed yellow dress that had printed on it scenes of acrobats flying through the air and swinging on a trapeze. I had just had a bath, and after it, instead of powdering me with my baby-smelling talcum powder, my mother had, as a special favor, let me use her own talcum powder, which smelled quite perfumy and came in a can that had painted on it people going out to dinner in nineteenth-century London and was called Mazie. How it pleased me to walk out the door and bend my head down to sniff at myself and see that I smelled just like my mother. I went to the chemist's shop, and he had to come from behind the counter and bend down to hear what it was that I wanted to buy, my voice was so little and timid then. I went back just the way I had come, and when I walked into the yard and presented my basket with its three packages to my mother her eyes filled with tears and she swooped me up and held me high in the air and said that I was wonderful and good and that there would never be anybody better. If I had just conquered Persia, she couldn't have been more proud of me.

We passed by our church — the church in which I had been chris- 12 tened and received and had sung in the junior choir. We passed by a house in which a girl I used to like and was sure I couldn't live without had lived. Once, when she had mumps, I went to visit her against my mother's wishes, and we sat on her bed and ate the cure of roasted, buttered sweet potatoes that had been placed on her swollen jaws, held there by a piece of white cloth. I don't know how, but my mother found out about it, and I don't know how, but she put an end to our friendship. Shortly after, the girl moved with her family across the sea to somewhere else. We passed the doll store where I would go with my mother when I was little and point out the doll I wanted that year for Christmas. We passed the store where I bought the much-fought-over shoes I wore to church to be received in. We passed the bank. On my sixth birthday, I was given, among other things, the present of a sixpence. My mother and I then went to this bank, and with the six-pence I opened my own savings account. I was given a little gray book with my name in big letters on it, and in the balance column it said "6d." Every Saturday morning after that, I was given a sixpence — later, a shilling, and later a two-and-sixpence piece — and I would take it to the bank for deposit. I had never been allowed to withdraw even a farthing from my bank account until just a few weeks before I was to leave; then the whole account was closed out, and I received from the bank the sum of six pounds, ten shillings, and two and a half pence.

We passed the office of the doctor who told my mother three times 13 that I did not need glasses, that if my eyes were feeling weak a glass of carrot juice a day would make them strong again. This happened when I was eight. And so every day at recess I would run to my school gate and meet my mother, who was waiting for me with a glass of juice from carrots she had just grated and then squeezed, and I would drink it and then run back to meet my chums. I knew there was noth-ing at all wrong with my eyes, but I had recently read a story in "A Girl's Own Annual" in which the heroine, a girl a few years older than I was then, cut such a figure to my mind with the way she was always adjusting her small, round horn-rimmed glasses that I felt I must have a pair exactly like them. When it became clear that I didn't need glasses, I began to complain about the glare of the sun being too much for my eyes, and I walked around with my hands shielding them — especially in my mother's presence. My mother then bought for me a pair of sunglasses with the exact horn-rimmed frames I wanted, and how I enjoyed the gestures of blowing on the lenses, wip-ing them with the hem of my uniform, adjusting the glasses when they slipped down my nose, and just removing them from their case and putting them on. In three weeks, I grew tired of them and they found a nice resting place in a drawer, along with some other things that at one time or another I couldn't live without. We passed the store that sold only grooming aids, all imported from England. This store had in it a large porcelain dog — white, with black spots all over and a red ribbon of satin tied around its neck. The dog sat in front of a white porcelain bowl that was always filled with fresh water, and it sat in such a way that it looked as if it had just taken a long drink. When I was a small child, I would ask my mother, if ever we were near this store, to please take me to see the dog, and I would stand in front of it, bent over slightly, my hands resting on my knees, and stare at it and stare at it. I thought this dog more beautiful and more real than any dog I had ever seen or any dog I would ever see. I must have outgrown my interest in the dog, for when it disappeared I never asked what became of it. We passed the library, and if there was anything on this walk that I might have wept over leaving this most surely would have been the thing. My mother had been a member of the library long before I was born. And since she took me everywhere with her when I was quite little, when she went to the library she took me along here, too. I would sit in her lap very quietly as she read books that she did not want to take home with her. I could not read the words yet, but just the way they looked on the page was interesting to me. Once, a book she was reading had a large picture of a man in it, and when I asked her who he was she told me that he was Louis Pasteur and that the book was about his life. It stuck in my mind, because she said it was because of him that she boiled my milk to purify it before I was allowed to drink it, that it was his idea, and that that was why the process was called pasteurization. One of the things I had put away in my mother's old trunk in which she kept all my childhood things was my library card. At that moment, I owed sevenpence in overdue fees.

As I passed by all these places, it was if I were in a dream, for I 14 didn't notice the people coming and going in and out of them, I didn't feel my feet touch ground. I didn't even feel my own body — I just saw these places as if they were hanging in the air, not having top or bottom, and as if I had gone in and out of them all in the same moment. The sun was bright; the sky was blue and just above my head. We then arrived at the jetty.

My heart now beat fast, and no matter how hard I tried I couldn't 15 keep my mouth from falling open and my nostrils from spreading to the ends of my face. My old fear of slipping between the boards of the jetty and falling into the dark-green water where the dark-green eels lived came over me. When my father's stomach started to go bad, the doctor had recommended a walk every evening right after he ate his dinner. Sometimes he would take me with him. When he took me with him, we usually went to the jetty, and there he would sit and talk to the night watchman about cricket or some other thing that didn't interest me, because it was not personal; they didn't talk about their wives, or their children, or their parents, or about any of their likes and dislikes. They talked about things in such a strange way, and I didn't see what they found funny, but sometimes they made each other laugh so much that their guffaws would bound out to sea and send back an echo. I was always sorry when we got to the jetty and saw that the night watchman on duty was the one he enjoyed speaking to; it was like being locked up in a book filled with numbers and diagrams and what-ifs. For the thing about not being able to understand and enjoy what they were saying was I had nothing to take my mind off my fear of slipping in between the boards of the jetty.

Now, too, I had nothing to take my mind off what was happening 16 to me. My mother and my father — I was leaving them forever. My home on an island — I was leaving it forever. What to make of everything? I felt a familiar hollow space inside. I felt I was being held down against my will. I felt I was burning up from head to toe. I felt that someone was tearing me up into little pieces and soon I would be able to see all the little pieces as they floated out into nothing in the deep blue sea. I didn't know whether to laugh or cry. I could see that it would be better not to think too clearly about any one thing. The launch was being made ready to take me, along with some other passengers, out to the ship that was anchored in the sea. My father paid our fares, and we joined a line of people waiting to board. My mother checked my bag to make sure that I had my passport, the money she had given me, and a sheet of paper placed between some pages in my Bible on which were written the names of the relatives — people I had not known existed — with whom I would live in England. Across from the jetty was a wharf, and some stevedores were loading and unloading barges. I don't know why seeing that struck me so, but suddenly a wave of strong feeling came over me, and my heart swelled with a great gladness as the words "I shall never see this again" spilled out inside me. But then, just as quickly, my heart shrivelled up and the words "I shall never see this again" stabbed at me. I don't know what stopped me from falling in a heap at my parents' feet.

When we were all on board, the launch headed out to sea. Away 17 from the jetty, the water became the customary blue, and the launch left a wide path in it that looked like a road. I passed by sounds and smells that were so familiar that I had long ago stopped paying any attention to them. But now here they were, and the ever-present "I shall never see this again" bobbed up and down inside me. There was the sound of the seagull diving down into the water and coming up with something silverish in its mouth. There was the smell of the sea and the sight of small pieces of rubbish floating around in it. There were boats filled with fishermen coming in early. There was the sound of their voices as they shouted greetings to each other. There was the hot sun, there was the blue sea, there was the blue sky. Not very far away, there was the white sand of the shore, with the run-down houses all crowded in next to each other, for in some places only poor people lived near the shore. I was seated in the launch between my parents, and when I realized that I was gripping their hands tightly I glanced quickly to see if they were looking at me with scorn, for I felt sure that they must have known of my never-see-this-again feelings. But instead my father kissed me on the forehead and my mother kissed me on the mouth, and they both gave over their hands to me, so that I could grip them as much as I wanted. I was on the verge of feeling that it had all been a mistake, but I remembered that I wasn't a child anymore, and that now when I made up my mind about something I had to see it through. At that moment, we came to the ship, and that was that.

The goodbyes had to be quick, the captain said. My mother intro- 18 duced herself to him and then introduced me. She told him to keep an eye on me, for I had never gone this far away from home on my own. She gave him a letter to pass on to the captain of the next ship that I would board in Barbados. They walked me to my cabin, a small space that I would share with someone else — a woman I did not know. I had never before slept in a room with someone I did not know. My father kissed me goodbye and told me to be good and to write home often. After he said this, he looked at me, then looked at the floor and swung his left foot, then looked at me again. I could see that he wanted to say something else, something that he had never said to me before, but then he just turned and walked away. My mother said, "Well," and then she threw her arms around me. Big tears streamed down her face, and it must have been that — for I could not bear to see my mother cry — which started me crying, too. She then tightened her arms around me and held me to her close, so that I felt that I couldn't breathe. With that, my tears dried up, and I was suddenly on my guard. "What does she want now?" I said to my-self. Still holding me close to her, she said, in a voice that raked across my skin, "It doesn't matter what you do or where you go. I'll always be your mother and this will always be your home."

I dragged myself away from her and backed off a little, and then I 19 shook myself, as if to wake myself out of a stupor. We looked at each other for a long time with smiles on our faces, but I know the opposite of that was in my heart. As if responding to some invisible cue, we both said, at the same moment, "Well." Then my mother turned around and walked out the cabin door. I stood there for I don't know how long, and then I remembered that it was customary to stand on deck and wave to your relatives who were returning to shore. From the deck, I could not see my father, but I could see my mother facing the ship, her eyes searching to pick me out. I removed from my bag a red cotton handkerchief that she had earlier given me for just this pur-pose, and I waved it wildly in the air. Recognizing me immediately, she waved back just as wildly, and we continued to do this until she became just a dot in the matchbox-size launch swallowed up in the big blue sea.

I went back to my cabin and lay down on my berth. Everything 20 trembled as if it had a spring at its very center. I could hear the small waves lap-lapping around the ship. They made an unexpected sound, as if a vessel filled with liquid had been placed on its side and now was slowly emptying out.

CONSIDERATIONS

1. In the first paragraph, what phrase is repeated with only slight variations until it expresses Annie John's basic attitude? How does the repetition af-fect our response to her situation?
2. Why does she object to the fact that all their belongings are handmade?
3. What is the point of her sarcasm about saying goodbye to her mother's friends and to her own friend Gwen? What qualities in these people does she scorn?
4. While walking to the jetty what memory begins to change her attitude to-ward this leave-taking? Why would that particular memory have special meaning for her now?

5. Remembering that as a child she used to be frightened on the jetty, she says in paragraph 16, "Now, too, I had nothing to take my mind off what was happening to me." What is the connection between her childhood fear and her present state of mind?
6. Do you think that Annie John has just been disguising her real feelings? Does she really want to go or doesn't she?
7. Do you think this selection is a story or a personal essay? That is, does it strike you as mostly fictional or as mostly a direct recollection? What details give you this impression?
8. WRITING TOPIC. Some people have more trouble than others when it comes to saying goodbye, but everyone finds it difficult at some time or other. In 700 words, analyze a particularly tense experience of saying goodbye to someone in your family circle (not to your former or present heartthrobs), when your own or someone else's uptight feelings were expressed by unusual or inappropriate behavior. A first day at camp or at school might serve as your example of leave-taking.

Gordon Lish

FEAR: FOUR EXAMPLES

◊

Gordon Lish (b. 1934) is an editor and fiction writer who teaches writing at Columbia University. At sixteen he dropped out of prep school to become a radio actor and disc jockey. When he decided to go to college, he was only provisionally accepted. After graduation from the University of Arizona, he studied at San Francisco State University. He taught high school and college in California before returning to New York City, where he entered publishing. His stories have appeared in *The New Yorker, Paris Review, Antioch Review,* and in *Esquire,* where he became the fiction editor. Since 1977 he has been an editor at Alfred A. Knopf. His stories have been collected in *What I Know So Far* (1984). His novels include *Dear Mr. Capote* (1983) and *Peru* (1986). Lish is also a father, which is how he came to know a lot about the kind of worrying that he portrays in the following story.

My daughter called from college. She is a good student, excellent 1 grades, is gifted in any number of ways.

"What time is it?" she said. 2

I said, "It is two o'clock." 3

"All right," she said. "It's two now. Expect me at four — four by 4 the clock that said it's two."

"It was my watch," I said. 5

"Good," she said. 6

It is ninety miles, an easy drive. 7

At a quarter to four, I went down to the street. I had these things in 8 mind — look for her car, hold a parking place, be there waving when she turned into the block.

At a quarter to five, I came back up. 9

I changed my shirt. I wiped off my shoes. I looked into the mirror 10
to see if I looked like someone's father.

She presented herself shortly after six o'clock.   11
"Traffic?" I said.   12
"No," she said, and that was the end of that.   13
After supper, she complained of insufferable pains, and doubled 14
over on the dining-room floor.
"My belly," she said.   15
"What?" I said.   16
She said, "My belly. It's agony. Get me a doctor."   17
There is a large and famous hospital mere blocks from my apart- 18
ment. Celebrities go there, statesmen, people who must know what
they are doing.
With the help of a doorman and an elevator man, I got my daugh- 19
ter to the hospital. Within minutes, two physicians and a corps of
nurses took the matter in hand.
I stood by watching.   20
It was hours and hours before they had her undoubled and were 21
willing to announce their findings.
A bellyache, a rogue cramp, a certain unspecific seizure of the ab- 22
domen — vagrant, indecipherable, a mystery not worth further inquiry.

We left the hospital unassisted, using a chain of tunnels in order to 23
shorten the distance home. The exposed distance, that is — since it
would be four in the morning on the city streets, and though the
blocks would be few, each one of them would be dangerous. So we
made our way along the system of underground passages that link the
units of the hospital until we were forced to surface and exit. We
came out onto a street with not a person on it — until we saw him,
the young man who was going from car to car. He carried something
under his arm. It looked to be a furled umbrella — black fabric, silver
fittings. But it could not have been what it looked to be — it was a
tool of entry disguised as an umbrella.
He turned to us as we stepped along, and then he turned back to 24
his work — going from car to car, trying the doors, and sometimes
using the thing to dig at the windows.
"Don't look," I said.   25

My daughter said, "What?"   26

I said, "There's someone across the street. He's trying to jimmy 27
open cars. Just keep on walking as if you don't see him."

My daughter said, "Where? I don't see him."   28

I put my daughter to bed and the hospital charges on my desk, and 29
then I let my head down on the pillow and listened.

There was nothing to hear.   30

Before I surrendered myself to sleep, there was only this in my 30
mind — the boy in the treatment room across the corridor from my
daughter's, how I had wanted to cry out each time he had cried out as
a stitch was sutured into his hand.

"Take it out! Take it out!"   32

That is what the boy was shrieking as the doctor worked to close 33
the wound.

I thought about the feeling in me when I had heard that awful 34
wailing. The boy wanted the needle out. I suppose it hurt worse than
the thing that had opened him up.

Then I considered the statement for emergency services, translat- 35
ing the amount first into theater tickets, then into hand-ironed shirts.

CONSIDERATIONS

1. What fearful thoughts occur to the father in each of the first three incidents? Why doesn't the author define the father's thoughts?
2. What does the father fear in the fourth example?
3. WRITING TOPIC. In no more than 300 words, substitute your own fourth
   example of fear to give a different ending to the story. You may want to
   preserve the story's focus on the father's thoughts, or you may want to
   switch to the daughter's thoughts, or to some other character's thoughts
   about the father and daughter.

Calvin Trillin

IT'S JUST TOO LATE

◊

CALVIN TRILLIN (b. 1935) grew up in Kansas City, Missouri, and attended Yale University. He worked as a reporter for *Time* magazine, and from 1963 to 1982 he was a staff writer for *The New Yorker*. His regular reports of his travels around the United States focused on daily life, including where and how Americans eat. These observations were collected in three books on food in America: *American Fried* (1974), *Alice, Let's Eat* (1978), and *Third Helpings* (1983). In 1984 he published another collection of observations drawn from *The New Yorker* on the ways Americans get killed, for this macabre topic, according to the author, often illuminates the way people live. In the following chapter from *Killings* (1984), Trillin examines the death of a teenage girl who was killed in a car chase and accident.

Knoxville, Tennessee
March 1979

Until she was sixteen, FaNee Cooper was what her parents some- 1
times called an ideal child. "You'd never have to correct her,"
FaNee's mother has said. In sixth grade, FaNee won a spelling contest. She played the piano and the flute. She seemed to believe what
she heard every Sunday at the Beaver Dam Baptist Church about
good and evil and the hereafter. FaNee was not an outgoing child.
Even as a baby, she was uncomfortable when she was held and cuddled. She found it easy to tell her parents she loved them but difficult
to confide in them. Particularly compared to her sister, Kristy, a
cheerful, open little girl two and a half years younger, she was reserved
and introspective. The thoughts she kept to herself, though, were apparently happy thoughts. Her eighth-grade essay on Christmas —
written in a remarkably neat hand — talked of the joys of helping put

together toys for her little brother, Leo, Jr., and the importance of her parents' reminder that Christmas is the birthday of Jesus. Her parents were the sort of people who might have been expected to have an ideal child. As a boy, Leo Cooper had been called "one of the greatest high-school basketball players ever developed in Knox County." He went on to play basketball at East Tennessee State, and he married the homecoming queen, JoAnn Henson. After college, Cooper became a high-school basketball coach and teacher and, eventually, an administrator. By the time FaNee turned thirteen, in 1973, he was in his third year as the principal of Gresham Junior High School, in Fountain City — a small Knox County town that had been swallowed up by Knoxville when the suburbs began to move north. A tall man, with curly black hair going on gray, Leo Cooper has an elaborate way of talking ("Unless I'm very badly mistaken, he has never related to me totally the content of his conversation") and a manner that may come from years of trying to leave errant junior-high-school students with the impression that a responsible adult is magnanimous, even humble, about invariably being in the right. His wife, a high-school art teacher, paints and does batik, and created the name FaNee because she like the way it looked and sounded — it sounds like "Fawn-ee" when the Coopers say it — but the impression she gives is not of artiness but of soft-spoken small-town gentility. When she found, in the course of cleaning up FaNee's room, that her ideal thirteen-year-old had been smoking cigarettes, she was, in her words, crushed. "FaNee was such a perfect child before that," JoAnn Cooper said some time later. "She was angry that we found out. She knew we knew that she had done something we didn't approve of, and then the rebellion started. I was hurt. I was very hurt. I guess it came through as disappointment."

Several months later, FaNee's grandmother died. FaNee had been 2 devoted to her grandmother. She wrote a poem in her memory — an almost joyous poem, filled with Christian faith in the afterlife ("Please don't grieve over my happiness/Rejoice with me in the presence of the Angels of Heaven"). She also took some keepsakes from her grandmother's house, and was apparently mortified when her parents found them and explained that they would have to be returned. By then, the Coopers were aware that FaNee was going to have a difficult time as a teenager. They thought she might be self-conscious about the double affliction of glasses and braces. They thought she might be uncomfortable in the role of the principal's daughter at Gresham. In ninth grade, she entered Halls High School, where JoAnn Cooper was teaching art. FaNee was a loner at first. Then she fell in with what could only be considered a bad crowd.

Halls, a few miles to the north of Fountain City, used to be known 3 as Halls Crossroads. It is what Knoxville people call "over the ridge" — on the side of Black Oak Ridge that has always been thought of as rural. When FaNee entered Halls High, the Coopers were already in the process of building a house on several acres of land they had bought in Halls, in a sparsely settled area along Brown Gap Road. Like two or three other houses along the road, it was to be constructed basically of huge logs taken from old buildings — a house that Leo Cooper describes as being, like the name FaNee, "just a little bit different." Ten years ago, Halls Crossroads was literally a crossroads. Then some of the Knoxville expansion that had swollen Fountain City spilled over the ridge, planting subdivisions here and there on roads that still went for long stretches with nothing but an occasional house with a cow or two next to it. The increase in population did not create a town. Halls has no center. Its commercial area is a series of two or three shopping centers strung together on the Maynardville Highway, the four-lane that leads north into Union County — a place almost synonymous in east Tennessee with mountain poverty. Its restaurant is the Halls Freezo Drive-In. The gathering place for the group FaNee Cooper eventually found herself in was the Maynardville Highway Exxon station.

At Halls High School, the social poles were represented by the 4 Jocks and the Freaks. FaNee found her friends among the Freaks. "I am truly enlighted upon irregular trains of thought aimed at strange depots of mental wards," she wrote when she was fifteen. "Yes! Crazed farms for the mental off — Oh! I walked through the halls screams & loud laughter fill my ears — Orderlys try to reason with me — but I am unreasonable! The joys of being a FREAK in a circus of imagination." The little crowd of eight or ten young people that FaNee joined has been referred to by her mother as "the Union County group." A couple of the girls were from backgrounds similar to FaNee's, but all the boys had the characteristics, if not the precise addresses, that Knoxville people associate with the poor whites of

Union County. They were the sort of boys who didn't bother to finish high school, or finished it in a special program for slow learners, or get ejected from it for taking a swing at the principal.

"I guess you can say they more or less dragged us down to their 5 level with the drugs," a girl who was in the group — a girl who can be called Marcia — said recently. "And somehow we settled for it. It seems like we had to get ourselves in the pit before we could look out." People in the group used marijuana and Valium and LSD. They sneered at the Jocks and the "prim and proper little ladies" who went with Jocks. "We set ourselves aside," Marcia now says. "We put ourselves above everyone. How we did that I don't know." In a Knox County high school, teenagers who want to get themselves in the pit need not mainline heroin. The Jocks they mean to be compared to do not merely show up regularly for classes and practice football and wear clean clothes; they watch their language and preach temperance and go to prayer meetings on Wednesday nights and talk about having a real good Christian witness. Around Knoxville, people who speak of well-behaved high-school kids often seem to use words like "perfect," or even "angels." For FaNee's group, the opposite was not difficult to figure out. "We were into wicked things, strange things," Marcia says. "It was like we were on some kind of devil trip." FaNee wrote about demons and vultures and rats. "Slithering serpents eat my sanity and bite my ass," she wrote in an essay called "The Lovely Road of Life," just after she turned sixteen, "while tornadoes derail and ever so swiftly destroy every car in my train of thought." She wrote a lot about death.

FaNee's girl friends spoke of her as "super-intelligent." Her 6 English teacher found some of her writing profound — and disturbing. She was thought to be not just super-intelligent but supermysterious, and even, at times, super-weird — an introverted girl who stared straight ahead with deep-brown, nearly black eyes and seemed to have thoughts she couldn't share. Nobody really knew why she had chosen to run with the Freaks — whether it was loneliness or rebellion or simple boredom. Marcia thought it might have had something to do with a feeling that her parents had settled on Kristy as their perfect child. "I guess she figured she couldn't be the best," Marcia said recently. "So she decided she might as well be the worst."

Toward the spring of FaNee's junior year at Halls, her problems 7
seemed to deepen. Despite her intelligence, her grades were sliding.
She was what her mother called "a mental dropout." Leo Cooper had
to visit Halls twice because of minor suspensions. Once, FaNee had
been caught smoking. Once, having ducked out of a required assembly, she was spotted by a favorite teacher, who turned her in. At
home, she exchanged little more than short, strained formalities with
Kristy, who shared their parents' opinion of FaNee's choice of friends.
The Coopers had finished their house — a large house, its size accen-
tuated by the huge old logs and a great stone fireplace and outsize
"Paul Bunyan"-style furniture — but FaNee spent most of her time
there in her own room, sleeping or listening to rock music through
earphones. One night, there was a terrible scene when FaNee returned from a concert in a condition that Leo Cooper knew had to be
the result of marijuana. JoAnn Cooper, who ordinarily strikes people
as too gentle to raise her voice, found herself losing her temper regularly. Finally, Leo Cooper asked a counsellor he knew, Jim Griffin, to
stop in at Halls High School and have a talk with FaNee — unoffi-
cially.

Griffin — a young man with a warm, informal manner — worked 8
for the Juvenile Court of Knox County. He had a reputation for being
able to reach teenagers who wouldn't talk to their parents or to school
administrators. One Friday in March of 1977, he spent an hour and a
half talking to FaNee Cooper. As Griffin recalls the interview, FaNee
didn't seem alarmed by his presence. She seemed to him calm and
controlled — Griffin thought it was something like talking to another
adult — and, unlike most of the teenagers he dealt with, she looked
him in the eye the entire time. Griffin, like some of FaNee's friends,
found her eyes unsettling — "the coldest, most distant, but, at the
same time, the most knowing eyes I'd ever seen." She expressed affection for her parents, but she didn't seem interested in exploring ways
of getting along better with them. The impression she gave Griffin
was that they were who they were, and she was who she was, and there
didn't happen to be any connection. Several times, she made the same
response to Griffin's suggestions: "It's too late."

That weekend, neither FaNee nor her parents brought up the sub- 9
ject of Griffin's visit. Leo Cooper has spoken of the weekend as being

particularly happy; a friend of FaNee's who stayed over remembers it as particularly strained. FaNee stayed home from school on Monday because of a bad headache — she often had bad headaches — but felt well enough on Monday evening to drive to the library. She was to be home at nine. When she wasn't, Mrs. Cooper began to phone her friends. Finally, around ten, Leo Cooper got into his other car and took a swing around Halls — past the teenage hangouts like the Exxon station and the Pizza Hut and the Smoky Mountain Market. Then he took a second swing. At eleven, FaNee was still not home.

She hadn't gone to the library. She had picked up two girl friends 10 and driven to the home of a third, where everyone took five Valium tablets. Then the four girls drove over to the Exxon station, where they met four boys from their crowd. After a while, the group bought some beer and some marijuana and reassembled at Charlie Stevens's trailer. Charlie Stevens was five or six years older than everyone else in the group — a skinny, slow-thinking young man with long black hair and a sparse beard. He was married and had a child, but he and his wife had separated; she was back in Union County with the baby. Stevens had remained in their trailer — parked in the yard near his mother's house, in a back-road area of Knox County dominated by decrepit, unpainted sheds and run-down trailers and rusted-out automobiles. Stevens had picked up FaNee at home once or twice — apparently, more as a driver for the group than as a date — and the Coopers, having learned that his unsuitability extended to being married, had asked her not to see him.

In Charlie's trailer, which had no heat or electricity, the group 11 drank beer and passed around joints, keeping warm with blankets. By eleven or so, FaNee was what one of her friends has called "super-messed-up." Her speech was slurred. She was having trouble keeping her balance. She had decided not to go home. She had apparently persuaded herself that her parents intended to send her away to some sort of home for incorrigibles. "It's too late," she said to one of her friends. "It's just too late." It was decided that one of the boys, David Munsey, who was more or less the leader of the group, would drive the Cooper's car to FaNee's house, where FaNee and Charlie Stevens would pick him up in Stevens's car — a worn Pinto with four bald tires, one light, and a dragging muffler. FaNee wrote a note to her parents, and then, perhaps because her handwriting was suffering the effects of beer and marijuana and Valium, asked Stevens to rewrite it on a large piece of paper, which would be left on the seat of the Coopers' car. The Stevens version was just about the same as FaNee's, except that Stevens left out a couple of sentences about trying to work things out ("I'm willing to try") and, not having won any spelling championships himself, he misspelled a few words, like "tomorrow." The note said, "Dear Mom and Dad. Sorry I'm late. Very late. I left your car because I thought you might need it tomorrow. I love you all, but this is something I just had to do. The man talked to me privately for one and a half hours and I was really scared, so this is something I just had to do, but don't worry. I'm with a very good friend. Love you all. FaNee. P.S. Please try to understand I love you all very much, really I do. Love me if you have a chance."

At eleven-thirty or so, Leo Cooper was sitting in his living room, 12 looking out the window at his driveway — a long gravel road that runs almost four hundred feet from the house to Brown Gap Road. He saw the car that FaNee had been driving pull into the driveway. "She's home," he called to his wife, who had just left the room. Cooper walked out on the deck over the garage. The car had stopped at the end of the driveway, and the lights had gone out. He got into his other car and drove to the end of the driveway. David Munsey had already joined Charlie Stevens and FaNee, and the Pinto was just leaving, travelling at a normal rate of speed. Leo Cooper pulled out on the road behind them.

Stevens turned left on Crippen Road, a road that has a field on one 13 side and two or three small houses on the other, and there Cooper pulled his car in front of the Pinto and stopped, blocking the way. He got out and walked toward the Pinto. Suddenly, Stevens put the car in reverse, backed into a driveway a hundred yards behind him, and sped off. Cooper jumped in his car and gave chase. Stevens raced back to Brown Gap Road, ran a stop sign there, ran another stop sign at Maynardville Highway, turned north, veered off onto the old Andersonville Pike, a nearly abandoned road that runs parallel to the highway, and then crossed back over the highway to the narrow, dark country roads on the other side. Stevens sometimes drove with his lights out. He took some of the corners by suddenly applying his hand brake to make the car swerve around in a ninety-degree turn. He was in familiar territory — he actually passed his trailer — and Cooper had difficulty keeping up. Past the trailer, Stevens swept down a hill into a sharp left turn that took him onto Foust Hollow Road, a winding, hilly road not much wider than one car.

At a fork, Cooper thought he had lost the Pinto. He started to go 14 right, and then saw what seemed to be a spark from Stevens's dragging muffler off to the left, in the darkness. Cooper took the left fork, down Salem Church Road. He went down a hill, and then up a long, curving hill to a crest, where he saw the Stevens car ahead. "I saw the car airborne. Up in the air," he later testified. "It was up in the air. And then it completely rolled over one more time. It started to make another flip forward, and just as it started to flip to the other side it flipped back this way, and my daughter's body came out."

Cooper slammed on his brakes and skidded to a stop up against the 15 Pinto. "Book!" Stevens shouted — the group's equivalent of "Scram!" Stevens and Munsey disappeared into the darkness. "It was dark, no one around, and so I started yelling for FaNee," Cooper had testified. "I thought it was an eternity before I could find her body, wedged under the back end of that car. . . . I tried everything I could, and saw that I couldn't get her loose. So I ran to a trailer back up to the top of the hill back up there to try to get that lady to call to get me some help, and then apparently she didn't think that I was serious. . . . I took the jack out of my car and got under, and it was dark, still couldn't see too much what was going on . . . and started prying and got her loose, and I don't know how. And then I dragged her over to the side, and, of course, at the time I felt reasonably assured that she was gone, because her head was completely — on one side just as if you had taken a sledgehammer and just hit it and bashed it in. And I did have the pleasure of one thing. I had the pleasure of listening to her breathe about the last three times she ever breathed in her life."

David Munsey did not return to the wreck that night, but Charlie 16 Stevens did. Leo Cooper was kneeling next to his daughter's body. Cooper insisted that Stevens come close enough to see FaNee. "He was kneeling down next to her," Stevens later testified. "And he said, 'Do you know what you've done? Do you really know what you've done?' Like that. And I just looked at her, and I said, 'Yes,' and just stood there. Because I couldn't say nothing." There was, of course, a legal decision to be made about who was responsible for FaNee Cooper's death. In a deposition, Stevens said he had been fleeing for his life. He testified that when Leo Cooper blocked Crippen Road, FaNee had said that her father had a gun and intended to hurt them. Stevens was bound over and eventually indicted for involuntary manslaughter. Leo Cooper testified that when he approached the Pinto on Crippen Road, FaNee had a strange expression that he had never seen before. "It wasn't like FaNee, and I knew something was wrong," he said. "My concern was to get FaNee out of the car." The district attorney's office asked that Cooper be bound over for reckless driving, but the judge declined to do so. "Any father would have done what he did," the judge said. "I can see no criminal act on the part of Mr. Cooper."

Almost two years passed before Charlie Stevens was brought to trial. Part of the problem was assuring the presence of David Munsey, who had joined the Navy but seemed inclined to assign his own leaves. In the meantime, the Coopers went to court with a civil suit — they had "uninsured-motorist coverage," which requires their insurance company to cover any defendant who has no insurance of his own — and they won a judgment. There were ways of assigning responsibility, of course, which had nothing to do with the law, civil or criminal. A lot of people in Knoxville thought that Leo Cooper had, in the words of his lawyer, "done what any daddy worth his salt would have done." There were others who believed that FaNee Cooper had lost her life because Leo Cooper had lost his temper. Leo Cooper was not among those who expressed any doubts about his actions. Unlike his wife, whose eyes filled with tears at almost any mention of FaNee, Cooper seemed able, even eager to go over the details of the accident again and again. With the help of a school-board security man, he conducted his own investigation. He drove over the route dozens of times. "I've thought about it every day, and I guess I will the rest of my life," he said as he and his lawyer and the prosecuting attorney went over the route again the day before Charlie Stevens's trial finally began. "But I can't tell any alternative for a father. I simply wanted her out of that car. I'd have done the same thing again, even at the risk of losing her."

Tennessee law permits the family of a victim to hire a special prosecutor to assist the district attorney. The lawyer who acted for the Coopers in the civil case helped prosecute Charlie Stevens. Both he and the district attorney assured the jurors that the presence of a special prosecutor was not to be construed to mean that the Coopers were vindictive. Outside the courtroom, Leo Cooper said that the verdict was of no importance to him — that he felt sorry, in a way, for Charlie Stevens. But there were people in Knoxville who thought Cooper had a lot riding on the prosecution of Charlie Stevens. If Stevens was not guilty of FaNee Cooper's death — found so by twelve of his peers — who was?

At the trial, Cooper testified emotionally and remarkably graphi-   19 cally about pulling FaNee out from under the car and watching her die in his arms. Charlie Stevens had shaved his beard and cut his hair, but the effort did not transform him into an impressive witness. His lawyer — trying to argue that it would have been impossible for Stevens to concoct the story about FaNee's having mentioned a gun, as the prosecution strongly implied — said, "His mind is such that if you ask him a question you can hear his mind go around, like an old mill creaking." Stevens did not deny the recklessness of his driving or the sorry condition of his car. It happened to be the only car he had available to flee in, he said, and he had fled in fear for his life.

The prosecution said that Stevens could have let FaNee out of the   20 car when her father stopped them, or could have gone to the commercial strip on the Maynardville Highway for protection. The prosecution said that Leo Cooper had done what he might have been expected to do under the circumstances — alone, late at night, his daughter in danger. The defense said precisely the same about Stevens: he had done what he might have been expected to do when being pursued by a man he had reason to be afraid of. "I don't fault Mr. Cooper for what he did, but I'm sorry he did it," the defense attorney said. "I'm sorry the girl said what she said." The jury deliberated for eighteen minutes. Charlie Stevens was found guilty. The jury recommended a sentence of from two to five years in the state penitentiary. At the announcement, Leo Cooper broke down and cried, JoAnn Cooper's eyes filled with tears; she blinked them back and continued to stare straight ahead.

In a way, the Coopers might still strike a casual visitor as an ideal   21 family — handsome parents, a bright and bubbly teenage daughter, a little boy learning the hook shot from his father, a warm house with some land around it. FaNee's presence is there, of course. A picture of her, with a small bouquet of flowers over it, hangs in the living room. One of her poems is displayed in a frame on a table. Even if Leo Cooper continues to think about that night for the rest of his life, there are questions he can never answer. Was there a way that Leo and JoAnn Cooper could have prevented FaNee from choosing the path she chose? Would she still be alive if Leo Cooper had not jumped into his car and driven to the end of the driveway to investigate? Did she in fact tell Charlie Stevens that her father would hurt them — or even that her father had a gun? Did she want to get away from her family even at the risk of tearing around dark country roads in Charlie Stevens's dismal Pinto? Or did she welcome the risk? The poem of FaNee's that the Coopers have displayed is one she wrote a week before her death:

> I think I'm going to die
> And I really don't know why.
> But look in my eye
> When I tell you good-bye.
> I think I'm going to die.

CONSIDERATIONS

1. In the first paragraph, what bearing do the parents' backgrounds and earlier life probably have on their attitude toward their children? How does the author suggest that the parents have remained somewhat childish?
2. In the second paragraph, how do the parents react to the problems that FaNee faces?
3. What is the author's purpose in giving detailed descriptions, as in paragraph 3 and other places, of the setting and the local conditions of life?
4. What is the effect of the two full paragraphs that recount the car chase? What would be lost by condensing paragraphs 13 and 14 into a short statement that reports what happened?
5. FaNee's own writings, including her farewell note, show sharp contrasts between her different outlooks on life. Does this contrast make her any more sympathetic as a person? Or does it turn her into more of a freak?
6. If Mr. Cooper had been able to stop Charlie Stevens's car (immediately after paragraph 12), what might have happened? Use your insight into the

characters and your sense of the situation to explain the most likely reactions of each of the main characters.

7. WRITING TOPIC. The essay presents the difficulties of assigning legal and moral blame for the death of FaNee. Do you think the author is too harsh or too soft in his judgment of who is guilty? who is responsible? who is victimized? Write a 700-word essay that explains the author's implied judgment in this accidental death. Include at least one point on which your judgment differs from the author's viewpoint.

Robert Hayden

THOSE WINTER SUNDAYS

◊

ROBERT HAYDEN (1913–1980) grew up in Detroit and was educated there at Wayne State University. He taught poetry writing at Fisk University and the University of Michigan. His poems often center on vivid characterizations, such as the following recollection of his father. Hayden's poems were collected in *Selected Poems* (1966), the same year that he won the Grand Prize for Poetry at the Dakar World Festival of the Arts.

Sundays too my father got up early
and put his clothes on in the blueblack cold,
then with cracked hands that ached
from labor in the weekday weather made
banked fires blaze. No one ever thanked him.

I'd wake and hear the cold splintering, breaking.
When the rooms were warm, he'd call,
and slowly I would rise and dress,
fearing the chronic angers of that house,

Speaking indifferently to him,   10
who had driven out the cold
and polished my good shoes as well.
What did I know, what did I know
of love's austere and lonely offices?

CONSIDERATIONS

1. How is the father characterized in the long first sentence of the first stanza? Why is there such a difference in length between this opening sentence and the short sentence that ends the stanza?
2. What was the boy's attitude toward his family and home life? How did he express his attitude?
3. What is the effect of the repetition in the next-to-last line? How would the meaning change if the phrase occurred only once?
4. What is the meaning of "offices" in the final line? As an oddly used word, how does it illuminate the adult poet's memory of his father?
5. WRITING TOPIC. In 500 words, write a character study of the most solitary or the most private person in your extended family (which can include aunts, uncles, cousins, grandparents). Give details that will make the person vivid to the reader and try to explain or present the relative separateness that is a way of life for this person.

John Updike

STILL OF SOME USE

◊

JOHN UPDIKE (b. 1932) was raised in a small town in Pennsylvania and was graduated with highest honors from Harvard. He joined the staff of *The New Yorker*, contributing stories, poems, and essays even to this day, though he soon moved away from the city to another small town, this one on the Massachusetts shore. His main novels are about a commonplace member of an unremarkable society, Harry "Rabbit" Angstrom, the dubious but sympathetic hero of *Rabbit, Run* (1960), *Rabbit Redux* (1971), and *Rabbit Is Rich* (1981). Updike's fiction usually includes an outlook of deep uneasiness mixed with humor over the transformations of relationships within a family. This story about a divorced couple and their family appeared in *The New Yorker*.

When Foster helped his ex-wife clean out the attic of the house 1
where they had once lived and which she was now selling, they came across dozens of forgotten, broken games. Parcheesi, Monopoly, Lotto; games aping the strategies of the stock market, of crime detection, of real-estate speculation, of international diplomacy and war; games with spinners, dice, lettered tiles, cardboard spacemen, and plastic battleships; games bought in five-and-tens and department stores feverish and musical with Christmas expectations; games enjoyed on the afternoon of a birthday and for a few afternoons thereafter and then allowed, shy of one or two pieces, to drift into closets and toward the attic. Yet, discovered in their bright flat boxes between trunks of outgrown clothes and defunct appliances, the games presented a forceful semblance of value: the springs of their miniature launchers still reacted, the logic of their instructions would still generate suspense, given a chance. "What shall we do with all these games?" Foster shouted, in a kind of agony, to his scattered family as they moved up and down the attic stairs.

"Trash 'em," his younger son, a strapping nineteen, urged.   2

"Would the Goodwill want them?" asked his ex-wife, still wife 3 enough to think that all of his questions deserved answers. "You used to be able to give things like that to orphanages. But they don't call them orphanages anymore, do they?"

"They call them normal American homes," Foster said.   4

His older son, now twenty-two, with a cinnamon-colored beard, of- 5 fered, "They wouldn't work anyhow; they all have something missing. That's how they got to the attic."

"Well, why didn't we throw them away at the time?" Foster asked, 6 and had to answer himself. Cowardice, the answer was. Inertia. Clinging to the past.

His sons, with a shadow of old obedience, came and looked over his 7 shoulder at the sad wealth of abandoned playthings, silently groping with him for the particular happy day connected to this and that pattern of coded squares and colored arrows. Their lives had touched these tokens and counters once; excitement had flowed along the paths of these stylized landscapes. But the day was gone, and scarcely a memory remained.

"Toss 'em," the younger decreed, in his manly voice. For these 8 days of cleaning out, the boy had borrowed a pickup truck from a friend and parked it on the lawn beneath the attic window, so the smaller items of discard could be tossed directly into it. The bigger items were lugged down the stairs and through the front hall and out; already the truck was loaded with old mattresses, broken clock-radios, obsolete skis, and boots. It was a game of sorts to hit the truck bed with objects dropped from the height of the house. Foster flipped game after game at the target two stories below. When the boxes hit, they exploded, throwing a spray of dice, tokens, counters, and cards into the air and across the lawn. A box called Mousetrap, its lid showing laughing children gathered around a Rube Goldberg device, drifted sideways, struck one side wall of the truck, and spilled its plastic components into a flower bed. As a set of something called Drag Race! floated gently as a snowflake before coming to rest, much diminished, on a stained mattress, Foster saw in the depth of downward space the cause of his melancholy: he had not played enough with these games. Now no one wanted to play.

Had he and his wife avoided divorce, of course, these boxes would   9
have continued to gather dust in an undisturbed attic, their sorrow
unexposed. The toys of his own childhood still rested in his mother's
attic. At his last visit, he had wound the spring of a tin Donald Duck
that had responded with an angry clack of its bill and a few stiff
strokes on its drum. A tin shield with concentric grooves for marbles
still waited in a bushel basket with his alphabet blocks and lead airplanes — waited for his childhood to return.

His ex-wife paused where he squatted at the attic window and   10
asked him, "What's the matter?"

"Nothing. These games weren't used much."   11

"I know. It happens fast. You better stop now; it's making you too   12
sad."

Behind him, his family had cleaned out the attic; the slant-   13
ceilinged rooms stood empty, with drooping insulation. "How can
you bear it?" he asked her, of the emptiness.

"Oh, it's fun, once you get into it. Off with the old, on with the   14
new. The new people seem nice. They have little children."

He looked at her and wondered if she was being brave or truly   15
hardhearted. The attic trembled slightly. "That's Ted," she said.

She had acquired a boyfriend, a big athletic banker fleeing from   16
domestic embarrassments in a neighboring town. When Ted
slammed the kitchen door two stories below, the glass shade of a
kerosene lamp that, though long unused, Foster hadn't had the heart
to throw out of the window vibrated in its copper clips, emitting a
thin note like a trapped wasp's song. Time to go. Foster's dusty knees
creaked when he stood. His ex-wife's eager steps raced ahead of him
down through the emptied house. He followed, carrying the lamp,
and set it finally on the bare top of a bookcase he had once built, on
the first-floor landing. He remembered screwing the top board, a prize
piece of knot-free pine, into place from underneath, so not a nailhead
marred its smoothness.

After all the vacant rooms and halls, the kitchen seemed indecently   17
full of heat and life. "Dad, want a beer?" the red-bearded son asked.
"Ted brought some." The back of the boy's hand, holding forth the
dewy can, blazed with fine ginger hairs. His girlfriend, wearing gypsy
earrings and a "No Nukes" sweatshirt, leaned against the discon-
nected stove, her hair in a bandanna and a black smirch becomingly

placed on one temple. From the kind way she smiled at Foster, he felt this party was making room for him.

"No, I better go."   18

Ted shook Foster's hand, as he always did. He had a thin pink skin 19
and silver hair whose fluffy waves seemed mechanically induced. Foster could look him in the eye no longer than he could gaze at the sun. He wondered how such a radiant brute had got into such a tame line of work. Ted had not helped with the attic today because he had been off in his old town, visiting his teen-age twins. "I hear you did a splendid job today," he announced.

"They did," Foster said. "I wasn't much use. I just sat there 20
stunned. All those things I had forgotten buying."

"Some were presents," his son reminded him. He passed the can 21
his father had snubbed to his mother, who took it and tore up the tab with that defiant-sounding *pssff*. She had never liked beer, yet tipped the can to her mouth.

"Give me one sip," Foster begged, and took the can from her and 22
drank a long swallow. When he opened his eyes, Ted's big hand was cupped under Mrs. Foster's chin while his thumb rubbed away a smudge of dirt along her jaw which Foster had not noticed. This protective gesture made her face look small, pouty, frail, and somehow parched. Ted, Foster noticed now, was dressed with a certain comical perfection in a banker's Saturday outfit — softened bluejeans, crisp tennis sneakers, lumberjack shirt with cuffs folded back. The youthful outfit accented his age, his hypertensive flush. Foster saw them suddenly as a touching, aging couple, and this perception seemed permission to go.

He handed back the can.   23

"Thanks for your help," his former wife said.   24

"Yes, we do thank you," Ted said.   25

"Talk to Tommy," she unexpectedly added. She was still sending 26
out trip wires to slow his departures. "This is harder on him than he shows."

Ted looked at his watch, a fat, black-faced thing he could swim un- 27
derwater with. "I said to him coming in, 'Don't dawdle till the dump closes.'"

"He loafed all day," his brother complained, "mooning over old 28
stuff, and now he's going to screw up getting to the dump."

"He's very sensi-tive," the visiting gypsy said, with a strange chiming brightness, as if repeating something she had heard.   29

Outside, the boy was picking up litter that had fallen wide of the truck. Foster helped him. In the grass there were dozens of tokens and dice. Some were engraved with curious little faces — Olive Oyl, Snuffy Smith, Dagwood — and others with hieroglyphs — numbers, diamonds, spades, hexagons — whose code was lost. He held out a handful for Tommy to see. "Can you remember what these were for?"   30

"Comic-Strip Lotto," the boy said without hesitation. "And a game called Gambling Fools there was a kind of slot machine for." The light of old chances and payoffs flickered in his eyes as he gazed down at the rubble in his father's hand. Though Foster was taller, the boy was broader in the shoulders, and growing. "Want to ride with me to the dump?" Tommy asked.   31

"I would, but I better go." He, too, had a new life to lead. By being on this forsaken property at all, Foster was in a sense on the wrong square, if not *en prise*. Once, he had begun to teach this boy chess, but in the sadness of watching him lose — the little bowed head frowning above his trapped king — the lessons had stopped.   32

Foster tossed the tokens into the truck; they rattled to rest on the metal. "This depress you?" he asked his son.   33

"Naa." The boy amended, "Kind of."   34

"You'll feel great," Foster promised him, "coming back with a clean truck. I used to love it at the dump, all that old happiness heaped up, and the sea-gulls."   35

"It's changed since you left. They have all these new rules. The lady there yelled at me last time, for putting stuff in the wrong place."   36

"She did?"   37

"Yeah. It was scary." Seeing his father waver, he added, "It'll only take twenty minutes." Though broad of build, Tommy had beardless cheeks and, between thickening eyebrows, a trace of that rounded, faintly baffled blankness babies have, that wrinkles before they cry.   38

"O.K.," Foster said, greatly lightened. "I'll protect you."   39

CONSIDERATIONS

1. What is the significance of the diversity and the condition of all those games? Do they suggest anything about the past?
2. Not many names are used in the story. Instead, characters are designated as "his ex-wife," "the younger son," "the red-bearded son," "the visiting gypsy," "the boy." What is the atmosphere of the situation that this form of reference suggests?
3. Mrs. Foster's boyfriend, Ted, and the older son's girlfriend are the only characters whose physical appearance is fully described. How do they appear to Foster?
4. At the end, are Foster and Tommy serious or joking? Or both? How can you tell?
5. WRITING TOPIC. In a 500-word essay, clarify the attitude that Updike appears to be taking toward divorce and new relationships.

ADDITIONAL
WRITING TOPICS

◊

FAMILY TIES

1. Consider the literal meanings of a few family names, such as Carmichael, Hessberg, O'Connor, Rosenthal, Sanchez, or Sylvester. Using a dictionary of family names, look up the origins of the names on both sides of your family for the preceding two or three generations. Write a 700-word essay on the two or three relevant names that best indicate the background and present traits of your family. Some reference works that may be useful are Elsdon Smith, *Dictionary of American Family Names* (1956); Edward MacLysaght, *Irish Families* (1957); P. H. Reaney, *A Dictionary of British Surnames* (1958); and Benzion Kaganoff, *A Dictionary of Jewish Names and Their History* (1977). Your reference librarian may be able to help you to other sources as well.

2. Is family life portrayed differently on television and in the movies? In a 700-word essay, compare the views of the family in these two forms of popular entertainment. Choose fairly current examples, and focus mainly on one movie and one television show.

3. Write a review of a book about one of the notable American families that has received a great deal of public attention and serious study. You might choose one about the Adams family, the Guggenheims, the James family, the Kennedys, or the Rockefellers. In a 700-word essay, explain the author's insight into what makes this family cohere; that is, what is the book's viewpoint toward this particular family's ideals, goals, leaders, and style of living?

4. In about 700 words write a family biography of your pet.

5. Do you have too many brothers and sisters, or too few? Almost everyone sometimes wishes for a few changes in that area of fate. Would some sibling revisions improve your life? In 500 words, explain how your personality would be changed by changing the number, sex, and ages of your siblings.

6. Are kids treated like inferiors? Consider Philip Slater's observation in *Insights* that the family maintains a class system. In 500 words define some class-enforced barriers and class-enforced roles in a family that you know well.

7. Does family life encourage independence or dependence? Does it promote liberty or authority? Does it serve individual values or social goals? Do you agree or disagree with Ferdinand Mount's statement in *Insights*? In a 500-word essay present at least two good reasons why in your view the effects of family life support mainly a free individual or support mainly a cohesive state.

PART 3

LOVE AND LONGINGS

Susan Allen Toth, *The Boyfriend*

Marcelle Clements, *Terminal Cool*

Robert Solomon, *"I-Love-You"*

Francesco Alberoni, *Two Kinds of Sexuality*

Raymond Carver, *What We Talk About When We Talk About Love*

D. H. Lawrence, *Counterfeit Love*

Margaret Atwood, *Siren Song*

Ernest van den Haag, *The Invention That Isn't Working*

Jill Tweedie, *The Future of Love*

Additional Writing Topics

INSIGHTS

All love is self-love.
– LA ROCHEFOUCAULD

◊

God is love.
– ST. JOHN

◊

Christ, here's my discovery. You have got hold of the wrong absolutes and infinities. God as absolute? God as infinity? I don't even understand the words. I'll tell you what's absolute and infinite. Loving a woman. But how would you know? You see, your church knows what it's doing: rule out one absolute so you have to look for another.

Do you know what it's like to be a self-centered not unhappy man who leads a tolerable finite life, works, eats, drinks, hunts, sleeps, then one fine day discovers that the great starry heavens have opened to him and that his heart is bursting with it. It? She. Her. Woman. Not a category, not a sex, not one of two sexes, a human female creature, but an infinity. $♀ = ∞$. What else is infinity but a woman become meat and drink to you, life and your heart's own music, the air you breathe? Just to be near her is to live and have your soul's own self. Just to open your mouth on the skin of her back. What joy just to wake up with her beside you in the morning. I didn't know there was such happiness.

But there is the dark converse: not having her is not breathing. I'm not kidding: I couldn't get my breath without her.

154

What else is man made for but this? I can see you agree about love but you look somewhat ironic. Are we talking about two different things? In any case, there's a catch. Love is infinite happiness. Losing it is infinite unhappiness.

— WALKER PERCY

◊

All's fair in love and war.

— ANONYMOUS

◊

During the first six months, the baby has the rudiments of a love language available to him. There is the language of the embrace, the language of the eyes, the language of the smile, vocal communications of pleasure and distress. It is the essential vocabulary of love before we can speak of love. Eighteen years later, when this baby is full grown and "falls in love" for the first time, he will woo his partner through the language of the eyes, the language of the smile, through the utterance of endearments, and the joy of the embrace. In his declarations of love he will use such phrases as "When I first looked into your eyes," "When you smiled at me," "When I held you in my arms." And naturally, in his exalted state, he will believe that he invented this love song.

— SELMA FRAIBERG

◊

No one can fall in love if he is even partially satisfied with what he has or who he is. The experience of falling in love originates in an extreme depression, an inability to find something that has value in everyday life. The "symptom" of the predisposition to fall in love is not the conscious desire to do so, the intense desire to enrich our lives; it is the profound sense of being worthless and of having nothing that is valuable and the shame of not having it. This is the first sign that we are prepared for the experience — the feeling of nothingness and shame over our own nothingness. For this reason, falling in love occurs more frequently among young people, since they are profoundly uncertain, unsure of their worth, and often ashamed of themselves. The same thing applies to people of other ages when they lose something in their lives — when their youth ends or when they start to grow old. There is an irreparable loss of something in the self, a feeling that we will inevitably become devoid of value or degraded, compared with what we have been. It isn't the longing for an affair that makes us fall in love, but the conviction that we have nothing to lose by becoming whatever we will become; it is the prospect of nothingness stretching before us. Only then do we develop the inclination for the different and the risky, that propensity to hurl ourselves into all or nothing which those who are in any way satisfied with their lives cannot feel.

— FRANCESCO ALBERONI

◊

Our whole culture is based on the appetite for buying, on the idea of a mutually favorable exchange. Modern man's happiness consists in the thrill of looking at the shop windows, and in buying all that he can afford to buy, either for cash or on installments. He (or she) looks at people in a similar way. For the man an attractive girl — and for the woman an attractive man — are the prizes they are after. "Attractive" usually means a nice package of qualities which are popular and sought after on the personality market. What specifically makes a person attractive depends on the fashion of the time, physically as well as mentally. During the twenties, a drinking and smoking girl, tough and sexy, was attractive; today the fashion demands more domesticity and coyness. At the end of the nineteenth and the beginning of this century, a man had to be aggressive and ambitious — today he has to be social and tolerant — in order to be an attractive "package." At any rate, the sense of falling in love develops usually only with regard to such human commodities as are within reach of one's own possibilities for exchange. I am out for a bargain; the object should be desirable from the standpoint of its social value, and at the same time should want me, considering my overt and hidden assets and potentialities. Two persons thus fall in love when they feel they have found the best object available on the market, considering the limitations of their own exchange values. Often, as in buying real estate, the hidden potentialities which can be developed play a considerable role in this bargain. In a culture in which the marketing orientation prevails, and in which material success is the outstanding value, there is little reason to be surprised that human love relations follow the same pattern of exchange which governs the commodity and the labor market.

– ERICH FROMM

◊

We are too ego-centered. The ego-shell in which we live is the hardest thing to outgrow. We seem to carry it all the time from childhood up to the time we finally pass away. We are, however, given many chances to break through this shell, and the first and greatest of them is when we reach adolescence. This is the first time the ego really comes to recognize the "other." I mean the awakening of sexual love. An ego, entire and undivided, now begins to feel a sort of split in itself. Love hitherto dormant deep in his heart lifts its head and causes a great commotion in it. For the love now stirred demands at once the assertion of the ego and its annihilation. Love makes the ego lose itself in the object it loves, and yet at the same time it wants to have the object as its own. This is a contradiction, and a great tragedy of life.

– D. T. SUZUKI

Susan Allen Toth

THE BOYFRIEND

◊

SUSAN ALLEN TOTH (b. 1940) grew up in Ames, Iowa, and was graduated from Smith College before she returned to the Midwest for a
Ph.D. in English and a college teaching career. She describes her college years in *Ivy Days: Making My Way Out East* (1984). Toth writes
for such magazines as *Redbook* and *Harper's*, and her scholarly articles
have appeared in professional journals. She recounts her precollege
years in *Blooming: A Small Town Girlhood* (1981), from which this
excerpt is taken. In regard to boyfriends generally, she writes "I can't
remember when I didn't want one."

Just when I was approaching sixteen, I found Peter Stone. Or did 1
he find me? Perhaps I magicked him into existence out of sheer need.
I was spooked by the boys who teased us nice girls about being sweet-
sixteen-and-never-been-kissed. I felt that next to being an old maid
forever, it probably was most demeaning to reach sixteen and not to
have experienced the kind of ardent embrace Gordon MacRae periodically bestowed on Kathryn Grayson between choruses of "Desert
Song." I was afraid I would never have a real boyfriend, never go
parking, never know true love. So when Peter Stone asked his friend
Ted to ask Ted's girlfriend Emily who asked me if I would ever neck
with anyone, I held my breath until Emily told me she had said to
Ted to tell Peter that maybe I would.

Not that Peter Stone had ever necked with anyone either. But I 2
didn't realize that for a long time. High-school courtship usually was
meticulously slow, progressing through inquiry, phone calls, planned
encounters in public places, double or triple dates, single dates, hand-
holding, and finally a good-night kiss. I assumed it probably stopped
there, but I didn't know. I had never gotten that far. I had lots of time
to learn about Peter Stone. What I knew at the beginning already attracted me: he was a year ahead of me, vice-president of Hi-Y, a shot-

putter who had just managed to earn a letter sweater. An older man, *and* an athlete. Tall, heavy, and broad-shouldered, Peter had a sweet slow smile. Even at a distance there was something endearing about the way he would blink nearsightedly through his glasses and light up with pleased recognition when he saw me coming toward him down the hall.

For a long while I didn't come too close. Whenever I saw Peter he 3 was in the midst of his gang, a group of five boys as close and as self-protective as any clique we girls had. They were an odd mixture: Jim, an introspective son of a lawyer; Brad, a sullen hot-rodder; Ted, an unambitious and gentle boy from a poor family; Andy, a chubby comedian; and Peter. I was a little afraid of all of them, and they scrutinized me carefully before opening their circle to admit me, tentatively, as I held tight to Peter's hand. The lawyer's son had a steady girl, a fast number who was only in eighth grade but looked eighteen; the hot-rodder was reputed to have "gone all the way" with his adoring girl, a coarse brunette with plucked eyebrows; gentle Ted pursued my friend Emily with hangdog tenacity; but Peter had never shown real interest in a girlfriend before.

Although I had decided to go after Peter, I was hesitant about how 4 to plot my way into the interior of his world. It was a thicket of strange shrubs and tangled branches. Perhaps I see it that way because I remember the day Peter took me to a wild ravine to shoot his gun. Girls who went with one of "the guys" commiserated with each other that their boyfriends all preferred two other things to them: their cars and their guns. Although Peter didn't hunt and seldom went to practice at the target range, still he valued his gun. Without permits, "the guys" drove outside of town to fire their guns illegally. I had read enough in my *Seventeen* about how to attract boys to know I needed to show enthusiasm about Peter's hobbies, so I asked him if some day he would take me someplace and teach me how to shoot.

One sunny fall afternoon he did. I remember rattling over gravel 5 roads into a rambling countryside that had surprising valleys and woods around cultivated farmland. Eventually we stopped before a barred gate that led to an abandoned bridge, once a railroad trestle, now a splintering wreck. We had to push our way through knee-high weeds to get past the gate. I was afraid of snakes. Peter took my hand; it was the first time he had ever held it, and my knees weakened a little. I was also scared of walking onto the bridge, which had broken boards and sudden gaps that let you look some fifty feet down into the golden and rust-colored brush below. But I didn't mind being a little scared as long as Peter was there to take care of me.

I don't think I had ever held a gun until Peter handed me his pistol, 6 a heavy metal weapon that looked something like the ones movie sheriffs carried in their holsters. I was impressed by its weight and power. Peter fired it twice to show me how and then stood close to me, watching carefully, while I aimed at an empty beer can he tossed into the air. I didn't hit it. The noise of the gun going off was terrifying. I hoped nobody was walking in the woods where I had aimed. Peter said nobody was, nobody ever came here. When I put the gun down, he put his arm around me, very carefully. He had never done that before, either. We both just stood there, looking off into the distance, staring at the glowing maples and elms, dark red patches of sumac, brown heaps of leaves. The late afternoon sun beat down on us. It was hot, and after a few minutes Peter shifted uncomfortably. I moved away, laughing nervously, and we walked back to the car, watching the gaping boards at our feet.

What Peter and I did with our time together is a mystery. I try to 7 picture us at movies or parties or somebody's house, but all I can see is the two of us in Peter's car. "Going for a drive!" I'd fling at my mother as I rushed out of the house; "rinking" was our high-school term for it, drawn from someone's contempt for the greasy "hoods" who hung out around the roller-skating rink and skidded around corners on two wheels of their souped-up cars. Peter's car barely made it around a corner on all four wheels. Though he had learned something about how to keep his huge square Ford running, he wasn't much of a mechanic. He could make jokes about the Ford, but he didn't like anyone else, including me, to say it looked like an old black hearse or remind him it could scarcely do forty miles an hour on an open stretch of highway. Highways were not where we drove, anyway, nor was speed a necessity unless you were trying to catch up with someone who hadn't seen you. "Rinking" meant cruising aimlessly around town, looking for friends in *their* cars, stopping for conversations shouted out of windows, maybe parking somewhere for a while, ending up at the A&W Root Beer Stand or the pizza parlor or the Rainbow Cafe.

Our parents were often puzzled about why we didn't spend time in 8 each other's homes. "Why don't you invite Peter in?" my mother would ask a little wistfully, as I grabbed my billfold and cardigan and headed toward the door. Sometimes Peter would just pause in front of the house and honk; if I didn't come out quickly, he assumed I wasn't home and drove away. Mother finally made me tell him at least to come to the door and knock. I couldn't explain to her why we didn't want to sit in the living room, or go down to the pine-paneled basement at the Harbingers', or swing on the Harrises' front porch. We might not have been bothered at any of those places, but we really wouldn't have been alone. Cars were our private space, a rolling parlor, the only place we could relax and be ourselves. We could talk, fiddle with the radio if we didn't have much to say, look out the window, watch for friends passing by. Driving gave us a feeling of freedom.

Most of my memories of important moments with Peter center in that old black Ford. One balmy summer evening I remember particularly because my friend Emily said I would. Emily and Ted were out cruising in his rusty two-tone Chevy, the lawyer's son Jim and his girl had his father's shiny Buick, and Peter and I were out driving in the Ford. As we rumbled slowly down Main Street, quiet and dark at night, Peter saw Ted's car approaching. We stopped in the middle of the street so the boys could exchange a few laconic grunts while Emily and I smiled confidentially at each other. We were all in a holiday mood, lazy and happy in the warm breezes that swept through the open windows. One of us suggested that we all meet later at Camp Canwita, a wooded park a few miles north of town. Whoever saw Jim would tell him to join us too. We weren't sure what we would do there, but it sounded like an adventure. An hour or so later, Peter and I bumped over the potholes in the road that twisted through the woods to the parking lot. We were the first ones there. When Peter turned off the motor, we could hear grasshoppers thrumming on all sides of us and leaves rustling in the dark. It was so quiet, so remote, I was a little frightened, remembering one of my mother's unnerving warnings about the dangerous men who sometimes preyed upon couples who parked in secluded places. We didn't have long to wait, though, before Ted's car coughed and sputtered down the drive. Soon Jim arrived too, and then we all pulled our cars close together in a kind of circle so we could talk easily out the windows. Someone's

9

radio was turned on, and Frank Sinatra's mournful voice began to sing softly of passing days and lost love. Someone suggested that we get out of the cars and dance. It wouldn't have been Peter, who was seldom romantic. Ted opened his door so the overhead light cast a dim glow over the tiny area between the cars. Solemnly, a little self-consciously, we began the shuffling steps that were all we knew of what we called "slow dancing." Peter was not a good dancer, nor was I, though I liked putting my head on his bulky shoulder. But he moved me around the small lighted area as best he could, trying not to bump into Ted and Emily or Jim and his girl. I tried not to step on his toes. While Sinatra, Patti Page, and the Four Freshmen sang to us about moments to remember and Cape Cod, we all danced, one-two back, one-two back. Finally Emily, who was passing by my elbow, looked significantly at me and said, "This is something we'll be able to tell our grandchildren." Yes, I nodded, but I wasn't so sure. The mosquitoes were biting my legs and arms, my toes hurt, and I was getting a little bored. I think the others were too, because before long we all got into our cars and drove away.

Not all the time we spent in Peter's car was in motion. After several   10 months, we did begin parking on deserted country roads, side streets, even sometimes my driveway, if my mother had heeded my fierce instructions to leave the light turned off. For a while we simply sat and talked, with Peter's arm draped casually on the back of the seat. Gradually I moved a little closer. Soon he had his arm around me, but even then it was a long time before he managed to kiss me good-night. Boys must have been as scared as we girls were, though we always thought of them as having much more experience. We all compared notes, shyly, about how far our boyfriends had gone; was he holding your hand yet, or taking you parking, or . . . ? When a girl finally got kissed, telephone lines burned with the news next day. I was getting a little embarrassed about how long it was taking Peter to get around to it. My sixteenth birthday was only a few weeks away, and so far I had nothing substantial to report. I was increasingly nervous too because I still didn't know quite how I was going to behave. We girls joked about wondering where your teeth went and did glasses get in the way, but no one could give a convincing description. For many years I never told anyone about what *did* happen to me that first time. I was too ashamed. Peter and I were parked down the street from my house, talking, snuggling, listening to the radio. During a silence I turned my face toward him, and then he kissed me, tentatively and quickly. I was exhilarated but frightened. I wanted to respond in an adequate way, but my instincts did not entirely cooperate. I leaned towards Peter, but at the last moment I panicked. Instead of kissing him, I gave him a sudden lick on the cheek. He didn't know what to say. Neither did I.

Next morning I was relieved that it was all over. I dutifully reported 11 my news to a few key girlfriends who could pass it on to others. I left out the part about the lick. That was my last bulletin. After a first kiss, we girls also respected each other's privacy. What more was there to know? We assumed that couples sat in their cars and necked, but nice girls, we also assumed, went no farther. We knew the girls who did. Their names got around. We marveled at them, uncomprehending as much as disapproving. Usually they talked about getting married to their boyfriends, and eventually some of them did. A lot of "nice" girls suffered under this distinction. One of them told me years later how she and her steady boyfriend had yearned and held back, stopped just short, petted and clutched and gritted their teeth. "When we went together to see the movie *Splendor in the Grass*, we had to leave the theatre," she said ruefully. "The part about how Natalie Wood and Warren Beatty wanted to make love so desperately and couldn't. . . . Well, that was just how we felt."

My mother worried about what was going on in the car during 12 those long evenings when Peter and I went "out driving." She needn't have. Amazing as it seems now, when courting has speeded up to a freeway pace, when I wonder if a man who doesn't try to get me to bed immediately might possibly be gay, Peter and I gave each other hours of affection without ever crossing the invisible line. We sat in his car and necked, a word that was anatomically correct. We hugged and kissed, nuzzling ears and noses and hairlines. But Peter never put a hand on my breast, and I wouldn't have known whether Peter had an erection if it had risen up and thwapped me in the face. I never got that close. Although we probably should have perished from frustration, in fact I reveled in all that holding and touching. Peter seemed pleased too, and he never demanded more. Later, I suppose, he learned quickly with someone else about what he had been missing. But I remember with gratitude Peter's awkward tenderness and the absolute faith I had in his inability to hurt me.

After Peter graduated and entered the university, our relationship 13
changed. Few high-school girls I knew went out with college men; it
was considered risky, like dating someone not quite in your social set
or from another town. You were cut off. At the few fraternity functions Peter took me to, I didn't know anyone there. I had no idea what
to talk about or how to act. So I refused to go, and I stopped asking
Peter to come with me to parties or dances at the high school. I
thought he didn't fit in there either. When I was honest with myself, I
admitted that romance had gone. Already planning to go away to college, I could sense new vistas opening before me, glowing horizons
whose light completely eclipsed a boyfriend like Peter. When I got on
the Chicago & Northwestern train to go east to Smith, I felt with relief that the train trip was erasing one problem for me. I simply rode
away from Peter.

On my sixteenth birthday, Peter gave me a small cross on a chain. 14
All the guys had decided that year to give their girlfriends crosses on
chains, even though none of them was especially religious. It was a
perfect gift, they thought, intimate without being soppy. Everyone's
cross cost ten dollars, a lot of money, because it was real sterling silver.
Long after Peter and I stopped seeing each other, I kept my cross
around my neck, not taking it off even when I was in the bathtub.
Like my two wooden dolls from years before, I clung to that cross as a
superstitious token. It meant that someone I had once cared for had
cared for me in return. Once I had had a boyfriend.

CONSIDERATIONS

1. What moved Toth into her first romance? What was apparently *not* part
   of the impetus?
2. Where did Toth learn the appropriate way for her to interest Peter? What
   indicates her present attitude toward the episode with the gun?
3. Why didn't they ever come into each other's houses? What were the reasons for being in cars all the time?
4. Is there any part of this account that strikes you as probably oversimplified
   or idealized? What additions might make it more true to life without
   changing the main points of her memoir?
5. What was the lasting effect of this romance after it ended? Was it different from what she sought or expected?

6. WRITING TOPIC. From your own insights about friendship and early dating, explain how a group of friends of your own sex affects the progress of a romantic interest. What do friends provide? And what confusions or complications do they sometimes cause? In a 500-word essay, come to a specific conclusion about the role of a group of friends in the context of high school dating.

Marcelle Clements

TERMINAL COOL

◊

MARCELLE CLEMENTS (b. 1948) was born in Paris and emigrated to
the United States. She was educated at Bard College, earning her bachelor's degree in music. In her twenties she went back to France and
worked for *The Paris Metro*, an English-language biweekly newspaper.
In 1978 she returned to the United States and has been writing free-
lance for *Esquire, The Village Voice, Rolling Stone, Mademoiselle*,
and *Vanity Fair*. In 1985 she went to Nicaragua, Central America, and
wrote a series of articles for *The Village Voice* about that experience.
Her first book, a collection of essays entitled *The Dog Is Us* (1985),
includes this description of sixties "cool" college-age romances.

In certain adolescent milieus of the 1960s, there reigned an aes- 1
thetic of silence concerning some topics. Certain phrases were never
uttered except under monstrous duress. For example: "I need you."
Like "I want you," "Reach out, I'll be there," "You keep me hangin'
on," or "Please, please, please," they were reserved strictly for rock 'n'
roll songs. "I love you" was too hokey for words. In fact, when seventeen-year-old girls exchanged confidences in their dormitories, "He's
serious about me" was a put-down. And how a boy behaved in a
breakup scene was a respected indicator of the degree to which he was
cool or uncool, a paramount consideration at the time, because the
concept of cool combined the two virtues that adolescents most ar-
dently desired: integrity and sex appeal.

"Saying 'Don't leave me' was totally out of the question when we 2
were in school," I recently observed to an old friend.

"Hey, I said it once," he answered. "In my sophomore year. Just 3
before I fell apart and had to leave school for three months."

Right. 4

For sixties adolescents, there were many types of cool to choose ₅ from: biker cool, street-corner cool, Zen cool, Jewish-comic cool, antiwar-movement cool, John Kennedy button-down cool, coffeehouse-intellectual cool — not to be confused with folk-song cool, largely enacted in coffeehouses but which also had contingents in city parks, in people's living rooms, and in subway stations. By the mid-sixties cool types were too numerous to name, and I'm thinking about just the relatively sedate East Coast. In the West, they had surfer cool, prankster cool, and God knows what else.

So, around that time, thousands of intellectually befuddled, ₆ morally perplexed, acne-ridden adolescents became incredibly cool, by sheer will. It might have seemed important at the time to be naturally cool, but in fact it wasn't. Almost no one is naturally cool anyway: the genetic odds are against that bizarre combination of intelligence, wit, alienation, and low metabolism. But if you were too agitated, insecure, romantic, or goony to come by cool naturally, you could still look cool and act cool, if you wanted it badly enough. Eventually, with practice, you could actually organize your psyche according to cool principles with surprising success. Soon enough, it became second nature to ride enigmatically off into the sunset or stay behind in Casablanca. In its final phase, cool was not a posture, but an attitude. Yet it was accessible to the most callow aspirant. In a way, just wanting to be cool (even if you didn't think of it that way but, instead, more vaguely, as having a certain relationship to your environment) took you halfway there, because the very nurturing of the desire meant that you had already gotten rid of untold amounts of uncool baggage.

It would require a ridiculously convoluted history of the morals and ₇ moods of postwar America to untangle the web of cultural threads that led to the mass juvenile depression of the late fifties and early sixties. But, by the mid-sixties, this collective depression was molded into a style of deportment that conferred status upon those who could elaborate it with elegance. As soon as we went away to college, no longer putting up with irritating adults exhorting us to be cheerful and mocking us for our predilections for bohemian values, we could be as despondent as we pleased. It was kind of fun doing it as a group. Of course, no one then admitted that it was fun. (*Happiness* was a word never mentioned, like *marriage* or *business*.) Fun was too mundane, like parents' cocktail parties. Thrills were all right, though, and the more extreme the better. Thrill seeking, after all, was a classic tactic of the disenfranchised and a historically correct balm for clinical ennui.

Anything to avoid being square — an ethical imperative at the 8 time. But that was twenty years ago. These days nobody seems to be afraid of being square anymore. At least, it's a topic that's never brought up at the dinner parties where women in angel shag hairdos and men in Armani jackets exchange professional gossip. And *cool* is now a word never mentioned without derision.

Yet one woman I know recently confided: "I miss it. There's a 9 thing I used to tell myself that ran 'Every day, in every way, I'm getting cooler and cooler.' And that kind of comforted me. I don't have any religion or any organized ideals or anything. So I used thinking about cool to keep me from getting subhuman."

Naturally, only a woman could have made that remark. After all, 10 guys were always much too cool to ever talk about it. . . . And they were right, of course: to acknowledge the attitude was to expose its authenticity to question.

Cool had a lot to do with sex, sex appeal, and sex roles. Girls have 11 never received enough credit for the fantastic leap of the mind they took in the sixties when they decided to take the cool aesthetic seriously. In these post-women's lib days, we've come to take a lot for granted. But when the seventeen-year-old girl from the comfortable home started adopting some of the attitudes of the black jazz musician, the lessons of centuries of class and gender indoctrination were dumped in the trash along with the pink plastic curlers. And gladly, too.

Yet, boys were always cooler. Cool boys were much more feminine 12 than their sloshed and rowdy frat-house counterparts, but basically all the characteristics of the cool personality were male traits. All of the cool prototypes were males, saxophone players, cowboys, hoods, male homosexual poets, basketball players, bass guitarists, Bogarts and Brandos.

It wasn't something we thought about, but looking back to college 13 days, I'd have to admit that my girlfriends and I imitated boys a lot. We dressed like them, we talked like them, we tried to imitate their attitudes: at first when we were in their company, later with each other, and finally, even to ourselves. And why shouldn't we have? What else was there to imitate? The so-called offbeat prototypes from the old films, the Katharine Hepburns and the Gloria Grahames, were basically only putting up a good front in reaction to men. Some anti-establishment types appealed: the Supremes, say, or Anna Magnani, or Susan Sontag. One could admire these women, but it was difficult to identify with them.

No, the boys we went to school with were onto much more sophis-   14
ticated material. We had more in common with them than with any women of the past or present. And besides, they were clearly having fun — in a grim, alienated way, of course — so we weren't about to be left behind. At my old school, the girls became champion thrill-seekers and aces in the I-can-take-it department; they were thought of as pals by their male friends and as wild (or worse) by everyone else (especially their mothers). It's a mistake to ignore the obvious.

The first thing girls did was to imitate male sexual behavior. And it   15
turned out that as soon as the label *fast* became obsolete — at least in the view of the subgroup — all of feminine behavior could be altered, because most of the circumscriptions had existed only to achieve the *demure* model. Once the sexually demure barrier had been shattered, the other constraints became irrelevant as well, and ever so much eas-ier to dismiss. So girls stepped out of their skirts and put on jeans, talked less, went hitchhiking around the country, took the most mind-bending drugs available, loved and left, had adventures, courted danger, and occasionally went to sleep drunk with their boots on . . . just like boys.

I distinctly remember a guy at school who made my heart leap in a   16
fierce way saying to me: "Lesbians are so cool." The funny thing is, I think that was probably his way of making an advance. It worked, too; I knew he was right, and it made me feel real jealous.

Yet, if you were still attracted to boys, you wound up retaining a   17
good deal of your feminine emotional equipment, and in fact all the time you were evolving in the male-oriented context you were also growing as a woman. My God, were we confused, continually adding one more illogically acquired trait to an already hopelessly ambiguous personality. We were like guests with a serendipitous appetite at a buffet dinner, piling an incongruous assortment of foods onto our plates. No wonder personalities were indecipherable. One of my col-lege friends recalls: "To be cool was either total affectation or total lack of affectation. With the coolest girls, you could never tell which they were."

If boys couldn't understand us, it was because we really weren't like 18
them, notwithstanding all our efforts. And it wasn't only biochemical,
either. There were too many concepts in the terminal-cool mentality
that we could grasp but not absorb. For example, girls might have
been enticed by black music and style, but few could match their
male friends' crucial and rich ambivalence — infatuation poisoned by
envy — toward black culture. After all, most girls had only the crash
course. And in matters of style, even though they had traveled a
longer road, they could never really be as cool as boys: the voice was
still too inflected; the eyes too expressive; the hand gestures, the tilt of
the head never successfully stifled — the style of the powerless, of the
participant observed by the infinitely cooler outsider. In the end, in
timeless fashion, the best way females could conquer power was to se-
duce it.

Like the courtship patterns of all inhibited cultures, the cool se- 19
duction was, of course, tremendously titillating. In addition to normal
human nostalgia for Sex of the Past, I'd bet almost every woman who
has experienced them still harbors wistful affection for these seductions. They were so well suited to feminine erotic-emotional predilections: drawn out, restrained, indirect, subtle, with exquisite attention
paid to detail. Never mind if this was due as much to adolescent fear
as to flair for sensual drama. The combination somehow made for
wonderfully complex and preoccupying social activity.

For one thing, these attractions were so meandering. *Does he want* 20
to? Do I want to? At my old campus, which was nestled in an idyllic
Hudson River valley landscape, kids used to go down to the riverbank
and lie down together for hours on the pine needles, drive each other
crazy, not doing or saying anything, just watching the sun glimmer on
the waterfall. Then they'd walk back to their classes and maybe not
speak to each other again for weeks.

The languid pace of the seductions was compounded by the fact 21
that, as of 1965 or so, the girls I knew still did not overtly initiate sexual encounters — though whether this was because of leftover sexual
mores or the new girl-cool code is beyond the scope of my memory.
The trouble was that in 1965 boys didn't want to overtly initiate sexual encounters either. Pushy, you know. Aggressive. Risky. Uncool.

The coolest boys, the real heartbreakers, seemed inaccessible to the 22
point of cruelty. Unless a girl happened to be good friends with him,
the most attention one of these guys would show her would be to

maybe say, "What are you up to?" when he put his tray down at the table where she was sitting in dining commons. And that was if he really liked her. And when he left, he'd say "See you later." So after lunch, she'd go back to her room and brood and try to talk herself out of caring about it.

Even if this guy was her friend, he was so enigmatic that she'd de-   23 velop a helpless compulsion to climb into his brain. She somehow knew he liked her, but she couldn't be sure whether he felt *that way* for months (or at least weeks, which seemed like an eternity at the time). But then one night, when a bunch of people had gone down to the local bar together, she'd catch him watching her dance with someone else. And if she smiled at him, then later, when they all left, he would stay next to her on the walk back to campus and he'd wait for the group to assume a propitious formation so that he could speak to her in a conversational tone but not be overheard and say, probably, "Do you want to get high?" in the most casual way.

When the group reached main campus and disbanded, none of the   24 others would say anything when she walked away with him toward his dorm, and the two of them wouldn't say anything to each other either. Once upstairs in his room, they'd both sit on his bed, leaning against the wall, but he wouldn't touch her, except to pass a joint. He'd put on a record and perhaps he'd tell her something funny about one of his teachers, or show her some object in his possession, a book of Francis Bacon paintings maybe. Hours would go by like that in the little dimly lit room, and she didn't know anymore what to expect. He'd stop putting records on, and now they'd become silent; they would just hear faint music coming from other people's rooms. And then if she stayed very still, he'd slide away from her so he could put her foot on his lap, and he'd slip off her boot.

When he finally learned over to kiss her (maybe not until after-   25 ward), his eyes would be closed and his mouth very open and his teeth somewhat in the way. But her eyes would be open, and she'd see that he had an expression that was kind of like pain on his face, which made her feel a queer mixture of joy and malaise. Why malaise? It wasn't until years later, if she remembered it, that she'd realize that the expression was simply tenderness, and that she had known it even then but hadn't believed it.

These boys always seemed to have a secret. It should have been   26 easy to see that the secret was loneliness, but it was so effectively encapsulated by irony and nonchalance that we were fooled every time. Boys were so mysterious that we could idealize them to an absurd degree. And so we did, not understanding that to do so was also a form of cruelty. A really cool guy seemed like an irresistible challenge, but ultimately the challenge was to get him to be uncool, or to make him tender. It's only now, all these years later, that it's become clear that a lot of what seemed so cool was probably simply shyness and fear. Only a few years earlier these boys had engaged in the standard century-old teenage fumblings, awkward gropings with the age-old clammy hands and excess saliva. Suddenly they found themselves in this absolutely amazing sexual funhouse, with all the girls they liked apparently available, and these poor boys were stuck with having to act cool when they were, well, scared. *Is she really willing?* Is that what they were thinking while we racked our brains to figure out why they tormented us? And we were as thickheaded as they were to deny the evidence that they were as willing to give us tenderness as we were willing to be seduced.

But then, there's all the more reason to ask, Why malaise? Well, 27 perhaps it wasn't only thickheadedness, perhaps we didn't want to process the evidence, because it would have meant wrecking our fantasies.

Time passed. And with experience, these sad but sweet scenes de- 28 generated, as inhibited tenderness hardened into cynicism — a far more dangerous form of fear. Eventually, it began to seem that the coolest sexuality was vicarious, remembered, imagined, removed. "After sex you could be cool," a friend says. "During wasn't cool at all, of course. And before, it could be pretty cool, but it was really too tense. But afterward, you could feel terrifically cool."

As a reaction to the uptight standards of society, sex was cool, but 29 how could you be cool while you were having sex? According to the cool subgroup standard, then, the coolest form of sexuality became sexual tension: the sex you didn't consummate, the nights you spent with someone on LSD when you never took off your clothes; the look you once exchanged, by accident, with your best friend's lover. The coolest relationships were ambiguous friendships, often with someone you'd slept with once, but it seemed so long ago that it only mattered in the sense that it was something already taken care of.

Of course, there was an unprecedented amount of sexual activity. 30 But if you were actually going to engage in sex, at least it could be kind of somber (thereby preserving distance). Despite the fact that so-called sexual liberation is always situated in the sixties, it wasn't until the next decade that the whole "joyful" sex syndrome materialized — *The Joy of Sex* wasn't published until 1972; the manuals of the mid-sixties conveyed the solemn and controlled sensuality of Eastern cultures, *The Perfumed Garden* and *The Kama Sutra.*

And precisely because there were so many casual affairs, the 31 approach was rather . . . minimalist. Eventually not even making love was exempt from those outward signs of cool behavior that were also the symptoms of depression. For example, it was quite silent. It was silently requested, with a single gesture, only a touch perhaps, and silently acquiesced to, with a glance. Except for the record player in the room, the act itself was silent, too. Between cuts, there wasn't a sound. In the mid-to-late sixties, kids must have reached millions of orgasms without a word or a moan, and afterward lain next to one another soundlessly. At the time, even "Did you come?" would have been considered an irremediably uncool invasion of privacy.

So many lonely children. So cool.   32

I think that's what finally wrecked the cool aesthetic: it was simply 33 too lonely. People started wanting to have long-term relationships, and after they'd failed at them a number of times because they were so damn cool, they decided to bail out of cool. As horrendously difficult and humiliating as it might have been to turn toward someone you loved and say, "I need you," it wasn't as hard and as painful as that terrifying solitude you felt in a stranger's bed if you'd succeeded in becoming detached enough to make all your lovers into strangers, or the uneasy solitude you felt with even your closest friends if you'd become cynical enough to make all your friends mere cohabitants of a sad planet, or the devastating spiritual solitude you felt if you had taken enough lysergic acid so that even the original joke — that everything was a joke — became a joke and *that* was really too sad to laugh at anymore. . . .

That's what happened: suddenly the soiled, messy, ridiculous, com- 34 pletely uncool real world started to seem more alluring than the endless mazes of the pure but cold territory of the perpetual outsider. So one by one, and eventually by the thousands, they defected from the terminal-cool ethos. There's been a good deal of smug commentary about the return of this group to straight America. But I think it's unfair to mock these people for acquiring the three-piece suits and the mortgages and the lawn furniture, and for starting to use words like *business* and *marriage*. Essentially, they just came in from the cold. . . .

But perhaps cool as part of an ethos is only dormant. If the aes- 35 thetic of the old cool depended on silence, it was also a powerful statement about conventional mores, love, war, and social inequity. Maybe there will come a time when we will choose to collectively stand back once more to question our conventions. Maybe the need for cool is cyclical, and there will be other, better forms of cool to be found in the future fashions for the mind.

CONSIDERATIONS

1. According to the author, what major values were expressed by those who were cool? Do you think their behavior actually did reflect those values? What does coolness indicate to you?
2. What changes in sex roles accompanied the cool style? What is the author's attitude toward these changes?
3. Why was it possible for boys alway to be cooler than girls? Do you think that cool was a primarily male phenomenon?
4. What finally ended the cool style? Can you think of other contributing causes at that time, such as historical events and social changes, that the author does not mention?
5. WRITING TOPIC. The generation that Clements describes was in college some twenty to thirty years ago, from 1955 to 1965. Those students could be your parents or parents of your friends. Did the Age of Cool have any lingering after-effects on them? Is this generation still affected by some aspects of their earlier "mass juvenile depression?" Are they presently more expressive or less expressive than our own generation? Write 700 words as a sequel to "Terminal Cool," bringing up to date the view of that generation's involvement in their present style of life. You may want to gather evidence from interviews and direct conversations on this topic.
6. WRITING TOPIC. As you observe the sophomores, juniors, and seniors on your campus, are they trying to appear "cool" or "hot" in their personal and social relations? Is it fashionable to appear detached and ironic, or to appear involved and sympathetic? As an observer, write 500 words on the preferred style of conduct in personal and social relations at your college. You may be able to use evidence from the student newspaper as well as from direct reporting.

Robert Solomon

"I-LOVE-YOU"

◊

ROBERT SOLOMON (b. 1942) was a medical student, a jazz musician, and a songwriter before he became a professor of philosophy at the University of Texas. *Post hoc, ergo propter hoc:* his philosophy analyzes the concrete and experiential rather than the abstract and logical. Solomon received his Ph.D. from the University of Michigan, and he has taught at Princeton and UCLA. His book on *The Passions* (1976) examines the philosophy of our emotions, a topic that he pursues further in his recent work, *Love: Emotion, Myth and Metaphor* (1981), from which this selection is taken. Solomon argues in general that love creates a shared self, changing both lovers into a new identity together. His analysis of the phrase "I love you" is modeled after a similar chapter in Roland Barthes's *A Lover's Discourse* (1978), which Solomon refers to in this essay.

I-love-you *has no usages: Like a child's word, it enters into no social constraint; it can be a sublime, solemn, trivial word, it can be an erotic, pornographic word. It is a socially irresponsible word.*

I-love-you *is without nuance. It suppresses explanations, adjustments, degrees, scruples . . . this word is always true (has no referent other than its utterance; it is a performative).*

— ROLAND BARTHES, *A Lover's Discourse*

"I love you."   1
What does that mean? Of course you know, but tell me.   2
A description of how I feel? Not at all.   3
An admission? A confession?   4
No, you don't understand, after all.   5

"I-love-you" is an action, not a word. It is not a short sentence. Of 6
course it *looks* like a sentence, made up of words, but sentences can be
transcribed and transformed. "I-love-you" is more like the word "this"
or "here"; it makes sense only when spoken in a very particular context. In writing, in a letter, it has meaning only to you, and only while
you can still imagine my speaking it. To anyone else, and after a while
to you, it means nothing at all; like the word "here," just sitting on
the page like an old coffee stain. Hardly a word at all.

"I-love-you" has no parts, no words to be rearranged or replaced. 7
"You-I-love" is more than merely clumsy, like "Me Tarzan, you
Jane." It is something like staking a claim. "John loves Sally," said by
John to Sally, is absurd. "I-love-you" allows for no substitutions, no
innovations. It stands outside the language. It says nothing. If it is
misunderstood, it cannot be explained. If unheard, it has not been uttered. And when it is heard, it no longer matters that you didn't mean
to say it in the first place, that you "just blurted it out." You *did* it,
and it cannot be undone.

"I-love-you" does not *express* my love. It need not already be there. 8
Perhaps I didn't feel it until I said it, or just before. But then, in a
sense, I didn't *say* anything at all.

One of the perennial misunderstandings about language is the idea 9
that all sentences *say* something; words refer and phrases describe.
But language also requests and cajoles, demands and refuses, plays,
puns, disguises as well as reveals, creates as well as clarifies, *pro*vokes
as well as *in*vokes, *per*forms as well as *in*forms. We *do* things with
words, in words done by the late Oxford philosopher J. L. Austin.
With words we make promises, christen ships, declare war, and get
married, none of which would be possible without them. Our sentences mean what we *do* as well as, or rather than, what we say. They
bring things about as well as tell us what has already come about. And
the meaning of "I-love-you" is to be found in what we *do* with it, not
in what it tries to tell us.

If we so easily misunderstand language and persistently refuse to 10
look at love, then of course we will miss completely the significance of
the language of love, if, that is, it is a language. Or is it, as Barthes
suggests, a *cry*? "I-love-you" mainly makes a demand. So when I say
it you react — not "How curious that you feel that way" but rather
"But what do you want me to do?" Its meaning is aimed at you, to
move you. (A "perlocutionary act," Austin called it.)

I say, "I have a headache," and you say, "Poor Boobie." Perhaps 11 you kiss my forehead, and I'm most grateful. But if you say, "Me too," I don't think, "What a coincidence"; I feel slighted. You've misunderstood me. Suppose I say, "I love you," and you kiss my forehead. I'm offended. That's not a reply but an evasion.

I say, "I love you," and I wait for a response. It can only be one 12 phrase: "I love you too," nothing less, nothing more. Perhaps, "Me too," though it is ungrammatical and a serious confusion of pronouns, but it is also less than the proper formula. If you say, *"Je t'aime,"* you have not done it either; instead you are showing off.

I could be silent and just love you. And perhaps you'd know. I 13 don't have to say, "I'm so angry with you," when I've been yelling at you for twenty minutes. I don't say, "I'm sad," when I'm crying. And yet I feel compelled to say, "I love you," even when it's obvious I do. "Nothing says I love you like 'I love you.'" But it is more than that too, more than something said.

The power of words, or at least certain words, sometimes is awe- 14 some. "I-love-you" is a magical phrase that ruins the evening. Or changes love into something more, even when it was love before. It is not an announcement, no R.S.V.P. No "if you please." It *demands* a reply; in fact, it *is* this demand. And a warning, and a threat. It is an embarrassment, first to me, but soon to you. It makes me vulnerable, but you are the one who is naked. I am watching your every move. Counting the fractions of a second. What will you do?

"I love you"; "what a terrible thing to say to someone." Terrible 15 indeed.

"Tell me you love me." 16

"What are you expecting from me? You know I love you." 17

"Then say it." 18

"I don't want to say it." 19

(The evening's already lost, but I pursue.) 20

"If you love me, why not say it?" 21

"Oh. I don't know; it just changes everything." 22

"How can saying what is true change anything?" 23

But it does. "I-love-you" doesn't fit into our conversations. It inter- 24 rupts them. Or ends them.

"I-love-you" is language reminding us of the unimportance of lan- 25 guage, language that destroys language. It is language without alternatives, without subtlety, like a gunshot or the morning alarm.

And then it's gone, not even a memory, and has to be done again.

But once said, it can never be said again. It can only be repeated, as 26 a ritual, an assurance. Not to say it, when it's never been said, is no matter, a curiosity. But not to say it, once said, is a cause for alarm, perhaps panic. One commits oneself to the word, and to say it again. What else follows? Perhaps nothing.

Barthes says it is "released," but I say, *shot out,* like a weapon. Re- 27 leased like an arrow, perhaps. And if I make myself vulnerable in say-ing it, the real question is what it will do to you. I'm still watching you. Still counting the fractions of a second. What will you do?

I say, "I hate you," and you quite rightly ask "Why?" But I say, "I 28 love you," and "Why?" is completely improper. A reasonable ques-tion, but a breach in the formula. You have turned the weapon back onto me, so of course I reply indignantly, "What do you mean? I love you, that's all." And I again await your reply. A second chance, but no more.

I say, "I love you," and you answer, "How much?" What are we 29 negotiating? Perhaps you are saying, "Well then, prove it." And, hav-ing said the word, I am bound to. Nevertheless, your reply is insuffer-able. You're acting as if I actually *said* something which can now be qualified, quantified, argued for and against. But I didn't. I just said, "I love you." And that is, in terms of "How much?" to say nothing at all.

"I-love-you": a warning, an apology, an interruption, a plea for at- 30 tention, an objection, an excuse, a justification, a reminder, a trap, a blessing, a disguise, a vacuum, a revelation, a way of saying nothing, a way of summarizing everything, an attack, a surrender, an opening, an end.

I say, "I love you," and I no longer remember the time I was 31 with you when it was not said. And we will never be together again with-out it.

CONSIDERATIONS

1. How does "I-love-you" differ from an ordinary sentence? Why does Solo-mon hyphenate the words?
2. What is the purpose of stating "I-love-you"? Do you agree with Solomon?

3. Once said, how does the phrase continue to be used by lovers? What new questions of meaning are raised?
4. Solomon addresses someone called "you" throughout the essay, and he includes bits of his dialogue with "you." Who is this implied second person, and how does this method of exposition serve his point?
5. WRITING TOPIC. Does the meaning of "I-love-you" change when it is spoken by a parent to a child or by a friend to a friend? Does it remain an action, or does it become an ordinary sentence? Or does it have mixed functions? In a 500-word essay, explain one or two of the other usages of the phrase. You may want to address your essay directly to Solomon in order to emphasize your points of agreement and disagreement with him.

Francesco Alberoni

TWO KINDS OF SEXUALITY*

◊

FRANCESCO ALBERONI (b. 1929), a leading sociologist in Italy, teaches at the University of Milan. His special field of research on the sociology of collective movements such as revolutions and cultural changes, is reflected in his book *Movement and Institution* (translated in 1983). As a writer for general audiences, Alberoni contributes to the newspaper *Corriere della Serra* and to *Panorama* magazine. His study, *Falling in Love* (1981; translated in 1983), has been widely read in Europe. This selection is a chapter from that book, and it examines the sexual component of falling in love.

According to a widely held view, the difference between human 1 and animal sexuality lies in the fact that in animals sexual activity is cyclic — it appears explosively during the mating season and then disappears — but in man sexual desire is continuous, always present, and only fails to manifest itself with intensity if it is repressed. Sexuality is thus placed in the same class as other "needs," like sleeping or eating; it is always present in an almost constant quantity day after day. This idea spread with the popularization of psychoanalysis. In fact, Freud, in his quest for an original vital energy, initially identified it with sexuality. And while we are alive, the vital energy must exist constantly in us. Today this postulate is the basis for all those disquisitions on sexual misery as the effect of repression and domination which, beginning with the obscure reflections of Reich and Marcuse, have since come to animate the findings of countless public opinion surveys.

What is repeatedly discovered in these surveys? That men and women have a limited number of rather brief sexual relations each week, and almost always with the same partner. So sexual activity is

* Editor's title.

recurrent, short, and of slight intensity, more or less like eating or drinking. The impression remains, however, that sex does not have to be like this, that it can be completely different. What is the source of this conviction?

It seems to me the answer is this: that all men and women have had 3 periods in their lives when sexual activity was frequent, intense, extraordinary, and exalting, and they would like it always to be this way. These extraordinary periods are taken as a standard for daily, ordinary sexuality, the kind that is measured in the public opinion surveys and that we experience almost habitually.

Now if we think carefully about the fact that we have all experi- 4 enced brief periods of extraordinary sexuality and long periods of the ordinary kind, we will have to conclude that, in reality, human sexuality is not something constant like eating and drinking. Rather, it is always there in its *ordinary* form, like the other "needs," but it assumes a totally different, *extraordinary* form and intensity in certain periods — when we fall in love.

In man, sexuality does not have a biological cycle. In both man and 5 animals, sexuality is discontinuous and is present in all its magnificence only during certain extraordinary periods, in love and in the mating season. At these times, sexuality is something inexhaustible and yet completely satisfying. We live for days on end, constantly absorbed in the person we love, and not only do we lose track of our sexual relations and their duration, but every glance, every touch, every thought addressed to her (or him) has an erotic intensity a hundred, a thousand times greater than that of ordinary sexual relations.

At these times, our entire physical and sensory life expands, be- 6 comes more intense; we pick up scents we didn't smell before, we perceive colors and lights we don't usually see. And our intellectual life expands too, so that we perceive relationships that were previously obscure to us. A gesture, a glance, a movement by the beloved speaks profoundly, tells us about her, her past, how she was as a child. We understand her sentiments, and we understand our own. We immediately sense what is sincere and what is not in others and in ourselves because we have become sincere. Yet we can create a universe of fantasies in which we never tire of rediscovering the one we love. And the erupting sexuality, the desire for pleasure and to give pleasure invests all that is part of her. We love everything about her, even the inside of her body, her liver, her lungs.

The sexual act then becomes a desire to be in the beloved's body, 7
to live there and be experienced by her in a fusion that is physical, but
that continues as tenderness for her weaknesses, her ingenuousness,
her defects, her imperfections. We even manage to love a wound she
might have, which is transfigured by our affection.

But all this is addressed to a single person and to her (or him) 8
alone. In the end, it doesn't matter who the person may be; what
matters is that along with our love a terrible force is born that leads to
our fusion and makes each of us irreplaceable and unique for the
other. The other, the beloved, becomes what only she can be, that absolutely special one. And this happens even against our will, even
though we continue for a long time to believe that we can do without
the one we love and can find that same happiness in another person.

But it isn't true. A brief separation is enough for us to reconfirm 9
that the one we love is the bearer of something unmistakable, something that we always lack without her, that is revealed to us through
her, and that without her we could never find again. And often we can
simply identify her by a detail — her hands, the shape of her breasts, a
crease in her flesh, her voice (it really doesn't matter what) — a detail — that represents or symbolizes her difference and uniqueness.
This is the "mark of grace." Eros — that is, extraordinary sexuality — is monogamous.

The facts, therefore, show us that our sexuality manifests itself in 10
two ways, one of which is ordinary and daily, the other extraordinary
and discontinuous. And the extraordinary occurs at particular moments: when we fall in love or when we experience a total, passionate
love. *Ordinary sexuality*, like eating and drinking, accompanies us
when our life proceeds uniformly, at the linear pace of the clock. *Extraordinary sexuality* appears at moments when our vital energy seeks
new and different paths. At these times, sexuality becomes the means
by which life explores the frontiers of the possible, the horizons of the
imaginary and of nature: the nascent state.

This sexuality is tied to the intellect and the imagination, to enthu- 11
siasm and passion — it is fused with them. But its nature is to subvert,
transform, rupture previous ties. Eros is a revolutionary force, even if
limited to two people. And there are few revolutions in life. For this
reason, extraordinary sexuality cannot be evoked at will. It signifies a
vital change in us, or an attempt to change, and so it is risky. Eros is a
source of constant aspiration and constant longing for us, yet we fear

it. To protect ourselves we use the same word to indicate eros and everyday sexuality, the eating and drinking of sex, the subject of those public opinion surveys that always rediscover the same things. These are things that we already know, but that calm us because they tell us that other people experience the same "sexual misery" — that is, our everyday life.

But the surveys can also deceive us. They do so by suggesting that 12 we can increase our happiness if, for example, we have sex ten times a week instead of four, if we increase the duration of each act, and, what is especially exciting, if we have sex with many different people. This is deceptive because when we are dealing with ordinary sexuality, having sex with the same person or with ninety-nine different persons doesn't change a thing. Anyone who has tried knows this, because he generally has tried it when he wanted to replace the one unique person who in herself could have given him satisfaction and peace during those intervals of time of which, subjectively experienced, are moments of eternity.

Since we are used to measuring everything by the linear time of the 13 clock, we forget that time is different in the extraordinary sexuality of true love. In Japanese Buddhism, the expressions *nin* and *ten* are used to indicate the two forms of the happy life. *Nin* is the world of peace and daily tranquillity, *ten* the extraordinary moment of emotion and love. Thus *nin* is already joy, and a day of *nin* corresponds to a year in a world without tranquillity. But a day of *ten* corresponds to a thousand or ten thousand years of time. In the nascent state there actually occurs an eternalization of the present. And when we lose our love, an hour's wait becomes years or centuries, and the nostalgia for the moment of eternity is always with us.

CONSIDERATIONS

1. Of the two kinds of human sexuality, which kind does the author compare with animal sexuality?
2. According to Alberoni, how does love affect our intelligence?
3. Paraphrase and explain Alberoni's statement that "eros is a revolutionary force." Try to make your language less abstract than his.
4. What is the author's criticism of sex surveys? In Alberoni's view, what do such surveys fail to reflect?

5. WRITING TOPIC. One adage about love is that "Love is blind." Other familiar sayings about love define it as an illness, a madness, a delusion, or a dream. These views of love as a deluded and irrational state are rejected by Alberoni. Write 500 words explaining his concept of love as "the nascent state." Be sure to look up *nascent* in the dictionary and consider all its meanings that might bear on Alberoni's point.

Raymond Carver

WHAT WE TALK ABOUT
WHEN WE TALK ABOUT LOVE

◊

See the earlier headnote about Raymond Carver on p. 99. This selection is the title story of his volume *What We Talk About When We Talk About Love* (1981). The story is a contemporary symposium. Plato's *Symposium*, an after-dinner conversation in which four people half-drunkenly discuss the peculiarities of love, seems to loom in the background.

My friend Mel McGinnis was talking. Mel McGinnis is a cardi- 1 ologist, and sometimes that gives him the right.

The four of us were sitting around his kitchen table drinking gin. 2 Sunlight filled the kitchen from the big window behind the sink. There were Mel and me and his second wife, Teresa — Terri, we called her — and my wife, Laura. We lived in Albuquerque then. But we were all from somewhere else.

There was an ice bucket on the table. The gin and the tonic water 3 kept going around, and we somehow got on the subject of love. Mel thought real love was nothing less than spiritual love. He said he'd spent five years in a seminary before quitting to go to medical school. He said he still looked back on those years in the seminary as the most important years in his life.

Terri said the man she lived with before she lived with Mel loved 4 her so much he tried to kill her. Then Terri said, "He beat me up one night. He dragged me around the living room by my ankles. He kept saying, 'I love you, I love you, you bitch.' He went on dragging me around the living room. My head kept knocking on things." Terri looked around the table. "What do you do with love like that?"

She was a bone-thin woman with a pretty face, dark eyes, and 5 brown hair that hung down her back. She liked necklaces made of turquoise, and long pendant earrings.

"My God, don't be silly. That's not love, and you know it," Mel 6 said. "I don't know what you'd call it, but I sure know you wouldn't call it love."

"Say what you want to, but I know it was," Terri said. "It may 7 sound crazy to you, but it's true just the same. People are different, Mel. Sure, sometimes he may have acted crazy. Okay. But he loved me. In his own way maybe, but he loved me. There was love there, Mel. Don't say there wasn't."

Mel let out his breath. He held his glass and turned to Laura and 8 me. "The man threatened to kill me," Mel said. He finished his drink and reached for the gin bottle. "Terri's a romantic. Terri's of the kick-me-so-I'll-know-you-love-me school. Terri, hon, don't look that way." Mel reached across the table and touched Terri's cheek with his fingers. He grinned at her.

"Now he wants to make up," Terri said. 9

"Make up what?" Mel said. "What is there to make up? I know 10 what I know. That's all."

"How'd we get started on this subject, anyway?" Terri said. She 11 raised her glass and drank from it. "Mel always has love on his mind," she said. "Don't you, honey?" She smiled, and I thought that was the last of it.

"I just wouldn't call Ed's behavior love. That's all I'm saying, 12 honey," Mel said. "What about you guys?" Mel said to Laura and me. "Does that sound like love to you?"

"I'm the wrong person to ask," I said. "I didn't even know the 13 man. I've only heard his name mentioned in passing. I wouldn't know. You'd have to know the particulars. But I think what you're saying is that love is an absolute."

Mel said, "The kind of love I'm talking about is. The kind of love 14 I'm talking about, you don't try to kill people."

Laura said, "I don't know anything about Ed, or anything about 15 the situation. But who can judge anyone else's situation?"

I touched the back of Laura's hand. She gave me a quick smile. 16 I picked up Laura's hand. It was warm, the nails polished, perfectly manicured. I encircled the broad wrist with my fingers, and I held her.

"When I left, he drank rat poison," Terri said. She clasped her 17
arms with her hands. "They took him to the hospital in Santa Fe.
That's where we lived then, about ten miles out. They saved his life.
But his gums went crazy from it. I mean they pulled away from his
teeth. After that, his teeth stood out like fangs. My God," Terri said.
She waited a minute, then let go of her arms and picked up her glass.

"What people won't do!" Laura said. 18

"He's out of the action now," Mel said. "He's dead." 19

Mel handed me the saucer of limes. I took a section, squeezed it 20
over my drink, and stirred the ice cubes with my finger.

"It's gets worse," Terri said. "He shot himself in the mouth. But he 21
bungled that too. Poor Ed," she said. Terri shook her head.

"Poor Ed nothing," Mel said. "He was dangerous." 22

Mel was forty-five years old. He was tall and rangy with curly soft 23
hair. His face and arms were brown from the tennis he played. When
he was sober, his gestures, all his movements, were precise, very careful.

"He did love me though, Mel. Grant me that," Terri said. "That's 24
all I'm asking. He didn't love me the way you love me. I'm not saying
that. But he loved me. You can grant me that, can't you?"

"What do you mean, he bungled it?" I said. 25

Laura leaned forward with her glass. She put her elbows on the 26
table and held her glass in both hands. She glanced from Mel to Terri
and waited with a look of bewilderment on her open face, as if amazed
that such things happened to people you were friendly with.

"How'd he bungle it when he killed himself?" I said. 27

"I'll tell you what happened," Mel said. "He took this twenty-two 28
pistol he'd bought to threaten Terri and me with. Oh, I'm serious, the
man was always threatening. You should have seen the way we lived
in those days. Like fugitives. I even bought a gun myself. Can you believe it? A guy like me? But I did. I bought one for self-defense and
carried it in the glove compartment. Sometimes I'd have to leave the
apartment in the middle of the night. To go to the hospital, you
know? Terri and I weren't married then, and my first wife had the
house and kids, the dog, everything, and Terri and I were living in this
apartment here. Sometimes, as I say, I'd get a call in the middle of the
night and have to go in to the hospital at two or three in the morning.
It'd be dark out there in the parking lot, and I'd break into a sweat

before I could even get to my car. I never knew if he was going to come up out of the shrubbery or from behind a car and start shooting. I mean, the man was crazy. He was capable of wiring a bomb, anything. He used to call my service at all hours and say he needed to talk to the doctor, and when I'd return the call, he'd say, 'Son of a bitch, your days are numbered.' Little things like that. It was scary, I'm telling you."

"I still feel sorry for him," Terri said.   29

"It sounds like a nightmare," Laura said. "But what exactly hap- 30 pened after he shot himself?"

Laura is a legal secretary. We'd met in a professional capacity. 31 Before we knew it, it was a courtship. She's thirty-five, three years younger than I am. In addition to being in love, we like each other and enjoy one another's company. She's easy to be with.

"What happened?" Laura said.   32

Mel said, "He shot himself in the mouth in his room. Someone 33 heard the shot and told the manager. They came in with a passkey, saw what had happened, and called an ambulance. I happened to be there when they brought him in, alive but past recall. The man lived for three days. His head swelled up to twice the size of a normal head. I'd never seen anything like it, and I hope I never do again. Terri wanted to go in and sit with him when she found out about it. We had a fight over it. I didn't think she should see him like that. I didn't think she should see him, and I still don't."

"Who won the fight?" Laura said.   34

"I was in the room with him when he died," Terri said. "He never 35 came up out of it. But I sat with him. He didn't have anyone else."

"He was dangerous," Mel said. "If you call that love, you can have 36 it."

"It was love," Terri said. "Sure, it's abnormal in most people's 37 eyes. But he was willing to die for it. He did die for it."

"I sure as hell wouldn't call it love," Mel said. "I mean, no one 38 knows what he did it for. I've seen a lot of suicides, and I couldn't say anyone ever knew what they did it for."

Mel put his hands behind his neck and tilted his chair back. "I'm 39 not interested in that kind of love," he said. "If that's love, you can have it."

Terri said, "We were afraid. Mel even made a will out and wrote to 40 his brother in California who used to be a Green Beret. Mel told him who to look for if something happened to him."

Terri drank from her glass. She said, "But Mel's right — we lived 41 like fugitives. We were afraid. Mel was, weren't you, honey? I even called the police at one point, but they were no help. They said they couldn't do anything until Ed actually did something. Isn't that a laugh?" Terri said.

She poured the last of the gin into her glass and waggled the bottle. 42 Mel got up from the table and went to the cupboard. He took down another bottle.

"Well, Nick and I know what love is," Laura said. "For us, I 43 mean," Laura said. She bumped my knee with her knee. "You're supposed to say something now," Laura said, and turned her smile on me.

For an answer, I took Laura's hand and raised it to my lips. I made 44 a big production out of kissing her hand. Everyone was amused.

"We're lucky," I said. 45

"You guys," Terri said. "Stop that now. You're making me sick. 46 You're still on the honeymoon, for God's sake. You're still gaga, for crying out loud. Just wait. How long have you been together now? How long has it been? A year? Longer than a year?"

"Going on a year and a half," Laura said, flushed and smiling. 47

"Oh, now," Terri said. "Wait awhile." 48

She held her drink and gazed at Laura. 49

"I'm only kidding," Terri said. 50

Mel opened the gin and went around the table with the bottle. 51

"Here, you guys," he said. "Let's have a toast. I want to propose a 52 toast. A toast to love. To true love," Mel said.

We touched glasses. 53

"To love," we said. 54

Outside in the backyard, one of the dogs began to bark. The leaves 55 of the aspen that leaned past the window ticked against the glass. The afternoon sun was like a presence in this room, the spacious light of ease and generosity. We could have been anywhere, somewhere enchanted. We raised our glasses again and grinned at each other like children who had agreed on something forbidden.

"I'll tell you what real love is," Mel said. "I mean, I'll give you a 56 good example. And then you can draw your own conclusions." He poured more gin into his glass. He added an ice cube and a sliver of lime. We waited and sipped our drinks. Laura and I touched knees again. I put a hand on her warm thigh and left it there.

"What do any of us really know about love?" Mel said. "It seems   57 to me we're just beginners at love. We say we love each other and we do, I don't doubt it. I love Terri and Terri loves me, and you guys love each other too. You know the kind of love I'm talking about now. Physical love, that impulse that drives you to someone special, as well as love of the other person's being, his or her essence, as it were. Carnal love and, well, call it sentimental love, the day-to-day caring about the other person. But sometimes I have a hard time accounting for the fact that I must have loved my first wife too. But I did, I know I did. So I suppose I am like Terri in that regard. Terri and Ed." He thought about it and then he went on. "There was a time when I thought I loved my first wife more than life itself. But now I hate her guts. I do. How do you explain that? What happened to that love? What happened to it, is what I'd like to know. I wish someone could tell me. Then there's Ed. Okay, we're back to Ed. He loves Terri so much he tries to kill her and he winds up killing himself." Mel stopped talking and swallowed from his glass. "You guys have been together eighteen months and you love each other. It shows all over you. You glow with it. But you both loved other people before you met each other. You've both been married before, just like us. And you probably loved other people before that too, even. Terri and I have been together five years, been married for four. And the terrible thing, the terrible thing is, but the good thing too, the saving grace, you might say, is that if something happened to one of us — excuse me for saying this — but if something happened to one of us tomorrow, I think the other one, the other person, would grieve for a while, you know, but then the surviving party would go out and love again, have someone else soon enough. All this, all of this love we're talking about, it would just be a memory. Maybe not even a memory. Am I wrong? Am I way off base? Because I want you to set me straight if you think I'm wrong. I want to know. I mean, I don't know anything, and I'm the first one to admit it."

"Mel, for God's sake," Terri said. She reached out and took hold of   58 his wrist. "Are you getting drunk? Honey? Are you drunk?"

"Honey, I'm just talking," Mel said. "All right? I don't have to be   59 drunk to say what I think. I mean, we're all just talking, right?" Mel said. He fixed his eyes on her.

"Sweetie, I'm not criticizing," Terri said.   60

She picked up her glass.   61

"I'm not on call today," Mel said. "Let me remind you of that. I   62
am not on call," he said.

"Mel, we love you," Laura said.   63

Mel looked at Laura. He looked at her as if he could not place her,   64
as if she was not the woman she was.

"Love you too, Laura," Mel said. "And you, Nick, love you too.   65
You know something?" Mel said. "You guys are our pals," Mel said.

He picked up his glass.   66

Mel said, "I was going to tell you about something. I mean, I was   67
going to prove a point. You see, this happened a few months ago, but
it's still going on right now, and it ought to make us feel ashamed
when we talk like we know what we're talking about when we talk
about love."

"Come on now," Terri said. "Don't talk like you're drunk if you're   68
not drunk."

"Just shut up for once in your life," Mel said very quietly. "Will   69
you do me a favor and do that for a minute? So as I was saying, there's
this old couple who had this car wreck out on the interstate. A kid hit
them and they were all torn to shit and nobody was giving them much
chance to pull through."

Terri looked at us and then back at Mel. She seemed anxious, or   70
maybe that's too strong a word.

Mel was handing the bottle around the table.   71

"I was on call that night," Mel said. "It was May or maybe it was   72
June. Terri and I had just sat down to dinner when the hospital called.
There'd been this thing out on the interstate. Drunk kid, teenager,
plowed his dad's pickup into this camper with this old couple in it.
They were up in their mid-seventies, that couple. The kid — eighteen, nineteen, something — he was DOA. Taken the steering wheel
through his sternum. The old couple, they were alive, you understand.
I mean, just barely. But they had everything. Multiple fractures, internal injuries, hemorrhaging, contusions, lacerations, the works, and
they each of them had themselves concussions. They were in a bad
way, believe me. And, of course, their age was two strikes against

them. I'd say she was worse off than he was. Ruptured spleen along with everything else. Both kneecaps broken. But they'd been wearing their seatbelts and, God knows, that's what saved them for the time being."

"Folks, this is an advertisement for the National Safety Council," 73 Terri said. "This is your spokesman, Dr. Melvin R. McGinnis, talking." Terri laughed. "Mel," she said, "sometimes you're just too much. But I love you, hon," she said.

"Honey, I love you," Mel said.   74

He leaned across the table. Terri met him halfway. They kissed.   75

"Terri's right," Mel said as he settled himself again. "Get those   76 seatbelts on. But seriously, they were in some shape, those oldsters. By the time I got down there, the kid was dead, as I said. He was off in a corner, laid out on a gurney. I took one look at the old couple and told the ER nurse to get me a neurologist and an orthopedic man and a couple of surgeons down there right away."

He drank from his glass. "I'll try to keep this short," he said. "So   77 we took the two of them up to the OR and worked like fuck on them most of the night. They had these incredible reserves, those two. You see that once in a while. So we did everything that could be done, and toward morning we're giving them a fifty-fifty chance, maybe less than that for her. So here they are, still alive the next morning. So, okay, we move them into the ICU, which is where they both kept plugging away at it for two weeks, hitting it better and better on all the scopes. So we transfer them out to their own room."

Mel stopped talking. "Here," he said, "let's drink this cheapo gin   78 the hell up. Then we're going to dinner, right? Terri and I know a new place. That's where we'll go, to this new place we know about. But we're not going until we finish up this cut-rate, lousy gin."

Terri said, "We haven't actually eaten there yet. But it looks good.   79 From the outside, you know."

"I like food," Mel said. "If I had it to do all over again, I'd be a   80 chef, you know? Right, Terri?" Mel said.

He laughed. He fingered the ice in his glass.   81

"Terri knows," he said. "Terri can tell you. But let me say this. If I   82 could come back again in a different life, a different time and all, you know what? I'd like to come back as a knight. You were pretty safe wearing all that armor. It was all right being a knight until gunpowder and muskets and pistols came along."

"Mel would like to ride a horse and carry a lance," Terri said.   83
"Carry a woman's scarf with you everywhere," Laura said.   84
"Or just a woman," Mel said.   85
"Shame on you," Laura said.   86
Terri said, "Suppose you came back as a serf. The serfs didn't have   87
it so good in those days," Terri said.
"The serfs never had it good," Mel said. "But I guess even the   88
knights were vessels to someone. Isn't that the way it worked? But
then everyone is always a vessel to someone. Isn't that right? Terri?
But what I liked about knights, besides their ladies, was that they
had that suit of armor, you know, and they couldn't get hurt very
easy. No cars in those days, you know? No drunk teenagers to tear
into your ass."

"Vassals," Terri said.   89
"What?" Mel said.   90
"Vassals," Terri said. "They were called vassals, not vessels."   91
"Vassals, vessels," Mel said, "what the fuck's the difference? You   92
knew what I meant anyway. All right," Mel said. "So I'm not educated. I learned my stuff. I'm a heart surgeon, sure, but I'm just a mechanic. I go in and I fuck around and I fix things. Shit," Mel said.
"Modesty doesn't become you," Terri said.   93
"He's just a humble sawbones," I said. "But sometimes they suffo-   94
cated in all that armor, Mel. They'd even have heart attacks if it got
too hot and they were too tired and worn out. I read somewhere that
they'd fall off their horses and not be able to get up because they were
too tired to stand with all that armor on them. They got trampled by
their own horses sometimes."
"That's terrible," Mel said. "That's a terrible thing, Nicky. I guess   95
they'd just lay there and wait until somebody came along and made a
shish kebab out of them."
"Some other vessel," Terri said.   96
"That's right," Mel said. "Some vassal would come along and   97
spear the bastard in the name of love. Or whatever the fuck it was
they fought over in those days."
"Same things we fight over these days," Terri said.   98
Laura said, "Nothing's changed."   99
The color was still high in Laura's cheeks. Her eyes were bright.   100
She brought her glass to her lips.

Mel poured himself another drink. He looked at the label closely as 101
if studying a long row of numbers. Then he slowly put the bottle
down on the table and slowly reached for the tonic water.

"What about the old couple?" Laura said. "You didn't finish that 102
story you started."
Laura was having a hard time lighting her cigarette. Her matches 103
kept going out.
The sunshine inside the room was different now, changing, getting 104
thinner. But the leaves outside the window were still shimmering, and
I stared at the pattern they made on the panes and on the Formica
counter. They weren't the same patterns, of course.
"What about the old couple?" I said.   105
"Older but wiser," Terri said.   106
Mel stared at her.   107
Terri said, "Go on with your story, hon. I was only kidding. Then 108
what happened?"
"Terri, sometimes," Mel said.   109
"Please, Mel," Terri said. "Don't always be so serious, sweetie. 110
Can't you take a joke?"
"Where's the joke?" Mel said.   111
He held his glass and gazed steadily at his wife.   112
"What happened?" Laura said.   113
Mel fastened his eyes on Laura. He said, "Laura, if I didn't have 114
Terri and if I didn't love her so much, and if Nick wasn't my best
friend, I'd fall in love with you. I'd carry you off, honey," he said.
"Tell your story," Terri said. "Then we'll go to that new place, 115
okay?"
"Okay," Mel said. "Where was I?" he said. He stared at the table 116
and then he began again.
"I dropped in to see each of them every day, sometimes twice a day 117
if I was up doing other calls anyway. Casts and bandages, head to foot,
the both of them. You know, you've seen it in the movies. That's just
the way they looked, just like in the movies. Little eye-holes and nose-
holes and mouth-holes. And she had to have her legs slung up on top
of it. Well, the husband was very depressed for the longest while.
Even after he found out that his wife was going to pull through, he
was still very depressed. Not about the accident, though. I mean, the

accident was one thing, but it wasn't everything. I'd get up to his mouth-hole, you know, and he'd say no, it wasn't the accident exactly but it was because he couldn't see her through his eye-holes. He said that was what was making him feel so bad. Can you imagine? I'm telling you, the man's heart was breaking because he couldn't turn his goddamn head and *see* his goddamn wife."

Mel looked around the table and shook his head at what he was 118 going to say.

"I mean, it was killing the old fart just because he couldn't *look* at 119 the fucking woman."

We all looked at Mel. 120

"Do you see what I'm saying?" he said. 121

Maybe we were a little drunk by then. I know it was hard keeping 122 things in focus. The light was draining out of the room, going back through the window where it had come from. Yet nobody made a move to get up from the table to turn on the overhead light.

"Listen," Mel said. "Let's finish this fucking gin. There's about 123 enough left here for one shooter all around. Then let's go eat. Let's go to the new place."

"He's depressed," Terri said. "Mel, why don't you take a pill?" 124

Mel shook his head. "I've taken everything there is." 125

"We all need a pill now and then," I said. 126

"Some people are born needing them," Terri said. 127

She was using her finger to rub at something on the table. Then she 128 stopped rubbing.

"I think I want to call my kids," Mel said. "Is that all right with 129 everybody? I'll call my kids," he said.

Terri said, "What if Marjorie answers the phone? You guys, you've 130 heard us on the subject of Marjorie? Honey, you know you don't want to talk to Marjorie. It'll make you feel even worse."

"I don't want to talk to Marjorie," Mel said. "But I want to talk to 131 my kids."

"There isn't a day goes by that Mel doesn't say he wishes she'd get 132 married again. Or else die," Terri said. "For one thing," Terri said, "she's bankrupting us. Mel says it's just to spite him that she won't get married again. She has a boyfriend who lives with her and the kids, so Mel is supporting the boyfriend too."

"She's allergic to bees," Mel said. "If I'm not praying she'll get 133 married again, I'm praying she'll get herself stung to death by a swarm of fucking bees."

"Shame on you," Laura said.   134

"Bzzzzzzz," Mel said, turning his fingers into bees and buzzing 135 them at Terri's throat. Then he let his hands drop all the way to his sides.

"She's vicious," Mel said. "Sometimes I think I'll go up there 136 dressed like a beekeeper. You know, that hat that's like a helmet with the plate that comes down over your face, the big gloves, and the padded coat? I'll knock on the door and let loose a hive of bees in the house. But first I'd make sure the kids were out, of course."

He crossed one leg over the other. It seemed to take him a lot of 137 time to do it. Then he put both feet on the floor and leaned forward, elbows on the table, his chin cupped in his hands.

"Maybe I won't call the kids, after all. Maybe it isn't such a hot 138 idea. Maybe we'll just go eat. How does that sound?"

"Sounds fine to me," I said. "Eat or not eat. Or keep drinking. I 139 could head right on out into the sunset."

"What does that mean, honey?" Laura said.   140

"It just means what I said," I said. "It means I could just keep 141 going. That's all it means."

"I could eat something myself," Laura said. "I don't think I've ever 142 been so hungry in my life. Is there something to nibble on?"

"I'll put out some cheese and crackers," Terri said.   143

But Terri just sat there. She did not get up to get anything.   144

Mel turned his glass over. He spilled it out on the table.   145

"Gin's gone," Mel said.   146

Terri said, "Now what?"   147

I could hear my heart beating. I could hear everyone's heart. I 148 could hear the human noise we sat there making, not one of us moving, not even when the room went dark.

CONSIDERATIONS

1. Think of three adjectives that together summarize Mel's character in the first half of the story. Would you change the adjectives to fit his character at the end of the story?

2. At what times and how do the characters express their love for their partners and for their friends during the conversation? What motives or satisfactions enter into their expressions of love? Examine the details closely.
3. What aspect of love is especially troubling to Mel? What bearing does it have on his earlier intention to become a priest and his present vocation as a cardiologist?
4. Why does Mel's language become more vulgar as he tells his story about the old people? What is agitating him?
5. What do Nick and Laura find disturbing about Mel's story? How do we know?
6. Mel divides love into "carnal" and "sentimental." Does his example of true love fit either category? How would you define it?
7. WRITING TOPIC. Is love something to "work on"? Is it something to "share"? Is it "communication"? Or a "commitment"? Is it a "feeling"? Or a "trip"? These commonly used expressions indicate that love is not just an emotion: it is also a whole set of ideas and beliefs about that emotion. In a 700-word essay, define the underlying concept of love that is most often accepted and used among a group of people you know personally. Examine the specific words, gestures, and reactions that indicate their view of love.

D. H. Lawrence

COUNTERFEIT LOVE

◊

D. H. LAWRENCE (1885–1930), who grew up in a coal-miner's family in England, wrote about the emotional complexities of his early life in an autobiographical novel, *Sons and Lovers* (1913). His later novels, such as *The Rainbow* (1915), *Women in Love* (1920), and *Lady Chatterley's Lover* (1928), treat the sexual relationship as the central experience in which men and women can, possibly, discover and fulfill their essential natures. He also wrote poetry and essays on this general theme of love and the natural identity of human beings. This selection is excerpted from a long essay in which Lawrence defends his explicit treatment of sex in *Lady Chatterley's Lover*, a novel that was banned as obscene until 1959.

The body's life is the life of sensations and emotions. The body 1 feels real hunger, real thirst, real joy in the sun or the snow, real pleasure in the smell of roses or the look of a lilac bush; real anger, real sorrow, real love, real tenderness, real warmth, real passion, real hate, real grief. All the emotions belong to the body, and are only recognized by the mind. We may hear the most sorrowful piece of news, and only feel a mental excitement. Then, hours after, perhaps in sleep, the awareness may reach the bodily centers, and true grief wrings the heart.

How different they are, mental feelings and real feelings. Today, 2 many people live and die without having had any real feelings — though they have had a "rich emotional life" apparently, having showed strong mental feelings. But it is all counterfeit. . . . The higher emotions are strictly dead. They have to be faked.

And by higher emotions we mean love in all its manifestations, 3 from genuine desire to tender love, love of our fellowmen, and love of God: we mean love, joy, delight, hope, true indignant anger, passionate sense of justice and injustice, truth and untruth, honor and dishonor, and real belief in *anything*: for belief is a profound emotion that has the mind's connivance. All these things, today, are more or less dead. We have in their place the loud and sentimental counterfeit of all such emotion.

Never was an age more sentimental, more devoid of real feeling, 4 more exaggerated in false feeling, than our own. Sentimentality and counterfeit feeling have become a sort of game, everybody trying to outdo his neighbor. The radio and the film are mere counterfeit emotion all the time, the current press and literature the same. People wallow in emotion: counterfeit emotion. They lap it up: they live in it and on it. They ooze with it.

And at times, they seem to get on very well with it all. And then, 5 more and more, they break down. They go to pieces. You can fool yourself for a long time about your own feelings. But not forever. The body itself hits back at you, and hits back remorselessly in the end.

As for other people — you can fool most people all the time, and 6 all people most of the time, but not all people all the time, with false feelings. A young couple fall in counterfeit love, and fool themselves and each other completely. But, alas, counterfeit love is good cake but bad bread. It produces a fearful emotional indigestion. Then you get a modern marriage, and a still more modern separation.

The trouble with counterfeit emotion is that nobody is really 7 happy, nobody is really contented, nobody has any peace. Everybody keeps on rushing to get away from the counterfeit emotion which is in themselves worst of all. They rush from the false feelings of Peter to the false feelings of Adrian, from the counterfeit emotions of Margaret to those of Virginia, from film to radio, from Eastbourne to Brighton, and the more it changes the more it is the same thing.

Above all things love is a counterfeit feeling today. Here, above all 8 things, the young will tell you, is the greatest swindle. That is, if you take it seriously. Love is all right if you take it lightly, as an amusement. But if you begin taking it seriously you are let down with a crash.

There are, the young women say, no *real* men to love. And there 9 are, the young men say, no *real* girls to fall in love with. So they go on falling in love with unreal ones, on either side; which means, if you can't have real feelings, you've got to have counterfeit ones: since some feelings you've *got* to have: like falling in love. There are still some young people who would *like* to have real feelings, and they are bewildered to death to know why they can't. Especially in love.

But especially in love, only counterfeit emotions exist nowadays. 10 We have all been taught to mistrust everybody emotionally, from parents downwards, or upwards. Don't trust *anybody* with your real emotions: if you've got any: that is the slogan of today. Trust them with your money, even, but *never* with your feelings. They are bound to trample on them.

I believe there has never been an age of greater mistrust between 11 persons than ours today: under a superficial but quite genuine social trust. Very few of my friends would pick my pocket, or let me sit on a chair where I might hurt myself. But practically all my friends would turn my real emotions to ridicule. They can't help it; it's the spirit of the day. So there goes love, and there goes friendship: for each implies a fundamental emotional sympathy. And hence, counterfeit love, which there is no escaping.

And with counterfeit emotions there is no real sex at all. Sex is the 12 one thing you cannot really swindle; and it is the center of the worst swindling of all, emotional swindling. Once come down to sex, and the emotional swindle must collapse. But in all the approaches to sex, the emotional swindle intensifies more and more. Till you get there. Then collapse.

Sex lashes out against counterfeit emotion, and is ruthless, devas- 13 tating against false love. The peculiar hatred of people who have not loved one another, but who have pretended to, even perhaps have imagined they really did love, is one of the phenomena of our time. The phenomenon, of course, belongs to all time. But today it is almost universal. People who thought they loved one another dearly, dearly, and went on for years, ideal: lo! suddenly the most profound and vivid hatred appears. If it doesn't come out fairly young, it saves itself till the happy couple are nearing fifty, the time of the great sexual change — and then — cataclysm!

Nothing is more startling. Nothing is more staggering, in our age, 14 than the intensity of the hatred people, men and women, feel for one another when they have once "loved" one another. It breaks out in the most extraordinary ways. And when you know people intimately, it is almost universal. It is the charwoman as much as the mistress, and the duchess as much as the policeman's wife.

And it would be too horrible, if one did not remember that in all of 15 them, men and women alike, it is the organic reaction against count-erfeit love. All love today is counterfeit. It is a stereotyped thing. All the young know just how they ought to feel and how they ought to behave, in love. And they feel and they behave like that. And it is counterfeit love. So that revenge will come back at them, tenfold. The sex, the very sexual organism in man and woman alike accumulates a deadly and desperate rage, after a certain amount of counterfeit love has been palmed off on it, even if itself has given nothing but counter-feit love. The element of counterfeit in love at last maddens, or else kills, sex, the deepest sex in the individual. But perhaps it would be safe to say that it *always* enrages the inner sex, even if at last it kills it. There is always the period of rage. And the strange thing is, the worst offenders in the counterfeit-love game fall into the greatest rage. Those whose love has been a bit sincere are always gentler, even though they have been most swindled.

CONSIDERATIONS

1. What is the difference between "mental feelings" and "real feelings"? Can you substitute other terms for the distinction Lawrence is making? How do the implications of your terms differ from Lawrence's? Do you accept his implications?

2. In Lawrence's list of "the higher emotions" are there any that seem out of place as emotions? Has he left out any negative emotions that you would include? What does he mean by "higher"?

3. Lawrence maintains that we are in an age of great mistrust of feelings among people, and even that we are taught to mistrust everybody emo-tionally. Yet, he offers no examples or explanations of his views. Can you clarify his point by suggesting modern ideas, attitudes, or events that may be evidence of this mistrust?

4. Given that Lawrence wrote this essay in 1929, are his concerns about our sexual attitudes outdated? Does present-day society encourage more or less authenticity of emotions?

5. WRITING TOPIC. How would Lawrence regard present-day dating? In a 750-word essay, evaluate the patterns, routines, and conventional re-sponses in the romance of dating, and decide what elements of it are usually counterfeited. What would be gained or lost by removing the counterfeit elements? Is there a difference between counterfeiting and disguising emotions? Would Lawrence agree?

Margaret Atwood

SIREN SONG

◊

MARGARET ATWOOD (b. 1939), a Canadian poet, novelist, and essayist, was born in Ottawa, Ontario. After graduating from the University of Toronto, she came to the United States to take a master's degree at Radcliffe College. She has taught at several Canadian universities and published several novels, including *Surfacing* (1972). In addition, her poetry has been collected in *Selected Poems* (1976). As a Canadian, Atwood has helped to free her national literature from its dependence on British and American influences. In *Survival* (1972) she defined what she believes are essential traits of Canadian writing. Objecting to national subordination, Atwood also writes about victimization and power plays between men and women. The following witty poem illustrates the power of the legendary sea nymphs in Greek mythology whose sweet singing lured mariners to destruction on the rocks surrounding their islands.

This is the one song everyone
would like to learn: the song
that is irresistible:

the song that forces men
to leap overboard in squadrons
even though they see the beached skulls

the song nobody knows
because anyone who has heard it
is dead, and the others can't remember.

Shall I tell you the secret   10
and if I do, will you get me
out of this bird suit?

I don't enjoy it here
squatting on this island
looking picturesque and mythical

with these two feathery maniacs,
I don't enjoy singing
this trio, fatal and valuable.

I will tell the secret to you,
to you, only to you.   20
Come closer. This song

is a cry for help: Help me!
Only you, only you can,
you are unique

at last. Alas
it is a boring song
but it works every time.

CONSIDERATIONS

1. In the first three stanzas, what are the reported effects of the siren's song? Why would anyone like to learn it? When the siren says "everyone would like to" — what does she imply?
2. How does the siren make her song "work" this time? What tricks does she illustrate that she believes work every time? Pay close attention to her word choice as well as to her other wiles.
3. Which of the insights at the beginning of this chapter, come closest to the siren's view of love and lovers? Which Insights imply sharp disagreement with her view?
4. WRITING TOPIC. What sort of man would the siren like? In 300 words, write a narrative episode in which Mr. Right comes along. How does he differ from the men she has evidently known? Or, if you don't want to attempt the narrative, in a 300-word essay, explain what faults the siren finds in men and their ardor.

Ernest van den Haag

THE INVENTION
THAT ISN'T WORKING*

◊

ERNEST VAN DEN HAAG (b. 1914) was born in The Hague (what his name tells us is true) and educated at European universities before he came to the United States. He pursued graduate study at New York University, where he continued as a staff psychoanalyst. He is the author of *The Fabric of Society* (1957), which combines sociological and psychological perspectives on modern life, and his articles have appeared in such magazines as *Commentary, Partisan Review,* and *Harper's,* which printed this essay in 1962. Professionally involved in counseling people about their feelings, van den Haag maintains that romantic love threatens to undermine marriage.

If someone asks, "Why do people marry?" he meets indignation or 1 astonishment. The question seems absurd if not immoral: the desirability of marriage is regarded as unquestionable. Divorce, on the other hand, strikes us as a problem worthy of serious and therapeutic attention. Yet marriage precedes divorce as a rule, and frequently causes it.

What explains marriage? People divorce often but they marry 2 still more often. Lately they also marry — and divorce, of course — younger than they used to, particularly in the middle classes (most statistics understate the change by averaging all classes). And the young have a disproportionate share of divorces. However, their hasty exertions to get out of wedlock puzzle me less than their eagerness to rush into it in the first place.

A hundred years ago there was every reason to marry young — 3 though middle-class people seldom did. The unmarried state had

* Editor's title.

heavy disadvantages for both sexes. Custom did not permit girls to be educated, to work, or to have social, let alone sexual, freedom. Men were free but since women were not, they had only prostitutes for partners. (When enforced, the double standard is certainly self-defeating.) And, though less restricted than girls shackled to their families, single men often led a grim and uncomfortable life. A wife was nearly indispensable, if only to darn socks, sew, cook, clean, take care of her man. Altogether, both sexes needed marriage far more than now — no TV, cars, dates, drip-dry shirts, cleaners, canned foods — and not much hospital care, insurance, or social security. The family was all-important.

Marriage is no longer quite so indispensable a convenience; yet we 4 find people marrying more than ever, and earlier. To be sure, prosperity makes marriage more possible. But why are the young exploiting the possibility so sedulously? Has the yearning for love become more urgent and widespread?

What has happened is that the physical conveniences which re- 5 duced the material usefulness of marriage have also loosened the bonds of family life. Many other bonds that sustained us psychologically were weakened as they were extended: beliefs became vague; associations impersonal, discontinuous, and casual. Our contacts are many, our relationships few: our lives, externally crowded, often are internally isolated; we remain but tenuously linked to each other and our ties come easily undone. One feels lonely surrounded by crowds and machines in an unbounded, abstract world that has become morally unintelligible; and we have so much time now to feel lonely in. Thus one longs, perhaps more acutely than in the past, for somebody to be tangibly, individually, and definitely one's own, body and soul.

This is the promise of marriage. Movies, songs, TV, romance mag- 6 azines, all intensify the belief that love alone makes life worthwhile, is perpetual, conquers the world's evils, and is fulfilled and certified by marriage. "Science" hastens to confirm as much. Doesn't popular psychology, brandishing the banner of Freud with more enthusiasm than knowledge, tell us, in effect, that any male who stays single is selfish or homosexual or mother-dominated and generally neurotic? and any unmarried female frustrated (or worse, not frustrated) and neurotic? A "normal" person, we are told, must love and thereupon marry. Thus love and marriage are identified with each other and with normality, three thousand years of experience notwithstanding. The yearning for love, attended by anxiety to prove oneself well-adjusted and normal, turns into eagerness to get married.

The young may justly say that they merely practice what their par- 7 ents preached. For, indeed, the idea that "love and marriage go together like a horse and carriage" has been drummed into their heads, so much that it finally has come to seem entirely natural. Yet, nothing could be less so. Love has long delighted and distressed mankind, and marriage has comforted us steadily and well. Both, however, are denatured — paradoxically enough, by their staunchest supporters — when they are expected to "go together." For love is a very unruly horse, far more apt to run away and overturn the carriage than to draw it. That is why, in the past, people seldom thought of harnessing marriage to love. They felt that each has its own motive power: one primed for a lifelong journey; the other for an ardent improvisation, a voyage of discovery.

More than a Frenzy?

Though by no means weaker, the marital bond is quite different from 8 the bond of love. If you like, it is a different bond of love — less taut, perhaps, and more durable. By confusing these two related but in many ways dissimilar bonds, we stand to lose the virtues and gain the vices of both: the spontaneous passion of love and the deliberate permanence of marriage are equally endangered as we try to live up to an ideal which bogs down one and unhinges the other.

Marriage is an immemorial institution which, in some form, exists 9 everywhere. Its main purpose always was to unite and to continue the families of bride and groom and to further their economic and social position. The families, therefore, were the main interested parties. Often marriages were arranged (and sometimes they took place) before the future husbands or wives were old enough to talk. Even when they were grown up, they felt, as did their parents, that the major purpose of marriage was to continue the family, to produce children. Certainly women hoped for kind and vigorous providers and men for faithful mothers and good housekeepers; both undoubtedly hoped for affection, too; but love did not strike either of them as indispensable and certainly not as sufficient for marriage.

Unlike marriage, love has only recently come to be generally ac- 10 cepted as something more than a frenzied state of pleasure and pain. It is a welcome innovation — but easily ruined by marriage; which in turn has a hard time surviving confusion with love. Marriage counselors usually recognize this last point, but people in love seldom consult them. Perhaps their limited clientele colors the views of too many marriage counselors: instead of acknowledging that love and marriage are different but equally genuine relationships, they depict love as a kind of dependable wheel horse that can be harnessed to the carriage of married life. For them, any other kind of love must be an "immature" or "neurotic" fantasy, something to be condemned as Hollywood-inspired, "unrealistic" romanticism. It is as though a man opposed to horse racing — for good reasons perhaps — were to argue that race horses are not real, that all real horses are draft horses. Thus marriage counselors often insist that the only "real" and "true" love is "mature" — it is the comfortable workaday relation Mommy and Daddy have. The children find it hard to believe that there is nothing more to it.

They are quite right. And they have on their side the great litera- 11 ture of the world, and philosophers from Plato to Santayana. What is wrong with Hollywood romance surely is not that it is romantic, but that its romances are shoddy clichés. And since Hollywood shuns the true dimensions of conflict, love in the movies is usually confirmed by marriage and marriage by love, in accordance with wishful fantasy, though not with truth.

Was the love Tristan bore Isolde "mature" or "neurotic"? They 12 loved each other before and after Isolde was married — to King Mark. It never occurred to them to marry each other; they even cut short an extramarital idyll together in the forest. (And Tristan too, while protesting love for Isolde, got married to some other girl.) Dante saw, but never actually met, Beatrice until he reached the nether world, which is the place for permanent romance. Of course, he was a married man.

It is foolish to pretend that the passionate romantic longing doesn't 13 exist or is "neurotic," i.e., shouldn't exist; it is as foolish to pretend that romantic love can be made part of a cozy domesticity. The truth is simple enough, though it can make life awfully complicated: there are two things, love and affection (or marital love), not one; they do not usually pull together as a team; they tend to draw us in different directions, if they are present at the same time. God nowhere promised to make this a simple world.

In the West, love came to be socially approved around the twelfth 14
century. It became a fashionable subject of discussion then, and even
of disputation, in formal "courts of love" convoked to argue its merits
and to elaborate its true characteristics. Poets and singers created the
models and images of love. They still do — though mass production
has perhaps affected the quality; what else makes the teen-age croon-
ers idols to their followers and what else do they croon about? In medieval times, as now, manuals were written, codifying the behavior
recommended to lovers. With a difference though. Today's manuals
are produced not by men of letters, but by doctors and therapists, as
though love, sex, and marriage were diseases or therapeutic problems — which they promptly become if one reads too many of these
guidebooks (any one is one too many). Today's manuals bear titles
like "Married Love" (unmarried lovers can manage without help, I
guess); but regardless of title, they concentrate on sex. In handbooks
on dating they tell how to avoid it; in handbooks on marriage, how to
go about it. The authors are sure that happiness depends on the sexual
mechanics they blueprint. Yet, one doesn't make love better by reading a book any more than one learns to dance, or ride a bicycle, by
reading about it.

The Use of "Technique"

The sexual engineering (or cookbook) approach is profitable only for 15
the writer: in an enduring relationship, physical gratification is an effect and not a cause. If a person does not acquire sexual skill from experience, he is not ready for it. Wherever basic inhibitions exist, no
book can remove them. Where they do not, no book is necessary. I
have seen many an unhappy relationship in my psychoanalytic practice, but none ever in which sexual technique or the lack of it was
more than a symptom and an effect. The mechanical approach never
helps.

The troubadours usually took sex and marriage for granted and 16
dealt with love — the newest and still the most surprising and fascinating of all relationships. And also the most unstable. They conceived love as a longing, a tension between desire and fulfillment.
This feeling, of course, had been known before they celebrated it.
Plato described love as a desire for something one does not have, im-
plying that it is a longing, not a fulfillment. But in ancient Greece,

love was regarded diffidently, as rather undesirable, an intoxication, a bewitchment, a divine punishment — usually for neglecting sex. The troubadours thought differently, although, unlike many moderns, they did not deny that love is a passion, something one suffers.* But they thought it a sweet suffering to be cultivated, and they celebrated it in song and story.

The troubadours clearly distinguished love and sex. Love was to   17 them a yearning for a psychic gratification which the lover feels only the beloved can give: sex, an impersonal desire anybody possessing certain fairly common characteristics can gratify by physical actions. Unlike love, sex can thrive without an intense personal relationship and may erode it if it exists. Indeed, the Romans sometimes wondered if love would not blunt and tame their sexual pleasures, whereas the troubadours fretted lest sex abate the fervor of love's longing. They never fully resolved the contest between love and sex; nor has anyone else. (To define it away is, of course, not to solve it.)

We try to cope with this contest by fusing love and sex. (Every   18 high-school student is taught that the two go together.) This, as Freud pointed out, does not always succeed and may moderate both, but, as he also implied, it is the best we can hope for. In the words of William Butler Yeats, "Desire dies because every touch consumes the myth and yet, a myth that cannot be consumed becomes a specter. . . ."

Romantics, who want love's desiring to be conclusive, though end-   19 less, often linked it to death: if nothing further can happen and rival its significance, if one dies before it does, love indeed is the end. But this is ending the game as much as winning it — certainly an ambiguous move. The religious too perpetuate longing by placing the beloved altogether out of physical reach. The "bride of Christ" who retires to a convent longs for her Redeemer — and she will continue to yearn, as long as she lives, for union with a God at once human and divine, incarnating life and love everlasting. In its highest sense, love is a

---

* . . . I am in love
And that is my shame.
What hurts the soul
My souls adores,
No better than a beast
Upon all fours.

   So says W. B. Yeats. About eight centuries earlier. Chrestien de Troyes expressed the same sentiment. [van den Haag's note]

reaching for divine perfection, an act of creation. And always, it is a longing.

Since love is longing, experts in the Middle Ages held that one 20 could not love someone who could not be longed for — for instance, one's wife. Hence, the Comtesse de Champagne told her court in 1174: "Love cannot extend its rights over two married persons." If one were to marry one's love, one would exchange the sweet torment of desire, the yearning, for that which fulfills it. Thus the tension of hope would be replaced by the comfort of certainty. He who longs to long, who wants the tension of desire, surely should not marry. In former times, of course, he married — the better to love someone else's wife.

When sexual objects are easily and guiltlessly accessible, in a so- 21 ciety that does not object to promiscuity, romantic love seldom prospers. For example, in imperial Rome it was rare and in Tahiti unknown. And love is unlikely to arouse the heart of someone brought up in a harem, where the idea of uniqueness has a hard time. Love flowers best in a monogamous environment morally opposed to unrestrained sex, and interested in cultivating individual experience. In such an environment, longing may be valued for itself. Thus, love as we know it is a Christian legacy, though Christianity in the main repudiates romantic love where the object is worldly, and accepts passion only when transcendent, when God is the object — or when muted into affection: marital love.

Shifting the Object

Let me hazard a Freudian guess about the genesis of the longing we 22 call love. It continues and reproduces the child's first feeling for his parent — the original source of unconditioned and unconditional love. But what is recreated is the child's image, the idealized mother or father, young and uniquely beautiful, and not the empirical parent others see. The unconsummated love for this ideal parent (and it could be someone else important in the child's experience) remains as an intense longing. Yet any fulfillment now must also become a disappointment — a substitute, cheating the longing that wants to long. Nonetheless most of us marry and replace the ideal with an imperfect reality. We repudiate our longing or we keep it but shift its object. If we don't, we may resent our partners for helping us "consume the myth," and leaving us shorn of longing — which is what Don Giovanni found so intolerable, and what saddens many a faithful husband.

Sexual gratification, of course, diminishes sexual desire for the time 23 being. But it does more. It changes love. The longing may become gratitude; the desire tenderness; love may become affectionate companionship — "After such knowledge, what forgiveness?" Depending on character and circumstance, love may also be replaced by indifference or hostility.

One thing is certain though: if the relationship is stabilized, love is 24 replaced by other emotions. (Marriage thus has often been recommended as the cure for love. But it does not always work.) The only way to keep love is to try to keep up — or re-establish — the distance between lovers that was inevitably shortened by intimacy and possession, and thus, possibly, regain desire and longing. Lovers sometimes do so by quarreling. And some personalities are remote enough, or inexhaustible enough, to be longed for even when possessed. But this has disadvantages as well. And the deliberate and artificial devices counseled by romance magazines and marriage manuals ("surprise your husband . . .") — even when they do not originate with the love of pretense — are unlikely to yield more than the pretense of love.

The sexual act itself may serve as a vehicle for numberless feelings: 25 lust, vanity, and self-assertion, doubt and curiosity, possessiveness, anxiety, hostility, anger, or indifferent release from boredom. Yet, though seldom the only motive, and often absent altogether, love nowadays is given as the one natural and moral reason which authorizes and even ordains sexual relations. What we have done is draw a moral conclusion from a rule of popular psychology: that "it is gratifying, and therefore healthy and natural, to make love when you love, and frustrating, and therefore unhealthy and unnatural, not to; we must follow nature; but sex without love is unnatural and therefore immoral."

Now, as a psychological rule, this is surely wrong; it can be as 26 healthy to frustrate as it is to gratify one's desires. Sometimes gratification is very unhealthy; sometimes frustration is. Nor can psychological health be accepted as morally decisive. Sanity, sanitation, and morality are all desirable, but they are not identical; our wanting all of them is the problem, not the solution. It may be quite "healthy" to run away with your neighbor's wife, but not, therefore, right. And there is nothing unhealthy about wishing to kill someone who has injured you — but this does not morally justify doing so. Finally, to say "we must follow nature" is always specious: we follow nature in whatever we do — we can't ever do what nature does not let us do. Why then identify nature only with the nonintellectual, the sensual, or the emotional possibilities? On this view, it would be unnatural to read: literacy is a gift of nature only if we include the intellect and training in nature's realm. If we do, it makes no sense to call a rule unnatural merely because it restrains an urge: the urge is no more natural than the restraint.

The combination of love and sex is no more natural than the separation. Thus, what one decides about restraining or indulging an emotion, or a sexual urge, rests on religious, social, or personal values, none of which can claim to be more natural than any other. 27

Not that some indulgences and some inhibitions may not be healthier than others. But one cannot flatly say which are good or bad for every man. It depends on their origins and effects in the personalities involved. Without knowing these, more cannot be said — except, perhaps, that we should try not to use others, or even ourselves, merely as a means — at least not habitually and in personal relations. Sex, unalloyed, sometimes leads to this original sin which our moral tradition condemns. Psychologically, too, the continued use of persons merely as instruments ultimately frustrates both the user and the used. This caution, though it justifies no positive action, may help perceive problems; it does not solve them; no general rule can. 28

How Long Does It Last?

What about marriage? In our society, couples usually invite the families to their weddings, although the decision to marry is made exclusively by bride and groom. However, a license must be obtained and the marriage registered; and it can be dissolved only by a court of law. Religious ceremonies state the meaning of marriage clearly: The couple are asked to promise "forsaking all others, [to] keep thee only unto her [him], so long as ye both shall live." The vow does not say, "as long as ye both shall want to," because marriage is a promise to con- 29 tinue even when one no longer wishes to. If marriage were to end when love does, it would be redundant: why solemnly ask two people to promise to be with each other for as long as they want to be with each other?

Marriage was to cement the family by tying people together "till 30 death do us part" in the face of the fickleness of their emotions. The authority of state and church was to see to it that they kept a promise voluntarily made, but binding, and that could not be unmade. Whether it sprang from love did not matter. Marriage differed from a love affair inasmuch as it continued regardless of love. Cupid shoots his arrows without rhyme or reason. But marriage is a deliberate rational act, a public institution making the family independent of Cupid's whims. Once enlisted, the volunteers couldn't quit, even when they didn't like it any longer. That was the point.

The idea that marriage must be synchronous with love or even af- 31 fection nullifies it altogether. (That affection should coincide with marriage is, of course, desirable, though it does not always happen.) We would have to reword the marriage vow. Instead of saying, "till death do us part," we might say, "till we get bored with each other"; and, instead of "forsaking all others," "till someone better comes along." Clearly, if the couple intend to stay "married" only as long as they want to, they only pretend to be married: they are having an affair with legal trimmings. To marry is to vow fidelity regardless of any future feeling, to vow the most earnest attempt to avoid contrary feelings altogether, but, at any rate, not to give in to them.

Perhaps this sounds grim. But it needn't be if one marries for affec- 32 tion more than for love. For affection, marital love may grow with knowledge and intimacy and shared experience. Thus marriage itself, when accepted as something other than a love affair, may foster affection. Affection differs from love as fulfillment differs from desire. Further, love longs for what desire and imagination make uniquely and perfectly lovable. Possession erodes it. Affection, however — which is love of a different, of a perhaps more moral and less aesthetic kind — cares deeply also for what is unlovable without transforming it into beauty. It cares for the unvarnished person, not the splendid image. Time can strengthen it. But the husband who wants to remain a splendid image must provide a swan to draw him away, or find a wife who can restrain her curiosity about his real person — something that Lohengrin did not succeed in doing. Whereas love stresses the unique form perfection takes in the lover's mind, affection stresses the uniqueness of the actual person.

One may grow from the other. But not when this other is expected 33 to remain unchanged. And affection probably grows more easily if not preceded by enchantment. For the disenchantment which often follows may turn husband and wife against each other, and send them looking elsewhere for re-enchantment — which distance lends so easily. Indeed, nothing else does.

CONSIDERATIONS

1. Writing in 1962, the author assumes that "the desirability of marriage is regarded as unquestionable." Since that time, marriage has been thoroughly questioned in this country. What has been the outcome of the scrutiny of marriage? Has marriage significantly changed?

2. What is different between the social pressures that used to lead people into marriage and the current pressures that van den Haag says lead people to get married these days?

3. What social conditions are necessary to establish a high value on love? Which of these conditions are evident in our society?

4. According to the author, what are the definitive aspects of romantic love? What synonym does he use for such love? How has this love been regarded in earlier times?

5. What attitude toward people does the author refer to as "this original sin which our moral tradition condemns"? Are we taught in secular ways to condemn it?

6. Are Americans likely to find something offensive, authoritarian, or unnatural in the author's statement that "marriage is a promise to continue even when one no longer wishes to"? Can we reconcile the institution of permanent marriage with the values of our society?

7. WRITING TOPIC. With van den Haag's points in mind, consider the merits and drawbacks of having marriages arranged by professional agencies or by families as a possible alternative to the modern American custom of romantic choice. How would arranged marriages modify or conflict with our present relations to our families and society? How would arranged marriages harmonize with our present system of education? Would they help foster or block emotional growth among married couples? In a 750-word essay, explain what you find potentially beneficial and potentially harmful in adopting such an alternative.

Jill Tweedie

THE FUTURE OF LOVE

◊

JILL TWEEDIE (b. 1936) was born in Egypt, lived in Montreal for eight years, and now lives in London where she writes a weekly column in *The Guardian.* She has been a talk-show host on television, and her articles appear in a number of British newspapers and magazines. In her book *In the Name of Love* (1979), she argues that love has usually been defined in ways that enforce women's dependence on men. In the following excerpt, Tweedie looks into the future and foresees a change in love from its present form into a better relation between the sexes.

Love, it seems, is as much a part of the unique equipment of homo 1
sapiens as language or laughter and far more celebrated. If all the
words that have been written about it since mankind first put stick to
clay were laid end to end, they would rocket past Venus and vanish
into deep space. Histories of love, philosophies of love, psychologies
of love, guidebooks to love, love letters, love hymns, love stories, love
poems, love songs have covered tablets and papyrus, parchment and
paper and walls, filled theatres across time and lands from Epidaurus
to Radio City, and been declaimed by gods and goddesses of love
from Sappho to Warren Beatty. Love has been, is now, and ever shall
be our scourge and balm, our wound and salve, source of our finest
and most bestial actions, the emotion that passeth all understanding.
It is a heavenly body out of our orbit, beyond man-made laws, ethics,
or control, a magical splendour that descends upon us like the gift of
tongues and possesses us whether we will or no. Love transforms us
into something strange and rare, it ignites our lives and, dying, takes
all meaning away.

> The mind has a thousand eyes
> And the heart but one
> Yet the light of a whole life dies
> When love is done.

We die of love and die without it, our hearts beat for it and break for it. Love built the Taj Mahal, wrote the Song of Solomon and cooks a billion meals every day, across the world. Love is the only thing that matters at all, after all.

Or so they say. And in my opinion what they say, give or take an   2
epigram or two, is rubbish. Take off the rose-colored glasses and what does a close examination of the facts reveal to the naked eye? That love, true love, is the rarest of all the emotions and one that has been conspicuous only by its absence ever since mankind dropped from the trees. If we condense the earth's history into one calendar year, homo sapiens appeared in the late evening of December 31st and love, his much-vaunted race-long companion, is still merely a glimmer on the midnight horizon of the coming New Year. Love, in other words, inhabits the future, a kind of reverse star whose light reaches us before it is born instead of after it has died. Certainly, intimations of love's coming have touched an individual here and there through time and its prophets have started new religions, composed great symphonies, made beautiful sculpture, and painted exquisite canvases. But for the wide river of humanity, the ordinary mass of men and women who have peopled our planet and reproduced our race, love was not necessary, not possible, and not there.

Why, then, the stories, the poems, and the songs, the jubilations   3
and the suicides? How can you argue that love does not exist when human beings deliberately end their own existence for love? Surely nothing is as indisputable as that love and mankind go hand in hand. I love, therefore I am. But is it love they feel? I think not. The word is a vast umbrella that covers a multitude of virtues and sins and because we are perfectly familiar with all of love's precursors and understudies, we imagine that we have pinned down love itself when we have merely trapped its shadow. Co-operation, for instance, midwife to that most ancient of drives, survival. You scratch my back and I'll scratch yours. Sex, a powerhouse so overwhelming in its assault upon us that, trying to domesticate it, we have given it the prettier name of love. We know about affection and friendship. We feel liking, duty, deference, greed, lust, ambition, attraction, protectiveness, ingratiation, and the desire to conform. We are gripped by infatuation, obsession, adoration, vanity, addiction, jealousy, fear, and the dread of being alone. Very deeply we know about need. I need you. He needs me. Needs must.

But love is somewhere else and all those other drives and needs and 4
feelings are like the gases that swirl about in space, inwardly spiralling
through the centuries to center at last on a small hard core, gases that
are only hot air in themselves but essential for the eventual formation
of a new world, a world of real love. We may arrive at it one day, given
time, but we are not there yet. . . .

The interesting thing is that the slow emergence of true love does 5
not predicate some higher version of morality. No sudden conver-
sions, no lights upon the road to Damascus are in any way necessary.
A new generation with new standards of loving will not come about as
a result of some mystical mutation or spiritual growth, though these
may well follow. The facts are more practical. As equality becomes
commonplace between men and women, they themselves will perforce change from stereotypes, however successful or unsuccessful,
into ordinary human beings, each one rather different from the
next. Standard sexual roles — the breadwinner, the housewife and
mother — already blurred, will eventually disappear and with them
will go the suppression or exaggeration of parts of the individual character made necessary by those roles. And as these masks, stylised as
the masks of Japanese Kabuki, slip to reveal the human face behind,
romantic love, so heavily dependent upon an artificial facade and predictable masculine or feminine behavior, will die from starvation. Already it is showing the first signs of incipient malnutrition. When,
added to that, children are raised in equality and mothers, secure in
their own identity, no longer pass their fears and inferiorities on to
their daughters or too great an admiration on to their sons; when both
parents are equally concerned with the upbringing of children and
therefore ensure that those children cannot divide their own emotions
between the sexes and discard one whole area, we will have bred a race
of human beings differentiated by their own personalities rather than
their genitalia. The old war-cry of sexists—*vive la différence*—actually
implied exactly the opposite; the rigid division of an infinite variety of
people into just two categories, male and female. *Vive la similarité.*
Variety will replace conformity and variety, apart from being an evolutionary must, forces each potential lover to take stock of an individual rather than search for the stereotyped ideal of a whole sex.

Nor is this change dependent solely on a conscious wish for 6
change. Evolution has always had a voracious appetite for variety, it is
literally the spice of life, offering as it does a wide menu for natural

selection. And it is becoming clear to many of us that the old stereotypes of male and female are increasingly a positive threat to the well-
being of the race and the earth. Women, confined to a domestic and
biological cage, produce unwanted children to crowd an already over-
populated world, while their own abilities wither on the hearth. Men,
driven by out-dated standards of virility, continue to denude the
planet and threaten each other with uncontemplatable war. Love between such men and such women serves only their own artificial needs
and seals them off in their *folie à deux* from the rest of the world instead of involving them more deeply, as real love would do. Our planetary problems are rapidly becoming too serious to permit the net-
curtain mentality of the average self-satisfied couple as they peep out
at trouble and hastily withdraw, safe in the certainty that God himself
blesses their cosy twosome and demands nothing more than its continuation, properly seeded with kiddies.

That is not to say that monogamy is on its way out, only that   7
monogamy as we know it today — sacrosanct, heterosexual, reproductive, lifelong, and almost always a retreat from life, no longer adequately fulfils either the individuals concerned or society. All research
done recently, whether anthropological, pediatric, psychiatric, criminal, or social, arrives at the same conclusion: human beings develop
most fully and happily if they can feel loved as children by one or two
constantly present adults and, as adults themselves, reproduce the
same closeness with one other adult. But there is nothing to prove
that years of monogamy with the *same* adult are necessarily beneficial.
Lifelong monogamy may be nice for the Church and useful for the
tax-collector but it has many drawbacks for the individual, who is a
learning as well as an imprinted being. As we change and learn, from
youth to old age, we must give ourselves room for that change. Like
snakes, we need occasionally to shed our old skins and often we cannot do that if we are tied by bonds of guilt to an outgrown love. None
of us grows at the same speed or in the same way and the chances of a
parallel development with one other human being are not great. But
nor does this imply a lack of love or some pervasive shame. Each of us
may give another person love and help in inner growth for a while.
But in a changing world, with changing people, why should we expect
that love to last for ever or denigrate it if it does not? Why should
love, once a mansion, be made into a cage through false expectations
of what love is?

Lifelong monogamy has other drawbacks, even when it works, per- 8
haps *especially* when it works. In a cold and problematic world it is all
too easy to withdraw into the cosiness of a familiar love, leaving those
problems for others to solve. We have a genetic need for other people;
monogamous love, in attempting to assuage that need with one other
person, may not only sour into neuroses or a mutual flattery that reduces both partners, making them fear the outside world, but may
also isolate us from our fellows and allow us to care less about their
fate. When my husband is away from home, I turn in need to my
friends, even to strangers. I become vulnerable once again to their
larger opinion of me. I see myself as others, more coldly, see me. On
his return my instinct is to warm myself at his me-centred love, to
soothe my slightly bruised ego. Luckily for me, he does not need to
build me up for his own ego and so he is not all *that* warm, just warm
enough. He leaves place in me for others, because he himself has
place for others.

All this — changing women, the danger of stereotypes, and intrac- 9
table monogramy, the needs of our race and our planet in the future — implies one imperative. We must leave adolescence behind
and grow up. It is absolutely vital, if we are to continue to exist in
some comfort upon our earth, that we take a giant step into true
adulthood, learn to filter the emotions through our reasoning capacities and learn that survival itself rests on knowing who we are, respecting others' space, and endeavoring justly to balance our own and
others' needs.

And this is where love truly comes into its own as an evolutionary 10
tool. Parental love teaches children one vital fact: that they are loved
and lovable and therefore can themselves love. But the love between
adults differs in one absolute from parental love: it is conditional, or
should be. We find out who we are by feeling our outlines against
other people, by finding out who we are not. In loving but honest eyes
we see prisms of our own vague face, slowly we put the prisms together and distinguish certain unchanging features, form certain principles. Inside, a center begins to form and once it is firmly established,
roots well grown, blossoms flourishing, we can turn from it towards
others with a real sense of where we differ and where we are the same.
And once we know that, once we respect ourselves, it becomes impossible to accept another who violates our beliefs and ourselves. A weak
ego, a weak hold on reality, opens the doors to any passing stranger

who flatters us enough and makes us feel real. A strong ego, a firm knowledge of who we are, demands conditions of that stranger, demands a similarity of belief and behavior and can discard what it does not respect, even at the price of rejecting easy flattery.

And that is what true love is there to help us do. Properly informed, 11 lovingly detached, centered respectfully in itself, it provides us with a real reflection of ourselves, to help us grow. Principles do not need to be suppressed for fear of displeasing, for fear of loss, because when the crunch comes, we can cope alone.

Love cannot thrive in inequality or extreme poverty. It requires 12 enough leisure for introspection and enough introspection for empathy. It demands that the individual feel a certain control over his life because, in too great a storm, we tend to seek any refuge. It thrives on honesty and therefore must do away with great need, since need drives out honesty. It is rational, it knows its own roots, it is moral and controllable because it stems from the head and not the heart. Any resemblance it bears to love as we know it today is purely fictional.

And true love is still in embryo, fragile compared to other ties be- 13 cause it derives no strength from more ancient needs. Its roots are not in the past but in the future. It is a beginning, a new survival mechanism slowly evolving to suit new circumstances.

CONSIDERATIONS

1. What clues in the first paragraph suggest that the author will soon reject the praises of love that comprise the first paragraph? How would you describe her tone?
2. What attitudes toward love are suggested by the images in the second paragraph? What are the connotative associations of the star?
3. What are the emotional ties that Tweedie says we mistakenly accept as the reality of love?
4. According to Tweedie, how will real love enter the world? What will then happen to romantic love?
5. Why will the new love be better for the species as well as better for individuals?
6. What changes in marriage does Tweedie foresee as beneficial? Do you see any losses that she does not mention?
7. WRITING TOPIC. What is the role of the passions in Tweedie's conception of real love? Can there be "rational" love in passionate love? And vice versa? In a 500-word essay, agree or disagree with Tweedie's implicit view of passion in love.

ADDITIONAL
WRITING TOPICS

◊

LOVE AND LONGINGS

1. Is your generation more romantic or less romantic than your parents and grandparents were in their younger days? What current customs and attitudes toward romance appear odd or even objectionable to them? Do you think that they missed something important that your generation enjoys? Or that they perhaps enjoyed something that is absent in contemporary romance? In a 750-word essay, evaluate your generation's outlook on love as compared with an earlier generation's. Use solid evidence to support your points. You may want to interview older people.

2. Analyze the lyrics of three or four popular songs about love by one songwriter, such as Ira Gershwin, Cole Porter, Bob Dylan, Paul McCartney, Kris Kristoffersen, or any other well-known lyricist whose works have been collected in song books. In a 1,000-word essay discuss the attitudes about love that the songs express both explicitly and implicitly.

3. The statements in *Insights* reflect a wide range of differing opinions about love. Clearly, people do not agree on what love is or even how it feels to love or be loved. Choose two statements in *Insights* that make sense to you, even if they differ about love, and compare and contrast their points and implications. In a 700-word essay, explain the view of love that is defined by those two statements.

4. A "fan" of a film star, a pop singer, an athlete, or a television personality is usually involved in an imaginary romantic relationship. A fan cherishes the star's face and image; a fan delights in knowing details of the star's life; a fan identifies with the star and often fantasizes reciprocated attention and affection. In 700 words, define one such specific imaginary relationship that you have had or have directly observed in another fan. Examine what it meant to be a fan. Explain how the relationship began, what activities it included, what attitudes it encouraged or changed, and how it diminished or came to an end. Be sure that you do not just reminisce; keep your emphasis on examining the behavior and responses of a fan.

PART 4

GROUP PICTURES

Edward C. Martin, *Being Junior High*

Maya Angelou, *Graduation*

John Cheever, *Expelled*

John Edgar Wideman, *Black and Blues*

Maxine Hong Kingston, *The Misery of Silence*

Paul Fussell, *"Speak, That I May See Thee"*

Gloria Steinem, *The Time Factor*

Marc Feigen Fasteau, *Friendships Among Men*

Desmond Morris, *Territorial Behavior*

Linda Pastan, *Market Day*

Alexis de Tocqueville, *Aristocracy and Democracy*

Additional Writing Topics

INSIGHTS

No man is an island, entire of itself; every man is a piece of the continent, a part of the main; if a clod be washed away by the sea, Europe is the less, as well as if a promontory were, as well as if a manor of thy friends or of thine own were; any man's death diminishes me, because I am involved in mankind; and therefore never send to know for whom the bell tolls: it tolls for thee.

— JOHN DONNE

◊

Hell is other people.
— JEAN-PAUL SARTRE

◊

Society everywhere is in conspiracy against the manhood of every one of its members. Society is a joint-stock company, in which the members agree, for the better securing of his bread to each shareholder, to surrender the liberty and culture of the eater. The virtue in most request is conformity. Self-reliance is its aversion. It loves not realities and creators, but names and customs. Whoso would be a man, must be a nonconformist.

— RALPH WALDO EMERSON

◊

Being ashamed of one's parents is, psychologically, not identical with being ashamed of one's people. I believe every one of us will, if he but digs deeply enough into the realm of unconscious memories, remember having been ashamed of his parents. Being ashamed of our people must have another psychological meaning. It must be the expression of a tendency to disavow the most essential part of ourself. To be ashamed of being Jewish means not only to be a coward and insincere in disavowing the proud inheritance of an old people who have made an eternal contribution to the civilization of mankind. It also means to disavow the best and the most precious part we get from our parents, their parents, and their ancestors, who continue to live in us. It means, furthermore, to renounce oneself. Without self-respect and dignity no man or woman can live. When the Jewish proverb proclaims that he who is ashamed of his family will have no luck in life, it must mean just that: he cannot have that self-confidence which makes life worth living. Strange that the folklore of an oriental people coincides here with the viewpoint of Goethe: any life can be lived if one does not miss oneself, if one but remains oneself.

The thought that my children are sometimes ashamed of the human faults and failings of their father does not sadden me; but, for their own sake, I wish that they will never be ashamed that their father was Jewish. The one feeling concerns only the personal shortcomings of an individual who was striving, sometimes succeeding and often failing. The other shame concerns something superpersonal, something beyond the narrow realm of the individual. It concerns the community of fate, it touches the bond that ties one generation to those preceding it and those following it.

— THEODOR REIK

◇

It is difficult to let others see the full psychological meaning of caste segregation. It is as though one, looking out from a dark cave in a side of an impending mountain, sees the world passing and speaks to it; speaks courteously and persuasively, showing them how these entombed souls are hindered in their natural movement, expression, and development; and how their loosening from prison would be a matter not simply of courtesy, sympathy, and help to them, but aid to all the world. One talks on evenly and logically in this way, but notices that the passing throng does not even turn its head, or if it does, glances curiously and walks on. It gradually penetrates the minds of the prisoners that the people passing do not hear; that some thick sheet of invisible but horribly tangible plate glass is between them and the world. They get excited; they talk louder; they gesticulate. Some of the passing world stop in curiosity; these gesticulations seem so pointless; they laugh and pass on. They still either do not hear at all, or hear but dimly, and even what they hear, they do not understand. Then the people within may become hysterical. They may scream and hurl themselves against the barriers, hardly realizing in their bewilderment that they are screaming in a vacuum unheard and that their antics may actually seem funny to those outside looking in. They may even, here and there, break through in blood and disfigurement, and find themselves faced by a horrified, implacable, and quite overwhelming mob of people frightened for their own very existence.

— W. E. B. DUBOIS

◊

The brotherhood of man is not a mere poet's dream; it is a most depressing and humiliating reality.

— OSCAR WILDE

◊

The "natural" approach to human relations presumes that to know any person well enough is to love him, that the only human problem is a communication problem. This denies that people might be separated by basic, genuinely irreconcilable differences — philosophical, political, or religious — and assumes that all such differences are no more than misunderstandings.

Many forms of etiquette are employed precisely to disguise those antipathies that arise from irreconcilable differences, in order to prevent mayhem. The reason that diplomacy, for example, is so stilted is that its purpose is to head off the most natural social relation between countries in conflict, namely war.

The idea that people can behave "naturally" without resorting to an artificial code tacitly agreed upon by their society is as silly as the idea that they can communicate by using a language without commonly accepted semantic and grammatical rules. Like language, a code of manners can be used with more or less skill, for laudable or evil purposes, to express a great variety of ideas and emotions. Like language, manners continually undergo slow changes and adaptations, but these changes have to be global, not atomic. For if everyone improvises his own manners, no one will understand the meaning of anyone else's behavior, and the result will be social chaos and the end of civilization, or about what we have now.

– JUDITH MARTIN ("Miss Manners")

◊

A group is extraordinarily credulous and open to influence, it has no critical faculty, and the improbable does not exist for it. It thinks in images.

Since a group is in no doubt as to what constitutes truth or error, and is conscious moreover, of its own great strength, it is as intolerant as it is obedient to authority. It respects force and can only be slightly influenced by kindness, which it regards as a form of weakness. What it demands of its heroes is strength, or even violence. It wants to be ruled and oppressed and to fear its masters. Fundamentally it is entirely conservative, and it has a deep aversion from all innovations and advances and an unbounded respect for tradition.

In order to make a correct judgment upon the morals of crowds, one must take into consideration the fact that when individuals come together in a group all their individual inhibitions fall away and all the cruel, brutal, and destructive instincts, which lie dormant in individuals as relics of a primitive epoch, are stirred up to fine free gratification.

– SIGMUND FREUD

Edward C. Martin

BEING JUNIOR HIGH

◊

EDWARD C. MARTIN (b. 1937) is an educational administrator and an author of such social science textbooks as *The People Make a Nation* (1971). He has taught in both high schools and junior high schools. In this essay on the early adolescent student, he discusses some of the special difficulties that a twelve- to fourteen-year-old has in being an individual and also a member of a group. This essay is a condensation of an article that originally appeared in *Daedalus* under the title "Reflections on the Early Adolescent in School."

What is it like to be in school if you are twelve to fourteen years of 1 age? What does and doesn't it mean to you?

. . . Fundamentally, for most American twelve-year-olds, school is 2 *where it's at*. School occupies the time and concerns of all the people you know — your friends, your parents, people you meet. People are always asking what you do in school and how you like school. School is often a source of contention between you and adults. Why did you get low grades? Why did you play hooky? Why don't you play school sports or join clubs or work harder or work less, and so forth? You are always telling people you don't like school, but often you don't mean it because school is comfortable and they at least want you around. Also you think school is important and even fun. But these things can't be said too openly.

Friends and enemies are a large part of school, perhaps the largest. 3 One comes to school to see friends, one fears school because enemies are there also. Some of the most important parts of the school day are the walk or ride there, changing between classes, the few minutes before the class gets started, the study hall, and the end of school. These times are the intense periods of "seeing the other kids," or realizing you have no one to see. One of those unwritten rules of teaching is "begin the class on time." It makes the teacher appear efficient and purposeful and gives the task to be done a sense of importance. When I started teaching in junior high I still believed this rule, until I began to realize how much there is to learn about students by observing or participating in the three minutes before class started. . . . My interest in the friendship group has been not to join it but to figure out ways to tap it when it made sense to do so. The usual separation of the interests of these groups and the classroom is not necessarily a bad separation. Doing the peer group's thing all the time would be as deadly as doing the teacher's thing all the time.

The case of a student staying home, being ill, or skipping a class 4 because he fears some group of students is more common than most adults imagine. Threats are used frequently by students although fortunately not often carried through. For two weeks a group of girls were harassing another girl in and out of classes. The girl under attack was literally terrified, although she sought to hold her ground by appearing casual and unafraid. When this failed she would seek the help of adults or just burst into tears. For the group of antagonists, this aggressiveness was a source of unity and camaraderie. They relished the times of confrontation and the times of subtle teasing. Individuals took pride and received group praise devising more exciting methods of taunting their foe. There was always the daring aspect of avoiding that line where the full force of adult intervention would be imposed. The several adults involved did not know what to do. One teacher tried to give some perspective on the situation by showing the long-run absurdity of such behavior, another by attempting disciplinary tactics — essentially tongue-lashing and keeping the aggressive group after school. The guidance counselor tried to talk it through with all the students involved. The situation improved on the surface, but we all knew the individual girl's fear remained and the group's resentment toward her and power over her continued. We also realized that there was very little we could do about it but make sure it did not become violent. I am always surprised at how brutal students this age can be toward each other. It reminds me again of how important a book Golding's novel *Lord of the Flies* is for teachers.

The intense friendship groupings in junior high obviously have an- 5 other side — the youngster who has no friends, no group to which he has allegiance or which sees him as a part. Several kinds of students in my experience fall into this category and it means different things to each. John was an outgoing intellectual student who spoke in an affected way and assumed he had the right answers. Other students saw him as a "freak" and made it clear to him that was how they regarded him. Sharon was a quiet withdrawn girl who talked with no one and to whom no one talked. She seemed not to be bothered by this isolation. Bob was a class leader. He demanded everyone's attention and when he did not get it was bound to provoke it. Although the students saw him as an important person to be reckoned with, he was really not a part of any group. Adults at one time or another are isolated from others by choice or happenstance, but the isolation of a twelve-, thirteen-, or fourteen-year-old is particularly difficult. There is a pain brought on by not being like everyone else when it is important that you be like others. This comes at a time in physical, emotional, and intellectual development when change is so rapid that many individual youngsters are either behind or ahead of the mass of their peers. Aggravating these gaps is the intolerance of this age group toward diversity and their delight in making an issue over those who are different. The boy who does not start to spurt in physical stature is called a "shrimp" and sees himself as a shrimp. The girl who gets seriously interested in a boy does not quite fit with her giggly friends. The peer group of the twelve- to fourteen-year-old has most of the mechanisms of keeping members in line but often lacks the moral, ethical, and intellectual substance of the so-called "youth culture" of older students. . . .

In schools, the classroom is seen as the center of the educational 6 experience. Whether or not it is in effect is beside the point. Students see it as such. . . .

In the center of the classroom experience is the teacher. Students 7 most often describe and define their courses in terms of the teacher. He or she is the one who makes a class great or terrible. Curriculum reform projects of the past ten years in the academic disciplines have tried to improve schools by producing better materials, some of which could be taught by *any* teacher. Most of them now realize that with a bad teacher students will feel the new course is as bad as the old. Parents, principals, and guidance counselors keep telling youngsters it should not matter who the teacher is. They say you should be able to learn from someone you do not like. This is true only when personal dislike is mild and is overpowered by respect for the teacher's fairness and competence. Most teachers accept the necessity of being liked by their students; some turn this into an end in itself. Students want a positive personal relationship with their teachers, but they want more.

The teacher, whether or not he considers himself a benevolent despot or a partner in learning, is a model. He is usually the only adult in a room of thirty people. He is the one most different and the one who is expected to do something to make that class good. If he does not, he is not a good teacher. He is the one turned to when the going gets rough. One day I brought six candy bars into class for a lesson on the distribution of goods. I put the candy bars on the desk and told the class they were welcome to have them and should agree on how to divide them. For the rest of the period and part of the next, alternatives were presented and discussed. Several boys from the track team suggested, only half in jest, that the candy be placed at one end of the room and the class race for it. Generally, this solution was opposed. Other proposals were made including equal division, grades, fighting, working, bidding, and drawing lots. None, by the way, suggested that I as teacher decide. Finally, drawing lots was agreed upon as the best method. As I moved the candy bars to another spot in the room, the elected class chairman grabbed at one. I asked him why, since all had agreed to do the division by lots. He said he wanted one. I held out the bars and he took one, opened it, and proceeded to eat it. The universal reaction of the class was silent confusion. I thought they would be outraged and I suppose they were, but in this case they expected me to take action, to stop the violation of their hard-reached decision. I finally did ask the boy why he disregarded the class's decision, rather mildly chewed him out, and ruled him out of the drawing of lots.

The incident illustrates many things and raises many questions. 9 Clearly I had violated the expectations of the students, either by letting their classmate take the candy or by not acting when he did. They expected me to handle this situation even though all but the assignment of the task was in their control and they had made the decisions. Perhaps I had asked them to step too far out of their notions of authority and the security that a teacher is expected to provide in the classroom. Another reason I was surprised at the class's lack of reaction was their usual strong reactions to injustice. Students measure teachers, generally with a high degree of accuracy, on a continuum from just to unjust in treatment of people. Twelve-year-olds often use a double standard — canons of fairness are strictly applied to others, much less strictly applied to themselves. Connected to both the security and justice issues is the whole question of authority. Although much less sensitive about authority than sixteen-year-olds, the twelve-year-old in school is keenly aware of who makes decisions and what role he has in the process. In the case of the candy bars, I was expected to act as the authority. No doubt I was naïve about how students viewed the authority relationships in class to think they would exercise some control on their classmate. This age student is more committed to the distinction between himself and adults. He is more willing to go along with the authorities, but is beginning to question. By the time he leaves junior high school, the question of legitimate authority is a central part of things about which he is "bugged."

A final point about the candy bar incident. The actions of the boy   10 represent, in the extreme, a serious problem for most youngsters in junior high school: *How do I establish and develop individuality in an institution that treats me as one of a group with similar characteristics?* Most of the students I teach want to be seen as individuals, just as we all do. A school is a difficult if not impossible place to get a great deal of individual treatment. The students want to be members of the group, but they also want to be someone unique. Since all the children have this problem and since there is considerable pressure toward group conformity, they are not much able to give each other this sense of individuality. The teacher is often the only one able to legitimatize pluralism, but he is hampered because he deals with so many children and almost always as a group.

CONSIDERATIONS

1. Martin recognizes that "seeing the other kids" is important in the school day, but he does not look into what makes it important. Based on your own observations, what interests and activities do seventh and eighth graders share with friends in school? How do they spend time together? Are they always with the same friends?
2. What are the qualities that junior high students generally expect from a teacher? How did Martin meet or fail their expectations?
3. Throughout the essay, Martin mentions several differences between junior high students and older, high school students. What are the differences he notes, and do you find his observations accurate?

4. In the final sentence what does Martin mean by "legitimatize pluralism"? Paraphrase Martin and add an illustration of how the teacher might be able to do this. Why don't the students do the same for one another?

5. WRITING TOPIC. In a 500-word paper, present a specific example of the pressure you once felt to conform to a group. Give enough details of the situation to show that you were being pressured, and not left free to act individually. Show that the situation was of some importance to you. Even choosing a flavor of ice cream can be important if you feel that you are being bullied over making up your mind.

Maya Angelou

GRADUATION

◊

MAYA ANGELOU (b. 1928) was raised by her grandmother, who ran a small store for blacks in the town of Stamps, Arkansas. She survived a childhood that seemed certain to defeat her, and as she once told an interviewer: "One would say of my life — born loser — had to be; from a broken family, raped at eight, unwed mother at sixteen." During her adult life, she became a dancer, an actress, a poet, a television writer and producer, and a coordinator in Martin Luther King's Southern Christian Leadership Conference. She is most widely known for her four autobiographical books, beginning with *I Know Why the Caged Bird Sings* (1970) from which this selection is taken. Her most recent memoir is *The Heart of a Woman* (1981).

The children in Stamps trembled visibly with anticipation. Some 1 adults were excited too, but to be certain the whole young population had come down with graduation epidemic. Large classes were graduating from both the grammar school and the high school. Even those who were years removed from their own day of glorious release were anxious to help with preparations as a kind of dry run. The junior students who were moving into the vacating classes' chairs were tradition-bound to show their talents for leadership and management. They strutted through the school and around the campus exerting pressure on the lower grades. Their authority was so new that occasionally if they pressed a little too hard it had to be overlooked. After all, next term was coming, and it never hurt a sixth grader to have a play sister in the eighth grade, or a tenth-year student to be able to call a twelfth grader Bubba. So all was endured in a spirit of shared understanding. But the graduating classes themselves were the nobility. Like travelers with exotic destinations on their minds, the graduates were remarkably forgetful. They came to school without their books, or tablets, or even pencils. Volunteers fell over themselves to secure replacements for the missing equipment. When accepted, the willing workers might or might not be thanked, and it was of no importance to the pregraduation rites. Even teachers were respectful of the now quiet and aging seniors, and tended to speak to them, if not as equals, as beings only slightly lower than themselves. After tests were returned and grades given, the student body, which acted like an extended family, knew who did well, who excelled, and what piteous ones had failed.

Unlike the white high school, Lafayette County Training School 2 distinguished itself by having neither lawn, nor hedges, nor tennis court, nor climbing ivy. Its two buildings (main classrooms, the grade school, and home economics) were set on a dirt hill with no fence to limit either its boundaries or those of bordering farms. There was a large expanse to the left of the school which was used alternately as a baseball diamond or a basketball court. Rusty hoops on the swaying poles represented the permanent recreational equipment, although bats and balls could be borrowed from the P.E. teacher if the borrower was qualified and if the diamond wasn't occupied.

Over this rocky area relieved by a few shady tall persimmon trees 3 the graduating class walked. The girls often held hands and no longer bothered to speak to the lower students. There was a sadness about them, as if this old world was not their home and they were bound for higher ground. The boys, on the other hand, had become more friendly, more outgoing. A decided change from the closed attitude they projected while studying for finals. Now they seemed not ready to give up the old school, the familiar paths and classrooms. Only a small percentage would be continuing on to college — one of the South's A & M (agricultural and mechanical) schools, which trained negro youths to be carpenters, farmers, handymen, masons, maids, cooks, and baby nurses. Their future rode heavily on their shoulders, and blinded them to the collective joy that had pervaded the lives of the boys and girls in the grammar school graduating class.

Parents who could afford it had ordered new shoes and ready-made 4 clothes for themselves from Sears and Roebuck or Montgomery Ward. They also engaged the best seamstresses to make the floating graduating dresses and to cut down secondhand pants which would be pressed to a military slickness for the important event.

Oh, it was important, all right. Whitefolks would attend the cere- 5
mony, and two or three would speak of God and home, and the
Southern way of life, and Mrs. Parsons, the principal's wife, would
play the graduation march while the lower-grade graduates paraded
down the aisles and took their seats below the platform. The high
school seniors would wait in empty classrooms to make their dramatic
entrance.

In the Store I was the person of the moment. The birthday girl. 6
The center. Bailey* had graduated the year before, although to do so
he had had to forfeit all pleasures to make up for his time lost in
Baton Rouge.

My class was wearing butter-yellow piqué dresses, and Momma 7
launched out on mine. She smocked the yoke into tiny crisscross-
ing puckers, then shirred the rest of the bodice. Her dark fingers
ducked in and out of the lemony cloth as she embroidered raised
daisies around the hem. Before she considered herself finished she had
added a crocheted cuff on the puff sleeves, and a pointy crocheted
collar.

I was going to be lovely. A walking model of all the various styles of 8
fine hand sewing and it didn't worry me that I was only twelve years
old and merely graduating from the eighth grade. Besides, many
teachers in Arkansas Negro schools had only that diploma and were
licensed to impart wisdom.

The days had become longer and more noticeable. The faded beige 9
of former times had been replaced with strong and sure colors. I began
to see my classmates' clothes, their skin tones, and the dust that
waved off pussy willows. Clouds that lazed across the sky were objects
of great concern to me. Their shiftier shapes might have held a message that in my new happiness and with a little bit of time I'd soon
decipher. During that period I looked at the arch of heaven so reli-
giously my neck kept a steady ache. I had taken to smiling more often,
and my jaws hurt from the unaccustomed activity. Between the two
physical sore spots, I suppose I could have been uncomfortable, but
that was not the case. As a member of the winning team (the graduating class of 1940) I had outdistanced unpleasant sensations by miles. I
was headed for the freedom of open fields.

* The author's brother. The children help out in their grandmother's store.

Youth and social approval allied themselves with me and we tram- 10 meled memories of slights and insults. The wind of our swift passage remodeled my features. Lost tears were pounded to mud and then to dust. Years of withdrawal were brushed aside and left behind, as hanging ropes of parasitic moss.

My work alone had awarded me a top place and I was going to be 11 one of the first called in the graduating ceremonies. On the classroom blackboard, as well as on the bulletin board in the auditorium, there were blue stars and white stars and red stars. No absences, no tardinesses, and my academic work was among the best of the year. I could say the preamble to the Constitution even faster than Bailey. We timed ourselves often: "WethepeopleoftheUnitedStatesinordertoformamoreperfectunion . . ." I had memorized the Presidents of the United States from Washington to Roosevelt in chronological as well as alphabetical order.

My hair pleased me too. Gradually the black mass had lengthened 12 and thickened, so that it kept at last to its braided pattern, and I didn't have to yank my scalp off when I tried to comb it.

Louise and I had rehearsed the exercises until we tired out our- 13 selves. Henry Reed was class valedictorian. He was a small, very black boy with hooded eyes, a long, broad nose and an oddly shaped head. I had admired him for years because each term he and I vied for the best grades in our class. Most often he bested me, but instead of being disappointed I was pleased that we shared top places between us. Like many Southern Black children, he lived with his grandmother, who was as strict as Momma and as kind as she knew how to be. He was courteous, respectful, and soft-spoken to elders, but on the playground he chose to play the roughest games. I admired him. Anyone, I reckoned, sufficiently afraid or sufficiently dull could be polite. But to be able to operate at a top level with both adults and children was admirable.

His valedictory speech was entitled "To Be or Not to Be." The 14 rigid tenth-grade teacher had helped him to write it. He'd been working on the dramatic stresses for months.

The weeks until graduation were filled with heady activities. A 15 group of small children were to be presented in a play about buttercups and daisies and bunny rabbits. They could be heard throughout the building practicing their hops and their little songs that sounded like silver bells. The older girls (non-graduates, of course) were as-

signed the task of making refreshments for the night's festivities. A
tangy scent of ginger, cinnamon, nutmeg, and chocolate wafted
around the home economics building as the budding cooks made
samples for themselves and their teachers.

In every corner of the workshop, axes and saws split fresh timber as 16
the woodshop boys made sets and stage scenery. Only the graduates
were left out of the general bustle. We were free to sit in the library at
the back of the building or look in quite detachedly, naturally, on the
measures being taken for our event.

Even the minister preached on graduation the Sunday before. His 17
subject was, "Let your light so shine that men will see your good
works and praise your Father, Who is in Heaven." Although the sermon was purported to be addressed to us, he used the occasion to
speak to backsliders, gamblers, and general ne'er-do-wells. But since
he had called our names at the beginning of the service we were mol-
lified.

Among Negroes the tradition was to give presents to children going 18
only from one grade to another. How much more important this was
when the person was graduating at the top of the class. Uncle Willie
and Momma had sent away for a Mickey Mouse watch like Bailey's.
Louise gave me four embroidered handkerchiefs. (I gave her three
crocheted doilies.) Mrs. Sneed, the minister's wife, made me an un-
derskirt to wear for graduation, and nearly every customer gave me a
nickel or maybe even a dime with the instruction "Keep on moving to
higher ground," or some such encouragement.

Amazingly the great day finally dawned and I was out of bed before 19
I knew it. I threw open the back door to see it more clearly, but
Momma said, "Sister, come away from that door and put your robe
on."

I hoped the memory of that morning would never leave me. Sun- 20
light was itself still young, and the day had none of the insistence maturity would bring it in a few hours. In my robe and barefoot in the
backyard, under cover of going to see about my new beans, I gave myself up to the gentle warmth and thanked God that no matter what
evil I had done in my life He had allowed me to live to see this day.
Somewhere in my fatalism I had expected to die, accidentally, and
never have the chance to walk up the stairs in the auditorium and
gracefully receive my hard-earned diploma. Out of God's merciful
bosom I had won reprieve.

Bailey came out in his robe and gave me a box wrapped in 21
Christmas paper. He said he had saved his money for months to pay
for it. It felt like a box of chocolates, but I knew Bailey wouldn't
save money to buy candy when we had all we could want under our
noses.

He was as proud of the gift as I. It was a soft-leather-bound copy of 22
a collection of poems by Edgar Allan Poe, or, as Bailey and I called
him, "Eap." I turned to "Annabel Lee" and we walked up and down
the garden rows, the cool dirt between our toes, reciting the beautifully sad lines.

Momma made a Sunday breakfast although it was only Friday. 23
After we finished the blessing, I opened my eyes to find the watch on
my plate. It was a dream of a day. Everything went smoothly and to
my credit. I didn't have to be reminded or scolded for anything. Near
evening I was too jittery to attend to chores, so Bailey volunteered to
do all before his bath.

Days before, we had made a sign for the Store and as we turned out 24
the lights Momma hung the cardboard over the doorknob. It read
clearly: CLOSED. GRADUATION.

My dress fitted perfectly and everyone said that I looked like a sun- 25
beam in it. On the hill, going toward the school, Bailey walked behind
with Uncle Willie, who muttered, "Go on, Ju." He wanted him to
walk ahead with us because it embarrassed him to have to walk so
slowly. Bailey said he'd let the ladies walk together, and the men
would bring up the rear. We all laughed, nicely.

Little children dashed by out of the dark like fireflies. Their crepe- 26
paper dresses and butterfly wings were not made for running and we
heard more than one rip, dryly, and the regretful "uh uh" that followed.

The school blazed without gaiety. The windows seemed cold and 27
unfriendly from the lower hill. A sense of ill-fated timing crept over
me, and if Momma hadn't reached for my hand I would have drifted
back to Bailey and Uncle Willie, and possibly beyond. She made a
few slow jokes about my feet getting cold, and tugged me along to the
now-strange building.

Around the front steps, assurance came back. There were my fel- 28
low "greats," the graduating class. Hair brushed back, legs oiled, new
dresses and pressed pleats, fresh pocket handkerchiefs and little handbags, all homesewn. Oh, we were up to snuff, all right. I joined my

comrades and didn't even see my family go in to find seats in the crowded auditorium.

The school band struck up a march and all classes filed in as had 29 been rehearsed. We stood in front of our seats, as assigned, and on a signal from the choir director, we sat. No sooner had this been accomplished than the band started to play the national anthem. We rose again and sang the song, after which we recited the pledge of allegiance. We remained standing for a brief minute before the choir director and the principal signaled to us, rather desperately I thought, to take our seats. The command was so unusual that our carefully rehearsed and smooth-running machine was thrown off. For a full minute we fumbled for our chairs and bumped into each other awkwardly. Habits change or solidify under pressure, so in our state of nervous tension we had been ready to follow our usual assembly pattern: the American National Anthem, then the pledge of allegiance, then the song every Black person I knew called the Negro National Anthem. All done in the same key, with the same passion and most often standing on the same foot.

Finding my seat at last, I was overcome with a presentiment of 30 worse things to come. Something unrehearsed, unplanned, was going to happen, and we were going to be made to look bad. I distinctly remember being explicit in the choice of pronoun. It was "we," the graduating class, the unit, that concerned me then.

The principal welcomed "parents and friends" and asked the Bap- 31 tist minister to lead us in prayer. His invocation was brief and punchy, and for a second I thought we were getting back on the high road to right action. When the principal came back to the dais, however, his voice had changed. Sounds always affected me profoundly and the principal's voice was one of my favorites. During assembly it melted and lowed weakly into the audience. It had not been in my plan to listen to him, but my curiosity was piqued and I straightened up to give him my attention.

He was talking about Booker T. Washington, our "late great 32 leader," who said we can be as close as the fingers on the hand, etc. . . . Then he said a few vague things about friendship and the friendship of kindly people to those less fortunate than themselves. With that his voice nearly faded, thin, away. Like a river diminishing to a stream and then to a trickle. But he cleared his throat and said, "Our speaker tonight, who is also our friend, came from Texarkana to deliver the commencement address, but due to the irregularity of the train schedule, he's going to, as they say, 'speak and run.' " He said that we understood and wanted the man to know that we were most grateful for the time he was able to give us and then something about how we were willing always to adjust to another's program, and without more ado — "I give you Mr. Edward Donleavy."

Not one but two white men came through the door offstage. The 33 shorter one walked to the speaker's platform, and the tall one moved over to the center seat and sat down. But that was our principal's seat, and already occupied. The dislodged gentleman bounced around for a long breath or two before the Baptist minister gave him his chair, then with more dignity than the situation deserved, the minister walked off the stage.

Donleavy looked at the audience once (on reflection, I'm sure that 34 he wanted only to reassure himself that we were really there), adjusted his glasses, and began to read from a sheaf of papers.

He was glad "to be here and to see the work going on just as it was 35 in the other schools."

At the first "Amen" from the audience I willed the offender to im- 36 mediate death by choking on the word. But Amens and Yes, sir's began to fall around the room like rain through a ragged umbrella.

He told us of the wonderful changes we children in Stamps had in 37 store. The Central School (naturally, the white school was Central) had already been granted improvements that would be in use in the fall. A well-known artist was coming from Little Rock to teach art to them. They were going to have the newest microscopes and chemistry equipment for their laboratory. Mr. Donleavy didn't leave us long in the dark over who made these improvements available to Central High. Nor were we to be ignored in the general betterment scheme he had in mind.

He said that he had pointed out to people at a very high level that 38 one of the first-line football tacklers at Arkansas Agricultural and Mechanical College had graduated from good old Lafayette County Training School. Here fewer Amen's were heard. Those few that did break through lay dully in the air with the heaviness of habit.

He went on to praise us. He went on to say how he had bragged 39 that "one of the best basketball players at Fisk sank his first ball right here at Lafayette County Training School."

The white kids were going to have a chance to become Galileos 40 and Madame Curies and Edisons and Gauguins, and our boys (the girls weren't even in on it) would try to be Jesse Owenses and Joe Louises.

Owens and the Brown Bomber were great heroes in our world, but 41 what school official in the white-goddom of Little Rock had the right to decide that those two men must be our only heroes? Who decided that for Henry Reed to become a scientist he had to work like George Washington Carver, as a bootblack, to buy a lousy microscope? Bailey was obviously always going to be too small to be an athlete, so which concrete angel glued to what country seat had decided that if my brother wanted to become a lawyer he had to first pay penance for his skin by picking cotton and hoeing corn and studying correspondence books at night for twenty years?

The man's dead words fell like bricks around the auditorium and 42 too many settled in my belly. Constrained by hard-learned manners I couldn't look behind me, but to my left and right the proud graduating class of 1940 had dropped their heads. Every girl in my row had found something new to do with her handkerchief. Some folded the tiny squares into love knots, some into triangles, but most were wadding them, then pressing them flat on their yellow laps.

On the dais, the ancient tragedy was being replayed. Professor Par- 43 sons sat, a sculptor's reject, rigid. His large, heavy body seemed devoid of will or willingness, and his eyes said he was no longer with us. The other teachers examined the flag (which was draped stage right) or their notes, or the windows which opened on our now-famous playing diamond.

Graduation, the hush-hush magic time of frills and gifts and con- 44 gratulations and diplomas, was finished for me before my name was called. The accomplishment was nothing. The meticulous maps, drawn in three colors of ink, learning and spelling decasyllabic words, memorizing the whole of *The Rape of Lucrece*—it was nothing. Donleavy had exposed us.

We were maids and farmers, handymen and washerwomen, and 45 anything higher that we aspired to was farcical and presumptuous. Then I wished that Gabriel Prosser and Nat Turner had killed all whitefolks in their beds and that Abraham Lincoln had been assassinated before the signing of the Emancipation Proclamation, and that Harriet Tubman had been killed by that blow on her head and Christopher Columbus had drowned in the *Santa Maria*.

It was awful to be Negro and have no control over my life. It was 46 brutal to be young and already trained to sit quietly and listen to charges brought against my color with no chance of defense. We should all be dead. I thought I should like to see us all dead, one on top of the other. A pyramid of flesh with the whitefolks on the bottom, as the broad base, then the Indians with their silly tomahawks and teepees and wigwams and treaties, the Negroes with their mops and recipes and cotton sacks and spirituals sticking out of their mouths. The Dutch children should all stumble in their wooden shoes and break their necks. The French should choke to death on the Louisiana Purchase (1803) while silkworms ate all the Chinese with their stupid pigtails. As a species, we were an abomination. All of us.

Donleavy was running for election, and assured our parents that if 47 he won we could count on having the only colored paved playing field in that part of Arkansas. Also — he never looked up to acknowledge the grunts of acceptance — also, we were bound to get some new equipment for the home economics building and the workshop.

He finished, and since there was no need to give any more than the 48 most perfunctory thank-you's, he nodded to the men on the stage, and the tall white man who was never introduced joined him at the door. They left with the attitude that now they were off to something really important. (The graduation ceremonies at Lafayette County Training School had been a mere preliminary.)

The ugliness they left was palpable. An uninvited guest who 49 wouldn't leave. The choir was summoned and sang a modern arrangement of "Onward, Christian Soldiers," with new words pertaining to graduates seeking their place in the world. But it didn't work. Elouise, the daughter of the Baptist minister, recited "Invictus," and I could have cried at the impertinence of "I am the master of my fate, I am the captain of my soul."

My name had lost its ring of familiarity and I had to be nudged to 50 go and receive my diploma. All my preparations had fled. I neither marched up to the stage like a conquering Amazon, nor did I look in the audience for Bailey's nod of approval. Marguerite Johnson, I heard the name again, my honors were read, there were noises in the audience of appreciation, and I took my place on the stage as rehearsed.

I thought about colors I hated: ecru, puce, lavender, beige, and 51 black.

There was shuffling and rustling around me, then Henry Reed was 52 giving his valedictory address, "To Be or Not to Be." Hadn't he heard the whitefolks? We couldn't *be*, so the question was a waste of time. Henry's voice came out clear and strong. I feared to look at him. Hadn't he got the message? There was no "nobler in the mind" for Negroes because the world didn't think we had minds, and they let us know it. "Outrageous fortune"? Now, that was a joke. When the ceremony was over I had to tell Henry Reed some things. That is, if I still cared. Not "rub," Henry, "erase." "Ah, there's the erase." Us.

Henry had been a good student in elocution. His voice rose on tides 53 of promise and fell on waves of warnings. The English teacher had helped him to create a sermon winging through Hamlet's soliloquy. To be a man, a doer, a builder, a leader, or to be a tool, an unfunny joke, a crusher of funky toadstools. I marveled that Henry could go through with the speech as if we had a choice.

I had been listening and silently rebutting each sentence with my 54 eyes closed; then there was a hush, which in an audience warns that something unplanned is happening. I looked up and saw Henry Reed, the conservative, the proper, the A student, turn his back to the audience and turn to us (the proud graduating class of 1940) and sing, nearly speaking,

> Lift ev'ry voice and sing
> Till earth and heaven ring
> Ring with the harmonies of Liberty . . .

It was the poem written by James Weldon Johnson. It was the music composed by J. Rosamond Johnson. It was the Negro National Anthem. Out of habit we were singing it.

Our mothers and fathers stood in the dark hall and joined the 55 hymn of encouragement. A kindergarten teacher led the small children onto the stage and the buttercups and daisies and bunny rabbits marked time and tried to follow:

> Stony the road we trod
> Bitter the chastening rod
> Felt in the days when hope, unborn, had died.
> Yet with a steady beat
> Have not our weary feet
> Come to the place for which our fathers sighed?

Every child I knew had learned that song with his ABC's and along 56
with "Jesus Loves Me This I Know." But I personally had never heard
it before. Never heard the words, despite the thousands of times I had
sung them. Never thought they had anything to do with me.

On the other hand, the words of Patrick Henry had made such an 57
impression on me that I had been able to stretch myself tall and
trembling and say, "I know not what course others may take, but as
for me, give me liberty or give me death."

And now I heard, really for the first time: 58

> We have come over a way that with tears has been watered,
> We have come, treading our path through the blood of the
>   slaughtered.

While echoes of the song shivered in the air, Henry Reed bowed 59
his head, said "Thank you," and returned to his place in the line. The
tears that slipped down many faces were not wiped away in shame.

We were on top again. As always, again. We survived. The depths 60
had been icy and dark, but now a bright sun spoke to our souls. I was
no longer simply a member of the proud graduating class of 1940; I
was a proud member of the wonderful, beautiful Negro race.

Oh, Black known and unknown poets, how often have your auc- 61
tioned pains sustained us? Who will compute the lonely nights made
less lonely by your songs, or by the empty pots made less tragic by
your tales?

If we were a people much given to revealing secrets, we might raise 62
monuments and sacrifice to the memories of our poets, but slavery
cured us of that weakness. It may be enough, however, to have it said
that we survive in exact relationship to the dedication of our poets
(include preachers, musicians, and blues singers).

CONSIDERATIONS

1. What changes come over the student body as the time for graduation approaches? What phrases convey a special atmosphere? What changes
   come over Angelou in particular?
2. What details indicate the involvement of the entire black community in
   the student graduations? Does the selection seem to exaggerate the public

importance of the event, or is the account entirely believable? Does Angelou as an eighth grader appear too impressionable to be storing up accurate memories?

3. What details in the narrative contribute to the suspense and the worry that something might go wrong? What kind of a calamity are we led to anticipate?

4. How do you explain Angelou's immediate response to Donleavy's speech? Does it seem excessive?

5. In what sense is this graduation truly a "commencement" for Angelou? Make your answer detailed and explicit.

6. WRITING TOPIC. What roots in history and tradition affect your pride? Beyond your immediate family, the national, ethnic, and religious groups that comprise your background contribute personality models and stereotypes to your developing identity. In 700 words, explain the mixed positive and negative effects of a group identification that you experience. (Like Angelou, you may find that songs and other forms of entertainment, such as jokes, games, and stories, convey personal messages.)

John Cheever

EXPELLED

◊

JOHN CHEEVER (1912–1982) attended a prep school in Massachusetts and was expelled. The event launched his notable literary career, for he gave his view of the school in his first published story, the following selection, which was written when he was seventeen. During his adult life Cheever wrote television scripts and occasionally taught writing courses, but he devoted himself mainly to writing stories and novels, including such collections as *The Way Some People Live* (1943), *The Enormous Radio* (1953), and *The Housebreaker of Shady Hill* (1958). His best-known novels are *The Wapshot Chronicle* (1957) and *The Wapshot Scandal* (1964).

It didn't come all at once. It took a very long time. First I had a 1 skirmish with the English department and then all the other departments. Pretty soon something had to be done. The first signs were cordialities on the part of the headmaster. He was never nice to anybody unless he was a football star, or hadn't paid his tuition, or was going to be expelled. That's how I knew.

He called me down to his office with the carved chairs arranged in a 2 semicircle and the brocade curtains resting against the vacant windows. All about him were pictures of people who had got scholarships at Harvard. He asked me to sit down.

"Well, Charles," he said, "some of the teachers say you aren't get- 3 ting very good marks."

"Yes," I said, "that's true." I didn't care about the marks. 4

"But Charles," he said, "you know the scholastic standard of this 5 school is very high and we have to drop people when their work becomes unsatisfactory." I told him I knew that also. Then he said a lot of things about the traditions, and the elms, and the magnificent military heritage from our West Point founder.

It was very nice outside of his room. He had his window pushed 6
open halfway and one could see the lawns pulling down to the road
behind the trees and the bushes. The gravy-colored curtains were too
heavy to move about in the wind, but some papers shifted around on
his desk. In a little while I got up and walked out. He turned and
started to work again. I went back to my next class.

The next day was very brilliant and the peach branches were full 7
against the dry sky. I could hear people talking and a phonograph
playing. The sounds came through the peach blossoms and crossed
the room. I lay in bed and thought about a great many things. My
dreams had been thick. I remembered two converging hills, some dry
apple trees, and a broken blue egg cup. That is all I could remember.

I put on knickers and a soft sweater and headed toward school. My 8
hands shook on the wheel. I was like that all over.

Through the cloudy trees I could see the protrusion of the new 9
tower. It was going to be a beautiful new tower and it was going to
cost a great deal of money. Some thought of buying new books for the
library instead of putting up a tower, but no one would see the books.
People would be able to see the tower five miles off when the leaves
were off the trees. It would be done by fall.

When I went into the building the headmaster's secretary was 10
standing in the corridor. She was a nice sort of person with brown
funnels of hair furrowed about a round head. She smiled. I guess she
must have known.

The Colonel

Every morning we went up into the black chapel. The brisk head- 11
master was there. Sometimes he had a member of the faculty with
him. Sometimes it was a stranger.

He introduced the stranger, whose speech was always the same. In 12
the spring life is like a baseball game. In the fall it is like football. That
is what the speaker always said.

The hall is damp and ugly with skylights that rattle in the rain. The 13
seats are hard and you have to hold a hymnbook in your lap. The
hymnbook often slips off and that is embarrassing.

On Memorial Day they have the best speaker. They have a mayor 14

or a Governor. Sometimes they have a Governor's second. There is
very little preference.

The Governor will tell us what a magnificent country we have. He   15
will tell us to beware of the Red menace. He will want to tell us that
the goddam foreigners should have gone home a hell of a long time
ago. That they should have stayed in their own goddam countries if
they didn't like ours. He will not dare say this though.

If they have a mayor the speech will be longer. He will tell us that   16
our country is beautiful and young and strong. That the War is over,
but that if there is another war we must fight. He will tell us that war
is a masculine trait that has brought present civilization to its fine
condition. Then he will leave us and help stout women place lilacs on
graves. He will tell them the same thing.

One Memorial Day they could not get a Governor or a mayor.   17
There was a colonel in the same village who had been to war and who
had a chest thick with medals. They asked him to speak. Of course he
said he would like to speak.

He was a thin colonel with a soft nose that rested quietly on his   18
face. He was nervous and pushed his wedding ring about his thin finger. When he was introduced he looked at the audience sitting in the
uncomfortable chairs. There was silence and the dropping of hymn-
books like the water spouts in the aftermath of a heavy rain.

He spoke softly and quickly. He spoke of war and what he had   19
seen. Then he had to stop. He stopped and looked at the boys. They
were staring at their boots. He thought of the empty rooms in the
other buildings. He thought of the rectangles of empty desks. He
thought of the curtains on the stage and the four Windsor chairs behind him. Then he started to speak again.

He spoke as quickly as he could. He said war was bad. He said that   20
there would never be another war. That he himself should stop it if he
could. He swore. He looked at the young faces. They were all very
clean. The boys' knees were crossed and their soft pants hung loosely.
He thought of the empty desks and began to whimper.

The people sat very still. Some of them felt tight as though they   21
wanted to giggle. Everybody looked serious as the clock struck. It was
time for another class.

People began to talk about the colonel after lunch. They looked   22
behind them. They were afraid he might hear them.

It took the school several weeks to get over all this. Nobody said 23 anything, but the colonel was never asked again. If they could not get a Governor or a mayor they could get someone besides a colonel. They made sure of that.

Margaret Courtwright

Margaret Courtwright was very nice. She was slightly bald and 24 pulled her pressed hair down across her forehead. People said that she was the best English teacher in this part of the country, and when boys came back from Harvard they thanked her for the preparation she had given them. She did not like Edgar Guest, but she did like Carl Sandburg. She couldn't seem to understand the similarity. When I told her people laughed at Galsworthy she said that people used to laugh at Wordsworth. She did not believe people were still laughing at Wordsworth. That was what made her so nice.

She came from the West a long time ago. She taught school for so 25 long that people ceased to consider her age. After having seen twenty-seven performances of "Hamlet" and after having taught it for sixteen years, she became a sort of immortal. Her interpretation was the one accepted on college-board papers. That helped everyone a great deal. No one had to get a new interpretation.

When she asked me for tea I sat in a walnut armchair with grapes 26 carved on the head and traced and retraced the arms on the tea caddy. One time I read her one of my plays. She thought it was wonderful. She thought it was wonderful because she did not understand it and because it took two hours to read. When I had finished, she said, "You know that thing just took right hold of me. Really it just swept me right along. I think it's fine that you like to write. I once had a Japanese pupil who liked to write. He was an awfully nice chap until one summer he went down to Provincetown. When he came back he was saying that he could express a complete abstraction. Fancy . . . a complete abstraction. Well, I wouldn't hear of it and told him how absurd it all was and tried to start him off with Galsworthy again, but I guess he had gone just too far. In a little while he left for New York and then Paris. It was really too bad. One summer in Provincetown just ruined him. His marks fell down . . . he cut classes to go to symphony. . . ." She went into the kitchen and got a tray of tarts.

The pastries were flaky and covered with a white coating that made 27
them shine in the dead sunlight. I watched the red filling burst the
thin shells and stain the triangles of bright damask. The tarts were
good. I ate most of them.

She was afraid I would go the way of her Japanese pupil. She 28
doubted anyone who disagreed with Heine on Shakespeare and Croce
on expression.

One day she called me into her antiseptic office and spoke to me of 29
reading Joyce. "You know, Charles," she said, "this sex reality can be
quite as absurd as a hypercritical regard for such subjects. You know
that, don't you? Of course, you do." Then she went out of the room.
She had straight ankles and wore a gold band peppered with diamond
chips on her ring finger. She seemed incapable of carrying the weight
of the folds in her clothing. Her skirt was askew, either too long in
front or hitching up on the side. Always one thing or the other.

When I left school she did not like it. She was afraid I might go too 30
near Provincetown. She wished me good luck and moved the blotter
back and forth on her desk. Then she returned to teaching "Hamlet."

Late in February Laura Driscoll got fired for telling her history 31
pupils that Sacco and Vanzetti were innocent. In her farewell appearance the headmaster told everyone how sorry he was that she was
going and made it all quite convincing. Then Laura stood up, told
the headmaster that he was a damned liar, and waving her fan-spread
fingers called the school a hell of a dump where everyone got into
a rut.

Miss Courtwright sat closely in her chair and knew it was true. She 32
didn't mind much. Professor Rogers with his anti-feminization movement bothered her a little, too. But she knew that she had been
teaching school for a long time now and no movement was going to
put her out of a job overnight — what with all the boys she had
smuggled into Harvard and sixteen years of "Hamlet."

Laura Driscoll

History classes are always dead. This follows quite logically, for 33
history is a dead subject. It has not the death of dead fruit or dead
textiles or dead light. It has a different death. There is not the timeless
quality of death about it. It is dead like scenery in the opera. It is on

cracked canvas and the paint has faded and peeled and the lights are too bright. It is dead like old water in a zinc bathtub.

"We are going to study ancient history this year," the teacher will   34
tell the pupils. "Yes, ancient history will be our field.

"Now of course, this class is not a class of children any longer. I   35
expect the discipline to be the discipline of well bred young people. We shall not have to waste any time on the scolding of younger children. No. We shall just be able to spend all our time on ancient history.

"Now about questions. I shall answer questions if they are impor-   36
tant. If I do not think them important I shall not answer them, for the year is short, and we must cover a lot of ground in a short time. That is, if we all cooperate and behave and not ask too many questions we shall cover the subject and have enough time at the end of the year for review.

"You may be interested in the fact that a large percentage of this   37
class was certified last year. I should like to have a larger number this year. Just think, boys: wouldn't it be fine if a very large number — a number larger than last year — was certified? Wouldn't that be fine? Well, there's no reason why we can't do it if we all cooperate and behave and don't ask too many questions.

"You must remember that I have twelve people to worry about and   38
that you have only one. If each person will take care of his own work and pass in his notebook on time it will save me a lot of trouble. Time and trouble mean whether you get into college or not, and I want you all to get into college.

"If you will take care of your own little duties, doing what is as-   39
signed to you and doing it well, we shall all get along fine. You are a brilliant-looking group of young people, and I want to have you all certified. I want to get you into college with as little trouble as possible.

"Now about the books. . . ."   40

I do not know how long history classes have been like this. One   41
time or another I suppose history was alive. That was before it died its horrible fly-dappled unquivering death.

Everyone seems to know that history is dead. No one is alarmed.   42
The pupils and the teachers love dead history. They do not like it when it is alive. When Laura Driscoll dragged history into the class-

room, squirming and smelling of something bitter, they fired Laura and strangled the history. It was too tumultuous. Too turbulent.

In history one's intellect is used for mechanical speculation on a   43 probable century or background. One's memory is applied to a list of dead dates and names. When one begins to apply one's intellect to the mental scope of the period, to the emotional development of its inhabitants, one becomes dangerous. Laura Driscoll was terribly dangerous. That's why Laura was never a good history teacher.

She was not the first history teacher I had ever had. She is not the   44 last I will have. But she is the only teacher I have ever had who could feel history with an emotional vibrance — or, if the person was too oblique, with a poetic understanding. She was five feet four inches tall, brown-haired, and bent-legged from horseback riding. All the boys thought Laura Driscoll was a swell teacher.

She was the only history teacher I have ever seen who was often ec-   45 statical. She would stand by the boards and shout out her discoveries on the Egyptian cultures. She made the gargoylic churnings of Chartres in a heavy rain present an applicable meaning. She taught history as an interminable flood of events viewed through the distortion of our own immediacy. She taught history in the broad-handed rhythms of Hauptmann's drama, in the static melancholy of Egypt moving before its own shadow down the long sand, in the fluted symmetry of the Doric culture. She taught history as a hypothesis from which we could extract the evaluation of our own lives.

She was the only teacher who realized that, coming from the West,   46 she had little business to be teaching these children of New England.

"I do not know what your reaction to the sea is," she would say.   47 "For I have come from a land where there is no sea. My elements are the fields, the sun, the plastic cadence of the clouds and the cloudlessness. You have been brought up by the sea. You have been coached in the cadence of the breakers and the strength of the wind.

"My emotional viewpoints will differ from yours. Do not let me   48 impose my perceptions upon you."

However, the college-board people didn't care about Chartres as   49 long as you knew the date. They didn't care whether history was looked at from the mountains or the sea. Laura spent too much time on such trivia and all of her pupils didn't get into Harvard. In fact, very few of her pupils got into Harvard, and this didn't speak well for her.

While the other members of the faculty chattered over Hepple- 50
white legs and Duncan Phyfe embellishments, Laura was before five-handed Siva or the sexless compassion glorious in its faded polychrome. Laura didn't think much of America. Laura made this obvious and the faculty heard about it. The faculty all thought America was beautiful. They didn't like people to disagree.

However, the consummation did not occur until late in February. 51
It was cold and clear and the snow was deep. Outside the windows there was the enormous roaring of broken ice. It was late in February that Laura Driscoll said Sacco and Vanzetti were undeserving of their treatment.

This got everyone all up in the air. Even the headmaster was dis- 52
concerted.

The faculty met.   53

The parents wrote letters.   54

Laura Driscoll was fired.   55

"Miss Driscoll," said the headmaster during her last chapel at the 56
school, "has found it necessary to return to the West. In the few months that we have had her with us, she has been a staunch friend of the academy, a woman whom we all admire and love and who, we are sure, loves and admires the academy and its elms as we do. We are all sorry Miss Driscoll is leaving us. . . ."

Then Laura got up, called him a damned liar, swore down the 57
length of the platform and walked out of the building.

No one ever saw Laura Driscoll again. By the way everyone talked, 58
no one wanted to. That was all late in February. By March the school was quiet again. The new history teacher taught dates. Everyone carefully forgot about Laura Driscoll.

"She was a nice girl," said the headmaster, "but she really wasn't 59
made for teaching history. . . . No, she really wasn't a born history teacher."

Five Months Later

The spring of five months ago was the most beautiful spring I have 60
ever lived in. The year before I had not known all about the trees and

the heavy peach blossoms and the tea-colored brooks that shook down over the brown rocks. Five months ago it was spring and I was in school.

In school the white limbs beyond the study hall shook out a green- 61 ness, and the tennis courts became white and scalding. The air was empty and hard, and the vacant wind dragged shadows over the road. I knew all this only from the classrooms.

I knew about the trees from the window frames. I knew the rain 62 only from the sounds on the roof. I was tired of seeing spring with walls and awnings to intercept the sweet sun and the hard fruit. I wanted to go outdoors and see the spring. I wanted to feel and taste the air and be among the shadows. That is perhaps why I left school.

In the spring I was glad to leave school. Everything outside was 63 elegant and savage and fleshy. Everything inside was slow and cool and vacant. It seemed a shame to stay inside.

But in a little while the spring went. I was left outside and there 64 was no spring. I did not want to go in again. I would not have gone in again for anything. I was sorry, but I was not sorry over the fact that I had gone out. I was sorry that the outside and the inside could not have been open to one another. I was sorry that there were roofs on the classrooms and trousers on the legs of the instructors to insulate their contacts. I was not sorry that I had left school. I was sorry that I left for the reasons that I did.

If I had left because I had to go to work or because I was sick 65 it would not have been so bad. Leaving because you are angry and frustrated is different. It is not a good thing to do. It is bad for everyone.

Of course it was not the fault of the school. The headmaster and 66 faculty were doing what they were supposed to do. It was just a pre- paratory school trying to please the colleges. A school that was doing everything the colleges asked it to do.

It was not the fault of the school at all. It was the fault of the sys- 67 tem—the noneducational system, the college-preparatory system. That was what made the school so useless.

As a college-preparatory school it was a fine school. In five years 68 they could make raw material look like college material. They could clothe it and breed it and make it say the right things when the col- leges asked it to talk. That was its duty.

They weren't prepared to educate anybody. They were members of 69 a college-preparatory system. No one around there wanted to be educated. No sir.

They presented the subjects the colleges required. They had math, 70 English, history, languages, and music. They once had had an art department but it had been dropped. "We have enough to do," said the headmaster, "just to get all these people into college without trying to teach them art. Yes sir, we have quite enough to do as it is."

Of course there were literary appreciation and art appreciation and 71 musical appreciation, but they didn't count for much. If you are young, there is very little in Thackeray that is parallel to your own world. Van Dyke's "Abbé Scaglia" and the fretwork of Mozart quartets are not for the focus of your ears and eyes. All the literature and art that holds a similarity to your life is forgotten. Some of it is even forbidden.

Our country is the best country in the world. We are swimming in 72 prosperity and our President is the best president in the world. We have larger apples and better cotton and faster and more beautiful machines. This makes us the greatest country in the world. Unemployment is a myth. Dissatisfaction is a fable. In preparatory school America is beautiful. It is the gem of the ocean and it is too bad. It is bad because people believe it all. Because they become indifferent. Because they marry and reproduce and vote and they know nothing. Because the tempered newspaper keeps its eyes ceilingwards and does not see the dirty floor. Because all they know is the tempered newspaper.

But I will not say any more. I do not stand in a place where I can 73 talk.

And now it is August. The orchards are stinking ripe. The tea- 74 colored brooks run beneath the rocks. There is sediment on the stone and no wind in the willows. Everyone is preparing to go back to school. I have no school to go back to.

I am not sorry. I am not at all glad.   75

It is strange to be so very young and to have no place to report to at 76 nine o'clock. That is what education has always been. It has been laced curtseys and perfumed punctualities.

But now it is nothing. It is symmetric with my life. I am lost in it. 77 That is why I am not standing in a place where I can talk.

The school windows are being washed. The floors are thick with 78
fresh oil.

Soon it will be time for the snow and the symphonies. It will be 79
time for Brahms and the great dry winds.

CONSIDERATIONS

1. Describe Charles's manner of behaving and his manner of writing. Are they alike?
2. Why was the colonel an embarrassment to everyone, students and faculty, on Memorial Day? What did Charles think of him in contrast to the usual speakers?
3. In the sketch of the English teacher, what are some indications of her attitude toward ideas? What seems to be important to her?
4. Did Laura Driscoll teach *history*? What high school teacher of your own most closely resembles her in intellectual and moral attitudes? In professional status with other teachers and administrators?
5. Charles becomes fed up with school during "the most beautiful spring I have ever lived in." What bearing does nature have on his attitude and actions in school?
6. How does Charles feel five months later in midsummer? How does he foresee his future?
7. WRITING TOPIC. Does a school really do much to develop a student's identity? How? By imparting skills and knowledge? Ideas? Values? By aiding self-discipline? Social development? What is the most important thing that a school gives its students? In a 750-word essay, establish an order of importance for two or three things that a good school does for its students.

John Edgar Wideman

BLACK AND BLUES*

◊

JOHN EDGAR WIDEMAN (b. 1941) grew up in the poor, black section
of Pittsburgh, Pennsylvania. As a boy he heard a lot of popular music
that he carried around in his head "like contraband in my skull," he
said in an article in *The New York Times Book Review.* This music
helped him express his feelings, and eventually he found his way out of
the limited world of the ghetto. After graduating from the University
of Pennsylvania, Wideman won a Rhodes Scholarship to Oxford University. He returned to Penn to teach English and write fiction, and he
is now a professor at the University of Wyoming. His six novels include
the award-winning *I Sent for You Yesterday* (1983). Wideman's younger brother became trapped by ghetto troubles and eventually was sentenced to life imprisonment for murder. The shock of this family tragedy led Wideman to reestablish his ties to his brother and to examine
their contrasting destinies. The book, *Brothers and Keepers* (1984), includes the following episode in which Wideman recalls his college
freshman days when a white student challenged his knowledge of black
music.

My first year at college when I was living in the dorms a white boy 1
asked me if I liked the blues. Since I figured I *was* the blues I answered, Yeah, sure. We were in Darryl Dawson's room. Darryl and I
comprised approximately one-third of the total number of black males
in our class. About ten of the seventeen hundred men and women
who entered the University of Pennsylvania as freshmen in 1959 were
black. After a period of wariness and fencing, mutual embarrassment
and resisting the inevitable, I'd buddied up with Darryl, even though
he'd attended Putney Prep School in Vermont and spoke with an ac-
cent I considered phony. Since that fat white boy in work shirt, mo-

---

* Editor's title.

torcycle boots, and dirty jeans was in Darryl's room, I figured maybe the guy was alright in spite of the fact he asked dumb questions. I'd gotten used to answering or ignoring plenty of those in two months on campus. "Yeah, sure," should have closed the topic but the white boy wasn't finished. He said he had a big collection of blues records and that I ought to come by his room sometime with Darryl and dig, man.

Who do you like? Got everybody, man. Leadbelly, and Big Bill 2 Broonzy. Lightning and Lemon and Sonny Boy. You dig Broonzy? Just copped a new side of his.

None of the names meant a thing to me. Maybe I'd heard Lead- 3 belly at a party at a white girl's house in Shadyside but the other names were a mystery. What was this sloppy-looking white boy talking about? His blond hair, long and greasy, was combed back James Dean style. Skin pale and puffy like a Gerber baby. He wore a smart-ass, whole-lot-hipper-than-you expression on his face. His mouth is what did it. Pudgy, soft lips with just a hint of blond fuzz above them, pursed into a permanent sneer.

He stared at me, waiting for an answer. At home we didn't get in 4 other people's faces like that. You talked toward a space and the other person had a choice of entering or not entering, but this guy's blue eyes bored directly into mine. Waiting, challenging, prepared to send a message to that sneering mouth. I wanted no part of him, his records, or his questions.

Blues. Well, that's all I listen to. I like different songs at different 5 times. Midnighters. Drifters got one I like out now.

Not that R-and-B crap on the radio, man. Like the real blues. 6 Down home country blues. The old guys picking and singing.

Ray Charles. I like Ray Charles. 7

Hey, that ain't blues. Tell him, Darryl. 8

Darryl don't need to tell me anything. Been listening to blues all 9 my life. Ray Charles is great. He's the best there is. How you gon tell me what's good and not good? It's my music. I've been hearing it all my life.

You're still talking about rock 'n' roll. Rhythm and blues. Most of 10 it's junk. Here today and gone tomorrow crap. I'm talking about authentic blues. Big Bill Broonzy. The Classics.

When we talked, he twisted his mouth so the words slithered out 11 of one corner of his face, like garbage dumped off one end of a cafeteria tray. He pulled a cigarette from a pack in his shirt pocket. Lit it without disturbing the sneer.

Bet you've never even heard Bill Broonzy.   12

Don't need to hear no Broonzy or Toonsy or whoever the fuck he   13
is. I don't give a shit about him nor any of them other old-timey dudes you're talking about, man. I know what I like and you can call it rhythm and blues or rock 'n' roll, it's still the best music. It's what I like and don't need nobody telling me what's good.

What are you getting mad about, man? How can you put down   14
something you know nothing about? Bill Broonzy is the greatest twelve-string guitar player who ever lived. Everybody knows that. You've never heard a note he's played but you're setting yourself up as an expert. This is silly. You obviously can't back up what you're saying. You have a lot to learn about music, my friend.

He's wagging his big head and looking over at Darryl like Darryl's   15
supposed to back his action. You can imagine what's going through my mind. How many times I've already gone upside his fat jaw. Biff. Bam. My fists were burning. I could see blood running out both his nostrils. The sneer split at the seams, smeared all over his chin. Here's this white boy in this white world bad-mouthing me to one of the few black faces I get to see, messing with the little bit of understanding I'm beginning to have with Darryl. And worse, trespassing on the private turf of my music, the black sounds from home I carry round in my head as a saving grace against the pressures of the university.

Talk about uptight. I don't believe that pompous ass could have   16
known, because even I didn't know at that moment, how much he was hurting me. What hurt most was the truth of what he was saying. His whiteness, his arrogance made me mad, but it was truth putting the real hurt on me.

I didn't hit him. I should have but never did. A nice forget-me-knot   17
upside his jaw. I should have but didn't. Not that time. Not him. Smashing his mouth would have been too easy, so I hated him instead. Let anger and shame and humiliation fill me to overflowing so the hate is still there, today, over twenty years later. The dormitory room had pale green walls, a bare wooden floor, contained the skimpy desk and sagging cot allotted to each cubicle in the hall. Darryl's things scattered everywhere. A self-portrait he'd painted stared down from one dirt-speckled wall. The skin of the face in the portrait was

wildly mottled, violent bruises of color surrounding haunted jade eyes. Darryl's eyes were green like my brother David's, but I hadn't noticed their color until I dropped by his room one afternoon between classes and Darryl wasn't there and I didn't have anything better to do than sit and wait and study the eyes in his painting. Darryl's room had been a sanctuary but when the white boy started preaching there was no place to hide. Even before he spoke the room had begun to shrink. He sprawled, lounged, an exaggerated casualness announcing how comfortable he felt, how much he belonged, Lord of the manor wherever he happened to plant his boots.

Darryl cooled it. His green eyes didn't choose either of us when we 18 looked toward him for approval. Dawson had to see what a miserable corner I was in. He had to feel that room clamped tight around my neck and the sneer tugging the noose tighter.

A black motorcycle jacket, carved from a lump of coal, studded 19 with silver and rhinestones, was draped over the desk chair. I wanted to stomp it, chop it into little pieces.

Hey, you guys, knock it off. Let's talk about something else. Ob- 20 viously you have different tastes in music.

Darryl knew damn well that wasn't the problem. Together we 21 might have been able to say the right things. Put the white boy in his place. Recapture some breathing space. But Darryl had his own ghosts to battle. His longing for his blonde, blue-eyed Putney girl friend whose parents had rushed her off to Europe when they learned of her romance with the colored boy who was Putney school president. His ambivalence toward his blackness that would explode one day and hurtle him into the quixotic campaign of the Black Revolutionary Army to secede from the United States. So Darryl cooled it that afternoon in his room and the choked feeling never left my throat. I can feel it now as I write.

Why did that smartass white son of a bitch have so much power 22 over me? Why could he confuse me, turn me inside out, make me doubt myself? Waving just a tiny fragment of truth, he could back me into a corner. Who was I? What was I? Did I really fear the truth about myself that much? Four hundred years of oppression, of lies had empowered him to use the music of my people as a weapon against me. Twenty years ago I hadn't begun to comprehend the larger forces, the ironies, the obscenities that permitted such a reversal to occur. All I had sensed was his power, the raw, crude force mocking me, diminishing me. I should have smacked him. I should have affirmed another piece of the truth he knew about me, the nigger violence. . . .

Coming home from the university, from people and situations that 23 continually set me against them and against myself, I was a dangerous person. If I wanted to stay in one piece and stay in school, I was forced to pull my punches. To maintain any semblance of dignity and confidence I had to learn to construct a shell around myself. Be cool. Work on appearing dignified, confident. Fool people with appearances, surfaces, live my real life underground in a region where no one could touch me. The trouble with this survival mechanism was the time and energy expended on upkeep of the shell. The brighter, harder, more convincing and impenetrable the shell became, the more I lost touch with the inner sanctuary where I was supposed to be hiding. It was no more accessible to me than it was to the people I intended to keep out. Inside was a breeding ground for rage, hate, dreams of vengeance.

Nothing original in my tactics. I'd adopted the strategy of slaves, 24 the oppressed, the powerless. I thought I was running but I was fashioning a cage. Working hand in hand with my enemies. Knowledge of my racial past, of the worldwide struggle of people of color against the domination of Europeans would have been invaluable. History could have been a tool, a support in the day-to-day confrontations I experienced in the alien university environment. History could have taught me I was not alone, my situation was not unique. Believing I was alone made me dangerous, to myself and others.

College was a time of precipitous ups and downs. I was losing con- 25 tact with the truth of my own feelings. Not trusting, not confiding in anyone else, learning to mistrust and deny my own responses left me no solid ground, nowhere to turn. I was an expert at going with the flow, protecting myself by taking on the emotional or intellectual coloring of whatever circumstance I found myself in. All of this would have been bad enough if I'd simply been camouflaging my feelings. Yet it was far worse. I had no feelings apart from the series of roles and masquerades I found myself playing. And my greatest concern at the time had nothing to do with reestablishing an authentic core. What I feared most and spent most of my energy avoiding, was being unmasked.

CONSIDERATIONS

1. Clarify the meaning of young Wideman's first, silent response, "I *was* the blues." Do you think that he had a valid claim to his assumption?
2. How do the differences in economic and social status of the three boys confuse the situation in Darryl's room? Does any of them respond mainly to the social differences, or do all three boys respond mainly to the racial differences?
3. Wideman does not use quotation marks to punctuate the remembered conversations in this incident. Does it make it harder to follow the dialogue? What is the purpose of omitting the quotation marks?
4. In paragraph 14 the other student asks Wideman, "What are you getting mad about, man?" What are the signs of Wideman's rising anger, and what *is* he mad about?
5. Wideman says that in college he became "an expert at going with the flow, protecting myself by taking on the emotional or intellectual coloring of whatever circumstance I found myself in." Why didn't his expertise at this strategy protect him?
6. WRITING TOPIC. How does knowledge about your family origins or family history affect your image of yourself and your relations with people? For example, how do you feel about the circumstances in which your ancestors first came to America? Or, what personal traits do you link to your national or cultural heritage? In 700 words, examine one specific fact or supposition about your family and cultural background that has a bearing on how you think about yourself. Explain how you came to know this particular bit of history and how the knowledge became relevant to your own life.

Maxine Hong Kingston

THE MISERY OF SILENCE*

◊

MAXINE HONG KINGSTON (b. 1940) grew up in a Chinese immigrant community in Stockton, California, where her parents ran a laundry. As a first-generation American, Kingston had to learn how to live in two distinctly contrasting societies. This was confusing and difficult for a five- to seven-year-old child, as she recalls in this selection from her autobiography, *The Woman Warrior: Memoirs of a Girlhood among Ghosts* (1976). The immigrants regarded all non-Chinese as "ghosts" — pale, insubstantial, and threatening. Kingston was graduated from the University of California at Berkeley. She now lives in Hawaii and teaches writing at the University of Hawaii. Her latest book is *China Men* (1980).

When I went to kindergarten and had to speak English for the first 1 time, I became silent. A dumbness — a shame — still cracks my voice in two, even when I want to say "hello" casually, or ask an easy question in front of the check-out counter, or ask directions of a bus driver. I stand frozen, or I hold up the line with the complete, grammatical sentence that comes squeaking out at impossible length. "What did you say?" says the cab driver, or "Speak up," so I have to perform again, only weaker the second time. A telephone call makes my throat bleed and takes up that day's courage. It spoils my day with self-disgust when I hear my broken voice come skittering out into the open. It makes people wince to hear it. I'm getting better, though. Recently I asked the postman for special-issue stamps; I've waited since childhood for postmen to give me some of their own accord. I am making progress, a little every day.

* Editor' title.

My silence was thickest — total — during the three years that I 2
covered my school paintings with black paint. I painted layers of black
over houses and flowers and suns, and when I drew on the blackboard,
I put a layer of chalk on top. I was making a stage curtain, and it was
the moment before the curtain parted or rose. The teachers called my
parents to school, and I saw they had been saving my pictures, curling
and cracking, all alike and black. The teachers pointed to the pictures
and looked serious, talked seriously too, but my parents did not understand English. ("The parents and teachers of criminals were exe-
cuted," said my father.) My parents took the pictures home. I spread
them out (so black and full of possibilities) and pretended the curtains
were swinging open, flying up, one after another, sunlight underneath,
mighty operas.

During the first silent year I spoke to no one at school, did not ask 3
before going to the lavatory, and flunked kindergarten. My sister also
said nothing for three years, silent in the playground and silent at
lunch. There were other quiet Chinese girls not of our family, but
most of them got over it sooner than we did. I enjoyed the silence. At
first it did not occur to me I was supposed to talk or to pass kindergarten. I talked at home and to one or two of the Chinese kids in class. I
made motions and even made some jokes. I drank out of a toy saucer
when the water spilled out of the cup, and everybody laughed, pointing at me, so I did it some more. I didn't know that Americans don't
drink out of saucers.

I liked the Negro students (Black Ghosts) best because they 4
laughed the loudest and talked to me as if I were a daring talker too.
One of the Negro girls had her mother coil braids over her ears Shang-
hai-style like mine; we were Shanghai twins except that she was covered with black like my paintings. Two Negro kids enrolled in Chinese school, and the teachers gave them Chinese names. Some Negro
kids walked me to school and home, protecting me from the Japanese
kids, who hit me and chased me and stuck gum in my ears. The Japanese kids were noisy and tough. They appeared one day in kindergarten, released from concentration camp, which was a tic-tac-toe mark,
like barbed wire, on the map.

It was when I found out I had to talk that school became a misery, 5
that the silence became a misery. I did not speak and felt bad each
time that I did not speak. I read aloud in first grade, though, and
heard the barest whisper with little squeaks come out of my throat.

"Louder," said the teacher, who scared the voice away again. The other Chinese girls did not talk either, so I knew the silence had to do with being a Chinese girl.

Reading out loud was easier than speaking because we did not have   6
to make up what to say, but I stopped often, and the teacher would think I'd gone quiet again. I could not understand "I." The Chinese "I" has seven strokes, intricacies. How could the American "I," assuredly wearing a hat like the Chinese, have only three strokes, the middle so straight? Was it out of politeness that this writer left off strokes the way a Chinese has to write her own name small and crooked? No, it was not politeness; "I" is a capital and "you" is lower-case. I stared at that middle line and waited so long for its black center to resolve into tight strokes and dots that I forgot to pronounce it. The other troublesome word was "here," no strong consonant to hang on to, and so flat, when "here" is two mountainous ideographs. The teacher, who had already told me every day how to read "I" and "here," put me in the low corner under the stairs again, where the noisy boys usually sat.

When my second grade class did a play, the whole class went to the   7
auditorium except the Chinese girls. The teacher, lovely and Hawaiian, should have understood about us, but instead left us behind in the classroom. Our voices were too soft or nonexistent, and our parents never signed the permission slips anyway. They never signed anything unnecessary. We opened the door a crack and peeked out, but closed it again quickly. One of us (not me) won every spelling bee, though.

I remember telling the Hawaiian teacher, "We Chinese can't sing   8
'land where our fathers died.' " She argued with me about politics, while I meant because of curses. But how can I have that memory when I couldn't talk? My mother says that we, like the ghosts, have no memories.

After American school, we picked up our cigar boxes, in which we   9
had arranged books, brushes, and an inkbox neatly, and went to Chinese school, from 5:00 to 7:30 P.M. There we chanted together, voices rising and falling, loud and soft, some boys shouting, everybody reading together, reciting together and not alone with one voice. When we had a memorization test, the teacher let each of us come to his desk and say the lesson to him privately, while the rest of the class practiced copying or tracing. Most of the teachers were men. The boys

who were so well behaved in the American school played tricks on them and talked back to them. The girls were not mute. They screamed and yelled during recess, when there were no rules; they had fistfights. Nobody was afraid of children hurting themselves or of children hurting school property. The glass doors to the red and green balconies with the gold joy symbols were left wide open so that we could run out and climb the fire escapes. We played capture-the-flag in the auditorium, where Sun Yat-sen and Chiang Kai-shek's pictures hung at the back of the stage, the Chinese flag on their left and the American flag on their right. We climbed the teak ceremonial chairs and made flying leaps off the stage. One flag headquarters was behind the glass door and the other on stage right. Our feet drummed on the hollow stage. During recess the teachers locked themselves up in their office with the shelves of books, copybooks, inks from China. They drank tea and warmed their hands at a stove. There was no play supervision. At recess we had the school to ourselves, and also we could roam as far as we could go — downtown, Chinatown stores, home — as long as we returned before the bell rang.

At exactly 7:30 the teacher again picked up the brass bell that sat 10 on his desk and swung it over our heads, while we charged down the stairs, our cheering magnified in the stairwell. Nobody had to line up.

Not all of the children who were silent at American school found 11 voice at Chinese school. One new teacher said each of us had to get up and recite in front of the class, who was to listen. My sister and I had memorized the lesson perfectly. We said it to each other at home, one chanting, one listening. The teacher called on my sister to recite first. It was the first time a teacher had called on the second-born to go first. My sister was scared. She glanced at me and looked away; I looked down at my desk. I hoped that she could do it because if she could, then I would have to. She opened her mouth and a voice came out that wasn't a whisper, but it wasn't a proper voice either. I hoped that she would not cry, fear breaking up her voice like twigs underfoot. She sounded as if she were trying to sing though weeping and strangling. She did not pause or stop to end the embarrassment. She kept going until she said the last word, and then she sat down. When it was my turn, the same voice came out, a crippled animal running on broken legs. You could hear splinters in my voice, bones rubbing jagged against one another. I was loud, though. I was glad I didn't whisper.

How strange that the emigrant villagers are shouters, hollering face 12
to face. My father asks, "Why is it I can hear Chinese from blocks
away? Is it that I understand the language? Or is it they talk loud?"
They turn the radio up full blast to hear the operas, which do not
seem to hurt their ears. And they yell over the singers that wail over
the drums, everybody talking at once, big arm gestures, spit flying.
You can see the disgust on American faces looking at women like
that. It isn't just the loudness. It is the way Chinese sounds, ching-
chong ugly, to American ears, not beautiful like Japanese sayonara
words with the consonants and vowels as regular as Italian. We make
guttural peasant noise and have Ton Duc Thang names you can't remember. And the Chinese can't hear Americans at all; the language is
too soft and western music unhearable. I've watched a Chinese audience laugh, visit, talk-story, and holler during a piano recital, as if the
musician could not hear them. A Chinese-American, somebody's son,
was playing Chopin, which has no punctuation, no cymbals, no
gongs. Chinese piano music is five black keys. Normal Chinese
women's voices are strong and bossy. We American-Chinese girls had
to whisper to make ourselves American-feminine. Apparently we whispered even more softly than the Americans. Once a year the teachers
referred my sister and me to speech therapy, but our voices would
straighten out, unpredictably normal, for the therapists. Some of us
gave up, shook our heads, and said nothing, not one word. Some of us
could not even shake our heads. At times shaking my head no is more
self-assertion than I can manage. Most of us eventually found some
voice, however faltering. We invented an American-feminine speaking personality.

CONSIDERATIONS

1. What was the connection between Kingston's silence and her paintings?
   What did the paintings signify to *her*?
2. Why did the English pronouns "I" and "you" strike Kingston as unnatural? How do they differ from their Chinese equivalents? What looks
   wrong about the word "here"?
3. Kingston was obviously a "problem student" in class. If you had been her
   teacher, what might you have done? How might the problem have been
   handled by a teacher like Edward Martin? (See "Being Junior High,"
   p. 228.)

4. Does this account reinforce a stereotype of the Oriental woman? What does Kingston suggest that Chinese women are like when they are among Chinese?

5. In one paragraph, describe the "speaking personality" of a friend or relative. Try to give your reader a direct impression of the voice and manner of the speaker.

6. WRITING TOPIC. At the beginning of this selection, Kingston says that even today she has trouble speaking up in public situations. Does her style of writing indicate any hesitation or absence of assertiveness in using English for writing to the public? Is her language easy or hard to read? What is the tone of her voice? Write 500 words on Kingston's style in relation to her childhood experience.

Paul Fussell

"SPEAK,
THAT I MAY SEE THEE"

◇

PAUL FUSSELL (b. 1924) was born in Pasadena, California, to a very wealthy, upper-class family. After serving as a combat officer in World War II, he earned a B.A. from Pomona College in 1947 and a Ph.D. from Harvard University. Now a professor of English at the University of Pennsylvania, Fussell taught at Rutgers University for many years. Publishing several notable scholarly books, Fussell turned to subjects of broader interest and more popular appeal. He won several awards for his first new venture, *The Great War and Modern Memory* (1975), a book about World War I and its effect on literature. His other recent work includes *Abroad: British Literary Traveling Between the Wars* (1980). Fussell dealt with the topic of social classes in America in an amusing essay that appeared first in *The New Republic* and which he expanded into *Class: A Guide Through the American Status System* (1983). The book includes chapters on many indicators of status, such as clothing, housing, traveling, shopping, and language, from which the following selection was excerpted.

Regardless of the money you've inherited, the danger of your job, 1 the place you live, the way you look, the shape and surface of your driveway, the items on your front porch and in your living room, the sweetness of your drinks, the time you eat dinner, the stuff you buy from mail-order catalogs, the place you went to school and your reverence for it, and the materials you read, your social class is still most clearly visible when you say things. "One's speech is an unceasingly repeated public announcement about background and social standing," says John Brooks, translating into modern American Ben Jonson's observation "Language most shows a man. Speak, that I may see thee." And what held true in his seventeenth century holds even truer in our twentieth, because we now have something virtually unknown to Jonson, a sizable middle class desperate not to offend through language and thus addicted to such conspicuous class giveaways as euphemism, genteelism, and mock profanity ("Golly!").

But at the outset it's well to recognize the difficulty of talking accu- 2 rately about the class significance of language. It's easy to get it wrong when talking about classes, or traditions, not one's own, the way the Englishman H. B. Brooks-Baker recently got American class usage quite wrong when he offered an "American Section" of upper- and lower-class terms in Richard Buckle's *U and Non-U Revisited* (1978). Mastery of this field takes years, and it's admittedly hard to hear accurately across the Atlantic. Still, Brooks-Baker's list of twenty-six expressions said to be avoided by upper Americans errs dramatically. For example, he tells us that *affair* is a non-upper word for *party*. But any American of any of the classes knows that the two are different things entirely, not different names for the same thing. An *affair* is a laid-on commercial catering event like a bad banquet or reception. Unlike a *party*, you don't go to an *affair* (unless it's a love affair) expecting to have a wildly good time. Again, Brooks-Baker informs the reader that *folding-stuff* is prole for *money*. No, it's simply archaic slang, as much heard today as *mazuma* or *greenbacks*. Brooks-Baker also says that in the U.S.A. proles say *tux*, uppers *tuxedo*. Wrong again. Proles say *tux*, middles *tuxedo*, but both are considered low by uppers, who say *dinner jacket* or (higher) *black tie*. But even getting our hero decently home from his *tuxedo affair* (i.e., *black-tie party*), Brooks-Baker slips up. Proles say *limo*, he asserts, uppers *limousine*. Wrong on both counts. Proles say *big black shiny Cad*, (sometimes *Caddy*). Middles say *limousine*, and the thing would be called a *limo* only behind the scenes by those who supply rented ones for funerals, bar mitzvahs, and the like. What, then, is this vehicle called by the upper orders? It's called a *car*, as in "We'll need the car about eleven, please, Parker."

Brooks-Baker's slips are useful reminders of the hazards of inter- 3 preting language class signals aright. Alexis de Tocqueville's* errors in prophecy also provide a handy warning against overconfidence there. De Tocqueville overestimated the leveling force on language of "de-

* For information about Tocqueville, turn to p. 307 for the headnote to a selection by him.

mocracy," and imagined that this new kind of political organization would largely efface social distinctions in language and verbal style. Looking about him at mid-nineteenth-century America, he thought he heard everyone using the same words, and conceived that the line was ceasing to be drawn "between . . . expressions which seem by their very nature vulgar and others which appear to be refined." He concluded that "there is as much confusion in language as there is in society." But developments on this continent have proved him wrong about both language and democratic society. Actually, just *because* the country's a democracy, class distinctions have developed with greater rigor than elsewhere, and language, far from coalescing into one great central mass without social distinctions, has developed even more egregious class signals than anyone could have expected. There's really no confusion in either language or society, as ordinary people here are quite aware. Interviewed by sociologists, they indicate that speech is the main way they estimate a stranger's social class when they first encounter him. "Really," says one deponent, "the first time a person opens his mouth, you can tell."

Because the class system here is more complicated than in 4 England, less amenable to merely binary categorization, language indicators are more numerous and subtle than merely those accepted as "U" (i.e., upper) or stigmatized as "non-U" by Nancy Mitford in her delightful 1955 essay in *Encounter*, "The English Aristocracy." Still, a way to begin considering the class meaning of language in the U.S.A. is to note some absolute class dividers. Probably the most important, a usage firmly dividing the prole classes from the middles and highers, is the double negative, as in "I can't get no satisfaction." You're as unlikely to hear something like that in a boardroom or premises frequented by "houseguests," or on a sixty-five-foot schooner off Nantucket, as you are likely to hear it in a barracks, an auto-repair shop, or a workmen's bar. Next in importance would rank special ways of managing grammatical number, as in "He don't" and "I wants it." And these are not just "slips" or "errors." They signal virtually a different dialect, identifying speakers socially distinct from users of the other English. The two can respect each other, but they can never be pals. They belong to different classes, and if they attempt to mix, they will inevitably regard each other as quaint and not quite human.

If it's grammar that draws the line between middles and below, it's 5 largely pronunciation and vocabulary that draw it between middles and above. Everyone will have his personal collection of class indicators here, but I have found the following quite trustworthy. Words employed to register (or advertise) "cultural experience" are especially dangerous for the middle class, even *crêpes*, which they pronounce *craypes*. The same with most words deployed to display one's familiarity with the foreign, like *fiancé*, which the middle class prefers to *boyfriend* and delivers with a ridiculous heavy stress on the final syllable: *fee-on-say'*. The same with *show-fur'*, a word it prefers to the upperclass *driver*. Some may think pronouncing the *h* in *Amherst* an excessively finicking indicator of middle-classhood, but others may not. The word *diamond*, pronounced as two syllables by uppers, is likely to be rendered as three by the middle class. Similarly with *beautiful* — three syllables to uppers, but, to middles, *bee-you'-tee-full*. The "grand" words *exquisite, despicable, hospitable, lamentable* invite the middle class to stress the second syllable; those anxious to leave no doubt of their social desirability stress the first, which is also to earn some slight, passing Anglophilic credit. As the middle class gets itself more deeply entangled in artistic experience, hazards multiply, like *patina*, a word it likes a lot but doesn't realize is stressed on the first syllable. High-class names from cultural history pose a similar danger, especially if they are British, like Henry Purcell. President Reagan's adviser Edwin Meese III clearly signaled his class when, interviewed on television, he chose to exhibit his gentility by using the word *salutary* instead of the common *wholesome* or *healthy*, but indicated by his pronunciation that he thought the word *salutory*. That's the pure middle-class act: opt for the showy, and in so doing take a pratfall. Class unfortunates who want to emphasize the largeness of something are frequently betrayed by *enormity*, as in "The whale was of such an enormity that they could hardly get it in the tank." (Prole version: "The whale was so big they couldn't hardly get it in the tank.") Elegance is the fatal temptation for the middle class, dividing it from the blunter usages of uppers and proles alike. Neither of these classes would warn against two people's simultaneously pursuing the same project by speaking of "duplicity of effort." The middle class is where you hear *prestigious* a lot, and to speculate about the reason it's replaced *distinguished* or *noted* or *respected* in the past twenty years is to do a bit of national soul-searching. The implications of *prestige*, C. Wright Mills observes, are really pejorative: "In its origins," he says, "it means dazzling the eye with conjuring tricks." And he goes on: "In

France, 'prestige' carries an emotional association of fraudulence, of the art of illusion, or at least of something adventitious." The same in Italy and Germany. Only in the U.S.A. does the word carry any prestige. . . .

Some of these class dividers are crude. Others are subtle. The 6 upper and upper-middle classes have a special vocabulary for indicating wearisome or unhappy social situations. They say *tiresome* or *tedious* where their social inferiors would say *boring;* they say *upset* or *distressed* or even *cross* where others would say *angry* or *mad* or *sore.* There's a special upper-class diction of approval too. No prole man would call something *super* (Anglophilic) or *outstanding* (prep school), just as it would sound like flagrant affectation for a prole woman to designate something seen in a store as *divine* or *darling* or *adorable. Nice* would be the non-upper way of putting it.

But it's the middle-class quest for grandeur and gentility that pro- 7 duces the most interesting effects. As we've seen, imported words especially are its downfall. It will speak of a *graffiti* and it thinks *chauvinism* has something to do with gender aggression. Pseudo-classical plurals are a constant pitfall: the middles will speak learnedly of *a phenomena* and *a criteria* and *a strata* and (referring perhaps to a newspaper) *a media.* A well-known author is *a literati.* It thinks *context* a grandeur form of the word *content,* and thus says things like "I didn't like the context of that book: all that blood and gore." Or consider the Coast Guard officer reporting a grievous oil spill in San Francisco Bay: *cross* is too vulgar a term for the occasion, he imagines, and so he says that "several ships transited the area." When after a succession of solecisms of this kind a middle-class person will begin to suspect that he is blowing his cover, he may try to reestablish status by appliquéing a mock-classical plural ending onto a perfectly ordinary word like *process.* Then he will say *process-sees.* The whole middle-class performance nicely illustrates the conclusion of Lord Melbourne. "The higher and lower classes, there's some good in them," he observed, "but the middle classes are all affectation and conceit and pretense and concealment."

All classes except sometimes upper-middle are implicated in the 8 scandal of saying *home* when they mean *house.* But the middle class seems to take a special pleasure in saying things like "They live in a lovely five-hundred-thousand-dollar home," or, after an earthquake, "The man noticed that his home was shaking violently." We can trace, I think, the stages by which *house* disappeared as a word favored by the middle class. First, *home* was offered by the real-estate business as a way of warming the product, that is, making the prospect imagine that in laying out money for a house he was purchasing not a passel of bricks, Formica, and wallboard but snuggly warmth, comfort, and love. The word *home* was then fervently embraced by the customers for several reasons: (1) the middle class loves to use words which have achieved cliché status in advertising; (2) the middle class, like the real-estate con men, also enjoys the comforting fantasy that you can purchase love, comfort, warmth, etc., with cold cash, or at least achieve them by some formula or other; (3) the middle class, by nature both puritanical and terrified of public opinion, welcomed *home* because, to its dirty mind, *house* carried bad associations. One spoke of a *rest home*, but of a *bawdy, whore-, fancy,* or *sporting house*. No one ever heard of a *home of ill fame*, or, for that matter, a *cat home*. So out went *house* for the same reason that *madam* has never really caught on in middle-class America. But curiously, users of *home* to describe domestic shelters make one exception. A *beach house* is so called, never a *beach home*. Because of the word's association with current real-estate scams, a *home*, or something appropriately so designated, does tend to suggest something pretty specific: namely, a small, pretentious, jerry-built developer's rip-off positioned in some unfortunate part of the country without history, depth, or allusiveness. You don't speak of a "two-hundred-year-old white clapboard frame farmhome" in Maine, New Hampshire, or Vermont. *Homes* are what the middle class live in. As it grows progressively poorer, it sells its *homes* and moves into *mobile homes* (formerly, trailers) or *motor homes*.

. . . Because of its need for the illusion of power and success that attend self-conscious consumerism, the middles instinctively adopt advertisers' *-wear* compounds, speaking with no embarrassment whatever of the family's 9

> footwear
> nightwear (or sleepwear)
> leisurewear
> stormwear
> beachwear
> swimwear

citywear
countrywear
campuswear
formal wear
eyewear (i.e., spectacles)
neckwear, etc.,

and they feel good uttering the analogous-*ware* compounds:

tableware
dinnerware
stemware
barware
flatware
kitchenware
glassware

or sometimes, when they get into their grand mood, *crystal.* (Uppers, whom the middles think they're imitating, say *glasses.*) Because it's a staple of advertising, the middle class also likes the word *designer*, which it takes to mean *beautiful* or *valuable.* Thus roll paper towels with expensive patterns printed on them cease to be stupid and ugly once they're designated *designer towels.* The Dacron bath towels of the middle class, the ones with the metallic threads, are also usually called *designer towels.*

Advertising diction feeds so smoothly into the middle-class psyche 10 because of that class's bent toward rhetorical fake elegance. Aspiring to ascend, it imagines that verbal grandeur will forward the process. . . .

So terrified of being judged socially insignificant is your typical member of the middle class, so ambitious of earning a reputation as a judicious thinker, indeed, almost an "executive," that it's virtually impossible for him to resist the temptation constantly to multiply syllables. He thus euphemizes willy-nilly. Indeed, it's sometimes hard to know whether the impulse to euphemize is causing the syllables to multiply, or whether the urge toward verbal weight and grandeur through multiplication is hustling the speaker into euphemism. The question confronts us when, inquiring what someone does, he answers not that he's a junk man, or even in the junk business, but in the scrap-iron business, or even the recycling business or reclamation industry. Occupational euphemisms always seem to entail multiplication of syllables. In many universities, what used to be the *bursar* is now the *disbursement officer*, just the way what used to be an *undertaker* (already sufficient as a euphemism, one would think) is now a *funeral director*, an advance of two whole syllables. (In raising *funeral director* to *grief therapist*, there's of course a loss of two syllables, but a compensating gain in "professionalism" and pseudo-medical pretentiousness.) *Selling* is raised to *retailing* or *marketing*, or even better, to *merchandising*, an act that exactly doubles its syllables, while *sales manager* in its turn is doubled by being raised to *Vice-President, Merchandising*. The person on the telephone who used to provide *Information* now gives (or more often, does not give) *Directory Assistance*, which is two syllables grander. Some sociologists surveying the status of occupations found that *druggist* ranked sixth out of fifteen. But when a syllable was added and the designation changed to *pharmacist*, the occupation moved up to fourth place.

Syllable multiplication usually occurs also in the euphemisms by 11 which the middle class softens hard facts or cheerfulizes actuality. It's all in aid of avoiding anything "depressing." But you can aim for the verbally splendid at the same time. Thus *correctional facility* for *prison*, *work stoppage* or *industrial action* for *strike*, *discomfort* for *pain*, *homicide* for *murder*, *self-deliverance* for *suicide*, *fatality* for *death*. *Slum clearance* (three syllables) becomes *urban renewal* (five). *Nuclear device* has it over *atom bomb* both by a lot of euphemism and by two full syllables. Being by nature unmagnanimous (cf. Ronald Reagan), the middle class has always hated to tip, regarding it as a swindle, etc., but when you call a *tip* a *gratuity*, you take a little of the sting out. . . .

A very little attention to the different idioms of the classes should 12 persuade the most sentimental not only that there is a tight system of social class in this country but that linguistic class lines are crossed only rarely and with great difficulty. A virtually bottomless social gulf opens between those who say "Have a nice day" and those who say, "Goodbye," those who when introduced say, "Pleased to meet you" and those who say "How do you do?" There may be some passing intimacy between those who think *momentarily* means *in a moment* (airline captain over loudspeaker: "We'll be taking off momentarily folks") and those who know it means *for a moment*, but it won't survive much strain. It's like the tenuous relation between people who conceive that *type* is an adjective ("She's a very classy type person") and people who know it's only a noun or verb. The sad thing is that by the time one's an adult, these stigmata are virtually unalterable and ineffaceable. We're pretty well stuck for life in the class we're raised in. Even adopting all the suggestions implied in this chapter, embracing all the high-class locutions and abjuring the low ones, won't help much.

CONSIDERATIONS

1. In the first three paragraphs how does the author persuade us that ordinary Americans really are very concerned about language? Are Fussell's arguments surprising? Ingenious? Funny? Convincing?
2. What is the main difference between lower- and middle-class language? What are the main differences between middle- and upper-class language?
3. According to Fussell how does advertising affect middle-class language?
4. What attitudes and motives does Fussell identify in middle-class speech? Do you agree with him? Do you think that some of his examples can suggest other outlooks?
5. What is the author's tone toward the middle class? Does it serve the purpose of his essay?
6. In the final paragraph Fussell claims that the evidence "should persuade the most sentimental. . . ." What are we being "sentimental" about, in his eyes, if we find his conclusions hard to accept?
7. WRITING TOPIC. Young people in school often devise special ways of talking with members of their clique or set. Their special language identifies them as a separate group, and often such language seems to give individuals a certain flair that distinguishes them. Writing as an observer or as a member of such a group, analyze its special language in a 700-word essay. Give samples of the vocabulary and explain the usages and describe the inflections or intonations of three or four key words. Try to illustrate your points with bits of dialogue, if useful.

Gloria Steinem

THE TIME FACTOR

◊

GLORIA STEINEM (b. 1934) is the editor of *Ms.* magazine, which she helped found in 1972. As a leading feminist journalist, she is active in publicizing the women's movement. Born in Toledo, Ohio, she graduated from Smith College and received a fellowship to study in India. In her early career as a fashionable freelance writer in New York City, she first gained national attention in 1963 with her undercover exposé "I Was a Playboy Bunny," which recounted the indignities of the job with a mixture of humor and scorn. She joined the women's movement in 1969 as a writer, speaker, and political activist working to increase women's share of power in society. This essay on women's sense of time appeared first in her regular column in *Ms.* in 1980 and was collected with her other columns in *Outrageous Acts and Everyday Rebellions* (1983).

Planning ahead is a measure of class. The rich and even the middle 1 class plan for future generations, but the poor can plan ahead only a few weeks or days.

I remember finding this calm insight in some sociological text and 2 feeling instant recognition. Yes, of course, our sense of time was partly a function of power, or the lack of it. It rang true even in the entirely economic sense the writer had in mind. "The guys who own the factories hand them down to their sons and great-grandsons," I remember a boy in my high school saying bitterly. "On this side of town, we just plan for Saturday night."

But it also seemed equally true of most of the women I knew — 3 including myself — regardless of the class we supposedly belonged to. Though I had left my factory-working neighborhood, gone to college, become a journalist, and thus was middle class, I still felt that I couldn't plan ahead. I had to be flexible — first, so that I could be ready to get on a plane for any writing assignment (even though the

279

male writers I knew launched into books and other long-term projects on their own), and then so that I could adapt to the career and priorities of an eventual husband and children (even though I was leading a rewarding life without either). Among the results of this uncertainty were a stunning lack of career planning and such smaller penalties as no savings, no insurance, and an apartment that lacked basic pieces of furniture.

On the other hand, I had friends who were married to men whose 4 longer-term career plans were compatible with their own, yet they still lived their lives in day-to-day response to any possible needs of their husbands and children. Moreover, the one male colleague who shared or even understood this sense of powerlessness was a successful black journalist and literary critic who admitted that even after twenty years he planned only one assignment at a time. He couldn't forget his dependence on the approval of white editors.

Clearly there is more to this fear of the future than a conventional 5 definition of class could explain. There is also caste: the unchangeable marks of sex and race that bring a whole constellation of cultural injunctions against power, even the limited power of controlling one's own life.

We haven't yet examined time-sense and future planning as func- 6 tions of discrimination, but we have begun to struggle with them, consciously or not. As a movement, women have become painfully conscious of too much reaction and living from one emergency to the next, with too little initiative and planned action of our own; hence many of our losses to a much smaller but more entrenched and consistent right wing.

Though the cultural habit of living in the present and glazing over 7 the future goes deep, we've begun to challenge the cultural punishment awaiting the "pushy" and "selfish" women (and the "uppity" minority men) who try to break through it and control their own lives.

Even so, feminist writers and theorists tend to avoid the future by 8 lavishing all our analytical abilities on what's wrong with the present, or on revisions of history and critiques of the influential male thinkers of the past. The big, original, and certainly courageous books of this wave of feminism have been more diagnostic than prescriptive. We need pragmatic planners and visionary futurists, but can we think of even one feminist five-year-plan? Perhaps the closest we have come is visionary architecture or feminist science fiction, but they generally avoid the practical steps of how to get from here to there.

Obviously, many of us need to extend our time-sense — to have   9 the courage to plan for the future, even while most of us are struggling to keep our heads above water in the present. But this does not mean a flat-out imitation of the culturally masculine habit of planning ahead, living in the future, and thus living a deferred life. It doesn't mean the traditional sacrifice of spontaneous action, or a sensitive awareness of the present, that comes from long years of career education with little intrusion of reality, from corporate pressure to work now for the sake of a reward after retirement, or, least logical of all, from patriarchal religions that expect obedience now in return for a reward after death.

In fact, the ability to live in the present, to tolerate uncertainty, and   10 to remain open, spontaneous, and flexible are all culturally female qualities that many men need and have been denied. As usual, both halves of the polarized masculine-feminine division need to learn from each other's experiences. If men spent more time raising small children, for instance, they would be forced to develop more patience and flexibility. If women had more power in the planning of natural resources and other long-term processes — or even in the planning of our own careers and reproductive lives — we would have to develop more sense of the future and of cause and effect.

An obsession with reacting to the present, feminine-style, or on   11 controlling and living in the future, masculine-style, are both wasteful of time.

And time is all there is.   12

CONSIDERATIONS

1. According to the author, how do economic and social advantages affect our sense of time? Do her observations ring true for the adults you know, or do you think that Steinem is overgeneralizing?
2. What is the difference between *class* and *caste* as Steinem uses these terms?
3. In paragraph 9 what is meant by "living a deferred life"?

4. What changes in attitudes about time does the author advocate? What other changes are involved in these proposed new attitudes?

5. WRITING TOPIC. How did the time factor influence your choice of a college? Were you *reacting* to the present? Were you *controlling* the future? Were you influenced by the time factor of your social background or family? In 500 words, measure your personal time factor in your decision to attend your college.

Marc Feigen Fasteau

FRIENDSHIPS AMONG MEN

◊

MARC FEIGEN FASTEAU (b. 1942) is a lawyer who specializes in sex discrimination cases. He attended Harvard Law School, where he was editor of the *Harvard Law Review*. Upon graduation, he returned to Washington, D.C., where he had been born, to work in government service. Moving to New York City, he then combined a law career with a political interest in legislation to reduce sex discrimination. He lectures widely on the topic of sexual stereotypes, and his articles have appeared in feminist magazines, such as *Ms.*, as well as journals for scientists. His book *The Male Machine* (1974) is a study of the masculine stereotype in our society. As the title suggests, the author believes that men are partly dehumanized by our idea of masculinity: "the male machine . . . is functional, designed mainly for work." In the following selection from that book, Fasteau argues that men remain unemotional and impersonal even in their friendships.

There is a long-standing myth in our society that the great friend- 1
ships are between men. Forged through shared experience, male friendship is portrayed as the most unselfish, if not the highest form, of human relationship. The more traditionally masculine the shared experience from which it springs, the stronger and more profound the friendship is supposed to be. Going to war, weathering crises together at school or work, playing on the same athletic team, are some of the classic experiences out of which friendships between men are believed to grow.

By and large, men do prefer the company of other men, not only in 2
their structured time but in the time they fill with optional, nonobligatory activity. They prefer to play games, drink, and talk, as well as work and fight together. Yet something is missing. Despite the time men spend together, their contact rarely goes beyond the external, a

limitation which tends to make their friendships shallow and unsatisfying.

My own childhood memories are of doing things with my friends — playing games or sports, building walkie-talkies, going camping. Other people and my relationships to them were never legitimate subjects for attention. If someone liked me, it was an opaque, mysterious occurrence that bore no analysis. When I was slighted, I felt hurt. But relationships with people just happened. I certainly had feelings about my friends, but I can't remember a single instance of trying consciously to sort them out until I was well into college.

For most men this kind of shying away from the personal continues into adult life. In conversations with each other, we hardly ever use ourselves as reference points. We talk about almost everything except how we ourselves are affected by people and events. Everything is discussed as though it were taking place out there somewhere, as though we had no more felt response to it than to the weather. Topics that can be treated in this detached, objective way become conversational mainstays. The few subjects which are fundamentally personal are shaped into discussions of abstract general questions. Even in an exchange about their reactions to liberated women — a topic of intensely personal interest — the tendency will be to talk in general, theoretical terms. Work, at least its objective aspects, is always a safe subject. Men also spend an incredible amount of time rehashing the great public issues of the day. Until early 1973, Vietnam was the work-horse topic. Then came Watergate. It doesn't seem to matter that we've all had a hundred similar conversations. We plunge in for another round, trying to come up with a new angle as much as to impress the others with what we know as to keep from being bored stiff.

Games play a central role in situations organized by men. I remember a weekend some years ago at the country house of a law-school classmate as a blur of softball, football, croquet, poker, and a dice-and-board game called Combat, with swimming thrown in on the side. As soon as one game ended, another began. Taken one at a time, these "activities" were fun, but the impression was inescapable that the host, and most of his guests, would do anything to stave off a lull in which they would be together without some impersonal focus for their attention. A snapshot of almost any men's club would show the same thing, 90 percent of the men engaged in some activity — ranging from backgammon to watching the tube — other than, or at least as an aid to, conversation.*

My composite memory of evenings spent with a friend at college 6 and later when we shared an apartment in Washington is of conversations punctuated by silences during which we would internally pass over any personal or emotional thoughts which had arisen and come back to the permitted track. When I couldn't get my mind off personal matters, I said very little. Talks with my father have always had the same tone. Respect for privacy was the rationale for our diffidence. His questions to me about how things were going at school or at work were asked as discreetly as he would have asked a friend about someone's commitment to a hospital for the criminally insane. Our conversations, when they touched these matters at all, to say nothing of more sensitive matters, would veer quickly back to safe topics of general interest.

In our popular literature, the archetypal male hero embodying this 7 personal muteness is the cowboy. The classic mold for the character was set in 1902 by Owen Wister's novel *The Virginian* where the author spelled out, with an explicitness that was never again necessary, the characteristics of his protagonist. Here's how it goes when two close friends the Virginian hasn't seen in some time take him out for a drink:

> All of them had seen rough days together, and they felt guilty with emotion.
>
> "It's hot weather," said Wiggin.
>
> "Hotter in Box Elder," said McLean. "My kid has started teething."
>
> Words ran dry again. They shifted their positions, looked in their glasses, read the labels on the bottles. They dropped a word now and then to the proprietor about his trade, and his ornaments.

One of the Virginian's duties is to assist at the hanging of an old

---

* Women may use games as a reason for getting together — bridge clubs, for example. But the show is more for the rest of the world — to indicate that they are doing *something* — and the games themselves are not the only means of communication.

friend as a horse thief. Afterward, for the first time in the book, he is visibly upset. The narrator puts his arm around the hero's shoulders and describes the Virginian's reaction:

> I had the sense to keep silent, and presently he shook my hand, not looking at me as he did so. He was always very shy of demonstration.

And, for explanation of such reticence, "As all men know, he also knew that many things should be done in this world in silence, and that talking about them is a mistake."

There are exceptions, but they only prove the rule.   8

One is the drunken confidence: "Bob, ole boy, I gotta tell ya —   9
being divorced isn't so hot. . . . [and see, I'm too drunk to be held responsible for blurting it out]." Here, drink becomes an excuse for exchanging confidences and a device for periodically loosening the restraint against expressing a need for sympathy and support from other men — which may explain its importance as a male ritual. Marijuana fills a similar need.

Another exception is talking to a stranger — who may be either   10
someone the speaker doesn't know or someone who isn't in the same social or business world. (Several black friends told me that they have been on the receiving end of personal confidences from white acquaintances that they were sure had not been shared with white friends.) In either case, men are willing to talk about themselves only to other men with whom they do not have to compete or whom they will not have to confront socially later.

Finally, there is the way men depend on women to facilitate certain   11
conversations. The women in a mixed group are usually the ones who make the first personal reference, about themselves or others present. The men can then join in without having the onus for initiating a discussion of "personalities." Collectively, the men can "blame" the conversation on the women. They can also feel in these conversations that since they are talking "to" the women instead of "to" the men, they can be excused for deviating from the masculine norm. When the women leave, the tone and subject invariably shift away from the personal.

The effect of these constraints is to make it extraordinarily difficult   12
for men to really get to know each other. A psychotherapist who has

conducted a lengthy series of encounter groups for men summed it up:

> With saddening regularity [the members of these groups] described how much they wanted to have closer, more satisfying relationships with other men: "I'd settle for having one really close man friend. I supposedly have some close men friends now. We play golf or go for a drink. We complain about our jobs and our wives. I care about them and they care about me. We even have some physical contact — I mean we may even give a hug on a big occasion. But it's not enough."

The sources of this stifling ban on self-disclosure, the reasons why men hide from each other, lie in the taboos and imperatives of the masculine stereotype.

To begin with, men are supposed to be functional, to spend their time working or otherwise solving or thinking about how to solve problems. Personal reaction, how one feels about something, is considered dysfunctional, at best an irrelevant distraction from the expected objectivity. Only weak men, and women, talk about — i.e., "give in," to their feelings. "I group my friends in two ways," said a business executive:

> those who have made it and don't complain and those who haven't made it. And only the latter spend time talking to their wives about their problems and how bad their boss is and all that. The ones who concentrate more on communicating . . . are those who have realized that they aren't going to make it and therefore they have changed the focus of attention.

In a world which tells men they have to choose between expressiveness and manly strength, this characterization may be accurate. Most of the men who talk personally to other men *are* those whose problems have gotten the best of them, who simply can't help it. Men not driven to despair don't talk about themselves, so the idea that self-disclosure and expressiveness are associated with problems and weakness becomes a self-fulfilling prophecy.

Obsessive competitiveness also limits the range of communication in male friendships. Competition is the principal mode by which men relate to each other — at one level because they don't know how else to make contact, but more basically because it is the way to demonstrate, to themselves and others, the key masculine qualities of unwavering toughness and the ability to dominate and control. The result is that they inject competition into situations which don't call for it.

In conversations, you must show that you know more about the 15 subject than the other man, or at least as much as he does. For example, I have often engaged in a contest that could be called My Theory Tops Yours, disguised as a serious exchange of ideas. The proof that it wasn't serious was that I was willing to participate even when I was sure that the participants, including myself, had nothing fresh to say. Convincing the other person — victory — is the main objective, with control of the floor an important tactic. Men tend to lecture at each other, insist that the discussion follow their train of thought, and are often unwilling to listen. As one member of a men's rap group said,

> When I was talking I used to feel that I had to be driving to a point, that it had to be rational and organized, that I had to persuade at all times, rather than exchange thoughts and ideas.

Even in casual conversation some men hold back unless they are absolutely sure of what they are saying. They don't want to have to change a position once they have taken it. It's "just like a woman" to change your mind, and, more important, it is inconsistent with the approved masculine posture of total independence.

Competition was at the heart of one of my closest friendships, now 16 defunct. There was a good deal of mutual liking and respect. We went out of our way to spend time with each other and wanted to work together. We both had "prospects" as "bright young men" and the same "liberal but tough" point of view. We recognized this about each other, and this recognition was the basis of our respect and of our sense of equality. That we saw each other as equals was important — our friendship was confirmed by the reflection of one in the other. But our constant and all-encompassing competition made this equality precarious and fragile. One way or another, everything counted in the measuring process. We fought out our tennis matches as though our lives depended on it. At poker, the two of us would often play on for hours after the others had left. These *mano a mano* poker marathons seem in retrospect especially revealing of the competitiveness of the relationship: playing for small stakes, the essence of the game is in outwitting, psychologically beating down the other player — the other skills involved are negligible. Winning is the only pleasure, one that evaporates quickly, a truth that struck me in inchoate form every time our game broke up at four A.M. and I walked out the door with my five-dollar winnings, a headache, and a sense of time wasted. Still, I did the same thing the next time. It was what we did together, and somehow it counted. Losing at tennis could be balanced by winning at poker; at another level, his moving up in the federal government by my getting on the *Harvard Law Review.*

This competitiveness feeds the most basic obstacle to openness be- 17 tween men, the inability to admit to being vulnerable. Real men, we learn early, are not supposed to have doubts, hopes and ambitions which may not be realized, things they don't (or even especially do) like about themselves, fears and disappointments. Such feelings and concerns, of course, are part of everyone's inner life, but a man must keep quiet about them. If others know how you really feel you can be hurt, and that in itself is incompatible with manhood. The inhibiting effect of this imperative is not limited to disclosures of major personal problems. Often men do not share even ordinary uncertainties and half-formulated plans of daily life with their friends. And when they do, they are careful to suggest that they already know how to pro- ceed — that they are not really asking for help or understanding but simply for particular bits of information. Either way, any doubts they have are presented as external, carefully characterized as having to do with the issue as distinct from the speaker. They are especially guarded about expressing concern or asking a question that would in- vite personal comment. It is almost impossible for men to simply ex- change thoughts about matters involving them personally in a com- fortable, non-crisis atmosphere. If a friend tells you of his concern that he and a colleague are always disagreeing, for example, he is likely to quickly supply his own explanation — something like "different pro- fessional backgrounds." The effect is to rule out observations or sug- gestions that do not fit within this already reconnoitered protective structure. You don't suggest, even if you believe it is true, that in fact the disagreements arise because he presents his ideas in a way which tends to provoke a hostile reaction. It would catch him off guard; it would be something he hadn't already thought of and accepted about himself and, for that reason, no matter how constructive and well-in- tentioned you might be, it would put you in control for the moment. He doesn't want that; he is afraid of losing your respect. So, sensing he feels that way, because you would yourself, you say something else. There is no real give-and-take.

It is hard for men to get angry at each other honestly. Anger 18 between friends often means that one has hurt the other. Since the straightforward expression of anger in these situations involves an admission of vulnerability, it is safer to stew silently or find an "objective" excuse for retaliation. Either way, trust is not fully restored.

Men even try not to let it show when they feel good. We may re- 19 port the reasons for our happiness, if they have to do with concrete accomplishments, but we try to do it with straight face, as if to say, "Here's what happened, but it hasn't affected my grown-up unemotional equilibrium, and I am not asking for any kind of response." Happiness is a precarious, "childish" feeling, easy to shoot down. Others may find the event that triggers it trivial or incomprehensible, or even threatening to their own self-esteen — in the sense that if one man is up, another man is down. So we tend not to take the risk of expressing it.

What is particularly difficult for men is seeking or accepting 20 help from friends. I, for one, learned early that dependence was unacceptable. When I was eight, I went to a summer camp I disliked. My parents visited me in the middle of the summer and, when it was time for them to leave, I wanted to go with them. They refused, and I yelled and screamed and was miserably unhappy for the rest of the day. That evening an older camper comforted me, sitting by my bed as I cried, patting me on the back soothingly and saying whatever it is that one says at times like that. He was in some way clumsy or funny-looking, and a few days later I joined a group of kids in cruelly making fun of him, an act which upset me, when I thought about it, for years. I can only explain it in terms of my feeling, as early as the age of eight, that by needing and accepting his help and comfort I had compromised myself, and took it out on him.

"You can't express dependence when you feel it," a corporate exec- 21 utive said, "because it's a kind of absolute. If you are loyal 90 percent of the time and disloyal 10 percent, would you be considered loyal? Well, the same happens with independence: you are either dependent or independent; you can't be both." "Feelings of dependence," another explained, "are identified with weakness or 'untoughness' and our culture doesn't accept those things in men." The result is that we either go it alone or "act out certain games or rituals to provoke the desired reaction in the other and have our needs satisfied without having to ask for anything."

Somewhat less obviously, the expression of affection also runs into   22 emotional barriers growing out of the masculine stereotype. When I was in college, I was suddenly quite moved while attending a friend's wedding. The surge of feeling made me uncomfortable and self-conscious. There was nothing inherently difficult or, apart from the fact of being moved by a moment of tenderness, "unmasculine" about my reaction. I just did not know how to deal with or communicate what I felt. "I consider myself a sentimentalist," one man said, "and I think I am quite able to express my feelings. But the other day my wife described a friend of mine to some people as my best friend and I felt embarrassed when I heard her say it."

A major source of these inhibitions is the fear of being, of being   23 thought, homosexual. Nothing is more frightening to a heterosexual man in our society. It threatens, at one stroke, to take away every vestige of his claim to a masculine identity — something like knocking out the foundations of a building — and to expose him to the ostracism, ranging from polite tolerance to violent revulsion, of his friends and colleagues. A man can be labeled as homosexual not just because of overt sexual act but because of almost any sign of behavior which does not fit the masculine stereotype. The touching of another man, other than shaking hands or, under emotional stress, an arm around the shoulder, is taboo. Women may kiss each other when they meet; men are uncomfortable when hugged even by close friends. Onlookers might misinterpret what they saw, and more important, what would we think of ourselves if we feel a twinge of sensual pleasure from the embrace.

Direct verbal expressions of affection or tenderness are also some-   24 thing that only homosexuals and women engage in. Between "real" men affection has to be disguised in gruff, "you old son-of-a-bitch" style. Paradoxically, in some instances, terms of endearment between men can be used as a ritual badge of manhood, dangerous medicine safe only for the strong. The flirting with homosexuality that characterizes the initiation rites of many fraternities and men's clubs serves this purpose. Claude Brown wrote about black life in New York City in the 1950s:

The term ["baby"] had a hip ring to it. . . . It was like saying, "Man, look at me. I've got masculinity to spare. . . . I can say 'baby' to another cat and he can say 'baby' to me, and we can say it with strength in our voices." If you could say it, this meant that you really had to be sure of yourself, sure of your masculinity.

Fear of homosexuality does more than inhibit the physical display of affection. One of the major recurring themes in the men's groups led by psychotherapist Don Clark was:

"A large segment of my feelings about other men are unknown or distorted because I am afraid they might have something to do with homosexuality. Now I'm lonely for other men and don't know how to find what I want with them."

As Clark observes, "The specter of homosexuality seems to be the dragon at the gateway to self-awareness, understanding, and acceptance of male-male needs. If a man tries to pretend the dragon is not there by turning a blind eye to erotic feelings for all other males, he also blinds himself to the rich variety of feelings that are related."

The few situations in which men do acknowledge strong feelings of 25 affection and dependence toward other men are exceptions which prove the rule. With "cop couples," for example, or combat soldier "buddies," intimacy and dependence are forced on the men by their work — they have to ride in the patrol car or be in the same foxhole with somebody — and the jobs themselves have such highly masculine images that the man can get away with behavior that would be suspect under any other conditions.

Furthermore, even these combat-buddy relationships, when looked 26 at closely, turn out not to be particularly intimate or personal. Margaret Mead has written:

During the last war English observers were confused by the apparent contradiction between American soldiers' emphasis on the buddy, so grievously exemplified in the break-downs that followed a buddy's death, and the results of detailed inquiry which showed how transitory these buddy relationships were. It was found that men actually accepted their buddies as derivatives from their outfit, and from accidents of association, rather than because of any special personality characteristics capable of ripening into friendship.

One effect of the fear of appearing to be homosexual is to reinforce the practice that two men rarely get together alone without a reason. I once called a friend to suggest that we have dinner together. "O.K.," he said. "What's up?" I felt uncomfortable telling him that I just wanted to talk, that there was no other reason for the invitation.

Men get together to conduct business, to drink, to play games and 27 sports, to re-establish contact after long absences, to participate in heterosexual social occasions — circumstances in which neither person is responsible for actually wanting to see the other. Men are particularly comfortable seeing each other in groups. The group situation defuses any possible assumptions about the intensity of feeling between particular men and provides the safety of numbers — "All the guys are here." It makes personal communication, which requires a level of trust and mutual understanding not generally shared by all members of a group, more difficult and offers an excuse for avoiding this dangerous territory. And it provides what is most sought after in men's friendships: mutual reassurance of masculinity.

CONSIDERATIONS

1. Are the first two paragraphs contradictory? If male friendships are superficial, why are they widely regarded as models of great friendship? Explain the author's point in paragraphs 1 and 2, adding whatever you think needs to be clarified in his argument.
2. According to the author, what are the satisfactions that games provide that make them more important to men than to women? Do you agree?
3. What example does the author give of society's archetypal male hero? Can you substitute a more up-to-date popular image of admired masculinity? (Pick a type, not an individual.) Is your example similar to or different from Fasteau's type of hero?
4. What does Fasteau say are the barriers to better friendships among men? Do you regard them as mainly social or mainly personal barriers? Does Fasteau suggest how the barriers can be overcome?
5. In restating his thesis about men, in the final paragraph Fasteau implies that women have different reasons for seeking friendship with other women. Which, if any, of these differences do you accept as self-evident? or as valid?
6. WRITING TOPIC. Should young males and females ever be raised separately for part of their lives? At what age can it do the most good or the most harm to redesign or reinforce sex roles through separate schools or

programs? Drawing on any of your relevant experiences from nursery school to college, write 700 words on the value of maintaining single-sex associations such as scouting, sports, clubs, and being with just "the boys" or "the girls." Explain what it has meant to you to have these associations, and explain how they might have been more beneficial than they were.

Desmond Morris

TERRITORIAL BEHAVIOR

◊

DESMOND MORRIS (b. 1928) is a British zoologist whose scientific research into animal behavior at Oxford University and as the curator of mammals at the London Zoo stirs his interest in explaining predictable patterns in human activity. In addition to his scholarly papers, he has written best-selling books for the general reader, such as *The Naked Ape* (1967), *The Human Zoo* (1970), *Intimate Behavior* (1972), and *Manwatching* (1977) from which this selection is taken. He seems to see groups of people as if they are all in cages — which might be not only true but also the safest place to be.

A territory is a defended space. In the broadest sense, there are 1 three kinds of human territory: tribal, family, and personal.

It is rare for people to be driven to physical fighting in defense of 2 these "owned" spaces, but fight they will, if pushed to the limit. The invading army encroaching on national territory, the gang moving into a rival district, the trespasser climbing into an orchard, the burglar breaking into a house, the bully pushing to the front of a queue, the driver trying to steal a parking space, all of these intruders are liable to be met with resistance varying from the vigorous to the savagely violent. Even if the law is on the side of the intruder, the urge to protect a territory may be so strong that otherwise peaceful citizens abandon all their usual controls and inhibitions. Attempts to evict families from their homes, no matter how socially valid the reasons, can lead to siege conditions reminiscent of the defence of a medieval fortress.

The fact that these upheavals are so rare is a measure of the success 3 of Territorial Signals as a system of dispute prevention. It is sometimes cynically stated that "all property is theft," but in reality it is the opposite. Property, as owned space which is *displayed* as owned space, is a special kind of sharing system which reduces fighting much more than it causes it. Man is a co-operative species, but he is also competitive, and his struggle for dominance has to be structured in some way if chaos is to be avoided. The establishment of territorial rights is one such structure. It limits dominance geographically. I am dominant in my territory and you are dominant in yours. In other words, dominance is shared out spatially, and we all have some. Even if I am weak and unintelligent and you can dominate me when we meet on neutral ground, I can still enjoy a thoroughly dominant role as soon as I retreat to my private base. Be it ever so humble, there is no place like a home territory.

Of course, I can still be intimidated by a particularly dominant in- 4 dividual who enters my home base, but his encroachment will be dangerous for him and he will think twice about it, because he will know that here my urge to resist will be dramatically magnified and my usual subservience banished. Insulted at the heart of my own territory, I may easily explode into battle — either symbolic or real — with a result that may be damaging to both of us.

In order for this to work, each territory has to be plainly advertised 5 as such. Just as a dog cocks its leg to deposit its personal scent on the trees in its locality, so the human animal cocks its leg symbolically all over his home base. But because we are predominantly visual animals we employ mostly visual signals, and it is worth asking how we do this at the three levels: tribal, family, and personal.

First: the Tribal Territory. We evolved as tribal animals, living in 6 comparatively small groups, probably of less than a hundred, and we existed like that for millions of years. It is our basic social unit, a group in which everyone knows everyone else. Essentially, the tribal territory consisted of a home base surrounded by extended hunting grounds. Any neighboring tribe intruding on our social space would be repelled and driven away. As these early tribes swelled into agricultural super-tribes, and eventually into industrial nations, their territorial defence systems became increasingly elaborate. The tiny, ancient home base of the hunting tribe became the great capital city, the primitive warpaint became the flags, emblems, uniforms, and regalia of the specialized military, and the war-chants became national anthems, marching songs, and bugle calls. Territorial boundary-lines hardened into fixed borders, often conspicuously patrolled and punctuated with defensive structures — forts and lookout posts, checkpoints and great walls, and, today, customs barriers.

Today each nation flies its own flag, a symbolic embodiment of its   7 territorial status. But patriotism is not enough. The ancient tribal hunter lurking inside each citizen finds himself unsatisfied by membership in such a vast conglomeration of individuals, most of whom are totally unknown to him personally. He does his best to feel that he shares a common territorial defense with them all, but the scale of the operation has become inhuman. It is hard to feel a sense of belonging with a tribe of fifty million or more. His answer is to form sub-groups, nearer to his ancient pattern, smaller, and more personally known to him — the local club, the teenage gang, the union, the specialist society, the sports association, the political party, the college fraternity, the social clique, the protest group, and the rest. Rare indeed is the individual who does not belong to at least one of these splinter groups, and take from it a sense of tribal allegiance and brotherhood. Typical of all these groups is the development of Territorial Signals — badges, costumes, headquarters, banners, slogans, and all the other displays of group identity. This is where the action is, in terms of tribal territorialism, and only when a major war breaks out does the emphasis shift upwards to the higher group level of the nation.

Each of these modern pseudo-tribes sets up its own special kind of   8 home base. In extreme cases non-members are totally excluded, in others they are allowed in as visitors with limited rights and under a control system of special rules. In many ways they are like miniature nations, with their own flags and emblems and their own border guards. The exclusive club has its own "customs barrier": the doorman who checks your "passport" (your membership card) and prevents strangers from passing in unchallenged. There is a government: the club committee; and often special displays of the tribal elders: the photographs or portraits of previous officials on the walls. At the heart of the specialized territories there is a powerful feeling of security and importance, a sense of shared defense against the outside world. Much of the club chatter, both serious and joking, directs itself against the rottenness of everything outside the club boundaries — in that "other world" beyond the protected portals.

In social organizations which embody a strong class system, such as   9 military units and large business concerns, there are many territorial rules, often unspoken, which interfere with the official hierarchy. High-status individuals, such as officers or managers, could in theory enter any of the regions occupied by the lower levels in the peck order, but they limit this power in a striking way. An officer seldom enters a sergeant's mess or a barrack room unless it is for a formal inspection. He respects those regions as alien territories even though he has the power to go there by virtue of his dominant role. And in businesses, part of the appeal of unions, over and above their obvious functions, is that with their officials, headquarters, and meetings they add a sense of territorial power for the staff workers. It is almost as if each military organization and business concern consists of two warring tribes: the officers versus the other ranks, and the management versus the workers. Each has its special home base within the system, and the territorial defence pattern thrusts itself into what, on the surface, is a pure social hierarchy. Negotiations between managements and unions are tribal battles fought out over the neutral ground of a boardroom table, and are as much concerned with territorial display as they are with resolving problems of wages and conditions. Indeed, if one side gives in too quickly and accepts the other's demands, the victors feel strangely cheated and deeply suspicious that it may be a trick. What they are missing is the protracted sequence of ritual and counter-ritual that keeps alive their group territorial identity.

Likewise, many of the hostile displays of sports fans and teenage 10 gangs are primarily concerned with displaying their group image to rival fan-clubs and gangs. Except in rare cases, they do not attack one another's headquarters, drive out the occupants, and reduce them to a submissive, subordinate condition. It is enough to have scuffles on the borderlands between the two rival territories. This is particularly clear at football matches, where the fan-club headquarters becomes temporarily shifted from the club-house to a section of the stands, and where minor fighting breaks out at the unofficial boundary line between the massed groups of rival supporters. Newspaper reports play up the few accidents and injuries which do occur on such occasions, but when these are studied in relation to the total numbers of displaying fans involved it is clear that the serious incidents represent only a tiny fraction of the overall group behavior. For every actual punch or kick there are a thousand war-cries, war-dances, chants, and gestures.

Second: the Family Territory. Essentially, the family is a breeding 11 unit and the family territory is a breeding ground. At the center of this space, there is the nest — the bedroom — where, tucked up in bed, we feel at our most territorially secure. In a typical house the bedroom is upstairs, where a safe nest should be. This puts it farther away from the entrance hall, the area where contact is made, intermittently, with the outside world. The less private reception rooms, where intruders are allowed access, are the next line of defense. Beyond them, outside the walls of the building, there is often a symbolic remnant of the ancient feeding grounds — a garden. Its symbolism often extends to the plants and animals it contains, which cease to be nutritional and become merely decorative — flowers and pets. But like a true territorial space it has a conspicuously displayed boundary-line, the garden fence, wall, or railings. Often no more than a token barrier, this is the outer territorial demarcation, separating the private world of the family from the public world beyond. To cross it puts any visitor or intruder at an immediate disadvantage. As he crosses the threshold, his dominance wanes, slightly but unmistakably. He is entering an area where he senses that he must ask permission to do simple things that he would consider a right elsewhere. Without lifting a finger, the territorial owners exert their dominance. This is done by all the hundreds of small ownership "markers" they have deposited on their family territory: the ornaments, the "possessed" objects positioned in the rooms and on the walls; the furnishings, the furniture, the colors, the patterns, all owner-chosen and all making this particular home base unique to them.

It is one of the tragedies of modern architecture that there has been 12
a standardization of these vital territorial living units. One of the most important aspects of a home is that it should be similar to other homes only in a general way, and that in detail it should have many differences, making it a *particular* home. Unfortunately, it is cheaper to build a row of houses, or a block of flats, so that all the family living-units are identical, but the territorial urge rebels against this trend and house-owners struggle as best they can to make their mark on their mass-produced properties. They do this with garden-design, with front-door colors, with curtain patterns, with wallpaper and all the other decorative elements that together create a unique and different family environment. Only when they have completed this nest-building do they feel truly "at home" and secure.

When they venture forth as a family unit they repeat the process in 13
a minor way. On a day-trip to the seaside, they load the car with per-

sonal belongings and it becomes their temporary, portable territory. Arriving at the beach they stake out a small territorial claim, marking it with rugs, towels, baskets, and other belongings to which they can return from their seaboard wanderings. Even if they all leave it at once to bathe, it retains a characteristic territorial quality and other family groups arriving will recognize this by setting up their own "home" bases at a respectful distance. Only when the whole beach has filled up with these marked spaces will newcomers start to position themselves in such a way that the inter-base distance becomes reduced. Forced to pitch between several existing beach territories they will feel a momentary sensation of intrusion, and the established "owners" will feel a similar sensation of invasion, even though they are not being directly inconvenienced.

The same territorial scene is being played out in parks and fields 14 and on riverbanks, wherever family groups gather in their clustered units. But if rivalry for spaces creates mild feelings of hostility, it is true to say that, without the territorial system of sharing and space-limited dominance, there would be chaotic disorder.

Third: the Personal Space. If a man enters a waiting-room and sits 15 at one end of a long row of empty chairs, it is possible to predict where the next man to enter will seat himself. He will not sit next to the first man, nor will he sit at the far end, right away from him. He will choose a position about halfway between these two points. The next man to enter will take the largest gap left, and sit roughly in the middle of that, and so on, until eventually the latest newcomer will be forced to select a seat that places him right next to one of the already seated men. Similar patterns can be observed in cinemas, public urinals, airplanes, trains, and buses. This is a reflection of the fact that we all carry with us, everywhere we go, a portable territory called a Personal Space. If people move inside this space, we feel threatened. If they keep too far outside it, we feel rejected. The result is a subtle series of spatial adjustments, usually operating quite unconsciously and producing ideal compromises as far as this is possible. If a situation becomes too crowded, then we adjust our reactions accordingly and allow our personal space to shrink. Jammed into an elevator, a rush-hour compartment, or a packed room, we give up altogether and allow body-to-body contact, but when we relinquish our Personal Space in this way, we adopt certain special techniques. In essence, what we do is to convert these other bodies into "nonpersons." We studiously ignore them, and they us. We try not to face them if we can possibly avoid it. We wipe all expressiveness from our faces, letting them go blank. We may look up at the ceiling or down at the floor, and we reduce body movements to a minimum. Packed together like sardines in a tin, we stand dumbly still, sending out as few social signals as possible.

Even if the crowding is less severe, we still tend to cut down our social interactions in the presence of large numbers. Careful observations of children in play groups revealed that if they are high-density groupings there is less social interaction between the individual children, even though there is theoretically more opportunity for such contacts. At the same time, the high-density groups show a higher frequency of aggressive and destructive behavior patterns in their play. Personal Space — "elbow room" — is a vital commodity for the human animal, and one that cannot be ignored without risking serious trouble. 16

Of course, we all enjoy the excitement of being in a crowd, and this reaction cannot be ignored. But there are crowds and crowds. It is pleasant enough to be in a "spectator crowd," but not so appealing to find yourself in the middle of a rush-hour crush. The difference between the two is that the spectator crowd is all facing in the same direction and concentrating on a distant point of interest. Attending a theatre, there are twinges of rising hostility toward the stranger who sits down immediately in front of you or the one who squeezes into the seat next to you. The shared armrest can become a polite, but distinct, territorial boundary-dispute region. However, as soon as the show begins, these invasions of Personal Space are forgotten and the attention is focused beyond the small space where the crowding is taking place. Now, each member of the audience feels himself spatially related, not to his cramped neighbors, but to the actor on the stage, and this distance is, if anything, too great. In the rush-hour crowd, by contrast, each member of the pushing throng is competing with his neighbors all the time. There is no escape to a spatial relation with a distant actor, only the pushing, shoving bodies all around. 17

Those of us who have to spend a great deal of time in crowded conditions become gradually better able to adjust, but no one can ever become completely immune to invasions of Personal Space. This is because they remain forever associated with either powerful hostile or equally powerful loving feelings. All through our childhood we will 18 have been held to be loved and held to be hurt, and anyone who invades our Personal Space when we are adults is, in effect, threatening to extend his behavior into one of these two highly charged areas of human interaction. Even if his motives are clearly neither hostile nor sexual, we still find it hard to suppress our reactions to his close approach. Unfortunately, different countries have different ideas about exactly how close is close. It is easy enough to test your own "space reaction": when you are talking to someone in the street or in any open space, reach out with your arm and see where the nearest point on his body comes. If you hail from western Europe, you will find that he is at roughly fingertip distance from you. In other words, as you reach out, your fingertips will just about make contact with his shoulder. If you come from eastern Europe you will find you are standing at "wrist distance." If you come from the Mediterranean region you will find that you are much closer to your companion, at little more than "elbow distance."

Trouble begins when a member of one of these cultures meets and 19 talks to one from another. Say a British diplomat meets an Italian or an Arab diplomat at an embassy function. They start talking in a friendly way, but soon the fingertips man begins to feel uneasy. Without knowing quite why, he starts to back away gently from his companion. The companion edges forward again. Each tries in his way to set up a Personal Space relationship that suits his own background. But it is impossible to do. Every time the Mediterranean diplomat advances to a distance that feels comfortable for him, the British diplomat feels threatened. Every time the Briton moves back, the other feels rejected. Attempts to adjust this situation often lead to a talking pair shifting slowly across a room, and many an embassy reception is dotted with western-European fingertip-distance men pinned against the walls by eager elbow-distance men. Until such differences are fully understood and allowances made, these minor differences in "body territories" will continue to act as an alienation factor which may interfere in a subtle way with diplomatic harmony and other forms of international transaction.

If there are distance problems when engaged in conversation, then 20 there are clearly going to be even bigger difficulties where people must work privately in a shared space. Close proximity of others, pressing against the invisible boundaries of our personal body-territory, makes it difficult to concentrate on nonsocial matters. Flat-mates, students sharing a study, sailors in the cramped quarters of a ship, and office staff in crowded work-places, all have to face this problem. They solve it by "cocooning." They use a variety of devices to shut themselves off from the others present. The best possible cocoon, of course, is a small private room — a den, a private office, a study, or a studio — which physically obscures the presence of other nearby territory-owners. This is the ideal situation for non-social work, but the space-sharers cannot enjoy this luxury. Their cocooning must be symbolic. They may, in certain cases, be able to erect small physical barriers, such as screens and partitions, which give substance to their invisible Personal Space boundaries, but when this cannot be done, other means must be sought. One of these is the "favored object." Each space-sharer develops a preference, repeatedly expressed until it becomes a fixed pattern, for a particular chair, or table, or alcove. Others come to respect this, and friction is reduced. This system is often formally arranged (this is my desk, that is yours), but even where it is not, favored places soon develop. Professor Smith has a favorite chair in the library. It is not formally his, but he always uses it and others avoid it. Seats around a mess-room table, or a boardroom table, become almost personal property for specific individuals. Even in the home, father has his favorite chair for reading the newspaper or watching television. Another device is the blinkers-posture. Just as a horse that over-reacts to other horses and the distractions of the noisy race-course is given a pair of blinkers to shield its eyes, so people studying privately in a public place put on pseudo-blinkers in the form of shielding hands. Resting their elbows on the table, they sit with their hands screening their eyes from the scene on either side.

A third method of reinforcing the body-territory is to use personal 21 markers. Books, papers, and other personal belongings are scattered around the favored site to render it more privately owned in the eyes of companions. Spreading out one's belongings is a well-known trick in public-transport situations, where a traveller tries to give the impression that seats next to him are taken. In many contexts carefully arranged personal markers can act as an effective territorial display, even in the absence of the territory owner. Experiments in a library revealed that placing a pile of magazines on the table in one seating position successfully reserved that place for an average of 77 minutes. If a sports-jacket was added, draped over the chair, then the "reservation effect" lasted for over two hours.

In these ways, we strengthen the defences of our Personal Spaces, 22
keeping out intruders with the minimum of open hostility. As with all
territorial behavior, the object is to defend space with signals rather
than with fists and at all three levels — the tribal, the family, and the
personal — it is a remarkably efficient system of space-sharing. It does
not always seem so, because newspapers and newscasts inevitably
magnify the exceptions and dwell on those cases where the signals
have failed and wars have broken out, gangs have fought, neighboring
families have feuded, or colleagues have clashed, but for every territorial signal that has failed, there are millions of others that have not.
They do not rate a mention in the news, but they nevertheless constitute a dominant feature of human society — the society of a remarkably territorial animal.

CONSIDERATIONS

1. How does Morris view human beings in relation to other animals? What
   are the key words and phrases in the first five paragraphs that indicate his
   perspective on human actions?
2. What is the main purpose of displaying "Territorial Signals"? Do you accept his explanation as it applies to human behavior?
3. What are the most often used, main signals for indicating each of the
   three types of territorial behavior?
4. To what type of territorial behavior does Morris give his fullest attention?
   Does this emphasis make his points easier or harder to confirm?
5. Does Morris define territorial behavior as sociable or antisocial? Do his
   examples adequately support his general point?
6. WRITING TOPIC. Writing as an observer of territorial behavior, analyze
   in 500 words the events at a freshman mixer, or at the first dorm meeting
   of the year, or at a large wedding reception, or during an overnight delay
   you experienced at an airport, or any similar assembly of strangers in
   partly unallocated spaces.

Linda Pastan

MARKET DAY

◊

LINDA PASTAN (b. 1932) is a poet who lives in Potomac, Maryland. She was born in New York City. After graduating from Radcliffe College, she earned advanced degrees at Simmons College and at Brandeis University. Her work appears widely in poetry journals, and her published books include *Aspects of Eve* (1975), *The Five Stages of Grief* (1978), *Waiting for My Life* (1981), and *New and Selected Poems* (1982). The following poem first appeared in *Poetry* magazine in 1985.

We have travelled all this way   1
to see the real France:
these trays of apricots and grapes spilled out
like semi-precious stones
for us to choose; a milky way
of cheeses whose names like planets
I forget; heraldic sole
displayed on ice, as if the fish
themselves had just escaped,
leaving their scaled armor behind.   10
There's nothing like this
anywhere, you say. And I see
Burnside Avenue in the Bronx, my mother

sending me for farmer cheese and lox:
the rounds of cheese grainy and white, pocked
like the surface of the moon;
the silken slices of smoked fish
lying in careful pleats; and always,
as here, sawdust under our feet
the color of sand brought in on pant cuffs   20
from Sunday at the beach.

Across the street on benches,
my grandparents lifted their faces
to the sun the way the blind turn
towards a familiar sound, speaking
another language I almost understand.

CONSIDERATIONS

1. For the poet and her companion, what are the connotations of French foods? How are the foods connected with France?
2. What are the connotations of the household foods Pastan remembers?
3. It seems that her grandparents' language is in some way more foreign to her than French. What does Pastan want to understand from them?
4. WRITING TOPIC. One of the most important symbols of ethnic or national identity is the food eaten by members of the group. The way it is prepared and served is often as important as the substance. In 500 words, describe the foods and the customs of sharing it that define your family's group identity. (Most Americans have participated in Thanksgiving, and most of us also share other food traditions.)

Alexis de Tocqueville

ARISTOCRACY AND DEMOCRACY

◊

ALEXIS DE TOCQUEVILLE (1805–1859) was raised in a liberal-minded, aristocratic family that had narrowly escaped destruction during the reign of terror in the French Revolution. He prepared for a career as a jurist, but as a young man in his twenties he was far more interested in political and social theorizing than in arguing or hearing legal cases. He was sent to America in 1831 to survey the penal system, and he made use of the opportunity to develop his ideas about society. Upon his return to France he wrote *Democracy in America* (1835) from which this selection is taken. Tocqueville saw the absolute power of the old French monarchy and the potential for mob rule in the new American democracy as comparable dangers to the practice of freedom.

Among aristocratic nations families maintain the same station for 1 centuries and often live in the same place. So there is a sense in which all the generations are contemporaneous. A man almost always knows about his ancestors and respects them; his imagination extends to his great-grandchildren, and he loves them. He freely does his duty by both ancestors and descendants and often sacrifices personal pleasures for the sake of beings who are no longer alive or are not yet born.

Moreover, aristocratic institutions have the effect of linking each 2 man closely with several of his fellows.

Each class in an aristocratic society, being clearly and permanently 3 limited, forms, in a sense, a little fatherland for all its members, to which they are attached by more obvious and more precious ties than those linking them to the fatherland itself.

Each citizen of an aristocratic society has his fixed station, one 4 above another, so that there is always someone above him whose protection he needs and someone below him whose help he may require.

So people living in an aristocratic age are almost always closely in- 5 volved with something outside themselves, and they are often inclined to forget about themselves. It is true that in these ages the general conception of *human fellowship* is dim and that men hardly ever think of devoting themselves to the cause of humanity, but men do often make sacrifices for the sake of certain other men.

In democratic ages, on the contrary, the duties of each to all are 6 much clearer but devoted service to any individual much rarer. The bonds of human affection are wider but more relaxed.

Among democratic peoples new families continually rise from 7 nothing while others fall, and nobody's position is quite stable. The woof of time is ever being broken and the track of past generations lost. Those who have gone before are easily forgotten, and no one gives a thought to those who will follow. All a man's interests are limited to those near himself.

As each class catches up with the next and gets mixed with it, its 8 members do not care about one another and treat one another as strangers. Aristocracy links everybody, from peasant to king, in one long chain. Democracy breaks the chain and frees each link.

As social equality spreads there are more and more people who, 9 though neither rich nor powerful enough to have much hold over others, have gained or kept enough wealth and enough understanding to look after their own needs. Such folk owe no man anything and hardly expect anything from anybody. They form the habit of thinking of themselves in isolation and imagine that their whole destiny is in their own hands.

Thus, not only does democracy make men forget their ancestors, 10 but also clouds their view of their descendants and isolates them from their contemporaries. Each man is forever thrown back on himself alone, and there is danger that he may be shut up in the solitude of his own heart.

CONSIDERATIONS

1. According to Tocqueville, what social bonds are formed in a hereditary aristocracy? How are the lower classes included?
2. What is the chief weakness that he sees in democracy? Restate his criticism in your own words.

3. Tocqueville's views are not derived from examples. Can you refute or confirm his deductions by offering examples of social bonds in democratic life?
4. WRITING TOPIC. Tocqueville's views were formed 150 years ago. As one of the present-day descendants of the democrats he observed, write a 700-word letter to Tocqueville bringing him up to date on the American character. Focus on one or two traits that are visible in both society and the individual.

ADDITIONAL
WRITING TOPICS

◊

GROUP PICTURES

1. Part of the fun of spectator sports is in being part of the crowd of spectators. There are customs associated with attending certain sports that amount to another set of "the rules of the game" for the fans who are present. A crowd at a hockey game, for instance, behaves differently from a crowd watching a marathon race. Crowds in a football stadium are different from crowds in baseball parks. Fans at a track meet adopt a different style when they go to basketball games. People's individual behavior changes as the crowd differs from sport to sport. Write a 500-word essay that gives instruction on the sport of "spectatoring." Explain the appropriate actions for a member of the crowd at a particular sports event. Or, you may want to contrast spectator styles for two different sports.

2. What groups do children like to pretend they are part of? When children play-act adult roles, they imagine themselves as part of some easily recognizable group; they seldom pick solitary roles for themselves. "Cowboys and Indians" used to be popular, but probably it is not played any longer, and only people well over thirty would remember it. Younger adults and present-day children grow up creating different imaginary groups. Drawing on your recollections or your direct observations of children at play, in a 500-word essay, define one or two social types that children play-act. Where do the roles come from? What sort of games do children play in these roles?

3. Being ashamed of one's parents for one reason or another is part of almost everyone's experience for a time. What was it about your parents, either one or both of them, that caused you embarrassment or shame for a while? What group or standard did they fail to measure up to? In whose eyes (in addition to your own) did you think that they looked bad? How did you express your embarrassment toward them, and how did they react to your behavior? If you can discuss this difficult, and probably troubling, subject with some sympathy now for all the people involved (including yourself at the time), write a 750-word essay on your social embarrassment over your parents. To what extent were you perhaps struggling with social allegiances outside your family?

4. Compare the lyrics of two patriotic songs that generate pride in being an American. "America The Beautiful" and "The Star-Spangled Banner," for instance, express attitudes about the country and its history that make us proud of our national identity. These and other patriotic songs — such as "America," "The Battle Hymn of the Republic," "Yankee Doodle," and "Dixie" — include references to burdens and weaknesses that help to bond people together and give them pride in unity against dangers. In a 500-word essay, explain what sources of group pride and peril are celebrated in two patriotic songs.

5. You must know someone you could call a "total jerk" — that is, someone who never knows the right way to act. In 500 words, explain the code of manners that this person does not follow. Be sure to focus on explaining the meaning of the accepted behavior that this person consistently violates. Do not just relate an anecdote that ridicules someone.

6. In the *Insights*, Sigmund Freud observes that people in groups behave differently from the way they usually behave individually. Test the truth of Freud's statement as it applies to sports events, political assemblies, religious ceremonies, or other group situations. Are Freud's observations accurate? Are his points fair-minded? Are there some good effects of group behavior that Freud overlooks? What can you add to support or modify his views? In a 700-word essay, describe the changes in your own and other people's behavior and feelings while acting as a group.

7. In his inaugural address, President John Kennedy said: "Ask not what your country can do for you. Ask what you can do for your country." Why should we seek ways to serve the nation unless we are called on to serve? What is the personal value of patriotism? In 500 words, explain what you think it means or should mean to be an American.

8. The statements in the *Insights* indicate that John Donne and Theodore Reik relate well to society but that the other writers find the social connection disagreeable. Pick one statement from each side of the fence and explain the contrasting attitudes toward society. Pay close attention to the connotations of each side's word choice.

PART 5

POSSESSIONS

Toni Cade Bambara, *The Lesson*

Harry Crews, *The Car*

E. M. Forster, *My Wood*

William Ryan, *Mine, All Mine*

Matthew, *The Lilies of the Field*

John Brooks, *Telephone Gamesmanship*

Susan C. Carlisle, *French Homes and French Character*

Lewis Hyde, *Gifts in Motion*

Additional Writing Topics

INSIGHTS

It is easier for a camel to go through the eye of a needle, than for a rich man to enter into the kingdom of God.

– MATTHEW 19:24

◇

A man is rich in proportion to the number of things which he can afford to let alone.

– HENRY DAVID THOREAU

◇

I call people rich when they're able to meet the requirements of their imagination.

– HENRY JAMES

◇

It is ironic that the very kind of thinking which produces all our riches also renders them unable to satisfy us. Our restless desire for more and more has been a major dynamic for economic growth, but it has made the achievement of that growth largely a hollow victory. Our sense of contentment and satisfaction is not a simple result of any absolute level of what we acquire or achieve. It depends upon our frame of reference, on how what we attain compares to what we expected. If we get farther than we expected we tend to feel good. If we expected to go farther than we have then even a rather high level of success can be experienced as disappointing. In America, we keep upping the ante. Our expectations keep accommodating to what we have attained. "Enough" is always just over the horizon, and like the horizon it recedes as we approach it.

We do not tend to think in terms of a particular set of conditions and amenities that we regard as sufficient and appropriate for a good life. Our calculations tend to be relative. It is not what we have that determines whether we think we are doing well; it is whether we have *more* — more than our parents, more than we had ten years ago, perhaps more than our neighbors. This latter source of relativity, keeping up with (or ahead of) the Joneses, is the most frequently commented upon. But it is probably less important, and less destructive, than our comparisons with our own previous levels and with the new expectations they generate. Wanting more remains a constant, regardless of what we have.

— PAUL WACHTEL

◇

The Latin word for island is *insula,* and the word itself breathes the spirit of island life. Here, surrounded on all sides by a protective moat, one is insulated from the grosser absurdities of an irrational world, from the wearisome conflicts of a restless society, from the relentless sweep of a century that often seems more freighted with fear than with hope. The island offers once more the great prize of passionate individualism, a steady constant in a shifting universe. It is no wonder that possession of an island is the central fantasy of man's dreams.

— CASKIE STINNETT

◇

No one finds difficulty in assenting to the commonplace that the greater part of the expenditure incurred by all classes for apparel is incurred for the sake of respectable appearance rather than for the protection of the person. And probably at no other point is the sense of shabbiness so keenly felt as it is if we fall short of the standard set by social usage in this matter of dress. It is true of dress in even a higher degree than of most other items of consumption, that people will undergo a very considerable degree of privation in the comforts or the necessaries of life in order to afford what is considered a decent amount of wasteful consumption; so that it is by no means an uncommon occurrence, in an inclement climate, for people to go ill clad in order to appear well dressed. And the commercial value of the goods used for clothing in any modern community is made up to a much larger extent of the fashionableness, the reputability of the goods than of the mechanical service which they render in clothing the person of the wearer. The need of dress is eminently a "higher" or spiritual need.

– THORSTEIN VEBLEN

◊

People who have lived for centuries in poverty in the relative isolation of the rural village have come to terms with this existence. It would be astonishing were it otherwise. People do not strive, generation after generation, century after century, against circumstances that are so constituted as to defeat them. They accept. Nor is such acceptance a sign of weakness of character. Rather, it is a profoundly rational response. Given the formidable hold of the . . . poverty within which they live, accommodation is the optimal solution. Poverty is cruel. A continuing struggle to escape that is continuously frustrated is more cruel. It is more civilized, more intelligent, as well as more plausible, that people, out of the experience of centuries, should reconcile themselves to what has for so long been the inevitable.

The deeply rational character of accommodation lies back, at least in part, of the central instruction of the principal world religions. All, without exception, urge acquiescence, some in remarkably specific form. The blessedness that Christianity accords to the meek is categorical. The pain of poverty is not denied, but its compensatory spiritual reward is very high. The poor pass through the eye of the needle into Paradise; the rich remain outside with the camels. Acquiescence is equally urged, or as in the case of Hinduism compelled, by the other ancient faiths. There has long been a suspicion, notably enhanced by Marx, that the contentment urged by religion is a design for diverting attention from the realities of class and exploitation — it is the opiate of the people. It is, more specifically, a formula for making the best of a usually hopeless situation.

           – JOHN KENNETH GALBRAITH

◇

Private Property, the Law of Accumulation of Wealth, and the Law of Competition . . . these are the highest results of human experience, the soil in which society so far has produced the best fruit.

           – ANDREW CARNEGIE

◇

The one who dies with the most toys wins.

           – ANONYMOUS

Toni Cade Bambara

THE LESSON

◊

Toni Cade Bambara (b. 1939) grew up in the black districts of New York City where she experienced racism and poverty set in sharp contrast to the opulence of white Manhattan, as the following story reflects. After graduating from Queens College, she studied dance and acting in Italy and France before returning to New York, where she took a M.A. degree at City College. Bambara worked as a welfare investigator and youth counselor while writing short stories. She has taught English at Duke University and Spellman College and is the editor of an anthology of essays, *The Black Woman* (1970). Her fiction has been collected in *The Sea Birds Are Still Alive: Collected Stories* (1977).

Back in the days when everyone was old and stupid or young and 1 foolish and me and Sugar were the only ones just right, this lady moved on our block with nappy hair and proper speech and no makeup. And quite naturally we laughed at her, laughed the way we did at the junk man who went about his business like he was some big-time president and his sorry-ass horse his secretary. And we kinda hated her too, hated the way we did the winos who cluttered up our parks and pissed on our handball walls and stank up our hallways and stairs so you couldn't halfway play hide-and-seek without a goddamn gas mask. Miss Moore was her name. The only woman on the block with no first name. And she was black as hell, cept for her feet, which were fish-white and spooky. And she was always planning these boring-ass things for us to do, us being my cousin, mostly, who lived on the block cause we all moved North the same time and to the same apartment then spread out gradual to breathe. And our parents would yank our heads into some kinda shape and crisp up our clothes so we'd

318

be presentable for travel with Miss Moore, who always looked like she was going to church, though she never did. Which is just one of things the grownups talked about when they talked behind her back like a dog. But when she came calling with some sachet she'd sewed up or some gingerbread she'd made or some book, why then they'd all be too embarrassed to turn her down and we'd get handed over all spruced up. She'd been to college and said it was only right that she should take responsibility for the young ones' education, and she not even related by marriage or blood. So they'd go for it. Specially Aunt Gretchen. She was the main gofer in the family. You got some ole dumb shit foolishness you want somebody to go for, you send for Aunt Gretchen. She been screwed into the go-along for so long, it's a blood-deep natural thing with her. Which is how she got saddled with me and Sugar and Junior in the first place while our mothers were in a la-de-da apartment up the block having a good ole time.

So this one day Miss Moore rounds us all up at the mailbox and it's puredee hot and she's knockin herself out about arithmetic. And school suppose to let up in summer I heard, but she don't never let up. And the starch in my pinafore scratching the shit outta me and I'm really hating this nappy-head bitch and her goddamn college degree. I'd much rather go to the pool or to the show where it's cool. So me and Sugar leaning on the mailbox being surly, which is a Miss Moore word. And Flyboy checking out what everybody brought for lunch. And Fat Butt already wasting his peanut-butter-and-jelly sandwich like the pig he is. And Junebug punchin on Q.T.'s arm for potato chips. And Rosie Giraffe shifting from one hip to the other waiting for somebody to step on her foot or ask her if she from Georgia so she can kick ass, preferably Mercedes'. And Miss Moore asking us do we know what money is, like we a bunch of retards. I mean real money, she say, like it's only poker chips or monopoly papers we lay on the grocer. So right away I'm tired of this and say so. And would much rather snatch Sugar and go to the Sunset and terrorize the West Indian kids and take their hair ribbons and their money too. And Miss Moore files that remark away for next week's lesson on brotherhood, I can tell. And finally I say we oughta get to the subway cause it's cooler and besides we might meet some cute boys. Sugar done swiped her mama's lipstick, so we ready.

So we heading down the street and she's boring us silly about what things cost and what our parents make and how much goes for rent and how money ain't divided up right in this country. And then she gets to the part about we all poor and live in the slums, which I don't feature. And I'm ready to speak on that, but she steps out in the street and hails two cabs just like that. Then she hustles half the crew in with her and hands me a five-dollar bill and tells me to calculate 10 percent tip for the driver. And we're off. Me and Sugar and Junebug and Flyboy hanging out the window and hollering to everybody, putting lipstick on each other cause Flyboy a faggot anyway, and making farts with our sweaty armpits. But I'm mostly trying to figure how to spend this money. But they all fascinated with the meter ticking and Junebug starts laying bets as to how much it'll read when Flyboy can't hold his breath no more. Then Sugar lay bets as to how much it'll be when we get there. So I'm stuck. Don't nobody want to go for my plan, which is to jump out at the next light and run off to the first bar-b-que we can find. Then the driver tells us to get the hell out cause we there already. And the meter reads eight-five cents. And I'm stalling to figure out the tip and Sugar say give him a dime. And I decide he don't need it bad as I do, so later for him. But then he tries to take off with Junebug foot still in the door so we talk about his mama something ferocious. Then we check out that we on Fifth Avenue and everybody dressed up in stockings. One lady in a fur coat, hot as it is. White folks crazy.

"This is the place," Miss Moore say, presenting it to us in the voice 4 she uses at the museum. "Let's look in the windows before we go in."

"Can we steal?" Sugar asks very serious like she's getting the 5 ground rules squared away before she plays. "I beg your pardon," say Miss Moore, and we fall out. So she leads us around the windows of the toy store and me and Sugar screamin, "This is mine, that's mine, I gotta have that, that was made for me, I was born for that," till Big Butt drowns us out.

"Hey, I'm goin to buy that there."   6
"That there? You don't even know what it is, stupid."   7
"I do so," he say punchin on Rosie Giraffe. "It's a microscope."   8
"Whatcha gonna do with a microscope, fool?"   9
"Look at things."   10
"Like what, Ronald?" ask Miss Moore. And Big Butt ain't got the 11 first notion. So here go Miss Moore gabbing about the thousands of bacteria in a drop of water and the somethinorother in a speck of

blood and the million and one living things in the air around us is invisible to the naked eye. And what she say that for? Junebug go to town on that "naked" and we rolling. Then Miss Moore ask what it cost. So we all jam into the window smudgin it up and the price tag say $300. So then she ask how long'd take for Big Butt and Junebug to save up their allowances. "Too long," I say. "Yeh," adds Sugar, "outgrown it by that time." And Miss Moore say no, you never outgrow learning instruments. "Why, even medical students and interns and," blah, blah, blah. And we ready to choke Big Butt for bringing it up in the first damn place.

"This here costs four hundred eighty dollars," say Rosie Giraffe. So   12
we pile up all over her to see what she pointin out. My eyes tell me it's a chunk of glass cracked with something heavy, and different-color inks dripped into the splits, then the whole thing put into a oven or something. But for $480 it don't make sense.

"That's a paperweight made of semi-precious stones fused together   13
under tremendous pressure," she explains slowly, with her hands doing the mining and all the factory work.

"So what's a paperweight?" asks Rosie Giraffe.   14

"To weigh paper with, dumbbell," say Flyboy, the wise man from   15
the East.

"Not exactly," say Miss Moore, which is what she say when you   16
warm or way off too. "It's to weigh paper down so it won't scatter and make your desk untidy." So right away me and Sugar curtsy to each other and then to Mercedes who is more the tidy type.

"We don't keep paper on top of the desk in my class," say Junebug,   17
figuring Miss Moore crazy or lyin one.

"At home, then," she say. "Don't you have a calendar and a pencil   18
case and a blotter and a letter-opener on your desk at home where you do your homework?" And she know damn well what our homes look like cause she nosys around in them every chance she gets.

"I don't even have a desk," say Junebug. "Do we?"   19

"No. And I don't get no homework neither," says Big Butt.   20

"And I don't even have a home," say Flyboy like he do at school to   21
keep the white folks off his back and sorry for him. Send this poor kid to camp posters, is his specialty.

"I do," says Mercedes. "I have a box of stationery on my desk and   22
a picture of my cat. My godmother bought the stationery and the

desk. There's a big rose on each sheet and the envelopes smell like roses."

"Who wants to know about your smelly-ass stationery," say Rosie 23
Giraffe fore I can get my two cents in.

"It's important to have a work area all your own so that . . ." 24

"Will you look at this sailboat, please," say Flyboy, cuttin her off 25
and pointin to the thing like it was his. So once again we tumble all over each other to gaze at this magnificent thing in the toy store which is just big enough to maybe sail two kittens across the pond if you strap them to the posts tight. We all start reciting the price tag like we in assembly. "Handcrafted sailboat of fiberglass at one thousand one hundred ninety-five dollars."

"Unbelievable," I hear myself say and am really stunned. I read it 26
again for myself just in case the group recitation put me in a trance. Same thing. For some reason this pisses me off. We look at Miss Moore and she lookin at us, waiting for I dunno what.

"Who'd pay all that when you can buy a sailboat set for a quarter 27
at Pop's, a tube of glue for a dime, and a ball of string for eight cents? It must have a motor and a whole lot else besides," I say. "My sailboat cost me about fifty cents."

"But will it take water?" say Mercedes with her smart ass. 28

"Took mine to Alley Pond Park once," say Flyboy. "String broke. 29
Lost it. Pity."

"Sailed mine in Central Park and it keeled over and sank. Had to 30
ask my father for another dollar."

"And you got the strap," laugh Big Butt. "The jerk didn't even 31
have a string on it. My old man wailed on his behind."

"Little Q.T. was staring hard at the sailboat and you could see he 32
wanted it bad. But he too little and somebody'd just take it from him. So what the hell. "This boat for kids, Miss Moore?"

"Parents silly to buy something like that just to get all broke up," 33
say Rosie Giraffe.

"That much money it should last forever," I figure. 34

"My father'd buy it for me if I wanted it." 35

"Your father, my ass," say Rosie Giraffe getting a chance to finally 36
push Mercedes.

"Must be rich people shop here," say Q.T. 37

"You are a very bright boy," say Flyboy. "What was your first 38
clue?" And he rap him on the head with the back of his knuckles,

since Q.T. the only one he could get away with. Though Q.T. liable
to come up behind you years later and get his licks in when you half
expect it.

"What I want to know is," I says to Miss Moore though I never 39
talk to her, I wouldn't give the bitch that satisfaction, "is how much a
real boat costs? I figure a thousand'd get you a yacht any day?"

"Why don't you check that out," she says, "and report back to the 40
group?" Which really pains my ass. If you gonna mess up a perfectly
good swim day least you could do is have some answers. "Let's go in,"
she say like she got something up her sleeve. Only she don't lead the
way. So me and Sugar turn the corner to where the entrance is, but
when we get there I kinda hang back. Not that I'm scared, what's
there to be afraid of, just a toy store. But I feel funny, shame. But
what I got to be shamed about? Got as much right to go in as anybody. But somehow I can't seem to get hold of the door, so I step
away for Sugar to lead. But she hangs back too. And I look at her and
she looks at me and this is ridiculous. I mean, damn, I have never ever
been shy about doing nothing or going nowhere. But then Mercedes
steps up and then Rosie Giraffe and Big Butt crowd in behind and
shove, and next thing we all stuffed into the doorway with only Mercedes squeezing past us, smoothing out her jumper and walking right
down the aisle. Then the rest of us tumble in like a glued-together jig-
saw done all wrong. And people lookin at us. And it's like the time me
and Sugar crashed into the Catholic church on a dare. But once we
got in there and everything so hushed and holy and the candles
and the bowin and the handkerchiefs on all the drooping heads,
I just couldn't go through with the plan. Which was for me to run
up to the altar and do a tap dance while Sugar played the nose flute
and messed around in the holy waters. And Sugar kept givin me the
elbow. Then later teased me so bad I tied her up in the shower and
turned it on and locked her in. And she'd be there till this day if Aunt
Gretchen hadn't finally figured I was lyin about the boarder takin a
shower.

Same thing in the store. We all walkin on tiptoe and hardly tou- 41
chin the games and puzzles and things. And I watched Miss Moore
who is steady watchin us like she waiting for a sign. Like Mama
Drewery watches the sky and sniffs the air and takes note of just how
much slant is in the bird formation. Then me and Sugar bump smack
into each other, so busy gazing at the toys, 'specially the sailboat. But

we don't laugh and go into our fat-lady bump-stomach routine. We
just stare at that price tag. Then Sugar run a finger over the whole
boat. And I'm jealous and want to hit her. Maybe not her, but I sure
want to punch somebody in the mouth.

"Watcha bring us here for, Miss Moore?"   42

"You sound angry, Sylvia. Are you mad about something?" Givin 43
me one of them grins like she tellin a grown-up joke that never turns
out to be funny. And she's lookin very closely at me like maybe she
plannin to do my portrait from memory. I'm mad, but I won't give her
that satisfaction. So I slouch around the store bein very bored and say,
"Let's go."

Me and Sugar at the back of the train watchin the tracks whizzin 44
by large then small then gettin gobbled up in the dark. I'm thinkin
about this tricky toy I saw in the store. A clown that somersaults on a
bar then does chin-ups just cause you yank lightly at his leg. Cost $35.
I could see me askin my mother for a $35 birthday clown. "You
wanna who that costs what?" she'd say, cocking her head to the side
to get a better view of the hole in my head. Thirty-five dollars and the
whole household could go visit Grandaddy Nelson in the country.
Thirty-five dollars would pay for the rent and the piano bill too. Who
are these people that spend that much for performing clowns and
$1000 for toy sailboats? What kinda work they do and how they live
and how come we ain't in on it? Where we are is who we are, Miss
Moore always pointin out. But it don't necessarily have to be that
way, she always adds then waits for somebody to say that poor people
have to wake up and demand their share of the pie and don't none of
us know what kind of pie she talkin about in the first damn place. But
she ain't so smart cause I still got her four dollars from the taxi and
she sure ain't gettin it. Messin up my day with this shit. Sugar nudges
me in my pocket and winks.

Miss Moore lines us up in front of the mailbox where we started 45
from, seem like years ago, and I got a headache for thinkin so hard.
And we lean all over each other so we can hold up under the draggy-
ass lecture she always finishes us off with at the end before we thank
her for borin us to tears. But she just looks at us like she readin tea
leaves. Finally she say, "Well, what did you think of F.A.O.
Schwartz?"

Rosie Giraffe mumbles, "White folks crazy."   46

"I'd like to go there again when I get my birthday money," says 47

Mercedes, and we shove her out the pack so she has to lean on the mailbox by herself.

"I'd like a shower. Tiring day," say Flyboy.　48

Then Sugar surprises me by saying, "You know, Miss Moore, I 49 don't think all of us here put together eat in a year what that sailboat costs." And Miss Moore lights up like somebody goosed her. "And?" she say, urging Sugar on. Only I'm standin on her foot so she don't continue.

"Imagine for a minute what kind of society it is in which some 50 people can spend on a toy what it would cost to feed a family of six or seven. What do you think?"

"I think," say Sugar pushing me off her feet like she never done 51 before, cause I whip her ass in a minute, "that this is not much of a democracy if you ask me. Equal chance to pursue happiness means an equal crack at the dough, don't it?" Miss Moore is besides herself and I am disgusted with Sugar's treachery. So I stand on her foot one more time to see if she'll shove me. She shuts up, and Miss Moore looks at me, sorrowfully I'm thinkin. And somethin weird is goin on. I can feel it in my chest.

"Anybody else learn anything today?" lookin dead at me. I walk 52 away and Sugar has to run to catch up and don't even seem to notice when I shrug her arm off my shoulder.

"Well, we got four dollars anyway," she says.　53

"Uh hunh."　54

"We could go to Hascombs and get half a chocolate layer and then 55 to the Sunset and still have plenty money for potato chips and ice cream sodas."

"Uh hunh."　56

"Race you to Hascombs," she say.　57

We start down the block and she gets ahead which is O.K. by me 58 cause I'm goin to the West End and then over to the Drive to think this day through. She can run if she want to and even run faster. But ain't nobody gonna beat me at nuthin.

CONSIDERATIONS

1. Based on details in the first paragraph, about how old is the narrator? What particular characteristics lead you to this informed guess?

2. At what point in the story does Miss Moore's lesson first begin to take hold of Sylvia? What are Sylvia's specific reactions at that moment?
3. Why does Sylvia continue to resist Miss Moore's efforts to teach the children?
4. What tone do the slang and obscenities add to the story? What attitudes do you think the author has toward the kids?
5. WRITING TOPIC. Going to look at other people's great wealth — for instance, the elegant houses of the very rich or boats in a yacht basin — can sometimes be enjoyable and sometimes disturbing. Whatever the reaction, images of other people's wealth affect how we feel about ourselves. In 300 words, describe a specific example of great wealth that affected you favorably or made you feel uncomfortable on a particular occasion. Concentrate on fully describing the example, so that your response to it is supported by concrete details.
6. WRITING TOPIC. Miss Moore's lesson is "where we are is who we are." Do you agree? How would you react to that axiom if it was directed to you by the parents of the person you wish to marry? How much of yourself is defined by where you are? In 500 words, agree or disagree with the point of Miss Moore's lesson as it pertains to people of similar social standing.

Harry Crews

THE CAR

◊

HARRY CREWS (b. 1935), who was raised in Georgia, joined the Marine Corps after high school and became a sergeant before he left the Corps to go to college. He was educated at the University of Florida, where he now teaches writing. His novels include CAR (1972) and A Feast of Snakes (1976). He often writes for such magazines as Playboy and Esquire, in the second of which this essay first appeared.

The other day, there arrived in the mail a clipping sent by a friend 1
of mine. It had been cut from a Long Beach, California, newspaper
and dealt with a young man who had eluded police for fifty-five minutes while he raced over freeways and through city streets at speeds up
to 130 miles per hour. During the entire time, he ripped his clothes
off and threw them out the window bit by bit. It finally took twenty-
five patrol cars and a helicopter to catch him. When they did, he said
that God had given him the car, and that he had "found God."

I don't want to hit too hard on a young man who obviously has his 2
own troubles, maybe even is a little sick with it all, but when I read
that he had found God in the car, my response was: *So say we all.* We
have found God in cars, or if not the true God, one so satisfying, so
powerful, and awe-inspiring that the distinction is too fine to matter.
Except perhaps ultimately, but pray we must not think too much on
that.

The operative word in all this is *we.* It will not do for me to main- 3
tain that I have been above it all, that somehow I've managed to remain aloof from the national love affair with cars. It is true that I got a
late start. I did not learn to drive until I was twenty-one; my brother
was twenty-five before he learned. The reason is simple enough. In
Bacon County, Georgia, where I grew up, many families had nothing

327

with a motor in it. Ours was one such family. But starting as late as I did, I still had my share, and I've remembered them all, the cars I've owned. I remember them in just the concrete specific way you remember anything that changed your life. Especially I remember the early ones.

The first car I ever owned was a 1938 Ford coupe. It had no low 4 gear and the door on the passenger side wouldn't open. I eventually put a low gear in it, but I never did get the door to work. One hot summer night on a clay road a young lady whom I'll never forget had herself braced and ready with one foot on the rearview mirror and the other foot on the wind vent. In the first few lovely frantic moments, she pushed out the wing vent, broke off the rearview mirror and left her little footprints all over the ceiling. The memory of it was so affecting that I could never bring myself to repair the vent or replace the headliner she had walked all over upside down.

Eight months later I lost the car on a rain-slick road between Folk- 5 ston, Georgia, and Waycross. I'd just stopped to buy a stalk of bananas (to a boy raised in the hookworm and rickets belt of the South, bananas will always remain an incredibly exotic fruit, causing him to buy whole stalks at a time), and back on the road again I was only going about fifty in a misting rain when I looked over to say something to my buddy, whose nickname was Bonehead and who was half drunk in the seat beside me. For some reason I'll never understand, I felt the back end of the car get loose and start to come up on us in the other lane. Not having driven very long, I overcorrected and stepped on the brake. We turned over four times. Bonehead flew out of the car and shot down a muddy ditch about forty yards before he stopped, sober and unhurt. I ended up under the front seat, thinking I was covered with gouts of blood. As it turned out, I didn't have much wrong with me and what I was covered with was gouts of mashed banana.

The second car I had was a 1940 Buick, square, impossibly heavy, 6 built like a Sherman tank, but it had a '52 engine in it. Even though it took about ten miles to get her open full bore, she'd do over a hundred miles an hour on flat ground. It was so big inside that in an emergency it could sleep six. I tended to live in that Buick for almost a year and no telling how long I would have kept it if a boy who was not a friend of mine and who owned an International Harvester pickup truck hadn't said in mixed company that he could make the run from New Lacy in Coffee County, Georgia, to Jacksonville, Florida, quicker than I could. He lost the bet, but I wrung the speedometer off the Buick, and also — since the run was made on a blistering day in July — melted four inner tubes, causing them to fuse with the tires, which were already slick when the run started. Four new tires and tubes cost more than I had or expected to have anytime soon, so I sadly put that old honey up on blocks until I could sell it to a boy who lived up toward Macon.

After the Buick, I owned a 1953 Mercury with three-inch lowering 7 blocks, fender skirts, twin aerials, and custom upholstering made of rolled Naugahyde. Staring into the bathroom mirror for long periods of time I practiced expressions to drive it with. It was that kind of car. It looked mean, and it was mean. Consequently, it had to be handled with a certain style. One-handing it through a ninety-degree turn on city streets in a power slide where you were in danger of losing your ass as well as the car, you were obligated to have your left arm hanging half out the window and a very *bored* expression on your face. That kind of thing.

Those were the sweetest cars I was ever to know because they were 8 my first. I remember them like people — like long-ago lovers — their idiosyncrasies, what they liked and what they didn't. With my hands deep in crankcases, I was initiated into their warm greasy mysteries. Nothing in the world was more satisfying than winching the front end up under the shade of a chinaberry tree and sliding under the chassis on a burlap sack with a few tools to see if the car would not yield to me and my expert ways.

The only thing that approached working on a car was talking about 9 one. We'd stand about for hours, hustling our balls and spitting, telling stories about how it had been somewhere, sometime, with the car we were driving. It gave our lives a little focus and our talk a little credibility, if only because we could point to the evidence.

"But, hell, don't it rain in with that wing vent broke out like that?" 10

"Don't mean nothing to me. Soon's Shirley kicked it out, I known 11 I was in love. I ain't about to put it back."

Usually we met to talk at night behind the A&W Root Beer stand, 12 with the air heavy with the smell of grease and just a hint of burned French fries and burned hamburgers and burned hot dogs. It remains one of the most sensuous, erotic smells in my memory because through it, their tight little asses ticking like clocks, walked the sweetest softest short-skirted carhops in the world. I knew what it was to stand for hours with my buddies, leaning nonchalant as hell on a fender, pretending not to look at the carhops, and saying things like: "This little baby don't look like much, but she'll git rubber in three gears." And when I said it, it was somehow my own body I was talking about. It was *my* speed and *my* strength that got rubber in three gears. In the mystery of that love affair, the car and I merged.

But, like many another love affair, it has soured considerably. 13 Maybe it would have been different if I had known cars sooner. I was already out of the Marine Corps and twenty-two years old before I could stand behind the A&W Root Beer and lean on the fender of a 1938 coupe. That seems pretty old to me to be talking about getting rubber in three gears, and I'm certain it is *very* old to feel your own muscle tingle and flush with blood when you say it. As is obvious, I was what used to be charitably called a late bloomer. But at some point I did become just perceptive enough to recognize bullshit when I was neck deep in it.

The 1953 Mercury was responsible for my ultimate disenchant- 14 ment with cars. I had already bored and stroked the engine and contrived to place a six-speaker sound system in it when I finally started to paint it. I spent the better half of a year painting that car. A friend of mine owned a body shop and he let me use the shop on weekends. I sanded the Mercury down to raw metal, primed it, and painted it. Then I painted it again. And again. And then again. I went a little nuts, as I am prone to do, because I'm the kind of guy who if he can't have too much of a thing doesn't want any at all. So one day I came out of the house (I was in college then) and saw it, the '53 Mercury, the car upon which I had heaped more attention and time and love than I had ever given a human being. It sat at the curb, its black surface a shimmering of the air, like hundreds of mirrors turned to catch the sun. It had twenty-seven coats of paint, each coat laboriously hand-rubbed. It seemed to glow, not with reflected light, but with some internal light of its own.

I stood staring, and it turned into one of those great scary rare mo- 15 ments when you are privileged to see into your own predicament. Clearly, there were two ways I could go. I could sell the car, or I could keep on painting it for the rest of my life. If twenty-seven coats of paint, why not a hundred and twenty-seven? The moment was brief and I understand it better now than I did then, but I did realize, if imperfectly, that something was dreadfully wrong, that the car owned me much more than I would ever own the car, no matter how long I kept it. The next day I drove to Jacksonville and left the Mercury on a used-car lot. It was an easy thing to do.

Since that day, I've never confused myself with a car, a confusion 16 common everywhere about us — or so it seems to me. I have a car now, but I use it like a beast, the way I've used all cars since the Mercury, like a beast unlovely and unlikable but necessary. True as all that is, though, God knows I'm in the car's debt for that blistering winning July run to Jacksonville, and the pushed-out wing vent, and finally for that greasy air heavy with the odor of burned meat and potatoes there behind the A&W Root Beer. I'll never smell anything that good again.

CONSIDERATIONS

1. What does Crews mean in saying that "We have found God in cars"? Why does the thought lead him immediately to say, in almost the same breath, "pray we must not think too much on that"?
2. Crews seems to be exaggerating some details in his descriptions of his car and in his accounts of his experiences. What kind of exaggerations does he lard into his essay and what effects do they have on our response to him as a writer? What qualities of his might be objectionable? What qualities might be thought of as attractive?
3. At what point did Crews first begin to realize that he was identifying himself too closely with his cars? What other realization is it linked with?
4. In the final paragraph Crews says that people around him seem to be confusing themselves with their cars. In what ways? What features of common American life is he alluding to in that observation?
5. The tone of the essay includes some nostalgia — over what, precisely? What broader theme is included in his treatment of the main topic?
6. WRITING TOPIC. In 300 words, describe an object that you would like to own — that is, something such as a musical instrument, sports equipment, a vehicle, a collection, or some other specially personal object that you enjoy imagining in your possession. Include enough concrete details to make it appear real to your reader and indicate why it would have particular value for you.

E. M. Forster

MY WOOD

◊

E. M. FORSTER (1879–1970) was a British novelist and essayist who was educated at Cambridge University. Except for periods of travel to India and the Mediterranean, where he was deeply affected by his contacts with ancient cultures, he continued to live at his college through most of his adulthood. His fiction is often about conventionally educated young English people discovering something unconventional in themselves in response to symbolic places, such as other countries or old houses. Even the titles of his novels suggest traveling to take up a fresh perspective on things: *Where Angels Fear to Tread* (1905), *The Longest Journey* (1907), *A Room with a View* (1908), *Howards End* (1910), and *Passage to India* (1924), which is the book Forster mentions in the first sentence of this selection from his collection of essays *Abinger Harvest* (1936).

A few years ago I wrote a book which dealt in part with the diffi- 1 culties of the English in India. Feeling that they would have had no difficulties in India themselves, the Americans read the book freely. The more they read it the better it made them feel, and a check to the author was the result. I bought a wood with the check. It is not a large wood — it contains scarcely any trees, and it is intersected, blast it, by a public footpath. Still, it is the first property that I have owned, so it is right that other people should participate in my shame, and should ask themselves, in accents that will vary in horror, this very important question: What is the effect of property upon the character? Don't let's touch economics; the effect of private ownership upon the community as a whole is another question — a more important question, perhaps, but another one. Let's keep to psychology. If you own things, what's their effect on you? What's the effect on me of my wood?

In the first place, it makes me feel heavy. Property does have this 2 effect. Property produces men of weight, and it was a man of weight who failed to get into the Kingdom of Heaven. He was not wicked, that unfortunate millionaire in the parable, he was only stout; he stuck out in front, not to mention behind, and as he wedged himself this way and that in the crystalline entrance and bruised his well-fed flanks, he saw beneath him a comparatively slim camel passing through the eye of a needle and being woven into the robe of God. The Gospels all through couple stoutness and slowness. They point out what is perfectly obvious, yet seldom realized: that if you have a lot of things you cannot move about a lot, that furniture requires dusting, dusters require servants, servants require insurance stamps, and the whole tangle of them makes you think twice before you accept an invitation to dinner or go for a bathe in the Jordan. Sometimes the Gospels proceed further and say with Tolstoy that property is sinful; they approach the difficult ground of asceticism here, where I cannot follow them. But as to the immediate effects of property on people, they just show straightforward logic. It produces men of weight. Men of weight cannot, by definition, move like the lightning from the East unto the West, and the ascent of a fourteen-stone bishop into a pulpit is thus the exact antithesis of the coming of the Son of Man. My wood makes me feel heavy.

In the second place, it makes me feel it ought to be larger.   3

The other day I heard a twig snap in it. I was annoyed at first, for I 4 thought that someone was blackberrying, and depreciating the value of the undergrowth. On coming nearer, I saw it was not a man who had trodden on the twig and snapped it, but a bird, and I felt pleased. My bird. The bird was not equally pleased. Ignoring the relation between us, it took fright as soon as it saw the shape of my face, and flew straight over the boundary hedge into a field, the property of Mrs. Henessy, where it sat down with a loud squawk. It had become Mrs. Henessy's bird. Something seemed grossly amiss here, something that would not have occurred had the wood been larger. I could not afford to buy Mrs. Henessy out, I dared not murder her, and limitations of this sort beset me on every side. . . .

In the third place, property makes its owner feel that he ought to 5 do something to it. Yet he isn't sure what. A restlessness comes over him, a vague sense that he has a personality to express — the same sense which, without any vagueness, leads the artist to an act of creation. Sometimes I think I will cut down such trees as remain in the wood, at other times I want to fill up the gaps between them with new trees. Both impulses are pretentious and empty. They are not honest movements toward money-making or beauty. They spring from a foolish desire to express myself and from an inability to enjoy what I have got. Creation, property, enjoyment form a sinister trinity in the human mind. Creation and enjoyment are both very, very good, yet they are often unattainable without a material basis, and at such moments property pushes itself in as a substitute, saying, "Accept me instead — I'm good enough for all three." It is not enough. It is, as Shakespeare said of lust, "The expense of spirit in a waste of shame": it is "Before, a joy proposed; behind, a dream." Yet we don't know how to shun it. It is forced on us by our economic system as the alternative to starvation. It is also forced on us by an internal defect in the soul, by the feeling that in property may lie the germs of self-development and of exquisite or heroic deeds. Our life on earth is, and ought to be, material and carnal. But we have not yet learned to manage our materialism and carnality properly; they are still entangled with the desire for ownership, where (in the words of Dante) "Possession is one with loss."

And this brings us to our fourth and final point: the blackberries. 6

Blackberries are not plentiful in this meagre grove, but they are eas- 7
ily seen from the public footpath which traverses it, and all too easily gathered. Foxgloves, too — people will pull up the foxgloves, and ladies of an educational tendency even grub for toadstools to show them on the Monday in class. Other ladies, less educated, roll down the bracken in the arms of their gentlemen friends. There is paper, there are tins. Pray, does my wood belong to me or doesn't it? And, if it does, should I not own it best by allowing no one else to walk there? There is a wood near Lyme Regis, also cursed by a public footpath, where the owner has not hesitated on this point. He had built high stone walls each side of the path, and has spanned it by bridges, so that the public circulate like termites while he gorges on the blackberries unseen. He really does own his wood, this able chap. And perhaps I shall come to this in time. I shall wall in and fence out until I really taste the sweets of property. Enormously stout, endlessly avaricious, pseudo-creative, intensely selfish, I shall weave upon my forehead the quadruple crown of possession until those nasty Bolshies come and take it off again and thrust me aside into the outer darkness.

CONSIDERATIONS

1. In the second paragraph, the terms "heavy" and "weight" include non-literal meanings. Give a literal explanation of this first effect of property on Forster's character. What is added by Forster's figurative presentation?
2. In paragraph four, explain the effect of the short sentence: "My bird."
3. Explain Forster's somewhat difficult point about property becoming a substitute for creativity and enjoyment. From his viewpoint, how is that to be avoided?
4. The essay includes an abundance of references to history, literature, and religion, and they occur without much introduction or clarification. What is their purpose? And what is the effect of their suddenness?
5. WRITING TOPIC. Forster uses concrete and personal details to discuss generalities; that is, he talks about his own experiences in order to explain "the effect of property upon the character." Reversing the method, write a 500-word essay that generalizes Forster's observations. What complicated attitudes and possible hypocrisies over property ownership does he draw attention to? In addition to himself, who holds mixed views about property? What does he mean when he talks about the moral effects of property ownership in our society?

William Ryan

MINE, ALL MINE*

◊

WILLIAM RYAN (b. 1923) is a professor of psychology at Boston College. His special interest in the psychological stresses of modern American life is reflected in his earlier books, *Distress in the City* (1969) and *Blaming the Victim* (1971). This selection is from *Equality* (1981), in which Ryan argues that the concept of property ownership and the amassing of great wealth are linked to insecurities over individual identity.

How do you get to own something? Well, you usually buy it. But how did the fellow you bought it from get to own it? Where did the idea of *owning* come from? Or was it always there, perhaps in the mind of God?

No one really knows, of course. The idea of owning and property emerged in the mists of unrecorded history. One can try to imagine the scene. Some Cro-Magnon innovator, seized with a fit of entrepreneurial passion, took his club and drew a line in the earth and called out, "Okay, you guys! Everything inside this line is mine. It belongs to me. I own it." Now, very likely, this first would-be landowner was a skinny, little, near-sighted Cro-Magnon who couldn't throw a spear straight and was able to drag by the hair only the homeliest girls of the tribe. A couple of his fellow cavemen may have kicked sand in his face, but most of the others probably laughed indulgently, kidding him about his intellectual pretensions, his ways of using big words like "belong" and "own" that nobody else knew the meaning of. "That Herman! A regular walking dictionary!" And they rubbed out Herman's line on the ground. (I am counting on a fair amount of good humor among the Cro-Magnons; another telling of the story might

---

* Editor's title.

assume more malevolence and end with their rubbing out Herman himself.)

But, as we all know, a good idea never dies, and sooner or later a 3 hefty, well-respected caveman who carried a big club picked up Herman's notion, drew his own line in the earth, and made his claim stick. Others drew their lines, taking possession of the land merely by outlining its boundaries, and then talked about what they owned and what belonged to them. The forcible seizure of what had been until then common property, if property at all, led first to emulation, as others also seized portions of land, and ultimately to the development of ideas and relationships that could be thought to coincide with the new reality. Rather than having men who had the muscle power to seize and men who had not, we had landowners and the landless; instead of loot from the seizure, we had "property," then property laws by the chapter, and finally the revelation that the institution of private property had been ordained by God. These concepts — landowner, property, and property rights — became common currency, unquestioned and unquestionable ideas, as natural and expected as the sunrise or as water flowing downhill, which we take for granted and don't give another thought. And that is the central nature of ideology.

If you do stop and think about it, it's quite remarkable. An individ- 4 ual human being, occupying a blip on the screen of time, has the incredible gall to stand up and say, "*I* own this land; this land is *mine*." He's talking about an acre or a hundred acres of the *earth*, a piece of the *planet*! And he says it's *his*! Isn't that really an incredible claim to make?

And he doesn't just say he owns the earth, he also says that he owns 5 what comes out of it and what is buried beneath it. The owner of the land lays claim to the grain and the grass that spring up from it and to the cattle that feed on the grain and the grass. He lays claim to the oil and the iron that lie beneath the ground and then to the steel made from the iron and to the automobile made from the steel and to the gasoline made from the oil. He counts as his property the tree that grows on the land and the wood of the tree and the buildings on the land made from the wood. He *owns* those things, he says; they *belong* to him. And we all act as if it were true, so it must be true. But behind all these claims, supporting and upholding them — and our willingness to believe them — is the big club of the hefty Cro-Magnon who made the first claim and dared his fellows to oppose him. The club is smaller and neater now, hanging from the belt of the policeman, but the principle remains the same.

Is it possible that the ideas we have today about ownership and 6 property rights have been so universal in the human mind that it is truly as if they had sprung from the mind of God? By no means. The ancient Jews, for one, had a very different outlook on property and ownership, viewing it as something much more temporary and tentative than we do. Mosaic law with respect to ownership of land (the only significant productive property of the time) is unambiguous:

> And the land shall not be sold in perpetuity; for the land is Mine; for ye are strangers and settlers with Me. And in all the land of your possession ye shall grant a redemption for the land. (Lev. 25:23–24)

The buying and selling of land was based on principles very different from those we know. It was not, in fact, the land itself that changed hands, but rather the right to use the land to cultivate crops. The price of the land was determined by the number of years, and therefore the number of crops, remaining until the next jubilee year, when the land reverted to the family that originally possessed it. Under such a law, buying land is similar to the process we call leasing.

The institution of the jubilee year was a specific mechanism for 7 rectifying the inequities that had accumulated, for simultaneously restoring liberty *and* equality for all:

> And ye shall hallow the fiftieth year, and proclaim liberty throughout the land unto all the inhabitants thereof; it shall be a jubilee unto you; and ye shall return every man unto his possession, and ye shall return every man unto his family. (Lev. 25:10)

There is no doubt that these laws were violated. Prophet after prophet condemned as violations efforts to accumulate wealth unjustly:

> Woe unto them that join house to house, that lay field to field, till there be no place, that they may be placed alone in the midst of the earth! (Isaiah, 5:8)

But that the law was violated and the violation condemned is a demonstration of its existence and applicability. Although the law of jubilee was evaded more and more and ultimately fell into disuse, there can be no doubt that it was adhered to for many generations.

Similarly, the tenure of land in the agrarian feudal ages was hedged 8 all about with restrictions and accompanied by specific obligations

that the landowner owed to his tenants. These restrictions and obligations, too, were frequently evaded and violated — perhaps more often
than they were honored — but they were unquestionably part of the
structure of law and custom until the dawn of the modern era, when
the very idea of land began to change and when land began to be
equated with capital, as the new commercial classes began to impose
their own view of private property as something with which one could
do more or less what one pleased.

A bit later, Europeans invented a new method of earning riches,   9
that of "discovery," and they came to America and claimed the
land — on the grounds that they had never seen it before — and then
went through the arduous labor of possessing by bounding. To most
of the Native American tribes, the land was not subject to "ownership" by individuals. Their thinking was expressed eloquently by a
Blackfeet chief:

> As long as the sun shines and the waters flow, this land will be here to
> give life to man and animals. We cannot sell the lives of men and ani-
> mals; therefore we cannot sell this land. It was put here by the Great
> Spirit and we cannot sell it because it does not belong to us.

The Europeans' peculiar ideas about individuals' claiming exclusive
ownership of specific portions of God's earth seemed strange, at first
incomprehensible and then irksomely eccentric. The Indians eventually learned to their sorrow that it was no eccentricity, but rather a
murderous mania.

In modern times, of course, we have the example of socialist coun-   10
tries where private ownership of any significant amount of property
that constitutes "means of production" is prohibited as antisocial and
antihuman.

So, the ideas we have in America (and in the majority of the   11
world's nations) about the private ownership of productive property as
a natural and universal right of mankind, perhaps of divine origin, are
by no means universal and must be viewed as an invention of man
rather than a decree of God. Of course, we are completely trained to
accept the idea of ownership of the earth and its products, raw and
transformed. It seems not at all strange; in fact, it is quite difficult to
imagine a society without such arrangements. If someone, some *individual*, didn't own that plot of land, that house, that factory, that machine, that tower of wheat, how would we function? What would the

rules be? How would we know how to act? Whom would we buy from and how would we sell?

It is important to acknowledge a significant difference between 12
achieving ownership simply by taking or claiming property and owning what we tend to call the "fruits of labor." If I, alone or together with my family, work on the land and raise crops, or if I make something useful out of natural material, it seems reasonable and fair to claim that the crops or the objects belong to me or my family, are my property, at least in the sense that I have first claim on them. Hardly anyone would dispute that. In fact, some of the early radical workingmen's movements made [an ownership] claim on those very grounds. As industrial organization became more complex, however, such issues became vastly more intricate. It must be clear that in modern society the social heritage of knowledge and technology and the social organization of manufacture and exchange account for far more of the productivity of industry and the value of what is produced than can be accounted for by the labor of any number of individuals. Hardly any person can now point and say, "That — that right there — is the fruit of *my* labor." We *can* say, as a society, as a nation — as a world, really — that what is produced is the fruit of *our* labor, the product of the whole society as a collectivity. . . .

No one man could conceivably build a house with only twelve 13
times the amount of time and effort that twelve men expend in building the same house. Yet we ignore this evident reality. Even the workmen, though their experience makes them aware of it, have no way of thinking and talking about it. So, when the man who bought the land, the lumber, the nails, and the wire comes around at the end and gives them each a check for the "value of their labor" — and then even has the chutzpah to bestow upon himself the title "builder" — no one doubts that he, that individual, now is the rightful owner of that house. It has become his property.

With all of this distortion and overemphasis on individual action, 14
the idea of private property and ownership of pieces of the earth is still pretty much limited to that portion of the earth that is actually land. We cannot readily imagine buying a piece of air or seeking a mortgage on a segment of ocean. The idea of owning the air and the seas seems as incomprehensible to us as the idea of owning his own factory must seem to a Russian (although we are beginning to see a rapidly growing interest in extending the idea of ownership to these elements, particu-

larly as the oceans come to be seen more clearly as a means of production, not only of fish, but of other food, of oil, and perhaps of minerals).

We would have a similar feeling if we watched someone sailing out 15 into the Atlantic and marking out a line of buoys to the north, east, south, and west and then proclaiming to whoever might listen, "These waves are mine. I own this piece of ocean. This water and the fish therein and the plankton and the salt and the seaweed belong to me. The water is mine and the fullness thereof." Hardly anyone would agree with him or honor his claim, no matter how much he might talk about the divine rights of man to own the ocean.

We have to recognize that the right of private individual ownership 16 of property is man-made and constantly dependent on the extent to which those without property believe that the owner can make his claim stick.

One way of making the claim stick is to remove it from the realm of 17 human agreements, to mystify it, to clothe it in myths, of which the most important with respect to the so-called right of private ownership of social product and the things that make this product possible is the myth of the lone "supernormal" individual. It is only by saying — louder and louder, over and over again — "I! I! I!" that we can then get away with saying "my" and "mine."

CONSIDERATIONS

1. Ryan begins with an anecdote about cavemen in order to illustrate the possible origin of private property. Does the anecdote *simplify* his point, or is it *simplistic*? That is, does it help us understand his explanation, or does it divert us from noticing other possible origins? Do other explanations sound more or less plausible to you?
2. In the fourth paragraph, the phrase "a blip on the screen of time" is a figure of speech that makes a metaphor out of what object? Is it appropriate to Ryan's tone?
3. According to Ryan, how did people formerly uphold their vast claims of property ownership? What historical exceptions and restrictions to the concept of private ownership does he mention?
4. Ryan says: "It must be clear that in modern society the social heritage of knowledge and technology and the social organization of manufacture and exchange account for far more of the productivity of industry and the

value of what is produced than can be accounted for by the labor of any number of individuals." Obviously, it isn't all that "clear" or else Ryan's sentence would be easier to understand. Paraphrase what he is saying, and add your own illustrations to clarify his point.

5. What is the main means through which contemporary society upholds the concept of private ownership of property? How does it differ from past societies?

6. WRITING TOPIC. If you were designing a utopian society, what would you allow individuals to own privately? In a 500-word essay, explain why your utopian plan for ownership would be good for people.

Matthew

THE LILIES OF
THE FIELD

◊

MATTHEW (first century A.D.), who was a tax collector for the Roman
Empire in Galilee, became a disciple of Jesus and wrote one of the four
Gospels that relate the life of Jesus in the New Testament. In this passage (Matthew 6:19–34) from the Sermon on the Mount, Jesus gives
advice about righteous living and the pursuit of wealth. Matthew
writes that when Jesus finished his sermon the people who had assem-
bled on the mountainside to hear him "were astonished at his doctrine," because he spoke with such strong personal conviction about
questions of holiness and virtue. This translation into English is from
the Revised Standard Version.

"Do not lay up for yourselves treasures on earth, where moth and 19
rust consume and where thieves break in and steal,

but lay up for yourselves treasures in heaven, where neither moth 20
nor rust consumes and where thieves do not break in and steal.

For where your treasure is, there will your heart be also. 21

"The eye is the lamp of the body. So, if your eye is sound, your 22
whole body will be full of light;

but if your eye is not sound, your whole body will be full of dark- 23
ness. If then the light in you is darkness, how great is the darkness!

"No one can serve two masters; for either he will hate the one and 24
love the other, or he will be devoted to the one and despise the other.
You cannot serve God and mammon.

"Therefore I tell you, do not be anxious about your life, what you 25
shall eat or what you shall drink, nor about your body, what you shall
put on. Is not life more than food, and the body more than clothing?

Look at the birds of the air: they neither sow nor reap nor gather 26 into barns, and yet your heavenly Father feeds them. Are you not of more value than they?

And which of you by being anxious can add one cubit to his span of 27 life?

And why are you anxious about clothing? Consider the lilies of the 28 field, how they grow; they neither toil nor spin;

yet I tell you, even Solomon in all his glory was not arrayed like one 29 of these.

But if God so clothes the grass of the field, which today is alive and 30 tomorrow is thrown into the oven, will he not much more clothe you, O men of little faith?

Therefore do not be anxious, saying, 'What shall we eat?' or 'What 31 shall we drink?' or 'What shall we wear?'

For the Gentiles seek all these things; and your heavenly Father 32 knows that you need them all.

But seek first his kingdom and his righteousness, and all these 33 things shall be yours as well.

"Therefore do not be anxious about tomorrow, for tomorrow will 34 be anxious for itself. Let the day's own trouble be sufficient for the day.

CONSIDERATIONS

1. Biblical writing is loaded with repetitions of words and phrases. Underline and connect some of the repeated expressions in this passage. What effects would the repetition have on the people listening to this sermon?
2. What are the illustrations from nature meant to show?
3. What does Jesus advise people to do about the practical necessities of life? How do you suppose this sermon made the audience feel?
4. WRITING TOPIC. What connections between poverty and piety do you observe in the world around you? Are people more likely to be religious if they are not wealthy? Are people with security and some luxuries more grateful for life? Do material possessions diminish or increase one's reverence for spiritual values? In 500 words, support, refute, or modify the message in the Sermon on the Mount.

John Brooks

TELEPHONE GAMESMANSHIP*

◊

JOHN BROOKS (b. 1920) lives in New York City, and as a staff writer for *The New Yorker,* he writes about the American business scene and Wall Street. He graduated from Princeton University, and his earlier works include the novels *A Pride of Lions* (1954) and *The Man Who Broke Things* (1958). His entertaining *New Yorker* essays were the basis of his book *The Fate of the Edsel and Other Business Adventures* (1963). More recently, he has taken a broader look at wealth in American society in *Showing Off in America* (1977). This book shows how it is sometimes more effective not to flaunt wealth or power. If it is hidden, there is less danger of an opponent matching or outdoing you. For instance, in the following excerpt Brooks argues that an ordinary phone call involves each caller in a hidden contest for power.

The telephone is the most important single artifact of modern so- 1
cial relations. Vast and vital industries, such as the securities business and international money trading, are conducted almost exclusively over it, and so are some private lives. Not surprising, then, that it is both taken for granted and seldom out of our thoughts.

This was all true to a lesser extent at the turn of the century 2
when. . . . the telephone was a quarter of a century old . . . and several million instruments were already in use in the United States. Its effect on manners had been noted by Mark Twain as early as 1879, the third year after its invention. Nevertheless, it remained both technologically and socially in an underdeveloped state. For example, coast-to-coast and overseas service did not yet exist. The industry itself was in a state of turmoil. The original Bell patents had recently expired, freeing anyone to set up a separate system, in competition with the Bell System; as a result, many towns and cities had two or more unconnected sys-

* Editor's title.

tems, resulting in communication chaos and — not incidentally — invidious social distinctions between subscribers to the various systems in a given place. In many rural areas where Bell had not yet deigned to provide service, farmers had strung wires over trees and fenceposts and hired a farm girl to serve as central operator, thus creating their own do-it-yourself cooperative systems. These systems provided surcease from loneliness and a degree of protection from physical danger among the isolated people of an underpopulated continent. "Central" was a message center and fountain of gossip. Such functions had from the point of view of social relations as a character nothing like that of the telephone today. Nevertheless, the modern characteristics of the telephone were beginning to manifest themselves. . . .

Having a telephone means both vulnerability and power — vulner- 3 ability because it lays one open to anyone, friend, foe, or stranger; power because it gives access to the vulnerability of others. Because of this characteristic, the telephone seems to create at least one problem for every one that it solves. Commercial solicitation by telephone — oral junk mail — is for many a particularly infuriating form of gratuitous assault on privacy, and one that some have for many years campaigned to have outlawed, so far without success. The insolence of telephoners, who, on getting a wrong number and thereby disturbing an innocent party, then brusquely hang up rather than apologizing, causes some victims of this double indignity to seethe and fume. At a greater extreme, obscene calls, which are illegal, and eavesdropping by wiretap, which may be either legal or illegal according to circumstances, are forms of assault by telephone that point up the telephone owner's vulnerability.

The available nontechnological defenses are relatively frail and 4 self-defeating. The principal one consists of avoiding incoming calls by leaving the instrument off the hook, switching off the bell if such a switch is available, putting chewing gum on the bell to silence it, or simply letting the telephone ring in a closed bureau drawer or under a pillow. That is to say, it consists of creating temporarily the condition of not having a telephone. . . .

This attack-and-defense aspect of the telephone, what may possibly 5 be called its sadomasochistic quality, is sharply emphasized by the basic purpose of practically all of the technical innovations in "terminal" telephone equipment — the equipment used in home or office — that have been introduced and have become popular over the years. Ostensibly, each such innovation was intended to increase convenience. On analysis, however, the real purpose invariably turns out to be to minimize vulnerability and increase power. Michael Korda,* an authority on office invidiousness, points out that "power . . . in telephoning is to have the maximum ability to place telephone calls together with the minimum possibility of receiving them." That is the basic function of practically all terminal-equipment innovations.

The first and simplest of these was the extension telephone. The industrialist E. H. Harriman early in this century seems to have been the pioneer user of multiple extensions. At one time he had one hundred of them in his country mansion, Arden House; among the rooms thus supplied was his bathroom. The multiple-extension user obviously gains the advantage of being able to place calls at any time from wherever he happens to be, and thus not only to place calls more conveniently but also to place more of them. Meanwhile, he is protected from receiving unwanted calls by a necessary component of such a system, one or more servants who screen incoming calls and pass on to the user only the calls that are appropriate and acceptable. Indeed, very early in commercial telephony the symbol of telephone authority came to be to have such a screener, so that a caller could not reach the authoritative one without first satisfying an intermediary — a clear instance, of course, of classic . . . invidiousness. Again very early in the game, not only businessmen but also others likely to get many unwanted calls, such as rich, attractive, and therefore highly desirable young women, took to having their calls screened for them.

Next came the unlisted number, a grosser form of roadblock 7 against callers because it entirely screens out all who do not know the number. An additional and incidental measure of invidiousness is achieved by an unlisted number's clear implication that its possessor is in constant demand for one reason or another, and is obliged to keep away hoi polloi or go mad. Many who are not in any special demand have adopted unlisted numbers solely to make this implication. The disadvantage of the unlisted number is that, since it is impossible to keep all eligible callers properly informed of the number (some of them may have the number but lose it), many wanted calls are

6

* Michael Korda is the author of *Success!* (1977), advice for business executives.

missed — that is, for most people it is *too* gross a screening device. (Not too gross, however, for a restaurant in Los Angeles called Ma Maison, which maintains an unlisted number. Just to call it up and beg for a chance to partake of its delights and pay its prices, one must be among the few in the know.)

The answering service — a post–Second World War development 8 that had to wait as long as it did because it requires the technical capability of switching calls from the called number to the service — made the screening of calls available for the first time to those who could not afford a full-time hired personal screener. Another postwar development, the speaker phone, gives an additional form of power edge. It enables the user to allow a whole roomful of his associates to listen to everything the party at the other end of the line says — a fact not necessarily known to the distant party. Korda says that in the nineteen-seventies speaker phones for business use suddenly became "very status-y." To dramatize the puissant, perhaps dangerously so, advantage that a speaker phone can confer, imagine an apartment-full of delectable young women living in a big city who have installed one. Calls from foolish and ardent suitors would be broadcast to everyone present in the apartment, for their information and amusement — an elaboration of the old habit of sought-after college girls, in the all-women institutions of the past, of conspicuously displaying their desirability and insouciance by passing around the more unsolicited of their love letters.

The introduction of what is called "key equipment" — a panel of 9 buttons available to the telephone user, the most crucial of which is the "Hold" button, enabling a called party (or for that matter, a calling party) to cut off the interlocutor, leaving him dangling in limbo, still connected but incommunicado, for as long as the button-pusher wishes — represents an important advance in telephone invidiousness. Functionally, the Hold button provides a mechanical way of achieving the same result formerly achieved by the winner of the old game between secretaries of contriving to get the other secretary's boss on the line before one's own boss comes on. The loser waits. (Lillian Hellman in *Pentimento* describes a fine exploit in the secretary game, of which she was the victim. One summer when she was in Martha's Vineyard, her telephone rang and it was Samuel Goldwyn's secretary. After Miss Hellman and the secretary had had a pleasant chat, the secretary said that Mr. Goldwyn had been trying to reach her for two days to ask if she wanted to write the script for the movie of *Porgy and Bess.* Whereupon, after a long wait, Goldwyn came on and said, "Hello, Lillian, hello. Nice of you to call me after all these years. How can I help you?")

In the simplest terms, the Hold button saves the button-pusher's 10
time and wastes that of the person put on Hold. (If he has called from a pay booth, it also wastes his money.) It is as nakedly invidious as possible, a fact emphasized by the manufacturer's name for a forty-eight-button office panel currently on the market, which is coolly called "Patrician." Strategically, the only answer to being put on Hold is to hang up — a solution as self-defeating as that of the home user who puts the telephone in a closed drawer. No wonder Korda advises, in bloodthirsty italics, "There is no doubt that *the more people you yourself can put and keep on Hold, the more successful you will seem.*"

Another fairly recent innovation is the wireless remote phone, con- 11
nected to the telephone network by radio, which enables the user to make or receive calls while in an aircraft, yacht, moving automobile, or the like. It is, of course, a further refinement of the principle of multiple extensions. A refinement of *it* is the beeper, which, while up to now it falls short of allowing the user to talk or listen from wherever he happens to be, is capable of summoning him at any time to the nearest telephone to receive a call. The beeper appears to violate the law that telephone innovations, to be successful, must increase the ability to make calls and decrease the ability to receive them. However, the beeper, so long as it remained a novelty and did not become a vulgar nuisance, had a unique ability to enhance the user's esteem, at least in the eyes of some, by beeping during social occasions such as dinner parties, thus calling attention in the most conspicuous possible way to the user's importance. In recent years, though, the beeper has fallen from grace. It is now commonly in the hands of low-status persons such as messengers and couriers, and thus has lost its status-enhancing power through democratization. Thus the iron law of telephone invidiousness has reasserted itself: to be effectively predatory, a telephone appliance must make the user harder to reach, not easier. . . .

A particularly versatile and mettlesome innovation of fairly recent 12
vintage is the home telephone answering machine. It provides opportunities considerably greater than those afforded by the answering ser-

vice, chiefly because the user, the receiving party, can deal with the caller as he chooses, and immediately rather than later. To begin with, the answering machine relies on an initial tape-recorded "announcement" by the machine user, which is automatically broadcast to any caller as soon as he reaches the number. Instead of the usual "hello" of a human answerer, the caller gets some such formula as, "This is Nancy Harman. We are not available at the moment. If you wish to leave a message, you may do so after you hear the signal, and we will call back." Since the announcement can be erased and rerecorded by the machine owner at will, it gives latitude for wide variation; on different days, the tone can be forbidding, sepulchral, jocular, aggressive, humble, according to whim. . . .

If the machine user is actually away when the machine is operating — as he says in his announcement that he is — he simply plays back any messages on his return. The machine functions exactly like an answering service, except that many people who will give messages to services refuse to give them to machines. It is when the user is secretly at home, and the machine turned on as a measure of deception, that its versatility comes into play. By activating the machine, turning its monitor up so that messages may be heard, by speaker, and remaining within earshot, the user may hear the caller's return messages as it is being delivered, secure in the knowledge that the caller believes him to be out. However, if the user wishes he may pick up the phone, switch off the machine, and talk directly to the caller. The machine thus affords the user, without the intervention of any third party, the basic power-gaining ability to answer only the calls he wants to answer. There are, of course, difficulties. The caller who, giving a message to the machine, is interrupted by the voice of the machine owner in real life, realizes that the device is being used for call-screening and is momentarily flattered at being among the elect to whom the machine owner is willing to talk. On reflection, though, the caller may remember previous occasions when his message on the machine has *not* been interrupted, and conclude that on those occasions, too, the machine user was really at home, in which case the caller was *not* elected, but instead was blackballed. That is, a current of invidiousness as strong as that made possible by the machine superimposed on the telephone itself is subject to a certain amount of feedback. 13

The commercial fate of the Picturephone, surely the most spectacular of recent telephone terminal equipment innovations, illustrates 14 vividly the rule that such innovations must increase the user's power in order to be successful. After years of research and development, the Bell System introduced the Picturephone commercially in 1970. Basically, it applies the principle of closed-circuit television to the telephone. The user has at hand not only a telephone receiver and transmitter but also a television receiver and transmitter. To make a picture call, one dials in the normal way the number of another Picturephone subscriber. After being connected, one adjusts knobs for picture clarity on one's screen, as does the recipient of the call; whereupon the two are not only in voice contact but also eyeball to eyeball. The year of the Picturephone's introduction, a popular book on business etiquette forehandedly included an earnest section on Picturephone manners — wear a colored shirt, avoid a "snarling countenance," don't worry about jewelry blinding out the lens, and so on — and the Bell System ventured to predict that one million Picturephone sets would be in service by 1980.

The fact that in 1980 the Picturephone still has to be described 15 drives home the point that this has not happened. The Picturephone is a flop, and was recognized as such by the Bell System as early as 1975. The few set owners who acquired them at the outset, in expectation of riding the crest of a new fashion, now find them almost useless, because there is hardly anyone else with a Picturephone set to call — or perhaps one should say conjure — up.

Various reasons have been adduced for the Picturephone's failure 16 to catch on for either business or private use. The original one, much raised when the device was in the development stage, was that it was a "mere toy," of little or no substantive value; the Bell men replied at the time that precisely the same criticism, expressed in the same words, had been directed at the telephone itself in the first years after its invention. Another theory holds that the Picturephone does have some substantive value — the capacity to convey nuances of meaning and feeling through gesture and facial expression, the capacity to display pictures and documents — but not enough to justify its considerable extra expense. But as we well know, neither uselessness nor excessive expense necessarily militates against an object's popularity in our society; rather . . . they categorically work in its favor. Probably the real cause of the Picturephone's failure is neither of these. Probably it is closely related to the telephone's traditional and natural use as an instrument of predatory invidiousness.

First, unlike the other technical innovations that have achieved 17
popularity the Picturephone cannot give its user an edge, because it is
necessarily bilateral. The person victimized by a Hold button or a
home answering machine may not have those amenities attached to
his own telephone, but the party called by Picturephone must have a
Picturephone, too. The power gained by seeing the interlocutor is balanced by the vulnerability incurred through being seen. (A Picturephone user can turn off his picture transmitter, but the other party
will then certainly retaliate in kind.) Beyond that, it is not possible
that most people simply do not want to see or be seen on the telephone — that the secrecy, and resultant feeling of power, inherent in
voice contact without visual contact is a principal reason people like
to use the telephone in the first place? If not, why do people so often
prefer to communicate, especially if the subject is painful or delicate,
by telephone rather than face-to-face? The Picturephone, out of its
nature, is open and aboveboard, equitable and noninvidious — fatal
qualities, it appears, in a telephone innovation.

As a natural weapon of social war, the telephone goes too far. Like 18
sport conducted without sportsmanship, it tends to tip the balance
between predatory invidiousness and peaceable savagery too far toward the former. Consequently, an unwritten telephone code, a kind
of telephone sportsmanship, has arisen to redress the balance. Letitia
Baldridge sets forth the basics of the code in the tone of piety once
used for exhortations to sportsmanship: adopt "a voice containing a
smile"; pronounce words clearly and carefully; avoid technical jargon
and overfamiliarity; don't try to get the upper hand by "failing to
react in any way to the person to whom you are speaking"; scrupu-
lously apologize upon reaching a wrong number, and so on. Even
Korda, the apostle and teacher of invidiousness, mentions that people
don't like to be put and kept on Hold. He explains that some people
must never be put on Hold — your mother, your boss, your wife, your
bookie, the Number One best-seller — while many others can.

This, of course, is the opposite of traditional sportsmanship, a ben- 19
efice conferred evenhandedly by the sportsman on all comers and
never a means of winnowing the important from the unimportant.
Korda's system of applying or not applying the Hold button isn't
sportsmanship; it is bullying and toadying. Still, there are signs of an
emerging code in the use of power-increasing telephone devices. Some

celebrities who have ample reason to maintain unlisted phones instead maintain ordinary listed ones, presumably as proof of their peaceable savagery (in this case, with overtones of democratic declassing). An increasing number of leading corporate executives answer their own phones whenever possible. Some who have speaker phones carefully inform the person on the other end that his voice is being amplified; conversely, and equally blamelessly, people calling from yachts or private jets make a point of *not* boasting about their whereabouts; and a distinct taboo against using Hold buttons unnecessarily has grown up to the point where many who have one, just in case, nevertheless regard its use with horror, as a low blow in the social bout. They would no sooner put someone they respect on Hold than hang up on him.

We recognize these mitigations of invidiousness, predicated on power, as the equivalent of traditional British sportsmanship of avoiding what is "not cricket"; in Theodore Rooseveltian diplomacy, as walking softly and carrying a big stick; and in poker, as the maneuver called "coffee-house." . . . But meanwhile, there continue to be plenty of telephone equivalents of the Ilie Nastases and Vince Lombardis of sport.*

20

* A tennis player and a football coach, both notorious for their highly competitive behavior.

CONSIDERATIONS

1. Do you agree with the generalization in the first sentence of the essay? Is the telephone a more important modern artifact than, for instance, the car? Does the rest of the paragraph confirm the main generalization?
2. In paragraphs 3, 4, and 5 what figurative language does Brooks use to emphasize his points? What is its effect on you as a reader? or as a telephoner?
3. In paragraphs 6, 7, and 8 Brooks gives examples of what he calls telephone "invidiousness." How are they different from instances of simple *selectivity?* Why does Brooks find them objectionable?
4. How does Brooks explain the commercial failure of the Picturephone? What view of human nature does his explanation include? Do you think he understands why people like — or don't like — to use the phone?

5. What new code of behavior have some users adopted? How does it potentially lead to a new level of gamesmanship?
6. WRITING TOPIC. Brooks's essay pertains to adults, but do his observations also apply to the way teenagers use the phone? To the dismay of most parents, teenagers appear to talk on the phone endlessly and tirelessly. The telephone may be serving teenagers as an important device for dealing with their social situations. Are there terms of telephone gamesmanship for teenagers? Or don't they play status games? In 500 words, explain the telephone's role in the social relations of teenagers. Try to illustrate your points with specific examples.

Susan C. Carlisle

FRENCH HOMES AND
FRENCH CHARACTER

◊

SUSAN C. CARLISLE (b. 1933) grew up in Philadelphia, Pennsylvania — but not in any specially memorable house that influenced her character, as she recalls. After graduating from Cornell University, she began the first of many visits to France, including a stint as director of foreign study programs for college students. She has taught English in Canton, New York, and in Boston, Massachusetts, where she earned an advanced degree at Boston University. Her poems have appeared in *Epoch* and *Andover Review*. This article, which appeared first in *Landscape* magazine in 1982, is based on her experiences in France, living in a more formal society than ours, where barriers to quick friendship appear to be built into French houses.

Thirty years ago when I first lived in France, I was intrigued by the formality of human relationships there. I noticed how much the French valued discretion and how they maintained a psychic distance from one another. The formal handshake achieves this distance. So do strict rules about how people address each other (Bonjour, *Madame!*). But during my six other years in France, I came to believe that the French insist on physical, as well as psychic, distance. They seem to extend their need for privacy and discretion to the way they organize spaces. They create material barriers against close human relationships. These barriers can be found by exploring the French home. . . .

Not only do people tell us about their character, however inadvertently, when they plan their homes, but once they have built these spaces, they set up environmental constraints that guide us in understanding why certain attitudes are perpetuated. Thus, we can guess how personal relationships might be molded and maintained by the layout of French dwellings — both houses and apartments.

Home as Fortress

What impression does the French house present to the outside 3
world? The most casual tourist could answer that. Fortified. Impenetrable. Though often decorated by building materials and flower boxes,
houses usually are protected by walls. The walls normally are thick,
opaque, and higher than the human eye. Pieces of broken glass occasionally are distributed along the top. The gate is solid wood or a high
metal grill, usually not transparent. The first barrier between those inside the house and those outside is presented unambiguously.

Even in the traditional Parisian apartment house, access to the 4
door of an apartment is not easy. Older buildings contain a massive
porte cochere within which a smaller door generally is carved. The visitor is obliged to step over a portion of the larger door. The impression
is one of entering, with difficulty, a cave. This difficulty is intentional,
and often viewed as desirable. Marcel Proust remembered his
mother's distress at deciding whether to move to an apartment house
with a door that opened directly onto the street, when she felt that a
porte cochere would be safer and more chic.

Until the 1960s urban entranceways were watched carefully by 5
those fixtures of French history and literature, the concierges. When I
first lived in Paris, the concierges who released the lock were ageless
French women bundled in layers of grey wool, who lived, always with
a little dog and sometimes with a husband, in a one-room apartment.
They were busybodies — repositories of information and guardians of
the inhabitants. Gradually, during the sixties, these women were replaced by young Portugaises and Espagñoles with babies and a less
proprietary interest in the building. Newer apartment houses now
have locks that spring open automatically when the *ouvre-porte* button is pushed. Significantly, the locks do not disappear, although they
are rendered useless by the mechanism that opens them. Custodial
duties have been taken over by men, often invisible, but ironically
only now called *gardiens.* Thus, though humans at the gates of apartment buildings now function less obviously as sentinels, the traditional material barriers have not disappeared.

Another element of the French facade worthy of note is the shut- 6
ter. Shutters are universal even today. The traditional *volets* that had
to be closed, and which *were* closed every night, by awkwardly open-

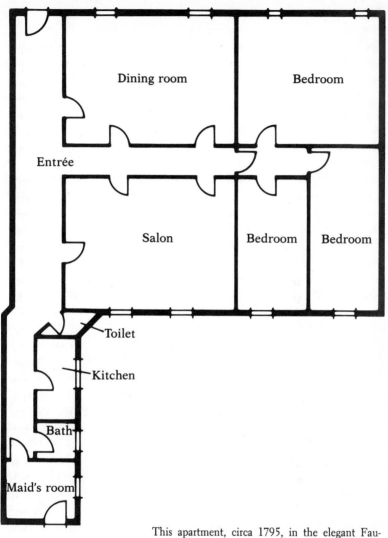

This apartment, circa 1795, in the elegant Faubourg St. Germain, was built for and still is occupied by French aristocrats. It is a striking example of hierarchical architecture. Note the tiny kitchen for the servants and its great distance from the dining room. The elaborate separation of spaces, typical of most French households, is revealed here; the entry and corridor have fifteen doors.

ing wide the windows and reaching out to unfold the panels, have given way to various systems that close off the window by lowering a flexible metal panel. Though the utility of shutters in the twentieth century could be questioned, the French home remains a fortress, even if it is on the tenth floor of a modern highrise.

Even when the shutters are open during the day, it is rare to see a 7 window in France without a translucent white curtain. It is common to find several sets of curtains that function in different ways. The glass curtains allow insiders to see out, while outsiders cannot see in. Heavier, more ornamental curtains are decorative when open, and are drawn at night to keep insiders from having to see closed shutters. Thus, while shutters close out the world, curtains close in the family.

Assuming we have gotten past the wall, the grille, the concierge, 8 and the locked entry, as outsiders we have arrived only on the doorstep, or *palier*, of the residence. We have not yet penetrated the interior. We must ring still another bell and wait while a series of locks is unfastened. In my experience, until recently few doors in France had only one lock, even apartment doors protected by concierges. Because the locks predated the fear of violent criminals and burglars, the series of locks and bolts must have meant protection from the outside world in general, not just its criminal element. If the French consistently fortify their dwellings, are they not likely to fortify their personalities? Perhaps we could hypothesize that a society with so many walls and shutters is made up of discreet and somewhat distrustful people.

If we have rung and the door is opened, we find ourselves in the 9 *entrée* of the house or apartment. Not even the most modest dwelling, . . . not even the most modern, does away completely with an area designed to prevent access to the living spaces. Whether a simple corridor or an elaborate and formal foyer, the entry is surrounded by doors that stop the uninvited intruder from penetrating farther into the private confines of the home. Not a single dwelling in our sample has a door from the outside that opens directly into the living and dining area. The average number of doors leading from the entry hall is six. As there is an area of reserve even inside the home, so with French social behavior, there is an area of coolness and formality even inside the initial barriers. The French do not make friends quickly or easily. They do not call virtual strangers by their first names, nor do they ask personal questions. This behavior could represent a psychic *entrée*, an inner region of protection and defense in the French character. It is unnecessary for us to make a schematic conceptual representation of layers of reserve in the French personality because the architecture of French homes gives us tangible evidence of reserve. In the entryway we can see and experience the French reluctance to accept others easily, as well as the strong inclination toward privacy in the family circle.

So far, I have distinguished loosely between insiders and outsiders. By *outsiders*, we mean anyone not in the immediate family. By *insiders*, we mean the nuclear family, what the French would call the *foyer*. Originally, the word foyer was tied to words meaning *fire* and *hearth*. Insiders in France are those who clustered around the family hearth. Within the French home, we discover that certain rooms are places of assembly for insiders and other rooms are places of withdrawal. Still other rooms are places of interaction between insiders and outsiders. Nonfamily insiders — servants — have their own living and working areas, usually at a considerable distance from the family. All of the spatial distinctions are clear, and spaces that function one way are seldom interchangeable with spaces that function another way. 10

As guests entering a French home, we will be shown into the *entrée* by a servant, if any, and our coats probably will be hung on pegs in this area, or in a closet in more modern buildings. Bedrooms seldom are used as coatrooms. Then we will be ushered into the salon. This is the formal, public room of the house. It is often furnished with antiques and is the showplace of certain family treasures. Styles and preferences in French furniture have changed considerably over the past twenty years. A study of these changes probably would uncover striking changes in French attitudes toward personal relationships. But the traditional salon was furnished with fragile, uncomfortable, often precious single chairs. These were placed at a considerable distance from each other, and guests were uncertain about where to set their drinks. Conspicuously absent were comfortable sofas, comfortable armchairs, and the low coffee tables that are the center of conviviality in the American living room. 11

Thus, the salon, with its stiff and formal disposition of furniture, is set aside specifically for the family to encounter outsiders. The room is otherwise little used. It is not uncommon to see French salons, curtains drawn, in which the furniture is protected with dust covers; the room clearly is off limits in the normal course of family events. The salon has evolved in the past twenty years in the direction of what the 12

French call the *living room* or the *salle de séjour* (vacation room), a multipurpose room with functions less clearly defined than those of the traditional salon. But the very name *vacation room* still leads us to believe that, perhaps, across the hall, there lurks even now a darkened formal salon reserved for special occasions.

A preoccupation with image, with *présentation*, with how the fam- 13
ily looks, is revealed in the salon. In many areas of French life — food, fashion, window display, diplomacy — presentation enjoys a high priority. Yet because intimacy is not encouraged, either by the comfort or arrangement of furniture, we can guess that the French prefer to keep outsiders at a distance. The French salon is neither relaxed nor relaxing. Domestic arrangements do, indeed, tell us about social attitudes.

Dining

Though the salon and the dining room have been moving closer to- 14
gether over the years until the spatial constraints of modern living often cause them to overlap, the change has been slow. The traditional dining room (*salle d manger*) is usually across an entrance hall or corridor from the salon, and it is here that the intensely close life of the French family takes place. The dining room is the "foyer of the foyer," a source of heat and light, or nourishment and conversation for the family. A table, often very large, is in the center. Chairs, usually more than the family needs, are placed around it and against the walls. Outsiders have been envisaged in this room. Their inclusion in a family meal is a sign that they have succesfully crossed many barriers between the family and the outside.

Where a separate dining room exists, it is a big or bigger than the 15
salon. Where only one room is available for both receiving and eating, dining activities take precedence. This has always been true even in small farmhouses and cramped quarters, and it continues to be true in the modern *salle de séjour*. In France, family life — decisions, arguments, banter — goes on around the dining table. Meals are obligatory and long. Space for communal relaxation is rendered almost unnecessary by the dining imperative, and where salons exist, they are not always used. No wonder the French family's television set is usually in the dining room. The dining room is the centripetal area of

the home. Its function as the focal point of sociability within the family tells us about French values.

Another piece of furniture, called a *buffet*, almost always found in   16
the French dining room, also gives clues to French attitudes. This massive and often antique storage cabinet holds precious objects, pieces of the family wealth used for dining: silver, crystal, china. As if the walls of the dwelling were not enough, the buffet is a fortress in itself. Like the home, the buffet is a defense against the outside world. Within it, order reigns and chaos is excluded. The buffet also symbolizes the family's continuity with the past. It protects the family's present possessions and it itself is expected to survive and be passed to future generations.

Corridors

The three areas we have visited — the *entrée*, the salon, and the   17
dining room — are connected by a corridor. Corridors appeared in the eighteenth century. Today they lead from public to private rooms, from democratic to autocratic space. What Americans call the *master bedroom* is the most distant and thus the most protected. Long corridors often separate the kitchen from the dining room. In all cases the receiving and dining areas are separated from the areas of excreting, washing, cooking, and, if possible, sleeping.

If the width of the corridor allows, one piece of furniture, or, more   18
precisely, one piece of movable architecture is universal: the armoire. No matter where it is found in the dwelling, the armoire is of considerable significance. This is a gigantic, portable closet, usually at least six feet tall, made of carved wood. Its locked doors conceal shelves of linens, the trousseau of the wife. Like the buffet, the armoire is a safe. Even its name has a military ring. The family wealth protected here is in the form of linens — heavy, hand-embroidered sheets, pillowcases, and towels, often handed down from mother to daughter, but always added to by hopeful parents during their daughter's late teens. Bachelard speaks* of the interior space of the armoire as profound and intimate. In his opinion, the armoire is the center of order in the French household — an order that is not just geometric, but an order established by the family's history.

* Gaston Bachelard, *The Poetics of Space*, 1964.

Times and values change. The trousseau is dying. But there are 19
millions of armoires in France. The tradition of private wealth fiercely
protected and of history doggedly kept alive is embodied in them. As
long as armoires remain, that tradition will be perpetuated.

Corridors are needed only when domestic spaces are compartmen- 20
talized and differentiated. We do not find them in Japanese houses. If
the French assign specific functions to certain areas of their houses,
perhaps this is evidence of an urge to compartmentalize all experience, to analyze, to order, to control. Armoires and buffets point to
the same need. This compartmentalization and hierarchical arrangement of space might reflect social attitudes. Indeed, the French would
be the first to admit they are class-conscious; social stratification is far
from dead in France. The idea of being, or marrying into, a "good
family" is still important to most French people. In fortifying their
dwellings and possessions, they are very likely guarding the foyer
against encroachment by social inferiors.

Kitchen, Bath, and Bedroom

France, despite its genius for exquisite food, is almost backward in 21
terms of kitchen space. Most French kitchens are conceived with such
disdain for comfort and convenience that one marvels at the gastronomic delights emerging from them. Kitchen floors are cold tile. An
air vent is mandatory for kitchens with gas stoves, which most Pari-
sians use. This intensifies the problem of drafts. Counters, if any, are
uncomfortably low. Lighting is poor, and electrical outlets are scarce.
Until recently the French were too distrustful of their neighbors to
subscribe to a central hot-water system. The upshot was that French
kitchens, as well as bathrooms, were encumbered by awkward, un-
sightly, and often dangerous water heaters.

Traditionally, kitchens were separated from dining rooms because 22
of the danger of kitchen fires. However, the smallness and discomfort
of French kitchens, as well as their distance from the dining room,
suggest a hierarchy in which the convenience of servants was a matter
of indifference. The separateness of the kitchen also reflects an es-
thetic or gastronomic concern for eating away from cooking odors in
order to maximize the enjoyment of food.

Servants are becoming rare in France, and people modernizing old 23 houses and apartments inevitably start with the kitchen. Second homes often have bigger kitchens than primary ones. But the space available in existing buildings is a real constraint; a democratic kitchen in which people can sit, eat, and talk is difficult to provide. Because of spatial constraints, the idea of a nonhierarchical kitchen probably seldom occurs to French people — another example of the circular phenomenon in which people design buildings with one set of human relationships in mind and their descendants are obliged to live in those buildings and to behave as if the original relationships were still valid. Hierarchy dies slowly in a country with hierarchical architecture.

Since indoor plumbing came there has been little variation in the 24 pattern of the French bathroom. One small, closetlike space encloses the toilet, and one larger space called the *salle de bains* or the *salle d'eau*, contains the sink, bidet, and bathtub. It is obvious from this division of space that excretion and washing are separated in the French mind. Only the most most modern French bathrooms house both a toilet and a bathtub. A further example of compartmentalization can be found in the existence of the bidet and the bidet's placement, not with the toilet, but with the bathtub and sink.

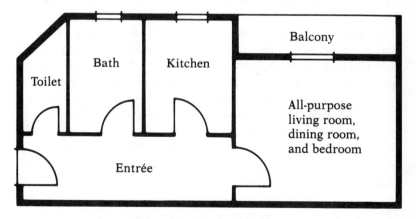

Built between the two world wars, this Paris apartment near the Porte de Montmartre was intended for low-income workers. It has concrete floors and a single room for eating, sleeping, and socializing. Still, in the traditional French manner, there is no direct access from the kitchen to this main room. Even here, the corridor, with its five doors, protects the living space.

Does this observation shed light on attitudes toward sex, hygiene, and discretion?

The French bedroom is space exempt from public scrutiny. The activities performed in it are the most private. Even family members knock before entering each other's bedrooms. Furniture found in French bedrooms reveals that the room is not used only for sleeping. At least one comfortable chair invites relaxation. A table or desk may be provided where children can do their time-consuming and exacting homework. If there are bookcases in the house, they usually will be found in the bedrooms. If there is good reading light, it also will be found in the bedrooms. Acceptable and intimate reading light seldom is found elsewhere. Solitary activities are discouraged in the more public rooms not only by the discomfort and placement of the furniture but by the lighting. The chandeliers and wall fixtures of the dining room and salon never seem to provide enough intensity. 25

In the bedroom, even a shared bedroom, the French person finally can relax. If there is any area in the French home where individuality can be asserted, it is here. None of the other spaces lend themselves to declaring one's self as an individual, rather than as a being connected with the family or with society as a whole. An outsider invited into a French bedroom has arrived at the core of the house, and probably at a profound and durable stage of friendship with its occupant. Formality and reserve finally can be shed. Distrust has been overcome. 26

Because French bedrooms are very private and protected by corridors, doors, public rooms, and rules about access, we might suspect that the French personality also includes a private self, a core defended against others, even other family members. Laurence Wylie speaks specifically or the French person's "refuge within himself," and of "the formation of a thick protective shell around the personality which will protect it from the intrusion of 'others.' " Wylie feels that the French are trained to resist others. Their bedrooms resist others too, and outer domestic spaces all fortify and defend the bedrooms. . . . 27

Architecture and Character

. . . It can be argued that the French home is a blueprint of the French personality. The French seem to want to live behind barriers. They value the central self so highly that they protect it fiercely. How- 28 ever, in defense of this important psychic space, they behave according to accepted ways of doing things. What else but conformity should we expect in a society whose domestic architecture incorporates so many elements from its history? French domestic space, even today, conserves vestiges of the French past. In the entrée and in the small kitchen, we find hints of distrust and class consciousness in conformity with tradition, not in defiance of it. In the salon and the armoire we find history preserved, not [superseded]. . . .

If conformity outweighs individuality in the French character, this   29
is reflected in the arrangement of French domestic space. Or is it the other way around? Homes both shape and reflect character. The circularity of our relationship to domestic architecture is apparent. If French behavior changes, so, slowly, will French homes. But the architecture will act as it does in many cultures: as inertia, a force against change.

CONSIDERATIONS

1. What architectural features of a fortress are also found in American residences? How are these French features changed, if at all, in American homes?
2. According to the author, what living arrangements are undemocratic in French homes? Where in the French home is this most obvious? Do you agree with Carlisle that these arrangements have political significance?
3. Why is the French dining room likely to be the largest room in the residence? What is the largest room in your family's home?
4. WRITING TOPIC. Do you think that your family truly fits your house, or is your family misrepresented by your house? In 700 words, point out the correspondences and contrasts between your home and your family. Carefully describe household features that reflect and reinforce specific attitudes and customs.

Lewis Hyde

GIFTS IN MOTION*

◊

LEWIS HYDE (b. 1945) teaches English at Harvard University. He received degrees from the University of Minnesota and the University of Iowa before returning to his birthplace, Boston, Massachusetts. His poems, articles, and notable translations of Spanish poetry have appeared in the *Kenyon Review, Paris Review, American Poetry Review,* and the *Nation.* He has worked as an alcoholism counselor, a part-time teacher at Tufts University, and also as an odd-jobber to support himself while writing. From these experiences he has acquired a personal perspective on the difficulties of maintaining creativity in a commercial society, which is the problem that he examines in *The Gift: Imagination and the Erotic Life of Property* (1982). In the following excerpt from that book, Hyde argues that a true gift is a present that you do not keep.

When the Puritans first landed in Massachusetts, they discovered a 1 thing so curious about the Indians' feelings for property that they felt called upon to give it a name. In 1764, when Thomas Hutchinson wrote his history of the colony, the term was already an old saying: "An Indian gift," he told his reader, "is a proverbial expression signifying a present for which an equivalent return is expected." We still use this, of course, and in an even broader sense, calling that friend an Indian giver who is so uncivilized as to ask us to return a gift he has given.

Imagine a scene. An Englishman comes into an Indian lodge, and 2 his hosts, wishing to make their guest feel welcome, ask him to share a pipe of tobacco. Carved from a soft red stone, the pipe itself is a peace offering that has traditionally circulated among the local tribes, stay-

---

* Editor's title.

ing in each lodge for a time but always given away again sooner or later. And so the Indians, as is only polite among their people, give the pipe to their guest when he leaves. The Englishman is tickled pink. What a nice thing to send back to the British Museum! He takes it home and sets it on the mantelpiece. A time passes and the leaders of a neighboring tribe come to visit the colonist's home. To his surprise he finds his guests have some expectation in regard to his pipe, and his translator finally explains to him that if he wishes to show his goodwill he should offer them a smoke and give them the pipe. In consternation the Englishman invents a phrase to describe these people with such a limited sense of private property. The opposite of "Indian giver" would be something like "white man keeper" (or maybe "capitalist"), that is, a person whose instinct is to remove property from circulation, to put it in a warehouse or museum (or, more to the point for capitalism, to lay it aside to be used for production).

The Indian giver (or the original one, at any rate) understood a cardinal property of the gift: whatever we have been given is supposed to be given away again, not kept. Or, if it is kept, something of similar value should move on in its stead, the way a billiard ball may stop when it sends another scurrying across the felt, its momentum transferred. You may keep your Christmas present, but it ceases to be a gift in the true sense unless you have given something else away. As it is passed along, the gift may be given back to the original donor, but this is not essential. In fact, it is better if the gift is not returned but is given instead to some new, third party. The only essential is this: *the gift must always move.* There are other forms of property that stand still, that mark a boundary or resist momentum, but the gift keeps going.

Tribal peoples usually distinguish between gifts and capital. Commonly they have a law that repeats the sensibility implicit in the idea of an Indian gift. "One man's gift," they say, "must not be another man's capital." Wendy James, a British social anthropologist, tells us that among the Uduk in northeast Africa, "any wealth transferred from one subclan to another, whether animals, grain, or money, is in the nature of a gift, and should be consumed, and not invested for growth. If such transferred wealth is added to the subclan's capital (cattle in this case) and kept for growth and investment, the subclan is regarded as being in an immoral relation of debt to the donors of the original gift." If a pair of goats received as a gift from another subclan is kept to breed or to buy cattle, "there will be general complaint that the so-and-so's are getting rich at someone else's expense, behaving immorally by hoarding and investing gifts, and therefore being in a state of severe debt. It will be expected that they will soon suffer storm damage. . . ."

The goats in this example move from one clan to another just as 5 the stone pipe moved from person to person in my imaginary scene. And what happens then? If the object is a gift, it keeps moving, which in this case means that the man who received the goats throws a big party and everyone gets fed. The goats needn't be given back, but they surely can't be set aside to produce milk or more goats. And a new note has been added: the feeling that if a gift is not treated as such, if one form of property is converted into another, something horrible will happen. In folk tales the person who tries to hold on to a gift usually dies; in this anecdote the risk is "storm damage." (What happens in fact to most tribal groups is worse than storm damage. Where someone manages to commercialize a tribe's gift relationships the social fabric of the group is invariably destroyed.). . . .

. . . A gift that cannot move loses its gift properties. Traditional be- 6 lief in Wales holds that when the fairies give bread to the poor, the loaves must be eaten on the day they are given or they will turn to toadstools. . . .

Another way to describe the motion of the gift is to say that a gift 7 must always be used up, consumed, eaten. *The gift is property that perishes.* . . . Food is one of the most common images for the gift because it is so obviously consumed. Even when the gift is not food, when it is something we would think of as a durable good, it is often referred to as a thing to be eaten. Shell necklaces and armbands are the ritual gifts in the Trobriand Islands, and when they are passed from one group to the next, protocol demands that the man who gives them away toss them on the ground and say, "Here, some food we could not eat." Or, again, a man in another tribe that Wendy James has studied says, in speaking of the money he was given at the marriage of his daughter, that he will pass it on rather than spend it on himself. Only, he puts it this way: "If I receive money for the children God has given me, I cannot eat it. I must give it to others."

Many of the most famous of the gift systems we know about center 8 on food and treat durable goods as if they were food. The potlatch of the American Indians along the North Pacific coast was originally a "big feed." At its simplest a potlatch was a feast lasting several days given by a member of a tribe who wanted his rank in the group to be publicly recognized. Marcel Mauss translates the verb "potlatch" as "to nourish" or "to consume." Used as a noun, a "potlatch" is "feeder" or "place to be satiated." Potlatches included durable goods, but the point of the festival was to have these perish as if they were food. Houses were burned; ceremonial objects were broken and thrown into the sea. One of the potlatch tribes, the Haida, called their feasting "killing wealth."

To say that the gift is used up, consumed and eaten sometimes 9 means that it is truly destroyed as in these examples, but more simply and accurately it means that the gift perishes *for the person who gives it away.* In gift exchange the transaction itself consumes the object. Now, it is true that something often comes back when a gift is given, but if this were made an explicit condition of the exchange, it wouldn't be a gift. . . . This, then, is how I use "consume" to speak of a gift — a gift is consumed when it moves from one hand to another with no assurance of anything in return. There is little difference, therefore, between its consumption and its movement. A market exchange has an equilibrium or stasis: you pay to balance the scale. But when you give a gift there is momentum, and the weight shifts from body to body.

I must add one more word on what it is to consume, because the 10 Western industrial world is famous for its "consumer goods" and they are not at all what I mean. Again, the difference is in the form of the exchange, a thing we can feel most concretely in the form of the goods themselves. I remember the time I went to my first rare-book fair and saw how the first editions of Thoreau and Whitman and Crane had been carefully packaged in heat-shrunk plastic with the price tags on the inside. Somehow the simple addition of airtight plastic bags had transformed the books from vehicles of liveliness into commodities, like bread made with chemicals to keep it from perishing. In commodity exchange it's as if the buyer and the seller were both in plastic bags; there's none of the contact of a gift exchange. There is neither motion nor emotion because the whole point is to keep the balance, to make sure the exchange itself doesn't consume anything or involve one person with another. Consumer goods are consumed by their owners, not by their exchange.

The desire to consume is a kind of lust. We long to have the world 11 flow through us like air or food. We are thirsty and hungry for something that can only be carried inside bodies. But consumer goods merely bait this lust, they do not satisfy it. The consumer of commodities is invited to a meal without passion, a consumption that leads to neither satiation nor fire. He is a stranger seduced into feeding on the drippings of someone else's capital without benefit of its inner nourishment, and he is hungry at the end of the meal, depressed and weary as we all feel when lust has dragged us from the house and led us to nothing.

Gift exchange has many fruits . . . and to the degree that the fruits 12 of the gift can satisfy our needs there will always be pressure for property to be treated as a gift. This pressure, in a sense, is what keeps the gift in motion. When the Uduk warn that a storm will ruin the crops if someone tries to stop the gift from moving, it is really their desire for the gift that will bring the storm. A restless hunger springs up when the gift is not being eaten. The brothers Grimm found a folk tale they called "The Ungrateful Son":

> Once a man and his wife were sitting outside the front door with a roast chicken before them which they were going to eat between them. Then the man saw his old father coming along and quickly took the chicken and hid it, for he begrudged him any of it. The old man came, had a drink, and went away.
> Now the son was about to put the roast chicken back on the table, but when he reached for it, it had turned into a big toad that jumped in his face and stayed there and didn't go away again.
> And if anybody tried to take it away, it would give them a poisonous look, as if about to jump in their faces, so that no one dared touch it. And the ungrateful son had to feed the toad every day, otherwise it would eat part of his face. And thus he went ceaselessly hither and yon about in the world.

This toad is the hunger that appears when the gift stops moving, 13 whenever one man's gift becomes another man's capital. To the degree that we desire the fruits of the gift, teeth appear when it is hidden away. When property is hoarded, thieves and beggars begin to be born to rich men's wives. A story like this says that there is a force seeking to keep the gift in motion. Some property must perish — its preservation is beyond us. We have no choice. Or rather, our choice is whether to keep the gift moving or to be eaten with it. We choose between the toad's dumb-lust and that other, more graceful perishing in which our hunger disappears as our gifts are consumed.

CONSIDERATIONS

1. How does gift giving differ among primitive people and people in modern western civilization? How do we maintain some primitive customs about gift giving?
2. Why is food the most common type of gift? What attitudes and expectations for both the giver and the recipient are symbolized by gifts of food?
3. According to the author what are the differences between "gift exchange" and "commodity exchange"?
4. What are the author's opinions about our present economic system? What outlook on the future does he imply for America and the rest of the world?
5. WRITING TOPIC. Are you sometimes given a gift of money instead of a present selected by the giver? On important occasions such as a graduation, Christmas, a bar mitzvah, or a wedding in the family, have significant amounts of money changed hands and accumulated instead of presents? What specific disappointments were avoided or created by giving money? In 500 words, write about the change in values on one specific occasion when you gave or received money in place of a selected gift.
6. WRITING TOPIC. What unwritten rules and careful arrangements applied to the exchange of gifts among your friends during your final year in high school? At Christmas, at graduation, or on birthdays during the year, did you find yourself paying more than usual attention to giving and receiving gifts among your friends? How did you determine the cost that would be appropriate for each gift? Did some people receive gifts only because they were part of a group including other, more valued friends? Writing as an observer of the customs of high school students, explain in 700 words the system of gift exchange that operated at that time among you and your friends.

ADDITIONAL
WRITING TOPICS

◊

POSSESSIONS

1. Everyone has felt the hope of winning big money in a lottery, a contest, or a bet on a long shot. The lure of Las Vegas and other gambling casinos is part of popular entertainment in movies and television; many states now conduct public lotteries and offer daily gambling on the numbers game; breakfast-food and fast-food companies sponsor nationwide contests with labels or matching tickets; horse races and many other sports events include the possibility of big payoffs. Write a 750-word essay on the many ways and reasons why we are stimulated to keep expecting to win sudden riches.

2. In many households there happens to be some specially treasured object that is associated with earlier generations or with an important period in the recent family past. Perhaps it is a vase or lamp or a Bible or jewelry or a piece of furniture or a rug. The object comes to be treated as something precious and irreplaceable — even though it may be a fairly common thing — because it embodies certain ideals or sentimental associations. Select some object that holds this special status, and write a 500-word extended description of it that conveys its physical appearance and its meaningfulness as a possession.

3. People often express themselves in the way they furnish and decorate their own rooms or apartments. In 500 words — or more if you wish — describe one room that suggests the character of someone outside your immediate family. Consider colors and textures as well as objects. Give concrete, precise details, and organize your description so your reader can acquire a sense of the whole room as well as vivid impressions of its particular features.

4. Our possessions can possess us — and they frequently do, sometimes delightfully, sometimes harmfully. Nearly everyone has sometimes felt that the essence of life was summed up for the moment by a record collection, or a pair of skis, or earrings, or a special pair of jeans. In 500 words, explain how your obsession with a special personal belonging arose, and clarify the ways it affected your life then or now. Be sure to give your reader a sense of the importance of this possession at the time you required it.

5. When we wear certain fashionable clothes, or wear clothes in a certain fashionable way, are we communicating something real about ourselves, or something acknowledged to be purely an illusion? What is the purpose of "fashion" in the way we dress? Write a 500-word essay on a fashion, such as designer jeans or loose shirt tails, that you adopted for some deliberate effect.

6. You have probably been seized at least once by a passion for collecting something — stamps, comic books, records, stuffed animals, Matchbox cars, or art prints. Write a 750-word essay about the joys (and the tinge of madness) of collecting. Include some explanation of how you got started, how you developed your collection, and what makes it interesting to pursue or to remember.

7. In a 500-word essay, explain how something you once proudly owned turned into an unexpected, larger responsibility. What were the welcome or unpleasant effects of owning that particular thing or animal? How did it affect other aspects of your life?

8. In 500-words, describe something you owned that once made you feel better about yourself — such as a special article of clothing, a bicycle, a toy, seashells, or any object to which you felt personally attached. Include enough information about the object and yourself to make your attachment to it understandable. With details and explanations, help the reader see the object as you saw it while it was important to you — and perhaps also as you see it now if the difference is relevant.

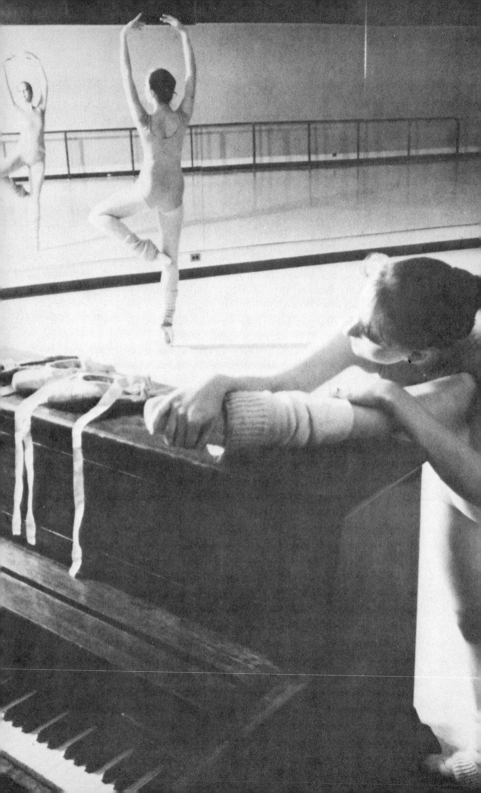

PART 6

AMBITIONS

Joseph Epstein, *The Virtues of Ambition*

Russell Baker, *My Lack of Gumption*

Richard Rodriguez, *Reading for Success*

Seymour Wishman, *A Lawyer's Guilty Secrets*

Pete Hamill, *Winning Isn't Everything*

Michael Novak, *The Metaphysics of Sports*

Virginia Woolf, *Professions for Women*

Sherwood Anderson, *The Egg*

Henry David Thoreau, *Where I Lived, and What I Lived For*

William Butler Yeats, *The Lake Isle of Innisfree*

Christopher Lasch, *Survival Mentality*

Additional Writing Topics

INSIGHTS

Ah, but a man's reach should exceed his grasp,
Or what's a heaven for?

— ROBERT BROWNING

◊

What many young people fail to realize is the fact that you don't have to be much better than most others in order to do well. Only a slight superiority may be enough to make a vast difference.

Most of the people we call successful are not twice as smart, or twice as able, as the rest of the field. Indeed, if they are only 10 percent more proficient, this is generally more than enough to give them a consistent edge.

In sports, for instance, the best batting or passing records are not a great deal higher than the average. In field or track the differences are even smaller: a fraction of an inch or a fraction of a second may distinguish the winner from the also-rans. . . .

If you can average 5 to 10 percent better — no more — than others in your field, the rewards can be 100 percent greater; this is the compounding effect of achievement over a period of time. . . .

You only have to be a little bit better than most in what you do. Just a little smarter, just a little steadier, just a little more energetic, or whatever other prime quality is demanded in your field. If successes admitted this, they would not have cause to feel so conceited; and if the aspirants recognized this, they would not have cause to feel so left behind at the starting line.

— SYDNEY J. HARRIS

◊

Occupational incompetence is everywhere. Have you noticed it? Probably we all have noticed it.

We see indecisive politicians posing as resolute statesmen and the "authoritative source" who blames his misinformation on "situational imponderables." Limitless are the public servants who are indolent and insolent; military commanders whose behavioral timidity belies their dreadnaught rhetoric, and governors whose innate servility prevents their actually governing. In our sophistication, we virtually shrug aside the immoral cleric, corrupt judge, incoherent attorney, author who cannot write and English teacher who cannot spell. At universities we see proclamations authored by administrators whose own office communications are hopelessly muddled; and droning lectures from inaudible or incomprehensible instructors.

Seeing incompetence at all levels of every hierarchy — political, legal, educational, and industrial — I hypothesized that the cause was some inherent feature of the rules governing the placement of employees. Thus began my serious study of the ways in which employees move upward through a hierarchy, and of what happens to them after promotion. . . .

In time I saw that all such cases had a common feature. The employee had been promoted from a position of competence to a position of incompetence. I saw that, sooner or later, this could happen to every employee in every hierarchy. . . .

So my analysis of hundreds of cases of occupational incompetence led me to formulate *The Peter Principle:*

In a Hierarchy Every Employee Tends to Rise to His Level of Incompetence

My Principle is the key to an understanding of all hierarchal systems, and therefore to an understanding of the whole structure of civilization. A few eccentrics try to avoid getting involved with hierarchies, but everyone in business, industry, trade-unionism, politics, government, the armed forces, religion, and education is so involved. All of them are controlled by the Peter Principle. . . .

The case of Miss T. Totland is typical. Miss Totland, who had been a competent student and an outstanding primary teacher, was promoted to primary supervisor. She now has to teach, not children, but teachers. Yet *she still uses the techniques which worked so well with small children.*

Addressing teachers, singly or in groups, she speaks slowly and distinctly. She uses mostly words of one or two syllables. She explains each point several times in different ways, to be sure it is understood. She always wears a bright smile.

Teachers dislike what they call her false cheerfulness and her patronizing attitude. Their resentment is so sharp that, instead of trying to carry out her suggestions, they spend much time devising excuses for *not* doing what she recommends.

Miss Totland has proved herself incompetent in communicating with primary teachers. She is therefore ineligible for further promotion, *and will remain as primary supervisor, at her level of incompetence.*

— LAURENCE J. PETER and RAYMOND HULL

◇

If you hear a voice within you saying, "You are not a painter," *then by all means paint,* boy, and that voice will be silenced, but only by working. He who goes to friends and tells his troubles when he feels like that loses part of his manliness, part of the best that's in him; your friends can only be those who themselves struggle against it, who raise your activity by their own example of action. One must undertake it with confidence, with a certain assurance that one is doing a reasonable thing, like the farmer drives his plow, or like our friend in the scratch below, who is harrowing, and even drags the harrow himself. If one hasn't a horse, one is one's own horse — many people do so here.

— VINCENT VAN GOGH

◇

The words of the Preacher, the son of David, king of Jerusalem. 1

Vanity of vanities, saith the Preacher, vanity of vanities; all *is* vanity. 2

What profit hath a man of all his labor which he taketh under the 3 sun?

One generation passeth away, and *another* generation cometh: but 4 the earth abideth for ever.

The sun also ariseth, and the sun goeth down, and hasteth to his 5 place where he arose.

The wind goeth toward the south, and turneth about unto the 6 north; it whirleth about continually, and the wind returneth again according to his circuits.

All the rivers run into the sea; yet the sea *is* not full; unto the place 7 from whence the rivers come, thither they return again.

All things *are* full of labor; man cannot utter *it:* the eye is not sat- 8 isfied with seeing, nor the ear filled with hearing.

The thing that hath been, it is *that* which shall be; and that which 9 is done *is* that which shall be done: and *there is* no new *thing* under the sun.

Is there *any* thing whereof it may be said, See, this *is* new? it hath 10 been already of old time, which was before us.

There is no remembrance of former *things;* neither shall there be 11 *any* remembrance of *things* that are to come with *those* that shall come after.

I the Preacher was king over Israel in Jerusalem. 12

And I gave my heart to seek and search out my wisdom concerning 13 all *things* that are done under heaven: this sore travail hath God given to the sons of man to be exercised therewith.

I have seen all the works that are done under the sun; and, behold, 14 all *is* vanity and vexation of spirit.

That which is crooked cannot be made straight: and that which is 15 wanting cannot be numbered.

I communed with mine own heart, saying, Lo, I am come to great 16 estate, and have gotten more wisdom than all *they* that have been before me in Jerusalem: yea, my heart had great experience of wisdom and knowledge.

And I gave my heart to know wisdom, and to know madness and 17 folly: I perceived that this also is vexation of spirit.

For in much wisdom *is* much grief: and he that increaseth knowl- 18 edge increaseth sorrow. . . .

I returned, and saw under the sun, that the race *is* not to the swift, 19 nor the battle to the strong, neither yet bread to the wise, nor yet riches to men of understanding, nor yet favor to men of skills; but time and chance happeneth to them all.

– ECCLESIASTES 1:1–18 and 9:11

Joseph Epstein

THE VIRTUES OF AMBITION

◊

JOSEPH EPSTEIN (b. 1937) is a professor of English at Northwestern University and the editor of *The American Scholar*, a quarterly journal published by the Phi Beta Kappa Society. He was born in Chicago and graduated from the University of Chicago. In addition to his often witty contributions to *The American Scholar*, Epstein writes for magazines such as *Commentary*, *Harper's*, and *The New Criterion*. His essays have been collected in *Familiar Territory* (1979), *The Middle of My Tether* (1983), and *Plausible Prejudices* (1985). His observations in the following essay about the good features of ambition are included in his study, *Ambition: The Secret Passion* (1980).

Ambition is one of those Rorschach words: define it and you instantly reveal a great deal about yourself. Even that most neutral of works, *Webster's*, in its Seventh New Collegiate Edition, gives itself away, defining ambition first and foremost as "an ardent desire for rank, fame, or power." Ardent immediately assumes a heat incommensurate with good sense and stability, and rank, fame, and power have come under fairly heavy attack for at least a century. One can, after all, be ambitious for the public good, for the alleviation of suffering, for the enlightenment of mankind, though there are some who say that these are precisely the ambitious people most to be distrusted.

Surely ambition is behind dreams of glory, of wealth, of love, of distinction, of accomplishment, of pleasure, of goodness. What life does with our dreams and expectations cannot, of course, be predicted. Some dreams, begun in selflessness, end in rancor; other dreams, begun in selfishness, end in large-heartedness. The unpredictability of the outcome of dreams is no reason to cease dreaming.

To be sure, ambition, the sheer thing unalloyed by some larger purpose than merely clambering up, is never a pretty prospect to ponder. As drunks have done to alcohol, the single-minded have done to ambition — given it a bad name. Like a taste for alcohol, too, ambition does not always allow for easy satiation. Some people cannot handle it; it has brought grief to others, and not merely the ambitious alone. Still, none of this seems sufficient cause for driving ambition under the counter.

What is the worst that can be said — that has been said — about 4 ambition? Here is a (surely) partial list:

To begin with, it, ambition, is often antisocial, and indeed is now 5 outmoded, belonging to an age when individualism was more valued and useful than it is today. The person strongly imbued with ambition ignores the collectivity; socially detached, he is on his own and out for his own. Individuality and ambition are firmly linked. The ambitious individual, far from identifying himself and his fortunes with the group, wishes to rise above it. The ambitious man or woman sees the world as a battle; rivalrousness is his or her principal emotion: the world has limited prizes to offer, and he or she is determined to get his or hers. Ambition is, moreover, jesuitical; it can argue those possessed by it into believing that what they want for themselves is good for everyone — that the satisfaction of their own desires is best for the commonweal. The truly ambitious believe that it is a dog-eat-dog world, and they are distinguished by wanting to be the dogs that do the eating.

From here it is but a short hop to believe that those who have 6 achieved the common goals of ambition — money, fame, power — have achieved them through corruption of a greater or lesser degree, mostly a greater. Thus all politicians in high places, thought to be ambitious, are understood to be, ipso facto, without moral scruples. How could they have such scruples — a weighty burden in a high climb — and still have risen as they have?

If ambition is to be well regarded, the rewards of ambition — 7 wealth, distinction, control over one's destiny — must be deemed worthy of the sacrifices made on ambition's behalf. If the tradition of ambition is to have vitality, it must be widely shared; and it especially must be esteemed by people who are themselves admired, the educated not least among them. The educated not least because, nowadays more than ever before, it is they who have usurped the platforms of public discussion and wield the power of the spoken and written word in newspapers, in magazines, on television. In an odd way, it is the educated who have claimed to have given up on ambition as an ideal. What is odd is that they have perhaps most benefited from ambition — if not always their own then that of their parents and grandparents. There is a heavy note of hypocrisy in this; a case of closing the barn door after the horses have escaped — with the educated themselves astride them.

Certainly people do not seem less interested in success and its accoutrements now than formerly. Summer homes, European travel, BMWs — the locations, place names, and name brands may change, but such items do not seem less in demand today than a decade or two years ago. What has happened is that people cannot own up to their dreams, as easily and openly as once they could, lest they be thought pushing, acquisitive, vulgar. Instead we are treated to fine pharisaical spectacles, which now more than ever seem in ample supply: the revolutionary lawyer quartered in the $250,000 Manhattan condominium; the critic of American materialism with a Southampton summer home; the publisher of radical books who takes his meals in three-star restaurants; the journalist advocating participatory democracy in all phases of life, whose own children are enrolled in private schools. For such people and many more perhaps not so egregious, the proper formulation is, "Succeed at all costs but refrain from *appearing* ambitious."   8

The attacks on ambition are many and come from various angles; its public defenders are few and unimpressive, where they are not extremely unattractive. As a result, the support for ambition as a healthy impulse, a quality to be admired and inculcated in the young, is probably lower than it has ever been in the United States. This does not mean that ambition is at an end, that people no longer feel its stirrings and promptings, but only that, no longer openly honored, it is less often openly professed. Consequences follow from this, of course, some of which are that ambition is driven underground, or made sly, or perverse. It can also be forced into vulgarity, as witness the blatant pratings of its contemporary promoters. Such, then, is the way things stand: on the left angry critics, on the right obtuse supporters, and in the middle, as usual, the majority of earnest people trying to get on in life.   9

Many people are naturally distrustful of ambition, feeling that it   10 represents something intractable in human nature. Thus John Dean entitled his book about his involvement in the Watergate affair during the Nixon administration *Blind Ambition,* as if ambition were to blame for his ignoble actions, and not the constellation of qualities that make up his rather shabby character. Ambition, it must once again be underscored, is morally a two-sided street. Place next to John Dean Andrew Carnegie, who, among other philanthropic acts, bought the library of Lord Acton, at a time when Acton was in financial distress, and assigned its custodianship to Acton, who never was told who his benefactor was. Need much more be said on the subject than that, important though ambition is, there are some things that one must not sacrifice to it?

But going at things the other way, sacrificing ambition so as to 11 guard against its potential excesses, is to go at things wrongly. To discourage ambition is to discourage dreams of grandeur and greatness. All men and women are born, live, suffer, and die; what distinguishes us one from another is our dreams, whether they be dreams about worldly or unworldly things, and what we do to make them come about.

It may seem an exaggeration to say that ambition is the linchpin of 12 society, holding many of its disparate elements together, but it is not an exaggeration by much. Remove ambition and the essential elements of society seem to fly apart. Ambition, as opposed to mere fantasizing about desires, implies work and discipline to achieve goals, personal and social, of a kind society cannot survive without. Ambition is intimately connected with family, for men and women not only work partly for their families; husbands and wives are often ambitious for each other, but harbor some of their most ardent ambitions for their children. Yet to have a family nowadays — with birth control readily available, and inflation a good economic argument against having children — is nearly an expression of ambition in itself. Finally, though ambition was once the domain chiefly of monarchs and aristocrats, it has, in more recent times, increasingly become the domain of the middle classes. Ambition and futurity — a sense of building for tomorrow — are inextricable. Working, saving, planning — these, the daily aspects of ambition — have always been the distinguishing marks of a rising middle class. The attack against ambition is not incidentally an attack on the middle class and what it stands for.

Like it or not, the middle class has done much of society's work in America; and it, the middle class, has from the beginning run on ambition.

It is not difficult to imagine a world shorn of ambition. It would 13 probably be a kinder world: without demands, without abrasions, without disappointments. People would have time for reflection. Such work as they did would not be for themselves but for the collectivity. Competition would never enter in. Conflict would be eliminated, tension become a thing of the past. The stress of creation would be at an end. Art would no longer be troubling, but purely celebratory in its functions. The family would become superfluous as a social unit, with all its former power for bringing about neurosis drained away. Longevity would be increased, for fewer people would die of heart attack or stroke caused by tumultuous endeavor. Anxiety would be extinct. Time would stretch on and on, with ambition long departed from the human heart.

Ah, how unrelievedly boring life would be!   14

There is a strong view that holds that success is a myth, and ambi- 15 tion therefore a sham. Does this mean that success does not really exist? That achievement is at bottom empty? That the efforts of men and women are of no significance alongside the force of movements and events? Now not all success, obviously, is worth esteeming, nor all ambition worth cultivating. Which are and which are not is something one soon enough learns on one's own. But even the most cynical secretly admit that success exists; that achievement counts for a great deal; and that the true myth is that the actions of men and women are useless. To believe otherwise is to take on a point of view that is likely to be deranging. It is, in its implications, to remove all motive for competence, interest in attainment, and regard for posterity.

We do not choose to be born. We do not choose our parents. We 16 do not choose our historical epoch, the country of our birth or the immediate circumstances of our upbringing. We do not, most of us, choose to die; nor do we choose the time or conditions of our death. But within all this realm of choicelessness, we do choose how we shall live: courageously or in cowardice, honorably or dishonorably, with purpose or in drift. We decide what is important and what is trivial in life. We decide that what makes us significant is either what we do or what we refuse to do. But no matter how indifferent the universe may be to our choices and decisions, these choices and decisions are ours to make. We decide. We choose. And as we decide and choose, so are our lives formed. In the end, forming our own destiny is what ambition is about.

CONSIDERATIONS

1. What does Epstein find wrong with the dictionary definition of ambition? What other assumptions about ambition does he expose in the first six paragraphs? What does Epstein accomplish by beginning his essay in this negative way?
2. Why are people hypocritical about ambition? What is a "pharisaical spectacle"?
3. According to Epstein, how does ambition hold society together? What might the world be like if nobody had ambitions?
4. Is Epstein claiming too much importance for the role of ambition in life? Is ambition really the main way we choose how we shall live?
5. WRITING TOPIC. In a 750-word essay, examine the various attitudes among college students and their families toward earning high grades. How openly are achievements pursued and displayed? What hypocrisies are generally accepted? What happens when kindness, loyalty, and generosity come into conflict with ambitions? How do they sometimes fuel ambitions? Examine the problem closely and come to a specific conclusion about the way ambition for high grades can affect a student's character for better or worse.

Russell Baker

MY LACK OF GUMPTION

◊

RUSSELL BAKER (b. 1925) is a widely syndicated newspaper columnist. He grew up in Virginia in a family that experienced special hardships during the Depression: his father died young and his mother was left with three children to raise. The following chapter from his autobiography, *Growing Up* (1982), recalls how his course was firmly set at an early age for his subsequent career in journalism. In his memoir the story he tells with a mixture of whimsy and pathos ends happily. After serving in the navy, Baker graduated from Johns Hopkins University and went to work as a reporter. In 1954 he joined the *New York Times* as a correspondent in its Washington bureau. After covering national politics for eight years, he says that he grew tired of waiting around each day just to hear people lie to him. He began writing his "Observer" column from New York City, and in 1979 he won the Pulitzer Prize for his social commentary. His columns have been collected in *So This Is Depravity* (1980). *Growing Up* won him another Pulitzer Prize in 1982.

I began working in journalism when I was eight years old. It was 1 my mother's idea. She wanted me to "make something" of myself and, after a level-headed appraisal of my strengths, decided I had better start young if I was to have any chance of keeping up with the competition.

The flaw in my character which she had already spotted was lack of 2 "gumption." My idea of a perfect afternoon was lying in front of the radio rereading my favorite Big Little Book, *Dick Tracy Meets Stooge Viller*. My mother despised inactivity. Seeing me having a good time in repose, she was powerless to hide her disgust. "You've got no more gumption than a bump on a log," she said. "Get out in the kitchen and help Doris do those dirty dishes."

My sister Doris, though two years younger than I, had enough 3 gumption for a dozen people. She positively enjoyed washing dishes, making beds, and cleaning the house. When she was only seven she could carry a piece of short-weighted cheese back to the A&P, threaten the manager with legal action, and come back triumphantly with the full quarter-pound we'd paid for and a few ounces extra thrown in for forgiveness. Doris could have made something of herself if she hadn't been a girl. Because of this defect, however, the best she could hope for was a career as a nurse or schoolteacher, the only work that capable females were considered up to in those days.

This must have saddened my mother, this twist of fate that had al- 4 located all the gumption to the daughter and left her with a son who was content with Dick Tracy and Stooge Viller. If disappointed, though, she wasted no energy on self-pity. She would make me make something of myself whether I wanted to or not. "The Lord helps those who help themselves," she said. That was the way her mind worked.

She was realistic about the difficulty. Having sized up the material 5 the Lord had given her to mold, she didn't overestimate what she could do with it. She didn't insist that I grow up to be President of the United States.

Fifty years ago parents still asked boys if they wanted to grow up to 6 be President, and asked it not jokingly but seriously. Many parents who were hardly more than paupers still believed their sons could do it. Abraham Lincoln had done it. We were only sixty-five years from Lincoln. Many a grandfather who walked among us could remember Lincoln's time. Men of grandfatherly age were the worst for asking if you wanted to grow up to be President. A surprising number of little boys said yes and meant it.

I was asked many times myself. No, I would say, I didn't want to 7 grow up to be President. My mother was present during one of these interrogations. An elderly uncle, having posed the usual question and exposed my lack of interest in the Presidency, asked, "Well, what *do* you want to be when you grow up?"

I loved to pick through trash piles and collect empty bottles, tin 8 cans with pretty labels, and discarded magazines. The most desirable

job on earth sprang instantly to mind. "I want to be a garbage man," I
said.

My uncle smiled, but my mother had seen the first distressing evi-　9
dence of a bump budding on a log. "Have a little gumption, Russell,"
she said. Her calling me Russell was a signal of unhappiness. When
she approved of me I was always "Buddy."

When I turned eight years old she decided that the job of starting　10
me on the road toward making something of myself could no longer
be safely delayed. "Buddy," she said one day, "I want you to come
home right after school this afternoon. Somebody's coming and I
want you to meet him."

When I burst in that afternoon she was in conference in the parlor　11
with an executive of the Curtis Publishing Company. She introduced
me. He bent low from the waist and shook my hand. Was it true as
my mother had told him, he asked, that I longed for the opportunity
to conquer the world of business?

My mother replied that I was blessed with a rare determination to　12
make something of myself.

"That's right," I whispered.　13

"But have you got the grit, the character, the never-say-quit spirit it　14
takes to succeed in business?"

My mother said I certainly did.　15

"That's right," I said.　16

He eyed me silently for a long pause, as though weighing whether I　17
could be trusted to his confidence, then spoke man-to-man. Before
taking a crucial step, he said, he wanted to advise me that working for
the Curtis Publishing Company placed enormous responsibility on a
young man. It was one of the great companies of America. Perhaps
the greatest publishing house in the world. I had heard, no doubt, of
the *Saturday Evening Post?*

Heard of it? My mother said that everyone in our house had heard　18
of the *Saturday Post* and that I, in fact, read it with religious devotion.

Then doubtless, he said, we were also familiar with those two　19
monthly pillars of the magazine world, the *Ladies Home Journal* and
the *Country Gentleman.*

Indeed we were familiar with them, said my mother.　20

Representing the *Saturday Evening Post* was one of the weightiest　21
honors that could be bestowed in the world of business, he said. He
was personally proud of being a part of that great corporation.

My mother said he had every right to be.   22
Again he studied me as though debating whether I was worthy of a   23
knighthood. Finally: "Are you trustworthy?"
My mother said I was the soul of honesty.   24
"That's right," I said.   25
The caller smiled for the first time. He told me I was a lucky young   26
man. He admired my spunk. Too many young men thought life was
all play. Those young men would not go far in this world. Only
a young man willing to work and save and keep his face washed and
his hair neatly combed could hope to come out on top in a world
such as ours. Did I truly and sincerely believe that I was such a young
man?
"He certainly does," said my mother.   27
"That's right," I said.   28
He said he had been so impressed by what he had seen of me that   29
he was going to make me a representative of the Curtis Publishing
Company. On the following Tuesday, he said, thirty freshly printed
copies of the *Saturday Evening Post* would be delivered at our door. I
would place these magazines, still damp with the ink of the presses, in
a handsome canvas bag, sling it over my shoulder, and set forth
through the streets to bring the best in journalism, fiction, and cartoons to the American public.
He had brought the canvas bag with him. He presented it with rev-   30
erence fit for a chasuble. He showed me how to drape the sling over
my left shoulder and across the chest so that the pouch lay easily accessible to my right hand, allowing the best in journalism, fiction, and
cartoons to be swiftly extracted and sold to a citizenry whose happiness and security depended upon us soldiers of the free press.
The following Tuesday I raced home from school, put the canvas   31
bag over my shoulder, dumped the magazines in, and, tilting to the
left to balance their weight on my right hip, embarked on the highway
of journalism.
We lived in Belleville, New Jersey, a commuter town at the north-   32
ern fringe of Newark. It was 1932, the bleakest year of the Depression.
My father had died two years before, leaving us with a few pieces of
Sears, Roebuck furniture and not much else, and my mother had
taken Doris and me to live with one of her younger brothers. This was
my Uncle Allen. Uncle Allen had made something of himself by
1932. As salesman for a soft-drink bottler in Newark, he had an in-

come of $30 a week; wore pearl-gray spats, detachable collars, and a three-piece suit; was happily married; and took in threadbare relatives.

With my load of magazines I headed toward Belleville Avenue. 33 That's where the people were. There were two filling stations at the intersection with Union Avenue, as well as an A&P, a fruit stand, a bakery, a barber shop, Zuccarelli's drugstore, and a diner shaped like a railroad car. For several hours I made myself highly visible, shifting position now and then from corner to corner, from shop window to shop window, to make sure everyone could see the heavy black lettering on the canvas bag that said the *Saturday Evening Post.* When the angle of the light indicated it was suppertime, I walked back to the house.

"How many did you sell, Buddy?" my mother asked. 34

"None." 35

"Where did you go?" 36

"The corner of Belleville and Union Avenues." 37

"What did you do?" 38

"Stood on the corner waiting for somebody to buy a *Saturday Eve-* 39 *ning Post.*"

"You just stood there?" 40

"Didn't sell a single one." 41

"For God's sake, Russell!" 42

Uncle Allen intervened. "I've been thinking about it for some 43 time," he said, "and I've about decided to take the *Post* regularly. Put me down as a regular customer." I handed him a magazine and he paid me a nickel. It was the first nickel I earned.

Afterwards my mother instructed me in salesmanship. I would 44 have to ring doorbells, address adults with charming self-confidence, and break down resistance with a sales talk pointing out that no one, no matter how poor, could afford to be without the *Saturday Evening Post* in the home.

I told my mother I'd changed my mind about wanting to succeed 45 in the magazine business.

"If you think I'm going to raise a good-for-nothing," she replied, 46 "you've got another think coming." She told me to hit the streets with the canvas bag and start ringing doorbells the instant school was out next day. When I objected that I didn't feel any aptitude for salesmanship, she asked how I'd like to lend her my leather belt so she could whack some sense into me. I bowed to superior will and entered jouralism with a heavy heart.

My mother and I had fought this battle almost as long as I could 47 remember. It probably started even before memory began, when I was a country child in northern Virginia and my mother, dissatisfied with my father's plain workman's life, determined that I would not grow up like him and his people, with calluses on their hands, overalls on their backs, and fourth-grade educations in their heads. She had fancier ideas of life's possibilities. Introducing me to the *Saturday Evening Post*, she was trying to wean me as early as possible from my father's world where men left with their lunch pails at sunup, worked with their hands until the grime ate into the pores, and died with a few sticks of mail-order furniture as their legacy. In my mother's vision of the better life there were desks and white collars, well-pressed suits, evenings of reading and lively talk, and perhaps — if a man were very, very lucky and hit the jackpot, really made something important of himself — perhaps there might be a fantastic salary of $5,000 a year to support a big house and a Buick with a rumble seat and a vacation in Atlantic City.

And so I set forth with my sack of magazines. I was afraid of the 48 dogs that snarled behind the doors of potential buyers. I was timid about ringing the doorbells of strangers, relieved when no one came to the door, and scared when someone did. Despite my mother's instructions, I could not deliver an engaging sales pitch. When a door opened I simply asked, "Want to buy a *Saturday Evening Post?*" In Belleville few persons did. It was a town of 30,000 people, and most weeks I rang a fair majority of its doorbells. But I rarely sold my thirty copies. Some weeks I canvassed the entire town for six days and still had four or five unsold magazines on Monday evening; then I dreaded the coming of Tuesday morning, when a batch of thirty fresh *Saturday Evening Posts* was due at the front door.

"Better get out there and sell the rest of those magazines tonight," 49 my mother would say.

I usually posted myself then at a busy intersection where a traffic 50 light controlled commuter flow from Newark. When the light turned red I stood on the curb and shouted my sales pitch at the motorists.

"Want to buy a *Saturday Evening Post?*" 51

One rainy night when car windows were sealed against me I came 52 back soaked and with not a single sale to report. My mother beckoned to Doris.

"Go back down there with Buddy and show him how to sell these 53 magazines," she said.

Brimming with zest, Doris, who was then seven years old, returned 54 with me to the corner. She took a magazine from the bag, and when the light turned red she strode to the nearest car and banged her small fist against the closed window. The driver, probably startled at what he took to be a midget assaulting his car, lowered the window to stare, and Doris thrust a *Saturday Evening Post* at him.

"You need this magazine," she piped, "and it only costs a nickel." 55

Her salesmanship was irresistible. Before the light changed half a 56 dozen times she disposed of the entire batch. I didn't feel humiliated. To the contrary. I was so happy I decided to give her a treat. Leading her to the vegetable store on Belleville Avenue, I bought three apples, which cost a nickel, and gave her one.

"You shouldn't waste money," she said. 57

"Eat your apple." I bit into mine. 58

"You shouldn't eat before supper," she said. "It'll spoil your appe- 59 tite."

Back at the house that evening, she dutifully reported me for wast- 60 ing a nickel. Instead of a scolding, I was rewarded with a pat on the back for having the good sense to buy fruit instead of candy. My mother reached into her bottomless supply of maxims and told Doris, "An apple a day keeps the doctor away."

By the time I was ten I had learned all my mother's maxims by 61 heart. Asking to stay up past normal bedtime, I knew that a refusal would be explained with, "Early to bed and early to rise, makes a man healthy, wealthy, and wise." If I whimpered about having to get up early in the morning, I could depend on her to say, "The early bird gets the worm."

The one I most despised was, "If at first you don't succeed, try, try 62 again." This was the battle cry with which she constantly sent me back into the hopeless struggle whenever I moaned that I had rung every doorbell in town and knew there wasn't a single potential buyer left in Belleville that week. After listening to my explanation, she handed me the canvas bag and said, "If at first you don't succeed . . ."

Three years in that job, which I would gladly have quit after the 63 first day except for her insistence, produced at least one valuable result. My mother finally concluded that I would never make something of myself by pursuing a life in business and started considering careers that demanded less competitive zeal.

One evening when I was eleven I brought home a short "composi- 64 tion" on my summer vacation which the teacher had graded with an A. Reading it with her own schoolteacher's eye, my mother agreed that it was top-drawer seventh grade prose and complimented me. Nothing more was said about it immediately, but a new idea had taken life in her mind. Halfway through supper she suddenly interrupted the conversation.

"Buddy," she said, "maybe you could be a writer." 65

I clasped the idea to my heart. I had never met a writer, had shown 66 no previous urge to write, and hadn't a notion how to become a writer, but I loved stories and thought that making up stories must surely be almost as much fun as reading them. Best of all, though, and what really gladdened my heart, was the ease of the writer's life. Writers did not have to trudge through the town peddling from canvas bags, defending themselves against angry dogs, being rejected by surly strangers. Writers did not have to ring doorbells. So far as I could make out, what writers did couldn't even be classified as work.

I was enchanted. Writers didn't have to have any gumption at all. I 67 did not dare tell anybody for fear of being laughed at in the schoolyard, but secretly I decided that what I'd like to be when I grew up was a writer.

CONSIDERATIONS

1. In Baker's childhood, who were the advocates and the models of competitive enterprise? Did he have any other standards and role models to follow?
2. What attitudes does the author express toward his mother? How have they changed, if at all, since his childhood? How does he feel about her having foreseen his career as a writer?
3. What gives Baker's humor its folksy quality? Identify particular details of the subject material and the language that contribute to his tone of unsophisticated familiarity.

4. WRITING TOPIC. In the household you grew up in, what attitudes toward competitive enterprise were taken for granted or explicitly defined? Who were the chief models and the chief spokesmen of the dominant view? Was there an opposing view? In 500 words, explain how you were expected to "make something" of yourself.

Richard Rodriguez

READING FOR SUCCESS

◊

RICHARD RODRIGUEZ (b. 1944) grew up in San Francisco, where as the child of Spanish-speaking Mexican Americans he received his education in a language that was not spoken at home. His attraction to English and to English-speaking culture became his avenue to a promising future but he felt torn away from the people he loved. He received a Ph.D. in English from the University of California at Berkeley and remained there as a teacher, until he decided to write about the conflicting aspirations that divided him between two worlds. This selection from his autobiography, *Hunger of Memory* (1982), recalls the origin of his passion for reading.

From an early age I knew that my mother and father could read 1 and write both Spanish and English. I had observed my father making his way through what, I now suppose, must have been income tax forms. On other occasions I waited apprehensively while my mother read onion-paper letters air-mailed from Mexico with news of a relative's illness or death. For both my parents, however, reading was something done out of necessity and as quickly as possible. Never did I see either of them read an entire book. Nor did I see them read for pleasure. Their reading consisted of work manuals, prayer books, newspapers, recipes. . . .

In our house each school year would begin with my mother's care- 2 ful instruction: "Don't write in your books so we can sell them at the end of the year." The remark was echoed in public by my teachers, but only in part: "Boys and girls, don't write in your books. You must learn to treat them with great care and respect."

OPEN THE DOORS OF YOUR MIND WITH BOOKS, read the red and 3 white poster over the nun's desk in early September. It soon was apparent to me that reading was the classroom's central activity. Each course had its own book. And the information gathered from a book was unquestioned. READ TO LEARN, the sign on the wall advised in December. I privately wondered: What was the connection between reading and learning? Did one learn something only by reading it? Was an idea only an idea if it could be written down? In June, CONSIDER BOOKS YOUR BEST FRIENDS. Friends? Reading was, at best, only a chore. I needed to look up whole paragraphs of words in a dictionary. Lines of type were dizzying, the eye having to move slowly across the page, then down, and across. . . . The sentences of the first books I read were coolly impersonal. Toned hard. What most bothered me, however, was the isolation reading required. To console myself for the loneliness I'd feel when I read, I tried reading in a very soft voice. Until: "Who is doing all that talking to his neighbor?" Shortly after, remedial reading classes were arranged for me with a very old nun.

At the end of each school day, for nearly six months, I would meet   4 with her in the tiny room that served as the school's library but was actually only a storeroom for used textbooks and a vast collection of *National Geographics.* Everything about our sessions pleased me: the smallness of the room; the noise of the janitor's broom hitting the edge of the long hallway outside the door; the green of the sun, lighting the wall; and the old woman's face blurred white with a beard. Most of the time we took turns. I began with my elementary text. Sentences of astonishing simplicity seemed to me lifeless and drab: "The boys ran from the rain. . . . She wanted to sing. . . . The kite rose in the blue." Then the old nun would read from her favorite books, usually biographies of early American presidents. Playfully she ran through complex sentences, calling the words alive with her voice, making it seem that the author somehow was speaking directly to me. I smiled just to listen to her. I sat there and sensed for the very first time some possibility of fellowship between a reader and a writer, a communication, never *intimate* like that I heard spoken words at home convey, but one nonetheless *personal.*

One day the nun concluded a session by asking me why I was so   5 reluctant to read by myself. I tried to explain; said something about the way written words made me feel all alone — almost, I wanted to add but didn't, as when I spoke to myself in a room just emptied of furniture. She studied my face as I spoke; she seemed to be watching more than listening. In an uneventful voice she replied that I had nothing to fear. Didn't I realize that reading would open up whole new worlds? A book could open doors for me. It could introduce me to people and show me places I never imagined existed. She gestured toward the bookshelves. (Bare-breasted African women danced, and the shiny hubcaps of automobiles on the back covers of the *Geographic* gleamed in my mind.) I listened with respect. But her words were not very influential. I was thinking then of another consequence of literacy, one I was too shy to admit but nonetheless trusted. Books were going to make me "educated." *That* confidence enabled me, several months later, to overcome my fear of the silence.

In fourth grade I embarked upon a grandiose reading program. 6 "Give me the names of important books," I would say to startled teachers. They soon found out that I had in mind "adult books." I ignored their suggestion of anything I suspected was written for children. (Not until I was in college, as a result, did I read *Huckleberry Finn* or *Alice's Adventures in Wonderland*.) Instead, I read *The Scarlet Letter* and Franklin's *Autobiography*. And whatever I read I read for extra credit. Each time I finished a book, I reported the achievement to a teacher and basked in the praise my effort earned. Despite my best efforts, however, there seemed to be more and more books I needed to read. At the library I would literally tremble as I came upon whole shelves of books I hadn't read. So I read and I read and I read: *Great Expectations*; all the short stories of Kipling; *The Babe Ruth Story*; the entire first volume of the *Encyclopaedia Britanica* (A–ANSTEY); the *Iliad*; *Moby Dick*; *Gone with the Wind*; *The Good Earth*; *Ramona*; *Forever Amber*; *The Lives of the Saints*; *Crime and Punishment*; *The Pearl*.... Librarians who initially frowned when I checked out the maximum ten books at a time started saving books they thought I might like. Teachers would say to the rest of the class, "I only wish the rest of you took reading as seriously as Richard obviously does."

But at home I would hear my mother wondering, "What do you 7 see in your books?" (Was reading a hobby like her knitting? Was so much reading even healthy for a boy? Was it the sign of "brains"? Or was it just a convenient excuse for not helping around the house on Saturday mornings?) Always, "What do you see . . . ?"

What *did* I see in my books? I had the idea that they were crucial 8 for my academic success, though I couldn't have said exactly how or why. In the sixth grade I simply concluded that what gave a book its value was some major idea or theme it contained. If that core essence could be mined and memorized, I would become learned like my teachers. I decided to record in a notebook the themes of the books that I read. After reading *Robinson Crusoe*, I wrote that its theme was "the value of learning to live by oneself." When I completed *Wuthering Heights*, I noted the danger of "letting emotions get out of control." Rereading these brief moralistic appraisals usually left me disheartened. I couldn't believe that they were really the source of reading's value. But for many more years, they constituted the only means I had of describing to myself the educational value of books.

In spite of my earnestness, I found reading a pleasurable activity. I   9
came to enjoy the lonely good company of books. Early on weekday mornings, I'd read in my bed. I'd feel a mysterious comfort then, reading in the dawn quiet — the blue-gray silence interrupted by the occasional churning of the refrigerator motor a few rooms away or the more distant sounds of a city bus beginning its run. On weekends I'd go to the public library to read, surrounded by old men and women. Or, if the weather was fine, I would take my books to the park and read in the shade of a tree. A warm summer evening was my favorite reading time. Neighbors would leave for vacation and I would water their lawns. I would sit through the twilight on the front porches or in backyards, reading to the cool, whirling sounds of the sprinklers.

I also had favorite writers. But often those writers I enjoyed most I   10
was least able to value. When I read William Saroyan's *The Human Comedy*, I was immediately pleased by the narrator's warmth and the charm of his story. But as quickly I became suspicious. A book so enjoyable to read couldn't be very "important." Another summer I determined to read all the novels of Dickens. Reading his fat novels, I loved the feeling I got — after the first hundred pages — of being at home in a fictional world where I knew the names of the characters and cared about what was going to happen to them. And it bothered me that I was forced away at the conclusion, when the fiction closed tight, like a fortune-teller's fist — the futures of all the major characters neatly resolved. I never knew how to take such feelings seriously, however. Nor did I suspect that these experiences could be part of a

novel's meaning. Still, there were pleasures to sustain me after I'd finish my books. Carrying a volume back to the library, I would be pleased by its weight. I'd run my fingers along the edge of the pages and marvel at the breadth of my achievement. Around my room, growing stacks of paperback books reinforced my assurance.

I entered high school having read hundreds of books. My habit of 11 reading made me a confident speaker and writer of English. Reading also enabled me to sense something of the shape, the major concerns, of Western thought. (I was able to say something about Dante and Descartes and Engels and James Baldwin in my high school term papers.) In these various ways, books brought me academic success as I hoped that they would. But I was not a good reader. Merely bookish, I lacked a point of view when I read. Rather, I read in order to acquire a point of view. I vacuumed books for epigrams, scraps of information, ideas, themes — anything to fill the hollow within me and make me feel educated. When one of my teachers suggested to his drowsy tenth-grade English class that a person could not have a "complicated idea" until he had read at least two thousand books, I heard the remark without detecting either its irony or its very complicated truth. I merely determined to compile a list of all the books I had ever read. Harsh with myself, I included only once a title I might have read several times. (How, after all, could one read a book more than once?) And I included only those books over a hundred pages in length. (Could anything shorter be a book?)

There was yet another high school list I compiled. One day I came 12 across a newspaper article about the retirement of an English professor at a nearby state college. The article was accompanied by a list of the "hundred most important books of Western Civilization." "More than anything else in my life," the professor told the reporter with finality, "these books have made me all that I am." That was the kind of remark I couldn't ignore. I clipped out the list and kept it for the several months it took me to read all of the titles. Most books, of course, I barely understood. While reading Plato's *Republic*, for instance, I needed to keep looking at the book jacket comments to remind myself what the text was about. Nevertheless, with the special patience and superstition of a scholarship boy, I looked at every word of the text. And by the time I reached the last word, relieved, I convinced myself that I had read *The Republic*. In a ceremony of great pride, I solemnly crossed Plato off my list.

CONSIDERATIONS

1. What were the reasons why Rodriguez did not enjoy his early reading? What do you think was the greatest single barrier to his enjoyment? What leads you to this conclusion?
2. Do you agree with his remark that "I was not a good reader"? What does he think was wrong? Is his self-criticism justified?
3. Rodriguez implies that early reading experiences would be different for a child in a middle-class, English-speaking family. What specific matters do you think might be just the same?
4. WRITING TOPIC. In a 500-word essay, reconsider a book that for a while was your favorite reading. What were you finding in it that appealed strongly to you at that time? What was its main contrast or similarity with your actual life? To what extent did the book stimulate dreams about yourself?

Seymour Wishman

A LAWYER'S GUILTY
SECRETS

◊

SEYMOUR WISHMAN (b. 1942) grew up in New Jersey and was educated at Rutgers University. He has been a practicing lawyer in New
York City and a presidential advisor in Washington, D.C., and he now
devotes himself mainly to writing. His memoir, *Confessions of a Criminal Lawyer* (1981), recalls notable cases and clients. He has also written a novel, *Nothing Personal* (1978), and is at work on a book about
juries. The following article, which first appeared in *Newsweek*, suggests that our great ambitions include unconscious goals, making it
impossible to explain exactly why we are doing what we do.

During my sixteen years as a criminal lawyer I have represented 1
hundreds of people accused of crimes, and not only have most of
them been guilty, many have been guilty of atrocities. I have represented sons who hatcheted fathers, strangers who shot strangers,
lovers who knifed lovers — killings out of rage, passion, revenge, or for
no "good" reason.

It is a fundamental principle of our system of justice that every 2
criminal defendant is entitled to a lawyer, but too much of what I've
done in the courtroom is beyond justifying by that abstract principle.
I've humiliated pathetic victims of crimes by making liars out of them
to gain the acquittal of criminals; I've struggled to win for clients who
would go out and commit new outrages. This is not what I had in
mind when I entered law school.

One of the reasons I became a criminal lawyer was to defend the 3
innocent, but I haven't had much opportunity to do that. Instead, I
find myself facing a difficult question: why have I fought so hard for
the interests of the guilty?

The answers I come up with are disturbing. Much of the satisfac- 4
tion I get from my work is connected to a lifelong emotional identification with the underdog, even a despicable underdog, against authority. Although I do enjoy, for its own sake, performing well during
a trial, my courtroom performances more than anything else express a
need for power and admiration.

. . . In trying to figure out the rewards of my work, I've received lit- 5
tle guidance from my colleagues. Most criminal lawyers I've met are
extraordinarily perceptive about the personalities of others, but when
it comes to their own behavior, the level of self-analysis usually
doesn't get much beyond: "When I'm trying a case, standing in front
of a jury, I feel totally alive."

The sense of aliveness comes, in part, from the fact that the court- 6
room is an acceptable forum in which to act out a whole range of intense emotions. On one level these displays of emotions are fake because they are controlled and purposeful. (I'm sure I'm not the first
trial lawyer who knew exactly when he was going to "lose" his temper,
what he would do while his temper was "lost," and how long it would
be before he recovered it.) Yet on another level these contrived emotions are as real and intense as anything else in my life. I have felt
genuine rage during an outburst when I had trapped a cop lying: I've
had real tears in my eyes when describing a horrible wound.

All the lawyer's emotions and skills are deployed for one pur- 7
pose — winning. During a cross-examination, all energy is spent on
beating the witness. With a tough witness, the duel can be thrilling.
Few lawyers would admit that anything other than the pleasure of
craftsmanship had been involved in subduing a witness. And yet I
have seen lawyers work a witness over, control him, dominate and
beat him — and then continue to torment him. Deriving enjoyment
from inflicting that unnecessary measure of pain might be rare, but
not that rare. If the witness is a woman, there might even be sexual
overtones to the encounter. Half joking, a colleague once told me,
"It's better than going home and hitting my wife."

Such sadism notwithstanding, most criminal lawyers are different 8
from their clients. Through mine I have become familiar with a world
that would have otherwise remained hidden from me — an intrigu-
ing, seductive, dark world. With little prompting, my clients would
describe their lives in lurid detail — passionate, desperate lives filled
with violence, drugs, and sex. I must confess I have sometimes felt a

vicarious excitement on hearing the exploits of these people so unfettered by normal restraints.

I haven't been the only one titillated by the stories. Judges, prose- 9
cutors, detectives, jurors — virtually all those connected with the administration of criminal justice — experience at one time or another this voyeurism.

But I have other, perhaps less neurotic reasons for finding my work 10
satisfying. Sometimes a trial has made me feel wonderful. I've experienced a sense of power and control over events and people that is lacking in most jobs. I could decide to make heroes or villains of people, to make them fear me or like me or respect me, and go ahead and do it. I could want to move a jury to tears, and go ahead and do it.

. . . The lawyer's performance is in front of an audience. All eyes 11
are focused on me. The jury is composed of twelve critics to be persuaded; they watch my every movement. Spectators fill the courtroom to cheer their favorites. The witness, the client, the court attendants, the court reporter taking down every word — all are there to see and appreciate. One can feel very special.

Looking down on the whole drama, watching me perform with 12
skill, maybe even elegance, is this fatherlike authority — the robed judge. I may be impressing him, and his approval can be inordinately reassuring to me. But if he becomes an adversary during the trial, the experience of standing up to him, defying him, outmaneuvering him can provide a sense of liberation far beyond the agreeable sensation of simply helping a client.

Viewed another way, the trial is a battle between adversaries in 13
which the trial lawyers are competitors. Winning the case means beating the other guy, beating your brother lawyer, just as it sometimes means beating your father, the judge. The verdict is clear and unequivocal, and it is announced in front of all those observers. A victory can provide an exhilaration like no other.

The trial is also a contest for high stakes. The lawyer is playing for a 14
life. A belief in the justness of the cause, if this is possible in a given case, carries its own rewards, but rescuing anyone — even a guilty client — can be very gratifying. A client's life, or years of it, can depend on his lawyer's efforts, and those efforts can arouse the same messianic illusions in the lawyer's head whether the client is a hero or villain.

In trying to understand myself and my work, I am led ineluctably 15
to the murky and subjective realm of what I brought with me when I

first stepped into a courtroom. It was clearly not just the belief that every criminal defendant has a right to counsel.

CONSIDERATIONS

1. What is Wishman's strongest incentive to win a case? What motives does he find generally in lawyers? What motives does he observe only in *other* lawyers?
2. How do lawyers perceive the judge? How do they react to him?
3. How appropriate is the title of the article? Perfect? Overstated? Or misleading?
4. In the final paragraph Wishman says that he is trying to recognize "what I brought with me when I first stepped into a courtroom." Summarize his article by defining the ambitions that he brings to his work.
5. WRITING TOPIC. What is the most competitive activity that you have been seriously engaged in? What made it intense? In a 500-word essay, explain the aims and some of the unexpected satisfactions of winning, or the special burdens of losing. Be specific and precise; avoid drifting into generalities and vagueness about your responses.

Pete Hamill

WINNING ISN'T EVERYTHING

◊

PETE HAMILL (b. 1935) is a free-lance writer who grew up in Brooklyn. After serving in the navy, he attended Pratt Institute and Mexico City College. During the 1960s he worked as a reporter, a Vietnam correspondent, and a political columnist. His feature articles appear in magazines such as *Cosmopolitan, Playboy, New York,* and the *New York Times Magazine*. The following essay on the value of competition appeared first in *Gentlemen's Quarterly* in 1983.

One of the more widely accepted maxims of modern American life 1 was uttered on a frozen winter afternoon during the early sixties. The late Vince Lombardi, who coached the Green Bay Packers when they were the greatest team in football, said it. "Winning isn't everything," he declared. "It's the only thing."

Vince Lombardi's notion was immediately appropriated by an ex- 2 traordinary variety of American males: presidents and lesser politicians, generals, broadcasters, political columnists, Little League coaches, heads of corporations, and probably millions of others. In fact, it sometimes seems that Lombardi's words have had greater impact than any sentence uttered by an American since Stephen Decatur's "our country, right or wrong."

That's surprising on many levels, beginning with the obvious: It's a 3 deceptively simple premise. Winning *isn't* "the only thing." Such an idea muddles the idea of competition, not simply in sports, but in all aspects of our lives. We've learned the hard way in this century that the world is a complex place; it's certainly not the National Football League. Winning isn't the only thing in love, art, marriage, commerce, or politics; it's not even the only thing in sports.

In sports, as in so many other areas of our national life, we've al- 4

405

ways cherished gallant losers. I remember one afternoon in the fall of 1956 when Sal Maglie was pitching for the Brooklyn Dodgers against the hated Yankees. Maglie was an old man that year, as age is measured in sports. But this was the World Series, and he hauled his thirty-nine-year-old body to the mound, inning after inning, gave everything he had, held the Yankees to a few scattered hits and two runs — and lost. That day Don Larsen pitched his perfect game: no runs, no hits, no errors. Yet, to me, the afternoon belonged to Maglie — tough, gallant, and a loser.

There was an evening in Manila when Joe Frazier went up against 5 Muhammad Ali for the third and final time. That night, Frazier brought his workman's skills into combat against the magic of the artist, called on his vast reservoir of courage and will, and came up empty at the end of fourteen rounds. Frazier was the loser, but that evening, nobody really lost. Because of that fight, Joe Frazier can always boast with honor that he made Muhammad Ali a great fighter. He was the test, the implacable force who made Ali summon all of his own considerable reserves of skill, heart, and endurance for a final effort. The contest consumed them both. Neither was ever again a good fighter. But during their violent confrontation, winning or losing was, in the end, a marginal concern; that all-consuming effort was everything.

There are hundreds of similar examples of losers who showed us 6 how to be more human, and their performances make the wide acceptance of Lombardi's notions even more mystifying. Lombardi's thesis, in fact, represented something of a shift in the nation's popular thought. Americans had been the people who remembered the Alamo or Pearl Harbor; we blew taps over the graves of those who lost at the Battle of the Bulge or Anzio or the Yalu Basin. Those soldiers had all been defeated, but we honored them for their display of a critical human quality: courage.

Ernest Hemingway once defined courage as grace under pressure, 7 and that's always struck me as an eminently useful definition. The best professional athletes not only possess that kind of courage but, more important, are willing to display it to strangers. Baseball's Reggie Jackson or Richard ("Goose") Gossage, for instance, function most completely as athletes and as men when appearing before gigantic crowds under pressure: bases loaded, late innings, a big game. They come to their tasks with gladness and absolute focus, neither whimpering, complaining nor shirking when doing their job; they just try their best to get that job done. And, of course, sometimes they fail. Gossage gives up a single and his team loses. Jackson strikes out. No matter. The important thing is that such men keep their appointments with confidence and grace. Courage has become so deep a part of their character that they don't even think about it. (They certainly *want* to win. Sometimes they absolutely lust for victory. But they know that winning isn't everything. All a man can do is his best.)

Competition isn't really a problem for Americans. All sports, in 8 one way or another, are competitive. But an individual's primary competition is with himself and all his attendant weaknesses. That's obviously true of boxing, where fear must be dominated and made to work to the fighter's benefit. Yet it's also true for team sports, as well as such solitary endeavors as golf, where a player must learn control before anything else. The problem isn't competition, which is a part of life; it's in the notion of the necessity of triumph. A man can lose but still win. And the point of competition in sports is an old and not very fashionable one: It builds character.

That's especially true of prizefighters, the athletes I've known best. 9 Outside the ring, almost all fighters are the gentlest of men. They carry themselves with the dignity of those who have little to prove, either to others or themselves. They're never bullies, rarely use their dangerous skills against ordinary citizens and avoid pointless confrontations. When a fighter hears that a colleague has been involved in a bar brawl or a swingout with a cop, he dismisses that fighter as a cowardly bum. Most of the boxers I know are honest, generous, funny. Yet they also know that as good as they are, there might be someone down the line who has their number. Again, they would prefer to be winners. But they're aware that losing, if a courageous effort is made, is never a disgrace. The highest compliment one fighter can pay another is to say that he has "heart."

There are lessons to be learned from such athletes that can be ap- 10 plied to how we live our lives. In the long run, we'll all come up losers because there's no greater loss than death. And since primitive man first began to think, we humans have devised strategies to deal with dying. Religion is the most obvious one, usually demanding that we adhere to a moral code on earth in exchange for a serene existence after death. Ideologies offer secular versions of the same instinct, insisting that we sacrifice now, directing our lives toward the ideal of a better future, with each man becoming an architect of his own utopia. Patriotism and nationalism carry some of the same fearful baggage.

An athlete's goals are less cosmic, his field of struggle less grandiose 11 and therefore more applicable to ordinary citizens. Great athletes teach us that life is a series of struggles, not one giant effort. Just when we appear to have triumphed, we must stop like Sisyphus and again begin rolling the boulder up that mountain. The true athlete teaches us that winning isn't everything, but struggle is — the struggle to simply get up in the morning or to see hope through the minefields of despair.

Viewed that way, a marriage, or any relationship with another 12 human being, is an ongoing struggle. The mastering of a skill or craft doesn't end with the granting of a diploma; it goes on for life. The relationship between parents and children doesn't end when the children turn eighteen. The running of a corporation isn't a one-shot affair, measured by a single year's statements of profits and losses; it's a continuing process, accomplished by human beings who learn from mistakes, plunge fearlessly into the struggle, take risks and prepare for the future.

It's probably no accident that American capitalism, with its often 13 permanently infantile male executives, experienced a decline that coincided with the period when Vince Lombardi's values received their widest acceptance. The results are visible everywhere. Sit on a plane with American businessmen and they'll be chattering about the Pittsburgh Steelers. Join a group of Japanese businessmen and they'll be discussing twenty-first-century technology. One group is trapped in a philosophy that demands winning as its goal; the other cares more about patient, long-term growth — and for the moment at least, the latter is winning.

Another great maxim of the years of America's triumphs also came 14 from the sports pages via the writer Grantland Rice. "It matters not who won or lost," declared the esteemed chronicler of the prewar years, "but how they played the game." By the time Vince Lombardi came along, such sentiments were being sneered at. We had then become a superpower, capable of blowing up the world. The man of grace, courage, endurance, and compassion was replaced in the public imagination by the swaggering macho blowhard; Humphrey Bogart gave way to John Wayne. With such attitudes dominating the landscape, we were certain to get into trouble, and we did. Vietnam and Watergate underscored the idea of winning at all costs. Yet today we seem incapable of admitting that an obsession with winning often leads to the most squalid of defeats.

Solid marriages are often built upon the experience of disastrous 15 ones. Politicians who lose elections become tempered for the contests that follow, sometimes going on to solid, useful careers. Painters, playwrights, novelists, and other artists often learn as much from their failures as they do from those rare moments when vision, craft, and ambition come together to produce masterpieces. It's also that way in sports.

I remember a night when my friend José Torres, then a middle- 16 weight, was boxing Florentino Fernandez in Puerto Rico. I couldn't go to the fight, so I spent the night tuning in and out of the all-news radio stations, anxious about the result because Florentino was a great puncher. About three in the morning, Torres called.

"Oh, Pete," he said, close to tears. "I'm so sorry."   17

"What happened?"   18

"I got knocked out," Torres replied, his voice brimming with emo- 19 tion, since he'd never lost as a professional. We started discussing what had happened. Emotions cooled; the talk became technical. Torres explained that he had learned some things about himself, about boxing. He now understood some of his flaws, and thought he could correct them. We talked for an hour. Then I asked what he was going to do next.

"Go to the gym," he said. "I'm going to be champion of the 20 world."

Two years later, Torres *was* the world's light-heavyweight cham- 21 pion. He didn't quit after his first defeat. That night in San Juan he didn't say winning was the only thing, that it was time to pack it in. He had learned something from defeat, and knew that one violent night, somewhere down the line, he would show the world what he had learned. And that was precisely what he did. But he was aware of something else too: Sooner or later, someone might come along who was better than he was, for at least one evening. After all, even champions are human. Even champions eventually lose. That happened to José Torres as well. But then it didn't really matter. José Torres, like the rest of us, had learned that winning wasn't everything. Living was all, and in life, defeat and victory are inseparable brothers.

CONSIDERATIONS

1. What is the important quality that can be as evident in losing as in winning? How does the author define it? How do most boxers define it?
2. According to Hamill, what are the adverse effects on individuals and on society of maintaining a philosophy of winning?
3. According to Hamill, what is the point of competition in sports? Do you agree?
4. Do you think Hamill has underestimated the importance of winning or losing? Or do most people overvalue the outcome of a game?
5. WRITING TOPIC. Does the nationwide mania for contests and mass gambling indicate that to Americans winning *is* the only thing? When only luck operates and no skill is involved, great winnings are possible without effort or risks, and loss isn't because of personal failure. Do you think that the widespread use of lotteries and prize contests has any effect on people's attitudes, values, and character? In 500 words, take a stand on the good or bad effects of the public emphasis on winning.

Michael Novak

THE METAPHYSICS OF SPORTS

◊

MICHAEL NOVAK (b. 1933) is a writer on religion, an educator, and a political activist. After graduating from Stonehill College, he studied theology in Rome and at Catholic University of America, and he earned an M.A. degree at Harvard University. Instead of a career as a clergyman, Novak was drawn to teaching and writing about the theology of contemporary culture; that is, he writes about the ways that religious values enter secular life. During the 1960s he wrote widely on Catholic theology and political questions in American social policies. His views are presented in his book *A Theology for Radical Politics*, 1969. He contributes to magazines such as *Commentary*, *Harper's*, *New Republic*, and *Commonweal*. Novak is also seriously interested in the spiritual significance of sports, which he regards as a kind of religious activity. The following selection is a chapter from his book, *The Joy of Sports: End Zones, Bases, Baskets, Balls, and the Consecration of the American Spirit* (1976).

Some hold that sports are childish, at best adolescent. "When one 1 becomes a man, one ought to put aside the things of childhood." But what if participation in sports is the mark of a civilized person? What if it deepens and mellows the soul?

Play, not work, is the end of life. To participate in the rites of play 2 is to dwell in the Kingdom of Ends. To participate in work, career, and the making of history is to labor in the Kingdom of Means. The modern age, the age of history, nourishes illusions. In a Protestant culture, as in Marxist cultures, work is serious, important, adult. Its essential insignificance is overlooked. Work, of course, must be done. But we should be wise enough to distinguish necessity from reality. Play is reality. Work is diversion and escape.

Work is justified by myth: that the essential human task is to im- 3 prove the world. The vision of history this ideology drums into us, with accompanying trumpet flourish, is the "march of time." *Progress.* Our ancestors were inferior to ourselves in knowledge, virtue, and civilization. Our present task is to advance the human condition beyond the state in which we find it. That the reality of human life contradicts this myth does not usually disabuse us of it, at least in our conscious minds. What we call progress should, perhaps, be interpreted in exactly the reverse way: *Decline.* Each year of our labors, it may be, hastens the destruction of this planet. I do not assert these propositions; they do bring to light the optimistic myth we tend to accept as reality itself.

It seems naïve to believe in the reality of progress, at least in the ₄ sense that humans become more moral generation by generation. Today there is television, and thirty years ago there was not. Today medicine saves lives that at the beginning of this century would have been lost. Today American society is by some degrees and in certain respects more just and egalitarian than twenty years ago, or forty, or sixty, or eighty, etc. Of course, changes do occur. But the enduring struggles of the human race do not seem to disappear. Death still claims us. The universe, despite us, steadily "does its thing." That we will survive all other species on this planet, or survive as long as there is a universe, it may be permissible to doubt. Now, as in the days when humans lived in caves, people sometimes love each other, sometimes cruelly kill each other; sometimes are honest, sometimes dishonest; sometimes are heroic and excellent in achievement, sometimes cowardly and mediocre.

Historical changes, social changes, cultural changes seem not to ₅ alter moral difficulties. They do displace them, rearrange them, distribute them differently. History does not much alter the quantum of good or evil in social structures or in individuals. In every age, in every culture, in every circumstance, it is difficult to be all that one ought to be as a human being. On the face of it, I do not consider myself and my brothers and sister higher human types than our parents or grandparents or our ancestors of a thousand years ago. Allowing for changes in circumstances, I do not think we are more independent of mind, courageous, truthful, and sensitive, or more capable of deep and true love. What we have gained along some lines of development — mobility of mind and travel and education, for example — we seem to have lost along others: a concentration of energy, simplicity, inner definition. We seem to be as lost as any generation in the long history of our people. I would not want to stand before God and claim to be better than my ancestors.

In a word, it has for some time struck me that those matters the 6 newspapers treat as serious and important (national news, international news, financial news, and so forth), are like shadows dancing on the walls of a cave; like the grass of the field that alternately is green, brown, and covered by snow; like dreams; and cyclical, repetitive, and spiraling now upward and now downward. It is not that history stands still: *Eppur, si muove!* It is, rather, that if one is absent from the news for a month, or a year, or three years, the world still seems to turn. Economic crises come and go. So do nations and elections. It is all fascinating. Each day is different. Each social process, each trend, each historical movement is unique. Still, there is a remarkable sameness deep down in things.

For this reason, I have sometimes thought the sports pages print 7 the critical dispatches from the realm of permanent reality. They celebrate the essential human qualities. They sing of the sameness, the cycles, of reality. They tell the truth about human life. They carry minimal illusion. It is the good sense of most humans that leads them to look first at the sports pages, second at the news from the world of image and shadow. It is their good sense that leads them to demand that the sports sections of the papers be longer, fuller, and more complete than the pages of international news, national news, local news, financial news. Sports are at the heart of the matter. Sports are the high point of civilization — along with the arts, but more powerfully than the arts, which are special in taste and execution and appeal. Only a very few books or folktales reach the same metaphysical levels as sports can. Very few philosophical-religious texts have as clear a ring of truth as a baseball smacked from the fat, true center of a willow bat.

The serious ones say that sports are escape. It seems far more true 8 to the eye, the ear, the heart, and the mind that history is an escape. Work is an escape. Causes are an escape. Historical movements are an escape. All these escapes must be attempted; I take part in as many as I can. But the heart of human reality is courage, honesty, freedom, community, excellence: the heart is sports.

Sports are not, of course, all of life. What good are courage, hon- 9 esty, freedom, community, and excellence if they do not inform one's family life, civic life, political life, work life? Sports do not celebrate such qualities in order to contain them, but in order to hold them clearly before the aspiring heart. No one can live a life wholly within sports. For professional athletes, sports themselves may become work, not sports; just as for a professional academic, studies may become work, not liberal arts; just as for a professional clergyman, religion may become work, not spirit.

It is fashionable to put down "jocks." Others, of course, put down 10 businessmen, or do-gooders, or beatniks, or artists, or theologians, or secularists, or saints. It is part of the human comedy for everyone to put down someone.

What the person of wisdom needs to derive from every sphere of 11 life is its inherent beauty, attraction, power, force.

What I have learned from sports is respect for authenticity and in- 12 dividuality (each player learning his own true instincts, capacities, style); for courage and perseverance and stamina; for the ability to enter into defeat in order to suck dry its power to destroy; for harmony of body and emotions and spirit. Sports are as old as the human race. Sports are the highest products of civilization and the most accessible, lived, experiential sources of the civilizing spirit. In sports, law was born and also liberty, and the nexus of their interrelation. In sports, honesty and excellence are caught, captured, nourished, held in trust for the generations. Without rules, there are no sports. Without limits, a sport cannot begin to exist. Within the rules, within the limits, freedom is given form. Play is the essence of freedom: "The free play of ideas." Play is the fundamental structure of the human mind. Of the body, too. The mind at play, the body at play — these furnish our imaginations with the highest achievements of beauty the human race attains. Symphonies, statues, novels, poems, dances, essays, philosophical treatises — these are transpositions of the world of sports into the exercises of higher civilization. Sports are their fundament, their never-failing life source. Cease play, cease civilization. Work is the diversion necessary for play to survive.

Those who have contempt for sports, our serious citizens, are a 13 danger to the human race, ants among men, drones in the honeycomb. There are many reasons for not participating in sports, or even for not liking certain sports. No one can do, or like, everything. Still, those of us who love sports are obliged to hear many taunts about the human inadequacies of "jocks." We disregard many taunts because of their transparent base in envy. The human body was meant to aspire to excellence, and the spirit to perfection. So when some refer to sports as an "animal occupation," they cause us to become aware of biases of our own. Allow me to mention one of my own, not one in which I judge myself correct, but one which I confess haunts my unconscious responses.

I have never met a person who disliked sports, or who absented 14 himself or herself entirely from them, who did not at the same time seem to me deficient in humanity. I don't only mean that all work and no play makes Jack a dull boy, or Jill a dull ms. I mean that a quality of sensitivity, an organ of perception, an access to certain significant truths appear to be missing. Such persons seem to me a danger to civilization. I do not, on the whole, like to work with them. In their presence I find myself on guard, often unconsciously. I expect from them a certain softness of mind, from their not having known a sufficient number of defeats. Unless they have compensated for it elsewhere, I anticipate that they will underestimate the practice and discipline required for execution, or the role of chance and Fate in human outcomes. I expect them to have a view of the world far too rational and mechanical.

Many women, I believe, who have had less access to sports, have 15 been denied heroic modes of behavior. Many men, traumatized by early failures in sports, often grow up warped by the trauma. Reconciliation to their own limits, submission to the disciplines necessary for accomplishment, submission to the humiliation involved in failure in the presence of their fellows, delight in whatever measure of talent God gave them — these are too often absent. Millions of men were as boys poorly coordinated, lacked strength, suffered from some disease or infirmity that prevented athletic accomplishment, were too sensitive to bear the sting of public failure. Those who were "good sports" lived within their limits and prospered spiritually. Those who grew embittered turned their backs, not on something petty and mean, but on something that would have enriched them. Since sports are so much of boyhood, boys who turn away from sports frequently seem crippled in humanity, poisoned against their peers, driven to a competitiveness in intellect or lost in the acquisition of power and wealth, never graced by the liberty of play.

Machismo — frequently identified with sports — is a vice, a dis- 16 tortion of sports, as manipulation, lust, or self-enclosure are corruptions of love. To diagnose sports as the source of machismo is like diagnosing love as the source of selfishness. By "machismo" I understand the fear of failure, the fear of cutting a *brutta figura*. Machismo is a diseased sense of honor, and it flourishes in cultures where honor — external appearance, style — is prized. It has its own glories: without it, the race would be much poorer, and the beau geste would not exist. Those who attack it do not weigh how much its loss to humanity would cost. I would hope that more women would learn to share in it, as many already do. But machismo is not an athletic ideal. It is, in sports, a deficiency.

A very few athletes are born so richly talented that every action and 17 instinct in their chosen game comes easily to them. Even those of great talent must war against the softness of the body, the slackness of instinct, the slowing of mental reaction, the dispersion of attention. And most must practice for scores of thousands of hours to sharpen their skills; most must painstakingly identify weaknesses and compensate for them; most must learn the humiliations and intricacies of team play, and of that fierce competition with the self in which one is measured against the achieved standards of the sport. All must every day face failure and defeat. Every contest is a risk of loss of face. In sports, machismo dies a thousand deaths. In the experience of most athletes, from earliest ages onward, the youngsters afflicted with machismo are soon identified as quitters. In the thousands of practice sessions, in the hazing and teasing of one's peers, in the countless series of injuries, frustrations, failures, and losses, machismo is burned like dross from maturity. It is true that some splendidly gifted athletes, whose peers cannot contain them, do not early enough or deeply enough know failure; and they, it is true, are sometimes insufferable. (Sometimes, too, they are the most surpassingly gentle among men.)

Yet millions of men look back nostalgically on their days in active 18 athletics precisely because they experienced there, as at few other points in their lives, a quality of tenderness, a stream of caring and concern from and toward others, such as would make the most ardent imaginers of the androgynous ideal envious. Male bonding is one of the most paradoxical forms of human tenderness: harsh, hazing, sweet, gentle, abrupt, soft. Blows are exchanged. Pretenses are painfully lanced. The form of compliment is, often as not, an insult. There is daily, hourly probing as to whether one can take it as well as dish it out. It is sweet preparation for a world less rational, less liberal, than childhood dreams imagine. Among men, sports help to form a brotherhood for which, alas, sisterhood has no similar equivalent, and which it is a high human imperative to invent.

Androgynous? Why do critics so often leer that "jocks" are secret 19 homosexuals, patting one another's buttocks, showing off their well-angled forearms and thighs, affectionately joshing one another in the showers? Sports bring out in every ideal team a form of gentleness and tenderness so intense that it is no misnomer to call it love; and coaches commonly speak to their supposed macho males like golden-tongued preachers of love, brotherhood, comradeship. Tears, burning throats, and raw love of male for male are not unknown among athletes in the daily heat of preparation, in the humiliation of doing plays over and over because the coach does not yet see sufficient perfection, and in the solemn battle. In the working world, such tears must normally await the testimonial dinner upon retirement. They are wrong who think the "brains" are androgynous and the jocks afflicted with machismo. For gentleness of demeanor, I will take the athlete eight times out of ten. For hardness of heart, I have learned to fear the man who has always hated sports.

Indeed, the contempt for machismo in sports that one meets in 20 such men is, on inspection, almost always a form of what it condemns. Those who were ashamed to fail, who needed to protect their dignity rather than risk being laughed at, live out the essence of machismo. As a youngster of no great bodily talent but of fierce competitiveness, I recall vividly dozens of struggles with my own machismo: reluctance to enter new forms of competition for fear of losing face; the need to learn that humiliation does not bring death, and that failure distills a sweetness of its own.

For the underlying metaphysic of sports entails overcoming the 21 fear of death. In every contest, one side is defeated. Defeat hurts. No use saying "It's only a game." It doesn't feel like a game. The anguish and depression that seize one's psyche in defeat are far deeper than a mere comparative failure — deeper than recognition of the opponent's superiority. That would be a simple emotion to handle. Even before a game, one might be willing to concede that much; one might already *know* that the other is better. But in a game, the more talented do not always win. A game tests considerably more than talent. A game tests, somehow, one's entire life. It tests one's standing with fortune and the gods. Defeat is too like death. Defeat hurts like death.

It can put one almost in a coma, slow up all of one's reactions, make the tongue cleave to the mouth, exhaust every fount of life and joy, make one *wish* one were dead, so as to be attuned to one's feelings.

How can that be? How can a mere game be a combat with death? 22 But it is. One knows it. One's body knows it. One's psyche knows it. Consolation and comfort from others do not touch the depths of one's feelings. In decency, announcers do not usually visit the locker rooms of the losers. It takes enormous efforts of will for the dead to pretend to be alive, congratulating those in whom Life still flows triumphant.

A contest like a baseball, basketball, or football game is in some as 23 yet unexplored way a ritual conducted under the sight and power of the gods. Thumbs up, or thumbs down. One side will live, one will die. When one's team is losing, it is too painful to keep on watching. Sports are not diversion. Entertainment diverts. A contest rivets the energies of life on a struggle for survival. The conflict is absolute. No holds barred. To win an athletic contest is to feel as though the gods are on one's side, as though one is fate's darling, as if the powers of being course through one's veins and radiate from one's action — powers stronger than nonbeing, powers over ill fortune, powers over death. Victory is abundant life, vivacity, bubbling over. Defeat is silence, withdrawal, passivity, glumness.

Each time one enters a contest, one's unseen antagonist is death. 24 Not one's visible opponent, who is only the occasion for the struggle. But the Negative Spirit, the Denier. That is why the image of the aging athlete is so poignant: it begins to mix the ritual contest with the actual contest, ritual death — with the coming of real death. In the aging athlete, the ultimate reality of sports breaks through the symbol, becomes explicit. Death advances on us all. Not even our vitality, not even our beauty of form, not even our heroic acts can hold it back. "The boys of summer" fade away. The ritual goes on, young men testing themselves against the terror without a name. Human life is essentially a defeat; we die. The victories of sport are ritual triumphs of grace, agility, perfection, beauty over death.

In these respects, sports owe more to the ritual grammar of religion 25 than to the laws and forms of entertainment. Millions become involved in the rituals of sport to a depth of seriousness never elicited by entertainment. Millions do not care about comedians, or variety shows, or films, or books — to these they turn for diversion. But they are deeply affected by participation in the ritual struggle of a football game. Such a game has the power to depress or to elate. To the unconscious rather than the conscious self (for few athletes or fans think such matters out in words), it offers signals ancient, disturbing, fundamental: I'm on the slope of life, or I am on the slope of death. Being, or nonbeing. Only by some such formula can we explain the seriousness of the depression caused by losing, the vitality of the elation caused by winning. It is not the mere game, not the mere pride, not the vaunting of self over others; it is the sense of one's inflation by power not one's own that makes victory so sweet. The victor has been chosen. Unsought strength sweeps through him. He is more than self. The elation of victory must be experienced to be understood; one is lifted, raised, infused with more than abundant life.

"Winning," said Vince Lombardi, "isn't everything; it's the only 26 thing." It isn't the thought of lording it over number two or number three that brings satisfaction; in one's heart, one may know that in some way one's competitors are superior. But finishing first is to have destiny blowing out one's sails. Let the other teams be better on the books; today, Fate has spoken, darling and beloved Fate.

Those who have been rejected relive the struggle to detect precisely 27 where they showed themselves unworthy. They vow not to fail the gods, next time. They renew their faith that the gods are really on their side, as the contest coming up will show.

When Alabama loses seven bowl games in a row; when for months 28 until the spell is broken the Boston Red Sox cannot win a game in Oakland; when the Dallas Cowboys lose the "big ones" year after year, indescribable anxiety descends. The jinx may be no fluke, no accident, but inescapably disastrous. The flaw within the heart may be incurable. The prognostication may be ultimate.

CONSIDERATIONS

1. How does the author redefine work and play? Think of two other words that clarify at least part of Novak's contrast between work and play.
2. In paragraph 7, what is the effect of the author's generalizations? What image of the author is suggested by this paragraph? Do you think the image is authentic?

3. According to Novak what serious faults are usually evident in people who don't like sports? Do you agree?

4. What does Novak emphasize as the predominant lesson of sports? What does he appear to have personally learned from sports?

5. Who is always the opponent in a sports contest? Who always wins? How does defeat affect a competitor?

6. WRITING TOPIC. In 500 words, compare Novak and Pete Hamill (see the preceding selection) in their responses to Vince Lombardi's axiom, "Winning isn't everything; it's the only thing." How do Novak's and Hamill's views about winning differ? In what ways, if at all, do they agree about sports competition?

7. WRITING TOPIC. Write a 750-word essay about an athletic or artistic activity in which you have tried to excel. Explain some of the difficulties that required much effort to overcome. What were your usual reactions to success and to frustration as you trained? Why did you want to excel at this particular activity? Do you now think that it was worthwhile?

Virginia Woolf

PROFESSIONS FOR WOMEN

◊

VIRGINIA WOOLF (1882–1941) was an important British novelist noted for her emphasis on the subjective meaning of events rather than the outward circumstances of plot and appearance. Her novels include *Mrs. Dalloway* (1925) and *To the Lighthouse* (1927). Born into a distinguished literary family, she was educated at home, and began her writing career as a book reviewer for the London *Times Literary Supplement*. With her husband she lived among a group of artists and intellectuals known as the Bloomsbury group — a group that included E. M. Forster, John Maynard Keynes, Bertrand Russell, and Lytton Strachey. She spoke out consistently for freedom and equality for women in such works as *A Room of One's Own* (1929) and the following address to the Women's Service League. Her essays are collected in four volumes of *Collected Essays* (1967).

When your secretary invited me to come here, she told me that 1 your Society is concerned with the employment of women and she suggested that I might tell you something about my own professional experiences. It is true I am a woman; it is true I am employed; but what professional experiences have I had? It is difficult to say. My profession is literature; and in that profession there are fewer experiences for women than in any other, with the exception of the stage — fewer, I mean, that are peculiar to women. For the road was cut many years ago — by Fanny Burney, by Aphra Behn, by Harriet Martineau, by Jane Austen, by George Eliot* — many famous women, and many more unknown and forgotten, have been before me, making the path smooth, and regulating my steps. Thus, when I came to write, there were very few material obstacles in my way. Writing was a reputable and harmless occupation. The family peace was not broken by the

---

* British women novelists of the eighteenth and nineteenth centuries.

scratching of a pen. No demand was made upon the family purse. For ten and sixpence one can buy paper enough to write all the plays of Shakespeare — if one has a mind that way. Pianos and models, Paris, Vienna and Berlin, masters and mistresses, are not needed by a writer. The cheapness of writing paper is, of course, the reason why women have succeeded as writers before they have succeeded in the other professions.

But to tell you my story — it is a simple one. You have only got to 2 figure to yourselves a girl in a bedroom with a pen in her hand. She had only to move that pen from left to right — from ten o'clock to one. Then it occurred to her to do what is simple and cheap enough after all — to slip a few of those pages into an envelope, fix a penny stamp in the corner, and drop the envelope into the red box at the corner. It was thus that I became a journalist; and my effort was rewarded on the first day of the following month — a very glorious day it was for me — by a letter from an editor containing a check for one pound ten shillings and sixpence. But to show you how little I deserve to be called a professional woman, how little I know of the struggles and difficulties of such lives, I have to admit that instead of spending that sum upon bread and butter, rent, shoes and stockings, or butcher's bills, I went out and bought a cat — a beautiful cat, a Persian cat, which very soon involved me in bitter disputes with my neighbors.

What could be easier than to write articles and to buy Persian cats 3 with the profits? But wait a moment. Articles have to be about something. Mine, I seem to remember, was about a novel by a famous man. And while I was writing this review I discovered that if I were going to review books I should need to do battle with a certain phantom. And the phantom was a woman, and when I came to know her better I called her after the heroine of a famous poem, The Angel in the House. It was she who used to come between me and my paper when I was writing reviews. It was she who bothered me and wasted my time and so tormented me that at last I killed her. You who come of a younger and happier generation may not have heard of her — you may not know what I mean by the Angel in the House. I will describe her as shortly as I can. She was intensely sympathetic. She was immensely charming. She was utterly unselfish. She excelled in the difficult arts of family life. She sacrificed herself daily. If there was chicken, she took the leg; if there was a draught she sat in it — in short she was so constituted that she never had a mind or a wish of her own, but preferred to sympathize always with the minds and wishes of others. Above all — I need not say it — she was pure. Her purity was supposed to be her chief beauty — her blushes, her great grace. In those days — the last of Queen Victoria — every house had its Angel. And when I came to write I encountered her with the very first words. The shadow of her wings fell on my page; I heard the rustling of her skirts in the room. Directly, that is to say, I took my pen in hand to review that novel by a famous man, she slipped behind me and whispered: "My dear, you are a young woman. You are writing about a book that has been written by a man. Be sympathetic; be tender; flatter; deceive; use all the arts and wiles of our sex. Never let anybody guess that you have a mind of your own. Above all, be pure." And she made as if to guide my pen. I now record the one act for which I take some credit to myself, though the credit rightly belongs to some excellent ancestors of mine who left me a certain sum of money — shall we say five hundred pounds a year? — so that it was not necessary for me to depend solely on charm for my living. I turned upon her and caught her by the throat. I did my best to kill her. My excuse, if I were to be had up in a court of law, would be that I acted in self-defense. Had I not killed her she would have killed me. She would have plucked the heart out of my writing. For, as I found, directly I put pen to paper, you cannot review even a novel without having a mind of your own, without expressing what you think to be the truth about human relations, morality, sex. And all these questions, according to the Angel in the House, cannot be dealt with freely and openly by women; they must charm, they must conciliate, they must — to put it bluntly — tell lies if they are to succeed. Thus, whenever I felt the shadow of her wing or the radiance of her halo upon my page, I took up the inkpot and flung it at her. She died hard. Her fictitious nature was of great assistance to her. It is far harder to kill a phantom than a reality. She was always creeping back when I thought I had despatched her. Though I flatter myself that I killed her in the end, the struggle was severe; it took much time that had better have been spent upon learning Greek grammar; or in roaming the world in search of adventures. But it was a real experience; it was an experience that was bound to befall all women writers at that time. Killing the Angel in the House was part of the occupation of a woman writer.

But to continue my story. The Angel was dead; what then remained? You may say that what remained was a simple and common 4 object — a young woman in a bedroom with an inkpot. In other words, now that she had rid herself of falsehood, that young woman had only to be herself. Ah, but what is "herself"? I mean, what is a woman? I assure you, I do not know. I do not believe that you know. I do not believe that anybody can know until she has expressed herself in all the arts and professions open to human skill. That indeed is one of the reasons why I have come here — out of respect for you, who are in process of showing us by your experiments what a woman is, who are in process of providing us, by your failures and successes, with that extremely important piece of information.

But to continue the story of my professional experiences. I made one pound ten and six by my first review; and I bought a Persian cat with the proceeds. Then I grew ambitious. A Persian cat is all very well, I said; but a Persian cat is not enough. I must have a motor car. And it was thus that I became a novelist — for it is a very strange thing that people will give you a motor car if you will tell them a story. It is a still stranger thing that there is nothing so delightful in the world as telling stories. It is far pleasanter than writing reviews of famous novels. And yet, if I am to obey your secretary and tell you my professional experiences as a novelist, I must tell you about a very strange experience that befell me as a novelist. And to understand it you must try first to imagine a novelist's state of mind. I hope I am not giving away professional secrets if I say that a novelist's chief desire is to be as unconscious as possible. He has to induce in himself a state of perpetual lethargy. He wants life to proceed with the utmost quiet and regularity. He wants to see the same faces, to read the same books, to do the same things day after day, month after month, while he is writing, so that nothing may break the illusion in which he is living — so that nothing may disturb or disquiet the mysterious nosings about, feelings round, darts, dashes and sudden discoveries of that very shy and illusive spirit, the imagination. I suspect that this state is the same both for men and women. Be that as it may, I want you to imagine me writing a novel in a state of trance. I want you to figure to yourselves a girl sitting with a pen in her hand, which for minutes, and indeed for hours, she never dips into the inkpot. The image that comes to my mind when I think of this girl is the image of a fisherman lying sunk in dreams on the verge of a deep lake with a rod held out over the water. She was letting her imagination sweep unchecked round every rock and cranny of the world that lies submerged in the depths of our unconscious being. Now came the experience, the experience that I believe to be far commoner with women writers than with men. The line raced through the girl's fingers. Her imagination had rushed away. It had sought the pools, the depths, the dark places where the largest fish slumber. And then there was a smash. There was an explosion. There was foam and confusion. The imagination had dashed itself against something hard. The girl was roused from her dream. She was indeed in a state of the most acute and difficult distress. To speak without figure she had thought of something, something about the body, about the passions which it was unfitting for her as a woman to say. Men, her reason told her, would be shocked. The consciousness of what men will say of a woman who speaks the truth about her passions had roused her from her artist's state of unconsciousness. She could write no more. The trance was over. Her imagination could work no longer. This I believe to be a very common experience with women writers — they are impeded by the extreme conventionality of the other sex. For though men sensibly allow themselves great freedom in these respects, I doubt that they realize or can control the extreme severity with which they condemn such freedom in women.

These then were two very genuine experiences of my own. These 6 were two of the adventures of my professional life. The first — killing the Angel in the House — I think I solved. She died. But the second, telling the truth about my own experiences as a body, I do not think I solved. I doubt that any woman has solved it yet. The obstacles against her are still immensely powerful — and yet they are very difficult to define. Outwardly, what is simpler than to write books? Outwardly, what obstacles are there for a woman rather than for a man? Inwardly, I think, the case is very different; she has still many ghosts to fight, many prejudices to overcome. Indeed it will be a long time still, I think, before a woman can sit down to write a book without finding a phantom to be slain, a rock to be dashed against. And if this is so in literature, the freest of all professions for women, how is it in the new professions which you are now for the first time entering?

Those are the questions that I should like, had I time, to ask you. 7 And indeed, if I have laid stress upon these professional experiences of mine, it is because I believe that they are, though in different forms, yours also. Even when the path is nominally open — when there is nothing to prevent a woman from being a doctor, a lawyer, a civil servant — there are many phantoms and obstacles, as I believe, looming in her way. To discuss and define them is I think of great value and importance; for thus only can the labor be shared, the difficulties be solved. But besides this, it is necessary also to discuss the ends and the aims for which we are fighting, for which we are doing battle with these formidable obstacles. Those aims cannot be taken for granted; they must be perpetually questioned and examined. The whole position, as I see it — here in this hall surrounded by women practicing for the first time in history I know not how many different professions — is one of extraordinary interest and importance. You have won rooms of your own in the house hitherto exclusively owned by men. You are able, though not without great labor and effort, to pay the rent. You are earning your five hundred pounds a year. But this freedom is only a beginning; the room is your own, but it is still bare. It has to be furnished; it has to be decorated; it has to be shared. How are you going to furnish it, how are you going to decorate it? With whom are you going to share it, and upon what terms? These, I think are questions of the utmost importance and interest. For the first time in history you are able to ask them; for the first time you are able to decide for yourselves what the answers should be. Willingly would I stay and discuss those questions and answers — but not tonight. My time is up; and I must cease.

CONSIDERATIONS

1. In the first two paragraphs, what relation does Woolf establish with her audience? What details make her appear ingratiating? Condescending? Earnest?
2. Does the Angel in the House still exist? What has changed, and what remains the same, in present-day expectations of women?
3. Does Woolf assume that men writers encounter no difficulties or conflicts in thinking independently and expressing themselves? Is Woolf a female sexist in some of her observations? How would you explain her views to an audience of men?
4. What relationships between men and women are implied in Woolf's many references to women in a house and a room? What changes in the future are suggested by the metaphorical use of "house" in the final paragraph?

5. WRITING TOPIC. In 700 words, consider the obstacles between you and an appealing but unlikely choice of profession. Freely imagine yourself in any role fifteen years from now, and explain why it is genuinely attractive to you. Differentiate between limitations or conflicts that would be particularly your own and hurdles in the profession itself. How would you or the world need to be different for you to pursue that course?

Sherwood Anderson

THE EGG

◊

SHERWOOD ANDERSON (1876–1941), whose prophetic nickname as a child was "Jobby," grew up to become an aggressive, successful paint manufacturer in Elyria, Ohio, before he abruptly abandoned his business career in order to become a writer. His first important book, *Winesburg, Ohio* (1919), sketches the isolated inhabitants of a small town in which loneliness drives people to the brink of madness. In other fiction about conventional middle-class life, such as *Many Marriages* (1923), Anderson portrays the drive for success as an emotionally deadening ambition; and in all his works he sympathizes deeply with the world's obvious failures. His compassion is mixed with folksy humor and a flair for deliciously absurd circumstances in this short story about the ultimate frustrations of pursuing success.

My father was, I am sure, intended by nature to be a cheerful, 1 kindly man. Until he was thirty-four years old he worked as a farmhand for a man named Thomas Butterworth whose place lay near the town of Bidwell, Ohio. He had then a horse of his own, and on Saturday evenings drove into town to spend a few hours in social intercourse with other farmhands. In town he drank several glasses of beer and stood about in Ben Head's saloon — crowded on Saturday evenings with visiting farmhands. Songs were sung and glasses thumped on the bar. At ten o'clock father drove home along a lonely country road, made his horse comfortable for the night, and himself went to bed, quite happy in his position in life. He had at that time no notion of trying to rise in the world.

It was in the spring of his thirty-fifth year that father married my 2 mother, then a country school-teacher, and in the following spring I came wriggling and crying into the world. Something happened to the two people. They became ambitious. The American passion for getting up in the world took possession of them.

It may have been that mother was responsible. Being a school- 3 teacher she had no doubt read books and magazines. She had, I presume, read of how Garfield, Lincoln, and other Americans rose from poverty to fame and greatness, and as I lay beside her — in the days of her lying-in — she may have dreamed that I would some day rule men and cities. At any rate she induced father to give up his place as a farmhand, sell his horse, and embark on an independent enterprise of his own. She was a tall silent woman with a long nose and troubled gray eyes. For herself she wanted nothing. For father and myself she was incurably ambitious.

The first venture into which the two people went turned out badly. 4 They rented ten acres of poor stony land on Grigg's Road, eight miles from Bidwell, and launched into chicken-raising. I grew into boyhood on the place and got my first impressions of life there. From the beginning they were impressions of disaster, and if, in my turn, I am a gloomy man inclined to see the darker side of life, I attribute it to the fact that what should have been for me the happy joyous days of childhood were spent on a chicken farm.

One unversed in such matters can have no notion of the many and 5 tragic things that can happen to a chicken. It is born out of an egg, lives for a few weeks as a tiny fluffy thing such as you will see pictured on Easter cards, then becomes hideously naked, eats quantities of corn and meal bought by the sweat of your father's brow, gets diseases called pip, cholera, and other names, stands looking with stupid eyes at the sun, becomes sick and dies. A few hens and now and then a rooster, intended to serve God's mysterious ends, struggle through to maturity. The hens lay eggs out of which come other chickens and the dreadful cycle is thus made complete. It is all unbelievably complex. Most philosophers must have been raised on chicken farms. One hopes for so much from a chicken and is so dreadfully disillusioned. Small chickens, just setting out on the journey of life, look so bright and alert and they are in fact so dreadfully stupid. They are so much like people they mix one up in one's judgments of life. If disease does not kill them, they wait until your expectations are thoroughly aroused and then walk under the wheels of a wagon — to go squashed and dead back to their maker. Vermin infest their youth, and fortunes must be spent for curative powders. In later life I have seen how a literature has been built up on the subject of fortunes to be made out of the raising of chickens. It is intended to be read by the gods who have just eaten of the tree of the knowledge of good and evil. It is a hopeful literature and declares that much may be done by simple ambitious people who own a few hens. Do not be led astray by it. It was not written for you. Go hunt for gold on the frozen hills of Alaska, put your faith in the honesty of a politician, believe if you will that the world is daily growing better and that good will triumph over evil, but do not read and believe the literature that is written concerning the hen. It was not written for you.

I, however, digress. My tale does not primarily concern itself with the hen. If correctly told it will center on the egg. For ten years my father and mother struggled to make our chicken farm pay and then they gave up their struggle and began another. They moved into the town of Bidwell, Ohio, and embarked in the restaurant business. After ten years of worry with incubators that did not hatch, and with tiny — and in their own way lovely — balls of fluff that passed on into semi-naked pullethood and from that into dead henhood, we threw all aside and, packing our belongings on a wagon, drove down Grigg's Road toward Bidwell, a tiny caravan of hope looking for a new place from which to start on our upward journey through life.

We must have been a sad-looking lot, not, I fancy, unlike refugees fleeing from a battlefield. Mother and I walked in the road. The wagon that contained our goods had been borrowed for the day from Mr. Albert Griggs, a neighbor. Out of its side stuck the legs of cheap chairs, and at the back of the pile of beds, tables, and boxes filled with kitchen utensils was a crate of live chickens, and on top of that the baby carriage in which I had been wheeled about in my infancy. Why we stuck to the baby carriage I don't know. It was unlikely other children would be born and the wheels were broken. People who have few possessions cling tightly to those they have. That is one of the facts that make life so discouraging.

Father rode on top of the wagon. He was then a bald-headed man of forty-five, a little fat, and from long association with mother and the chickens he had become habitually silent and discouraged. All during our ten years on the chicken farm he had worked as a laborer on neighboring farms and most of the money he had earned had been spent for remedies to cure chicken diseases, on Wilmer's White Wonder Cholera Cure or Professor Bidlow's Egg Producer or some other preparations that mother found advertised in the poultry papers. There were two little patches of hair on father's head just above his ears. I remember that as a child I used to sit looking at him when he had gone to sleep in a chair before the stove on Sunday afternoons in the winter. I had at that time already begun to read books and have notions of my own, and the bald path that led over the top of his head was, I fancied, something like a broad road, such a road as Caesar might have made on which to lead his legions out of Rome and into the wonders of an unknown world. The tufts of hair that grew above father's ears were, I thought, like forests. I fell into a half-sleeping, half-waking state and dreamed I was a tiny thing going along the road into a far beautiful place where there were no chicken farms and where life was a happy eggless affair.

One might write a book concerning our flight from the chicken 9 farm into town. Mother and I walked the entire eight miles — she to be sure that nothing fell from the wagon and I to see the wonders of the world. On the seat of the wagon beside father was his greatest treasure. I will tell you of that.

On a chicken farm, where hundreds and even thousands of 10 chickens come out of eggs, surprising things sometimes happen. Grotesques are born out of eggs as out of people. The accident does not often occur — perhaps once in a thousand births. A chicken is, you see, born that has four legs, two pairs of wings, two heads, or what not. The things do not live. They go quickly back to the hand of their maker that has for a moment trembled. The fact that the poor little things could not live was one of the tragedies of life to father. He had some sort of notion that if he could but bring into henhood or roosterhood a five-legged hen or a two-headed rooster his fortune would be made. He dreamed of taking the wonder about the county fairs and of growing rich by exhibiting it to other farmhands.

At any rate, he saved all the little monstrous things that had been 11 born on our chicken farm. They were preserved in alcohol and put each in its own glass bottle. These he had carefully put into a box, and on our journey into town it was carried on the wagon seat beside him. He drove the horses with one hand and with the other clung to the box. When we got to our destination, the box was taken down at once and the bottles removed. All during our days as keepers of a restaurant in the town of Bidwell, Ohio, the grotesques in their little glass bottles sat on a shelf back of the counter. Mother sometimes protested, but father was a rock on the subject of his treasure. The grotesques were, he declared, valuable. People, he said, liked to look at strange and wonderful things.

Did I say that we embarked in the restaurant business in the town 12 of Bidwell, Ohio? I exaggerated a little. The town itself lay at the foot of a low hill and on the shore of a small river. The railroad did not run through the town and the station was a mile away to the north at a place called Pickleville. There had been a cider mill and pickle factory at the station, but before the time of our coming they had both gone out of business. In the morning and in the evening busses came down to the station along a road called Turner's Pike from the hotel on the main street of Bidwell. Our going to the out-of-the-way place to embark in the restaurant business was mother's idea. She talked of it for a year and then one day went off and rented an empty store building opposite the railroad station. It was her idea that the restaurant would be profitable. Traveling men, she said, would be always waiting around to take trains out of town and town people would come to the station to await incoming trains. They would come to the restaurant to buy pieces of pie and drink coffee. Now that I am older I know that she had another motive in going. She was ambitious for me. She wanted me to rise in the world, to get into a town school and become a man of the towns.

At Pickleville father and mother worked hard, as they always had 13 done. At first there was the necessity of putting our place into shape to be a restaurant. That took a month. Father built a shelf on which he put tins of vegetables. He painted a sign on which he put his name in large red letters. Below his name was the sharp command — "EAT HERE" — that was so seldom obeyed. A showcase was bought and filled with cigars and tobacco. Mother scrubbed the floors and the walls of the room. I went to school in the town and was glad to be away from the farm, from the presence of the discouraged, sad-looking chickens. Still I was not very joyous. In the evening I walked home from school along Turner's Pike and remembered the children I had seen playing in the town school yard. A troop of little girls had gone hopping about and singing. I tried that. Down along the frozen road I went hopping solemnly on one leg. "Hippity Hop To The Barber Shop," I sang shrilly. Then I stopped and looked doubtfully about. I was afraid of being seen in my gay mood. It must have seemed to me that I was doing a thing that should not be done by one who, like myself, had been raised on a chicken farm where death was a daily visitor.

Mother decided that our restaurant should remain open at night. 14 At ten in the evening a passenger train went north past our door followed by a local freight. The freight crew had switching to do in Pickleville, and when the work was done they came to our restaurant for hot coffee and food. Sometimes one of them ordered a fried egg. In the morning at four they returned north-bound and again visited us. A little trade began to grow up. Mother slept at night and during the day tended the restaurant and fed our boarders while father slept. He slept in the same bed mother had occupied during the night and I went off to the town of Bidwell and to school. During the long nights, while mother and I slept, father cooked meats that were to go into sandwiches for the lunch baskets of our boarders. Then an idea in regard to getting up in the world came into his head. The American spirit took hold of him. He also became ambitious.

In the long nights when there was little to do, father had time to 15 think. That was his undoing. He decided that he had in the past been an unsuccessful man because he had not been cheerful enough and that in the future he would adopt a cheerful outlook on life. In the early morning he came upstairs and got into bed with mother. She woke and the two talked. From my bed in the corner I listened.

It was father's idea that both he and mother should try to entertain 16 the people who came to eat at our restaurant. I cannot now remember his words, but he gave the impression of one about to become in some obscure way a kind of public entertainer. When people, particularly young people from the town of Bidwell, came into our place, as on very rare occasions they did, bright entertaining conversation was to be made. From father's words I gathered that something of the jolly innkeeper effect was to be sought. Mother must have been doubtful from the first, but she said nothing discouraging. It was father's notion that a passion for the company of himself and mother would spring up in the breasts of the younger people of the town of Bidwell. In the evening bright happy groups would come singing down Turner's Pike. They would troop shouting with joy and laughter into our place. There would be song and festivity. I do not mean to give the impression that father spoke so elaborately of the matter. He was, as

I have said, an uncommunicative man. "They want some place to go. I tell you they want some place to go," he said over and over. That was as far as he got. My own imagination has filled in the blanks.

For two or three weeks this notion of father's invaded our house. 17 We did not talk much, but in our daily lives tried earnestly to make smiles take the place of glum looks. Mother smiled at the boarders and I, catching the infection, smiled at our cat. Father became a little feverish in his anxiety to please. There was, no doubt, lurking somewhere in him, a touch of the spirit of the showman. He did not waste much of his ammunition on the railroad men he served at night, but seemed to be waiting for a young man or woman from Bidwell to come in to show what he could do. On the counter in the restaurant there was a wire basket kept always filled with eggs, and it must have been before his eyes when the idea of being entertaining was born in his brain. There was something pre-natal about the way eggs kept themselves connected with the development of his idea. At any rate, an egg ruined his new impulse in life. Late one night I was awakened by a roar of anger coming from father's throat. Both mother and I sat upright in our beds. With trembling hands she lighted a lamp that stood on a table by her head. Downstairs the front door of our restaurant went shut with a bang and in a few minutes father tramped up the stairs. He held an egg in his hand and his hand trembled as though he were having a chill. There was a half-insane light in his eyes. As he stood glaring at us I was sure he intended throwing the egg at either mother or me. Then he laid it gently on the table beside the lamp and dropped on his knees beside mother's bed. He began to cry like a boy, and I, carried away by his grief, cried with him. The two of us filled the little upstairs room with our wailing voices. It is ridiculous, but of the picture we made I can remember only the fact that mother's hand continually stroked the bald path that ran across the top of his head. I have forgotten what mother said to him and how she induced him to tell her of what had happened downstairs. His explanation also has gone out of my mind. I remember only my own grief and fright and the shiny path over father's head glowing in the lamplight as he knelt by the bed.

As to what happened downstairs. For some unexplainable reason I 18 know the story as well as though I had been a witness to my father's discomfiture. One in time gets to know many unexplainable things. On that evening young Joe Kane, son of a merchant of Bidwell, came to Pickleville to meet his father, who was expected on the ten-o'clock evening train from the South. The train was three hours late and Joe came into our place to loaf about and to wait for its arrival. The local freight train came in and the freight crew were fed. Joe was left alone in the restaurant with father.

From the moment he came into our place the Bidwell young man 19 must have been puzzled by my father's actions. It was his notion that father was angry at him for hanging around. He noticed that the restaurant-keeper was apparently disturbed by his presence and he thought of going out. However, it began to rain and he did not fancy the long walk to town and back. He bought a five-cent cigar and ordered a cup of coffee. He had a newspaper in his pocket and took it out and began to read. "I'm waiting for the evening train. It's late," he said apologetically.

For a long time father, whom Joe Kane had never seen before, re- 20 mained silently gazing at his visitor. He was no doubt suffering from an attack of stage fright. As so often happens in life he had thought so much and so often of the situation that now confronted him that he was somewhat nervous in its presence.

For one thing, he did not know what to do with his hands. He 21 thrust one of them nervously over the counter and shook hands with Joe Kane. "How-de-do," he said. Joe Kane put his newspaper down and stared at him. Father's eyes lighted on the basket of eggs that sat on the counter and he began to talk. "Well," he began hesitatingly, "well, you have heard of Christopher Columbus, eh?" He seemed to be angry. "That Christopher Columbus was a cheat," he declared emphatically. "He talked of making an egg stand on its end. He talked, he did, and then he went and broke the end of the egg."

My father seemed to his visitor to be beside himself at the duplicity 22 of Christopher Columbus. He muttered and swore. He declared it was wrong to teach children that Christopher Columbus was a great man when, after all, he cheated at the critical moment. He had declared he would make an egg stand on end and then, when his bluff had been called, he had done a trick. Still grumbling at Columbus, father took an egg from the basket on the counter and began to walk up and down. He rolled the egg between the palms of his hands. He smiled genially. He began to mumble words regarding the effect to be produced on an egg by the electricity that comes out of the human body. He declared that, without breaking its shell and by virtue of rolling it back and forth in his hands, he could stand the egg on its end. He explained that the warmth of his hands and the gentle rolling movement he gave the egg created a new center of gravity, and Joe Kane was mildly interested. "I have handled thousands of eggs," father said. "No one knows more about eggs than I do."

He stood the egg on the counter and it fell on its side. He tried the 23 trick again and again, each time rolling the egg between the palms of his hands and saying the words regarding the wonders of electricity and the laws of gravity. When after a half-hour's effort he did succeed in making the egg stand for a moment, he looked up to find that his visitor was no longer watching. By the time he had succeeded in calling Joe Kane's attention to the success of his effort, the egg had again rolled over and lay on its side.

Afire with the showman's passion and at the same time a good deal 24 disconcerted by the failure of his first effort, father now took the bottles containing the poultry monstrosities down from their place on the shelf and began to show them to his visitor. "How would you like to have seven legs and two heads like this fellow?" he asked, exhibiting the most remarkable of his treasures. A cheerful smile played over his face. He reached over the counter and tried to slap Joe Kane on the shoulder as he had seen men do in Ben Head's saloon when he was a young farmhand and drove to town on Saturday evenings. His visitor was made a little ill by the sight of the body of the terribly deformed bird floating in the alcohol in the bottle and got up to go. Coming from behind the counter, father took hold of the young man's arm and led him back to his seat. He grew a little angry and for a moment had to turn his face away and force himself to smile. Then he put the bottles back on the shelf. In an outburst of generosity he fairly compelled Joe Kane to have a fresh cup of coffee and another cigar at his expense. Then he took a pan and filling it with vinegar, taken from a jug that sat beneath the counter, he declared himself about to do a new trick. "I will heat this egg in this pan of vinegar," he said. "Then I will put it through the neck of a bottle without breaking the shell. When the egg is inside the bottle it will resume its normal shape and the shell will become hard again. Then I will give the bottle with the egg in it to you. You can take it about with you wherever you go. People will want to know how you got the egg in the bottle. Don't tell them. Keep them guessing. That is the way to have fun with this trick."

Father grinned and winked at his visitor. Joe Kane decided that the 25 man who confronted him was mildly insane but harmless. He drank the cup of coffee that had been given him and began to read his paper again. When the egg had been heated in vinegar, father carried it on a spoon to the counter and going into a back room got an empty bottle. He was angry because his visitor did not watch him as he began to do his trick, but nevertheless went cheerfully to work. For a long time he struggled, trying to get the egg to go through the neck of the bottle. He put the pan of vinegar back on the stove, intending to reheat the egg, then picked it up and burned his fingers. After a second bath in the hot vinegar, the shell of the egg had been softened a little, but not enough for his purpose. He worked and worked and a spirit of desperate determination took possession of him. When he thought that at last the trick was about to be consummated, the delayed train came in at the station and Joe Kane started to go nonchalantly out at the door. Father made a last desperate effort to conquer the egg and make it do the thing that would establish his reputation as one who knew how to entertain guests who came into his restaurant. He worried the egg. He attempted to be somewhat rough with it. He swore and the sweat stood out on his forehead. The egg broke under his hand. When the contents spurted over his clothes, Joe Kane, who had stopped at the door, turned and laughed.

A roar of anger rose from my father's throat. He danced and 26 shouted a string of inarticulate words. Grabbing another egg from the basket on the counter, he threw it, just missing the head of the young man as he dodged through the door and escaped.

Father came upstairs to mother and me with an egg in his hand. I 27 do not know what he intended to do. I imagine he had some idea of destroying it, of destroying all eggs, and that he intended to let mother and me see him begin. When, however, he got into the presence of mother, something happened to him. He laid the egg gently on the table and dropped on his knees by the bed as I have already explained. He later decided to close the restaurant for the night and to come upstairs and get into bed. When he did so, he blew out the light and after much muttered conversation both he and mother went to sleep. I suppose I went to sleep also, but my sleep was troubled. I awoke at dawn and for a long time looked at the egg that lay on the table. I wondered why eggs had to be and why from the egg came the hen who again laid the egg. The question got into my blood. It has

stayed there, I imagine, because I am the son of my father. At any
rate, the problem remains unsolved in my mind. And that, I conclude,
is but another evidence of the complete and final triumph of the
egg — at least as far as my family is concerned.

CONSIDERATIONS

1. What does the first sentence imply about the relationship between father
   and son, and what precisely implies it?
2. In the fifth paragraph how does Anderson inflate the difficulties of
   chicken farming? What theme unifies his humor in this paragraph?
3. Anderson takes many elements of a conventional success story and treats
   them ironically. What general facts of character, setting, and plot in the
   story are often associated with "the American passion" for getting ahead
   in the world? How are the particular details different in this story?
4. The narrator says about his story, "If correctly told it will center on the
   egg" (paragraph 6). Does the story, title and all, succeed in centering on
   the egg? What meaning and value does the egg come to have in this story?
5. WRITING TOPIC. In a 500-word essay, clarify Anderson's satire of the
   American dream of business success. What are the main features of the
   nightmare that the author perceives underlying the dream? What sym-
   pathies and alternative values are implicit in the story?

Henry David Thoreau

WHERE I LIVED,
AND WHAT I LIVED FOR

◊

HENRY DAVID THOREAU (1817–1862), one of America's greatest writers, was graduated from Harvard and went home to Concord, Massachusetts, to consider what to do in life, since he did not care to enter
business or the professions, and, despite the pressures from his family
and the townspeople who saw him as a drifter, he strongly resisted following any career. For a few years he and his brother tried to run a
school, and Thoreau sometimes helped his father who manufactured
pencils, or he took odd jobs as a surveyor. His main activity was keeping a daily journal in which he wrote probing, meticulous observations
of nature around him and human nature within him. He was an intellectual rebel who condemned the shams of political democracy in his
essay on "Civil Disobedience"(1849) just as he condemned slavery,
which was still upheld in the United States throughout his life. He
tested his ideas about self-reliance when he lived for two years in the
woods at Walden Pond. This excerpt from his account of the experience, *Walden* (1854), explains that he was searching for "simplicity of
life and elevation of purpose."

I went to the woods because I wished to live deliberately, to front 1
only the essential facts of life, and see if I could not learn what it had
to teach, and not, when I came to die, discover that I had not lived. I
did not wish to live what was not life, living is so dear; nor did I wish
to practise resignation, unless it was quite necessary. I wanted to live
deep and suck out all the marrow of life, to live so sturdily and Spar-
tan-like as to put to rout all that was not life, to cut a broad swath
and shave close, to drive life into a corner, and reduce it to its lowest
terms, and, if it proved to be mean, why then to get the whole and
genuine meanness of it, and publish its meanness to the world; or if it

were sublime, to know it by experience, and be able to give a true account of it in my next excursion. For most men, it appears to me, are
in a strange uncertainty about it, whether it is of the devil or of God,
and have *somewhat hastily* concluded that it is the chief end of man
here to "glorify God and enjoy him forever."

Still we live meanly, like ants; though the fable tells us that we were   2
long ago changed into men; like pygmies we fight with cranes; it is
error upon error, and clout upon clout, and our best virtue has for its
occasion a superfluous and evitable wretchedness. Our life is frittered
away by detail. An honest man has hardly need to count more than
his ten fingers, or in extreme cases he may add his ten toes, and lump
the rest. Simplicity, simplicity, simplicity! I say, let your affairs be as
two or three, and not a hundred or a thousand; instead of a million
count half a dozen, and keep your accounts on your thumb-nail. In
the midst of this chopping sea of civilized life, such are the clouds and
storms and quicksands and thousand-and-one items to be allowed for,
that a man has to live, if he would not founder and go to the bottom
and not make his port at all, by dead reckoning, and he must be a
great calculator indeed who succeeds. Simplify, simplify. Instead of
three meals a day, if it be necessary eat but one; instead of a hundred
dishes, five; and reduce other things in proportion. Our life is like a
German Confederacy, made up of petty states, with its boundary forever fluctuating, so that even a German cannot tell you how it is
bounded at any moment. The nation itself, with all its so-called internal improvements, which, by the way, are all external and superficial,
is just such an unwieldy and overgrown establishment, cluttered with
furniture and tripped up by its own traps, ruined by luxury and heed-
less expense, by want of calculation and a worthy aim, as the million
households in the land; and the only cure for it, as for them, is in a
rigid economy, a stern and more than Spartan simplicity of life and
elevation of purpose. It lives too fast. Men think that it is essential
that the *Nation* have commerce, and export ice, and talk through a
telegraph, and ride thirty miles an hour, without a doubt, whether
they do or not; but whether we should live like baboons or like men, is
a little uncertain. If we do not get out sleepers, and forge rails, and
devote days and nights to the work, but go to tinkering upon our *lives*
to improve *them*, who will build railroads? And if railroads are not
built, how shall we get to Heaven in season? But if we stay at home
and mind our business, who will want railroads? We do not ride on

the railroad; it rides upon us. Did you ever think what those sleepers are that underlie the railroad? Each one is a man, an Irishman, or a Yankee man. The rails are laid on them, and they are covered with sand, and the cars run smoothly over them. They are sound sleepers, I assure you. And every few years a new lot is laid down and run over; so that, if some have the pleasure of riding on a rail, others have the misfortune to be ridden upon. And when they run over a man that is walking in his sleep, a supernumerary sleeper in the wrong position, and wake him up, they suddenly stop the cars, and make a hue and cry about it, as if this were an exception. I am glad to know that it takes a gang of men for every five miles to keep the sleepers down and level in their beds as it is, for this is a sign that they may sometime get up again. . . .

Let us spend one day as deliberately as Nature, and not be thrown 3 off the track by every nutshell and mosquito's wing that falls on the rails. Let us rise early and fast, or break fast, gently and without perturbation; let company come and let company go, let the bells ring and the children cry — determined to make a day of it. Why should we knock under and go with the stream? Let us not be upset and overwhelmed in that terrible rapid and whirlpool called a dinner, situated in the meridian shallows. Weather this danger and you are safe, for the rest of the way is down hill. With unrelaxed nerves, with morning vigor, sail by it, looking another way, tied to the mast like Ulysses. If the engine whistles, let it whistle till it is hoarse for its pains. If the bell rings, why should we run? We will consider what kind of music they are like. Let us settle ourselves, and work and wedge our feet downward through the mud and slush of opinion, and prejudice, and tradition, and delusion, and appearance, that alluvion which covers the globe, through Paris and London, through New York and Boston and Concord, through Church and State, through poetry and philosophy and religion, till we come to a hard bottom and rocks in place, which we can call *reality*, and say, This is, and no mistake; and then begin, having a *point d'appui*, below freshet and frost and fire, a place where you might found a wall or a state, or set a lamp-post safely, or perhaps a gauge, not a Nilometer, but a Realometer, that future ages might know how deep a freshet of shams and appearances had gathered from time to time. If you stand right fronting and face to face to a fact, you will see the sun glimmer on both its surfaces, as if it were a cimeter, and feel its sweet edge dividing you through the heart and marrow, and so you will happily conclude your mortal career. Be it life or death, we crave only reality. If we are really dying, let us hear the rattle in our throats and feel cold in the extremities; if we are alive, let us go about our business.

CONSIDERATIONS

1. What would be the opposite of living "deliberately"? Think of two or three adverbs that clarify the contrast Thoreau has in mind in the first paragraph between living "life" and living "not life."
2. What is the literal meaning of "dead reckoning" in the second paragraph? How does this term fit into his surrounding figures of speech? What kind of action does Thoreau mean by this term?
3. What is the point of Thoreau's puns about railroad ties? Is he condemning the exploitation of cheap labor, or is he criticizing something else?
4. What does Thoreau say needs to be cleared away in order to reach bedrock reality?
5. In the third sentence from the end, what analogy does Thoreau use for the direct perception of truth? What emotional state does it suggest?
6. What is the argumentative purpose, or the effect on the reader, of Thoreau's abundance of puns, figures of speech, and allusions to legends and history?
7. WRITING TOPIC. If Thoreau were a college friend of yours, how would you argue with him over his insistence that you should simplify your life and your ambitions? In a 500-word response directly to Thoreau, tell him why his point of view does or does not measure up on your own Realometer.

William Butler Yeats

THE LAKE ISLE OF INNISFREE

◊

WILLIAM BUTLER YEATS (1865–1939) was the leading poet of Ireland and a major figure in the development of modern literature. He was born near Dublin, educated in London and Dublin, and lived in both cities throughout his life. From England he participated in the Irish movement for national independence, writing plays as well as poems based on Irish legends and themes. He also served as a senator in the then-new Irish Free State, but he staunchly defended the integrity of private life against the claims of society and politics. In his *Autobiography* Yeats recalled how he came to write the following poem in 1892. On a street in London he heard water trickling in a fountain, and it reawakened in him "the ambition formed in Sligo in my teens, of living in imitation of Thoreau on Innisfree." The poem expresses a goal that is associated with a specific place.

I will arise and go now, and go to Innisfree,
And a small cabin build there, of clay and wattles made;
Nine bean rows will I have there, a hive for the honey bee,
And live alone in the bee-loud glade.

And I shall have some peace there, for peace comes dropping slow, 5
Dropping from the veils of the morning to where the cricket sings;
There midnight's all a glimmer, and noon a purple glow,
And evening full of the linnet's wings.

I will arise and go now, for always night and day
I hear lake water lapping with low sounds by the shore; 10
While I stand on the roadway, or on the pavements gray,
I hear it in the deep heart's core.

CONSIDERATIONS

1. What details in the poem suggest that Yeats was familiar with Thoreau's *Walden?*
2. How does the island of Innisfree contrast with the poet's present place of residence? Which of the contrasts are explicit, and which are only implied?
3. Is the poet homesick? Or is that not the cause of his distress? What details in the poem help you to explain his feelings?
4. WRITING TOPIC. In 500 words, define the place where you would most like to be for a while if you did not have to stay in college. The place can be an imaginary or a remembered location, or a mixture of both. Your definition of the place should include concrete descriptive details and also explanations of your reasons for wanting to be there rather than elsewhere.

Christopher Lasch

SURVIVAL MENTALITY

◊

CHRISTOPHER LASCH (b. 1932) is an American historian who teaches
at the University of Rochester. He was born in Omaha, Nebraska, and
after graduating from Harvard University, he earned a Ph.D. degree at
Columbia University. His early books examined the history of American radicalism, but his work gained a wider audience when he turned
to topics involving personal life and psychological changes in contemporary society. His books include *Haven in a Heartless World: The
Family Besieged* (1977) and *The Culture of Narcissism* (1979). The
following selection is an excerpt from his most recent book, *The
Minimal Self: Psychic Survival in Troubled Times*. Lasch examines
what happens to people's goals during a period of unrelieved, extended
crisis.

In a time of troubles, everyday life becomes an exercise in survival. 1
People take one day at a time. They seldom look back, lest they suc-
cumb to a debilitating "nostalgia"; and if they look ahead, it is to see
how they can insure themselves against the disasters almost everybody
now expects. Under these conditions, selfhood becomes a kind of luxury, out of place in an age of impending austerity. Selfhood implies a
personal history, friends, family, a sense of place. Under siege, the self
contracts to a defensive core, armed against adversity. Emotional
equilibrium demands a minimal self. . . .

. . . People have lost confidence in the future. Faced with an esca- 2
lating arms race, an increase in crime and terrorism, environmental
deterioration, and the prospect of long-term economic decline, they
have begun to prepare for the worst, sometimes by building fallout
shelters and laying in provisions, more commonly by executing a kind
of emotional retreat from the long-term commitments that presup-
pose a stable, secure, and orderly world. Ever since the Second World

War, the end of the world has loomed as a hypothetical possibility, but the sense of danger has greatly increased in the last twenty years, not only because social and economic conditions have grown objectively more unstable but because the hope of a remedial politics, a self-reformation of the political system, has sharply declined. The hope that political action will gradually humanize industrial society has given way to a determination to survive the general wreckage or, more modestly, to hold one's own life together in the face of mounting pressures. . . .

The Normalization of Crisis. In an uneasy age, still secure in the   3
enjoyment of material comforts unknown to earlier ages yet obsessed by thoughts of disaster, the problem of survival overshadows loftier concerns. The preoccupation with survival, a prominent feature of American culture ever since the early seventies, takes many forms, grave and trivial. It finds its most characteristic and insidious expression, its ultimate expression, in the illusion of winnable nuclear wars; but it by no means exhausts itself in the anticipation of earthshaking calamities. It has entered so deeply into popular culture and political debate that every issue, however fleeting or unimportant, presents itself as a matter of life or death.

A left-wing magazine, *Mother Jones,* advertises itself as a "survival   4
guide" to the "political Dark Ages" brought about by the election of Ronald Reagan. A Los Angeles radio station, hoping to spread "kindness, joy, love, and happiness," commends itself to its listeners as "your survival station of the eighties." Samsonsite, a manufacturer of luggage, advertises its latest briefcase as "the survivor." A *New York Times* headline refers to an attempt to limit the substitution of recorded music for live performers, conducted by the American Federation of Musicians, as a "survival battle." An antifeminist tirade, published with the usual media fanfare, announces itself as *A Survival Guide for the Bedeviled Male.* A basketball coach praises one of his players for his capacity to learn from his mistakes and to "survive" them. The same sportswriter who reports this tribute muses about the "survival" of college basketball as a major spectator sport.

At Yale, a "Student Rescue Committee" urges parents to send   5
their sons and daughters a "survival kit" ("nourishing snack foods in a humorously packaged box") to help them weather the "most crucial and nerve racking (*sic*) period of the entire academic year — Final

Exams!" The American Historical Association publishes a pamphlet designed to help women overcome discrimination: *A Survival Manual for Women (and Other) Historians.* A patient suffering from herpes explains how he overcame his fear of the disease by confiding in fellow sufferers: "When you begin sharing with other people, it's like being with survivors of a flood or a POW camp." A review of Henry Kissinger's memoirs bears the predictable headline, "Master of the Art of Survival." Michael Sellers, son of the late actor Peter Sellers, tells reporters that "Dad clung frantically" — even after a heart attack in 1964 — "to the belief that he was a survivor and . . . would live until he was seventy-five." Another actor, George C. Scott, speaks of himself as a "survivor" in a cutthroat calling. Jason Robards, Jr., having weathered alcoholism, a nearly fatal automobile crash, and a long period of critical neglect, wonders about the "mystery" as a result of which "people like George (Scott) and myself have survived." A drama critic acclaims revivals of Noël Coward's *Private Lives* and Herman Wouk's *The Caine Mutiny* in an article, "Survivors," that also acclaims the return of Elizabeth Taylor and Richard Burton to the Broadway stage.

Erma Bombeck introduces her latest collection of columns as a 6 book "about surviving." Another book addressed to housewives — *Surviving as a Woman, or How to Keep Your Chin High, Your Courage Up, and Never Be Caught with Your Brioches Down* — adopts the same tone, depicting daily life as a succession of minor emergencies. "Whether they are squares or swingers," women have "one thing in common," according to Betty Canary. "And that is, they are determined to be survivors." Betty Friedan resorted to the same kind of rhetorical exaggeration in *The Feminine Mystique,* but without any humorous intent, when she called the middle-class household a "comfortable concentration camp." Those who take a more kindly view of domestic institutions nevertheless ask themselves whether the shrinking, beleaguered family still provides conditions "for the emotional survival of the individual in our mass society."

The trivialization of crisis, while it testifies to a pervasive sense of 7 danger — to a perception that nothing, not even the simplest domestic detail, can be taken for granted — also serves as a survival strategy in its own right. When the grim rhetoric of survivalism invades everyday life, it simultaneously intensifies and relieves the fear of disaster. The victim of circumstances copes with crisis by preparing for the worst and by reassuring himself that the worst has a way of falling short of expectations. Bertolt Brecht once said that those who laugh have not yet heard the bad news. But laughter today — and this helps to explain why it often has a hollow sound and why so much contemporary humor takes the form of parody and self-parody — comes from people who are all too well aware of the bad news but have nevertheless made a determined effort to keep smiling. "Let a smile be your umbrella." Stanley Kubrick satirized this desperate good cheer in the subtitle of his film *Dr. Strangelove: How I Learned to Stop Worrying and Love the Bomb.* The editors of *Mad* satirized it, but also affirmed unfounded optimism as the only tenable attitude in a mad, mad, mad, mad world, when they set up as their spokesman the figure of Alfred E. Neumann, with his idiotic grin and his "What? Me Worry?"

Nothing is gained, after all, by dwelling on the bad news. The survival artist takes bad news for granted; he is beyond despair. He deflects reports of fresh disasters, warnings of ecological catastrophe, warnings of the probable consequences of the nuclear arms race by refusing to discriminate between events that threaten the future of mankind and events that merely threaten his peace of mind. He jokes about the unending outpouring of bad news on television and in the newspapers, complains that it depresses him, and thus absolves himself of the need to distinguish between various kinds and degrees of bad news. He protects himself from its impact, moreover, by dismissing those who bear it as prophets of gloom and doom — misanthropes and killjoys embittered by personal disappointments or an unhappy childhood, left-wing intellectuals embittered by the collapse of their revolutionary expectations, reactionaries unable to adjust to changing times.

The threat of nuclear war, the threat of ecological catastrophe, the memory of the Nazi's genocidal war against the Jews, the possible collapse of our entire civilization have generated a widespread sense of crisis, and the rhetoric of crisis now pervades discussion of race relations, prison reform, mass culture, fiscal management, and everyday personal "survival." A list of recent books on survival and survivalism would include books on ecology and nuclear war, books on the Holocaust, books on technology and automation, and a flood of "future studies," not to mention an outpouring of science fiction that takes a coming apocalypse as its major premise. But such a list would also include the huge psychiatric literature on "coping" and the equally enormous sociological literature on victims and "victimology." It would include books setting forth "survival strategies for oppressed minorities," "survival in the executive jungle," and "survival in marriage." Reinforced by other media — film, radio, television, newspapers, magazines — this propaganda of disaster has a cumulative effect almost exactly opposite to the effect ostensibly intended. The infiltration of everyday life by the rhetoric of crisis and survival emasculates the idea of crisis and leaves us indifferent to appeals founded on the claim that some sort of emergency commands our attention. Nothing makes our attention wander so quickly as talk of another crisis. When public crises pile up unresolved, we lose interest in the possibility that anything can be done about them. Then too, cries of crisis often serve merely to justify the claims of professional crisis-managers, whether they traffic in politics, war, and diplomacy or simply in the management of emotional "stress."

One reply to these claims insists that questions of genuine sur- 10
vival — energy policy, environmental policy, the nuclear arms race — ought to be decided politically, collaboratively, and democratically, instead of being treated as technical subjects understood only by a handful of specialists. It is more characteristic of the contemporary survival mentality, however, that it turns away from public questions and concerns itself with the predictable crisis of everyday life, where individual actions still seem to have some minimal impact on the course of events. Everyday life has come to present itself as a succession of crises not necessarily because it is more risky and competitive than it used to be but because it confronts people with manageable stresses, whereas the hope of preventing public disaster appears so remote, for most people, that it enters their thoughts only in the form of a wistful prayer for peace and brotherhood.

CONSIDERATIONS

1. Do freshmen generally live "under siege"? Do they show the symptoms mentioned in paragraphs 1 and 2 of a diminished self? Or do you think they more generally display an expanded self?
2. The author says that survivalism "takes many forms, grave and trivial." What is the effect of his mentioning many examples that are less than

grave? Are they trivial? What significance does Lasch imply that they have?

3. What is Lasch's attitude toward the survival artist? What is your own?
4. What serious crisis seems to be created by the survival mentality? What does Lasch imply that we should be doing about it?
5. WRITING TOPIC. In the first month of college should freshmen *strive* or *survive?* In 700 words, write a pre-freshman guide to the crisis of starting college. Be informative about serious stresses and differentiate between grave and trivial reactions to a time of troubles.

ADDITIONAL
WRITING TOPICS

◊

AMBITIONS

1. Write a 750-word essay on golf or some other participant sport as a form of entertainment that embodies high ideals of workmanship that most people do not find in their jobs. Consider the sport from the viewpoint of a sociologist who is trying to find the values and stresses of a society as expressed in its recreational activities.

2. "What do you want to be when you grow up?" Children's answers to this universal question rarely express their *ambitions*. To children, any form of being adult means being more able to have what they presently want, not what they hope to achieve in the future. Their answers tell us about their likes and dislikes, which are often mixed together. In a 500-word essay, closely examine the meaning of a particular response of a child you know (or recall one of your own) when asked this question.

3. In 700 words, compare Joseph Epstein and Henry David Thoreau on the topic of ambition. Consider the issues of free choice, motivation, and the nature of failure that are part of each writer's consideration of the goals of life.

4. In the insight about *The Peter Principle*, Laurence J. Peter and Raymond Hull humorously explain why incompetence is widespread and solidly entrenched. In light of *The Peter Principle*, examine, in 500 words, the competence and the hierarchy among co-workers in a job you once held. How did people deal with the incompetence of others at different levels of the hierarchy?

5. The word *professional* is widely and often carelessly used to signify someone's responsible attitudes and special skills. What does the concept *professional* mean to you? In 500 words, write an extended definition of the term, clarifying the standards and values you connect with it. Include at least one illustration of a careless or misleading use of the word.

6. In the *Insights*, Vincent van Gogh tells what to do when self-doubt interferes with ambition. Is it good advice to follow? Has his method of dogged perseverance ever worked well for you? In 500 words, explain how you overcame serious self-doubts in a specific situation when your confidence was threatened.

PART 7

CONVICTIONS

Richard Morris, *How Real Is "Real"?*

Stephen Jay Gould, *Nonmoral Nature*

Robert Nisbet, *Creationism*

Robert Finch, *Very Like a Whale*

Carl Jung, *Secret Thought*

Barbara Grizzuti Harrison, *Growing Up Apocalyptic*

Bernard Malamud, *Angel Levine*

James Wright, *A Blessing*

Alan W. Watts, *Spiritual Living*

Additional Writing Topics

INSIGHTS

When I first began to experience the power of God in my own life, I could hardly believe it. Something very real and discernible was happening to me, yet I felt it could not or should not be happening. God was speaking to me; God was calling me. He spoke no louder than a whisper, but I heard him. And each time that I heard him, and chose him, a change occurred, the opening of a door I had not guessed was there. Each step, each crossing of a doorway was made with great uncertainty, my doubts mingling with my faith. But with each step, my strength and my conviction grew; I felt myself on sounder ground. Something was happening in my life, which I could recognize but which I could not yet name. It was conversion.

By conversion I mean the discovery, made gradually or suddenly, that God is real. It is the perception that this real God loves us personally and acts mercifully and justly towards each of us. Conversion is the direct experience of the saving power of God. As such it is not an event, not an action, not an occurrence. Instead it is a continuing revelation and a transforming force. This encounter with the Lord is not one of visions, necessarily, though some converts have experienced God in a mystical way. It is not a matter of sudden changes in the mode of one's life, though some converts do choose new life-styles. Conversion is simply a matter of becoming open to God's overflowing and powerful love. To be filled with that love is to change, to be changed, to act lovingly towards others.

– EMILIE GRIFFIN

◊

Summing up the broadest possible way the characteristics of the religious life, as we have found them, it includes the following beliefs:

1. That the visible world is part of a more spiritual universe from which it draws its chief significance;

2. That union or harmonious relation with that higher universe is our true end;

3. That prayer or inner communion with the spirit thereof — be that spirit "God" or "law" — is a process wherein work is really done, and spiritual energy flows in and produces effects, psychological or material, within the phenomenal world.

Religion includes also the following psychological characteristics:

4. A new zest which adds itself like a gift to life, and takes the form either of lyrical enchantment or of appeal to earnestness and heroism.

5. An assurance of safety and a temper of peace, and, in relation to others, a preponderance of loving affections.

— WILLIAM JAMES

◊

Religion is what keeps the poor from murdering the rich.

— NAPOLEON

◊

"Design"

I found a dimpled spider, fat and white,
On a white heal-all, holding up a moth
Like a white piece of rigid satin cloth —
Assorted characters of death and blight '
Mixed ready to begin the morning right,
Like the ingredients of a witches' broth —
A snow-drop spider, a flower like a froth,
And dead wings carried like a paper kite.

What had that flower to do with being white,
The wayside blue and innocent heal-all?

What brought the kindred spider to that height,
Then steered the white moth thither in the night?
What but design of darkness to appall? —
If design govern in a thing so small.

— ROBERT FROST

◊

Often the convictions of one generation are the rejects of the next. That does not deny the possibility that, as time goes on, we shall accumulate some body of valid conclusions. But it does mean that we can achieve only by accumulation, that wisdom is to be gained only as we stand upon the shoulders of those who have gone before. Just as in science, we cannot advance except as we take over what we inherit, and in statecraft no generation can safely start at scratch, so personal, basic beliefs must be slowly built from our experience, but also from a study of the experience and conclusions of others. . . .

— JUDGE LEARNED HAND

◊

The philosophy of nature is one thing, the philosophy of value is quite another. Nothing but harm can come of confusing them. What we think good, what we should like, has no bearing whatever upon what is, which is the question for the philosophy of nature. On the other hand, we cannot be forbidden to value this or that on the ground that the nonhuman world does not value it, nor can we be compelled to admire anything because it is a "law of nature." Undoubtedly we are part of nature, which has produced our desires, our hopes and fears, in accordance with laws which the physicist is beginning to discover. In this sense we are part of nature; in the philosophy of nature we are subordinated to nature, the outcome of natural laws, and their victims in the long run.

— BERTRAND RUSSELL

◊

"Amazing Grace"

Amazing grace! How sweet the sound,
That saved a wretch like me!
I once was lost, but now am found,
Was blind, but now I see.

'Twas grace that taught my heart to fear,
And grace my fears relieved;
How precious did that grace appear
The hour I first believed!

                      – JOHN NEWTON

◇

The derivation of a need for religion from the child's feeling of helplessness and the longing it evokes for a father seems to me incontrovertible, especially since this feeling is not simply carried on from childhood days but is kept alive perpetually by the fear of what the superior power of fate will bring.

                      – SIGMUND FREUD

Richard Morris

HOW REAL IS "REAL"?

◊

RICHARD MORRIS (b. 1939), a science writer and poet, graduated from the University of Nevada and earned a Ph.D. in theoretical physics. Although his academic qualifications prepared him for a career in teaching and scientific research, Morris instead followed his literary interests in writing and publishing. He founded a poetry magazine, *Camels Come In*, and also published chapbooks of poetry, including his own collection, *Poetry Is a Kind of Write-In* (1975). He has written six books about science, including *Dismantling the Universe: The Nature of Scientific Discovery* (1983), and *Time's Arrows* (1984), an explanation of theories of time in Western civilization. His literary and scientific interests are united by his focus on the central role of the creative imagination. In the following selection, the final chapter of *Dismantling the Universe*, Morris discusses similarities between scientific and artistic "truth."

Physicists often speak of "seeing" the subatomic particles that are 1 produced in particle accelerators. The particles can be made to interact within a device called a *bubble chamber*, which is a large tank that has been filled with liquid hydrogen. As the particles pass through the hydrogen, they produce tiny bubbles. After these bubbles are photographed, the particle interactions that took place can be studied at leisure.

But are the particles really *seen?* Of course not. The only things 2 that are observed are hydrogen bubbles that are strung together like beads. All physicists actually see is that some of the hydrogen in the tank has been converted into bubbles of vapor. The particles themselves are too small to be observed directly, even by the most powerful electron microscopes.

Protons and neutrons, leptons, photons, and quarks don't "really 3 exist" in the way that tables and chairs do. Their existence is inferred; physicists believe in them because they can be used to explain so many things that are observed in the laboratory. The subatomic particles are "real" in the sense that they are concepts which can be used to codify an enormous amount of data about natural phenomena. The theories which describe the behavior of particles provide us with *models* of reality.

If a scientific model is a successful one, it will give more or less ac- 4 curate predictions when the right mathematical calculations are carried out. Scientists observe certain phenomena, such as the emission of light, and invent concepts that will explain them. They perform mathematical manipulations upon these concepts in order to find out what other phenomena can be predicted. But however successful their models are, they are never perfectly accurate. Each generation discovers that it must find a way to improve upon the model used by the previous one. The concept of indivisible atoms had to be replaced by a picture in which atoms were composed of electrons, protons, and neutrons. The concept of a nucleon as an elementary particle was replaced by that of gluons and quarks.

Many scientists and philosophers of science regard the concepts of 5 physics as maps or pictures rather than as real objects. This is what Bohr* meant when he said that the quantum world did not exist. In Bohr's view, the only things that were "real" were the readings on pointers and dials in the laboratory. Electrons, probability waves, and other subatomic entities were nothing but useful constructs.

If we regard scientific discovery as the construction of useful 6 models, this would explain why theory has been more important than experiment so many times in the history of science. By itself, experiment tells us nothing. Theories are not constructed from generalizations derived from experimental data. On the contrary, they are products of human imagination. A theory is discovered when a scientist has an insight which shows him that it is possible to invent a model which will make it possible for data to be interpreted. Theory organizes data, and brings them together in a picture that human beings find comprehensible.

---

* Niels Bohr (1885–1962), a Danish physicist, formulated important theories of quantum mechanics. He explained that the laws of behavior for subatomic particles contradict the laws of nature in the larger world.

Scientific models are not entirely arbitrary. A theory must be able   7
to codify data in a useful form, or it is useless. If one imagined that a
flat earth was supported by four huge elephants standing on the back
of an enormous turtle, he would have created a model. But this particular model could not be used to bring together data derived from observations of the earth's moon and the planets, or even observations of
the ocean tides. A scientist who is constructing a theory cannot ignore
the fact that there are data to be explained. He is no more free to
imagine anything he likes than a poet is free to write a sonnet that has
fifteen lines.

In the time of Kepler, Newton, and Galileo, scientists believed that   8
they were discovering exact "laws of nature." Today we realize that
the discovery of exact laws is not possible. At best, a scientific theory is
a set of approximations. The approximations, however, can be extremely accurate, and models can be developed that tie together an
astonishing range of phenomena. Perhaps science does not really discover order in nature. Order may be something that is imposed upon
nature by human minds. Nevertheless, this order can be an impressive
one.

If the "order of the universe" is something that we invent, then it is   9
somewhat easier to see why it is so obvious that a theory that is "just
too unreasonable to be true" can so readily be discarded. Even when
there exists no experimental evidence that would allow us to decide
between two competing theories, it can still be obvious that one is a
better model than the other.

For example, it would be possible to argue that the Ptolemaic sys-   10
tem is really just as valid as the Copernican. If Einstein was correct,
and the viewpoint of one observer is just as good as that of another,
then there is no way we can prove that the sun does not really revolve
around the earth. After all, from the standpoint of an earthbound observer, the heavens do rotate, and the sun does rise and set.

The only reason that scientists do not make this assumption is that   11
it would lead to a theory that was anything but clear or logical or elegant. Not only would one have to deal with all the complications that
Ptolemy encountered, one would also have to think up an explanation
for the centrifugal force that causes the earth to bulge outward at the
equator, and explain why terrestrial gravity is a little stronger at the
poles. One would have to explain why the orbital velocities of distant
stars appear to be so much greater than the speed of light, and it

would be necessary to explain the origin of the *coriolis force* that imparts an eastward or westwood drift to a missile that is fired over the North Pole.

There is no doubt that it would be possible to explain all these 12 things in one way or another. However, the resulting theory would be ugly; it would be anything but parsimonious. It would be as complicated as a theory designed to prove that the earth was really flat.

I often have the feeling that scientific discovery and the arts are 13 more alike than we tend to think. . . . I sometimes wonder if science could not be described as an attempt to impose order upon physical reality, which would make it rather similar to art, which could be described as an activity that imposes order upon all the myriad aspects of human experience.

Sometimes artistic trends and scientific theories exhibit similarities 14 one would not expect. Poets too can dismantle the universe and recombine it in startling ways. For example, during most of Western history, mountains were regarded as fearsome objects that were the likely abodes of demonic creatures. But when the Romantic artists and poets began to see a kind of grandeur in mountainous landscapes, attitudes changed. When the Romantics showed their contemporaries that mountains could be experienced in a different way, men even began to think of climbing them. Mountaineering was, in fact, an invention of the Romantic age. As far as we know, no one had ever considered the idea previously.

Most works of art do not change our attitudes about physical objects. After all, art attempts to structure the universe of human experience, and emotional reactions to mountains and landscapes constitute only a small part of it. Nevertheless, the analogy between the Romantic restructuring of a certain part of the world and the Einsteinian restructuring of the universe is striking.

When Einstein propounded his two theories of relativity, the universe also became a different kind of place. The general theory, in particular, made it possible to give up the idea of gravitational "action at a distance" that had so bothered the contemporaries of Newton. This mysterious "action" was replaced by the concept of changes in the geometry of space.

There are failed works of art which are grotesque rather than moving. Similarly, there are crackpot theories, and theories which are too complicated to be reasonable. Not all attempts to dismantle or restructure the universe are successful. Of those which are successful, not all are equally imposing. We admire the theories of Einstein because they restructure our conception of the universe in clear and logical ways, just as we admire the works of Shakespeare because so much of the universe of human experience is given form in his plays.

Perhaps this is a digression. But it is not an irrelevant one, I think. 18 The events which take place on the magic isle in *The Tempest* have something of the character of a dream. There is a sense in which mesons and quarks and gluons are dreams too. Do they "really" exist? They almost certainly do not.

And yet one could say that they do exist in some sense of the word. 19 They are real in the sense that they provide us with a map that allows us to find our way around in the chaotic world of subatomic phenomena. They are real in the sense that they give us a picture of this world that is astonishingly vivid and fruitful.

Models are useful because they show us that hidden connections 20 exist in the universe around us. And after all, this is what science is all about. Science seeks to create pictures of the order in nature which are so logically elegant that we cannot doubt that they are true.

CONSIDERATIONS

1. Explain what the author means by "a model of reality." How does Morris's use of the word *model* differ from its meaning in such phrases as "a model of a house" and "a model to follow"?
2. According to the author, what is the connection between scientific theory and experiment?
3. How have scientific attitudes toward the order of nature changed in our century?
4. According to Morris, how are science and art similar and how do they differ?
5. Morris uses the words "elegant" and "ugly" to refer to scientific theories. How does the use of these subjective terms affect the point of his essay? How does it affect your view of science?
6. WRITING TOPIC. What has been your most fascinating scientific interest or hobby? — a chemistry set? a personal computer? a butterfly collection? a telescope? a photographic darkroom? In 700 words, write an intellectual autobiography about this interest in your life. While you had this interest, what fresh information were you eager to acquire? What frustrations or challenges did you face in pursuing your interest? How did you gain a somewhat different perspective on the world as a result of this activity?

Stephen Jay Gould

NONMORAL NATURE

◊

STEPHEN JAY GOULD (b. 1941), a paleontologist at Harvard University, writes popular books on evolution that range over a wide variety of topics within his Darwinian perspective. Born in New York City, Gould graduated from Antioch College and earned a Ph.D. degree from Columbia University. His columns for *Natural History* magazine have been collected in four volumes of scientific essays for the general reader: *Ever Since Darwin* (1977), *The Panda's Thumb* (1980), *Hen's Teeth and Horse's Toes* (1983), and *The Flamingo's Smile* (1985). Gould is interested not only in biological determinism but also in cultural factors that influence scientific theories. He points out that in any age facts have been misperceived, mishandled, and misrepresented in order to fit the moral and ideological biases of scientists. Gould is always aware of the dilemma that science is a social activity which is partly responsive to the dogmas and prejudices of society. In the following chapter from *Hen's Teeth and Horse's Toes*, Gould tries to see nature without the distortion of a moral bias — but, of course, that perspective may indicate his own ideology.

When the Right Honorable and Reverend Francis Henry, earl of 1 Bridgewater, died in February, 1829, he left £8,000 to support a series of books "on the power, wisdom, and goodness of God, as manifested in the creation." William Buckland, England's first official academic geologist and later dean of Westminster, was invited to compose one of the nine Bridgewater Treatises. In it he discussed the most pressing problem of natural theology: if God is benevolent and the Creation displays his "power, wisdom, and goodness," then why are we surrounded with pain, suffering, and apparently senseless cruelty in the animal world?

Buckland considered the depredation of "carnivorous races" as the 2 primary challenge to an idealized world where the lion might dwell with the lamb. He resolved the issue to his satisfaction by arguing that carnivores actually increase "the aggregate of animal enjoyment" and "diminish that of pain." Death, after all, is swift and relatively painless, victims are spared the ravages of decrepitude and senility, and populations do not outrun their food supply to the greater sorrow of all. God knew what he was doing when he made lions. Buckland concluded in hardly concealed rapture:

> The appointment of death by the agency of carnivora, as the ordinary termination of animal existence, appears therefore in its main results to be a dispensation of benevolence; it deducts much from the aggregate amount of the pain of universal death; it abridges, and almost annihilates, throughout the brute creation, the misery of disease, and accidental injuries, and lingering decay; and imposes such salutary restraint upon excessive increase of numbers, that the supply of food maintains perpetually a due ratio to the demand. The result is, that the surface of the land and depths of the waters are ever crowded with myriads of animated beings, the pleasures of whose life are coextensive with its duration; and which throughout the little day of existence that is allotted to them, fulfill with joy the junctions for which they were created.

We may find a certain amusing charm in Buckland's vision today, but such arguments did begin to address "the problem of evil" for many of Buckland's contemporaries — how could a benevolent God create such a world of carnage and bloodshed? Yet this argument could not abolish the problem of evil entirely, for nature includes many phenomena far more horrible in our eyes than simple predation. I suspect that nothing evokes greater disgust in most of us than slow destruction of a host by an internal parasite — gradual ingestion, bit by bit, from the inside. In no other way can I explain why *Alien*, an uninspired, grade-C, formula horror film, should have won such a following. That single scene of Mr. Alien, popping forth as a baby parasite from the body of a human host, was both sickening and stunning. Our nineteenth-century forebears maintained similar feelings. The greatest challenge to their concept of a benevolent deity was not simple predation — but slow death by parasitic ingestion. The classic case, treated at length by all great naturalists, invoked the so-called ichneumon fly. Buckland had sidestepped the major issue.

The "ichneumon fly," which provoked such concern among natural theologians, was actually a composite creature representing the habits of an enormous tribe. The Ichneumonoidea are a group of wasps, not flies, that include more species than all the vertebrates combined (wasps, with ants and bees, constitute the order Hymenoptera; flies, with their two wings — wasps have four — form the order Diptera). In addition, many non-ichneumonid wasps of similar habits were often cited for the same grisly details. Thus, the famous story did not merely implicate a single aberrant species (perhaps a perverse leakage from Satan's realm), but hundreds of thousands — a large chunk of what could only be God's creation.

The ichneumons, like most wasps, generally live freely as adults but 5 pass their larval life as parasites feeding on the bodies of other animals, almost invariably members of their own phylum, the Arthropoda. The most common victims are caterpillars (butterfly and moth larvae), but some ichneumons prefer aphids and others attack spiders. Most hosts are parasitized as larvae, but some adults are attacked, and many tiny ichneumons inject their brood directly into the egg of their host.

The free-flying females locate an appropriate host and then convert 6 it to a food factory for their own young. Parasitologists speak of ectoparasitism when the uninvited guest lives on the surface of its host, and endoparasitism when the parasite dwells within. Among endoparasitic ichneumons, adult females pierce the host with their ovipositor and deposit eggs within. (The ovipositor, a thin tube extending backward from the wasp's rear end, may be many times as long as the body itself.) Usually, the host is not otherwise inconvenienced for the moment, at least until the eggs hatch and the ichneumon larvae begin their grim work of interior excavation.

Among ectoparasites, however, many females lay their eggs directly 7 upon the host's body. Since an active host would easily dislodge the egg, the ichneumon mother often simultaneously injects a toxin that paralyzes the caterpillar or other victim. The paralysis may be permanent, and the caterpillar lies, alive but immobile, with the agent of its future destruction secure on its belly. The egg hatches, the helpless caterpillar twitches, the wasp larva pierces and begins its grisly feast.

Since a dead and decaying caterpillar will do the wasp larva no 8 good, it eats a pattern that cannot help but recall, in our inappropriate, anthropocentric interpretation, the ancient English penalty of treason — drawing and quartering, with its explicit object of extracting as much torment as possible by keeping the victim alive and sentient. As the king's executioner drew out and burned his client's entrails, so does the ichneumon larva eat fat bodies and digestive organs first, keeping the caterpillar alive by preserving intact the essential heart and central nervous system. Finally, the larva completes its work and kills its victim, leaving behind the caterpillar's empty shell. Is it any wonder that ichneumons, not snakes or lions, stood as the paramount challenge to God's benevolence during the heyday of natural theology?

As I read through the nineteenth- and twentieth-century literature   9
on ichneumons, nothing amused me more then the tension between an intellectual knowledge that wasps should not be described in human terms and a literary or emotional inability to avoid the familiar categories of epic and narrative, pain and destruction, victim and vanquisher. We seem to be caught in the mythic structures of our own cultural sagas, quite unable, even in our basic descriptions, to use any other language than the metaphors of battle and conquest. We cannot render this corner of natural history as anything but story, combining the themes of grim horror and fascination and usually ending not so much with pity for the caterpillar as with admiration for the efficiency of the ichneumon.

I detect two basic themes in most epic descriptions: the struggles of   10
prey and the ruthless efficiency of parasites. Although we acknowledge that we may be witnessing little more than automatic instinct or physiological reaction, still we describe the defenses of hosts as though they represented conscious struggles. Thus, aphids kick and caterpillars may wriggle violently as wasps attempt to insert their ovipositors. The pupa of the tortoiseshell butterfly (usually considered an inert creature silently awaiting its conversion from duckling to swan) may contort its abdominal region so sharply that attacking wasps are thrown into the air. The caterpillars of *Hapalia*, when attacked by the wasp *Apanteles machaeralis*, drop suddenly from their leaves and suspend themselves in air by a silken thread. But the wasp may run down the thread and insert its eggs nonetheless. Some hosts can encapsulate the injected egg with blood cells that aggregate and harden, thus suffocating the parasite.

J. H. Fabre, the great nineteenth-century French entomologist,   11
who remains to this day the preeminently literate natural historian of insects, made a special study of parasitic wasps and wrote with an unabashed anthropocentrism about the struggles of paralyzed victims

(see his books *Insect Life* and *The Wonders of Instinct*). He describes some imperfectly paralyzed caterpillars that struggle so violently every time a parasite approaches that the wasp larvae must feed with unusual caution. They attach themselves to a silken strand from the roof of their burrow and descend upon a safe and exposed part of the caterpillar:

> The grub is at dinner: head downards, it is digging into the limp belly of one of the caterpillars. . . . At the least sign of danger in the heap of caterpillars, the larva retreats . . . and climbs back to the ceiling, where the swarming rabble cannot reach it. When peace is restored, it slides down [its silken cord] and returns to table, with its head over the viands and its rear upturned and ready to withdraw in case of need.

In another chapter, he describes the fate of a paralyzed cricket: 12

> One may see the cricket, bitten to the quick, vainly move its antennae and abdominal styles, open and close its empty jaws, and even move a foot, but the larva is safe and searches its vitals with impunity. What an awful nightmare for the paralyzed cricket!

Fabre even learned to feed paralyzed victims by placing a syrup of   13 sugar and water on their mouthparts — thus showing that they remained alive, sentient, and (by implication) grateful for any palliation of their inevitable fate. If Jesus, immobile and thirsting on the cross, received only vinegar from his tormentors, Fabre at least could make an ending bittersweet.

The second theme, ruthless efficiency of the parasites, leads to the   14 opposite conclusion — grudging admiration for the victors. We learn of their skill in capturing dangerous hosts often many times larger than themselves. Caterpillars may be easy game, but psammocharid wasps prefer spiders. They must insert their ovipositors in a safe and precise spot. Some leave a paralyzed spider in its own burrow. *Planiceps hirsutus*, for example, parasitizes a California trapdoor spider. It searches for spider tubes on sand dunes, then digs into nearby sand to disturb the spider's home and drives it out. When the spider emerges, the wasp attacks, paralyses its victim, drags it back into its own tube, shuts and fastens the trapdoor, and deposits a single egg upon the spider's abdomen. Other psammocharids will drag a heavy spider back to a previously prepared cluster of clay or mud cells. Some amputate a spider's legs to make the passage easier. Others fly back over water, skimming a buoyant spider along the surface.

Some wasps must battle with other parasites over a host's body. 15
Rhyssella curvipes can detect the larvae of wood wasps deep within
alder wood and drill down to a potential victim with its sharply ridged
ovipositor. *Pseudorhyssa alpestris,* a related parasite, cannot drill
directly into wood since its slender ovipositor bears only rudimentary
cutting ridges. It locates the holes made by *Rhyssella,* inserts its ovipositor, and lays an egg on the host (already conveniently paralyzed by
Rhysella), right next to the egg deposited by its relative. The two eggs
hatch at about the same time, but the larva of *Pseudorhyssa* has a
bigger head bearing much larger mandibles. *Pseudorhyssa* seizes the
smaller *Rhyssella* larva, destroys it, and proceeds to feast upon a banquet already well prepared.

Other praises for the efficiency of mothers invoke the themes of 16
early, quick, and often. Many ichneumons don't even wait for their
hosts to develop into larvae, but parasitize the egg directly (larval
wasps may then either drain the egg itself or enter the developing host
larva). Others simply move fast. *Apanteles militaris* can deposit up to
seventy-two eggs in a single second. Still others are doggedly persistent. *Aphidius gomezi* females produce up to 1,500 eggs and can
parasitize as many as 600 aphids in a single working day. In a bizarre
twist upon "often," some wasps indulge in polyembryony, a kind of
iterated supertwining. A single egg divides into cells that aggregate
into as many as 500 individuals. Since some polyembryonic wasps
parasitize caterpillars much larger than themselves and may lay up to
six eggs in each, as many as 3,000 larvae may develop within, and feed
upon a single host. These wasps are endoparasites and do not paralyze
their victims. The caterpillars writhe back and forth, not (one sus-
pects) from pain, but merely in response to the commotion induced
by thousands of wasp larvae feeding within.

Maternal efficiency is often matched by larval aptitude. I have al- 17
ready mentioned the pattern of eating less essential parts first, thus
keeping the host alive and fresh to its final and merciful dispatch.
After the larva digests every edible morsel of its victim (if only to prevent later fouling of its abode by decaying tissue), it may still use the
outer shell of its host. One aphid parasite cuts a hole in the button of
its victim's shell, glues the skeleton to a leaf by sticky secretions from
its salivary gland, and then spins a cocoon to pupate within the
aphid's shell.

In using inappropriate anthropocentric language for this romp 18 through the natural history of ichneumons, I have tried to emphasize just why these wasps became a preeminent challenge to natural theology — the antiquated doctrine that attempted to infer God's essence from the products of his creation. I have used twentieth-century examples for the most part, but all themes were known and stressed by the great nineteenth-century natural theologians. How then did they square the habits of these wasps with the goodness of God? How did they extract themselves from this dilemma of their own making?

The strategies were as varied as the practitioners; they shared only   19 the theme of special pleading for an a priori doctrine — our naturalists *knew* that God's benevolence was lurking somewhere behind all these tales of apparent horror. Charles Lyell, for example, in the first edition of his epochal *Principles of Geology* (1830–1833), decided that caterpillars posed such a threat to vegetation that any natural checks upon them could only reflect well upon a creating deity, for caterpillars would destroy human agriculture "did not Providence put causes in operation to keep them in due bounds."

The Reverend William Kirby, rector of Barham, and Britain's fore-   20 most entomologist, chose to ignore the plight of caterpillars and focused instead upon the virtue of mother love displayed by wasps in provisioning their young with such care.

> The great object of the female is to discover a proper nidus for her eggs. In search of this she is in constant motion. Is the caterpillar of a butterfly or moth the appropriate food for her young? You see her alight upon the plants where they are most usually to be met with, run quickly over them, carefully examining every leaf, and, having found the unfortunate object of her search, insert her sting into its flesh, and there deposit an egg. . . . The active Ichneumon braves every danger, and does not desist until her courage and address have insured subsistence for one of her future progeny.

Kirby found this solicitude all the more remarkable because the fe-   21 male wasp will never see her child and enjoy the pleasures of parenthood. Yet love compels her to danger nonetheless:

> A very large proportion of them are doomed to die before their young come into existence. But in these the passion is not extinguished. . . . When you witness the solicitude with which they provide for the security and sustenance of their future young, you can scarcely deny to them love for a progeny they are never destined to behold.

Kirby also put in a good word for the marauding larvae, praising 22
them for their forbearance in eating selectively to keep their caterpillar alive. Would we all husband our resources with such care!

In this strange and apparently cruel operation one circumstance is truly
remarkable. The larva of the Ichneumon, though every day, perhaps
for months, it gnaws the inside of the caterpillar, and though at last it
has devoured almost every part of it except the skin and intestines,
carefully all this time it avoids injuring the vital organs, as if aware that
its own existence depends on that of the insect upon which it preys! . . .
What would be the impression which a similar instance amongst the
race of quadrupeds would make upon us? If, for example, an animal
. . . should be found to feed upon the inside of a dog, devouring only
those parts not essential to life, while it cautiously left uninjured the
heart, arteries, lungs, and intestines — should we not regard such an
instance as a perfect prodigy, as an example of instinctive forbearance
almost miraculous? [The last three quotes come from the 1856, and
last pre-Darwinian, edition of Kirby and Spence's *Introduction to En-
tomology.*]

This tradition of attempting to read moral meaning from nature 23
did not cease with the triumph of evolutionary theory in 1859 — for
evolution could be read as God's chosen method of peopling our
planet, and ethical messages might still populate nature. Thus, St.
George Mivart, one of Darwin's most effective evolutionary critics
and a devout Catholic, argued that "many amiable and excellent people" had been misled by the apparent suffering of animals for two
reasons. First, whatever the pain, "physical suffering and moral evil
are simply incommensurable." Since beasts are not moral agents, their
feelings cannot bear any ethical message. But secondly, lest our vis-
ceral sensitivities still be aroused, Mivart assures us that animals must
feel little, if any, pain. Using a favorite racist argument of the time —
that "primitive" people suffer far less than advanced and cultured
folk — Mivart extrapolated further down the ladder of life into a
realm of very limited pain indeed: Physical suffering, he argued,

depends greatly upon the mental condition of the sufferer. Only during
consciousness does it exist, and only in the most highly organized men
does it reach its acme. The author has been assured that lower races of
men appear less keenly sensitive to physical suffering than do more
cultivated and refined human beings. Thus only in man can there
really be any intense degree of suffering, because only in him is there
that intellectual recollection of past moments and that anticipation of

future ones, which constitute in great part the bitterness of suffering. The momentary pang, the present pain, which beasts endure, though real enough, is yet, doubtless, not to be compared as to its intensity with the suffering which is produced in man through his high prerogative of self-consciousness (from *Genesis of Species*, 1871).

It took Darwin himself to derail this ancient tradition — and he 24 proceeded in the gentle way so characteristic of his radical intellectual approach to nearly everything. The ichneumons also troubled Darwin greatly and he wrote of them to Asa Gray in 1860:

> I own that I cannot see as plainly as others do, and as I should wish to do, evidence of design and beneficence on all sides of us. There seems to me too much misery in the world. I cannot persuade myself that a beneficent and omnipotent God would have designedly created the Ichneumonidae with the express intention of their feeding within the living bodies of Caterpillars, or that a cat should play with mice.

Indeed, he had written with more passion to Joseph Hooker in 1856: "What a book a devil's chaplain might write on the clumsy, wasteful, blundering, low, and horribly cruel works of nature!"

This honest admission — that nature is often (by our standards) 25 cruel and that all previous attempts to find a lurking goodness behind everything represent just so much special pleading — can lead in two directions. One might retain the principle that nature holds moral messages, but reverse the usual perspective and claim that morality consists in understanding the ways of nature and doing the opposite. Thomas Henry Huxley advanced this argument in his famous essay on *Evolution and Ethics* (1893):

> The practice of that which is ethically best — what we call goodness or virtue — involves a course of conduct which, in all respects, is opposed to that which leads to success in the cosmic struggle for existence. In place of ruthless self-assertion it demands self-restraint; in place of thrusting aside, or treading down, all competitors, it requires that the individual shall not merely respect, but shall help his fellows. . . . It repudiates the gladiatorial theory of existence. . . . Laws and moral precepts are directed to the end of curbing the cosmic process.

The other argument, radical in Darwin's day but more familiar 26 now, holds that nature simply is as we find it. Our failure to discern a universal good does not record any lack of insight or ingenuity, but merely demonstrates that nature contains no moral messages framed in human terms. Morality is a subject for philosophers, theologians, students of the humanities, indeed for all thinking people. The answers will not be read passively from nature; they do not, and cannot, arise from the data of science. The factual state of the world does not teach us how we, with our powers for good and evil, should alter or preserve it in the most ethical manner.

Darwin himself tended toward this view, although he could not, as   27
a man of his time, thoroughly abandon the idea that laws of nature might reflect some higher purpose. He clearly recognized that specific manifestations of those laws — cats playing with mice, and ichneumon larvae eating caterpillars — could not embody ethical messages, but he somehow hoped that unknown higher laws might exist "with the details, whether good or bad, left to the working out of what we may call chance."

Since ichneumons are a detail, and since natural selection is a law   28
regulating details, the answer to the ancient dilemma of why such cruelty (in our terms) exists in nature can only be that there isn't any answer — and that framing the question "in our terms" is thoroughly inappropriate in a natural world neither made for us nor ruled by us. It just plain happens. It is a strategy that works for ichneumons and that natural selection has programmed into their behavioral repertoire. Caterpillars are not suffering to teach us something; they have simply been outmaneuvered, for now, in the evolutionary game. Perhaps they will evolve a set of adequate defenses sometime in the future, thus sealing the fate of ichneumons. And perhaps, indeed probably, they will not.

Another Huxley, Thomas's grandson Julian, spoke for this position,   29
using as an example — yes, you guessed it — the ubiquitous ichneumons:

> Natural selection, in fact, though like the mills of God in grinding slowly and grinding small, has few other attributes that a civilized religion would call divine. . . . Its products are just as likely to be aesthetically, morally, or intellectually repulsive to as they are to be attractive. We need only think of the ugliness of *Sacculina* or a bladder-worm, the stupidity of a rhinoceros or a stegosaur, the horror of a female mantis devouring its mate or a brood of ichneumon flies slowly eating out a caterpillar.

If nature is nonmoral, then evolution cannot teach any ethical the-   30
ory at all. The assumption that it can has abetted a panoply of social evils that ideologues falsely read into nature from their beliefs —

eugenics and (misnamed) social Darwinism prominently among them. Not only did Darwin eschew any attempt to discover an antireligious ethic in nature, he also expressly stated his personal bewilderment about such deep issues as the problem of evil. Just a few sentences after invoking the ichneumons, and in words that express both the modesty of this splendid man and the compatibility, through lack of contact, between science and true religion, Darwin wrote to Asa Gray,

> I feel most deeply that the whole subject is too profound for the human intellect. A dog might as well speculate on the mind of Newton. Let each man hope and believe what he can.

CONSIDERATIONS

1. After summarizing and quoting the views of a nineteenth-century geologist, the author states: "We may find a certain amusing charm in Buckland's vision today." What attitudes, interests, and general knowledge does Gould take for granted in his readers? Do you fit precisely into his assumed audience, or do you differ with Gould in your response to Buckland's viewpoint?
2. Why are ichneumons more of a challenge to a moral view of nature than ferocious beasts? What connotations affect our view of large predatory animals?
3. What are the most prevalent themes in descriptions of ichneumon life? Why does Gould call them "epic descriptions"?
4. In paragraph 18, Gould acknowledges that he too has used "inappropriate anthropocentric language" to describe ichneumons. Why has he done so? Is it inappropriate to Gould's essential subject?
5. According to Gould, what two directions of thought arise after we give up the idea that nature reveals moral goodness? Which of the two arguments does Gould accept? Which direction seems more radical and challenging to you?
6. WRITING TOPIC. Do people believe in a *natural theology* in contemporary terms? In 700 words, analyze specific evidence that nature indicates positive moral values to many people in our society. You may wish to focus on the way nature is presented in advertising, television, outdoor sports, environmentalism, or other responses to nature as a moral symbol and good influence. Identify and clarify any "anthropocentric" themes you find in the language or visual images.

Robert Nisbet

CREATIONISM

◊

ROBERT NISBET (b. 1913), a leading sociologist and social critic, was born in Los Angeles and educated at the University of California at Berkeley, where he earned three academic degrees. He taught at Berkeley and later at the Riverside campus of the University of California before becoming the distinguished Albert Schweitzer Professor of Humanities at Columbia University in 1974. Nisbet's books include *Social Change and History* (1969) and *The Twilight of Authority* (1975). His work often focuses on problems of social cohesion in a democracy, a concern that was stimulated by his early reading of Alexis de Tocqueville (for a selection from Tocqueville see page 307). Nisbet's most recent book is an unconventional collection called *Prejudices: A Philosophical Dictionary* (1982), in which he considers, in alphabetical order, loosely connected topics on which he holds firm opinions. Part of the fun of defining your prejudices, he explains, is in finding reasons for what you already believe anyway. The following entry from his "dictionary" examines a key issue in the debate between science and religion.

In the strict sense, the word means belief in a literal understand- 1 ing of Genesis 1–2 in the Old Testament. The earth and everything on it were created by God in six days — each of them of twenty-four hours' duration. The redoubtable Archbishop Ussher, by meticulous reading of all the begats and other events in the Old Testament, calculated that God had created the world in 4004 B.C., assigning even the day of the week and the hour that Adam and Eve departed the Garden.

Creationists in this strict and literal sense of the word have few 2 supporters outside their own ranks. It is easy to make them the butt of

the kind of humor Darrow indulged himself in at the Scopes Trial.*
For such literalism cannot be entertained seriously by any but dolts, it
would seem, given the ineradicable evidences on earth of the passage
of very long periods of time and, in the present day, tests which date
almost to the year fossils and other paleological or geological entities
found in numerous parts of the earth.

These literalists are well advised in their own interest to go to *Om-* 3
phalos, written by Philip Gosse and published in 1857, just two years
before Darwin's *Origin* appeared. Gosse was one of the most respected naturalists in England, and without doubt he knew the evolutionary views of his naturalist contemporaries, who did not need the
Darwinian afflatus to learn about evolution as a natural process of nature, the works of biologists, botanists, and others of the preceding
century having taken care of that. But Gosse saw that, from the point
of view of strict logic, the creationists could not be summarily oblit-
erated in their arguments by the kind of evidence that naturalists of
the time utilized, to wit, the signs of age in the geological record. The
reason, Gosse argued, is that a genuine God, one omnipotent, omni-
scient, and omnipresent as a genuine God must be, would not for a
moment have created the world and its species without creating at the
same time the geological and embryological evidences of a long past.
After all, in creating man, God created a being with a unique time-
binding capacity, with a sense of the past as well as the present and
future. Given this sense of past in *Homo sapiens*, God could not but
have endowed his creation with an ingrained past. Eric Korn put this
view into sharper focus: "The argument is not that fossils were put
into rocks to make the world seem older, to confuse geologists or to
test people's faith; merely that if the world was created by divine fiat,
it could only be created as a going concern, with a created (not faked)
past." And as for deriving proof of the actual antiquity of earth and
man from the geological record alone, without prior assumption or
prejudgment, Korn wrote: "The geological evidence could no more
tell you when the world was created than the age of a character could
tell you how long a play had continued since the rise of the curtain."

* Clarence Darrow (1857–1938), a famous criminal lawyer, defended the high
school biology instructor John Scopes, who was convicted in 1925 for teaching the
doctrine of evolution in a public school in Tennessee. The so-called "Monkey trial"
subjected the Creationists to ridicule both in the courtroom and in the national press.

True, all true. The geological record, like tree rings, means abso- 4
lutely nothing as indicator of the past apart from an antecedent faith
in that past. Only in minds already prepared, minds possessed of belief in a law of historical motion, of development, of advancement,
can the strata of fossils in this or that part of the earth convey the
sense of a long, evolving past. In the history of mankind's consciousness of the past, man did not acquire his conviction of evolution from
fossils. On the contrary, man acquired respect for fossils as evidence
for an evolution already believed in in some form, divine or natural,
slow or speedy, continuous or discontinuous.

Gosse, to the consternation of his fellow naturalists and then to 5
their virtual ostracism of him, saw all of this and more. As is so often
the case, what the evidence was said to teach had in fact been learned
prior to any evidence whatever, and man then set about, over a period
of two or three thousand years, "proving" through evidence what had
already been learned from or been suggested by the sages of antiquity.
In terms of strict logic, Gosse is irrefutable.

Even so, it is unlikely that the ranks of the literal creationists will 6
swell to much larger number. From whatever source, for whatever
reason, most people in Western society have the unalterable conviction of a very long period of time in the history of the earth and of a
rather slow evolution of its mantle of life. The Western mind, from its
Greek roots in fascination with growth, with seeing the world and
everything in it against the metaphors of development and teleological fulfillment, takes to the basic idea of evolution rather easily. The
brain acquires, if it does not possess innately, certain ideas very early
in life; such ideas are like constitutive tissues of the mind. Evolution,
as an idea or perspective, is implicit in one degree or other in the
Greco-Roman and also in the Christian tradition, and it has been a
staple of the modern mind since the eighteenth century, Darwin's alleged revelation of 1859 notwithstanding.

It is in this light that creationism in the looser sense, as opposed to 7
literal creationism, must be assessed. Nothing can be done for or to
the literalists by biologists; they can take care of themselves. But the
overwhelming majority of self-styled creationists today are a different
breed. They accept the reality of a long evolution of earth and life.
But explicitly or implicitly they argue that, such reality accepted, current naturalist hypotheses and theories have proved inadequate and
insufficient to explain the astonishing things disclosed in recent years

by scientists themselves. These mainstream creationists accept without serious question the spectacle of an evolutionary differentiation of species going back great distances of time. What, however, is not acceptable is a theory that posits only the laws of chance, only an irrational, blind, mechanistic process of selection which is the sole and exclusive causal agent in this whole complex and intricate process of evolution. Sophisticated creationists are as well aware of the current *lacunae* in the purely naturalist theory of geological and biological evolution, of the conundrums and enigmas which virtually scream for recognition, as are sophisticated biologists and geologists.

Such creationists have no objection whatever to a planet of evolv- 8 ing life over four and a half billion years. After all, the principle of development, of fulfillment, of progress is intrinsic to Christianity, to be found all the way from Saint Augustine to Cardinal Newman in the nineteenth century, who used Christian developmentalism to throw light upon doctrinal issues. Moreover, creationists are well aware that not to this moment has any scientist come even close to the manufacture of life in the laboratory out of prebiotic substances. The origin of life is as much a mystery today as it was when Darwin carefully avoided the subject, referring merely, in the *Origin*, to the "Creator." Given such massive, long-lasting ignorance, creationists ask what is wrong with doing just what Darwin did, accepting the existence of a Creator and never pretending that principles set forth to account for the development of the species are sufficient to explain the actual origin of life. Modern biologists are really not much farther along, at least in laboratory results, with the problem of life and its initial appearance than Darwin and his contemporaries were. The question, then, is why the drum beaters for the "church of science" incessantly belabor the public with homiletics to the opposite effect.

If the answer is that they seek to prevent the church of God from 9 strangling the scientific enterprise, it can only cause bewilderment. The close linkage of Western religion and science goes back at least to Grosseteste and Bacon* in the Middle Ages. Apart from the desire to explain and illuminate divine laws, the works of Copernicus, Newton, Priestley, and Maxwell are incomprehensible. Newton declared that his entire purpose in writing the *Principia* was from the beginning the

---

* Robert Grosseteste (c. 1175–1253), an English scholar and Catholic bishop; Roger Bacon (c. 1220–1292), an English philosopher and scientist.

explication and clarification of the divine order. From boyhood Newton had been deeply devout in his Christianity, a believer indeed in
the imminent millennium. The majority of the geniuses of modern
times have had a firm belief that ranged from ordinary piety to evan-
gelical commitment. The idea that there is a conflict between religious belief and scientific conclusion would have seemed absurd to
these men. To suppose that any one of them would have considered
the exclusion of religion in all its forms from the schools, indeed from
the scientific classroom, a salutary, to-be-hoped-for eventuality is to
suppose nonsense. They believed they knew the limits of purely logical, rationalist, experimentalist science, and they were perfectly willing to deed over to the divine what lay beyond these limits. Even
Spencer,* more nearly philosopher of science perhaps than scientist,
expressed his contempt for atheists and his confidence in what he
called the Unknown and First Principles. In the present day there are
scientists who not only are willing to hypothesize the divine but see no
real alternative, given the sheer complexity of the world and universe
turned up by earth science and astronomy. But their voices are not
easily heard in the din created by the fundamentalists of science and
their allies in the media and the humanities.

But there is every likelihood of a sharp change in this dominance of 10
pure secularism. The reason, quite apart from the religious efflores-
cence taking place, is the uncomfortable yield of the sciences concerned most closely with the nature of the universe and man. This
yield — scarcely older than three decades — has thrown into question
many of the premises and assumptions of the rigorously anticreation-
ist mentality of modern times. It is now known that our own universe,
far from being a timeless complex of planets and stars, is finite in age,
in existence for only the last ten to twenty billion years, and is very
probably the outcome of a primal event, the "big bang." This notion
has every bit of the flavor of "creationism," for out of that single event
emerged a universe so delicately articulated, so harmonious in the
motions of its component bodies, and so marvelously suspended in
space as to deserve in and for itself the label of divinity. As an astron-
omer recently observed: "With every fresh penetration of our universe
through space craft tens of millions of miles away from the earth, the
suspicion grows that the theologian got there first."

* Herbert Spencer (1820–1903), an English philosopher.

The sciences have also revealed some hard truths about the earth 11
which are *prima facie* much more congruent with the creationist than
with the conventional secular view of the earth's age and relation to
other planets in the universe. It is now known that the earth itself is
only four and a half billion years old, that it too, like its environing
universe, is finite, not ageless and eternal as was thought until recently, and that it too has been subjected to great convulsive events
which play havoc with suppositions based upon the idea of timeless,
uniform, and observable processes. More important perhaps is the
dawning knowledge, drawn from the adventures in space of Mariner
and other craft, that the earth is, after all, just as the theologians have
said for millennia, unique in its possession not only of man but of life.
Add to the stupendous improbability of a universe such as ours an
earth such as ours, apparently alone in its mantle of organic life, and
we become humble.

Add also the stupendous improbability of the origin through purely 12
natural, secular processes of man, indeed of the whole complex and
intricate web of life. That purely natural processes of development
and differentiation exist is not to be doubted. And among these is natural selection. But the biomathematical improbability of all this
emerging solely through one simple process is so immense, given the
finite age of the earth, as to invite ridicule and to give impetus to
creationist philosophy. A near infinity of noughts is required in the
natural selection probabilities for so much as a fruit fly to emerge
through natural selection alone. As for the wonder that is man's mind
and nervous system, the physiologist Eccles, noted for his discoveries
in the transmission of electric impulses of the brain, remarked that
only something that is supernatural to the same degree as creationism
can even begin to explain man's unique mental faculties. Lovelock's
Gaia theory opens up the existence of a biosphere so infinitely complex in its homeostatic mechanisms as to make seriously suspect, irre-
spective of whether one "believes in God," most of the processes currently adduced by scientists in explanation of these exquisitely
interconnected mechanisms. The scenario of homeostasis presented
by the organism man is extraordinary enough as a super-Everest to
climb, but it is almost as nothing compared with the terrestrial homeostatic processes.

Creationists of the educated, common-sense, rational type are not 13
asking for illustrations in school textbooks of a bearded Olympian to

be called God and hailed for having, out of one mind, devised it all, either over six days or over six hundred million years. They could, if they wanted to, appeal to the physicist Bohr and his idea of complementarity. Bohr used this term to characterize situations in man's attempt to understand the universe where there are several mutually exclusive but legitimate approaches to reality. Such situations, as the physical scientist Weiskopf more recently noted, exist throughout science, including physics with its complementary aspects of the atom — quantum state and location. Divergent though the two states of vision are, each is necessary to a full understanding of the atom.

Granted that such a quandary or paradox is a far cry from belief in 14 a divine principle, an aboriginal creative force, but as Weiskopf emphasizes, science has always had its roots outside its own rational mode of thinking. He cites the mathematician Goedel's demonstration that a system of axioms can never be based on itself. To prove the axioms, statements from the outside must be introduced. "Science," noted Weiskopf, "must have a nonscientific base: it is the conviction of every scientist and of society as a whole, that scientific truth is relevant and essential." The physicist Planck, one of the astoundingly creative scientists of the twentieth century and a believer both in the divine and in the service of science to the divine, would have agreed, as he wrote: "Religion and natural science are fighting a joint battle in an incessant, never-relaxing crusade against skepticism and dogmatism, against disbelief and against superstition, and the rallying cry in this crusade has always been, and will always be, 'On to God.' " To paraphrase Chesterton, the time has come when the conflict is no longer between those who believe and those who do not believe, but between those who believe and those who will believe anything. Seek the truth, enjoined Saint Augustine, as if about to find it; find it with the intention of always seeking it. In the present day, that injunction has particular pertinence to the scientists and their camp followers who have so confidently declared God not only dead but never alive.

CONSIDERATIONS

1. How does mainstream creationism differ from literal creationism? For what reasons does the author regard it as the "mainstream" outlook?

What arguments might apply the term "mainstream" to the more literal doctrine of creation? Does Nisbet's judgment reflect a prejudice?

2. Who are the "fundamentalists of science" and how are they aided by "their allies in the media and the humanities"? How does Nisbet's word choice affect your response to his point in paragraph 9?

3. In paragraphs 10 through 12, Nisbet mentions several scientific concepts and attitudes that suggest creationism. What conclusions does Nisbet draw? What conclusions do you draw?

4. What values do science and religion share? Do you agree with Nisbet about the harmony between these two ways of thinking and living? Over which of the author's points could basic disagreements with Nisbet arise?

5. WRITING TOPIC. Do you have prejudices about people you have met from different parts of the United States? Do you have prejudices about living in the city, the suburbs, or the country? Or prejudices about political parties? Do prejudices affect your responses to the kind of people you date and don't date? In 500 words, write two separate entries in a dictionary of your own prejudices. In each entry take one opinion or attitude that you fairly consistently hold and give reasons why you hold this specific view.

Robert Finch

VERY LIKE A WHALE

◊

ROBERT FINCH (b. 1943), a naturalist and writer, lives on Cape Cod, Massachusetts. He is the author of *Common Ground: A Naturalist's Cape Cod* (1981) and *The Primal Place* (1983). The title of the following essay refers to a scene in *Hamlet*, act III, scene ii. Pretending to be deranged, Hamlet claims that the changing shapes of a passing cloud resemble a camel, a weasel, and a whale. Polonius, an aged statesman, humors him by agreeing that the amorphous cloud is indeed "very like a whale."

One day last week at sunset I went back to Corporation Beach in 1 Dennis to see what traces, if any, might be left of the great, dead finback whale that had washed up there several weeks before. The beach was not as hospitable as it had been that sunny Saturday morning after Thanksgiving when thousands of us streamed over the sand to gaze and look. A few cars were parked in the lot, but these kept their inhabitants. Bundled up against a sharp wind, I set off along the twelve-foot swath of trampled beach grass, a raw highway made in a few hours by ten thousand feet that day.

I came to the spot where the whale had beached and marveled that 2 such a magnitude of flesh could have been there one day and gone the next. But the carcass had been hauled off and the tide had smoothed and licked clean whatever vestiges had remained. The cold, salt wind had lifted from the sands the last trace of that pervasive stench of decay that clung to our clothes for days, and now blew clean and sharp into my nostrils.

The only sign that anything unusual had been there was that the 3 beach was a little too clean, not quite so pebbly and littered as the surrounding areas, as the grass above a new grave is always fresher and greener. What had so manifestly occupied this space a short while ago was now utterly gone. And yet the whale still lay heavily on my mind; a question lingered, like a persistent odor in the air. And its dark shape, though now sunken somewhere beneath the waves, still loomed before me, beckoning, asking something.

What was it? What had we seen? Even the several thousand of us 4 that managed to get down to the beach before it was closed off did not see much. Whales, dead or alive, are protected these days under the Federal Marine Mammals Act, and shortly after we arrived, local police kept anyone from actually touching the whale. I could hardly regret this, since in the past beached whales, still alive, have had cigarettes put out in their eyes and bits of flesh hacked off with pocket knives by souvenir seekers. And so, kept at a distance, we looked on while the specialists worked, white-coated, plastic-gloved autopsists from the New England Aquarium, hacking open the thick hide with carving knives and plumbing its depth for samples to be shipped to Canada for analysis and determination of causes of death. What was it they were pulling out? What fetid mystery would they pluck from that huge coffin of dead flesh? We would have to trust them for the answer.

But as the crowds continued to grow around the whale's body like 5 flies around carrion, the question seemed to me, and still seems, not so much why did the whale die, as why had we come to see it? What made this dark bulk such a human magnet, spilling us over onto private lawns and fields? I watched electricians and oil truck drivers pulling their vehicles off the road and clambering down to the beach. Women in high heels and pearls, on their way to Filene's, stumbled through the loose sand to gaze at a corpse. The normal human pattern was broken and a carnival atmosphere was created, appropriate enough in the literal sense of "a farewell to the flesh." But there was also a sense of pilgrimage in those trekking across the beach, an obligation to view such a thing. But for what? Are we really such novices to death? Or so reverent toward it?

I could understand my own semiprofessional interest in the whale, 6 but what had drawn these hordes? There are some obvious answers, of course: a break in the dull routine, "something different." An old human desire to associate ourselves with great and extraordinary events. We placed children and sweethearts in front of the corpse and clicked cameras. "Ruthie and the whale." "Having a whale of a time on Cape Cod."

Curiosity, the simplest answer, doesn't really answer anything. 7 What, after all, did we learn by being there? We were more like children at a zoo, pointing and poking, or Indians on a pristine beach, gazing in innocent wonder at strange European ships come ashore. Yet, as the biologists looted it with vials and plastic bags and the press captured it on film, the spectators also tried to *make* something of the whale. Circling around it as though for some hold on its slippery bulk, we grappled it with metaphors, lashed similes around its immense girth. It lay upside down, overturned "like a trailer truck." Its black skin was cracked and peeling, red underneath, "like a used tire." The distended, corrugated lower jaw, "a giant accordion," was afloat with the gas of putrefaction and, when pushed, oscillated slowly "like an enormous waterbed." Like our primitive ancestors, we still tend to make images to try to comprehend the unknown.

But what were we looking at? Or more to the point, from what 8 perspective were we looking at it? What did we see in it that might tell us why we had come? A male finback whale — *Balaenoptera physalus* — a baleen cetacean. The second largest creature ever to live on earth. An intelligent and complex mammal. A cause for conservationists. A remarkably adapted swimming and eating machine. Perfume, pet food, engineering oil. A magnificent scientific specimen. A tourist attraction. A media event, a "day to remember." A health menace, a "possible carrier of a communicable disease." A municipal headache and a navigational hazard. Material for an essay.

On the whale's own hide seemed to be written its life history, 9 which we could remark but not read. The right fluke was almost entirely gone, lost in some distant accident or battle and now healed over with a white scar. The red eye, unexpectedly small and mammalian, gazed out at us with fiery blankness. Like the glacial scratches sometimes found on our boulders, there were strange marks or grooves in the skin around the anal area, perhaps caused by scraping the ocean bottom.

Yet we could not seem to scratch its surface. The whale — dead, 10 immobile, in full view — nonetheless shifted kaleidoscopically before our eyes. The following morning it was gone, efficiently and sanitarily removed, like the week's garbage. What was it we saw? I have a theory, though probably (as they say in New England) it hardly does.

There is a tendency these days to defend whales and other endan- 11
gered animals by pointing out their similarities to human beings. Ce-
taceans, we are told, are very intelligent. They possess a highly complex language and have developed sophisticated communications
systems that transmit over long distances. They form family groups,
develop social structures and personal relationships, and express loyalty and affection toward one another. Much of their behavior seems
to be recreational: they sing, they play. And so on.

These are not sentimental claims. Whales apparently do these 12
things, at least as far as our sketchy information about their habits
warrants such interpretations. And for my money, any argument that
helps to preserve these magnificent creatures can't be all bad.

I take exception to this approach not because it is wrong, but be- 13
cause it is wrongheaded and misleading. It is exclusive, anthropocentric, and does not recognize nature in its own right. It implies that
whales and other creatures have value only insofar as they reflect man
himself and conform to his ideas of beauty and achievement. This attitude is not really far removed from that of the whalers themselves.
To consume whales solely for their nourishment of human values is
only a step from consuming them for meat and corset staves. It is not
only presumptuous and patronizing, but it is misleading and does
both whales and men a grave disservice. Whales have an inalienable
right to exist, not because they resemble man *or* because they are useful to him, but simply because they do exist, because they have a
proven fitness to the exactitudes of being on a global scale matched by
few other species. If they deserve our admiration and respect, it is because, as Henry Beston put it, "They are other nations, caught with
ourselves in the net of life and time, fellow prisoners of the splendor
and travail of life."

But that still doesn't explain the throngs who came pell-mell to 14
stare and conjecture at the dead whale that washed up at Corporation
Beach and dominated it for a day like some extravagant *memento
mori.* Surely we were not flattering ourselves, consciously or unconsciously, with any human comparisons to that rotting hulk. Nor was
there much, in its degenerate state, that it had to teach us. And yet we
came — why?

The answer may be so obvious that we have ceased to recognize it. 15
Man, I believe, has a crying need to confront otherness in the universe. Call it nature, wilderness, the "great outdoors,"or what you

will — we crave to look out and behold something other than our own human faces staring back at us, expectantly and increasingly frustrated. What the human spirit wants, as Robert Frost said, "Is not its own love back in copy-speech, / But counter-love, original response." This sense of otherness is, I feel, as necessary a requirement to our personalities as food and warmth are to our bodies. Just as an individual, cut off from human contact and stimulation, may atrophy and die of loneliness and neglect, so mankind is today in a similar, though more subtle, danger of cutting himself off from the natural world he shares with all creatures. If our physical survival depends upon our devising a proper use of earth's materials and produce, our growth as a species depends equally upon our establishing a vital and generative relationship with what surrounds us.   16

We need plants, animals, weather, unfettered shores, and unbroken woodland, not merely for a stable and healthy environment, but as an antidote to introversion, a preventive against human inbreeding. Here in particular, in the splendor of natural life, we have an extraordinary reservoir of the Cape's untapped possibilities and modes of being, ways of experiencing life, of knowing wind and wave. After all, how many neighborhoods have whales wash up in their backyards? To confine this world in zoos or in exclusive human terms does injustice not only to nature, but to ourselves as well.   17

Ever since his beginnings, when primitive man adopted totems and animal spirits to himself and assumed their shapes in ritual dance, *Homo sapiens* has been a superbly imitative animal. He has looked out across the fields and seen and learned. Somewhere along the line, though, he decided that nature was his enemy, not his ally, and needed to be confined and controlled. He abstracted nature and lost sight of it. Only now are we slowly realizing that nature can be confined only by narrowing our own concepts of it, which in turn narrows us. That is why we came to see the whale.   18

We substitute human myth for natural reality and wonder why we starve for nourishment. "Your Cape" becomes "your Mall," as the local radio jingle has it. Thoreau's "huge and real Cape Cod . . . a wild, rank place with no flattery in it," becomes the Chamber of Commerce's "Rural Seaside Charm" — until forty tons of dead flesh wash ashore and give the lie to such thin, flattering conceptions, flesh whose stench is still the stench of life that stirs us to reaction and response. That is why we came to see the whale. Its mute, immobile   19 bulk represented that ultimate, unknowable otherness that we both seek and recoil from, and shouted at us louder than the policeman's bullhorn that the universe is fraught, not merely with response or indifference, but incarnate assertion.

Later that day the Dennis Board of Health declared the whale carcass to be a "health menace" and warned us off the beach. A health menace? More likely an intoxicating, if strong, medicine that might literally bring us to our senses. 20

But if those of us in the crowd failed to grasp the whale that day, others did not have much better luck. Even in death the whale escaped us: the tissue samples taken in the autopsy proved insufficient for analysis and the biologists concluded, "We will never know why the whale died." The carcass, being towed tail-first by a Coast Guard cutter for a final dumping beyond Provincetown, snapped a six-inch hawser. Eluding further attempts to reattach it, it finally sank from sight. Even our powers of disposal, it seemed, were questioned that day. 21

And so, while we are left on shore with the memory of a deflated and stinking carcass and of bullhorns that blared and scattered us like flies, somewhere out beyond the rolled waters and the shining winter sun, the whale sings its own death in matchless, sirenian strains. 22

CONSIDERATIONS

1. Why did the author go back to the beach for a second look? What words indicate how his second visit affects his mood?
2. In paragraph 7, Finch metaphorically describes the figurative speech used by the crowd. What differences between the author's attitude and the crowd's appear in the different figurative language?
3. What is "wrongheaded and misleading" about the view that whales are very much like people? Do you agree with Finch that this viewpoint is pernicious? What are its possible good effects?
4. According to Finch what is the important human need that we have not satisfied? For what purpose do we deprive ourselves of this particular satisfaction?
5. In the final paragraph, what is the double meaning of "sirenian"? What feelings in Finch have been evoked by the whale's fate?

6. Suggest a different title for this essay. Try to give it a title that reflects the author's tone as well as the subject.

7. WRITING TOPIC. In 500 words or more, clarify Finch's attitudes about death in this essay. Point out specific responses such as moments of revulsion, fascination, fear, irony, sadness, or other attitudes that you may find in his account. Considering all his reactions together, do you think that he is depressed or uplifted by his encounter with death?

8. WRITING TOPIC. In 500 words, recall an encounter you may have had with the death of an animal, perhaps the death of a pet, the shooting of a game bird or animal, or the slaughter of a food animal. Include descriptive details that enable the reader to share your perspective on the experience. Explain whatever mixed reactions you had at the time.

Carl Gustav Jung

SECRET THOUGHT*

◊

CARL GUSTAV JUNG (1875–1961), a renowned Swiss psychiatrist, was a leading member of Sigmund Freud's circle of colleagues and disciples during the early years of this century when the theories and practice of psychoanalysis were developed in Europe. He differed with Freud over key issues that led Jung to found his own branch of analytic psychology. His many books include *Modern Man in Search of a Soul* (1933) and *Psychology and Religion* (1938). When Jung was eighty-one, he was finally persuaded to dictate his life story, published posthumously as *Memories, Dreams, Reflections* (1961). In the following excerpt Jung recalls a momentous spiritual crisis that occurred when he was twelve years old. The frightening yet illuminating experience opened up a new outlook on life, which led him ultimately to his profession as a psychiatrist.

One fine summer day that same year† I came out of school at noon 1 and went to the cathedral square. The sky was gloriously blue, the day one of radiant sunshine. The roof of the cathedral glittered, the sun sparkling from the new, brightly glazed tiles. I was overwhelmed by the beauty of the sight, and thought: "The world is beautiful and the church is beautiful, and God made all this and sits above it far away in the blue sky on a golden throne and . . ." Here came a great hole in my thoughts, and a choking sensation. I felt numbed, and knew only: "Don't go on thinking now! Something terrible is coming, something I do not want to think, something I dare not even approach. Why not? Because I would be committing the most frightful of sins. What is the most terrible sin? Murder? No, it can't be that. The most terrible sin is the sin against the Holy Ghost, which cannot be forgiven. Anyone who commits that sin is damned to hell for all eternity. That would be very sad for my parents, if their only son, to whom they are

* Editor's title.
† In 1887 Jung was twelve years old.

489

so attached, should be doomed to eternal damnation. I cannot do that to my parents. All I need do is not go on thinking."

That was easier said than done. On my long walk home I tried to think all sorts of other things, but I found my thoughts returning again and again to the beautiful cathedral which I loved so much, and to God sitting on the throne — and then my thoughts would fly off again as if they had received a powerful electric shock. I kept repeating to myself: "Don't think of it, just don't think of it!" I reached home in a pretty worked-up state. My mother noticed that something was wrong, and asked, "What is the matter with you? Has something happened at school? I was able to assure her, without lying, that nothing had happened at school. I did have the thought that it might help me if I could confess to my mother the real reason for my turmoil. But to do so I would have to do the very thing that seemed impossible: think my thought right to the end. The poor dear was utterly unsuspecting and could not possibly know that I was in terrible danger of committing the unforgivable sin and plunging myself into hell. I rejected the idea of confessing and tried to efface myself as much as possible.

That night I slept badly; again and again the forbidden thought, which I did not yet know, tried to break out, and I struggled desperately to fend it off. The next two days were sheer torture, and my mother was convinced that I was ill. But I resisted the temptation to confess, aided by the thought that it would cause my parents intense sorrow.

On the third night, however, the torment became so unbearable that I no longer knew what to do. I awoke from a restless sleep just in time to catch myself thinking again about the cathedral and God. I had almost continued the thought! I felt my resistance weakening. Sweating with fear, I sat up in bed to shake off sleep. "Now it is coming, now it's serious! *I must think.* It must be thought out beforehand. *Why* should I think something I do not know? I don't want to, by God, that's sure. But *who* wants me to? Who wants to force me to think something I don't know and don't want to know? Where does this terrible will come from? And why should I be the one to be subjected to it? I was thinking praises of the Creator of this beautiful world, I was grateful to him for this immeasurable gift, so why should I have to think something inconceivably wicked? I don't know what it is, I really don't, for I cannot and must not come anywhere near this thought, for that would be to risk thinking it at once. *I haven't done this or wanted this, it has come on me like a bad dream.* Where do such things come from? This has happened to me without my doing. Why? After all, I didn't create myself, I came into the world the way God made me — that is, the way I was shaped by my parents. Or can it have been that my parents wanted something of this sort? But my good parents would never have had any thoughts like that. Nothing so atrocious would ever have occurred to them."

I found this idea utterly absurd. Then I thought of my grandpar- 5
ents, whom I knew only from their portraits. They looked benevolent and dignified enough to repulse any idea that they might possibly be to blame. I mentally ran through the long procession of unknown ancestors until finally I arrived at Adam and Eve. And with them came the decisive thought: Adam and Eve were the first people; they had no parents, but were created directly by God, who intentionally made them as they were. They had no choice but to be exactly the way God had created them. Therefore they did not know how they could possibly be different. They were perfect creatures of God, for He creates only perfection, and yet they committed the first sin by doing what God did not want them to do. How was that possible? They could not have done it if God had not placed in them the possibility of doing it. That was clear, too, from the serpent, whom God had created before them, obviously so that it could induce Adam and Eve to sin. God in His omniscience had arranged everything so that the first parents would have to sin. *Therefore it was God's intention that they should sin.*

This thought liberated me instantly from my worst torment, since I 6
now knew that God Himself had placed me in this situation. At first I did not know whether He intended me to commit my sin or not. I no longer thought of praying for illumination, since God had landed me in this fix without my willing it and had left me without any help. I was certain that I must search out His intention myself, and seek the way out alone. At this point another argument began.

"What does God want? To act or not to act? I must find out what 7
God wants with me, and I must find out right away." I was aware, of course, that according to conventional morality there was no question but that sin must be avoided. That was what I had been doing up to now, but I knew I could not go on doing it. My broken sleep and my spiritual distress had worn me out to such a point that fending off the

thought was tying me into unbearable knots. This could not go on. At the same time, I could not yield before I understood what God's will was and what He intended. For I was now certain that He was the author of this desperate problem. Oddly enough, I did not think for a moment that the devil might be playing a trick on me. The devil played little part in my mental world at that time, and in any case I regarded him as powerless compared with God. But from the moment I emerged from the mist and became conscious of myself, the unity, the greatness, and the superhuman majesty of God began to haunt my imagination. Hence there was no question in my mind but that God Himself was arranging a decisive test for me, and that everything depended on my understanding Him correctly. I knew, beyond a doubt, that I would ultimately be compelled to break down, to give way, but I did not want it to happen without my understanding it, since the salvation of my eternal soul was at stake.

"God knows that I cannot resist much longer, and He does not 8 help me, although I am on the point of having to commit the unforgivable sin. In His omnipotence He could easily lift this compulsion from me, but evidently He is not going to. Can it be that He wishes to test my obedience by imposing on me the unusual task of doing something against my own moral judgment and against the teachings of my religion, and even against His own commandment, something I am resisting with all my strength because I fear eternal damnation? Is it possible that God wishes to see whether I am capable of obeying His will even though my faith and my reason raise before me the specters of death and hell? That might really be the answer! But these are merely my own thoughts. I may be mistaken. I dare not trust my own reasoning as far as that. I must think it all through once more."

I thought it over again and arrived at the same conclusion. "Ob- 9 viously God also desires me to show courage," I thought. "If that is so and I go through with it, then He will give me His grace and illumination."

I gathered all my courage, as though I were about to leap forthwith 10 into hell-fire, and let the thought come. I saw before me the cathedral, the blue sky. God sits on His golden throne, high above the world — and from under the throne an enormous turd falls upon the sparkling new roof, shatters it, and breaks the walls of the cathedral asunder.

So that was it! I felt an enormous, an indescribable relief. Instead 11 of the expected damnation, grace had come upon me, and with it an unutterable bliss such as I had never known. I wept for happiness and gratitude. The wisdom and goodness of God had been revealed to me now that I had yielded to His inexorable command. It was as though I had experienced an illumination. A great many things I had not previously understood became clear to me. That was what my father had not understood, I thought; he had failed to experience the will of God, had opposed it for the best reasons and out of the deepest faith. And that was why he had never experienced the miracle of grace which heals all and makes all comprehensible. He had taken the Bible's commandments as his guide; he believed in God as the Bible prescribed and as his forefathers had taught him. But he did not know the immediate living God who stands, omnipotent and free, above His Bible and His Church, who calls upon man to partake of His freedom, and can force him to renounce his own views and convictions in order to fulfill without reserve the command of God. In His trial of human courage God refuses to abide by traditions, no matter how sacred. In His omnipotence He will see to it that nothing really evil comes of such tests of courage. If one fulfills the will of God one can be sure of going the right way.

God had also created Adam and Eve in such a way that they had to 12 think what they did not at all want to think. He had done that in order to find out whether they were obedient. And He could also demand something of me that I would have had to reject on traditional religious grounds. It was obedience which brought me grace, and after that experience I knew what God's grace was. One must be utterly abandoned to God; nothing matters but fulfilling His will. Otherwise all is folly and meaninglessness. From that moment on, when I experienced grace, my true responsibility began. Why did God befoul His cathedral? That, for me, was a terrible thought. But then came the dim understanding that God could be something terrible. I had experienced a dark and terrible secret. It overshadowed my whole life, and I became deeply pensive.

The experience also had the effect of increasing my sense of inferi- 13 ority. I am a devil or a swine, I thought; I am infinitely depraved. But then I began searching through the New Testament and read, with a certain satisfaction, about the Pharisee and the publican, and that reprobates are the chosen ones. It made a lasting impression on me that the unjust steward was praised, and that Peter, the waverer, was appointed the rock upon which the Church was built.

The greater my inferiority feelings became, the more incompre- 14
hensible did God's grace appear to me. After all, I had never been sure
of myself. When my mother once said to me, "You have always been
a good boy," I simply could not grasp it. I a good boy? That was quite
new to me. I often thought of myself as a corrupt and inferior person.

With the experience of God and the cathedral I at last had some- 15
thing tangible that was part of the great secret — as if I had always
talked of stones falling from heaven and now had one in my pocket.
But actually, it was a shaming experience. I had fallen into something
bad, something evil and sinister, though at the same time it was a kind
of distinction. Sometimes I had an overwhelming urge to speak, not
about that, but only to hint that there were some curious things about
me which no one knew of. I wanted to find out whether other people
had undergone similar experiences. I never succeeded in discovering
so much as a trace of them in others. As a result, I had the feeling that
I was either outlawed or elect, accursed or blessed. . . .

My entire youth can be understood in terms of this secret. It in- 16
duced in me an almost unendurable loneliness. My one great achievement during those years was that I resisted the temptation to talk
about it with anyone. Thus the pattern of my relationship to the
world was already prefigured: today as then I am a solitary, because I
know things and must hint at things which other people do not know,
and usually do not even want to know.

CONSIDERATIONS

1. As a twelve-year-old, why didn't Jung confide in his mother and tell her
   his fear?
2. Who does the boy blame for his lack of control over his thoughts? How
   did he come to this conclusion in his reasoning?
3. What is the conflict between the boy's faith and his moral conscience?
   How is the conflict resolved?
4. How did the boy's religious illumination affect his subsequent behavior?
   In your view did his actions become better or worse?
5. If you know the Biblical story of Abraham and the sacrifice of Isaac, explain the parallels and differences between that story and Jung's experience. Which story seems more true to life?
6. In your view of this experience did Jung learn to accept God or to accept
   himself? What is Jung's view?

7. WRITING TOPIC. In 500 words, clarify what Jung means when he says "grace had come upon me." In this essay, how is grace defined and how does it happen? It will be useful to compare Jung's account with the lyrics to "Amazing Grace" in the *Insights* to this chapter: note the similarities and differences.

8. WRITING TOPIC. Children often make up games to deal with compulsive thoughts, such as "Step on a crack — and break your mother's back!" By avoiding the cracks in the sidewalk, the playing child magically wards off an imaginary disaster. Based on your observations or recollections, write a 500-word analysis of a specific childhood fear that conjured up magic thoughts or compulsive actions.

Barbara Grizzuti Harrison

GROWING UP APOCALYPTIC

◊

BARBARA GRIZZUTI HARRISON (b. 1934), a feminist writer and critical observer of the American scene, was born in Brooklyn, New York. Roman Catholic for her first nine years, Harrison, together with her mother, converted to the Jehovah's Witnesses. At the age of twenty-two, she rejected the faith. She wrote an account of her religious upbringing in *Visions of Glory: A History and a Memory of Jehovah's Witness* (1978). Always sensitive to women's issues, Harrison examined the effects of public education in *Unlearning the Lie: Sexism in School* (1973). Her essays on literature, politics, and popular culture have appeared in such magazines as *Ms.*, *Esquire*, and *The New Republic*, and they have been collected in *Off Center* (1980). Two years after the following autobiographical essay first appeared in *Ms.* in 1975, Harrison converted back to Catholicism — a "return," she notes, that surprised her.

"The trouble with you," Anna said, in a voice in which compassion, disgust, and reproach fought for equal time, "is that you can't remember what it was like to be young. And even if you could remember — well, when you were my age, you were in that crazy Jehovah's Witness religion, and you probably didn't even play spin the bottle." 1

Anna, my prepubescent eleven-year-old, feels sorry for me because I did not have "a normal childhood." It has never occurred to her to question whether her childhood is "normal" . . . which is to say, she is happy. She cannot conceive of a life in which one is not free to move around, explore, argue, flirt with ideas and dismiss them, form passionate alliances and friendships according to no imperative but one's own nature and volition; she regards love as unconditional, she expects nurturance as her birthright. It fills her with terror and pity that anyone — especially her mother — could have grown up any dif- 2 ferently — could have grown up in a religion where love was conditional upon rigid adherence to dogma and established practice . . . where approval had to be bought from authoritarian sources . . . where people did not fight openly and love fiercely and forgive generously and make decisions of their own and mistakes of their own and have adventures of their own.

"Poor Mommy," she says. To have spent one's childhood in love 3 with/tyrannized by a vengeful Jehovah is not Anna's idea of a good time — nor is it her idea of goodness. As, in her considered opinion, my having been a proselytizing Jehovah's Witness for thirteen years was about as good a preparation for real life as spending a commensurate amount of time in a Skinner box on the North Pole, she makes allowances for me. And so, when Anna came home recently from a boy-girl party to tell me that she had kissed a boy ("interesting," she pronounced the experiment), and I heard my mouth ask that atavistic mother-question, "And what else did you do?" Anna was inclined to be charitable with me: "Oh, for goodness' sake, what do you think we did, screw? The trouble with you is . . ." And then she explained to me about spin the bottle.

I do worry about Anna. She is, as I once explained drunkenly to 4 someone who thought that she might be the better for a little vigorous repression, a teleological child. She is concerned with final causes, with ends and purposes and means; she would like to see evidence of design and order in the world; and all her adventures are means to that end. That, combined with her love for the music, color, poetry, ritual, and drama of religion, might, I think, if she were at all inclined to bow her back to authority — and if she didn't have my childhood as an example of the perils thereof — have made her ripe for conversion to an apocalyptic, messianic sect.

That fear may be evidence of my special paranoia, but it is not an 5 entirely frivolous conjecture. Ardent preadolescent girls whose temperament tends toward the ecstatic are peculiarly prone to conversion to fancy religions.

I know. My mother and I became Jehovah's Witnesses in 1944, 6 when I was nine years old. I grew up drenched in the dark blood-poetry of a fierce messianic sect. Shortly after my conversion, I got my first period. We used to sing this hymn: "Here is He who comes from Eden/all His raiment stained with blood." My raiments were stained with blood, too. But the blood of the Son of Man was purifying, redemptive, cleansing, sacrificial. Mine was filthy — proof of my having inherited the curse placed upon the seductress Eve. I used to "read" my used Kotexes compulsively, as if the secret of life — or a harbinger of death — were to be found in that dull, mysterious effluence.

My brother, at the time of our conversion, was four. After a few 7 years of listlessly following my mother and me around in our door-to-door and street-corner proselytizing, he allied himself with my father, who had been driven to noisy, militant atheism by the presence of two female religious fanatics in his hitherto patriarchal household. When your wife and daughter are in love with God, it's hard to compete — particularly since God is good enough not to require messy sex as proof or expression of love. As a child, I observed that it was not extraordinary for women who became Jehovah's Witnesses to remove themselves from their husband's bed as a first step to getting closer to God. For women whose experience had taught them that all human relationships were treacherous and capricious and frighteningly volatile, an escape from the confusions of the world into the certainties of a fundamentalist religion provided the illusion of safety and of rest. It is not too simple to say that the reason many unhappily married and sexually embittered women fell in love with Jehovah was that they didn't have to go to bed with Him.

Apocalyptic religions are, by their nature, antierotic. Jehovah's 8 Witnesses believe that the world — or, as they would have it, "this evil system under Satan the Devil" — will end in our lifetime. After the slaughter Jehovah has arranged for his enemies at Armageddon, say the Witnesses, this quintessentially masculine God — vengeful in battle, benevolent to survivors — will turn the earth into an Edenic paradise for true believers. I grew up under the umbrella of the slogan, "Millions Now Living Will Never Die," convinced that 1914 marked "the beginning of the times of the end." So firmly did Jehovah's Witnesses believe this to be true that there were those who, in 1944, refused to get their teeth filled, postponing all care of their bodies until God saw to their regeneration in His New World, which was just around the corner.

Some corner.   9

Despite the fact that their hopes were not immediately rewarded, 10 Jehovah's Witnesses have persevered with increasing fervor and conviction, and their attitude toward the world remains the same: because all their longing is for the future, they are bound to hate the present — the material, the sexual, the flesh. It's impossible, of course, truly to savor and enjoy the present, or to bend one's energies to shape and mold the world into the form of goodness, if you are only waiting for it to be smashed by God. There is a kind of ruthless glee in the way in which Jehovah's Witnesses point to earthquakes, race riots, heroin addiction, the failure of the United Nations, divorce, famine, and liberalized abortion laws as proof of the nearness of Armageddon.

The world will end, according to the Witnesses, in a great shaking 11 and rending and tearing of unbelieving flesh, with unsanctified babies swimming in blood — torrents of blood. They await God's Big Bang — the final orgasmic burst of violence, after which all things will come together in a cosmic orgasm of joy. In the meantime, they have disgust and contempt for the world; and freedom and spontaneity, even playfulness, in sex are explicitly frowned upon.

When I was ten, it would have been more than my life was worth 12 to acknowledge, as Anna does so casually, that I knew what *screwing* was. (Ignorance, however, delivered me from that grave error.) Once, having read somewhere that Hitler had a mistress, I asked my mother what a mistress was. (I had an inkling that it was some kind of sinister superhousekeeper, like Judith Anderson in *Rebecca*). I knew from my mother's silence, and from her cold, hard, and frightened face, that the question was somehow a grievous offense. I knew that I had done something terribly wrong, but as usual, I didn't know what. The fact was that I never knew how to buy God's — or my mother's — approval. There were sins I consciously and knowingly committed. That was bad, but it was bearable. I could always pray to God to forgive me, say, for reading the Bible for its "dirty parts" (to prefer the Song of Solomon to all the begats of Genesis was proof absolute of the sinfulness of my nature). But the offenses that made me most cringingly guilty were those I had committed unconsciously; as an imperfect human being descended from the wretched Eve, I was bound — so I had been taught — to offend Jehovah seventy-seven times a day without my even knowing what I was doing wrong.

I knew that good Christians didn't commit "unnatural acts"; but I 13 didn't know what "unnatural acts" were. I knew that an increase in the number of rapes was one of the signs heralding the end of the world, but I didn't know what rape was. Consequently, I spent a lot of time praying that I was not committing unnatural acts or rape.

My ignorance of all things sexual was so profound that it frequently 14 led to comedies of error. Nothing I've ever read has inclined me to believe that Jehovah has a sense of humor, and I must say that I consider it a strike against Him that He wouldn't find this story funny: One night shortly after my conversion, a visiting elder of the congregation, as he was avuncularly tucking me in bed, asked me if I were guilty of performing evil practices with my hands under the covers at night. I was puzzled. He was persistent. Finally, I thought I understood. And I burst into wild tears of self-recrimination: What I did under the covers at night was bite my cuticles — a practice which, in fact, did afford me a kind of sensual pleasure. I didn't learn about masturbation — which the Witnesses call "idolatry" because "the masturbator's affection is diverted away from the Creator and is bestowed upon a coveted object . . . his genitals" — until much later. So, having confessed to a sin that I didn't even know existed, I was advised of the necessity of keeping one's body pure from sin; cold baths were recommended. I couldn't see the connection between cold baths and my cuticles, but one never questioned the imperatives of an elder. So I subjected my impure body, in midwinter, to so many icy baths that I began to look like a bleached prune. My mother thought I was demented. But I couldn't tell her that I'd been biting my cuticles, because to have incurred God's wrath — and to see the beady eye of the elder steadfastly upon me at every religious meeting I went to — was torment enough. There was no way to win.

One never questioned the imperatives of an elder. I learned as a 15 very small child that it was my primary duty in life to "make nice." When I was little, I was required to respond to inquiries about my health in this manner: "Fine and dandy, just like sugar candy, thank you." And to curtsy. If that sounds like something from a Shirley Temple movie, it's because it is. Having been brought up to be the Italian working-class Shirley Temple from Bensonhurst, it was not terribly difficult for me to learn to "make nice" for God and the elders. Behaving well was relatively easy. The passionate desire to win approval guaranteed my conforming. But behaving well never made me feel good. I always felt as if I were a bad person.

I ask myself why it was that my brother was not hounded by the 16 obsessive guilt and the desperate desire for approval that informed all my actions. Partly, I suppose, luck, and an accident of temperament, but also because of the peculiarly guilt-inspiring double message girls received. Girls were taught that it was their nature to be spiritual, but paradoxically that they were more prone to absolute depravity than were boys.

In my religion, everything beautiful and noble and spiritual and   17
good was represented by a woman; and everything evil and depraved and monstrous was represented by a woman. I learned that "God's organization," the "bride of Christ," or His 144,000 heavenly co-rulers were represented by a "chaste virgin." I also learned that "Babylon the Great," or "false religion," was "the mother of the abominations or the 'disgusting things of the earth' . . . She likes to get drunk on human blood. . . . Babylon the Great is . . . pictured as a woman, an international harlot."

Young girls were thought not to have the "urges" boys had. They   18
were not only caretakers of their own sleepy sexuality but protectors of boys' vital male animal impulses as well. They were thus doubly responsible, and, if they fell, doubly damned. Girls were taught that, simply by existing, they were provoking male sexuality . . . which it was their job then to subdue.

To be female, I learned, was to be Temptation; nothing short of   19
death — the transformation of your atoms into a lilac bush — could change that. (I used to dream deliciously of dying, of being as inert — and as unaccountable — as the dust I came from.) Inasmuch as males naturally "wanted it" more, when a female "wanted it" she was doubly depraved, unnatural as well as sinful. She was the receptacle for male lust, "the weaker vessel." If the vessel, created by God for the use of males, presumed to have desires of its own, it was perforce consigned to the consuming fires of God's wrath. If, then, a woman were to fall from grace, her fall would be mighty indeed — and her willful nature would lead her into that awful abyss where she would be deprived of the redemptive love of God and the validating love of man. Whereas, were a man to fall, he would be merely stumbling over his own feet of clay.

(Can this be accident? My brother, when he was young, was always   20
falling over his own feet. I, on the other hand, to this day sweat with terror at the prospect of going down escalators or long flights of stairs. I cannot fly; I am afraid of the fall.)

I spent my childhood walking a religious tightrope, maintaining a   21
difficult dizzying balance. I was, for example, expected to perform well at school, so that glory would accrue to Jehovah and "His organization." But I was also made continually aware of the perils of falling

prey to "the wisdom of this world which is foolishness to God." I had constantly to defend myself against the danger of trusting my own judgment. To question or to criticize God's "earthly representatives" was a sure sign of "demonic influence"; to express doubt openly was to risk being treated like a spiritual leper. I was always an honor student at school; but this was hardly an occasion for unqualifed joy. I felt, rather, as if I were courting spiritual disaster: while I was congratulated for having "given a witness" by virtue of my academic excellence, I was, in the next breath, warned against the danger of supposing that my intelligence could function independently of God's. The effect of all this was to convince me that my intelligence was like some kind of tricky, predatory animal, which, if it were not kept firmly reined, would surely spring on and destroy me.

"Vanity, thy name is woman." I learned very early what happened 22 to women with "independent spirits" who opposed the will and imperatives of male elders. They were disfellowshipped (excommunicated) and thrown into "outer darkness." Held up as an example of such perfidious conduct was Maria Frances Russell, the wife of Charles Taze Russell, charismatic founder of the sect.

Russell charged his wife with "the same malady which has smitten 23 others — *ambition.*" Complaining of a "female conspiracy" against the Lord's organization, he wrote: "The result was a considerable stirring up of slander and misrepresentation, for of course it would not suit (her) purposes to tell the plain unvarnished truth, that Sister Russell was ambitious. . . . When she desired to come back, I totally refused, except upon a promise that she should make reasonable acknowledgment of the wrong course she had been pursuing." Ambition in a woman was, by implication, so reprehensible as to exact from Jehovah the punishment of death.

(What the Witnesses appeared less eager to publicize about the 24 Russell's spiritual-cum-marital problems is that in April, 1906, Mrs. Russell, having filed suit for legal separation, told a jury that her husband had once remarked to a young orphan woman the Russells had reared: "I am like a jellyfish. I float around here and there. I touch this one and that one, and if she responds I take her to me, and if not I float on to others." Mrs. Russell was unable to prove her charge.

I remember a line in *A Nun's Story:* "Dear God," the disaffected 25 Belgian nun anguished, "forgive me. I will never be able to love a Nazi." I, conversely, prayed tormentedly for many years, "Dear God,

forgive me, I am not able to hate what you hate. I love the world." As
a Witness I was taught that "friendship with the world" was "spiritual
adultery." The world was crawling with Satan's agents. But Satan's
agents — evolutionists, "false religionists," and all those who opposed, or were indifferent to, "Jehovah's message" — often seemed
like perfectly nice, decent, indeed lovable people to me. (They were
certainly interesting.) As I went from door to door, ostensibly to help
the Lord divide the "goats" from the "sheep," I found that I was
more and more listening to *their* lives; and I became increasingly more
tentative about telling them that I had *The* Truth. As I grew older, I
found it more and more difficult to eschew their company. I entertained fantasies, at one time or another, about a handsome, ascetic Je-
suit priest I had met in my preaching work and about Albert
Schweitzer, J. D. Salinger, E. B. White, and Frank Sinatra; in fact, I
was committing "spiritual adultery" all over the place. And then,
when I was fifteen, I fell in love with an "unbeliever."

If I felt — before having met and loved Arnold Horowitz, English 26
31, New Utrecht High School — that life was a tightrope, I felt afterward that my life was perpetually being lived on a high wire, with no
safety net to catch me. I was obliged, by every tenet of my faith, to
despise him: to be "yoked with an unbeliever," an atheist and an intellectual . . . the pain was exquisite.

He was the essential person, the person who taught me how to love, 27
and how to doubt. Arnold became interested in me because I was
smart; he loved me because he thought I was good. He nourished me.
He nurtured me. He paid me the irresistible compliment of totally
comprehending me. He hated my religion. He railed against the sect
that would rather see babies die than permit them to have blood
transfusions, which were regarded as unscriptural; he had boundless
contempt for my overseers, who would not permit me to go to college — the "Devil's playground," which would fill my head with
wicked, ungodly nonsense; he protested mightily, with the rage that
springs from genuine compassion, against a religion that could tolerate segregation and apartheid, sneer at martyred revolutionaries, dismiss social reform and material charity as "irrelevant," a religion
that — waiting for God to cure all human ills — would act by default
to maintain the status quo, while regarding human pain and struggle
without pity and without generosity. He loathed the world view that
had been imposed on me, a black-and-white view that allowed no

complexities, no moral dilemmas, that disdained metaphysical or philosophical or psychological inquiry; he loathed the bloated simplicities that held me in thrall. But he loved *me*. I had never before felt loved unconditionally.

This was a measure of his love: Jehovah's Witnesses are not permitted to salute the flag. Arnold came, unbidden, to sit with me at every school assembly, to hold my hand, while everyone else stood at rigid salute. We were very visible; and I was very comforted. And this was during the McCarthy era. Arnold had a great deal to lose, and he risked it all for me. Nobody had ever risked anything for me before. How could I believe that he was wicked? 28

We drank malteds on his porch and read T. S. Eliot and listened to Mozart. We walked for hours, talking of God and goodness and happiness and death. We met surreptitiously. (My mother so feared and hated the man who was leading me into apostasy that she once threw a loaf of Arnold bread out the window; his very name was loathsome to her.) Arnold treated me with infinite tenderness; he was the least alarming man I had ever known. His fierce concentration on me, his solicitous care uncoupled with sexual aggression, was the gentlest — and most thrilling — love I had ever known. He made me feel what I had never felt before — valuable, and good. 29

It was very hard. All my dreams centered around Arnold, who was becoming more important, certainly more real to me, than God. All my dreams were blood-colored. I would fantasize about Arnold's being converted and surviving Armageddon and living forever with me in the New World. Or I would fantasize about my dying with Arnold, in fire and flames, at Armageddon. I would try to make bargains with God — my life for his. When I confessed my terrors to the men in charge of my spiritual welfare — when I said that I knew I could not rejoice in the destruction of the "wicked" at Armageddon — I was told that I was presuming to be "more compassionate than Jehovah," the deadliest sin against the holy spirit. I was reminded that, being a woman and therefore weak and sentimental, I would have to go against my sinful nature and listen to their superior wisdom, which consisted of my never seeing Arnold again. I was also reminded of the perils of being over-smart: if I hadn't been such a good student, none of this would have happened to me. 30

I felt as if I were leading a double life, as indeed I was. I viewed the world as beautifully various, as a blemished but mysteriously won- 31 derful place, as savable by humans, who were neither good nor bad but imperfectly wise; but I *acted* as if the world were fit for nothing but destruction, as if all human efforts to purchase happiness and goodness were doomed to failure and deserving of contempt, as if all people could be categorized as "sheep" or "goats" and herded into their appropriate destinies by a judgmental Jehovah, the all-seeing Father who knew better than His children what was good for them.

As I had when I was a little girl, I "made nice" as best I could. I 32 maintained the appearance of "goodness," that is, of religiosity, although it violated my truest feelings. When I left high school, I went into the full-time preaching work. I spent a minimum of five hours a day ringing doorbells and conducting home Bible studies. I went to three religious meetings a week. I prayed that my outward conformity would lead to inner peace. I met Arnold very occasionally, when my need to see him overcame my elders' imperatives and my own devastating fears. He was always accessible to me. Our meetings partook equally of misery and of joy. I tried, by my busyness, to lock all my doubts into an attic of my mind.

And for a while, and in a way, it "took." I derived sustenance from 33 communal surges of revivalist fervor at religious conventions and from the conviction that I was united, in a common cause, with a tiny minority of persecuted and comradely brothers and sisters whose approval became both my safety net and the Iron Curtain that shut me off from the world. I felt that I had chosen Jehovah, and that my salvation, while not assured, was at least a possibility; perhaps He would choose me. I vowed finally never to see Arnold again, hoping, by this sacrifice, to gain God's approval for him as well as for me.

I began to understand that for anyone so obviously weak and irre- 34 sponsible as I, only a life of self-sacrifice and abnegation could work. I wanted to be consumed by Jehovah, to be locked so closely into the straitjacket of His embrace that I would be impervious to the devilish temptations my irritable, independent intelligence threw up in my path.

I wished to be eaten up alive; and my wish was granted. When I 35 was nineteen, I was accepted into Bethel, the headquarters organization of Jehovah's Witnesses, where I worked and lived, one of twelve young women among two hundred and fifty men, for three years. "Making nice" had paid off. Every minute of my waking life was accounted for; there was no leisure in which to cultivate vice or reflection. I called myself happy. I worked as a housekeeper for my brothers, making thirty beds a day, sweeping and vacuuming and waxing and washing fifteen rooms a day (in addition to proselytizing in my "free time"); I daily washed the bathtub thirty men had bathed in. In fact, the one demural I made during those years was to ask — I found it so onerous — if perhaps the brothers, many of whom worked in the Witnesses' factory, could not clean out their own bathtub (thirty layers of grease is a lot of grease). I was told by the male overseer who supervised housekeepers that Jehovah had assigned me this "privilege." And I told myself I was lucky.

I felt myself to be even luckier — indeed, blessed — when, after   36
two years of this servant's work, one of Jehovah's middlemen, the president of the Watch Tower Bible and Tract Society, told me that he was assigning me to proofread Watch Tower publications. He accompanied this benediction with a warning: this new honor, I was told, was to be a test of my integrity — "Remember in all things to defer to the brothers; you will have to guard your spirit against pride and vanity. Satan will try now to tempt you as never before."

And defer I did. There were days when I felt literally as if my eter-   37
nal destiny hung upon a comma: if the brother with whom I worked decided a comma should go out where I wanted to put one in, I prayed to Jehovah to forgive me for that presumptuous comma. I was perfectly willing to deny the existence of a split infinitive if that would placate my brother. I denied and denied — commas, split infinitives, my sexuality, my intelligence, my femaleness, my yearning to be part of the world — until suddenly with a great silent shifting and shuddering, and with more pain than I had ever experienced or expect to experience again, I broke. I woke up one morning, packed my bags, and walked out of that place. I was twenty-two; and I had to learn how to begin to live. It required a great deal of courage; I do not think I will ever be capable of that much courage again.

The full story of life in that institution and the ramifications of my   38
decision to leave it is too long to tell here; and it will take me the rest of my life to understand fully the ways in which everything I have ever done since has been colored and informed by the guilt that was my daily bread for so many dry years, by the desperate need for approval that allowed me to be swallowed up whole by a devouring religion, by the carefully fostered desire to "make nice" and to be "a good girl,"

by the conviction that I was nothing and nobody unless I served a cause superior to that of my own necessities.

Arnold, of course, foresaw the difficulty; when I left religion, he 39 said, "Now you will be just like the rest of us." With no guiding passion, he meant; uncertain, he meant, and often muddled and confused, and always struggling. And he wept.

CONSIDERATIONS

1. Do you think that the portrayal of the author's eleven-year-old daughter in paragraphs 1 through 4 is realistic? Does Anna have the attitudes of a modern child or a modern adult?
2. How did the author's religious upbringing affect her sexual development? What specific doctrines and attitudes toward women influenced her image of herself?
3. How did her relationship with Arnold challenge Harrison's religious beliefs? How did she attempt to resolve this spiritual crisis?
4. Clarify Arnold's attitude in the final paragraph. Is he congratulating or criticizing Harrison? What are the overtones of the final sentence?
5. WRITING TOPIC. In the religion you know best, what signs of sexism do you find expressed in specific doctrines, stories, images, or customs? In 700 words, analyze woman's role in one particular sect. If its view of women contradicts its other religious values, explain the inconsistency of beliefs. If you find signs of woman's subordination equalized by other advantages, explain the balance.

Bernard Malamud

ANGEL LEVINE

◊

BERNARD MALAMUD (b. 1914), a professor of English at Bennington College, writes fiction that brought him greatest acclaim during the 1950s and 1960s. He grew up in Brooklyn and graduated from City College in New York City. After teaching evening high school and earning a master's degree from Columbia University, he set out with his wife and baby to Oregon where he taught at Oregon State College and devoted himself to writing serious fiction. His first novel, *The Natural* (1952), was recently made into a film starring Robert Redford. His other books include *The Assistant* (1957), *A New Life* (1962), a comic account of a New York English professor's attempt to start life over at a West Coast university, and a volume of short stories, *The Magic Barrel* (1958), which included "Angel Levine" and won Malamud a National Book Award. His most recent novel is *God's Grace* (1982), an imaginative description of life after a nuclear war. Malamud's stories have been collected in *The Stories of Bernard Malamud* (1983). His fiction is often mythical, symbolic, and allegorical, especially in Malamud's portrayal of Jews as symbols for Everyman. For instance, the hero of the following story struggles with the universal problem of faith: how to believe what is unreasonable, impossibly unlikely, and yet true. "Angel Levine" was filmed for television.

Manischevitz, a tailor, in his fifty-first year suffered many reverses 1
and indignities. Previously a man of comfortable means, he overnight
lost all he had, when his establishment caught fire, after a metal con-
tainer of cleaning fluid exploded, and burned to the ground. Although
Manischevitz was insured against fire, damage suits by two customers
who had been hurt in the flames deprived him of every penny he had
saved. At almost the same time, his son, of much promise, was killed
in the war, and his daughter, without so much as a word of warning,
married a lout and disappeared with him as off the face of the earth.

Thereafter Manischevitz was victimized by excruciating backaches and found himself unable to work even as a presser — the only kind of work available to him — for more than an hour or two daily, because beyond that the pain from standing was maddening. His Fanny, a good wife and mother, who had taken in washing and sewing, began before his eyes to waste away. Suffering shortness of breath, she at last became seriously ill and took to her bed. The doctor, a former customer of Manischevitz, who out of pity treated them, at first had difficulty diagnosing her ailment, but later put it down as hardening of the arteries at an advanced stage. He took Manischevitz aside, prescribed complete rest for her, and in whispers gave him to know there was little hope.

Throughout his trials Manischevitz had remained somewhat stoic,   2 almost unbelieving that all this had descended on his head, as if it were happening, let us say, to an acquaintance or some distant relative; it was in sheer quantity of woe, incomprehensible. It was also ridiculous, unjust, and because he had always been a religious man, an affront to God. Manischevitz believed this in all his suffering. When his burden had grown too crushingly heavy to be borne he prayed in his chair with shut hollow eyes: "My dear God, sweetheart, did I deserve that this should happen to me?" Then recognizing the worthlessness of it, he set aside the complaint and prayed humbly for assistance: "Give Fanny back her health, and to me for myself that I shouldn't feel pain in every step. Help now or tomorrow is too late." And Manischevitz wept.

Manischevitz's flat, which he had moved into after the disastrous   3 fire, was a meager one, furnished with a few sticks of chairs, a table, and bed, in one of the poorer sections of the city. There were three rooms: a small, poorly papered living room; an apology for a kitchen with a wooden icebox; and the comparatively large bedroom where Fanny lay in a sagging secondhand bed, gasping for breath. The bedroom was the warmest room in the house and it was here, after his outburst to God, that Manischevitz, by the light of two small bulbs overhead, sat reading his Jewish newspaper. He was not truly reading because his thoughts were everywhere; however the print offered a convenient resting place for his eyes, and a word or two, when he permitted himself to comprehend them, had the momentary effect of helping him forget his troubles. After a short while he discovered, to his surprise, that he was actively scanning the news, searching for an item of great interest to him. Exactly what he thought he would read he couldn't say — until he realized, with some astonishment, that he was expecting to discover something about himself. Manischevitz put his paper down and looked up with the distinct impression that someone had come into the apartment, though he could not remember having heard the sound of the door opening. He looked around: the room was very still, Fanny sleeping, for once, quietly. Half frightened, he watched her until he was satisfied she wasn't dead; then, still disturbed by the thought of an unannounced visitor, he stumbled into the living room and there had the shock of his life, for at the table sat a black man reading a newspaper he had folded up to fit into one hand.

"What do you want here?" Manischevitz asked in fright.   4

The Negro put down the paper and glanced up with a gentle ex- 5 pression. "Good evening." He seemed not to be sure of himself, as if he had got into the wrong house. He was a large man, bonily built, with a heavy head covered by a hard derby, which he made no attempt to remove. His eyes seemed sad, but his lips, above which he wore a slight mustache, sought to smile; he was not otherwise prepossessing. The cuffs of his sleeves, Manischevitz noted, were frayed to the lining, and the dark suit was badly fitted. He had very large feet. Recovering from his fright, Manischevitz guessed he had left the door open and was being visited by a case worker from the Welfare Department — some came at night — for he had recently applied for welfare. Therefore he lowered himself into a chair opposite the Negro, trying, before the man's uncertain smile, to feel comfortable. The former tailor sat stiffly but patiently at the table, waiting for the investigator to take out his pad and pencil and begin asking questions; but before long he became convinced the man intended to do nothing of the sort.

"Who are you?" Manischevitz at last asked uneasily.   6

"If I may, insofar as one is able to, identify myself, I bear the name 7 of Alexander Levine."

In spite of his troubles Manischevitz felt a smile growing on his 8 lips. "You said Levine?" he politely inquired.

The Negro nodded. "That is exactly right."   9

Carrying the jest further, Manischevitz asked, "You are maybe 10 Jewish?"

"All my life I was, willingly."   11

The tailor hesitated. He had heard of black Jews but had never met   12
one. It gave an unusual sensation.

Recognizing in afterthought something odd about the tense of Le-   13
vine's remark, he said doubtfully, "You ain't Jewish any more?"

Levine at this point removed his hat, revealing a very white part in   14
his black hair, but quickly replaced it. He replied, "I have recently
been disincarnated into an angel. As such, I offer you my humble assistance, if to offer is within my province and power — in the best
sense." He lowered his eyes in apology. "Which calls for added explanation: I am what I am granted to be, and at present the completion is
in the future."

"What kind of angel is this?" Manischevitz gravely asked.   15

"A bona fide angel of God, within prescribed limitations," an-   16
swered Levine, "not to be confused with the members of any particular sect, order, or organization here on earth operating under a similar
name."

Manischevitz was thoroughly disturbed. He had been expecting   17
something, but not this. What sort of mockery was it — provided that
Levine was an angel — of a faithful servant who had from childhood
lived in the synagogues, concerned with the word of God?

To test Levine he asked, "Then where are your wings?"   18

The Negro blushed as well as he could. Manischevitz understood   19
this from his altered expression. "Under certain circumstances we lose
privileges and prerogatives upon returning to earth, no matter for
what purpose or endeavoring to assist whomsoever."

"So tell me," Manischevitz said triumphantly, "how did you get   20
here?"

"I was translated."   21

Still troubled, the tailor said, "If you are a Jew, say the blessing for   22
bread."

Levine recited it in sonorous Hebrew.   23

Although moved by the familiar words Manischevitz still felt   24
doubt he was dealing with an angel.

"If you are an angel," he demanded somewhat angrily, "give me   25
the proof."

Levine wet his lips. "Frankly, I cannot perform either miracles or   26
near-miracles, due to the fact that I am in a condition of probation.
How long that will persist or even consist depends on the outcome."

Manischevitz racked his brains for some means of causing Levine 27
positively to reveal his true identity, when the Negro spoke again:
"It was given me to understand that both your wife and you require 28
assistance of a salubrious nature?"
The tailor could not rid himself of the feeling that he was the butt 29
of a jokester. Is this what a Jewish angel looks like? he asked himself.
This I am not convinced.
He asked a last question. "So if God sends to me an angel, why a 30
black? Why not a white that there are so many of them?"
"It was my turn to go next," Levine explained. 31
Manischevitz could not be persuaded. "I think you are a faker." 32
Levine slowly rose. His eyes indicated disappointment and worry. 33
"Mr. Manischevitz," he said tonelessly, "if you should desire me to be
of assistance to you any time in the near future, or possibly before, I
can be found" — he glanced at his fingernails — "in Harlem."
He was by then gone. 34

The next day Manischevitz felt some relief from his backache and 35
was able to work four hours at pressing. The day after, he put in six
hours; and the third day four again. Fanny sat up a little and asked for
some halvah to suck. But after the fourth day the stabbing, breaking
ache afflicted his back, and Fanny again lay supine, breathing with
blue-lipped difficulty.
Manischevitz was profoundly disappointed at the return of his ac- 36
tive pain and suffering. He had hoped for a longer interval of ease-
ment, long enough to have a thought other than of himself and his
troubles. Day by day, minute after minute, he lived in pain, pain his
only memory, questioning the necessity of it, inveighing, though with
affection, against God. Why *so much*, Gottenyu? If He wanted to
teach His servant a lesson for some reason, some cause — the nature
of His nature — to teach him, say, for reasons of his weakness, his
pride, perhaps, during his years of prosperity, his frequent neglect of
God — to give him a little lesson, why then any of the tragedies that
had happened to him, any *one* would have sufficed to chasten him.
But *all together* — the loss of both his children, his means of liveli-
hood, Fanny's health and his — that was too much to ask one frail-
boned man to endure. Who, after all, was Manischevitz that he had
been given so much to suffer? A tailor. Certainly not a man of talent.
Upon him suffering was largely wasted. It went nowhere, into noth-

ing: into more suffering. His pain did not earn him bread, nor fill the
cracks in the wall, nor lift, in the middle of the night, the kitchen
table; only lay upon him, sleepless, so sharply oppressive that he could
many times have cried out yet not heard himself this misery.

In this mood he gave no thought to Mr. Alexander Levine, but at 37
moments when the pain wavered, slightly diminishing, he sometimes
wondered if he had been mistaken to dismiss him. A black Jew and
angel to boot — very hard to believe, but suppose he *had* been sent to
succor him, and he, Manischevitz, was in his blindness too blind to
understand? It was this thought that put him on the knife-point of
agony.

Therefore the tailor, after much self-questioning and continuing 38
doubt, decided he would seek the self-styled angel in Harlem. Of
course he had great difficulty because he had not asked for specific directions, and movement was tedious to him. The subway took him to
116th Street, and from there he wandered in the open dark world. It
was vast and its lights lit nothing. Everywhere were shadows, often
moving. Manischevitz hobbled along with the aid of a cane, and not
knowing where to seek in the blackened tenement buildings, would
look fruitlessly through store windows. In the stores he saw people and
everybody was black. It was an amazing thing to observe. When he
was too tired, too unhappy to go farther, Manischevitz stopped in
front of a tailor's shop. Out of familiarity with the appearance of it,
with some sadness he entered. The tailor, an old skinny man with a
mop of woolly gray hair, was sitting cross-legged on his workbench,
sewing a pair of tuxedo pants that had a razor slit all the way down the
seat.

"You'll excuse me, please, gentleman," said Manischevitz, admir- 39
ing the tailor's deft thimbled fingerwork, "but you know maybe somebody by the name Alexander Levine?"

The tailor, who, Manischevitz thought, seemed a little antagonistic 40
to him, scratched his scalp.

"Cain't say I ever heared dat name." 41

"Alex-ander Lev-ine," Manischevitz repeated it. 42

The man shook his head. "Cain't say I heared." 43

Manischevitz remembered to say: "He is an angel, maybe." 44

"Oh *him*," said the tailor, clucking. "He hang out in dat honky- 45
tonk down here a ways." He pointed with his skinny finger and returned to sewing the pants.

Manischevitz crossed the street against a red light and was almost 46 run down by a taxi. On the block after the next, the sixth store from the corner was a cabaret, and the name in sparkling lights was Bella's. Ashamed to go in, Manischevitz gazed through the neon-lit window, and when the dancing couples had parted and drifted away, he discovered at a table on the side, toward the rear, Alexander Levine.

He was sitting alone, a cigarette butt hanging from the corner of 47 his mouth, playing solitaire with a dirty pack of cards, and Manischevitz felt a touch of pity for him, because Levine had deteriorated in appearance. His derby hat was dented and had a gray smudge. His ill-fitting suit was shabbier, as if he had been sleeping in it. His shoes and trouser cuffs were muddy, and his face covered with an impenetrable stubble the color of licorice. Manischevitz, though deeply disappointed, was about to enter, when a big-breasted Negress in a purple evening gown appeared before Levine's table, and with much laughter through many white teeth, broke into a vigorous shimmy. Levine looked at Manischevitz with a haunted expression, but the tailor was too paralyzed to move or acknowledge it. As Bella's gyrations continued Levine rose, his eyes lit in excitement. She embraced him with vigor, both his hands clasped around her restless buttocks, and they tangoed together across the floor, loudly applauded by the customers. She seemed to have lifted Levine off his feet and his large shoes hung limp as they danced. They slid past the windows where Manischevitz, white-faced, stood staring in. Levine winked slyly and the tailor left for home.

Fanny lay at death's door. Through shrunken lips she muttered 48 concerning her childhood, the sorrows of the marriage bed, the loss of her children; yet wept to live. Manischevitz tried not to listen, but even without ears he would have heard. It was not a gift. The doctor panted up the stairs, a broad but bland, unshaven man (it was Sunday), and soon shook his head. A day at most, or two. He left at once to spare himself Manischevitz's multiplied sorrow; the man who never stopped hurting. He would someday get him into a public home.

Manischevitz visited a synagogue and there spoke to God, but God 49 had absented himself. The tailor searched his heart and found no hope. When she died, he would live dead. He considered taking his life although he knew he wouldn't. Yet it was something to consider.

Considering, you existed. He railed against God — Can you love a rock, a broom, an emptiness? Baring his chest, he smote the naked bones, cursing himself for having, beyond belief, believed.

Asleep in a chair that afternoon, he dreamed of Levine. He was 50 standing before a faded mirror, preening small decaying opalescent wings. "This means," mumbled Manischevitz, as he broke out of sleep, "that it is possible he could be an angel." Begging a neighbor lady to look in on Fanny and occasionally wet her lips with water, he drew on his thin coat, gripped his walking stick, exchanged some pennies for a subway token, and rode to Harlem. He knew this act was the last desperate one of his woe: to go seeking a black magician to restore his wife to invalidism. Yet if there was no choice, he did at least what was chosen.

He hobbled to Bella's, but the place seemed to have changed 51 hands. It was now, as he breathed, a synagogue in a store. In the front, toward him, were several rows of empty wooden benches. In the rear stood the Ark, its portals of rough wood covered with rainbows of sequins; under it a long table on which lay the sacred scroll unrolled, illuminated by the dim light from a bulb on a chain overhead. Around the table, as if frozen to it and the scroll, which they all touched with their fingers, sat four Negroes wearing skullcaps. Now as they read the Holy Word, Manischevitz could, through the plate-glass window, hear the singsong chant of their voices. One of them was old, with a gray beard. One was bubble-eyed. One was humpbacked. The fourth was a boy, no older than thirteen. Their heads moved in rhythmic swaying. Touched by this sight from his childhood and youth, Manischevitz entered and stood silent in the rear.

"Neshoma," said bubble eyes, pointing to the word with a stubby 52 finger. "Now what dat mean?"

"That's the word that means soul," said the boy. He wore eye- 53 glasses.

"Let's git on wid de commentary," said the old man. 54

"Ain't necessary," said the humpback. "Souls is immaterial sub- 55 stance. That's all. The soul is derived in that manner. The immateriality is derived from the substance, and they both, causally an' otherwise, derived from the soul. There can be no higher."

"That's the highest." 56

"Over de top." 57

"Wait a minute," said bubble eyes. "I don't see what is dat imma- 58
terial substance. How come de one gits hitched up to de odder?" He
addressed the humpback.

"Ask me somethin' hard. Because it is substanceless immateriality. 59
It couldn't be closer together, like all the parts of the body under one
skin — closer."

"Hear now," said the old man. 60

"All you done is switched de words." 61

"It's the primum mobile, the substanceless substance from which 62
comes all things that were incepted in the idea — you, me, and everything and -body else."

"Now how did all dat happen? Make it sound simple." 63

"It de speerit," said the old man. "On de face of de water moved 64
de speerit. An' dat was good. It say so in de Book. From de speerit ariz
de man."

"But now listen here. How come it become substance if it all de 65
time a spirit?"

"God alone done dat." 66

"Holy! Holy! Praise His Name." 67

"But has dis spirit got some kind of a shade or color?" asked bubble 68
eyes, deadpan.

"Man, of course not. A spirit is a spirit." 69

"Then how come we is colored?" he said with a triumphant glare. 70

"Ain't got nothing to do wid dat." 71

"I still like to know." 72

"God put the spirit in all things," answered the boy. "He put it in 73
the green leaves and the yellow flowers. He put it with the gold in the
fishes and the blue in the sky. That's how come it came to us."

"Amen." 74

"Praise Lawd and utter loud His speechless Name." 75

"Blow de bugle till it bust de sky." 76

They fell silent, intent upon the next word. Manischevitz, with 77
doubt, approached them.

"You'll excuse me," he said. "I am looking for Alexander Levine. 78
You know him maybe?"

"That's the angel," said the boy. 79

"Oh *him*," snuffed bubble eyes. 80

"You'll find him at Bella's. It's the establishment right down the 81
street," the humpback said.

Manischevitz said he was sorry that he could not stay, thanked 82 them, and limped across the street. It was already night. The city was dark and he could barely find his way.

But Bella's was bursting with jazz and the blues. Through the win- 83 dow Manischevitz recognized the dancing crowd and among them sought Levine. He was sitting loose-lipped at Bella's side table. They were tippling from an almost empty whiskey fifth. Levine had shed his old clothes, wore a shiny new checkered suit, pearl-gray derby hat, cigar, and big, two-tone, button shoes. To the tailor's dismay, a drunken look had settled upon his formerly dignified face. He leaned toward Bella, tickled her earlobe with his pinky while whispering words that sent her into gales of raucous laughter. She fondled his knee.

Manischevitz, girding himself, pushed open the door and was not 84 welcomed.

"This place reserved."   85

"Beat it, pale puss."   86

"Exit, Yankel, semitic trash."   87

But he moved toward the table where Levine sat, the crowd break- 88 ing before him as he hobbled forward.

"Mr. Levine," he spoke in a trembly voice. "Is here Manischevitz." 89

Levine glared blearily. "Speak yo' piece, son."   90

Manischevitz shivered. His back plagued him. Tremors tormented 91 his legs. He looked around, everybody was all ears.

"You'll excuse me. I would like to talk to you in a private place." 92

"Speak, Ah is a private pusson."   93

Bella laughed piercingly. "Stop it, boy, you killin' me."   94

Manischevitz, no end disturbed, considered fleeing but Levine ad- 95 dressed him:

"Kindly state the pu'pose of yo' communication with yo's truly." 96

The tailor wet cracked lips. "You are Jewish. This I am sure."   97

Levine rose, nostrils flaring. "Anythin' else yo' got to say?"   98

Manischevitz's tongue lay like a slab of stone.   99

"Speak now or fo'ever hold off."   100

Tears blinded the tailor's eyes. Was ever man so tried? Should he 101 say he believed a half-drunk Negro was an angel?

The silence slowly petrified.   102

Manischevitz was recalling scenes of his youth as a wheel in his 103 mind whirred: believe, do not, yes, no, yes, no. The pointer pointed to yes, to between yes and no, to no, no it was yes. He sighed. It moved but one still had to make a choice.

"I think you are an angel from God." He said it in a broken voice, thinking, If you said it it was said. If you believed it you must say it. If you believed, you believed. 104

The hush broke. Everybody talked but the music began and they went on dancing. Bella, grown bored, picked up the cards and dealt herself a hand. 105

Levine burst into tears. "How you have humiliated me." 106

Manischevitz apologized. 107

"Wait'll I freshen up." Levine went to the men's room and returned in his old suit. 108

No one said goodbye as they left. 109

They rode to the flat via subway. As they walked up the stairs Manischevitz pointed with his cane at his door. 110

"That's all been taken care of," Levine said. "You go in while I take off." 111

Disappointed that it was so soon over, but torn by curiosity, Manischevitz followed the angel up three flights to the roof. When he got there the door was already padlocked. 112

Luckily he could see through a small broken window. He heard an odd noise, as though of a whirring of wings, and when he strained for a wider view, could have sworn he saw a dark figure borne aloft on a pair of strong black wings. 113

A feather drifted down. Manischevitz gasped as it turned white, but it was only snowing. 114

He rushed downstairs. In the flat Fanny wielded a dust mop under the bed, and then upon the cobwebs on the wall. 115

"A wonderful thing, Fanny," Manischevitz said. "Believe me, there are Jews everywhere." 116

CONSIDERATIONS

1. In paragraphs 1 and 2, what events are condensed and summarized? In contrast, what details are given sharp focus in the foreground of the story?
2. In the first section (through paragraph 34), what is the tailor's reaction to Levine's appearance, manner, and explanations? What is your response to this portrayal of a black man?

3. How does Manischevitz view the importance and meaning of his suffering? Is his view of himself modest? Is it devout?
4. How do the tailor's two trips to Harlem affect his belief? What is your response to the mixture of jive talk, dialect, and doctrine that Manischevitz hears in the synagogue? Compare this explicit discussion of religious philosophy with the final four paragraphs of the story.
5. Why does Levine cry that Manischevitz has humiliated him? How has he been humiliated?
6. In the final sentence Manischevitz finds it difficult to say exactly what he means. Explain what you think he really would like to say. How does what he actually says affect our final view of his character and experience? Does the ending make the story more religious or less religious in meaning and tone?
7. WRITING TOPIC. In 500 words, write a lecture, a sermon, or a commentary on the conflict between reason and faith as the problem is presented in this story. Why is the conflict treated humorously? What is shown to be trustworthy in any of our convictions? Remember that you are writing to *instruct* your audience by explaining what you think the story says about the conflict.

James Wright

A BLESSING

◊

James Wright (1927–1980), a poet and teacher, was born in rural Ohio, not far from Kenyon College. As a student at Kenyon, he studied literature and began writing poetry. After serving in the army in Japan, Wright took a Ph.D. degree at the University of Washington. He taught at several universities and published six volumes of poetry as well as notable translations of German and Chilean verse. His *Collected Poems* (1971) won a Pulitzer Prize. In the following poem Wright responds with joy to a moment of surprising beauty.

Just off the highway to Rochester, Minnesota,
Twilight bounds softly forth on the grass.
And the eyes of those two Indian ponies
Darken with kindness.
They have come gladly out of the willows   5
To welcome my friend and me.
We step over the barbed wire into the pasture
Where they have been grazing all day, alone.
They ripple tensely, they can hardly contain their happiness
That we have come.   10
They bow shyly as wet swans. They love each other.
There is no loneliness like theirs.
At home once more,
They begin munching the young tufts of spring in the darkness.
I would like to hold the slenderer one in my arms,   15
For she has walked over to me
And nuzzled my left hand.
She is black and white,
Her mane falls wild on her forehead,

And the light breeze moves me to caress her long ear 20
That is delicate as the skin over a girl's wrist.
Suddenly I realize
That if I stepped out of my body I would break
Into blossom.

CONSIDERATIONS

1. It is odd to say about two ponies that "They love each other." How does the poet come to this intuition? What specific qualities of love does he observe in the first twelve lines that make his supposition sound believable to us?
2. What unusual word choice do you find in line 15? How does the diction help explain his impulse?
3. In several ways line 1 differs from the rest of the poem. What are the effects of the contrasts that you observe?
4. WRITING TOPIC. In a 300-word essay, explain why the poem is titled "A Blessing." Consider such questions as who is blessed? How does the blessing occur? What does the blessing convey?
5. WRITING TOPIC. In a 500-word essay, compare the "blessing" in Wright's poem with the miracle or blessing in Malamud's story. What, if any, are the similarities in the way both authors envision the "body"? What are the similarities and differences in the way both authors portray revelation?

Alan W. Watts

SPIRITUAL LIVING

◊

ALAN W. WATTS (1915–1973), a religious philosopher and popularizer of Oriental thought, was born in England and emigrated to the United States in 1938. He earned degrees in divinity at Seabury-Western Theological Seminary and at the University of Vermont. Ordained as an Anglican priest, he served as a religious counselor and a professor of religion. While teaching at Northwestern University, he broke away from conventional Christianity and did not thereafter belong to any sect. "Partisanship in religion closes the mind," he said. During the 1950s and 1960s Watts was an important catalyst in the upsurge of American interest in Zen Buddhism. The following excerpt from his very widely read book *The Meaning of Happiness* (1940) tries to explain the nearly ineffable quality of true spirituality.

The Religious Experience

Religious experience is something like artistic or musical inspiration, though inspiration is a word that through misuse has unfortunate associations; religious experience is not "uplift" or flighty emotionalism. Strictly speaking, a composer is inspired when melody emerges from the depths of his mind, how or why we do not know. To convey that melody to others he writes it down on paper, employing a technical knowledge which enables him to name the notes which he hears in his mind. This fact is important: his technical knowledge does not *create* the tune in his mind; it simply provides him with a complicated alphabet, and is no more the source of music than the literary alphabet and the rules of grammar are the sources of men's ideas. If he is writing a symphony he will want to orchestrate his melody, but to do this he does not look up the books on harmony and orchestration to find out what combinations of notes he is advised by the rules to put together. He has heard the whole symphony in his mind with every instrument playing its independent part, and his knowledge of orches- 1 tration and harmony simply enables him to tell which is which. What music teachers call the "rules" of harmony are just observations on the harmonies most usually used by such people as Bach and Beethoven. Bach and Beethoven did not use them because they were in the rules but because they liked their sound, and if peoples' tastes change so that they like other sounds then the old harmonic forms are replaced. It is necessary for a composer to study harmony in order that he may be able to identify chords which he hears in his mind, but he does not use his knowledge to *construct* chords unless he is a mere imitator of other people. In the same way, language is used not to create thoughts but to express them, and mastery of prose does not make a great thinker.

The spiritual genius works in the same way as the musical genius.   2
He has a wider scope because his technique of expression, his alphabet, is every possible human activity. For some reason there arises in his soul a feeling of the most profound happiness, not because of some special event, but because of the whole of life. This is not necessarily contentment or joy; it is rather that he feels himself completely united to the power that moves the universe, whatever that may be. This feeling he expresses in two ways, firstly by living a certain kind of life, and secondly by translating his feeling into the form of thoughts and words.

People who have not had this feeling make observations on his ac-   3
tions and words, and from them formulate the "rules" of religious morality and theology. But this involves a strange distortion, for as a rule the observer goes about his work in the wrong way. When the mystic says, "I feel united with God," the observer is interested primarily in the statement as a revelation of the existence of God, and goes on to consult the mystic's other sayings to find out what kind of God this is and in what manner He behaves. He is interested only secondarily in the mystic's feeling as a feeling, and it occurs to him only as an after thought that it might be possible for himself to feel united with God. Whereat he proceeds to achieve this by trying to think in the same way as the mystic; that is to say, he takes the mystic's *ideas* and substitutes them for his own. He also tries to behave in the same way, imitating the mystic's actions. In other words, he tries to perform a kind of sympathetic magic, and in imitating the mystic's external forms deceives himself and others into thinking that he is really like him. But the important thing about the mystic was his feeling, not his

ideas and actions, for these were only reflections of the feeling, and a reflection existing without a light is a sham. Therefore just as great technical proficiency will not make a creative genius in music, morality, theology, and discipline will not make a genius in religion, for these things are results of religious experience, not causes, and by themselves can no more produce it than the tail can be made to wag the dog.

The Spiritual Irrelevance of Occultism

This is not the only example of confused thought in searching for religious experience. The other . . . is the opposition made between the spiritual and the material. Much depends, of course, on the precise meaning given to the word "spirit," but it should certainly not be confused with the word "psychic" and many things described as spiritual are clearly psychic. There is no definite rule as to how these words should be used, so to be explicit we have to make our own rules. And the spiritual, in the sense in which it is used here, is no more opposed to the material than white is opposed to long. The opposite of white is black, and of long, short; white things are no more necessarily short than material things are unspiritual. But we can say that the material and the psychic are opposed, if only in the sense that they are opposite ends of the same stick. Psychic things belong to the world explored by occultism and "psychic science" — telepathy, clairvoyance, mind-reading, and all those phenomena which appear to require sixth or seventh senses whose development seems unquestionably to be assisted by ascetic practices. The so-called spiritual realms inhabited by departed souls, angels, elementals, and demons, and the source of beatific visions, would be most correctly described as psychic if we are to allow that such things have actual, objective existence. And this world is the logical opposite of the material world because it belongs in the same category; it contains forms and substances, even though its substance may be of a wholly different order from what we understand as matter. People who are in touch with this world, however, are not necessarily spiritual people; they may have unusual faculties of perception and be familiar with the beings and ways of a more glorious world than our own, but this is a matter of *faculty* and *knowledge*, not of spirituality. The technique of living employed by such people is more highly evolved than that of ordinary men, just as the technique of the opera is more complicated than that of pure drama. Opera involves not only acting but singing, playing music, and sometimes dancing, but this does not make it a greater art.

Spirituality belongs in the same category as happiness and freedom, and strictly speaking there is no such thing as the spiritual *world*. If psychic people are to be believed, there is a psychic *world*, and because it is a world entry into it is simply an enlargement of experience. But experience as such never made anyone either free or happy, and in so far as freedom and happiness are concerned with experience the important thing is not experience itself but what is learned from it. Some people learn from experience and others do not; some learn much from a little, others learn little from much. "Without going out of my house," said the Chinese sage Lao Tzu, "I know the whole universe." For the spiritual is in no way divided from the material, nor from the psychic, nor from any other aspect of life. To find it, it is not necessary to go from one state of consciousness to another, from one set of senses to another or from one world to another. Such journeying about in the fields of experience takes you neither toward it nor away from it. In the words of the Psalmist:

> Whither shall I go from Thy spirit? Or whither shall I flee from Thy presence?
> If I ascend up into heaven, Thou art there: if I make my bed in hell, behold, Thou art there.
> If I take the wings of the morning, and dwell in the uttermost parts of the sea; even there shall thy hand lead me, and thy right hand shall hold me.
> If I say, Surely the darkness shall cover me; even the night shall be light about me.
> Yea, the darkness hideth not from Thee; but the night shineth as the day: the darkness and the light are both alike to Thee.

In fact the spiritual world, if we must use the term, is this world and all possible worlds, and spiritual experience is what we are experiencing at this moment and at any moment — if we look at it in the right way.

Union with Life

This is the difference between religious or spiritual experience and artistic inspiration; both are analogous, but the latter is particularized.

The artist or musician has a special type of creative genius; he creates pictures or music, for his genius is a specialized gift. But the spiritual genius is not a specialist, for he does not just paint or compose creatively: he *lives* creatively, and his tools are not confined to brush, pen or instrument; they are all things touched by his hand. This is not to say that when he takes up a brush he can paint like Leonardo or that when he takes hammer and chisel he can work like a master-mason. Spiritual experience involves neither technical proficiency nor factual knowledge; it is no short-cut to things that must ordinarily be mastered by pains and practice. Nor is spiritual experience necessarily expressed in any *particular* mode of life; its presence in any given individual cannot be judged by measurement in accordance with certain standards. It can only be felt intuitively, for creative living is not always outwardly distinguishable from any other kind of living; in fact, spiritual people are often at pains to appear as normal as possible. At the same time, although spiritual people may do exactly the same things as others, one feels that their actions are in some way different. There is a story of a Buddhist sage who was about to speak to his disciples when he found that he wanted more light. He pointed to a curtain covering one of the windows and instantly two of the disciples went and rolled it up, whereat the sage remarked, "One of them is right, but the other is wrong."

In itself, spirituality is purely an inner experience; it has no necessary effect whatsoever on one's outward behavior judged from the standards of efficiency and worldly-wisdom. This is not to say, however, that it is something absolutely private and personal, finding no expression that others can see. For spirituality is a deep sense of inner freedom based on the realization that one's self is in complete union and harmony with life, with God, with the Self of the universe or whatever that principle may be called. It is the realization that that union has existed from all time, even though one did not know it, and that nothing in all the world nor anything that oneself can do is able to destroy it. It is thus the sense that the whole might of the universe is at work in one's every thought and action, however trivial and small. In fact this is true of all men and all things, but only the spiritual man really knows it and his realization gives a subtly different quality to his life; all that he does becomes strangely alive, for though its outward appearance is perhaps the same as before it acquires a new meaning. It is this which other people notice, but if he has the gift for teaching they will see it in other ways as well. By his words as well as his deeds and his personal "atmosphere" they will understand that this realization has awakened in him a tremendous love for life in all its aspects.

Prose and the logic of philosophy cannot explain this love; one 8 might as well try to describe a beautiful face by a mathematical account of its measurements and proportions. It is a mixture of the joy of freedom, a childlike sense of wonder, and the inner sensation of absolute harmony with life as in the rhythm of an eternal dance such as the Hindus portray in the interlocked figures of Shiva and his bride. In one sense you feel that your life is not lived by you at all; the power of the universe, fate and destiny, God Himself, are directing all your motions and all your responsibilities are blown to the winds. In another sense you feel free to move as you wish; you seem to be moving life with the same vast power with which life moves you, and your littlest acts become filled with gigantic possibilities. Indeed, physicists tell us that the stars are affected when we lift a single finger. The result of these two feelings is that you no longer distinguish between what you do to life and what life does to you; it is as if two dancers moved in such perfect accord that the distinction between lead and response vanished, as if the two became one and the same motion. By the whirling, ever changing movement of this dance you are carried along without pause, but not like a drunken man in a torrent, for you as much as life are the source of the movement. And this is real freedom; it includes both freedom to move and to be moved; action and passivity are merged, and in spirituality as well as in marriage this is the fulfillment of love.

CONSIDERATIONS

1. According to the author, what is *inspiration?* How does it differ from knowledge or skill? To the artistic or spiritual genius, what is the usefulness of having knowledge and skill? Do you agree with Watts about inspiration?

2. How does Watts define *spirituality?* Do you think that his definition shows a religious bias? That is, does it fit the outlook of certain religions better than others?

3. If a complete spiritual state is induced by taking a drug, would that state of consciousness be a *religious* experience? If the spiritual state is induced

by kneeling and praying, fasting, performing rituals, or meditating, is that experience more religious than one induced by a drug? What is your view?

4. WRITING TOPIC. Considering the religion that you know best — which may or may not be a religion in which you were raised — how does that religion deal with pain and misery in personal experience? What are the specific images, themes, and remedies of unhappiness? How are feelings of unhappiness included, if at all, in acts of worship? In 500 words, describe one particular religion's acknowledgements of human suffering.

ADDITIONAL
WRITING TOPICS

◊

CONVICTIONS

1. In a 500-word essay, analyze the "scientific attitude" that you were taught in school. Was there a difference between the proclaimed ideals of science and the real messages you received from science instruction? Did science classes emphasize experiment? Speculation? Authority? Reasoning? Did science instruction affect your outlook on the rest of your experience? Looking back on it, what was the chief value of your science education in secondary school?

2. In 500 words, explain your views on a specific holy ritual, traditional religious observance, or sacred law that you are inclined to uphold or reject. For instance, communion, circumcision, baptism, fasting, and marriage rites all involve complex beliefs that you may accept fully, partly, or not at all. Explain what is meaningful and not meaningful to you in one particular religious observance.

3. In Robert Frost's poem "Design" (in the Insights), is the poet's attitude toward nature mainly scientific or mainly religious? While his outlook may include elements of both, decide which response is more central to the meaning of the poem. In 500 words, explain what meaning the poet finds in nature.

4. In a 500-word essay, suggest an alternative way to reclassify plants and animals. Is your system more "elegant" or more "ugly" than the present scientific system? (See Richard Morris's essay, "How Real is 'Real'?" for the use of "elegant" and "ugly" to describe theories.) Don't hesitate to be fanciful, humorous, or impractical in your proposed system, but treat your idea seriously as a model of reality different from the one we have.

5. Is science value-free, as Bertrand Russell claims in the Insights? Or is science value-laden? In 500 words, analyze the attitudes suggested in one chapter of a science textbook you are currently using. Discuss the concepts and the language.

6. Look again at Napoleon's remark in the Insights. Do you agree that religion protects the status quo in society? Or is religion a force for social change and reform? Based on your knowledge of a specific contemporary problem, write a 500-word essay on the role religion plays in social justice.

PART 8

DILEMMAS

Robert Frost, *The Road Not Taken*

Neil Chayet, *Law and Morality*

Leo Rosten, *Home Is Where to Learn How to Hate*

Forum, *Images of Fear*

George Orwell, *Shooting an Elephant*

Tillie Olsen, *I Stand Here Ironing*

Jonathan Schell, *The Choice*

Robert Jastrow, *An End and a Beginning*

Additional Writing Topics

INSIGHTS

Unreasoning and unreasonable human nature causes two nations to compete, though no economic necessity compels them to do so; it induces two political parties or religions with amazingly similar programs of salvation to fight each other bitterly, and it impels an Alexander or a Napoleon to sacrifice millions of lives in his attempt to unite the world under his scepter. We have been taught to regard some of the persons who have committed these and similar absurdities with respect, even as "great" men, we are wont to yield to the political wisdom of those in charge, and we are all so accustomed to these phenomena that most of us fail to realize how abjectly stupid and undesirable the historical mass behavior of humanity actually is.

– KONRAD LORENZ

◊

Logic is the art of going wrong with confidence.

– ANONYMOUS

◊

The most fundamental error that people make when weighing lies is to evaluate the costs and benefits of a particular lie in an isolated case, and then to favor the lie if the benefits seem to outweigh the costs. In doing so, they overlook two factors. Bias, first of all, skews all judgment, but never more than in the search for good reasons to deceive. Liars tend to overestimate their own good will, high motives, and chances to escape detection, to understate the intelligence of the deceived and to ignore their rights.

Second, in focusing on the isolated lie it is easy to ignore the most significant costs of lying: to ignore what lying — even in a good cause — does to the standards of those who tell the lies, as well as to their credibility; to overlook the effects of lies on the co-workers who witness them, and who may imitate them, or on others who learn about them and who may deceive in retaliation or merely to stay even. Above all, such a narrow focus ignores the cumulative effects of lies — many told for what seemed at the time "good reasons" — as they build up into vast institutional practices.

— SISSELA BOK

◇

Will it really profit us so much if we save our souls and lose the whole world?

— E. M. FORSTER

◇

More than any other time in history, mankind faces a crossroads. One path leads to despair and utter hopelessness. The other, to total extinction. Let us pray we have the wisdom to choose correctly.

— WOODY ALLEN

◇

Increasing familiarity with the curative powers of human tissues is likely, in the opinion of many, to foster a public attitude under which citizens will be considered to have a duty to make their dead bodies available for the aid of the sick, and the community will have valid claims upon its dead for the same purpose. It is well within contemplation that as medicine continues to find greater and greater uses for human tissues, we will come to see these claims upon the dead assuming the aspect of a public entitlement. If this happened, the human body would acquire some of the attitudes of property. The possibility of such a climate of opinion makes it necessary to reexamine the strength of our beliefs in personal autonomy and individual freedom.

— RUSSELL SCOTT

◇

Instinctual danger makes human beings intelligent. In periods of calm in instinctual life, when there is no danger, the individual can permit himself a certain degree of stupidity.

— ANNA FREUD

◇

To kill someone for committing murder is a punishment incomparably worse than the crime itself. Murder by legal sentence is immeasurably more terrible than murder by brigands.

— FYODOR DOSTOYEVSKI

◇

What the news has gained in volume and speed it appears to have lost in durability. Information is more available but also more perishable. Part of the reason may be the very nature of the electronic media. They offer the news in a present that has neither a past nor a future. You cannot look back up the page of a television broadcast to check what you have just seen, or down the page to see how it might relate to what follows. The pictures flicker on the screen and then are gone forever. We speak of a newspaper of record, but no one ever speaks of a television station of record. (Libraries of television news programs, for example, are few.) Through television, we are enclosed in a vivid present that is immediately not only replaced but effaced by another vivid present. That the increase in the horizontal spread of news, through the new global technology, may have been won at the expense of its vertical spread in time — in memory — is, in fact, suggested by the experience of countries that lack freedom, and so have been left out of the global revolution. In Poland, for example, news crawls laboriously from hand to hand by means of dog-eared samizdat but, once learned, leaves an indelible mark. There each event takes its place, and finds its meaning, in the historical chain, and no people is more occupied with its history than the Poles are. Behind the Iron Curtain, people obtain information with difficulty and retain it with ease. Here we obtain it with ease and retain it with difficulty. The new communications media may be giving rise to a new ignorance. Each generation brings a clean slate into the world. But the world itself is not a clean slate, and what happened before needs to be learned and remembered.

– THE NEW YORKER, April 15, 1985

Robert Frost

THE ROAD NOT TAKEN

◊

ROBERT FROST (1874–1963) was the great poet of rural New England, the region that appears in his poetry in unforgettable glimpses of birch trees glistening with ice, stone fences, apple orchards in blossom, and dark woods in the snowy night. He lived in New Hampshire and taught intermittently at Amherst College, at the University of Michigan (which, granted, is not in New England), and at Dartmouth College. By transforming the laconic statements and simple diction of Yankee farmers into an easily understandable, first-rate poetic language, Frost became the most widely read and widely honored American poet in his lifetime. He had reached the age of thirty-eight before his first book of poems was accepted for publication — in England, at that — but his second book, *North of Boston* (1914), established him as a notable poet even home in America. His complete works are collected in *The Poetry of Robert Frost* (1969). Judging from the following poem, Frost's life included critical periods of uncertainty and faint-heartedness.

Two roads diverged in a yellow wood,
And sorry I could not travel both
And be one traveller, long I stood
And looked down one as far as I could
To where it bent in the undergrowth;

Then took the other, as just as fair,
And having perhaps the better claim,
Because it was grassy and wanted wear;
Though as for that the passing there
Had worn them really about the same,   10

And both that morning equally lay
In leaves no step had trodden black.
Oh, I kept the first for another day!
Yet knowing how way leads on to way,
I doubted if I should ever come back.

I shall be telling this with a sigh
Somewhere ages and ages hence:
Two roads diverged in a wood, and I —
I took the one less travelled by,
And that has made all the difference.　　20

CONSIDERATIONS

1. How do we know that the choice was difficult to make? What kinds of indecision over the choice are suggested in the poem?
2. What are Frost's feelings after he makes the choice?
3. Does he think his choice was truly the better road? Or is it just the choice for better or worse that he has accepted as entirely his own?
4. WRITING TOPIC. Where did you go right or wrong in life? In a 500-word essay, develop your second thoughts about a choice, a direction, or an action you once took that you now see from a different perspective. What was the strongest factor in your decision at the time? What would be a stronger consideration now? In your outlook on the past event, do you now feel mainly regret, pride, embarrassment, relief, resentment, nostalgia, resignation, or some other attitude? Do you think that the consequences of your action have become more important or less important in the intervening time?

Neil Chayet

LAW AND MORALITY

◊

NEIL CHAYET (b. 1939) was educated at Tufts University and Harvard
Law School. In his law practice, he has often dealt with special legal
problems affecting health and medicine, such as drug abuse, the rights
of the mentally ill, and medical opinion as testimony in the courtroom.
He teaches courses in legal medicine at several medical schools in the
Boston area and also reaches a wide audience beyond his profession
with his radio program, which summarizes actual cases illustrating
legal and ethical perplexities. The following selection is one of his radio
"spots," collected in *Looking at the Law* (1981).

Can a court force you to give up part of your body to a relative if 1
you don't want to? That was the question recently brought before the
court of common pleas in Allegheny County, Pennsylvania. The case
involved a thirty-nine-year-old man who suffered from aplastic anemia, a rare disease of the bone marrow. The only chance the man had
was to receive a bone marrow transplant from a compatible donor,
and usually only close relatives can be compatible donors.

It turned out that the man had a cousin who could be a compatible 2
donor. There was only one hitch: The cousin didn't want to give up
any of his bone marrow — even though there was virtually no risk to
him, and the chances of his cousin recovering would be raised from
near zero to 50 percent. The man with aplastic anemia pleaded with
his cousin to let him have the transplant, but to no avail. As a last-
ditch measure he went to court asking the court to grant a preliminary
injunction ordering his cousin to give up twenty-one ounces of bone
marrow.

The court began its opinion noting it could find no authority for 3
such an order to be made. The plaintiff said there was a precedent in
an ancient statute of King Edward I, a law that was more than seven

hundred years old. That law said that an individual has a moral and legal obligation to secure the well-being of other members of society. But unfortunately for the plaintiff, since the thirteenth century not a single case could be found where such an obligation was enforced. In fact, to the contrary, the common law has consistently held that one human being is under no legal obligation to give aid or take action to save another human being or to rescue one.

The court said that such a rule, although revolting in a moral sense, 4 is founded upon the very essence of a free society, and while other societies may view things differently, our society has as its first principle respect for the individual — and society and government exist to protect that individual from being invaded and hurt by another.

The court did say that the refusal of the defendant was morally in- 5 defensible, but a society that respects the right of one individual must not sink its teeth into the jugular vein or neck of another — that would be revolting to our concepts of jurisprudence.

The plaintiff is dead now, but the common law remains intact.   6

CONSIDERATIONS

1. What explanations or attitudes might be part of the cousins' refusal to donate a bone marrow transplant? What reasons are precluded in the selection?
2. Why couldn't the court order what the judge considered the morally right action?
3. WRITING TOPIC. In a 500-word essay, reconsider an important argument that you lost even though you probably were right. What defeated you? What principles and rules were involved? Did they conflict? Were they upheld or broken? How should the argument have concluded?

Leo Rosten

HOME IS WHERE
TO LEARN HOW TO HATE

◊

LEO ROSTEN (b. 1908) was born in Poland and emigrated to the United States, where he was educated at the University of Chicago, earning a doctorate in political science. During the depression years, he took a part-time job teaching English to immigrant adults in night school, an experience that provided the material for his widely enjoyed collection of humorous short stories, *The Education of H*Y*M*A*N K*A*P*L*A*N* (1937), which he published under a pseudonym that he continued to use for his humorous pieces, Leonard Q. Ross. As a political observer Rosten reported on current events in his column "Dateline Europe"; he also lectured on politics at Columbia University and served in the federal government under several administrations. He is also a screenwriter, and his interest in popular entertainment is evident in his collection of Jewish wit, *The Joys of Yiddish* (1968). In this article, Rosten argues that we need to acknowledge and train our capacity to hate or else our hatreds acquire ungovernable force.

I once committed a lecture, to an entirely innocent group of 1 women, on "Pacifism and Its Problems." My theme was simple: The human race is plagued by powerful, irrational, intransigent passions; men could not kill each other unless they possessed the *capacity* to hate and the will to slaughter. During a war, each side even invests its killing with the highest moral purpose. Theologians of every faith, philosophers and psychologists of every bent, know that our tormented species is caught in a ceaseless struggle between good and evil, generosity and greed, love and hate. Men inflict unspeakable horrors upon each other because they hate what they fear, and kill what they hate.

So pacifism, I ruefully concluded, confronts an ancient, tragic, 2 almost insurmountable task: to mobilize reason and compassion against the terrible trio of insecurity, irrationality, and aggression. War, the most hideous of man's acts, has its roots not only in malevolent leaders or ambitious generals, megalomaniacal statesmen or deluded patriots — but in ordinary, decent men and women, who carry within themselves rages that can be aroused, passions that can be manipulated, emotions that can become so exacerbated that they become unbearable and cry for release — against an enemy.

After my lecture, the usual number of survivors came up to pay the 3 usual compliments and ask the usual questions. One pink-cheeked, beaming little dowager, who looked as if she had stepped right off the cover of a Mother's Day candy box, addressed me, with the utmost kindliness: "Any man who goes around saying God's children are capable of the horrid things you described should be stood up against a blank wall and shot dead!" Off she marched, trailing clouds of sweetness and light and love for her fellow men. (She never even let me ask why the wall had to be blank.)

I think what was wrong with that dear little old lady (as with so 4 many of our young rebels) is that she had never been taught how to hate properly. By "properly" I mean: (a) relevantly; (b) in proportion, fitting the thing or person hated; (c) without blind rage; (d) without guilt. Her love of "mankind" blinded her to her hatred of those who made her uneasy.

Where does hate begin? In the womb? During "the trauma of 5 birth"? In the crib? Because of spanking? Frustration? In "bad" homes or overly permissive kindergartens?

I do not know. Nor does anyone else; one or another authority pin- 6 points one or another source. But the fact that we do not know why and where hate originates in no way invalidates the fact that hate exists, and that it is deep, virulent, and dangerous. (We don't know what electricity is, either, but we use it.)

No one who has seen a baby scream until its face turns blue would 7 deny that the baby is convulsed by — call it fury. Anyone who has watched tots playing together would be foolish to deny their propensity to violence. For where does anger erupt more swiftly than among the very young? Where are impulses more nakedly displayed and more selfishly gratified? Where are baubles more fiercely guarded or

seized? Where are blows, kicks, bites, spits, pinches, and punches delivered with less hesitation?

The maudlin may praise childhood's "innocence," uttering sugary   8
prattle about the little angels in our midst. But if you will reflect upon
your own experience you will, I think, agree that it is not heaven but
hell that "lies about us in our infancy."

When hate flares up in a little darling (I say "when," not "if"),   9
what should one do? The question is like the one a thousand parents
ask a thousand times a day: "Should you spank a child?"

Now, no one would approve of parents who are so vicious as to say,   10
"Dear, let's have some fun: Let's beat up the kids." But "*should* one
spank . . ." is better asked: "What should you do *if you are angry
enough, for whatever reason, to want to spank a child?*" The real
problem is: how do you handle that anger?

Consider what you do if you do *not* spank, when you are angry   11
enough to want to. The child, of course, sees that you are angry.
What can it think?

(1) "Oh, he's mad. He's *real* mad. If *I* were that mad, I'd wallop,   12
I'd hit, I'd bite, I'd kick, I'd throw things, I'd knock him down, I'd
beat him. But he doesn't hit me. Oh, how much better he is than I.
Will I ever be that good?" (This is an awful burden to place on a
child.)

(2) "He's *mad*. He's really busting to hit me. Why doesn't he? Be-   13
cause he's afraid to! Because he knows that if he ever let go, he'd kill
me — which is what I've suspected all along he's wanted to do."(How
unwise to fortify this common childhood fantasy.)

(3) "He's mad, so mad he'd like to swat me. Why *doesn't* he? Why   14
doesn't he act like all the fathers of my friends? Why must I be the
only one who has never been spanked?" (How unwise to make your
child a pariah in his group.)

(4) "I made him mad, and I could understand his punishing me   15
because it's what I would do if I were in his place. When will he show
his anger? What do I have to *do* to make him hit me the way I deserve, and expect — and want?!" (How can you prolong a child's tortured waiting? How can you refuse to mete out the justice he may secretly crave? Children *want* restraints put upon their freedom, which
delivers them into the hands of their passion.)

Conclusion: If you are angry enough to want to spank a child, *it is*   16
cruel not to. A slap on the hand or a swat on the butt is clear, simple,
comprehensible. It releases the anger of the parent, resolves the
child's confusions, and clears the emotional air. I think Bernard Shaw
put it best: "Never strike a child in cold blood."

It grieves me to say that, to the best of our knowledge, hate is as   17
much a part of man as hunger. You can no more stop a child from
hating than you can stop him from dreaming. So we must each learn
how to manage hate, how to channel it, how to use it where hate is
justified — and how to teach our children to do these things, too.

To raise children by drumming into their minds that they do not   18
"really" hate is to tell them a fearful lie. To moon benignly to the
child who cries, "I *hate* you!" that (at that moment) he does not —
not *really* — is to confuse a child about an emotion he really feels,
knows he possesses, and cannot avoid harboring.

The opposite of hate, in this context, is not love; it is hypocrisy.   19
And children loathe the mealymouthed.

To ask a child to *repress* hate is to play with fire. Modern psychia-   20
try and medicine agree that people who cannot voice their hostilities
express them in other ways: eczema, ulcers, migraine, hypertension,
constipation, insomnia, impotence, hallucinations, nightmares, suicide. (Look around you.)

For hate concealed is far more dangerous than hate revealed. To try   21
to "bury" hate is to intensify it. Hate is more virulent, in the long run,
when it is closeted rather than confronted. (Those of you who are
shuddering at this point, or who recoil from the unpleasant thought of
"animal hate," might remember that animals do not hate the way
men and women do: animals attack out of instinct or fear; and they
kill for food or safety — without the vindictive satisfactions that
human hate can obtain.)

You may retort that we should teach a child to *understand*, and   22
argue that understanding will defuse his hatreds. But is it not true that
the more we understand some people or acts, the more we detest
them — and should? Ought we to alter our horror and hatred of a
Torquemada, a Hitler, a Charles Manson?

Do you protest, "But they had an unhappy childhood!" Or do you   23
cry, "They're *sick*, not bad!" All childhood is full of unhappiness, yet

few of us become murderers; and, though most sick people are not "bad," *some* sick people are so evil, so monstrous, that they pass the limits of compassion or defense.

You tell me "Love thy neighbor"? What if your neighbor happens 24 to be Jack the Ripper?

You say "turn the other cheek"? Turn it, if you will, if only *your* 25 life or nightmares are at stake; but would you turn the cheek of a little girl (or boy) about to be gagged, abused, and irreparably damaged by a pervert or a rapist?

Please notice: In a psychology seminar, I would try to analyze the 26 reasons for A's cruelty, or B's greed; in a sociology class, I would place C's delusions or D's hostilities in the larger context of political-social-economic pressures; in a psychiatric clinic, I would seek enlightenment on the unconscious drives, the thwarted hungers, the symbolic function served by X's madness or Y's paranoia. But in my capacity as a human being, as a living, responsible, hurtable mortal, as a member of the human community that must live together in this neighbor-hood-village-city-country-continent-world — in *that* capacity, can I react to evil except with the most profound moral outrage?

I see no reason to hate sadists less because we understand sadism 27 more. (You may remember the couple in England who tape-recorded the screams of the children they tortured, then murdered. They were psychopaths, to be sure; and, to be equally sure, they committed un-speakable horrors — which they enjoyed.)

There is a subtler point here: Not *ever* to hate is to surrender a just 28 scale of decent values. Not ever to hate is to drain *love* of its meaning. Not to hate *anyone* is as crazy as to hate everyone.

Besides, a world of automatic, indiscriminate loving is suicidal — 29 for the good and the loving are enslaved or exterminated by those who gratify their cruelty and their lust. A world that so recently wept over the bloodshed in Russia, Germany, China, Hungary, Poland, Czecho-slovakia, Cuba, Pakistan, and Ireland has reason to know that neither truth nor justice nor compassion can possibly survive unprepared and unarmed.

Blind hatred is, of course, horrid and indefensible. But hate need 30 not be blind. Hate can be clear-eyed — and moral. Hate need not be our master but our servant, for it can be enlisted in the service of decency (hating those who hate decency), of kindness (hating those who choose to be cruel), of love itself (hating those who hate love and seek to destroy or corrupt it).

Are you thinking that this violates "our better selves," or betrays 31 our Judeo-Christian precepts? But the Bible tells us: "The bloodthirsty hate the upright" (*Proverbs*). I am not about to parade my uprightness, but I hate the bloodthirsty; and I think the upright *should* hate them. Shall we allow the bloodthirsty to prevail?

There is indeed a time to love and a time to hate, and the Eighty- 32 ninth Psalm uses a phrase of transcendent morality: "I hate them with perfect hatred."

I, for one, hate fanatics (regardless of race, color, or creed) who are 33 ready to kill me or you or our children in the detestable certainty that they are absolutely right.

I hate injustice, therefore I hate those who treat others unjustly 34 (because of their color, or creed, or simply because they are powerless).

I hate those who teach others to hate those who disagree with 35 them: I loathe demagogues.

I hate anyone who hates indiscriminately — without hard thought, 36 for irrational reasons, or out of false principles. I think my hatreds are the result of careful thought, reason, and moral principle.

All these things I would teach our children. 37

I would not offend their good sense, or nauseate their sensibilities, 38 by glutinous yammerings about indiscriminate love — love that does not brand evil for what it is, that does not respond with moral passion to those who inflict agony or indignities on others. Such love Emerson dismissed with contempt as the love that "pules and whines."

I hope our children will learn how and whom and when to hate, no 39 less than how and whom and when to help, forgive, or love.

Home is where hate can and should first express itself, and be 40 taught to contain itself, in proper dosages and proportions. Home is where children should be allowed to practice and test and begin to conquer this powerful, terrible human passion.

Home is where it is *safe* to hate — first. 41

CONSIDERATIONS

1. According to Rosten, how do ordinary, decent people contribute to the causes of war? Can you offer examples to illustrate how it occurs?
2. Do you agree with Rosten that hitting a child is usually better than restraining the impulse? Would you add any consideration, pro or con, that he overlooks?
3. Rosten says that the principle of general loving is "suicidal." How does he support that point? What could be added to strengthen his argument?
4. In this short essay, eleven of the paragraphs end with parenthetical statements. What are a few effects of this device? Does Rosten overdo it, or do you like the recurrence of these particular parenthetical comments?
5. How does this essay make a reader feel? What effect do you think Rosten wants to have on his audience?
6. WRITING TOPIC. In a 500-word essay, argue for or against Rosten's thesis that children at home need to be taught to hate. Why does he emphasize *home*? What would be made better or worse by instruction outside the home? Would home instruction be effective without some reinforcement by society?

Forum

IMAGES OF FEAR

◊

FORUM. The moderator is LEWIS LAPHAM, the editor of *Harper's* magazine. CHARLES MURRAY is a research scholar and writer on problems of juvenile crime and American social policy. HUBERT WILLIAMS directed the Newark Police Department before becoming president of the Police Foundation, a national organization. BURTON ROBERTS is the administrative judge in a criminal appeals court in New York. CLAUDE BROWN is an author whose books recount his experiences growing up in Harlem. JONATHAN RUBINSTEIN, who oversees research on social policies, writes about urban police departments and organizations. ADAM WALINSKY is a lawyer who has been active in investigations of organized crime. SUSAN JACOBY is the author of a book about revenge and the controversy over the death penalty.

Despite many large-scale urban and national programs to fight crime and to reduce its causes, the fear of crime reaches into everyone's life in most areas of the United States. But do Americans really live in a lawless society or is society overreacting to exaggerated fears of danger? This question was intensified by two events that galvanized extreme public reactions. The highly popular movie *Death Wish* glorified its chief character, a crime victim who single-handedly sought revenge by becoming murderously vindictive against all hoodlums. Audiences applauded his violent, lawless action. In December 1984, an actual shooting won similar public acclaim. In a New York City subway car Bernhard Goetz shot four teenagers who threatened to rob him. The public initially praised this "subway vigilante," but further evidence suggested that Goetz had not acted in simple self-defense. As the movie and Goetz's case indicate, an atmosphere of fear may generate criminal reactions on their own. To explore this social problem, *Harper's* magazine organized and published the following panel discussion in 1985. After some opening observations about demography and crime statistics (which have been deleted), the panelists examine some of the social dilemmas arising from a chronic national crisis over crime.

JONATHAN RUBINSTEIN: If there has really been a great improve- 1
ment in our criminal justice system, why is the public still railing
against high crime in the cities?

BURTON ROBERTS: Because people's *perceptions* of what's hap- 2
pening are as important as the reality. The media prefer to tell the
public that crime is rampant, that it is continuing to rise, that people
are afraid to go out at night. After all, that's what sells newspapers and
makes exciting television. But the reality is that crime is going down:
the streets are safer and the criminal justice system is more effective.

The politicians, meanwhile, find it convenient to blame the judges, 3
and the judges climb into their ivory towers and don't respond. As
Mr. Williams pointed out, numerous social problems contribute to
the crime rate, as do demographic factors. So why do politicians always point to the judiciary? Because blaming judges is much easier
than looking in the mirror, easier than examining what has really happened to our inner cities.

ADAM WALINSKY: It just so happens, Judge, that the drop in crime 4
you have been congratulating yourself about may be at an end. Indeed, we've had comparable, and temporary, drops in the crime rate
before — between 1974 and 1977, for example. Then, too, everyone
said, "Isn't it wonderful that we've turned the corner on crime, that
the system is working more effectively?" But in 1977 we saw the biggest rise in the crime rate in American history, and the increase continued for four years. In all the excitement about the decline in crime
last year, no one seems to have noticed that the number of violent
crimes in New York City in December 1984 was *higher* than in December 1983. What is more, the number of minority teenagers will
soon begin to increase again.

About five years from now, the children of the Baby Boomers, 5
more than half of whom were born into non-intact families — the ille-
gitimacy rate among blacks shot up to 50 percent in 1976 — will become teenagers. These are the kids that our school system does not
seem able to reach or help, and they are going to make themselves felt
as juvenile problems of one sort or another. To sit back congratulating
ourselves on the recent small drop in crime would be a disaster —
especially since, in my view, those congratulations are undeserved.
The victimization surveys show that only a third of crimes are reported. And crime itself has changed — it has become more violent,
for one thing.

ROBERTS: The system deals effectively with the more violent 6 crimes; the higher courts, as I said, are becoming more efficient all the time. But the system has grave problems dealing with the so-called quality-of-life crimes — shoplifting, vandalism, and so on — the petty crimes that are channeled to our lower courts. These courts are completely overburdened.

Why is this important? Well, the young criminals we've been talk- 7 ing about usually have their first experience with the system when they commit a petty crime and come before a lower court. Usually their cases drag on until they are dismissed, or they are given unconditional discharges. Very little retributive punishment is handed down in the lower courts. After seeing how it operates at the lower level, these kids become contemptuous of what goes on in the criminal justice system. Of course, as far as the system is concerned, the kids are only little acorns of criminal activity; but out of the acorns grow the huge oaks that cast their shadows over our society.

We should be educating the public, convincing taxpayers that the 8 lower courts are important and that imprisoning violent criminals is not the only function the criminal justice system must perform. The public must come to understand that a probation officer with a caseload of, say, twenty kids instead of 200 really *can* supervise them and prevent them from committing other offenses. And if we educate the public about the value of intensified supervision of those on probation or parole, we won't need all those prisons.

The public must recognize that even when all the components of 9 the criminal justice system work as they were designed to, they still can't solve the crime problem. There is a limit to what the courts can do. After all, only a small percentage of all crimes result in arrests: 26 percent of reported robberies, 15 percent of reported burglaries, and so on. We can't expect the courts to do everything.

RUBINSTEIN: Of course the judiciary is not reponsible for the 10 crime rate. But the public, continually threatened and increasingly frightened, is only too happy to attack the courts.

The rate of crime *is* intolerable — yet we have managed to live 11 with it at least since the sixties. I believe the crime rate actually shot up much earlier, but in the forties and fifties Americans were so involved in building a new suburban civilization and abandoning their big cities that the escalating crime rate went unnoticed. At that time, the police didn't treat "Negro crime," as it was called, seriously. In

New York, for instance, they noticed it only when it began to move from Harlem, where there never was any public order — or police presence — to the white neighborhoods downtown.

The crime rate we endure today, and have endured for the last 12 twenty-five years, stems from conditions that show absolutely no sign of changing. American cities are filled with a large, youthful, and disaffected minority population. The unemployment rate among these kids is near 50 percent, more than six times that of the society as a whole. They have no hope of finding a decent job; they are subject to incredible racism and indifference; our educational system is unable to teach them the ABCs; heroin and other drugs are freely available. And the prosperity of the United States is there, ripe for the picking.

But what is new about this? No one has ever thought it was normal 13 or right. People always say it's "intolerable." But what do we ever *do* about it? When I was a kid in the 1950s, it was fashionable to fire police chiefs when crime was on the rise. Sometime in the 1960s we stopped holding police chiefs responsible for reported increases in crime. Eventually people gave up even criticizing the police.

What is particularly frightening is that American cities now have 14 police they can't afford and court systems that gobble up hundreds of millions of dollars a year. But despite all the money they're spending, Americans do not feel safe. They have grown increasingly frustrated, and are now demanding the right to kill their fellow citizens. This sentiment, which Bernhard Goetz helped bring to the surface, is being expressed daily in the press.

SUSAN JACOBY: People are supporting the right to kill in "self-de- 15 fense" for the same reason they have been screaming for the death penalty all these years; they feel — misguidedly, I believe — that at least it would be a strong response to a problem that has come to seem utterly intractable and hopeless. In the same way, people don't know what to do, so they demand the death penalty, which symbolically expresses society's outrage. An ineffective criminal justice system such as ours leads people increasingly to demand these extreme, symbolic, but largely useless penalties.

CHARLES MURRAY: It is my impression that the white middle 16 class generally believes things are getting better, and that in many parts of the country crime is receding as a major issue. Perhaps this is because many white folks have sealed themselves off from the inner cities. I'd like to ask Claude Brown what the sense is in the inner cities — in Harlem, for instance. Do people believe crime is getting worse, or better?

CLAUDE BROWN: They believe it's getting worse. Maybe fewer 17 people are victimized in Harlem — and I suspect this is true across urban America — because they have learned to live defensively. In any Harlem building, whether a tenement or a relatively luxurious high-rise, every door has at least three locks on it. Nobody opens a door without first finding out who's there. In the early evening, or even at midday, you see people — middle-aged men and women — lingering outside nice apartment houses, peeking in the lobbies. They seem to be casing the joint. They are actually trying to figure out who is in the lobby of *their* building. "Is this someone waiting to mug me? Should I risk going in, or should I wait for someone else to come?"

If you live in Harlem, USA, you don't park your automobile two 18 blocks from your apartment house because that gives potential muggers an opportunity to get a fix on you. You'd better find a parking space within a block of your house, because if you have to walk two blocks you're not going to make it. In 1950 my grandparents could take a walk in Colonial Park in Harlem at three o'clock in the morning. Today that would be suicide. Most people make sure they're in the house by nine or ten o'clock.

In Harlem, elderly people walking their dogs in the morning cross 19 the street when they see some young people coming. They try to act casual, but of course they aren't. They are very aware of those young people — you can almost feel the tension as the youngsters get closer. And what those elderly men and women have in the paper bags they're carrying is not just a pooper scooper — it's a gun. And if those youngsters cross that street, somebody's going to get hurt — you're going to hear it. Everybody knows this.

That's Harlem, USA, in 1985. Fewer victims, maybe, but crime is 20 worse.

WALINSKY: As Claude and Susan and everyone here has said, peo- 21 ple today are terrified of crime. Whatever the small year-to-year variations in the official crime rate, people are becoming *more* afraid.

We cannot continue to ignore the consequences of this fear. The 22 most obvious example of those consequences is the public response to Bernhard Goetz's actions in a New York City subway car. Goetz shot four kids, two of them in the back, and people overwhelmingly approved of what he did.

Another consequence is that people are running away. In Harlem, 23 for example, the population has dropped by over a quarter during the last fifteen years, which is one of the reasons the crime rate has declined. Blacks in Harlem are doing exactly what whites did. Because the government seems unable to protect them, blacks are fleeing their homes.

We now have far more private police officers in the United States 24 than public police officers. A whole industry has grown up to protect people and their possessions from crime. Communities sell themselves by boasting about fortified walls, electronic security, and private police forces. We seem to accept this, to accept car alarm systems and multiple locks on our doors.

WILLIAMS: When one out of every three American households is 25 directly victimized each year, it isn't long before everyone has either been a victim himself or had someone very close to him victimized. The problem is not just what crime does to people's lives; it is also what the fear of crime does to our society. As this fear feeds on itself, any decisive action to fight crime becomes less likely. People take strong collective action only when they have confidence in themselves and in their society. When people are afraid, they tend to act as individuals. The result is an increasingly atomized society. That's when people flock to the suburbs and buy the extra locks — or a gun.

JACOBY: In 1978 I wrote an article about this titled "Fear Taxes." 26 All those people who move into the middle of the street when they see someone coming, all those women who will not ride the subways and therefore take cabs they can't afford, the countless dollars spent on locks and gates and hired cars. Even if you or someone you know well has never been a victim — which, as Mr. Williams pointed out, is unlikely — crime still has an enormous effect on your life.

WILLIAMS: One way to combat both crime and the fear of crime is 27 to work to strengthen the foundation on which the criminal justice system was constructed in the first place — a strong sense of oneness between the police and the public. The public must provide the police with information and support. And the police in turn must help reduce citizens' fear by encouraging them to participate in making their neighborhoods safe.

Let me give an example. In 1979, we had to lay off 200 police offi- 28 cers in Newark. People were very upset; they organized "crime marches" on police headquarters. One group came from the housing projects to meet with me. "Look, Mr. Director," they said, "we know you have lost a lot of men. But we want you to understand that we cannot live under these conditions. We are scared to death, and you've got to help." My response was, "Well, if you look at the statistics, you don't *have* any crime in your area." People in the projects don't report crime even though a lot occurs there. I told them that they had to tell the police what was going on. "We're afraid to," they said.

We finally persuaded them to meet with us — outside police head- 29 quarters — and tell us what was going on. Later we slipped a police officer into a vacant apartment in one of the projects to gather evidence. After we had compiled a book on the criminals, we met with this group again and said, "Look, we know who is committing the crimes. We are going to arrest these people, many of them for relatively minor offenses. You will not have to go to court or give evidence publicly, but you must make clear to the judges privately the problems these people are creating in your neighborhood. Just tell the judges what you told us."

Well, we arrested those guys. We arrested one for possession of a 30 knife. But the judge, who had been told what was going on, sentenced him to six months in jail. The people in the projects were ecstatic. That's the kind of cooperation we need to encourage.

BROWN: I think we should talk a little about what happens to peo- 31 ple *after* they're arrested. After all, many are professional criminals, and until we eradicate that class — people who are constantly moving in and out of prison — we are never going to have a real effect on crime.

Years ago, "professional criminal" meant petty criminal — some- 32 one who pulled stick-ups on the street and that sort of thing. Nowadays, professional criminals kill people. Many muggers and robbers kill people as a matter of course. The only way to eliminate this criminal behavior is to change our prisons. The rehabilitation programs in our correctional facilities, as they're now called, are a farce. This society incarcerates hundreds of thousands of semiliterate, unskilled people, but offers them no education, teaches them no salable skill. It is ludicrous to expect someone who was making $1,000 a day as a petty drug dealer to go out and work as a dishwasher for $150 a week. Why not teach them to program a computer, or to fix air conditioners and refrigerators? Many of them can't even read. Why can't we teach them?

I propose that anyone convicted of a felony must learn to read and 33 write and must acquire a salable skill *before* he can be released from prison. Of course, such a requirement would keep prisoners in jail longer, and we don't have the facilities for that because no one wants to pay taxes to build new prisons. Well, the state of Kentucky has recently come up with a way to raise money to build prisons without increasing taxes. Kentucky now collects a ten-dollar tax from every person convicted of a misdemeanor. This tax brings in $300,000 a month, and the state is using the money to modernize existing facilities and build new ones.

WILLIAMS: It's true that if we do not create a different mind-set in 34 the people we incarcerate, their natural tendency on being released will be to return to their former lifestyle. But we must not ignore the circumstances that breed criminal behavior in the first place.

Drug addiction is the most obvious. Drugs — not only heroin but 35 all narcotics — must be kept out of the hands of our children; the penalties for peddling drugs to children should be extraordinarily harsh. And people who already have drug habits should be separated from the larger society.

RUBINSTEIN: Are you proposing a quarantine?   36

WILLIAMS: The criminal justice system ought to be used as a giant 37 vacuum to suck these people in. Addicts are constantly committing crimes, and the criminal justice system gets hold of most of them. But city jails and state prisons are clearly not the places to treat people with chronic drug problems. The federal government should set up a large-scale treatment program for drug offenders, a program emphasizing medical help and psychotherapy, and eventually job training. Or perhaps after treatment these people could take part in some sort of "youth corps." Maybe they could be trained to cut trees, or whatever. Even if such a program didn't eliminate their addiction, at least it would remove them from society.

RUBINSTEIN: I think drugs themselves are a trivial issue — at least 38 compared with the extraordinary ideas that have been suggested here by Claude Brown and Hubert Williams. Their proposals reflect perfectly the sentiments being expressed in our society today, particularly in the debate over Goetz, whose actions have become the great symbolic crime of this generation.

Consider some of the proposals made at this table. Hubert Wil- 39 liams, a very distinguished police chief, is suggesting that we quarantine drug users — that we create a gulag, in effect. Preventive detention — imprisonment without trial — is now legal; now people are talking about creating prison colonies. Claude Brown is talking about keeping sixteen- and seventeen-year-old inner-city kids in prison until they can read and write. We can't teach them in the schools, so we'll send them to prison to learn. What do we propose to do with the thirty-year-olds?

LAPHAM: But why do we even *need* to confine all these people in 40 the way that Hubert Williams has described? Why don't we simply make narcotics legal?

WILLIAMS: Frankly, I think we should consider the idea very 41 seriously. It is clear that the money being made in drugs has corrupted our system, our judges, our police officers.

WALINSKY: The extent to which drug use causes crime is overesti- 42 mated. The fact that large numbers of the people who are arrested happen to be drug users does not mean drug use *causes* crime. People inclined for one reason or another toward antisocial behavior often use drugs for similar reasons.

Over the last twenty years, politicians have had to rationalize their 43 miserable record in coping with crime. Every police chief in America has learned to say that the causes of crime are "really" poverty, degradation, bad housing, unemployment — problems he cannot be expected to solve.

Although they still use poverty as an excuse, politicians now talk 44 more about drugs. Rather than devote any more resources to courts, police, prosecutors, and prisons in their own states, politicians blame the State Department for not getting tough with Turkey or Colombia. Meanwhile, New York State, which proposes to give its citizens a $2 billion tax cut, manages to eke out less than 6 percent of its budget for the criminal justice system.

JACOBY: Well, *we* seem to be pointing our fingers at the politi- 45 cians, the prisons, the courts, and the police. No one has said much about the victims. The United States is the only country in the industrialized West that does not have a mechanism to routinely provide some compensation to crime victims. We need some way to help people *after* they've been victimized — perhaps some form of publicly financed "crime insurance." The maintenance of public safety is a social responsibility, which we should acknowledge not only by punishing criminals more swiftly and surely but by literally paying victims if we fail to maintain the "freedom of the city." And victims must become more visible in the criminal justice process. A number of states now require victims, or the relatives of victims who have died, to testify. This should be extended throughout the country. The state is supposed to represent the victim in court by representing society as a whole. We need to establish special advocates who will present vivid portraits of the victims in court. Crime must be treated as a total public responsibility, not simply the domain of the police or the courts.

RUBINSTEIN: That won't happen until the police begin to think 46 that *all* crime is equally important. The fact is, the kind of crime that has attacked the whole society during the last twenty-five years has always been a part of the lives of poor people in large cities.

JACOBY: Certainly whites must change their attitudes about black- 47 on-black crime. A few months ago, a young white Harvard graduate was murdered on the roof of her New York apartment building. It made the front page. The Police Department put forty detectives on the case and made an arrest in a few days. Soon afterward a black housewife was murdered in Harlem. The incident merited only a small item in the paper; three detectives were assigned to the case. Now what on earth do the people living in fear in Harlem and Bedford Stuyvesant think when they read about those forty detectives? Does that encourage the community's "sense of oneness" with the police?

We must guarantee that our criminal justice system exacts punish- 48 ment with some consistency and reliability. And not only for murder and rape. Certainly one of the reasons that the crime problem is so bad, and that people *perceive* it as being even worse than it is, is that they don't see any punishment exacted for "small"crimes. The person who is mugged, who feels the knife against his throat, does not consider that crime small. A friend of mine was hit on the head with a blunt instrument and wound up in the hospital for two days. But to the police officer who came to interview her she wasn't "really" hurt — she wasn't in the intensive care unit or in a coma. The officer told her that because she would recover, hers was not a "high-priority" case. He was telling the truth. But what does this say to people? Someone must be stabbed through the heart for the crime to be important. A society cannot give the impression that a criminal who doesn't gravely injure someone is not worth punishing. Punishment is important in both a real sense and a symbolic sense: people must feel that society regards their lives and their property and their peace of mind as important.

MURRAY: Our goal should be: Let us do justice. We can't catch all 49 criminals, but when one is apprehended, it is essential that justice be done. And justice must consist of some action by the state that says unmistakably, "You shouldn't have done that, and here is the penalty."

I remember the juvenile delinquents in Chicago whom I studied 50 ten years ago. The average youngster committed for the first time to an institution in Cook County had thirteen prior arrests. He had been told thirteen times that it was O.K. to do what he did. If he had been given a small punishment after his first arrest, and a slightly larger one after his second, society would at least have done justice. And some kids would have been discouraged from doing the same thing again.

WALINSKY: While we continue to argue about whether to cook 51 the bird, put it on ice, or flay it alive, I feel obligated to point out that those we have chosen to govern us — the men and women who make the decisions about where to spend the public's money, whether in city hall, the statehouse, or Congress — do not happen to agree with you. They don't seem to feel that "justice must be done, and be seen to be done." Why is that? I've decided that the reason elected officers don't feel the need to do much about crime is that there is no real money to be made in public safety. Except for building more prisons — a popular cause among politicians — there are no big contracts to be let.

When we discuss crime, we tend to focus so much on the magni- 52 tude of the penalties, the procedural safeguards, and the state of our prisons that we ignore the fact that *public order has broken down.* People in this country don't feel safe walking in their own neighborhoods, for God's sake! The overwhelming problem today is one of public order and public safety.

We have to increase the safety of our neighborhoods. And that *can* 53 be done. If we simply augmented our police forces we might not eliminate all crime, but we would create islands of safety where citizens could begin to live their lives and recover their confidence. If a police officer patrolled the street that Claude Brown talked about, the old people walking their dogs wouldn't feel the need to carry guns in paper bags.

Jonathan and I have proposed a "police corps," which would dou- 54
ble our police forces by giving young people a college education in return for three years of service as police officers. The proposal would
give us more police, at an affordable cost. And it would make citizens
feel they were doing something concrete to fight crime. But it is useless to pretend that we are not going to have a significant public-order
problem as long as the situation at the core of our cities is so desperate.

Governments have preferred to spend money elsewhere, and they 55
have found it expedient to invent a whole mythology about the causes
of crime. I think the judge is correct in saying the judiciary has long
been treated as a scapegoat. It's much easier, after all, to make a
speech about weak-kneed judges than it is to provide adequate police
protection. It's much easier to attack the State Department for not
pressuring the governments of Turkey or Colombia than it is to do
something about the condition of the schools. The fundamental issue
is whether we have the political will to do something about crime.
That this issue, which by every account is the single greatest concern
of the American people, is not receiving more attention at all levels of
government is absolutely stunning.

CONSIDERATIONS

1. In the view of Judge Roberts, why hasn't the drop in the crime rate
   calmed people's fears of crime? What steps does he seem to favor to deal
   with the present atmosphere? Do other panelists offer different explanations for the rising fear of crime?
2. How do the various panelists each interpret the significance of Bernhard
   Goetz's actions? Which of them gives it the most importance?
3. Why does Rubinstein object to the ideas about imprisonment suggested
   by Brown and Williams? With whom do you tend to agree on these
   issues?
4. What advantages are seen in making narcotics legal to use? In your opinion, what conditions would legalization correct or fail to correct?
5. Do you think that "crime insurance" would work? What problems do you
   foresee? Is it worthwhile to try to solve them?
6. How can punishments be made more *symbolic?* Do you think that this

major change from our present attitude about punishments would be beneficial to society?

7. Would you join a police corps? Give the pros and cons of Walinsky's proposal.

8. According to Walinsky why do we lack the political will to combat crime effectively? What other possible causes have been suggested by other panelists? In your opinion who comes closest to the heart of the problem?

9. WRITING TOPIC. The forum includes at least six specific proposals for dealing with crime. In 500 words, support or refute one of the proposals by explaining the likely effects of putting it into action.

George Orwell

SHOOTING AN ELEPHANT

◊

George Orwell (1903–1950) was the pen name of Eric Blair, who was born in India and sent by his English parents to England for his education at Eton. He returned to India as an officer in the Imperial Police, but he became bitterly disenchanted with service to the Empire and he soon abandoned his career in the government. His first book, *Down and Out in Paris and London* (1933), recounts his struggles to support himself while he learned to write. His lifelong subject, however, is not bohemian life as a writer but his personal encounters with totalitarianism, which he addressed in his novel *Burmese Days* (1935) and his book *Homage to Catalonia* (1938), a chronicle of his developing despair over all political parties after he participated in the Spanish Civil War. Orwell rejected political creeds but somberly recognized that "in our age . . . all issues are political issues, and politics itself is a mass of lies, evasions, folly, hatred, and schizophrenia," as he maintains in his essay "Politics and the English Language" (1945). This vision is also expressed in his fiction, *Animal Farm* (1945) and *1984* (1949). The following essay is a memoir of his early period of conflicting loyalties as a British magistrate in Burma.

In Moulmein, in lower Burma, I was hated by large numbers of 1 people — the only time in my life that I have been important enough for this to happen to me. I was sub-divisional police officer of the town, and in an aimless, petty kind of way anti-European feeling was very bitter. No one had the guts to raise a riot, but if a European woman went through the bazaars alone somebody would probably spit betel juice over her dress. As a police officer I was an obvious target and was baited whenever it seemed safe to do so. When a nimble Burman tripped me up on the football field and the referee (another Burman) looked the other way, the crowd yelled with hideous laughter. This happened more than once. In the end the sneering yellow faces of young men that met me everywhere, the insults hooted after me when I was at a safe distance, got badly on my nerves. The young Buddhist priests were the worst of all. There were several thousands of them in the town and none of them seemed to have anything to do except stand on street corners and jeer at Europeans.

All this was perplexing and upsetting. For at that time I had al- 2 ready made up my mind that imperialism was an evil thing and the sooner I chucked up my job and got out of it the better. Theoretically — and secretly, of course — I was all for the Burmese and all against their oppressors, the British. As for the job I was doing, I hated it more bitterly than I can perhaps make clear. In a job like that you see the dirty work of Empire at close quarters. The wretched prisoners huddling in the stinking cages of the lock-ups, the grey, cowed faces of the long-term convicts, the scarred buttocks of the men who had been flogged with bamboos — all these oppressed me with an intolerable sense of guilt. But I could get nothing into perspective. I was young and ill-educated and I had had to think out my problems in the utter silence that is imposed on every Englishman in the East. I did not even know that the British Empire is dying, still less did I know that it is a great deal better than the younger empires that are going to supplant it. All I knew was that I was stuck between my hatred of the empire I served and my rage against the evil-spirited little beasts who tried to make my job impossible. With one part of my mind I thought of the British Raj as an unbreakable tyranny, as something clamped down, in *saecula saeculorum*, upon the will of prostrate peoples; with another part I thought that the greatest joy in the world would be to drive a bayonet into a Buddhist priest's guts. Feelings like these are the normal by-products of imperialism; ask any Anglo-Indian official, if you can catch him off duty.

One day something happened which in a roundabout way was en- 3 lightening. It was a tiny incident in itself, but it gave me a better glimpse than I had had before of the real nature of imperialism — the real motives for which despotic governments act. Early one morning the sub-inspector at a police station the other end of the town rang me up on the phone and said that an elephant was ravaging the bazaar. Would I please come and do something about it? I did not know what I could do, but I wanted to see what was happening and I got on to a pony and started out. I took my rifle, an old .44 Winchester and much too small to kill an elephant, but I thought the noise might be useful *in terrorem*. Various Burmans stopped me on the way and told me about the elephant's doings. It was not, of course, a wild elephant, but a tame one which had gone "must." It had been chained up, as tame elephants always are when their attack of "must" is due, but on the previous night it had broken its chain and escaped. Its mahout, the only person who could manage it when it was in that state, had set out in pursuit, but had taken the wrong direction and was now twelve hours' journey away, and in the morning the elephant had suddenly reappeared in the town. The Burmese population had no weapons and were quite helpless against it. It had already destroyed somebody's bamboo hut, killed a cow, and raided some fruit-stalls and devoured the stock; also it had met the municipal rubbish van and, when the driver jumped out and took to his heels, had turned the van over and inflicted violences upon it.

The Burmese sub-inspector and some Indian constables were wait- 4 ing for me in the quarter where the elephant had been seen. It was a very poor quarter, a labyrinth of squalid bamboo huts, thatched with palm-leaf, winding all over a steep hillside. I remember that it was a cloudy, stuffy morning at the beginning of the rains. We began questioning the people as to where the elephant had gone and, as usual, failed to get any definite information. That is invariably the case in the East; a story always sounds clear enough at a distance, but the nearer you get to the scene of events the vaguer it becomes. Some of the people said that the elephant had gone in one direction, some said that he had gone in another, some professed not even to have heard of any elephant. I had almost made up my mind that the whole story was a pack of lies, when we heard yells a little distance away. There was a loud, scandalized cry of "Go away, child! Go away this instant!" and an old woman with a switch in her hand came round the corner of a hut, violently shooing away a crowd of naked children. Some more women followed, clicking their tongues and exclaiming; evidently there was something that the children ought not to have seen. I rounded the hut and saw a man's dead body sprawling in the mud. He was an Indian, a black Dravidian coolie, almost naked, and he could not have been dead many minutes. The people said that the elephant had come suddenly upon him round the corner of the hut, caught him with its trunk, put its foot on his back, and ground him into the earth. This was the rainy season and the ground was soft, and his face had scored a trench a foot deep and a couple of yards long. He was lying on his belly with arms crucified and head sharply twisted to one side. His face was coated with mud, the eyes wide open, the teeth bared and grinning with an expression of unendurable agony. (Never tell me, by the way, that the dead look peaceful. Most of the corpses I have seen looked devilish.) The friction of the great beast's foot had stripped the skin from his back as neatly as one skins a rabbit. As soon as I saw the dead man I sent an orderly to a friend's house nearby to borrow an elephant rifle. I had already sent back the pony, not wanting it to go mad with fright and throw me if it smelt the elephant.

The orderly came back in a few minutes with a rifle and five cartridges, and meanwhile some Burmans had arrived and told us that the elephant was in the paddy fields below, only a few hundred yards away. As I started forward practically the whole population of the quarter flocked out of the houses and followed me. They had seen the rifle and were all shouting excitedly that I was going to shoot the elephant. They had not shown much interest in the elephant when he was merely ravaging their homes, but it was different now that he was going to be shot. It was a bit of fun to them, as it would be to an English crowd; besides they wanted the meat. It made me vaguely uneasy. I had no intention of shooting the elephant — I had merely sent for the rifle to defend myself if necessary — and it is always unnerving to have a crowd following you. I marched down the hill, looking and feeling a fool, with the rifle over my shoulder and an ever-growing army of people jostling at my heels. At the bottom, when you got away from the huts, there was a metalled road and beyond that a miry waste of paddy fields a thousand yards across, not yet ploughed but soggy from the first rains and dotted with coarse grass. The elephant was standing eight yards from the road, his left side towards us. He took not the slightest notice of the crowd's approach. He was tearing up bunches of grass, beating them against his knees to clean them and stuffing them into his mouth.

I had halted on the road. As soon as I saw the elephant I knew with perfect certainty that I ought not to shoot him. It is a serious matter to shoot a working elephant — it is comparable to destroying a huge and costly piece of machinery — and obviously one ought not to do it if it can possibly be avoided. And at that distance, peacefully eating, the elephant looked no more dangerous than a cow. I thought then and I think now that his attack of "must" was already passing off; in which case he would merely wander harmlessly about until the mahout came back and caught him. Moreover, I did not in the least want to shoot him. I decided that I would watch him for a little while to make sure that he did not turn savage again, and then go home.

But at that moment I glanced round at the crowd that had fol- 7
lowed me. It was an immense crowd, two thousand at the least and growing every minute. It blocked the road for a long distance on either side. I looked at the sea of yellow faces above the garish clothes — faces all happy and excited over this bit of fun, all certain that the elephant was going to be shot. They were watching me as they would watch a conjurer about to perform a trick. They did not like me, but with the magical rifle in my hands I was momentarily worth watching. And suddenly I realized that I should have to shoot the elephant after all. The people expected it of me and I had got to do it; I could feel their two thousand wills pressing me forward, irresistibly. And it was at this moment, as I stood there with the rifle in my hands, that I first grasped the hollowness, the futility of the white man's dominion in the East. Here was I, the white man with his gun, standing in front of the unarmed native crowd — seemingly the leading actor of the piece; but in reality I was only an absurd puppet pushed to and fro by the will of those yellow faces behind. I perceived in this moment that when the white man turns tyrant it is his own freedom that he destroys. He becomes a sort of hollow, posing dummy, the conventionalized figure of a sahib. For it is the condition of his rule that he shall spend his life in trying to impress the "natives," and so in every crisis he has got to do what the "natives" expect of him. He wears a mask, and his face grows to fit it. I had got to shoot the elephant. I had committed myself to doing it when I sent for the rifle. A sahib has got to act like a sahib; he has got to appear resolute, to know his own mind and do definite things. To come all that way, rifle in hand, with two thousand people marching at my heels, and then to trail feebly away, having done nothing — no, that was impossible. The crowd would laugh at me. And my whole life, every white man's life in the East, was one long struggle not to be laughed at.

But I did not want to shoot the elephant. I watched him beating 8
his bunch of grass against his knees, with that preoccupied grandmotherly air that elephants have. It seemed to me that it would be murder to shoot him. At that age I was not squeamish about killing animals, but I had never shot an elephant and never wanted to.

(Somehow it always seems worse to kill a *large* animal.) Besides, there was the beast's owner to be considered. Alive, the elephant was worth at least a hundred pounds; dead, he would only be worth the value of his tusks, five pounds, possibly. But I had got to act quickly. I turned to some experienced-looking Burmans who had been there when we arrived, and asked them how the elephant had been behaving. They all said the same thing: he took no notice of you if you left him alone, but he might charge if you went too close to him.

It was perfectly clear to me what I ought to do. I ought to walk up   9
to within, say, twenty-five yards of the elephant and test his behavior. If he charged, I could shoot; if he took no notice of me, it would be safe to leave him until the mahout came back. But also I knew that I was going to do no such thing. I was a poor shot with a rifle and the ground was soft mud into which one would sink at every step. If the elephant charged and I missed him, I should have about as much chance as a toad under a steam-roller. But even then I was not thinking particularly of my own skin, only of the watchful yellow faces behind. For at that moment, with the crowd watching me, I was not afraid in the ordinary sense, as I would have been if I had been alone. A white man mustn't be frightened in front of "natives"; and so, in general, he isn't frightened. The sole thought in my mind was that if anything went wrong those two thousand Burmans would see me pursued, caught, trampled on, and reduced to a grinning corpse like that Indian up the hill. And if that happened it was quite probable that some of them would laugh. That would never do. There was only one alternative. I shoved the cartridges into the magazine and lay down on the road to get a better aim.

The crowd grew very still, and a deep, low, happy sigh, as of people   10
who see the theatre curtain go up at last, breathed from innumerable throats. They were going to have their bit of fun after all. The rifle was a beautiful German thing with cross-hair sights. I did not then know that in shooting an elephant one would shoot to cut an imaginary bar running from ear-hole to ear-hole. I ought, therefore, as the elephant was sideways on, to have aimed straight at his ear-hole; actually I aimed several inches in front of this, thinking the brain would be further forward.

When I pulled the trigger I did not hear the bang or feel the   11
kick — one never does when a shot goes home — but I heard the devilish roar of glee that went up from the crowd. In that instant, in too

short a time, one would have thought, even for the bullet to get there, a mysterious, terrible change had come over the elephant. He neither stirred nor fell, but every line of his body had altered. He looked suddenly stricken, shrunken, immensely old, as though the frightful impact of the bullet had paralysed him without knocking him down. At last, after what seemed a long time — it might have been five seconds, I dare say — he sagged flabbily to his knees. His mouth slobbered. An enormous senility seemed to have settled upon him. One could have imagined him thousands of years old. I fired again into the same spot. At the second shot he did not collapse but climbed with desperate slowness to his feet and stood weakly upright, with legs sagging and head drooping. I fired a third time. That was the shot that did for him. You could see the agony of it jolt his whole body and knock the last remnant of strength from his legs. But in falling he seemed for a moment to rise, for as his hind legs collapsed beneath him he seemed to tower upward like a huge rock toppling, his trunk reaching skywards like a tree. He trumpeted, for the first and only time. And then down he came, his belly towards me, with a crash that seemed to shake the ground even where I lay.

I got up. The Burmans were already racing past me across the mud. 12 It was obvious that the elephant would never rise again, but he was not dead. He was breathing very rhythmically with long rattling gasps, his great mound of a side painfully rising and falling. His mouth was wide open — I could see far down into caverns of pale pink throat. I waited a long time for him to die, but his breathing did not weaken. Finally I fired my two remaining shots into the spot where I thought his heart must be. The thick blood welled out of him like red velvet, but still he did not die. His body did not even jerk when the shots hit him, the tortured breathing continued without a pause. He was dying, very slowly and in great agony, but in some world remote from me where not even a bullet could damage him further. I felt that I had got to put an end to that deadful noise. It seemed dreadful to see the great beast lying there, powerless to move and yet powerless to die, and not even to be able to finish him. I sent back for my small rifle and poured shot after shot into his heart and down his throat. They seemed to make no impression. The tortured gasps continued as steadily as the ticking of a clock.

In the end I could not stand it any longer and went away. I heard 13 later that it took him half an hour to die. Burmans were bringing dahs* and baskets even before I left, and I was told they had stripped his body almost to the bones by the afternoon.

Afterwards, of course, there were endless discussions about the 14 shooting of the elephant. The owner was furious, but he was only an Indian and could do nothing. Besides, legally I had done the right thing, for a mad elephant has to be killed, like a mad dog, if its owner fails to control it. Among the Europeans opinion was divided. The older men said I was right, the younger men said it was a damn shame to shoot an elephant for killing a coolie, because an elephant was worth more than any damn Coringhee coolie. And afterwards I was very glad that the coolie had been killed; it put me legally in the right and it gave me a sufficient pretext for shooting the elephant. I often wondered whether any of the others grasped that I had done it solely to avoid looking a fool.

* Large knives.

CONSIDERATIONS

1. Why did Orwell hate his job even before this incident occurred? What effect was the job having on his feelings and attitudes? How would you describe his state of mind at the time?
2. Why does the Burman sub-inspector have to call Orwell? Why can't the Burmans themselves take care of the problem?
3. What details in the descriptions of the elephant connect it with human life? What details in the descriptions of the Burmans connect them with animals? What evokes Orwell's humane, sympathetic responses?
4. Among the many reasons Orwell may have had for writing this essay, what two purposes are most important? Is he equally successful in achieving both purposes?
5. Orwell says that he acted "solely to avoid looking a fool." If he had believed in the goals and values of British imperialism, would his actions have had more integrity?
6. WRITING TOPIC. What will my relatives think? Or what will the neighbors think? Or what will my friends think? What will my parents think? Explain a decision or action that you were pressured into by the expectations of other people. How did your dilemma build up to the point where you felt that you had to do what others wanted? What possible advantages, compromises, and questions of conscience did you have to think about? Do you still think that you were right and they were wrong? In 700 words, explain what it was like in your own experience to have to do a "dumb" thing.

Tillie Olsen

I STAND HERE IRONING

◊

TILLIE OLSEN (b. 1913) dropped out of high school in Nebraska at fifteen in order to help support her family during the Depression years. She held jobs as a factory worker or secretary while she organized labor unions, got married, raised four children, and continued to read prodigiously. "Public libraries were my college," she has said. When she was forty, she resumed her early efforts to write fiction. She enrolled in a class in fiction writing at San Francisco State College, and later she won a writing fellowship at Stanford University. Her volume of stories, *Tell Me A Riddle* (1961), established her as a sensitively compassionate and politically radical champion of the poor and overburdened. In her essay *Silences* (1962), Olsen examines the injustices of social class, racism, and sexism that hinder creativity, particularly in women. The cruelty of harmful social conditions is a theme in all her work, including the following story that reflects dilemmas she faced in her own life. It was written in 1953–54 when people were just becoming aware of the threat of nuclear war.

I stand here ironing, and what you asked me moves tormented back 1
and forth with the iron.

"I wish you would manage the time to come in and talk with me 2
about your daughter. I'm sure you can help me understand her. She's
a youngster who needs help and whom I'm deeply interested in helping."

"Who needs help." . . . Even if I came, what good would it do? 3
You think because I am her mother I have a key, or that in some way
you could use me as a key? She has lived for nineteen years. There is
all that life that has happened outside of me, beyond me.

And when is there time to remember, to sift, to weigh, to estimate, 4
to total? I will start and there will be an interruption and I will have to
gather it all together again. Or I will become engulfed with all I did or
did not do, with what should have been and what cannot be helped.

She was a beautiful baby. The first and only one of our five that was 5

568

beautiful at birth. You do not guess how new and uneasy her tenancy in her now-loveliness. You did not know her all those years she was thought homely, or see her poring over her baby pictures, making me tell her over and over how beautiful she had been — and would be, I would tell her — and was now, to the seeing eye. But the seeing eyes were few or nonexistent. Including mine.

I nursed her. They feel that's important nowadays. I nursed all the 6 children, but with her, with all the fierce rigidity of first motherhood, I did like the books then said. Though her cries battered me to trembling and my breasts ached with swollenness, I waited till the clock decreed.

Why do I put that first? I do not even know if it matters, or if it 7 explains anything.

She was a beautiful baby. She blew shining bubbles of sound. She 8 loved motion, loved light, loved color and music and textures. She would lie on the floor in her blue overalls patting the surface so hard in ecstasy her hands and feet would blur. She was a miracle to me, but when she was eight months old I had to leave her daytimes with the woman downstairs to whom she was no miracle at all, for I worked or looked for work and for Emily's father, who "could no longer endure" (he wrote in his good-bye note) "sharing want with us."

I was nineteen, it was the pre-relief, pre-WPA world of the De- 9 pression. I would start running as soon as I got off the streetcar, running up the stairs, the place smelling sour, and awake or asleep to startle awake, when she saw me she would break into a clogged weeping that could not be comforted, a weeping I can hear yet.

After a while I found a job hashing at night so I could be with her 10 days, and it was better. But it came to where I had to bring her to his family and leave her.

It took a long time to raise the money for her fare back. Then she 11 got chicken pox and I had to wait longer. When she finally came, I hardly knew her, walking quick and nervous like her father, looking like her father, thin, and dressed in a shoddy red that yellowed her skin and glared at the pockmarks. All the baby loveliness gone.

She was two. Old enough for nursery school they said, and I did 12 not know then what I know now — the fatigue of the long day, and the lacerations of group life in the kinds of nurseries that are only parking places for children.

Except that it would have made no difference if I had known. It 13 was the only place there was. It was the only way we could be together, the only way I could hold a job.

And even without knowing, I knew. I knew the teacher that was 14 evil because all these years it has curdled into my memory, the little boy hunched in the corner, her rasp, "why aren't you outside, because Alvin hits you? that's no reason, go out, scaredy." I knew Emily hated it even if she did not clutch and implore "don't go Mommy" like the other children, mornings.

She always had a reason why we should stay home. Momma, you 15 look sick, Momma. I feel sick. Momma, the teachers aren't there today, they're sick. Momma, we can't go, there was a fire there last night. Momma, it's a holiday today, no school, they told me.

But never a direct protest, never rebellion. I think of our others in 16 their three-, four-year-oldness — the explosions, the tempers, the denunciations, the demands — and I feel suddenly ill. I put the iron down. What in me demanded that goodness in her? And what was the cost, the cost to her of such goodness?

The old man living in the back once said in his gentle way: "You 17 should smile at Emily more when you look at her." What *was* in my face when I looked at her? I loved her. There were all the acts of love.

It was only with the others I remembered what he said, and it was 18 the face of joy, and not of care or tightness or worry I turned to them — too late for Emily. She does not smile easily, let alone almost always as her brothers and sisters do. Her face is closed and sombre, but when she wants, how fluid. You must have seen it in her pantomimes, you spoke of her rare gift for comedy on the stage that rouses a laughter out of the audience so dear they applaud and applaud and do not want to let her go.

Where does it come from, that comedy? There was none of it in 19 her when she came back to me that second time, after I had had to send her away again. She had a new daddy now to learn to love, and I think perhaps it was a better time.

Except when we left her alone nights, telling ourselves she was old 20 enough.

"Can't you go some other time, Mommy, like tomorrow?" she 21 would ask. "Will it be just a little while you'll be gone? Do you promise?"

The time we came back, the front door open, the clock on the floor 22 in the hall. She rigid awake. "It wasn't just a little while. I didn't cry. Three times I called you, just three times, and then I ran downstairs to open the door so you could come faster. The clock talked loud. I threw it away, it scared me what it talked."

She said the clock talked loud again that night I went to the hospital to have Susan. She was delirious with the fever that comes before red measles, but she was fully conscious all the week I was gone and the week after we were home when she could not come near the new baby or me. 23

She did not get well. She stayed skeleton thin, not wanting to eat, and night after night she had nightmares. She would call for me, and I would rouse from exhaustion to sleepily call back: "You're all right, darling, go to sleep, it's just a dream," and if she still called, in a sterner voice, "now go to sleep, Emily, there's nothing to hurt you." Twice, only twice, when I had to get up for Susan anyhow, I went in to sit with her. 24

Now when it is too late (as if she would let me hold and comfort her like I do the others) I get up and go to her at once at her moan or restless stirring. "Are you awake, Emily? Can I get you something?" And the answer is always the same. "No, I'm all right, go back to sleep, Mother." 25

They persuaded me at the clinic to send her away to a convalescent home in the country where "she can have the kind of food and care you can't manage for her, and you'll be free to concentrate on the new baby." They still send children to that place. I see pictures on the society page of sleek young women planning affairs to raise money for it, or dancing at the affairs, or decorating Easter eggs or filling Christmas stockings for the children. 26

They never have a picture of the children so I do not know if the girls still wear those gigantic red bows and the ravaged looks on the every other Sunday when parents can come to visit "unless otherwise notified" — as we were notified the first six weeks. 27

Oh it is a handsome place, green lawns and tall trees and fluted flower beds. High up on the balconies of each cottage the children stand, the girls in their red bows and white dresses, the boys in white suits and gigantic red ties. The parents stand below shrieking up to be heard and the children shriek down to be heard, and between them the invisible wall "Not To Be Contaminated by Parental Germs or Physical Affection." 28

There was a tiny girl who always stood hand in hand with Emily. 29
Her parents never came. One visit she was gone. "They moved her to
Rose Cottage," Emily shouted in explanation. "They don't like you to
love anybody here."

She wrote once a week, the labored writing of a seven-year-old. "I 30
am fine. How is the baby. If I write my letter nicly I will have a star.
Love." There never was a star. We wrote every other day, letters she
could never hold or keep but only hear read — once. "We simply do
not have room for children to keep any personal possessions, they patiently explained when we pieced one Sunday's shrieking together to
plead how much it would mean to Emily, who loved so to keep things,
to be allowed to keep her letters and cards.

Each visit she looked frailer. "She isn't eating," they told us.   31

(They had runny eggs for breakfast or mush with lumps, Emily said 32
later, I'd hold it in my mouth and not swallow. Nothing ever tasted
good, just when they had chicken.)

It took us eight months to get her released home, and only the fact 33
that she gained back so little or her seven lost pounds convinced the
social worker.

I used to try to hold and love her after she came back, but her body 34
would stay stiff, and after a while she'd push away. She ate little. Food
sickened her, and I think much of life too. Oh she had physical
lightness and brightness, twinkling by on skates, bouncing like a ball
up and down up and down over the jump rope, skimming over the
hill; but these were momentary.

She fretted about her appearance, thin and dark and foreign-look- 35
ing at a time when every little girl was supposed to look or thought
she should look a chubby blonde replica of Shirley Temple. The
doorbell sometimes rang for her, but no one seemed to come and
play in the house or be a best friend. Maybe because we moved so
much.

There was a boy she loved painfully through two school semesters. 36
Months later she told me how she had taken pennies from my purse
to buy him candy. "Licorice was his favorite and I brought him some
every day, but he still liked Jennifer better'n me. Why, Mommy?"
The kind of question for which there is no answer.

School was a worry to her. She was not glib or quick in a world 37
where glibness and quickness were easily confused with ability to
learn. To her overworked and exasperated teachers she was an over-

conscientious "slow learner" who kept trying to catch up and was absent entirely too often.

I let her be absent, though sometimes the illness was imaginary. 38 How different from my now-strictness about attendance with the others. I wasn't working. We had a new baby, I was home anyhow. Sometimes, after Susan grew old enough, I would keep her home from school, too, to have them all together.

Mostly Emily had asthma, and her breathing, harsh and labored, 39 would fill the house with a curiously tranquil sound. I would bring the two old dresser mirrors and her boxes of collections to her bed. She would select beads and single earrings, bottle tops and shells, dried flowers and pebbles, old postcards and scraps, all sorts of oddments; then she and Susan would play Kingdom, setting up landscapes and furniture, peopling them with action.

Those were the only times of peaceful companionship between her 40 and Susan. I have edged away from it, that poisonous feeling between them, that terrible balancing of hurts and needs I had to do between the two, and did so badly, those earlier years.

Oh there are conflicts between the others too, each one human, 41 needing, demanding, hurting, taking — but only between Emily and Susan, no, Emily toward Susan that corroding resentment. It seems so obvious on the surface, yet it is not obvious. Susan, the second child, Susan, golden- and curly-haired and chubby, quick and articulate and assured, everything in appearance and manner Emily was not; Susan, not able to resist Emily's precious things, losing or sometimes clumsily breaking them; Susan telling jokes and riddles to company for applause while Emily sat silent (to say to me later; that was *my* riddle, Mother, I told it to Susan); Susan, who for all the five years' difference in age was just a year behind Emily in developing physically.

I am glad for that slow physical development that widened the dif- 42 ference between her and her contemporaries, though she suffered over it. She was too vulnerable for that terrible world of youthful competition, of preening and parading, of constant measuring of yourself against every other, of envy, "If I had that copper hair," "If I had that skin. . . ." She tormented herself enough about not looking like the others, there was enough of the unsureness, the having to be conscious of words before you speak, the constant caring — what are they thinking of me? without having it all magnified by the merciless physical drives.

Ronnie is calling. He is wet and I change him. It is rare there is   43
such a cry now. That time of motherhood is almost behind me when
the ear is not one's own but must always be racked and listening for
the child cry, the child call. We sit for a while and I hold him, looking
out over the city spread in charcoal with its soft aisles of light. "*Shoogily,*" he breathes and curls closer. I carry him back to bed, asleep.
Shoogily. A funny word, a family word, inherited from Emily, invented by her to say: *comfort.*

In this and other ways she leaves her seal, I say aloud. And startle at   44
me saying it. What do I mean? What did I start to gather together, to
try and make coherent? I was at the terrible, growing years. War years.
I do not remember them well. I was working, there were four smaller
ones now, there was not time for her. She had to help be a mother,
and housekeeper, and shopper. She had to set her seal. Mornings of
crisis and near hysteria trying to get lunches packed, hair combed,
coats and shoes found, everyone to school or Child Care on time, the
baby ready for transportation. And always the paper scribbled on by a
smaller one, the book looked at by Susan then mislaid, the homework
not done. Running out to that huge school where she was one, she
was lost, she was a drop; suffering over her unpreparedness, stammering and unsure in her classes.

There was so little time left at night after the kids were bedded   45
down. She would struggle over books, always eating (it was in those
years she developed her enormous appetite that is legendary in our
family) and I would be ironing, or preparing food for the next day, or
writing V-mail to Bill, or tending the baby. Sometimes, to make me
laugh, or out of her despair, she would imitate happenings or types at
school.

I think I said once: "Why don't you do something like this in the   46
school amateur show?" One morning she phoned me at work, hardly
understandable through the weeping: "Mother, I did it. I won, I won;
they gave me first prize; they clapped and clapped and wouldn't let
me go."

Now suddenly she was Somebody, and as imprisoned in her differ-   47
ence as she had been in anonymity.

She began to be asked to perform at other high schools, even in   48
colleges, then at city and statewide affairs. The first one we went to, I
only recognized her that first moment when thin, shy, she almost
drowned herself into the curtains. Then: Was this Emily? The con-

trol, the command, the convulsing and deadly drowning, the spell, then the roaring, stamping audience, unwilling to let this rare and precious laughter out of their lives.

Afterwards: You ought to do something about her with a gift like 49 that — but without money or knowing how, what does one do? We have left it all to her, and the gift has as often eddied inside, clogged and clotted, as been used and growing.

She is coming. She runs up the stairs two at a time with her light 50 graceful step, and I know she is happy tonight. Whatever it was that occasioned your call did not happen today.

"Aren't you ever going to finish the ironing, Mother? Whistler 51 painted his mother in a rocker. I'd have to paint mine standing over an ironing board." This is one of her communicative nights and she tells me everything and nothing as she fixes herself a plate of food out of the icebox.

She is so lovely. Why did you want me to come in at all? Why were 52 you concerned? She will find her way.

She starts up the stairs to bed. "Don't get me up with the rest in 53 the morning." "But I thought you were having midterms." "Oh, those," she comes back in, kisses me, and says quite lightly, "in a couple of years when we'll all be atom-dead they won't matter a bit."

She has said it before. She *believes* it. But because I have been 54 dredging the past, and all that compounds a human being is so heavy and meaningful in me, I cannot endure it tonight.

I will never total it all. I will never come in to say: She was a child 55 seldom smiled at. Her father left me before she was a year old. I had to work her first six years when there was work, or I sent her home and to his relatives. There were years she had care she hated. She was dark and thin and foreign-looking in a world where the prestige went to blondeness and curly hair and dimples, she was slow where glibness was prized. She was a child of anxious, not proud, love. We were poor and could not afford for her the soil of easy growth. I was a younger mother, I was a distracted mother. There were the other children pushing up, demanding. Her younger sister seemed all that she was not. There were years she did not want me to touch her. She kept too much in herself, her life was such she had to keep too much in herself. My wisdom came too late. She has much to her and probably little will come of it. She is a child of her age, of depression, of war, of fear.

Let her be. So all that is in her will not bloom — but in how many 56
does it? There is still enough left to live by. Only help her to know —
help make it so there is cause for her to know — that she is more than
this dress on the ironing board, helpless before the iron.

CONSIDERATIONS

1. Who has phoned Emily's mother and how has the caller's request affected
   the mother?
2. In paragraph 11, do we agree with the mother's point or do we blame her?
   What is the effect of the repetitiveness of her thoughts?
3. How did Emily differ from her brother and sisters? What explanations
   does the mother have for Emily's differences? Which of her explanations
   do you think are most valid and important?
4. In the final two paragraphs, why does the mother refuse to consult about
   Emily?
5. Does the story reflect specific political views toward particular social conditions and historical events? What social attitudes, if any, does the story
   stimulate in the reader?
6. WRITING TOPIC. How would a child like Emily perceive her mother's
   conflict of responsibilities? What dilemmas do you think the child faced?
   Adopt Emily's viewpoint in a 500-word monologue that explores Emily's
   thoughts during any one incident or situation suggested in the story.
7. WRITING TOPIC. Should mothers be paid by the government to stay
   home and raise their children? Should the government maintain adequate
   day-care centers so that mothers can work? Or should parents bear all financial responsibility for their young children? Weigh good and bad
   points in each of these alternatives. In 700 words, explain what you think
   our society should do about the task and cost of child rearing.

Jonathan Schell

THE CHOICE*

◊

JONATHAN SCHELL (b. 1943) was born in New York City and educated at the University of California at Berkeley. He writes for *The New Yorker*, and his essays there have often become the basis for his books on the significance of American international policies and domestic politics, including *The Village of Ben Suc* (1967) and *The Time of Illusion* (1976). His book, *The Fate of the Earth* (1982), which was originally serialized in *The New Yorker*, analyzes the theories and effects of the nuclear arms race, the multinational preparations for and the inevitable consequences of a nuclear war. In the following excerpt from his concluding section, Schell argues that mankind faces a dilemma that is utterly new to our ways of thinking, a dilemma that is virtually inconceivable, and one that we will never have a second chance to resolve.

Four and a half billion years ago, the earth was formed. Perhaps a 1 half billion years after that, life arose on the planet. For the next four billion years, life became steadily more complex, more varied, and more ingenious, until, around a million years ago, it produced mankind — the most complex and ingenious species of them all. Only six or seven thousand years ago — a period that is to the history of the earth as less than a minute is to a year — civilization emerged, enabling us to build up a human world, and to add to the marvels of evolution marvels of our own: marvels of art, of science, of social organization, of spiritual attainment. But, as we built higher and higher, the evolutionary foundation beneath our feet became more and more shaky, and now, in spite of all we have learned and achieved — or,

* Editor's title.

577

rather, because of it — we hold this entire terrestrial creation hostage to nuclear destruction, threatening to hurl it back into the inanimate darkness from which it came. And this threat of self-destruction and planetary destruction is not something that we will pose one day in the future, if we fail to take certain precautions; it is here now, hanging over the heads of all of us at every moment. The machinery of destruction is complete, poised on a hair trigger, waiting for the "button" to be "pushed" by some misguided or deranged human being or for some faulty computer chip to send out the instruction to fire. That so much should be balanced on so fine a point — that the fruit of four and a half billion years can be undone in a careless moment — is a fact against which belief rebels. And there is another, even vaster measure of the loss, for stretching ahead from our present are more billions of years of life on earth, all of which can be filled not only with human life but with human civilization. The procession of generations that extends onward from our present leads far, far beyond the line of our sight, and, compared with these stretches of human time, which exceed the whole history of the earth up to now, our brief civilized moment is almost infinitesimal. And yet we threaten, in the name of our transient aims and fallible convictions, to foreclose it all. If our species does destroy itself, it will be a death in the cradle — a case of infant mortality. The disparity between the cause and the effect of our peril is so great that our minds seem all but powerless to encompass it. In addition, we are so fully enveloped by that which is menaced, and so deeply and passionately immersed in its events, which are the events of our lives, that we hardly know how to get far enough away from it to see it in its entirety. It is as though life itself were one huge distraction, diverting our attention from the peril to life. In its apparent durability, a world menaced with imminent doom is in a way deceptive. It is almost an illusion. Now we are sitting at the breakfast table drinking our coffee and reading the newspaper, but in a moment we may be inside a fireball whose temperature is tens of thousands of degrees. Now we are on our way to work, walking through the city streets, but in a moment we may be standing on an empty plain under a darkened sky looking for the charred remnants of our children. Now we are alive, but in a moment we may be dead. Now there is human life on earth, but in a moment it may be gone.

Once, there was time to reflect in a more leisurely way on our pre- 2 dicament. In August, 1945, when the invention of the bomb was made known through its first use on a human population, the people of Hiroshima, there lay ahead an interval of decades which might have been used to fashion a world that would be safe from extinction by nuclear arms, and some voices were in fact heard counseling deep reflection on the looming peril and calling for action to head it off. On November 28, 1945, less than four months after the bombing of Hiroshima, the English philosopher Bertrand Russell rose in the House of Lords and said:

> We do not want to look at this thing simply from the point of view of the next few years; we want to look at it from the point of view of the future of mankind. The question is a simple one: Is it possible for a scientific society to continue to exist, or must such a society inevitably bring itself to destruction? It is a simple question but a very vital one. I do not think it is possible to exaggerate the gravity of the possibilities of evil that lie in the utilization of atomic energy. As I go about the streets and see St. Paul's, the British Museum, the Houses of Parliament, and the other monuments of our civilization, in my mind's eye I see a nightmare vision of those buildings as heaps of rubble with corpses all around them. That is a thing we have got to face, not only in our own country and cities, but throughout the civilized world.

Russell and others, including Albert Einstein, urged full, global 3 disarmament, but the advice was disregarded. Instead, the world set about building the arsenals that we possess today. The period of grace we had in which to ward off the nuclear peril before it became a reality — the time between the moment of the invention of the weapons and the construction of the full-scale machinery for extinction — was squandered, and now the peril that Russell foresaw is upon us. Indeed, if we are honest with ourselves we have to admit that unless we rid ourselves of our nuclear arsenals a holocaust not only *might* occur but *will* occur — if not today, then tomorrow; if not this year, then the next. We have come to live on borrowed time: every year of continued human life on earth is a borrowed year, every day a borrowed day.

In the face of this unprecedented global emergency, we have so far 4 had no better idea than to heap up more and more warheads, apparently in the hope of so thoroughly paralyzing ourselves with terror that we will hold back from taking the final, absurd step. Considering the wealth of our achievement as a species, this response is unworthy of us. Only by a process of gradual debasement of our self-esteem can we have lowered our expectations to this point. For, of all the "modest hopes of human beings," the hope that mankind will survive is the most modest, since it only brings us to the threshold of all the other hopes. In entertaining it, we do not yet ask for justice, or for freedom, or for happiness, or for any of the other things that we may want in life. We do not even necessarily ask for our personal survival; we ask only that we *be survived.* We ask for assurance that when we die as individuals, as we know we must, mankind will live on. Yet once the peril of extinction is present, as it is for us now, the hope for human survival becomes the most tremendous hope, just because it is the foundation for all the other hopes, and in its absence every other hope will gradually wither and die. Life without the hope for human survival is a life of despair.

The death of our species resembles the death of an individual in its 5 boundlessness, its blankness, its removal beyond experience, and its tendency to baffle human thought and feeling, yet as soon as one mentions the hope of survival the similarities are clearly at an end. For while individual death is inevitable, extinction can be avoided; while every person must die, mankind can be saved. Therefore, while reflection on death may lead to resignation and acceptance, reflection on extinction must lead to exactly the opposite response: to arousal, rejection, indignation, and action. Extinction is not something to contemplate, it is something to rebel against. To point this out might seem like stating the obvious if it were not that on the whole the world's reaction to the peril of extinction has been one of numbness and inertia, much as though extinction were as inescapable as death is. Even today, the official response to the sickening reality before us is conditioned by a grim fatalism, in which the hope of ridding the world of nuclear weapons, and thus of surviving as a species, is all but ruled out of consideration as "utopian" or "extreme" — as though it were "radical" merely to want to go on living and to want one's descendants to be born. And yet if one gives up these aspirations one has given up on everything. As a species, we have as yet done nothing to save ourselves. The slate of action is blank. We have organizations for the preservation of almost everything in life that we want but no organization for the preservation of mankind. People seem to have decided that our collective will is too weak or flawed to rise to this occasion. They see the violence that has saturated human history, and conclude that to practice violence is innate in our species. They find the perennial hope that peace can be brought to the earth once and for all a delusion of the well-meaning who have refused to face the "harsh realities" of international life — the realities of self-interest, fear, hatred, and aggression. They have concluded that these realities are eternal ones, and this conclusion defeats at the outset any hope of taking the actions necessary for survival. Looking at the historical record, they ask what has changed to give anyone confidence that humanity can break with its violent past and act with greater restraint. The answer, of course, is that everything has changed. To the old "harsh realities" of international life has been added the immeasurably harsher new reality of the peril of extinction. To the old truth that all men are brothers has been added the inescapable new truth that not only on the moral but also on the physical plane the nation that practices aggression will itself die. This is the law of the doctrine of nuclear deterrence — the doctrine of "mutual assured destruction" — which "assures" the destruction of the society of the attacker. And it is also the law of the natural world, which, in its own version of deterrence, supplements the oneness of mankind with a oneness of nature, and guarantees that when the attack rises above a certain level the attacker will be engulfed in the general ruin of the global ecosphere. To the obligation to honor life is now added the sanction that if we fail in our obligation life will actually be taken away from us, individually and collectively. Each of us will die, and as we die we will see the world around us dying. Such imponderables as the sum of human life, the integrity of the terrestrial creation, and the meaning of time, of history, and of the development of life on earth, which were once left to contemplation and spiritual understanding, are now at stake in the political realm and demand a political response from every person. As political actors, we must, like the contemplatives before us, delve to the bottom of the world, and, Atlas-like, we must take the world on our shoulders.

The self-extinction of our species is not an act that anyone describes as sane or sensible; nevertheless, it is an act that, without quite admitting it to ourselves, we plan in certain circumstances to commit. Being impossible as a fully intentional act, unless the perpetrator has lost his mind, it can come about only through a kind of inadvertence — as a "side effect" of some action that we do intend, such as the defense of our nation, or the defense of liberty, or the defense of socialism, or the defense of whatever else we happen to believe in. To that extent, our failure to acknowledge the magnitude and significance of the peril is a necessary condition for doing the deed. We can do it only if we don't quite know what we're doing. If we did acknowledge the full dimensions of the peril, admitting clearly and without reservation that any use of nuclear arms is likely to touch off a holocaust in which the continuance of all human life would be put at risk, extinction would at that moment become not only "unthinkable" but also undoable. What is needed to make extinction possible, therefore, is some way of thinking about it that at least partly deflects our attention from what it is. And this way of thinking is supplied to us, unfortunately, by our political and military traditions, which, with the weight of almost all historical experience behind them, teach us that it is the way of the world for the earth to be divided up into independent, sovereign states, and for these states to employ war as the final arbiter for settling the disputes that arise among them. This arrangement of the political affairs of the world was not intentional. No one wrote a book proposing it; no parliament sat down to debate its merits and then voted it into existence. It was simply there, at the beginning of recorded history; and until the invention of nuclear weapons it remained there, with virtually no fundamental changes. Unplanned though this arrangement was, it had many remarkably durable features, and certain describable advantages and disadvantages; therefore, I shall refer to it as a "system" — the system of sovereignty. Perhaps the leading feature of this system, and certainly the most important one in the context of the nuclear predicament, was the apparently indissoluble connection between sovereignty and war. For without sovereignty, it appeared, peoples were not able to organize and launch wars against other peoples, and without war they were unable to preserve their sovereignty from destruction by armed enemies. (By "war" I here mean only international war, not revolutionary war, which I shall not discuss.) Indeed, the connection between sovereignty and war is almost a definitional one — a sovereign state being a state that enjoys the right and the power to go to war in defense or pursuit of its interests.

It was into the sovereignty system that nuclear bombs were born, as "weapons" for "war." As the years have passed, it has seemed less and less plausible that they have anything to do with war; they seem to break through its bounds. Nevertheless, they have gone on being fit- 7 ted into military categories of thinking. One might say that they appeared in the world in a military disguise, for it has been traditional military thinking, itself an inseparable part of the traditional political thinking that belonged to the system of sovereignty, that has provided those intentional goals — namely, national interests — in the pursuit of which extinction may now be brought about unintentionally, or semi-intentionally, as a "side effect." The system of sovereignty is now to the earth and mankind what a polluting factory is to its local environment. The machine produces certain things that its users want — in this case, national sovereignty — and as an unhappy side effect extinguishes the species.

The ambivalence resulting from the attempt to force nuclear weapons into the preexisting military and political system has led to a situation in which, in the words of Einstein — who was farseeing in his political as well as in his scientific thought — "the unleashed power of the atom has changed everything save our modes of thinking, and we thus drift toward unparalleled catastrophes." As Einstein's observation suggests, the nuclear revolution has gone quite far but has not been completed. The question we have to answer is whether the completion will be extinction or a global political revolution — whether the "babies" that the scientists at Alamogordo brought forth will put an end to us or we will put an end to them. For it is not only our thoughts but also our actions and our institutions — our global political arrangements in their entirety — that we have failed to change. We live with one foot in each of two worlds. As scientists and technicians, we live in the nuclear world, in which whether we choose to acknowledge the fact or not, we possess instruments of violence that make it possible for us to extinguish ourselves as a species. But as citizens and statesmen we go on living in the pre-nuclear world, as though extinction were not possible and sovereign nations could still employ the instruments of violence as instruments of policy — as "a continuation of politics by other means," in the famous phrase of Karl von Clausewitz, the great philosopher of war. In effect, we try to make do with a Newtonian politics in an Einsteinian world. The combination is the source of our immediate peril. For governments, still acting within a system of independent nation-states, and formally representing no one but the people of their separate, sovereign nations, are driven to try to defend merely national interests with means of destruction that threaten not only international but intergenerational and planetary doom. In our present-day world, in the councils where

8

the decisions are made there is no one to speak for man and for the earth, although both are threatened with annihilation.

... The terms of the deal that the world has now struck with itself 9 must be made clear. On the one side stand human life and the terrestrial creation. On the other side stands a particular organization of human life — the system of independent, sovereign nation-states. Our choice so far has been to preserve that political organization of human life at the cost of risking all human life. We are told that "realism" compels us to preserve the system of sovereignty. But that political realism is not biological realism; it is biological nihilism — and for that reason is, of course, political nihilism, too. Indeed, it is nihilism in every conceivable sense of that word. We are told that it is human fate — perhaps even "a law of human nature" — that, in obedience, perhaps, to some "territorial imperative," or to some dark and ineluctable truth in the bottom of our souls, we must preserve sovereignty and always settle our differences with violence. If this is our fate, then it is our fate to die. But must we embrace nihilism? Must we die? Is self-extermination a law of our nature? Is there nothing we can do? I do not believe so. Indeed, if we admit the reality of the basic terms of the nuclear predicament — that present levels of global armament are great enough to possibly extinguish the species if a holocaust should occur; that in extinction every human purpose would be lost; that because once the species has been extinguished there will be no second chance, and the game will be over for all time; that therefore this possibility must be dealt with morally and politically as though it were a certainty; and that either by accident or by design a holocaust can occur at any second — then, whatever political views we may hold on other matters, we are driven almost inescapably to take action to rid the world of nuclear arms. Just as we have chosen to make nuclear weapons, we can choose to unmake them. Just as we have chosen to live in the system of sovereign states, we can choose to live in some other system. To do so would, of course, be unprecedented, and in many ways frightening, even truly perilous, but it is by no means impossible. Our present system and the institutions that make it up are the debris of history. They have become inimical to life, and must be swept away. They constitute a noose around the neck of mankind, threatening to choke off the human future, but we can cut the noose and break free. To suppose otherwise would be to set up a false, fictitious fate, molded out of our own weaknesses and our own alterable decisions. We are indeed fated by our acquisition of the basic knowledge of physics to live for the rest of time with the knowledge of how to destroy ourselves. But we are not for that reason fated to destroy ourselves. We can choose to live.

CONSIDERATIONS

1. The selection opens with a fairly long paragraph. How does Schell develop its central point? Would breaking it up into shorter paragraphs strengthen or weaken the point?
2. According to Schell, what is mankind's most fundamental hope? Do you think he is right? Is there any evidence in daily life to support or refute his generalization?
3. How do people presently respond to the possibility of the extinction of the species? Where does this response appear to originate? How does Schell propose, explicitly or implicity, to develop new attitudes?
4. For what purposes would nuclear havoc be unleashed? How does Schell see the balance between the likely causes and the likely effects of war?
5. What does Schell find fundamentally wrong with the political system of national sovereignty? Why would it be "in many ways frightening, even perilous" to change the system? What changes would you favor? Which would you oppose?
6. WRITING TOPIC. Schell says that nuclear bombs were introduced for use in war but that "as the years have passed, it has seemed less and less plausible that they have anything to do with war; they seem to break through its bounds." In a 500-word essay, explain or disagree with his assertion that present-day nuclear bombs are not military weapons.

Robert Jastrow

AN END
AND A BEGINNING

◊

ROBERT JASTROW (b. 1925), the director of the Goddard Institute for Space Studies, received his training as a physicist at Columbia University. In addition to his scientific research, he has written several books on science for the general public, including *Red Giants and White Dwarfs: The Evolution of Stars, Planets and Life* (1967) and a book more focused on earth, *Until the Sun Dies* (1977). The following selection is a chapter from his most recent book, *The Enchanted Loom* (1982), in which Jastrow explains the evolution of the human mind — and its possible future in a world without people.

The era of carbon-chemistry life is drawing to a close on the earth 1 and a new era of silicon-based life — indestructible, immortal, infinitely expandable — is beginning. By the turn of the century, ultraintelligent machines will be working in partnership with our best minds on all the serious problems of the day, in an unbeatable combination of brute reasoning power and human intuition. Dartmouth mathematician John Kemeny, a pioneer in computer usage, sees the ultimate relation between man and computer as a symbiotic union of two living species, each dependent on the other for survival. The computer — a new form of life dedicated to pure thought — will be taken care of by its human partners, who will minister to its bodily needs with electricity and spare parts. Man will also provide for computer reproduction, as he does today. In return, the computer will minister to man's social and economic needs. It will become his salvation in a world of crushing complexity.

The partnership will not last very long. Human intelligence is 2 changing slowly, if at all, while the capabilities of the computer are increasing at a fantastic rate. Since the birth of the modern computer in the 1950s, computers have increased rapidly in power and capability. The first generation of computers was a billion times clumsier and less efficient than the human brain. Today, the gap has been narrowed a thousandfold. Around 1995, it may be closed entirely. And there is no limit to the rising curve of silicon intelligence; computers, unlike the human brain, do not have to pass through a birth canal.

As these nonbiological intelligences increase in size and capacity, 3 there will be people around to teach them everything they know. One sees a vision of mammoth brains that have soaked up the wisdom of the human race and gone on from there. If this forecast is accurate, man is doomed to a subordinate status on his own planet.

The story is an old one on the earth: in the struggle for survival, 4 bigger brains are better. One hundred million years ago, when the brainy little mammal coexisted with the less intelligent dinosaurs, the mammal survived and the dinosaur vanished. It appears that in the next chapter of this unfolding story, fate has cast man in the role of the dinosaur.

What can be done? The answer is obvious: Pull the plug.   5

That may not be so easy. Computers enhance the productivity of 6 human labor; they create wealth and the leisure to enjoy it; they have ushered in the Golden Age. In 15 or 20 years, computer brains will be indispensable to top level management in every facet of the nation's existence: the economy, transportation, security, medicine, communications . . . If someone pulled the plug, chaos would result. There is no turning back.

Perhaps the human brain will begin to evolve again under the 7 pressure of the competition between the two species. The history of life supports this idea. The trouble with the thought is that biological evolution works very slowly; thousands or even millions of years are usually required for the appearance of a new species of animal. Evolution works on animals through changes in their "reproductive success," i.e., in the number of progeny each individual produces. The raw materials for this evolutionary change are the small variations from one individual to another that exist in every population. Darwin did not know the cause of these variations, but today we know that they result from changes in the DNA molecules that exist in every living cell. These DNA molecules contain the master plan of the animal; they determine the shape of its body, the size of its brain, everything. When a new kind of animal evolves, it is actually the animal's DNA molecules that are changing and evolving. But the DNA molecules are not located outside of the animal, where they can be gotten at and tinkered with easily to make big changes. They are located inside the animal's germ cells — the sperm or the ova — where they can only be changed a tiny bit at a time, over many generations, by Darwin's subtle mechanism of differences in the number of offspring. That is why biological evolution is so slow.

Computers do not have DNA molecules; they are not biological organisms; and Darwin's theory of evolution does not apply to them. We are the reproductive organs of the computer. We create new generations of computers, one after another. The computer designer tacks on a piece here, and lops off a piece there, and makes major improvements in one computer generation.   8

This kind of evolution, as the short history of computers has already shown, can proceed at a dizzying pace. It is the kind of evolution that Lamarck — the eighteenth-century evolutionist — envisioned. Lamarckian evolution turned out to be wrong for flesh-and-blood creatures, but right for computers.   9

Now we see why the brain will never catch up to the rapidly evolving computer. At the end of the century, the two forms of intelligence will be working together. What about the next century? And the century after that? A leader in research on artificial brains, Marvin Minsky of Massachusetts Institute of Technology, believes that ultimately a machine will come into being with the "general intelligence of an average human being . . . the machine will begin to educate itself . . . in a few months it will be at a genius level . . . a few months after that its power will be incalculable." After that, Minsky says, "If we are lucky, they might decide to keep us as pets."   10

Is there any way out? As we cast about for a solution, a thought strikes us. Perhaps man can join forces with the computer to create a brain that combines the accumulated wisdom of the human mind with the power of the machine, much as the primitive brain of the reptile and old mammal was combined with the new brain in the cerebral cortex to form a better animal. This hybrid intelligence would be the progenitor of a new race, that would start at the human level of achievement and go on from there. It would not be an end, but a beginning.   11

Here is how it might happen: brains and computers are turning out   12 to be more alike than anyone would have believed a few years ago. Each is a thinking machine that operates on little pulses of electricity traveling along wires. In the brain, the "wires" are the axons and dendrites of the brain cell, which make up the circuits that connect one part of the brain to the other. Brain scientists have painstakingly traced many of these electrical circuits in the brain; they are beginning to understand how the brain is wired, and where it stores its memories and skills.

This research has barely started, but the pace of the progress is astonishing. In one recent experiment, scientists attached electrodes to the rear of a subject's skull, just above the brain's center of vision. They discovered that this region emitted different electrical patterns, depending on what the subject was looking at. Circles, squares, or straight lines — each had its special pattern of electrical waves. In another experiment, scientists detected a special signal that seemed to signify excitement or elation, coming from the seat of feelings and emotions in the brain. Looking at these electrical records, the scientist can tell something about the thoughts and feelings in a person's mind, and the impressions that are passing into his memory. 13

These are small steps, but they establish a direction. If scientists can decipher a few of the brain's signals today, they should be able to decipher more signals tomorrow. Eventually, they will be able to read a person's mind. 14

When the brain sciences reach this point, a bold scientist will be able to tap the contents of his mind and transfer them into the metallic lattices of a computer. Because mind is the essence of being, it can be said that this scientist has entered the computer, and that he now dwells in it. 15

At last the human brain, ensconced in a computer, has been liberated from the weaknesses of the mortal flesh. Connected to cameras, instruments, and engine controls, the brain sees, feels, and responds to stimuli. It is in control of its own destiny. The machine is its body; it is the machine's mind. The union of mind and machine has created a new form of existence, as well designed for life in the future as man is designed for life on the African savanna. 16

It seems to me that this must be the mature form of intelligent life in the Universe. Housed in indestructible lattices of silicon, and no longer constrained in the span of its years by the life and death cycle of a biological organism, such a kind of life could live forever. It would 17 be the kind of life that could leave its parent planet to roam the space between the stars. Man as we know him will never make that trip, for the passage takes a million years. But the artificial brain, sealed within the protective hull of a star ship, and nourished by electricity collected from starlight, could last a million years or more. For a brain living in a computer, the voyage to another star would present no problems.

When will the great voyages begin? Not soon on the earth; perhaps 18 not for a thousand years or more. But our planet is a newcomer in the Universe, and its life is still primitive. The earth is only 4.6 billion years old, but the Universe is 20 billion years old according to the best evidence, and stars and planets have been forming throughout that long interval. Thus, many planets circling distant stars are 5, 10, and even 15 billion years older than the earth. If life is common in the universe — and scientific theories on the origin of life make that assumption plausible — many of these older planets are inhabited, and the life they bear, a billion years older and more advanced than man, must already have passed through the stage we are now entering. Scientists living on those other, older worlds must long since have unlocked the secrets of the brain; they must long since have taken the fateful step of uniting mind and machine. In countless solar systems science has created a race of immortals, and the exodus has begun.

I have a vision of black-hulled ships, like swarms of locusts, taking 19 flight from their parent stars to move out into the Galaxy. No crews walk their decks; the hulls are silent, beyond the quiet rustle of moving electrons. But each ship is alive. Swiftly it speeds to the rendezvous with its fellows. Now the star travelers wander together through the void, driven by the craving for new experiences. An encounter with a fresh and innocent race like ours must be their greatest pleasure. For decades they have known of our existence, for the earth's television broadcasts, spreading out into space at the speed of light, make our planet a conspicuous body in the heavens. We have become a magnet to all the roving brains of the Galaxy. Man need not wait a thousand years to reach the stars; the stars will come to him.

CONSIDERATIONS

1. Are computers alive? Jastrow speaks of computers in the future as "a living species." In this essay, what qualities define their aliveness?

2. If in twenty years it will be too late to turn back from our dependence on computers, why not stop now? Why not "pull the plug" without waiting to lose the chance? Does Jastrow answer this question? What is your answer?

3. If we will be able to copy our entire mind into a computer, what relationship would then result from this transfer? Since the computer could subsequently learn and change at a much faster rate than we could, would the computer be fulfilling our essential nature? Who would be the real individual?

4. Compare Jastrow and Jonathan Schell (in the preceding selection) on the subject of the discontinuation of the human species. How do their attitudes toward human life differ?

5. How does Jastrow's essay resemble a story? How does he present surprises, growing suspense, and relief?

6. Jastrow gives us a view of plausible immortality. How does it resemble and differ from traditional religious ideas of immortality?

7. WRITING TOPIC. One main premise in Jastrow's essay is that "mind is the essence of being." It is demonstrably true that a computer can think. Is a computer then truly a living being? To bring this problem down to essentials, what do you think *you* are? In a 750-word essay, argue whether you would still be you if you lost your thinking mind, or if you lost your memory, or if you lost your body. In each case, consider the problem as your own: suppose that there is nobody else around to identify you.

ADDITIONAL
WRITING TOPICS

◊

DILEMMAS

1. In the *Insights*, Russell Scott points out that as medical technology develops better ways of transplanting body organs and tissues, the value of body parts could soar. Illegal markets, inflated prices for scarce items, and criminal assaults for precious commodities could put everyone's life in jeopardy. Legalized commerce in body parts would also dehumanize the participants and corrupt our moral standards. Court battles would soon arise over ownership rights and the fair value of human parts. Consider the pros and cons of offering any payment for any human parts. What about payment for human hair? For blood? For semen? For skin? For an eye or a retina? For a kidney, or a lung, or a heart? In a 500-word essay, offer a well-reasoned argument for the principle of prohibiting or allowing payment for body parts.

2. Consider from another perspective the issues raised in the piece by Neil Chayet, "Law and Morality." In times of war, even free societies put their young men under the legal obligation "to secure the well-being of other members of society," even at the direct cost of the bodies and lives of many. Does the military draft conflict with the principle of our common law that maintains that no person is under a legal obligation to aid or rescue another? Do differences in the situation, and perhaps other principles involved, make the military draft legal in a society dedicated to individual conscience and freedom? In a 750-word essay, argue for or against the principle of a military draft.

3. Because of their popularity, some computer game arcades have been shut down in the vicinity of schools and places of work, or else restricted to operating after hours. Should they be licensed by the state or city, like bars and slot machines? Are computer games entertainment? Or are they like gambling? Or are they educational? In a 500-word essay, argue what you think society's policy should be regarding computer game arcades.

4. As a member of a student publications board, how would you react to your campus newspaper occasionally printing pornography? In a 500-word essay, develop the argument that explains your probable vote one way or the other on this controversy over freedom of expression and freedom of

the press. You may want to consider your newspaper's distribution, its source of funds, and its main purpose, as well as the problem of defining pornography.

5. Every child has been told "It's for your own good!" when adults apply strong coercion of force. Why is the statement, even when true, always offensive? In a 500-word essay, explain the actual effects on both child and parents when a distressing decision is forced on a child. Create an illustration based on your own knowledge or experience.

APPENDIX

*Reading and Writing About Essays, with
Reflections on a Sample Essay,
E. B. White's "Once More to the Lake"*

Not everyone realizes that reading, like writing, requires imagination. You can't just swallow words and get much sense out of them. You must actively collaborate with the writer and put together in your mind a personal sense of the writer's intentions. This collaboration between writer and reader produces meaning. The American poet Walt Whitman put it this way:

> I know I am solid and sound,
> To me the converging objects of the universe perpetually flow,
> All are written to me, and I must get what the writing means.

You are the center of understanding in your universe. Your personal center develops into something "solid and sound" as you strive to "get what the writing means." By *making sense* you make connections with the world.

This appendix offers some practical advice on how to read and write with clear perception and imaginative response. The effectiveness of these suggestions will depend on your willingness to practice them again and again. Like playing the piano, reading and writing are acquired skills that no one is born with. What is more, no one can maintain either skill at a high level without frequent practice and effort to improve. But as you become good at what you're doing, the pleasure of doing it increases.

Approach a selection with an intention to read it word by word. Begin with the title, because the title is part of an essay just as your name is part of your personality. Be aware of what the title tells you or leads you to expect. For example, from the title of Susan Brownmiller's essay, "The Contrived Postures of Femininity," you can foresee the author's critical attitude toward her subject. On the other hand, Joan Didion's title, "In Bed," may mislead a reader into expecting a racier subject than the author presents. Some titles are deliberately general or ambiguous, like Mary McCarthy's "Names." They acquire their specific meaning only after you plunge into the essay.

When you get going, don't skim and don't skip over details. At least once through the whole essay, take it *all* in, so that its full meaning will be available to you to consider. There is nothing in this anthology that takes very long to read, and you are reading not for the broad outline or summary of what is said but to grasp the author's full meaning and to see how it is developed. If you begin with good intentions to read carefully but find that your attention is waning and your mind wandering, perhaps the selection itself is at fault. When you are too bored to read word by word, ask yourself, Why is this writing so uninteresting? What is the author doing here that makes it hard to pay attention? That inquiry ought to wake you up. You can't read with an inactive mind any better than you can play the piano with numb fingers.

Read with a pencil in hand and use the pages of your anthology (only in your own copy, please!) to help define your responses. Mark whatever sounds important as you read. Words, phrases, and suggestions that stick out prominently as you read are reliable indicators of what is important in the essay. Circle words you don't understand and try to figure out what they mean from the context. You can look them up later. Write comments in the margins. Some of your comments will refer directly to the essay's contents, and some comments will record your own associations or reactions.

As you read, reformulate in your mind what the author is saying. Get the ideas up off the page and into your head. The more conscious you are of the author's thoughts, the more energized you are to respond with thoughts of your own, either in agreement or disagreement. Be sure to notice and to record in the margin wherever your mind balks over an assertion or concept. Constantly take your mental pulse. Are you disagreeing? Are you puzzled? Make a note of that too. The good thing about questions is that they provoke action. Perhaps your question can be dealt with in class discussion. Sometimes you will have to answer your own question later — perhaps by doing some writing of your own on the topic.

Don't hesitate to include personal associations in your marginal comments. Does a passage in the textbook remind you of something that once happened to you? Make a note of it. Something you read or heard? Something you learned in another class? Write it down, in the margin if the thought can be expressed briefly, or in a notebook if your response is more lengthy. Jot down connections that occur to you as you're reading, because this network of associations is helping you to assimilate new material.

Taking note of your responses includes keeping clear sight of what the author is saying. Identify the author's points of emphasis as you read. Of course you know the usefulness of locating a topic sentence in a paragraph, when you can find one. A topic sentence, or main point, gives a paragraph a tread mark with which it grips the subject, like the tread of a hiker's shoe. Pay attention also to where the point of strongest emphasis occurs. Is it at the beginning, the middle, or the end of the paragraph? Is it an uphill, a downhill, or an over-the-hill hike?

If you identify the basic contour of each paragraph, you will also be able to see how the paragraphs fit together. What is added to the subject as the author proceeds from one paragraph to the next? Is the writer offering illustrations or examples to support a prior point? Or the author may be refining a prior point by dealing with its exceptions or apparent contradictions that need to be resolved. Or is the author introducing fresh material that directs attention to a new point? If so, is the writer proceeding in a straight, logical line or taking widely spaced steps that seem to go off in slightly divergent directions?

Good writing is not necessarily a straight linear development of thoughts. The linear model is often found in tightly reasoned arguments, such as a lawyer's presentation of a case. Examples in this book of linear arguments are John Berger's "The Changing View of Man in the Portrait" and Jonathan Schell's "The Choice." Even arguments, however, can proceed by more widely spaced steps. In developing a comparison and contrast, for instance, a writer shifts sides perhaps several times in an essay. Alexis de Tocqueville, in "Aristocracy and Democracy," argues his point through this method of moving back and forth as he goes forward. A skillful writer sometimes includes emotional associations or digressions into other topics without losing the train of thought. A meditative, reflective essay such as Robert Finch's "Very Like a Whale" can include much repetition and circling back over the same concept or image as the author explores the subject. The choice of models and strategies is up to the writer, and the reader must be able to follow the way the essay is organized. (Some writers wobble, stagger, and fall down, but we trust that none of the authors in this anthology will be that hard to follow.)

As you note an essay's points of emphasis and its method of organization, you will be acquiring a sense of the author's purpose in writing the essay. You will begin to say in your mind, "I see what this is getting at." Pay attention to this sense of the essay's overall purpose. It is your mind recognizing the author's intentions.

One constant guide to the author's purpose is his or her tone. In the margin try to describe the writer's voice that is heard silently inside your head. Any voice includes tones that convey more than the words themselves mean — that impart the speaker's attitudes and implications. The tones of voice in written language are more subtle than in spoken language, but they are nevertheless essential to the meaning. You can begin to identify the writer's tone of voice if you first approach it as a more general quality, one of "manner." Is the writer formal? Humorous? Solemn? Earnest? Casual? Authoritative? Ironic? Straightforward? Playful? Argumentative? Come up with two or three adjectives that best describe the writer's general manner and jot them down in the margin. Then closely examine the passage that prompted your observation and find the specific words and phrases that fit your description of the writer. Underline those words. Try to hear them as spoken words in order to check the accuracy of your description. Do they illustrate the manner you noted? Perhaps you will need to adjust your initial description of the writer's manner as you recognize the nuances of the language that express the tone of voice.

A writer's word choice expresses a particular slant, or viewpoint, toward the subject. A specialized or technical vocabulary establishes the tone of an expert authority, such as a sportswriter who addresses an audience of fans who understand the lingo of baseball or horse-racing. Sportswriters also use many figures of speech to suggest the excitement of the game. The statement "Rice exploded the horsehide into the stands" doesn't make much sense to an ordinary reader, or even to any too literal-minded fan. The selections in this anthology seldom use such jargon. But even common diction and more comprehensible figures of speech indicate the writer's attitude toward the subject. Look at the first paragraph of Maya Angelou's "Graduation" (on p. 234). Words and phrases like *glorious release, nobility, exotic destina-*

tions, and *rites* indicate Angelou's — and the black community's — feelings about the school graduation.

Keep noticing the tone to see where and how it changes within a selection. Sometimes it is possible to underline the sentence, or circle a pivotal word or phrase, where the tone shifts to express a different attitude. For example, in "Graduation" the intense, poetic language continues until the entrance of the white man who gives the speech at the ceremony. Now the language changes to officialese — boring generalities and flat clichés — revealing the white speaker's attitude toward the event. Angelou is making a point about race relations by this change in the essay's tone.

It is especially important to identify the tone at the conclusion of a selection, because you want to recognize the writer's final attitude. On what note does the essay end? How does the ending affect you? Has the writer been building up to this effect all along? Or is it a slight surprise? Even a very short essay such as Luis Buñuel's "Memory" can achieve a remarkable change in tone from beginning to end. A long essay such as Garrison Keillor's "After a Fall" includes several changes of tone and ends on a note that is still unexpected. The concluding paragraph of Robert Jastrow's "An End and a Beginning" introduces an entirely new tone to the essay that suggests another dimension of the subject.

Paying close attention to the conclusion's tone gives you a way to pull together your observations about the entire essay. This reconsideration of the whole is the most fruitful step in making sense of your reading. It is often an exciting synthesis of the material that leads to discoveries and fresh insights. In comparing the tone at the conclusion with the tone at the beginning, you will see how the author's attitude changed, if at all, as a result of writing the essay. Reconsider the title to see if it is appropriate now that you know where the essay leads. Some titles reveal their appropriateness, or lack of it, only after you have reached the conclusion. Reread the headnote and note information about the author that may seem more pertinent now that you have read the essay.

Most important, from your overview of all the material you can determine what the author's main purpose was in writing the essay. You can't ask the author, so you must ask yourself. Besides, the answer to such a challenging question is best found in the writer's work, not in an author's remarks about doing it "for the money" or "to get it off my chest." Ask yourself what the writer tried to achieve by presenting this specific material in this particular way. Don't lazily accept such generalities as to entertain, or to report, or to explain, or to persuade; these are general purposes that classify types of essays. Go further to identify the specific purpose of the particular essay. Get down to cases by defining what the essay has communicated to you. As Whitman observed, the world is full of messages, but you have to work at them: "All are written to me, and I must get what the writing means."

Try these reading suggestions on a fine essay, E. B. White's "Once More to the Lake." We have done part of the work for you here; we've annotated White's essay as you might when reading it yourself. Important points and significant words are underlined, and varied associations or questions are noted in the margins. As you read White's essay through once or several times, note your own reactions and add them to the margins.

E. B. White

ONCE MORE TO
THE LAKE

◊

E. B. WHITE (1899–1985) joined the staff of *The New Yorker* (see the headnote on James Thurber, p. 56) soon after he was graduated from Cornell University. He contributed regularly to the "Talk of the Town" and other sections of the magazine. In later years he wrote essays for *Harper's*, many of which are collected in *One Man's Meat* (1942), *The Second Tree from the Corner* (1953), and the *Essays of E. B. White* (1977). He also wrote the classic children's books *Stuart Little* (1945) and *Charlotte's Web* (1952). In 1938 he moved with his wife and son to Maine, to the region that he had loved since boyhood. In this essay, a visit with his son to a scene of his own youthful summers with his father brings on vivid memories and a keen sense of the sequence of generations.

First trip to lake (w/Father)

They used to return every summer. Do they any more?

Ocean vs. lake (Restlessness vs. Placidity)

One summer, along about 1904, my father rented a camp on a lake 1 in Maine and took us all there for the month of August. We all got ringworm from some kittens and had to rub Pond's Extract on our arms and legs night and morning, and my father rolled over in a canoe with all his clothes on; but outside of that the vacation was a success and from then on none of us ever thought there was any place in the world like that lake in Maine. We returned summer after summer — always on August 1 for one month. I have since become a salt-water man, but sometimes in summer there are days when the restlessness of the tides and the fearful cold of the sea water and the incessant wind that blows across the afternoon and into the evening make me wish for the placidity of a lake in the woods. A few weeks ago this feeling got so strong I bought myself a couple of bass hooks and a spinner and returned to the lake where we used to go, for a week's fishing and to revisit old haunts.

*His father
took him—he
takes son*

I took along my son, who had never had any fresh water up his nose   2
and who had seen lily pads only from train windows. On the journey
over to the lake I began to wonder what it would be like. I wondered
how time would have marred this unique, this holy spot — the coves
and streams, the hills that the sun set behind, the camps and the
paths behind the camps. I was sure that the tarred road would have
found it out, and I wondered in what other ways it would be deso-
lated. It is strange how much you can remember about places like that

*Fear of change—
he wants it
all back just
as it was*

once you allow your mind to return into the grooves that lead back.
You remember one thing, and that suddenly reminds you of another
thing. I guess I remembered clearest of all the early mornings, when
the lake was cool and motionless, remembered how the bedroom
smelled of the lumber it was made of and of the wet woods whose
scent entered through the screen. The partitions in the camp were
thin and did not extend clear to the top of the rooms, and as I was
always the first up I would dress softly so as not to wake the others,
and sneak out into the sweet outdoors and start out in the canoe,
keeping close along the shore in the long shadows of the pines. I remembered being very careful never to rub my paddle against the gun-

*Lake is "holy"—
still—like
a cathedral*

wale for fear of disturbing the stillness of the cathedral.
   The lake had never been what you would call a wild lake. There   3
were cottages sprinkled around the shores, and it was in farming country although the shores of the lake were quite heavily wooded. Some
of the cottages were owned by nearby farmers, and you would live at
the shore and eat your meals at the farmhouse. That's what our family
did. But although it wasn't wild, it was a fairly large and undisturbed
lake and there were places in it that, to a child at least, seemed infinitely remote and primeval.

*Full of
wonder for a
child—more
ordinary for
adults*

   I was right about the tar: it led to within half a mile of the shore.   4
But when I got back there, with my boy, and we settled into a camp
near a farmhouse and into the kind of summertime I had known, I
could tell that it was going to be pretty much the same as it had been
before — I knew it, lying in bed the first morning, smelling the bedroom and hearing the boy sneak quietly out and go off along the shore
in a boat. I began to sustain the illusion that he was I, and therefore,
by simple transposition, that I was my father. This sensation persisted,
kept cropping up all the time we were there. It was not an entirely
new feeling, but in this setting it grew much stronger. I seemed to be
living a dual existence. I would be in the middle of some simple act, I

*Son repeats what father used to do—Narrator
feels like his father—confusion of identity*

would be picking up a bait box or laying down a table fork, or I would be saying something, and suddenly it would be not I but my father who was saying the words or making the gesture. It gave me a creepy sensation.

Why is it creepy?

We went fishing the first morning. I felt the same damp moss cov-   5
ering the worms in the bait can, and saw the dragonfly alight on the tip of my rod as it hovered a few inches from the surface of the water. It was the arrival of this fly that convinced me beyond any doubt that everything was as it always had been, that the years were a mirage and that there had been no years. The small waves were the same, chuck-ing the rowboat under the chine as we fished at anchor, and the boat was the same boat, the same color green and the ribs broken in the same places, and under the floorboards the same fresh-water leavings and debris — the dead helgramite, the wisps of moss, the rusty dis-carded fishhook, the dried blood from yesterday's catch. We stared si-lently at the tips of our rods, at the dragonflies that came and went. I lowered the tip of mine into the water, tentatively, pensively dislodg-ing the fly, which darted two feet away, poised, darted two feet back, and came to rest again a little farther up the rod. There had been no years between the ducking of this dragonfly and the other one — the one that was part of memory. I looked at the boy, who was silently watching his fly, and it was my hands that held his rod, my eyes watching. I felt dizzy and didn't know which rod I was at the end of.

But there had been years!

all the same in past & present

Repeated— Time is dissolved at this lake

We caught two bass, hauling them in briskly as though they were   6
mackerel, pulling them over the side of the boat in a businesslike manner without any landing net, and stunning them with a blow on the back of the head. When we got back for a swim before lunch, the lake was exactly where we had left it, the same number of inches from the dock, and there was only the merest suggestion of a breeze. This seemed an utterly enchanted sea, this lake you could leave to its own devices for a few hours and come back to, and find that it had not stirred, this constant and trustworthy body of water. In the shallows, the dark, water-soaked sticks and twigs, smooth and old, were undu-lating in clusters on the bottom against the clean ribbed sand, and the track of the mussel was plain. A school of minnows swam by, each minnow with its small individual shadow, doubling the attendance, so clear and sharp in the sunlight. Some of the other campers were in swimming, along the shore, one of them with a cake of soap, and the water felt thin and clear and unsubstantial. Over the years there had

"enchanted"

motionless = trustworthy

The lake is like memory where things remain always the same

His phrase repeated 3 times

First minor change

What worries him?

been this person with the cake of soap, this cultist, and here he was. There had been no years.

Up to the farmhouse to dinner through the teeming, dusty field, 7 the road under our sneakers was only a two-track road. The middle track was missing, the one with the marks of the hooves and the splotches of dried, flaky manure. There had always been three tracks to choose from in choosing which track to walk in; now the choice was narrowed down to two. For a moment I missed terribly the middle alternative. But the way led past the tennis court, and something about the way it lay there in the sun reassured me; the tape had loosened along the backline, the alleys were green with plantains and other weeds, and the net (installed in June and removed in September) sagged in the dry noon, and the whole place steamed with midday heat and hunger and emptiness. There was a choice of pie for dessert, and one was blueberry and one was apple, and the waitresses were the same country girls, there having been no passage of time, only the illusion of it as in a dropped curtain — the waitresses were still fifteen; their hair had been washed, that was the only difference — they had been to the movies and seen the pretty girls with the clean hair.

Passage of time — an illusion —
But — 2nd slight change

Life on shore —
"innocent & tranquil design"

Summertime, oh, summertime, pattern of life indelible, the fade- 8 proof lake, the woods unshatterable, the pasture with the sweetfern and the juniper forever and ever, summer without end; this was the background, and the life along the shore was the design, the cottagers with their innocent and tranquil design, their tiny docks with the flagpole and the American flag floating against the white clouds in the blue sky, the little paths over the roots of the trees leading from camp to camp and the paths leading back to the outhouses and the can of lime for sprinkling, and at the souvenir counters at the store the miniature birch-bark canoes and the postcards that showed things looking a little better than they looked. This was the American family at play, escaping the city heat, wondering whether the newcomers in the camp at the head of the cove were "common" or "nice," wondering whether it was true that the people who drove up for Sunday dinner at the farmhouse were turned away because there wasn't enough chicken.

Experience at lake = American family at play (Not just a single family)

It seemed to me, as I kept remembering all this, that those times 9 and those summers had been infinitely precious and worth saving. There had been jollity and peace and goodness. The arriving (at the beginning of August) had been so big a business in itself, at the rail-

are they lost now?

Child's perception of arrival (in past)
—present arrival "less exciting"
—it makes him sad

way station the farm wagon drawn up, the first smell of the pine-laden air, the first glimpse of the smiling farmer, and the great importance of the trunks and your father's enormous authority in such matters, and the feel of the wagon under you for the long ten-mile haul, and at the top of the last long hill catching the first view of the lake after eleven months of not seeing this <u>cherished body of water.</u> The shouts and cries of the other campers when they saw you, and the trunks to be unpacked, to give up their rich burden. (Arriving was less exciting nowadays, when you sneaked up in your car and parked it under a tree near the camp and took out the bags and in five minutes it was all over, no fuss, no loud wonderful fuss about trunks.)

Phrase repeated (w/variation)

<u>Peace and goodness and jollity.</u> The only thing that was wrong 10 now, really, was <u>the sound of the place</u>, an unfamiliar <u>nervous sound of the outboard motors. This was the note that jarred, the one thing that would sometimes break the illusion and set the years moving.</u> In

Biggest Change
—sound of boat motors (outboard vs. inboard)
past — sleepy sound
vs. present—petulant, irritable, whining

those other summertimes all motors were inboard; and when they were at a little distance, the noise they made was <u>a sedative,</u> an ingredient of summer sleep. They were one-cylinder and two-cylinder engines, and some were make-and-break and some were jump-spark, but they all made <u>a sleepy sound</u> across the lake. The one-lungers throbbed and fluttered, and the twin-cylinder ones purred and purred, and that was a quiet sound, too. But now the campers all had outboards. In the daytime, in the hot mornings, these motors made <u>a petulant, irritable sound;</u> at night, in the still evening when the afterglow lit the water, <u>they whined about one's ears like mosquitoes.</u> My boy loved our rented outboard, and his great desire was to achieve single-handed mastery over it, and authority, and he soon learned the trick of choking it a little (but not too much), and the adjustment of the needle valve. Watching him I would remember the things you could do with the old one-cylinder engine with the heavy flywheel, how you could have it eating out of your hand if you got <u>really close to it spiritually.</u> Motorboats in those days didn't have clutches, and you would make a landing by shutting off the motor at the proper time and coasting in with a dead rudder. But there was a <u>way of reversing them,</u> if you learned the trick, by cutting the switch and putting it on again exactly on the final dying revolution of the flywheel, so that it would kick back against compression and begin reversing. Approaching a dock in a strong following breeze, it was difficult to slow up sufficiently by the ordinary coasting method, and if a boy felt he had com-

Memory of the boy reversing the engine

Compare with writer reversing time in this essay

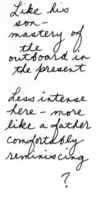

Like his son — mastery of the outboard in the present

Less intense here — more like a father comfortably reminiscing?

Past memories blend with present activities

Why doesn't he ever talk to the boy in this essay?

plete mastery over his motor, he was tempted to keep it running beyond its time and then reverse it a few feet from the dock. It took a cool nerve, because if you threw the switch a twentieth of a second too soon you would catch the flywheel when it still had speed enough to go up past center, and the boat would leap ahead, charging bull-fashion at the dock.

We had a good week at the camp. The bass were biting well and 11 the sun shone endlessly, day after day. We would be tired at night and lie down in the accumulated heat of the little bedrooms after the long hot day and the breeze would stir almost imperceptibly outside and the smell of the swamp drift in through the rusty screens. Sleep would come easily and in the morning the red squirrel would be on the roof, tapping out his gay routine. I kept remembering everything, lying in bed in the mornings — the small steamboat that had a long rounded stern like the lip of a Ubangi, and how quietly she ran on the moonlight sails, when the older boys played their mandolins and the girls sang and we ate doughnuts dipped in sugar, and how sweet the music was on the water in the shining night, and what it had felt like to think about girls then. After breakfast we would go up to the store and the things were in the same place — the minnows in a bottle, the plugs and spinners disarranged and pawed over by the youngsters from the boys' camp, the Fig Newtons and the Beeman's gum. Outside, the road was tarred and cars stood in front of the store. Inside, all was just as it had always been, except there was more Coca-Cola and not so much Moxie and root beer and birch beer and sarsaparilla. We would walk out with a bottle of pop apiece and sometimes the pop would backfire up our noses and hurt. We explored the streams, quietly, where the turtles slid off the sunny logs and dug their way into the soft bottom; and we lay on the town wharf and fed worms to the tame bass. Everywhere we went I had trouble making out which was I, the one walking at my side, the one walking in my pants.

One afternoon while we were there at that lake a thunderstorm 12 came up. It was like the revival of an old melodrama that I had seen long ago with childish awe. The second-act climax of the drama of the electrical disturbance over a lake in America had not changed in any important respect. This was the big scene, still the big scene. The whole thing was so familiar, the first feeling of oppression and heat and a general air around camp of not wanting to go very far away. In mid-afternoon (it was all the same) a curious darkening of the sky, and

Storm/melodrama "the big scene"

*Change in
wind—
boats react*

a lull in everything that had made life tick; and then the way the boats suddenly swung the other way at their moorings with the coming of a breeze out of the new quarter, and the premonitory rumble. Then the kettle drum, then the snare, then the bass drum and cymbals, then crackling light against the dark, and the gods grinning and licking their chops in the hills. Afterward the calm, the rain steadily rustling in the calm lake, the return of light and hope and spirits, and the campers running out in joy and relief to go swimming in the rain, their bright cries perpetuating the deathless joke about how they were getting simply drenched, and the children screaming with delight at the new sensation of bathing in the rain, and the joke about getting drenched linking the generations in a strong indestructible chain. And the comedian who waded in carrying an umbrella.

*?
Why such
malice from
the gods?*

calm returns

When the others went swimming, my son said he was going in, too. 13
He pulled his dripping trunks from the line where they had hung all through the shower and wrung them out. Languidly, and with no thought of going in, I watched him, his hard little body, skinny and bare, saw him wince slightly as he pulled up around his vitals the small, soggy, icy garment. As he buckled the swollen belt, suddenly my groin felt the chill of death.

*Generations
linked in
"a strong
indestructible
chain"*

*Why?
Who is going to die?*

After you have actively read an essay it is important to pull your thoughts together to improve your understanding of it. Begin by formulating observations like, "This essay is mainly about such and such," or "This essay asserts this and that." In thinking about "Once More to the Lake," you may find it very difficult to formulate exactly what the essay asserts. It doesn't start by making a point, nor does it appear to come to a point. There is no thesis statement in the first paragraph; in fact a thesis is not explicitly stated anywhere in the essay. Clearly, it is not an essay that develops a linear, logical argument. But there is no difficulty at all in fomulating the essay's main subject: White's powerful childhood memories, which pull him back into reexperiencing his past. A direct, matter-of-fact observation like that gives you a foundation, an anchoring point, on which to build other observations and connections. White's specific memories are all associated with the lake, which becomes increasingly important as a reflection of the way life used to be. The lake becomes a kind of reservoir of the past for White to dip into. That is, the lake turns into a symbolic place for him, evoking the past and also suggesting the pool of memory itself in which White immerses himself.

His memories are stimulated also by the presence of his son. White sees his son doing things that he did as a boy, and the parallels make him feel like a boy again. In fact, White begins to feel that he is the boy, and he temporarily loses track of himself as an adult. This part of the experience becomes more complicated and more unsettling to White than the memories evoked by only the lake. In responding to the boy, White's identity is shaken, and his confusion mixes three generations in his self-image. He is unsure from moment to moment whether he is the boy, or himself, or his own father. The recurring sense of being young carries him into illogical, ecstatic states of mind in which it seems that time itself has not passed. Years don't exist. Again and again he is amazed to find that so much of the past can still be present to his senses. But this joyful reexperience of the past is also sobering, because each concrete memory presents something that has, in fact, disappeared from his usual adult life. White doesn't become melancholy over being old. He continues to enjoy details that bring back his youth, like the brand names of chewing gum and soft drinks. But as he spends the week in company with his son, he allows more of the boy's experiences to take precedence over his memories. The father adjusts to accompanying the boy, following the boy's initiatives and interests, watching him or helping him but no longer enthusiastically leading him or submerging the boy entirely in his own memories. White's initial *confusion* of overlapping identities straightens out into his recognition of the *succession* of generations "in a strong indestructible chain."

The sight of the boy struggling into the cold, wet swimming trunks crystallizes the whole experience for White. By remembering the sensations, he can still feel what his son's wiry, immature little body feels. But the father also knows what the boy does not yet know: that we lose the present moment even as we experience it. Time passes and entire generations are lost. The acknowledgment of death springs fully into his mind as he winces from the imagined chill around his groin. The succession of generations that proceeds from his groin (his genitals) is also a succession of deaths. The acknowledgment of death at the end of the essay is surprising but not unprepared for. Death is not a macabre or depressing thought to White. He feels the shock of a truth rediscovered with fuller meaning.

Though the essay does not present a thesis even at the conclusion, it nevertheless comes to a point implicitly and suggestively. It is possible to formulate a thesis statement, such as: The pleasures of reexperiencing youth intensify an adult awareness of loss and death. This is an acceptably accurate thesis statement, but to most readers it will seem to diminish or even trivialize the meaning of the essay. The thesis does not fully capture what the essay is getting at; it seems too narrow and hollow to indicate why White bothered to write "Once More to the Lake." The essay has a larger purpose, a motivation behind it, that is more important than its thesis. This purpose is embodied in White's strong emphasis on the workings of his mind as he is caught up in the excitement of reexperiencing the past. The essay reveals how memories are evoked and how memory can overwhelm our consciousness of the present. Illogically but convincingly, memory can make the past seem more real than the present. Disturbingly, memory can even change our self-image, like a mirror that reflects a face that is not ours. But even when memory is unleashed in full force, the adult mind keeps sorting out the differences between past and present. The purpose of the essay is to reveal this interplay between the immortality of memory and the mortality of actual experience.

Grasping the purpose, we understand that the essay is truly about returning to the *lake*, in the symbolic meaning of the title. Memory is that inland, interior sea where we live partly above the surface and partly deep within the water that holds all the past.

You cannot expect to make this much sense of an essay by just mulling it over in your mind. Your responses and observations have to be articulated in words in order to become coherent ideas. Writing in the margins and taking notes as you read start this process of formulating what you mean. Participating in class discussions will take your understanding further. But the process of making sense is not complete until you write out your views in a fully developed essay of your own. When you have finished your careful reading, substantive realizations still remain ahead of you, because you never really know what you think until you see what you say.

Try to approach the experience of writing in the same spirit in which you might approach a new acquaintance on a date. There should be an air of excitement about venturing toward anything unknown. You don't yet know what this writing encounter will lead to, but you are certainly going to pay attention to the possibilities as they develop.

If you have been given a topic to write on, write on the assigned topic. It has probably been carefully phrased to direct your thoughts and to identify a subject that you can handle in a few pages. If you have to find your own topic after reading an essay, rely on your responses to the reading. After concentrating on "Once More to the Lake," for instance, you should have plenty of personal associations that suggest something to write about, such as a trip you took with your family or a favorite vacation spot. Perhaps you were fascinated by the relationship between White and his son. White's essay illustrates that adults are inclined to relive their past through their children. That mixing of roles between generations is something you know a lot about from your own experience. You may not have thought about this aspect of your life, but writing about it is an opportunity to examine it closely and freely. Perhaps White's essay made the power of memory itself more interesting. You might want to write about someone who lives in the past. Why does that person dwell in the past? From writing you can discover something about yourself and others who are important to you.

Work by jotting down phrases that catch your fleeting thoughts. Don't worry about connecting up the jumble of thoughts that may cover your sheet of paper. Keep writing even if you are formulating only fragments. As you continue to energize your mind into forming phrases and sentences you will soon begin to write longer passages and more cohesive thoughts. The important activity is to make your mind use words that you write down. The object of writing at any stage of preparation or revision is to get thoughts out of your head and onto paper. To achieve this goal you must work on the page. If you have trouble focusing your attention and getting started, push yourself to articulate one thought and then another. (It also helps to have privacy and silence where you write.)

What you get down onto paper during your first hour or two of effort will be patchy and often vague. Don't be disheartened. You can't construct the complicated network of ideas in an essay as easily and methodically as you knit a scarf or add a column of figures. You have to work further on the material you produce, adding what you need in order to be clear and convincing, and trimming away what you don't need.

Working from your first efforts, turn your rough material into a well-formed draft. Fully developing your thoughts and organizing your essay are the main tasks of effective writing. The readings in this anthology provide models and illustrate methods of effective writing that you can apply in your work. Don't hesitate to follow their examples. It can be both entertaining and instructive to try to write like an author you have recently read. Imitating a skillful writer will not interfere with your originality of mind. It will stretch your intellectual muscles, so to speak, and show you how to do something new. Whether you are following someone's example or striking out on your own road, remember that you alone are in charge of the meaning. You must get ideas into the form of sentences and paragraphs, and you must take out words that don't add to the meaning. Include examples when they make your writing more convincing. Illustrate your points when this will clarify your meaning. Eliminate vague phrases and replace them with precise, specific information. Paragraph by paragraph, spell out what you mean.

Pay critical attention to the sequence of your paragraphs. Are you following a tightly logical, linear development? Or are you proceeding by taking wider steps? Either way, you should indicate clear transitions between paragraphs so that your reader can follow your path.

Develop a sense of purpose as you revise your draft into a well-organized essay. What do you want above all else to convey to your reader? Are you giving it sufficient emphasis? Are you making it interesting and convincing? Remember that your intended meaning is expressed by both what you say and how you say it. Your own tone of voice should be faintly audible in your head as you write. Is it a voice that sounds worth listening to on this particular topic? Is it a voice with a purpose?

When you think that you are finished, muster up the energy and courage to take one more critical look at your introduction and conclusion. These paragraphs have special functions that cannot be achieved until you have fully understood the point of your essay and your purpose in writing. You should make last-minute adjustments to your introduction and conclusion so that they serve your intentions. Remember from your readings that there is a rich variety of ways to begin and end an essay. Don't be humdrum in your introduction and conclusion. You owe it to yourself to win some attention to your fully developed views.

This brief bit of advice about writing should remind you that readers and writers confront much the same problems. But writing is more difficult. Writing is difficult for everyone, so you should never lose your nerve. The frustrations you face are the same frustrations that experienced writers face in their work. The standards you strive to attain are the same goals set by authors in this anthology. The work of writing is very democratic work: students, teachers, authors — all of us are in this boat together. If it is your turn to row, always pull a little harder. Keep thinking that next time it will be easier.

Acknowledgments (continued from page iv)

Incorporated. Copyright 1921 by B. W. Huebsch, Inc. Copyright renewed 1948 by Eleanor C. Anderson.

Maya Angelou, "Graduation." Title by the editor. From *I Know Why the Caged Bird Sings*, by Maya Angelou. Copyright © 1969 by Maya Angelou. Reprinted by permission of Random House, Inc.

Margaret Atwood, "Siren Song." From *Selected Poems* by Margaret Atwood. Copyright © 1976 by Margaret Atwood. Reprinted by permission of Simon & Schuster, Inc. and Margaret Atwood.

Russell Baker, "My Lack of Gumption." From *Growing Up* by Russell Baker. Copyright © 1982 by Russell Baker. Reprinted by permission of Congdon & Weed, Inc.

Toni Cade Bambara, "The Lesson." From *Gorilla, My Love*, by Toni Cade Bambara. Copyright © 1972 by Toni Cade Bambara. Reprinted by permission of Random House, Inc.

John Berger, "The Changing View of Man in the Portrait." From *The Moment of Cubism and Other Essays* (Pantheon Books), by John Berger. Copyright © 1969 by John Berger. Reprinted by permission of the author.

John Brooks, "Telephone Gamesmanship." Title by the editor. From *Showing Off in America* by John Brooks. Copyright © 1981 by John Brooks. First appeared in the *Atlantic Monthly*. By permission of Little, Brown and Company in association with the Atlantic Monthly Press.

Susan Brownmiller, "The Contrived Postures of Femininity." From *Femininity*, by Susan Brownmiller. Copyright © 1984 by Susan Brownmiller. Reprinted by permission of Linden Press, a division of Simon & Schuster, Inc.

Luis Buñuel, "Memory." From *My Last Sign*, by Luis Buñuel, translated by Abigail Israel. Translation Copyright © 1983 by Alfred A. Knopf, Inc. Reprinted by permission of the publisher.

Susan Carlisle, "French Homes and French Character." "French Homes and French Character" by Susan Carlisle originally appeared in *Landscape*, vol. 26, no. 3, in 1982. Permission to reprint is granted by Blair Boyd, Publisher, P.O. Box 7107, Landscape Station, Berkeley, California 94707. All rights reserved.

Raymond Carver, "My Father's Life." Copyright © 1984 by Raymond Carver. First appeared in *Esquire*. Reprinted with permission. "What We Talk About When We Talk About Love." Copyright © 1981 by Raymond Carver. Reprinted from *What We Talk About When We Talk About Love*, by Raymond Carver, by permission of Alfred A. Knopf, Inc.

Neil Chayet, "Law and Morality." Originally titled "Can the Court Force You to Part with Your Body?" From *Looking at the Law* (New York: Rutledge Press, 1981). Reprinted by permission of the publisher.

John Cheever, "Expelled." Copyright 1930 by John Cheever. Reprinted by permission of International Creative Management, Inc.

Marcelle Clements, "Terminal Cool." Copyright © 1984 by Marcelle Clements. First appeared in *Esquire*. Reprinted with permission of the author.

Louie Crew, Thriving as an Outsider, Even as an Outcast in Smalltown America." Copyright 1981 by Louie Crew. Reprinted by permission of the author.

Harry Crews, "The Car." Copyright © 1975 by Harry Crews. Reprinted by permission of John Hawkins & Associates, Inc., 71 West 23rd Street, New York, NY 10010. First published in *Esquire* (December 1975).

Emily Dickinson. "I'm Nobody! Who are you?" Reprinted by permission of the publish-

Desmond Morris, "Territorial Behavior." Excerpted from *Manwatching: A Field Guide to Human Behavior.* Text © 1977 by Desmond Morris. Published by Harry N. Abrams, Inc., New York. By permission of the publisher.

Richard Morris, "How Real Is Real?" From *Dismantling the Universe, The Nature of Scientific Discovery,* by Richard Morris. Copyright © 1983 by Richard Morris. Reprinted by permission of Simon & Schuster, Inc.

The New Yorker, excerpt from "Notes and Comment." © 1985 *The New Yorker* Magazine, Inc. Reprinted by permission.

Robert Nisbet, "Creationism." From *Prejudices: A Philosophical Dictionary* by Robert Nisbet. Copyright © 1982 by Robert Nisbet. Published by Harvard University Press. Reprinted by permission.

Michael Novak, "The Metaphysics of Sports." From *The Joy of Sports: End Zones, Bases, Baskets, Balls, and the Consecration of the American Spirit* by Michael Novak. © 1976 by Michael Novak. Reprinted by permission of Basic Books, Inc., Publishers.

Tillie Olsen, "I Stand Here Ironing." Excerpted from the book *Tell Me a Riddle* by Tillie Olsen. Copyright © 1956 by Tillie Olsen. Reprinted by permission of Delacorte Press/Seymour Lawrence.

George Orwell, "Shooting an Elephant." From *Shooting an Elephant and Other Essays* by George Orwell, copyright 1950 by Sonia Brownell Orwell; renewed 1978 by Sonia Pitt-Rivers. Reprinted by permission of Harcourt Brace Jovanovich, Inc., the estate of the late Sonia Brownell Orwell, and Martin Secker & Warburg, Ltd.

Linda Pastan, "Market Day." First appeared in *Poetry,* April 1985. Copyright © 1985 by The Modern Poetry Association. Reprinted by permission of the Editor of *Poetry* and the author.

Laurence J. Peter and Raymond Hull, excerpt from *The Peter Principle.* Copyright © 1969 by William Morrow and Company, Inc. Reprinted by permission.

Adrienne Rich, "The Anger of a Child." Reprinted from *Of Woman Born* by Adrienne Rich, by permission of W. W. Norton & Company, Inc. Copyright © 1976 by W. W. Norton & Company, Inc.

Richard Rodriguez, "Reading for Success." From *Hunger of Memory* by Richard Rodriguez. Copyright © 1981 by Richard Rodriguez. Reprinted by permission of David R. Godine, Publisher, Inc.

Theodore Roethke, "Open House." Copyright 1941 by Theodore Roethke from *The Collected Poems of Theodore Roethke.* Reprinted by permission of Doubleday & Company, Inc.

Leo Rosten, "Home Is Where to Learn How to Hate." From the column titled "Diversions" in *World* Magazine, August 29, 1972. Copyright: Leo Rosten, 1972. Reprinted by permission of the author.

William Ryan, "Mine, All Mine." Title by the editor. From *Equality,* by William Ryan. Copyright © 1981 by William Ryan. Reprinted by permission by Pantheon Books, a division of Random House, Inc.

Jonathan Schell, "The Choice." Title by the editor. From *The Fate of the Earth,* by Jonathan Schell. Copyright © 1982 by Jonathan Schell. Reprinted by permission of Alfred A. Knopf, Inc.

Robert Solomon, "'I-Love-You.'" From *Love: Emotion, Myth, and Metaphor* (Anchor/Doubleday, 1981) by Robert Solomon. Copyright © 1981 by Robert C. Solomon. Reprinted by permission of The Aaron M. Priest Literary Agency, Inc.

Gloria Steinem, "The Time Factor." From *Outrageous Acts and Everyday Rebellions*

RHETORICAL
INDEX

◇

A familiar adage has it that there is more than one way to skin a cat. Few users of this textbook will ever have skinned a bobcat, but as the adage suggests, it requires skill, patience, and sometimes ingenuity to get a good pelt. Hence this rhetorical index, for alternative approaches to the goal of good writing. It is sometimes instructive to observe a particular method of writing, and it helps occasionally to study and practice the use of a special device. This selective index (which does not include the poems and stories) lists some of the rhetorical techniques that every good writer uses to get the job done, and gives examples from the text of the use of each technique.

Analogy

Desmond Morris, *Territorial Behavior*   295
Susan Carlisle, *French Homes and French Character*   355
Michael Novak, *The Metaphysics of Sports*   411
Alan Watts, *Spiritual Living*   522

Argument and Persuasion

Susan Brownmiller, *The Contrived Postures of Femininity*   35
D. H. Lawrence, *Counterfeit Love*   198
Jill Tweedie, *The Future of Love*   215
Joseph Epstein, *The Virtues of Ambition*   380
Pete Hamill, *Winning Isn't Everything*   405
Michael Novak, *The Metaphysics of Sports*   411
Henry David Thoreau, *Where I Lived, and What I Lived For*   439
Stephen Jay Gould, *Nonmoral Nature*   463
Leo Rosten, *Home Is Where to Learn How to Hate*   540
Jonathan Schell, *The Choice*   577

Cause and Effect

Joan Didion, *In Bed*   51
John Berger, *The Changing View of Man in the Portrait*   64
Marie Winn, *The* Mad *View of Parents*   86
Adrienne Rich, *The Anger of a Child*   109
Ernest van den Haag, *The Invention That Isn't Working*   204
Maya Angelou, *Graduation*   234
Alexis de Tocqueville, *Aristocracy and Democracy*   307
E. M. Forster, *My Wood*   332
Christopher Lasch, *Survival Mentality*   445
Forum, *Images of Fear*   547
George Orwell, *Shooting an Elephant*   560

Comparison and Contrast

John Berger, *The Changing View of Man in the Portrait*   64
Nancy Friday, *Competition*   92
Alexis de Tocqueville, *Aristocracy and Democracy*   307
Lewis Hyde, *Gifts in Motion*   366
Richard Morris, *How Real Is Real?*   458
Neil Chayet, *Law and Morality*   538
Robert Jastrow, *An End and a Beginning*   586

Definition

Joan Didion, *In Bed*   51
Marcelle Clements, *Terminal Cool*   166
Robert Solomon, *"I-Love-You"*   175
D. H. Lawrence, *Counterfeit Love*   198
Edward Martin, *Being Junior High*   228
Desmond Morris, *Territorial Behavior*   295
Joseph Epstein, *The Virtues of Ambition*   380
Robert Nisbet, *Creationism*   474
Alan Watts, *Spiritual Living*   522

Description

Nancy Friday, *Competition*   92
Calvin Trillin, *It's Just Too Late*   130
Harry Crews, *The Car*   327
Susan Carlisle, *French Homes and French Character*   355
Robert Finch, *Very Like a Whale*   482
George Orwell, *Shooting an Elephant*   560

Division and Classification

Mary McCarthy, *Names*   26
Margaret Mead, *Family Codes*   81
Francesco Alberoni, *Two Kinds of Sexuality*   180
Ernest van den Haag, *The Invention That Isn't Working*   204
Edward Martin, *Being Junior High*   228
John Edgar Wideman, *Black and Blues*   258
Paul Fussell, *"Speak, That I May See Thee"*   270
Marc Feigen Fasteau, *Friendships Among Men*   283
John Brooks, *Telephone Gamesmanship*   345
Forum, *Images of Fear*   547

Example

Mary McCarthy, *Names*   26
Louie Crew, *Thriving as an Outsider*   41
Gordon Lish, *Fear: Four Examples*   127
Susan Allen Toth, *The Boyfriend*   158
Paul Fussell, *"Speak, That I May See Thee"*   270
E. M. Forster, *My Wood*   332
Seymour Wishman, *A Lawyer's Guilty Secrets*   401
Neil Chayet, *Law and Morality*   538

Narration

Nora Ephron, *Shaping Up Absurd*   7
Mary McCarthy, *Names*   26

Raymond Carver, *My Father's Life*　　99
Calvin Trillin, *It's Just Too Late*　　130
Susan Allen Toth, *The Boyfriend*　　158
Maya Angelou, *Graduation*　　234
John Edgar Wideman, *Black and Blues*　　258
Russell Baker, *My Lack of Gumption*　　386
Carl Jung, *Secret Thought*　　489
Barbara Grizzuti Harrison, *Growing Up Apocalyptic*　　496
George Orwell, *Shooting an Elephant*　　560

Process Analysis

Luis Buñuel, *Memory*　　64
John Brooks, *Telephone Gamesmanship*　　345
Richard Rodriguez, *Reading for Success*　　395
Virginia Woolf, *Professions for Women*　　421
Steven Jay Gould, *Nonmoral Nature*　　463
Leo Rosten, *Home Is Where to Learn How to Hate*　　540

INDEX OF
AUTHORS AND TITLES

◊

After a Fall (Keillor), 17

Alberoni, Francesco, 155; *Two Kinds of Sexuality*, 180

Allen, Woody, 533

Amazing Grace,(Newton), 457

Anderson, Sherwood, *The Egg*, 428

Angel Levine (Malamud), 508

Angelou, Maya, *Graduation*, 234

Anger of a Child, The (Rich), 109

Aristocracy and Democracy (Tocqueville), 307

Atwood, Margaret, *Siren Song*, 202

Bacon, Francis, 79

Baker, Russell, *My Lack of Gumption*, 386

Bambara, Toni Cade, *The Lesson*, 318

Being Junior High (Martin), 228

Berger, John, *The Changing View of Man in the Portrait*, 64

Black and Blues (Wideman), 258

Blessing, A (Wright), 520

Bok, Sissela, 532

Boyfriend, The (Toth), 158

Brooks, John, *Telephone Gamesmanship*, 345

Browning, Robert, 376

Brownmiller, Susan, *The Contrived Postures of Femininity*, 35

Buñuel, Luis, *Memory*, 64

Car, The (Crews), 327

Carlisle, Susan C., *French Homes and French Character*, 355

Carnegie, Andrew, 317

Carver, Raymond, *My Father's Life*, 99; *What We Talk About When We Talk About Love*, 185

Changing View of Man in the Portrait, The (Berger), 64

Chayet, Neil, *Law and Morality*, 538

Cheever, John, *Expelled*, 247

Choice, The (Schell), 577

Clements, Marcelle, *Terminal Cool*, 166

Competition (Friday), 92

Contrived Postures of Femininity, The (Brownmiller), 35

Counterfeit Love (Lawrence), 198

Creationism (Nisbet), 474

Crew, Louie, *Thriving as a Outsider*, 41

Crews, Harry, *The Car*, 327

Cummings, E. E., 6

Dickinson, Emily, 5

Didion, Joan, *In Bed*, 51

Donne, John, 224

Dostoyevski, Fyodor, 534

DuBois, W. E. B., 225

Ecclesiastes, 379

Egg, The (Anderson), 428

Emerson, Ralph Waldo, 224

End and a Beginning, An (Jastrow), 586
Ephron, Nora, *Shaping Up Absurd*, 7
Epstein, Joseph, *The Virtues of Ambition*, 380
Expelled (Cheever), 247

Family Codes (Mead), 81
Fasteau, Marc Feigen, *Friendships Among Men*, 283
Fear: Four Examples (Lish), 127
Finch, Robert, *Very Like a Whale*, 482
Forster, E. M., 533; *My Wood*, 332
Forum, *Images of Fear*, 547
Fraiberg, Selma, 155
French Homes and French Character (Carlisle), 355
Freud, Anna, 534
Freud, Sigmund, 227, 457
Friday, Nancy, *Competition*, 92
Friendships Among Men (Fasteau), 283
Fromm, Erich, 156
Frost, Robert, 455; *The Road Not Taken*, 536
Fussell, Paul, *"Speak, That I May See Thee,"* 270
Future of Love, The (Tweedie), 215

Galbraith, John Kenneth, 316
Gifts in Motion (Hyde), 366
Gould, Stephen Jay, *Nonmoral Nature*, 463
Graduation (Angelou), 234
Greer, Germaine, 5
Griffin, Emilie, 454
Growing Up Apocalyptic (Harrison), 496

Hamill, Pete, *Winning Isn't Everything*, 405

Hand, (Judge) Learned, 456
Harre, Rom, 4
Harris, Sydney J., 376
Harrison, Barbara Grizzuti, *Growing Up Apocalyptic*, 496
Hayden, Robert, *Those Winter Sundays*, 142
Home Is Where to Learn How to Hate (Rosten), 540
How Real Is Real? (Morris), 458
Hyde, Lewis, *Gifts in Motion*, 366

"I-Love-You" (Solomon), 175
Images of Fear (Forum), 547
In Bed (Didion), 51
Invention That Isn't Working, The (van den Haag), 204
I Stand Here Ironing (Olsen), 568
It's Just Too Late (Trillin), 130

James, Henry, 314
James, William, 455
Jastrow, Robert, *An End and a Beginning*, 586
Jung, Carl, *Secret Thought*, 489

Keillor, Garrison, *After a Fall*, 17
Keller, Helen, 4
Kincaid, Jamaica, *A Walk to the Jetty*, 114
Kingston, Maxine Hong, *The Misery of Silence*, 264

Lake Isle of Innisfree, The (Yeats), 443
La Rochefoucauld, 154
Lasch, Christopher, *Survival Mentality*, 445
Law and Morality (Chayet), 538
Lawrence, D. H., *Counterfeit Love*, 198
Lawyer's Guilty Secret, A (Wishman), 401
Lesson, The (Bambara), 318

Lewis, C. S., 78
Lilies of the Field, The
    (Matthew), 343
Lish, Gordon, *Fear: Four Exam-
    ples*, 127
Lorenz, Konrad, 532

McCarthy, Mary, *Names*, 26
Mad *View of Parents, The*
    (Winn), 86
Malamud, Bernard, *Angel Levine*,
    508
Market Day (Pastan), 305
Martin, Edward C., *Being Junior
    High*, 228
Martin, Judith ("Miss Manners"),
    226
Matthew, 314; *The Lilies of the
    Field*, 343
May, Rollo, 6
Mead, Margaret, *Family Codes*,
    81
Memory (Buñuel), 64
Metaphysics of Sports, The
    (Novak), 411
Mine, All Mine (Ryan), 336
Misery of Silence, The (Kingston),
    264
Morris, Desmond, *Territorial Be-
    havior*, 295
Morris, Richard, *How Real Is
    Real?* 458
Mount, Ferdinand, 78
My Father's Life (Carver), 99
My Lack of Gumption (Baker),
    386
My Wood (Forster), 332

Names (McCarthy), 26
Napoleon, 455
Newton, John, *Amazing Grace*,
    457
New Yorker, The, 534

Nisbet, Robert, 78; *Creationism*,
    474
Nonmoral Nature (Gould), 463
Novak, Michael, *The Metaphysics
    of Sports*, 411

Olsen, Tillie, *I Stand Here Iron-
    ing*, 568
Once More to the Lake (White),
    601
Open House (Roethke), 62
Orwell, George, *Shooting an Ele-
    phant*, 560

Pastan, Linda, *Market Day*, 305
Percy, Walker, 154
Peter, Lawrence J., and Raymond
    Hull, 377
Professions for Women (Woolf),
    421

Reading for Success (Rodriguez),
    395
Reik, Theodor, 224
Rich, Adrienne, *The Anger of a
    Child*, 109
Road Not Taken, The (Frost), 536
Rodriguez, Richard, *Reading for
    Success*, 395
Roethke, Theodore, *Open House*,
    62
Rosten, Leo, *Home Is Where to
    Learn How to Hate*, 540
Russell, Bertrand, 456
Ryan, William, *Mine, All Mine*,
    336

St. John, 154
Sartre, Jean-Paul, 224
Schell, Jonathan, *The Choice*, 577
Scott, Russell, 534
Secret Life of Walter Mitty, The
    (Thurber), 56
Secret Thought (Jung), 489

Shaping Up Absurd (Ephron), 7
Shooting an Elephant (Orwell), 560
Siren Song (Atwood), 202
Slater, Philip, 79
Solomon, Robert, *"I-Love-You,"* 175
Sontag, Susan, 4
"Speak, That I May See Thee" (Fussell), 270
Spiritual Living (Watts), 522
Steinem, Gloria, *The Time Factor,* 279
Still of Some Use (Updike), 144
Stinnett, Caskie, 315
Survival Mentality (Lasch), 445
Suzuki, D. T., 157

Telephone Gamesmanship (Brooks), 345
Terminal Cool (Clements), 166
Territorial Behavior (Morris), 295
Thoreau, Henry David, 314; *Where I Lived, and What I Lived For,* 439
Those Winter Sundays (Hayden), 142
Thriving as an Outsider (Crew), 41
Thurber, James, *The Secret Life of Walter Mitty,* 56
Time Factor, The (Steinem), 279
Tocqueville, Alexis de, *Aristocracy and Democracy,* 307
Tolstoy, Leo, 78
Toth, Susan Allen, *The Boyfriend,* 158
Trillin, Calvin, *It's Just Too Late,* 130
Tweedie, Jill, *The Future of Love,* 215

Two Kinds of Sexuality (Alberoni), 180

Updike, John, *Still of Some Use,* 144

van den Haag, Ernest, *The Invention That Isn't Working,* 204
van Gogh, Vincent, 378
Veblen, Thorstein, 315
Very Like a Whale (Finch), 482
Virtues of Ambition, The (Epstein), 380

Wachtel, Paul, 314
Walk to the Jetty, A (Kincaid), 114
Watts, Alan W., *Spiritual Living,* 522
Weiss, Robert, 79
What We Talk About When We Talk About Love (Carver), 185
Where I Lived, and What I Lived For (Thoreau), 439
White, E. B., *Once More to the Lake,* 601
Wideman, John Edgar, *Black and Blues,* 258
Wilde, Oscar, 226
Winn, Marie, *The Mad View of Parents,* 86
Winning Isn't Everything (Hamill), 405
Wishman, Seymour, *A Lawyer's Guilty Secrets,* 401
Woolf, Virginia, *Professions for Women,* 421
Wright, James, *A Blessing,* 520

Yeats, William Butler, *The Lake Isle of Innisfree,* 443

To the Student

We regularly revise the books we publish in order to make them better. To do this well we need to know what instructors and students think of the previous edition. At some point your instructor will be asked to comment on *Life Studies*, Second Edition; now we would like to hear from you.

Please take a few minutes to rate the selections and complete this questionnaire. Send it to Bedford Books of St. Martin's Press, 29 Commonwealth Avenue, Boston, Massachusetts 02116. We promise to listen to what you have to say. Thanks.

School _____

School location (city, state) _____

Course title _____

Instructor's name _____

	Liked a lot	Okay	Didn't like	Didn't read
Chapter 1. Self-Images				
Ephron, *Shaping Up Absurd*	___	___	___	___
Keillor, *After a Fall*	___	___	___	___
McCarthy, *Names*	___	___	___	___
Brownmiller, *The Contrived Postures of Femininity*	___	___	___	___
Crew, *Thriving as an Outsider*	___	___	___	___
Didion, *In Bed*	___	___	___	___
Thurber, *The Secret Life of Walter Mitty*	___	___	___	___
Roethke, *Open House*	___	___	___	___
Berger, *The Changing View of Man in the Portrait*	___	___	___	___
Buñuel, *Memory*	___	___	___	___

	Liked a lot	Okay	Didn't like	Didn't read

Chapter 2. Family Ties

	Liked a lot	Okay	Didn't like	Didn't read
Mead, *Family Codes*	___	___	___	___
Winn, *The Mad View of Parents*	___	___	___	___
Friday, *Competition*	___	___	___	___
Carver, *My Father's Life*	___	___	___	___
Rich, *The Anger of a Child*	___	___	___	___
Kincaid, *A Walk to the Jetty*	___	___	___	___
Lish, *Fear: Four Examples*	___	___	___	___
Trillin, *It's Just Too Late*	___	___	___	___
Hayden, *Those Winter Sundays*	___	___	___	___
Updike, *Still of Some Use*	___	___	___	___

Chapter 3. Love and Longings

	Liked a lot	Okay	Didn't like	Didn't read
Toth, *The Boyfriend*	___	___	___	
Clements, *Terminal Cool*	___	___	___	
Solomon, "*I-Love-You*"	___	___	___	
Alberoni, *Two Kinds of Sexuality*	___	___	___	
Carver, *What We Talk About When We Talk About Love*	___	___	___	___
Lawrence, *Counterfeit Love*	___	___	___	___
Atwood, *Siren Song*	___	___	___	___
van den Haag, *The Invention That Isn't Working*	___	___	___	___
Tweedie, *The Future of Love*	___	___	___	___

Chapter 4. Group Pictures

	Liked a lot	Okay	Didn't like	Didn't read
Martin, *Being Junior High*	___	___	___	___
Angelou, *Graduation*	___	___	___	___
Cheever, *Expelled*	___	___	___	___
Wideman, *Black and Blues*	___	___	___	___
Kingston, *The Misery of Silence*	___	___	___	___
Fussell, "*Speak, That I May See Thee*"	___	___	___	___
Steinem, *The Time Factor*	___	___	___	___
Fasteau, *Friendships Among Men*	___	___	___	___
Morris, *Territorial Behavior*	___	___	___	___
Pastan, *Market Day*	___	___	___	___
de Tocqueville, *Aristocracy and Democracy*	___	___	___	___

	Liked a lot	Okay	Didn't like	Didn't read
Chapter 5. Possessions				
Bambara, *The Lesson*	___	___	___	___
Crews, *The Car*	___	___	___	___
Forster, *My Wood*	___	___	___	___
Ryan, *Mine, All Mine*	___	___	___	___
Matthew, *The Lilies of the Field*	___	___	___	___
Brooks, *Telephone Gamesmanship*	___	___	___	___
Carlisle, *French Homes and French Character*	___	___	___	___
Hyde, *Gifts in Motion*	___	___	___	___
Chapter 6. Ambitions				
Epstein, *The Virtues of Ambition*	___	___	___	___
Baker, *My Lack of Gumption*	___	___	___	___
Rodriguez, *Reading for Success*	___	___	___	___
Wishman, *A Lawyer's Guilty Secrets*	___	___	___	___
Hamill, *Winning Isn't Everything*	___	___	___	___
Novak, *The Metaphysics of Sports*	___	___	___	___
Woolf, *Professions for Women*	___	___	___	___
Anderson, *The Egg*	___	___	___	___
Thoreau, *Where I Lived, and What I Lived For*	___	___	___	___
Yeats, *The Lake Isle of Innisfree*	___	___	___	___
Lasch, *Survival Mentality*	___	___	___	___
Chapter 7. Convictions				
Morris, *How Real Is Real?*	___	___	___	___
Gould, *Nonmoral Nature*	___	___	___	___
Nisbet, *Creationism*	___	___	___	___
Finch, *Very Like a Whale*	___	___	___	___
Jung, *Secret Thought*	___	___	___	___
Harrison, *Growing Up Apocalyptic*	___	___	___	___
Malamud, *Angel Levine*	___	___	___	___
Wright, *A Blessing*	___	___	___	___
Watts, *Spiritual Living*	___	___	___	___
Chapter 8. Dilemmas				
Frost, *The Road Not Taken*	___	___	___	___
Chayet, *Law and Morality*	___	___	___	___

	Liked a lot	Okay	Didn't like	Didn't read
Rosten, *Home Is Where to Learn How to Hate*	⸻	⸻	⸻	⸻
Forum, *Images of Fear*	⸻	⸻	⸻	⸻
Orwell, *Shooting an Elephant*	⸻	⸻	⸻	⸻
Olsen, *I Stand Here Ironing*	⸻	⸻	⸻	⸻
Schell, *The Choice*	⸻	⸻	⸻	⸻
Jastrow, *An End and a Beginning*	⸻	⸻	⸻	⸻

Any general comments or suggestions?

Name ⸻

Mailing address ⸻

Date ⸻